Andrew Pickens

"I leave it to my country to say whether in my public transactions I have discharged the duty assigned me with honesty and fidelity and whether I have been an humble instrument in the hand of Providence, to its advantages, But whatever the public sentiment may be, I have a witness within myself that my public life and conduct have been moved and actuated by an ardent zeal for the welfare and happiness of my beloved country."—
Andrew Pickens

Andrew Pickens

*South Carolina Patriot
in the Revolutionary War*

WILLIAM R. REYNOLDS, JR.

McFarland & Company, Inc., Publishers
Jefferson, North Carolina, and London

LIBRARY OF CONGRESS CATALOGUING-IN-PUBLICATION DATA

Reynolds, William R., 1945–
Andrew Pickens : South Carolina patriot
in the Revolutionary War / William R. Reynolds, Jr.
      p.   cm.
Includes bibliographical references and index.

ISBN 978-0-7864-6694-8
softcover : acid free paper ∞

1. Pickens, Andrew, 1739–1817.
2. Generals—United States—Biography.
3. United States—History—Revolution, 1775–1783.
4. United States. Congress. House—Biography.
5. South Carolina—History—Revolution, 1775–1783.
6. South Carolina—Militia—Biography.
I. Title.

E207.P63R49 2012   975.7'030292—dc23   [B]   2012026508

BRITISH LIBRARY CATALOGUING DATA ARE AVAILABLE

© 2012 William R. Reynolds, Jr. All rights reserved

*No part of this book may be reproduced or transmitted in any form
or by any means, electronic or mechanical, including photocopying
or recording, or by any information storage and retrieval system,
without permission in writing from the publisher.*

On the cover: General Andrew Pickens;
background © 2012 Clipart.com and Shutterstock

Manufactured in the United States of America

*McFarland & Company, Inc., Publishers
Box 611, Jefferson, North Carolina 28640
www.mcfarlandpub.com*

To:
My wife, Diane.
My mother, Shirley Calton.
My children, Lynne Hathaway, Jonathan, Kelley Gregory,
Melody Thomas, William, Jared, Melissa Mendoza,
Torry Mendoza, and Sally Mendoza.
My grandchildren, Christina, Zeniff, Bobby, Aaron,
Kyrra, Tashina, Joshua, Matthew, William Rudy, Hunter,
Amon, Xela, Brigham, Gabriella, Brenden, Nathan,
Emmalee, Joseph, Elizabeth, Grace, and Veronica.
My great-grandchildren, Sylvia, Willow, Thomas, and Damon.

Table of Contents

Acknowledgments	vii
Preface	1
Prologue	7
1 — The Early Days (1740–1765)	11
2 — Edging Toward War (1765–1775)	27
3 — Pickens Sees Action (1775)	46
4 — Here Come the Redcoats! Here Come the Cherokee! (1776)	55
5 — The Backcountry Heats Up (1777–1778)	81
6 — Georgia Explodes! (1779)	99
7 — South Carolina in Jeopardy (1780)	134
8 — It Comes Apart for Britain (1780)	167
9 — Cowpens! (1781)	189
10 — Taking Control of South Carolina (1781)	233
11 — The Siege of Augusta (1781)	255
12 — The Siege of Ninety Six (1781)	262
13 — Cleaning Up the Backcountry (1781 and Later)	290
Epilogue	301
Appendices	
A: South Carolina Legislature Bill of 2007	307
B: Civil Records	308
Will of Andrew Pickens, Sr.	308
Estate Inventory of Andrew Pickens, Sr.	308
Abstracts of Augusta County, Virginia, Records	309
Will of Robert Gouedy	309
C: 1755 Anson County, North Carolina, Militia	310
D: 1778 Constitution of South Carolina	312
E: Pension Claims	318
F: Pickens, Hillhouse and the Cherokee Ancestry of the Author	345
G: Articles from Revolutionary Era Publications	348
Chapter Notes	363
Bibliography	379
Index	383

Acknowledgments

I owe a debt of gratitude to many people who provided not only material and information but also inspiration and support. One person cannot write a book without participation in many forms by many people. It is hard to find the words that express how thankful I am for the assistance and guidance.

I would first like to thank my wife, Diane Robinson, for her love, encouragement, support, and understanding of the time I needed to spend on this project. Additionally, Diane provided a valuable service. She was the primary editor of the book and is well-qualified for the task. She is a published author, retired editor by profession, retired instructor of English, grammar, and writing at several small colleges, and has judged many writing competitions. Diane unselfishly devoted many hours of editing for this publication.

I would also like to thank my mother, Shirley Calton, who lives in Missouri, for her interest and support of this endeavor. It is through her line that I trace my ancestry to Captain Joseph Pickens, General Andrew Pickens' brother.

I need to express thanks to my children, grandchildren, and great grandchildren for the inspiration I receive just knowing they are here. Living descendants provide a strong incentive for one to explore ancestry. Genealogy provided a great opportunity for me to learn of my progenitors, and I am convinced that knowing my ancestors helps me to understand who I am. I sincerely hope this book will provide my progeny the desire to learn more of their ancestry. My grown children and grandchildren also provided much moral support during the writing process. It helped me immeasurably, and kept me up to the task, as they asked for periodic updates and expressed their pride in my effort.

My friends at the Monday Writers' Group provided an invaluable service. Each week I read four to six double-spaced pages as the members patiently listened and offered appropriate helpful critique. My thanks to members Ginger Allen, Nancy Altman, Barbara Breunig, George Cetinich, Lou Chandler, Brian Dowell, Terry Frost, Mary Gory, Bill Hart, Steve Herndon, Julius Jortner, Jim Kesey, Mary Lou McMillen, Jewell Miller, Virginia Prowell, Diana Sears, Jackie Shank, and Rhonda Valet.

I am thankful for Andrew and Joseph Pickens, for what they sacrificed, and for what they accomplished in a most historic and troubled era. During research I learned of their unbelievable scruples and their intense focus on the task before them. They truly were a force for American Independence. I sincerely believe that, if our leaders exhibited a like strength of character, we would have no worries about the future of our nation.

I must also express thanks for another line of my ancestry — the Cherokee. I wrote this book from the perspective of Andrew Pickens and his Whig neighbors, but I do recognize the plight of the Cherokee tribe in the 18th century. I tried to represent the Cherokee Nation, and the chiefs including Dragging Canoe, in a realistic manner. I know that to do the tribe justice I must follow this book with another that fully represents the same period of time from the Cherokee point of view.

There are several people that provided specific material assistance, and proper acknowledgment is given to them throughout the document. I must especially recognize Henry Fulmer, the curator of manuscripts at South Caroliniana Library, University of South Carolina, for his assistance with the original William Tennent papers in their possession. The South Caroliniana Library holds a wealth of information for a researcher in South Carolina history.

I must also recognize D. Ray Smith who is a valuable authority on Cherokee tribal history and provided me the drawing of Cherokee War Chief Dragging Canoe (by artist Mike Smith) that is used in this book. He runs an interesting and informative website (see the bibliography).

Mary Clyde Reid Mungo deserves special thanks for providing two old photographs of the Old Waxhaw Presbyterian Church in Lancaster, South Carolina. Old pictures add mystique to history that keeps one wanting to learn more.

There is one last group of individuals that provided an invaluable service to this work — the authors listed in the bibliography. I believe it important to describe the atmosphere that surrounded the Pickens brothers throughout the era discussed and specific authors, some of whom have passed on, deserve special notice for providing much of the required reference material. These individuals are (in alphabetical order): Lawrence E. Babits; Robert D. Bass; Edwin C. Bearss; John Buchanan; Kate Pickens Day; Lyman C. Draper; John Ferling; Monica Mary Gardner; R. W. Gibbes; John W. Gordon; George Washington Greene; Jerome A. Greene; Richard J. Hooker (editor of Charles Woodmason's journal); Washington Irving; William Johnson; J. B. O. Landrum; Henry Lumpkin; A.L. Pickens; G. M. Sharp; Christine R. Swager; and Alice Noble Waring.

Preface

Independence! Such a simple-sounding word to us; yet, try to imagine how improbable this concept must have been to Whigs (Patriots) in the days leading up to the Revolutionary War. American independence was certainly an impossible thought to the leaders of Europe. How could, from the haughty Europeans' point of view, a ragtag bunch of heathens from the backwoods possibly compete with the most powerful military on earth and declare themselves sovereign? The large numbers of American Tories (Loyalists) able and eager to impede the progress of the Whigs further added to the incredibility.

I use the terms Whigs and Patriots interchangeably in this book as I do Tories and Loyalists. The Patriots called themselves Whigs after 1768 because they identified with members of the liberal British Whig party who favored more tolerant colonial policies. Thus, the Loyalists became Tories because their conservative beliefs aligned with the conviction of the British Tory party members who desired firm British control over the colonies. After the Declaration of Independence was signed, the Whigs became generally identified as Americans or rebels while the Tories continued to be called Tories or Loyalists.

The odds were extremely small that South Carolina would meet its destiny as the foundation for the Patriots' success. During the early days of the war the British and the rebels had come to a standstill in the north. Therefore, the British had to put such strong emphasis upon controlling South Carolina that, during the latter part of the conflict, the core of the British army focused the thrust of its efforts within that provincial boundary. Odds were further reduced because the pivotal part of South Carolina was the backcountry (or upcountry) that consisted of the western two-thirds of the province. Within this area, for a time, there was no law save for locally-assigned regulators, not unlike the vigilantes of the old west. Indeed, the Tories and the Whigs each had groups meting out justice from their own positions, and the Tories outnumbered the Whigs in this part of the colony by nearly two to one during the majority of the war. Later, each group commissioned its own militias to supplement the regular British and Continental armies. The brunt of Whig power was initially established in the lowcountry from the coast to the edge of the backcountry. Early in the war the Whigs established a provincial government to rival that of the formal Royal Governor.

So much was dependent upon each group's attempt to gain control in the backcountry that relationships among neighbors, and sometimes families, deteriorated into extremely bitter associations. Heroes were required, and found, as the situation became tenuous for the Whigs. Those heroes put their personal lives on hold when battle pressed heavily upon them in their own back yards. Those dedicated men stepped forward to lead and inspire other brave men to take up arms even though their families would be forced to contend with constant danger from those around them.

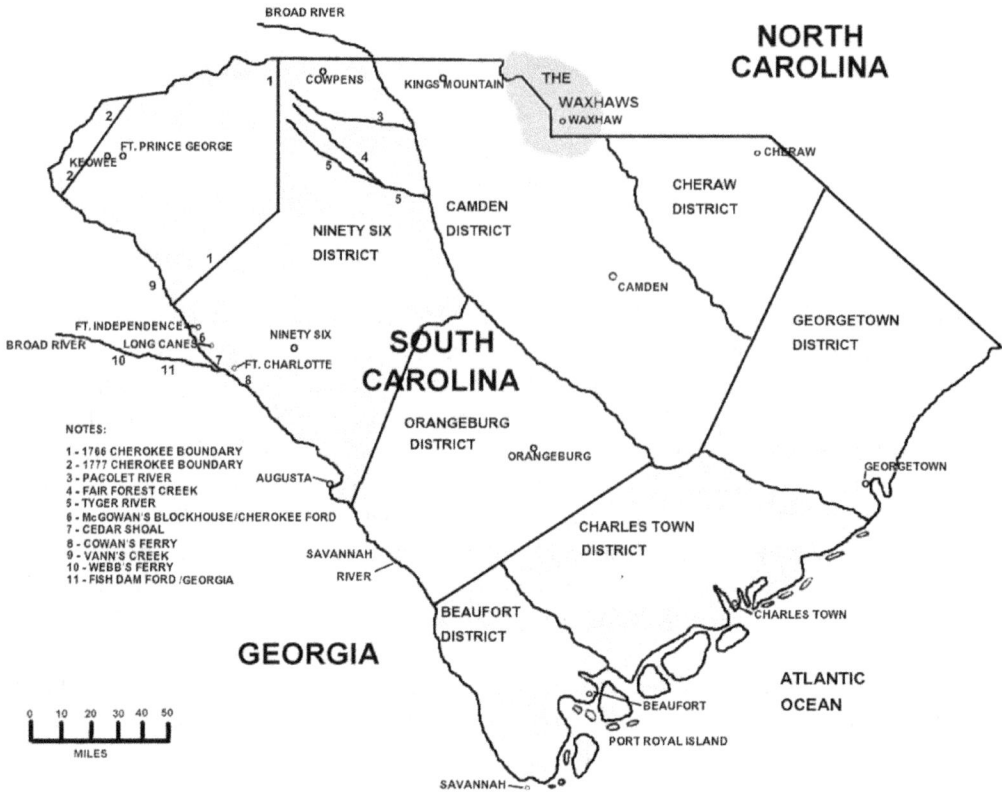

South Carolina points of interest pre–1776.

Heroes! What makes a hero? Many of us had heroes as we grew up; some were Revolutionary War icons. I remember when several of my friends and I ran around and sang "Swamp Fox, Swamp Fox, tail on his hat! Nobody knows where the Swamp Fox' at..." as we pretended to be Francis Marion.

As a teenager in Kansas City, Missouri, I belonged to a Boy Scouts of America explorer post. Our post's project was target shooting 22 caliber rifles, and we challenged other posts to contests at our indoor rifle range. The other posts in the city had other primary projects so we had a distinct advantage. We always won! Indeed, my score and Scout Merrill Watt's combined would usually defeat all five-man teams from the other posts. We called ourselves "The Swamp Fox Patrol," and we wore 'coonskin hats and fringed leather shirts at the annual Boy Scouts of America show.

Many boyhood heroes, like Francis "Swamp Fox" Marion, were well known to us for several reasons. They were often flamboyant or, like Henry "Light Horse Harry" Lee, they wrote memoirs. The better known ones, of course, had catchy nicknames. A few had extreme egos that helped them become famous. Whatever the cause for their renown, they were the ones that would likely have biographies written or movies made about them.

Other heroes were quieter, unpretentious, and did not write memoirs. These men simply fulfilled their responsibilities, and did not seek the fame and fortune that might be due them because of their great accomplishments during the war. They are often overlooked or receive minimal attention in the many excellent modern references that relate to the Revolutionary War or its specific major engagements. I do not denigrate any Patriot who became famous through memoirs or political activity; each deserved the fame achieved. My purpose is to note that the lack of such attention does not disqualify one from being a hero.

Each Patriot had a great impact on the establishment of this independent nation — an impact so important that, had any one of these individuals failed in his actions, the cause may well have been totally lost, and we might likely today be subjects of Britain. A number of great individuals were active in the southern campaigns, especially in Georgia and the Carolinas. Fully a third of the Revolutionary War engagements were fought in South Carolina. I strongly believe that the Whig successes in the Carolinas and Georgia compelled the victory at Yorktown.

This book deals with one of the more humble and unassuming of these heroes. This sober Patriot is Brigadier General Andrew Pickens of the Ninety Six Militia Regiment and the South Carolina State Troops. He is not as well known as Marion, Lee, Thomas "Gamecock" Sumter, Major General Nathanael Greene, or Brigadier General Daniel Morgan except within the general area of his activity.

I must admit that I had never heard of Andrew Pickens until, as an adult, I delved into my genealogical roots. During my research I found that Pickens' actions had as much impact on the final outcome of the war as those of any other Patriot; debatably, even more than some that are highly acknowledged.

Andrew Pickens may be well-recognized only by historians that deal extensively with the southern campaigns, to students of Revolutionary War detail, or to Pickens family members. Some of the reason for that may be the character of the man. General Pickens, though a competent individual, was not a man of high ego nor did he seek fame or fortune. Indeed, he did not entertain any thought of writing his memoirs. While not at all bashful, Pickens was confident in his abilities, yet extremely unpretentious.

There have been few biographical writings that detail Andrew Pickens' Revolutionary War actions. Two of the better-known biographies tagged him with his only nicknames. They are *Skyagunsta, The Border Wizard Owl* by Dr. Andrew L. Pickens and *The Fighting Elder: Andrew Pickens (1739–1817)* by Alice N. Waring. However, those books have been out of print for years and, while well known among historians, they are not readily available to the general public. Typically, reliable contemporary texts about the southern campaigns devote no more than two or three sentences to Andrew Pickens' efforts. It is understandable that, because these distinguished references deal with the macrocosm of the southern campaigns (or a particular battle within a campaign), some detail will be lacking. However, because of Pickens' extraordinarily valuable contributions to the outcome of the American Revolution, his nearly complete omission from written history is neglectful.

An updated reference that details Pickens' important contributions to American independence is necessary. I will stress that the victory at Cowpens, South Carolina, in 1781 heavily influenced the battle at Yorktown. Furthermore, the actions of Andrew Pickens and the South Carolina militias were pivotal to the victory at Cowpens. Pickens likely would not have, as a colonel, been assigned a general's command at Cowpens if he had not proven his worthiness; indeed, he had consistently received promotions resultant from several previous engagements since he first attained captaincy in 1761.

This book addresses Andrew Pickens' life from his early years to his final days. My ancestry continues to drive my interest in this effort. I learned, through thirty years of genealogical research, that Captain Joseph William Pickens, brother to Andrew Pickens, is my seventh great-grandfather. Joseph, also a hero, gave his life for the cause at the Siege of

Ninety Six on June 17, 1781. Joseph is my designated Patriot ancestor for membership in Sons of the American Revolution (SAR). My research into the Pickens family has inspired me to publicize the record and render a comprehensive history of General Andrew Pickens available to the public. Pickens was markedly valuable to the southern campaign and to the finality of the war.

I have included herein many individual tributes and accolades that were awarded to, but not sought by, Andrew Pickens. While a Colonel and a General through the later conflicts in South Carolina, he often commanded great men such as Henry Lee and Francis Marion. When he was not assigned the command, he acquiesced without qualm or tantrum to other chosen commanders such as Sumter or Marion, and he followed strict military discipline throughout.

Andrew Pickens was not a man given to humor or a boisterous nature. Even his looks were grim and severe. His militiamen, however, found him a very fair, while stoic and stern, leader. He gained much respect among local farmers, millers, and other inhabitants of the Carolina backcountry; so much that Pickens had little trouble when he recruited a local volunteer militia. This was extremely important because of the lack of men in the Southern Department of the Continental Army. Pickens' success in raising a militia, time and again throughout the war, is a tribute to his leadership capabilities.

I have also included details regarding the following areas where other texts have either provided misinformation or insufficient specifics:

1. The relative ages of Joseph and Andrew Pickens.
2. The identities of the Pickenses listed on the Colonial Militia Roster of 1755.
3. The reason for Andrew Pickens' visit to Long Canes after the Grant expedition of 1761.
4. A letter written on August 4, 1776, from Andrew Williamson to W. H. Drayton is mistakenly included in Gibbes History as being written on August 4, 1775, from Colonel William Thomson to W. H. Drayton.
5. Robert Anderson fought at Kings Mountain so likely did not take parole with Andrew Pickens.
6. The rank of Joseph Pickens between 1776 and 1779.
7. The "legend" of a second "ring fight" in 1779 almost identical to the original of 1776.
8. Brigadier General Andrew Williamson's appearance, or lack thereof, at Savannah in 1779.
9. The incarceration of Andrew Pickens by the British after the fall of Charles Town.
10. The part played by Andrew Pickens in General Morgan's decision to stay and fight at Cowpens rather than cross the Broad River.
11. The topography of the battlefield at Cowpens.
12. What became of Captain Henry Connelly and his North Carolina State Troops at the Battle of Cowpens?
13. The circumstances surrounding the death of Joseph Pickens.
14. The date of the death of Andrew's brother, John Pickens.

Some of these errors originated with an interviewee's comments recorded in *The Draper Manuscripts* by Lyman C. Draper.

I am an historian primarily in the sense that I deal in family history, a fairly specialized field and certainly not all-encompassing. Therefore, as I developed this reference, I sought "atmosphere" from genealogical resources, public records, and previously published texts concerning the Revolutionary War. I visited the battle sites where the Pickens brothers fought, so I could obtain a better understanding for what they experienced. I continued herein to record the regional war effort, even during periods when Pickens was relative inactive, to maintain the atmosphere that impacted his life.

During my research, I intently examined the histories of Cowpens and Ninety Six National Battlefields. I have led informal tours of those parks and lectured about them to members of local Sons of the American Revolution (SAR) chapters. I am in awe of the many Patriots who sacrificed so much for the ideal that existed within their hearts, minds and souls. My hope is for readers of this reference to experience the spirit of, and be thankful for, Andrew Pickens' efforts during that extremely important period of our nation's history.

Prologue

Joseph William Pickens was born to Andrew and Nancy Ann (Davis) Pickens February 1, 1737,[1] in Paxton Township, Lancaster County, Pennsylvania. His brother Andrew Pickens, later General Pickens, was born September 19, 1739,[2] also in Paxton Township. I will refer to the elder Andrew Pickens as Andrew Pickens, Sr., to distinguish between him and his son. At the time, the Pickens brothers' birth dates probably seemed like any other. Now I look back, and almost envision heralds proclaiming, "Hark! Hark! Britain's tyranny over this land is coming to an end, and a new free country will rise up to claim its destiny!"

An exaggeration, you may say. Well, perhaps I took some liberty with that opening, but Andrew Pickens and his older brother, Joseph William, did have a huge impact upon the success of the Patriots in the Revolutionary War. They were well-prepared for the coming effort by virtue of their birth to a poor, honest, righteous, and totally devout family. Their ancestry consisted of hardy stock with a history that foreshadows the rigors the Pickens brothers would come to experience.

In 1896, the Cowpens Centennial Committee published in *Cowpens Centennial, 1781–1881*:

> Andrew Pickens, of a lineage traced back through the centuries to that sad procession of half a million French Protestant refugees ... exiles for liberty of religious opinions; for some a temporary resting place in Scotland; another sojourn in North of Ireland, where our hero's parents were born; then the yearning for absolute liberty ... brought the Pickens family across the wide Atlantic.[3]

The Pickens family was part of the overall migration of Scots-Irish Presbyterians. They desired religious autonomy as well as the right to work at a labor of their own choosing and to peacefully live where they desired. The Pickens' religion was supremely important to their lives. Not a joyful denomination in those days, theirs stressed obedience to and fear of God. They dressed inconspicuously in bland, unornamented clothing and worshipped in unadorned meeting halls. Celebrations, while not unheard of, were few and far between, usually occurring for only the most special events.[4] General Andrew Pickens, 28 years after the war's end, wrote General Henry "Light Horse Harry" Lee, "My father and mother came from Ireland. My father's progenitors emigrated from France after the revocation of the Edict of Nantes."[5] Robert Andrew Pickens, a cousin of Joseph and Andrew, was interviewed by Lyman C. Draper in 1833 and stated, "The grandfather of General Pickens emigrated from Ireland about the commencement of the 18th Century."[6]

The history of the lowland Scottish, including their relocation to Ireland and then as Scots-Irish to America, had a substantial impact upon the War of Independence from Britain, especially to the final stages of the war in South Carolina. A review of the European phase of that history is necessary for an understanding of its influence upon the Scots-

Irish. Many of their ancestors' experiences seemed to have come full circle. It was important that they not continue to be subjected to the same tyrannies as their forefathers. This review makes abundantly clear what inspired their great enthusiasm to resist continuing British control in the New World and why many Scots-Irish, Andrew Pickens being a prime example, took a leadership role in the Revolutionary War.

In 1521, Martin Luther was declared a heretic for his religious beliefs because any deviation from the Catholic Church was considered blasphemous. There followed severe conflicts between devoutly Presbyterian lowland Scottish, living on the border with England, and highland Scottish and English who were just as devoutly Catholic. These conflicts continued in the late 1500s and early 1600s even though the Church of England (Anglican) had displaced Catholicism as Britain's State Church. The Anglicans considered themselves to be Catholic in thought and Protestant only in lineage of authority; therefore the fully Protestant religions were "beneath" them.

The Scottish Presbyterians were treated harshly because they were extremely contrary to the rule of the Church of England. They formed very rugged and fearsome border guerrilla bands called "Border Reevers" as they were intent upon defending themselves against any religious persecution.

Calvinist Protestants, known as Huguenots in Catholic-dominated France, had experienced similar religious intolerance until April 13, 1598, when King Henry IV issued the Edict of Nantes. Henry was determined to unify the French. His edict established civil rights for the Protestants, so they were no longer treated as heretics. Tolerance amid secularism was established — exactly what the Scottish Presbyterians desired.

Several of the Scottish Presbyterians departed for France shortly after the edict was issued. A man named Robert Picken (Picon), who is the accepted great-great-grandfather of Andrew Pickens, Sr., went with them. Theoretically, he was the descendant of a Norman named Piccen, who was a contemporary of William the Conqueror, and is entered in the Domesday Book, a census ordered by William in 1086. Robert had three brothers named Johnne, Andrew, and Peter who had remained in the lowlands while Robert was in France. Robert Picken held a diplomatic position on the royal court until King Henry IV was assassinated in 1610. Henry's wife, Marie de' Medici, acted as regent for their son, Louis XIII, for five years until he became of age at 13. The Edict of Nantes remained in force during his reign.

Meanwhile, King James VI of Scotland inherited the English throne as King James I in 1603. He wanted to strengthen the authority of the Church of England by displacing the remaining heretics from Britain and Scotland.

In 1609, King James' advisors developed the Plantation of Ulster and convinced the King of its merits. The plan was initiated and provided that properties owned by Irish chieftains, the O'Neills and O'Donnells and their supporters, were confiscated and used to settle colonists. The Irish chieftains owned, and left behind, an estimated 500,000 acres when they departed for Spain to enlist help for a rebellion against Britain. Several previous rebellions had been unsuccessful, and indeed had proven to make life much more difficult for the Irish citizens.

The "British Tenants," a term applied to the colonists, most of whom came from Scotland and England, were required to be English–speaking and Protestant. The Scottish colonists were primarily lowland Presbyterians, especially the Border Reevers, whom the English typically persecuted as dissenters from the Church of England.

The atmosphere of the Scottish lowlands settled down and became a safer place after

William Penn signs treaty with Indians. Unknown engraver, 1883.

the Plantation of Ulster because a majority of ruffians had departed. There no longer remained a serious threat to the Church of England since King James was, after all, Scottish. Robert Picken returned to Scotland after King Henry's assassination. He married and, in 1624, had a son named Andrew. Charles I became King of England in 1625 and immediately began again to persecute the lowland Scottish. Robert was known as a diplomat with an exemplary reputation, so he was able to safely remain in Scotland with his family.

In 1644, Andrew Pickens had a son named Robert. Andrew, as his father had done, moved to France where Robert married Esther Jean (Jane) Benoit, a widowed Huguenot. Robert's and Esther Jean's children included William Henry Pickens who was born in France in 1669. In October 1685 Louis XIV, grandson of King Henry IV, issued the Edict of Fontainebleau that is also known as the Revocation of the Edict of Nantes. Religious tolerance in France, which had been established by edict rather than popularity, was tenuous at best. Louis XIV expected universal adherence to Catholicism; hence, since heretics didn't fit within his ideal autocracy, some 400,000 Huguenots left France.

The Pickens family returned to Scotland but found that their relatives had already departed for Ireland. They followed, and William Henry married Margaret Pike there in 1693. Their children, including Andrew Pickens, Sr., were born in Ireland.

Originally, King James and his advisors had a second goal in mind with the Plantation of Ulster. It was to serve as a venture to pacify and civilize Ulster and to assure Ireland would not be destroyed by any further rebellion. However, the devoutly Catholic Irish were involved in a severe conflict with the Church of England. This antagonism had been the root of those previously unsuccessful rebellions, so the Irish viewed the settlers, whether English or Scottish, as intruders. It made no difference that the settlers did not belong to the Church of England.[7]

The Scottish, who were individualists and believed in human rights, were sorely vexed. They were subjected to a caste system in Ireland that disallowed them to own land or to hold any public office. They paid exorbitant rent on property then owned by the English gentry. Additionally, England had placed an exorbitant tax on textiles imported from Ireland to avoid a competitive burden on weavers in England. The Scottish were excellent weavers and raised sheep for wool, so they were definitely targeted by, and suffered because of, this tax.

The Scottish continued to endure substantial religious persecution. They did not believe in strict authoritarianism. Their individualistic beliefs required that they rely on their local pastors for leadership. When the Church of England discredited all sacraments performed by any clergy other than its own, that was the last straw for the Scots. The Church of England already required a full tithe from anyone living in Ireland, regardless of individual church affiliations. Later, circa 1700, the Church of England declared anyone other than members of the Church to be dissenters. Thus marriages, baptisms, communions, and burial services performed by Presbyterian clergy were illegal. Indeed, clergymen were arrested if they tried to administer those rites.[8]

Several hundred thousand Scots-Irish immigrated to America from 1700 until the English began to heavily control shipping to the colonies in the 1770s. William Henry Pickens followed the trail of Presbyterian migration and moved his family to Pennsylvania in the spring of 1719.[9]

Many Scots-Irish came to the colonies as indentured servants, which practice earned them training in a trade. Many of them were agrarian and settled in western Pennsylvania among the Germans. The Scots-Irish practiced a very mobile type of agriculture. They would plant a property until it became overused, and they would then move on to another. The Germans in the area, better farmers, were frugal and industrious; therefore, they did not understand the Scots-Irish approach to land use. The area became heavily populated, and the Scots-Irish tended to move further into the wilderness. They did not want to be subjected to many rules and often extended themselves well past legal boundaries that had been established by the Penn family. Their moves to less-populated areas allowed them to live their desired lifestyle and practice their religion unencumbered. However, it also meant they became a buffer between the rest of Pennsylvania and the Indians. This experience would prove to be valuable for them a few short years later.

Eventually, these Presbyterians continued to improve their lives by moving down the Great Wagon Road (see Chapter 1) to rich and fertile new areas in Virginia and the Carolinas.[10] This relocation put Andrew and Joseph on the road to their destiny and to that of America's independence from Britain.

1

The Early Days (1740–1765)

The Church of England began to subject the lowland Scottish Presbyterians to much religious persecution in the 16th century. In the 17th century, the oppressed Scottish were a part of the Plantation of Ulster. The Pickens family had followed Andrew Pickens' great-grandparents to Ireland in 1690. There Andrew's grandfather, William Henry Pickens, married Margaret Pike. They soon began a family that included Andrew Pickens, Sr. Those lowland Scottish, now called Scots-Irish (also Scotch-Irish), had received no rest from tyranny while in Ireland. Indeed, their torment was worsened by the actions of the Church of England.

Throughout the 18th century, as the Scots-Irish migrated to America, many settled in Pennsylvania. William Henry Pickens and his family were among those that arrived in the spring of 1719.

The Pennsylvania Scots-Irish Presbyterians had become a hardy group because of their experience in Europe. They were capable of forging a life in a new land and could skillfully defend themselves. In Pennsylvania, they had lived in a buffer zone between Indians and other settlers. That challenging situation further hardened them to their environment.

Fearsome as their ancestors the Border Reevers had been, these new Americans did not appear overly forbidding. They led a frugal and hardworking lifestyle. The men wore the same clothes for labor as for fighting. They dressed in homespun breeches and blouses with hand-tooled leather vests. Their boots were sturdy but often patched with ragged scraps. They discovered early that homemade leather moccasins were best worn to track game or scout potential threats in the forest. These settlers were a motley group that appeared harmless. Their foes, however, quickly learned that first impressions might be inaccurate.

The General Assembly of the Colony of Virginia established Frederick and Augusta Counties November 1, 1738. These counties were formally organized in 1745. Augusta had been formed from Orange County and bordered the Indian frontier. Virginia Lieutenant Governor Sir William Gooch (acting for absentee Royal Virginia Governor Willem Anne van Keppel, 2nd Earl of Albemarle) was familiar with the Scots-Irish. Gooch knew they were well-suited for this new land. Edmund Burke, 18th century British Parliamentarian, orator, political philosopher, and author of *Reflections on the Revolution in France*, described "their religion [as] a refinement on the principle of resistance; it was the dissidence of dissent—the Protestantism of the Protestant religion!" The text expanded on Burke's comment with, "They had crossed the ocean for expanded opportunity: for liberty of development, and the chance of a more rewarding work. Their sons after them kept their stern fidelity to this moral conviction, and that frugal, hardy, courageous temper, which came to them easily, as an ancestral inheritance."[1] Lieutenant Governor Gooch offered the Scots-Irish tempting incentives, mostly land, for them to settle, and these Scots-Irish accepted this opportunity to achieve their ideals.[2]

Many of these Pennsylvania Presbyterians began to move down the Great Wagon Road by the middle of the 18th century. The road was originally an Indian trail that cattlemen later used to drive stock from the backcountry to market in Pennsylvania. Andrew Pickens, Sr., and his wife, Nancy Ann, were a part of the Great Wagon Road migration. They and their children, Catherine, Joseph William, Andrew, daughter Jean, and John, arrived in Augusta County, Virginia, by 1740. Some family references indicate that there may have been two older sons, William and James, who presumably came at least as far as Augusta County with the family. The best verifications for the existence of these two sons are from the writings of Dr. A. L. Pickens in *Skyagunsta, The Border Wizard Owl*, and from the genealogical collection of Thomas Mason Monroe Pickens as recorded by Kate Pickens Day in *Cousin Monroe's History of the Pickens Family*. (See "Research Regarding William Pickens" in Appendix C.)

Gabriel, John, and Lucy (who had married John Kerr while in Pennsylvania) Pickens, three of Andrew Sr.'s siblings, arrived in Augusta County close to the same time. William, another brother, arrived sometime later. The remaining brother, Robert Pike Pickens, seems initially to have settled in Frederick County, Virginia.[3]

The relative ages of Andrew and Joseph Pickens have been incorrectly published in other historical volumes. Their birth dates (February 1, 1737, for Joseph and September 19, 1739, for Andrew) clearly show that Joseph was the older of the two; yet, it has been recently written that Joseph was the younger brother. This inaccuracy is widespread because Robert Andrew Pickens, a first cousin of Andrew and Joseph, declared in his 1833 interview with Lyman C. Draper, "General Piickens [sic] was the eldest son of Andrew, then Joseph and John."[4] Historians would not readily question Draper's writings because he is respected, well read, and widely cited. The information he recorded for posterity is valuable to researchers.

A later annotation states, "EDITOR's NOTE: ...He (Draper) was also mistaken about Andrew, the General being the oldest child of Andrew Pickens the pioneer. Bible records show that Capt. Joseph was the older."[5] This note indicates that Draper was the one mistaken. However, Robert Andrew's faulty recollection was the cause of the misinformation; an understandable error since he was 88 years old at the time of the interview and was some 15 years younger than Andrew and Joseph. Lyman C. Draper simply quoted the recollections of Robert Andrew verbatim, an acceptable recording practice used to preserve historical knowledge. (Robert Andrew Pickens was commonly known as Andrew Pickens; therefore, he will be hereafter designated as Robert Andrew Pickens to avoid confusion with General Andrew Pickens).

Contemporary historians would not likely question Robert Andrew's statement because Andrew Pickens quickly advanced to a colonel's rank at the height of the American Revolution, and later to general. Joseph was a captain by his death in 1781 and was often directly subordinate to Andrew in the Ninety Six Militia Regiment. This gave the appearance that Andrew was the older because it was common for younger brothers to hold a lower military rank. Regardless, the achieved ranks of Andrew and Joseph were direct results of their respective military capabilities and individual personalities, rather than their ages. While each was a respected leader of men, Andrew Pickens was an extraordinary bellwether and superb military tactician who could develop comprehensive battle plans on the fly. Joseph's leadership ability was also excellent but not quite as impressive as Andrew's. Joseph performed admirably as a captain because he could precisely follow a battle plan and effectively lead a company of men through an important military action. Andrew was patient and studious when faced with a challenge and could quickly rationalize the expected results. While Joseph capably made good decisions, he was more rash, brash, and inclined to charge in. (Their differing responsibilities and importance to the Revolutionary War in South Carolina is made obvious in the following chapters.)

The aforementioned interview shows that errors are not uncommon when an historian cites a source. The age difference between Andrew and Joseph is simply one of several examples of contemporary misinformation briefly covered within this book.

Referring to the interviewee, Robert Andrew Pickens, Draper records, "Andrew Pickens, now of Fayete [sic] County, Tennessee, born near Staunton, Virginia on December 10, 1753."[6] This is also later annotated by, "EDITOR's NOTE: ...Draper was mistaken on birth date of Andrew Pickens above, as being December 10, 1753. Pickens Bible records give the date as January 6, 1853."[7] The correction is interesting because Robert Andrew Pickens' birth date is actually January 6, 1753; thus, the annotation itself includes either a typographical error or was incorrectly recorded in the Bible. Pickens certainly could not have given an interview to Draper in 1833 if he had been born in 1853.

Civil records indicate that the Pickens family settled eight miles west of Beverly Mills Place, now Staunton, Virginia.[8] They worshipped at the Old Stone Presbyterian Church eight miles northeast of Staunton in what today is Fort Defiance, Virginia.[9] Catherine, the oldest daughter of Andrew, Sr., married Major William Davis there in 1747. (William Davis was a nephew of Nancy Ann Davis, wife of Andrew Pickens, Sr.)

The Staunton settlement likely not only contained the church, but also structures wherein blacksmiths, merchants, clerks, and other professional people labored. The goods sold in the stores were expensive; consequently, settlers made everything they possibly could. Their clothing was created from homespun materials as women had acquired the skills to weave, spin, and sew. Girls began early to contribute to such tasks, usually beginning by combing and dying flax. Women even made flannel hunting shirts and cotton hunting breeches for their men, and the men fashioned fringed leather jackets, breeches, moccasins, and leggings from deerskin. They often cast their own ammunition balls and created their own gunpowder. Only when absolutely necessary did the settlers purchase items on credit or borrow money for things they could neither make nor obtain in trade.[10]

New rituals were gradually introduced by immigrants and varied from one religious background to another. Some marriages were performed in the settlers' native languages; i.e., German and Dutch. The Quakers would marry themselves in their meetinghouses, using vows they had written. Catherine Pickens and William Davis would have published their banns in the Presbyterian Church to notify all villagers among the regional settlements, so they could attend the forthcoming wedding in the Old Stone Church. Subsequent festivities included a gathering at the parental home. A wedding celebration provided a rare opportunity for the staunch Scots-Irish to revel in a bit of merriment.[11]

Abstracts of Augusta County Virginia records show several entries for Andrew Pickens, Sr., and his brother John. They each served the county as Justice of the Peace. Additionally, Andrew served as coroner and road committee member while John also served as sheriff.[12] (See Appendix B for details of these appointments along with several land transactions and other civil actions.)

There has been conjecture as to when Andrew Pickens, Sr., relocated from Augusta County, Virginia, to the Waxhaws of the Carolinas. Some sources state he relocated in 1749[13] while others have written he did so in 1750.[14] General Andrew Pickens wrote in a letter to General Henry Lee in 1811, "My father removed with his family when I was very young to

Virginia ... and in the year 1752 or 3 removed to the Waxhaws and was amongst the first settlers of that part of South Carolina."[15]

Andrew Pickens, Sr., was heard at the New Berne, North Carolina, Council Chamber on October 1, 1751, regarding the purchase of an 800–acre farm in the Waxhaws, and a deed was recorded the same day at Wadesboro, Anson County, North Carolina.[16] Also, in the Augusta County abstracts mentioned above, it is recorded that Andrew Pickens, Sr., granted a power of attorney to William McPheeters in August of 1751, and then sold 400 acres to McPheeters in November. These events indicate that the physical transition likely took place no earlier than late 1751 or, at the very latest, early 1752.

On April 13, 1752, Pickens received an additional grant of 500 acres on the north side of Waxhaw Creek. The grant was recorded in Anson County, North Carolina, but appears to exist in what is now Lancaster County, South Carolina. Confusion about the locations of events in those days results from many changes to the border between the two Carolinas, so it is likely that Pickens owned property that crossed the border into each province. Livestock, tools and some furnishings were included in the 1752 acquisition.[17]

One of the first activities, indeed a necessity wherever the Scots-Irish relocated, was to organize a Presbyterian Church. The church in the Waxhaws was established in 1752, and the Old Waxhaw Presbyterian Church building was erected under the supervision of, and on land owned by, Andrew Pickens, Sr.[18]

Hugh McAden, a missionary evangelist, held the first meeting in the building on November 23, 1755. Robert Miller and his wife, Jean, then owned the property and deeded it to the Waxhaw congregation on March 9, 1758. Miller, who had been a Scottish school master, was called as the congregation's first minister.[19] (Jean Miller is Jean Pickens, the youngest daughter of Andrew Pickens, Sr., and a sister of Andrew and Joseph William Pickens. She deeded the property to the church one and one half years after her father's death).

Anson County was new when Andrew Pickens, Sr., arrived. Once again he was in the role of pioneer. He was immediately named to a committee to establish the site for the county's first courthouse, and he was one of the first county building commissioners.[20] His brothers, John Pickens, Sr., and Robert Pike Pickens, followed him from Virginia in October 1754.[21]

Andrew Pickens, Sr., was also named Captain of an Anson County colonial militia company.[22] A roster of this company in 1755 (see Appendix C) showed a William, a Joseph, and a John Pickens all single; also an Andrew Pickens that was married. (Refer to Appendix F for the Pickens family tree.)

It is important to correct conjecture surrounding the identities of the Pickenses that were listed on the roster. Some contemporaries have mistakenly surmised that the listed Joseph, John, and Andrew were all sons of Captain Andrew Pickens, Sr.; however, Joseph was the only one of these three to be his son. Pickens' son, John, was only ten years old at the time. Furthermore, his son Andrew was only fifteen and, while possibly old enough to join the militia, was not yet married as was the Andrew indicated on the roster.

There is an obvious choice for the John Pickens listed on the roster. Revolutionary War Captain John Pickens was eighteen in 1755, the son of John Pickens, Sr., and brother to Robert Andrew Pickens (the Andrew interviewed by Lyman C. Draper). This John was also the brother of Eleanor Baskin Pickens, a cousin to Andrew and Joseph Pickens, who became Joseph Pickens' wife.

The best option for the Andrew Pickens on this roster is the son of Robert Pike Pickens and brother of Revolutionary War Captain Robert Pickens. This Andrew was nineteen in 1755, had been married since 1753, and was also a cousin to Andrew and Joseph Pickens.

The identity of William, the only other Pickens on the roster, is more of a challenge. It is likely that William was an older son of Andrew Pickens, Sr. There is no record that he ever followed the family to Long Canes. William was killed early in the Revolutionary War; little information can be obtained regarding him. He probably fought for either the regular army or a militia unit from North Carolina. (See Appendix C for more information regarding William Pickens research.)

Andrew Pickens, Sr., must have been promoted to his final rank of Colonel in the colonial militia shortly after the issuance of the roster. He died within two years.[23]

In February of 1756, another important family to South Carolina's future arrived in the Waxhaws: brothers James, Ezekial, William, and Patrick Calhoun with their wives and children. Their sister, Mary, and their mother, Catherine, accompanied them. The Calhouns became an integral part of the Revolutionary War in the backcountry of South Carolina, and their lives intertwined so closely with the Pickenses that they became as one large family.[24] The two families remained very close for generations, and their descendants relocated westward together and settled in Missouri.

Andrew Pickens, Sr., authored a will dated November 5, 1756[25] (see Appendix B). He died shortly thereafter. His memorial in the old Waxhaw Presbyterian Church Cemetery bears the inscription:

TO THE MEMORY OF COL. ANDREW PICKENS SR. C. 1690–1756
AND WIFE ANN DAVIS PICKENS
PARENTS OF GEN. ANDREW PICKENS HERO OF THE REVOLUTION

He designated his wife, Nancy (Ann), and his son-in-law, William Davis, as his executors. He specifically left 551 acres of land to his sons, Andrew and Joseph, but also provided that Andrew would obtain land for John (the youngest of the children), at his earliest convenience. John Pickens, Sr., was among the witnesses to the signature of his brother, Andrew Pickens, Sr. Andrew also left livestock and other belongings to his wife and his youngest daughter, Jean. There is no mention of anything being left to Catherine, James, or William. As mentioned earlier, Catherine was already married, well established and had probably received any endowment he had planned for her. James may have already been deceased as mentioned by "Cousin" Monroe, and William was probably as established as Catherine. Jean was married near the time of her father's death, but probably a few months later. She was only sixteen and was included in his will, "And to my daughter JENA [JEAN], a black meare [mare] called Bonney and a saddle and bridle with all the other tinge [sic] called her property."

North Carolina Colonial Records show that "ANN PICKENS, widow of COL. ANDREW PICKENS, Sr., and Maj. William Davis presented an inventory of the estate of Col. PICKENS for record in the office of the Clerk of Court of Anson County in 1757, Col. PICKENS owned eight hundred acres of land along what is now the line between the two Carolinas." (See Appendix B for further details of the inventory.)

Joseph was nearly 20 years of age, and Andrew was barely 17 at the time of their father's death. John, the youngest brother, was 11 years old. The death of their father put a burden of responsibility upon young Joseph and Andrew. They were now to be the male role models for, and the supporters of, their mother and younger siblings.

Andrew, Sr., provided for his wife, Nancy Ann, "all ye benefits of ye plantation and all ye movables thereon during her life: and after her departure to be ye property of my son

Andrew." This mention of his wife and the plantation could account for the difference of what was initially purchased and finally granted; i.e., 551 specific acres mentioned in the will plus 800 acres mentioned in the inventory. The remaining acreage may have included the estate house. Whatever Nancy Ann received was specified to go to Andrew following her death. Therefore, it was likely not the exact same property left to Andrew outright. As discussed earlier, Jean had later given some of the land to the church, so possibly Nancy Ann provided some land for Jean after she was married.

Andrew, exceptionally well-provided-for in the will, had received more land from his father than did Joseph, but he also received more responsibility. The will expressly provided Andrew 300 of the 551 acres willed to the two brothers, and left Andrew bound to secure a land interest for John. Andrew learned well from his father. He must have been an exceptional 17-year-old, and Andrew, Sr., had apparently recognized his aptitude for leadership and propensity for reliability.

Andrew and Joseph enjoyed great wealth with their inherited acreage; however, it was not likely that much of the land had been cleared. Settlers cleared land by girdling the trees. The farmer would cut a notch in the bark around the tree. That piece would be pulled off, causing the tree to no longer grow sprouts, and causing all the small limbs to become decayed. The farmer would plant a new sprout where the sunlight filtered through the branches. In time the remains of the dead tree would meet the ax and ultimately be burned. If the farmer had a team of oxen, the stumps would be pulled from the earth; otherwise, they would rot in the field.

If a farm had no age-old hedges or prominent ditches to define its boundaries, the farmer might erect a post-and-rail fence that would be strong enough to pen a pig and contain a bull. Because it would have been improbable to fence animals in, the farmer instead would fence in his crops to keep livestock out. A post-and-rail fence consisted of vertical posts that were inserted into the ground. They were then nailed with cross beams. The construction of such fencing was time-consuming, laborious, and costly. Other farmers determined that post-and-rail construction was not worth the effort. Instead they adopted the puncheon (split rail) zigzag fence designed in the Chesapeake region. The puncheons would be crisscrossed over one another in a snake-like formation. This necessitated only a slanted post at each intertwined corner to hold them fast. Such fencing was much easier to make, required little skill in the making, went up quickly, was enduring, and was effortless to repair or reassemble.

Few farm tools were available as Joseph and Andrew worked their acreage. They would have been fortunate enough to have a number of plows, as well as sufficient oxen or horses to pull the plows. They used hoe, shovel, and mattock to cultivate their land. They also had slaves to work the fields, and any available family members were to help.

Pickens, as did every farmer, planted corn and the family used the entire plant as a basic necessity. Corn was not only used for cooking and eating; its stalks fed the livestock in winter. Cornhusks were used to stuff mattresses, and corncobs were especially useful for making handles for gardening implements and hand tools. They were also used to create bowls for corncob pipes and to stop jugs and bottles. Other crops consisted of wheat, millet, flaxseed, and tobacco, as well as root vegetables for the family's larder. Some of their crops were exported to the coast along with other produce, such as, wheat, cornmeal (created by pounding dried corn with a hominy block), butter and tallow.[26]

It has been shown that Andrew, Sr., had many civic responsibilities, so it is likely that Andrew, Jr., managed a major portion of the family farm at his tender age. Joseph also was responsible to oversee a smaller and less critical portion of the enterprise. Andrew and Joseph, being close-knit, would have counseled together and discussed major decisions under the watchful eye of their father. Their training and responsibility would later serve the Pickens brothers well, albeit on a much larger scale, in the service of South Carolina and America, in the Revolutionary War.

Andrew and Joseph were not only extremely devoted to one another, but were also very close to their uncle, Robert Pike Pickens, whom they greatly respected.[27] He was available as a trusted source of advice for the brothers after Andrew, Sr.'s death. Robert Pike Pickens' example was also an important factor in their development as they progressed toward their destiny.

Others had begun to recognize Andrew's ability to rationally solve problems. He was extremely bright despite a lack of formal education, and family tradition indicates there were plans for him to eventually have attended college. Those plans, of course, were out of the question after his father's death. Andrew wrote over 50 years later, "As I was raised on the frontiers of New Settlement and my father dying when I was young, I had not an opportunity of receiving even a good english education."[28]

Although Andrew and Joseph were propelled into an early maturity, they were not alone. Throughout history, many young frontiersmen shared similar situations that thrust them into the role of family leader. It was a matter of survival. Important traits for responsible men of any age were trustworthiness and accountability. Rough backgrounds and tough experiences amounted to training grounds for many men who led the fight to secure independence from Britain.

One of the advantages that Andrew had over Joseph, and a reason for his expanded responsibility at an early age, was his ability to focus. He was extremely serious-minded, portrayed as an uncommonly dour man who never smiled, who kept to himself, and who engaged in little discourse.[29] Indeed, at times Andrew needed to counsel and gently chide his older brother to correct his manner. Civil War General Robert E. Lee wrote:

> He [Andrew] was a sincere believer in the Christian religion, and a devout observer of the Presbyterian form of worship. His frame was sinewy and active; his habits were simple, temperate, and industrious. His characteristics were taciturnity and truth, prudence and decision, modesty and courage, disinterestedness and public spirit.[30]

Andrew's seriousness is often described as shyness. However, while Andrew was quiet and brief with his opinions during the war, he was far from timid. None misunderstood the intent of his words when he did speak.

The Calhoun family did not stay in the Waxhaws very long. They became the pioneers of a new area. They established Long Canes in 1758, the first major settlement in the Ninety Six District near present-day Abbeville, South Carolina. Long Canes was located on the border between South Carolina and the Cherokee Nation. The Calhouns' relocation was important to the Pickenses who followed them a few years later.[31]

The Cherokee Indians who frequented the area resided mainly in their "lower villages" of northwest South Carolina. Their towns were located along the headwaters of the Savannah and Chattahoochee Rivers. The Cherokee were numerous; they covered an area from these lower villages to "over mountain" villages located in the Tennessee Appalachians. One of the nearest of the lower villages to Ninety Six was Keowee, located along the Keowee River and considered the gateway to Cherokee country.[32]

The name of Ninety Six appears on a 1744 land grant to Thomas Brown. The grant describes the land as located "96 miles from the Cherokee Nation." A portion of this land later became the site of the village called Ninety Six. Brown died in 1747. In 1749, the land passed by grant to William Livingston and then through the ownership of John Hamilton who sold to William Simpson and Dr. John Murray in 1755.[33]

In the 1750s the community amounted to scattered homesteads that extended for several miles. One of the early settlers, Andrew Williamson, became a military leader and was important to the military progression of Andrew Pickens. Williamson worked as a cattle drover for John Murray in those early days.

In 1751, Robert Gouedy, who had traded with the Cherokee for many years, saw an opportunity to settle just south of Murray's land. Considered the halfway point between Charles Town and Keowee, this was obviously a prime location for a trading post, and Gouedy was up to the task. In 1753, he constructed what became one of the most popular trading posts of that era. There for 22 years he supplied cloth, tools, gunpowder, lead, rum, sleeping accommodations, and meals to soldiers, Indians, slaves, settlers and even representatives of the British colonial government. Many passed through Ninety Six on their way to or from Charles Town and the Cherokee villages.[34]

In October 1753, South Carolina Royal Governor James Glen laid out a fort to be built on land ceded by the Cherokee. It was built on the Cherokee Path and was located across the Keowee River from the village of Keowee. (The original site is submerged under present-day Lake Keowee created in 1971.)

The structure was called Fort Prince George in honor of the young prince who would soon become King George III. The Cherokee had requested the fort for protection from the French and Iroquois, and they had promised to assist the British with its construction. This gave the British an opportunity to further their own interests in the Cherokee Nation, and to strengthen bonds with a potentially necessary ally.

Governor Glen visited the Cherokee in person to arrange for the fort. Most of his dealings were with Attakulla Kulla (Little Carpenter, so named for his skill at crafting treaty language acceptable to all) who, along with Oconostota, Old Tassel, and Savanooka, was a principle chief of the Cherokee. Chief Attakulla Kulla was a great diplomat and was second in authority only to War Chief Oconostota (his uncle and father-in-law). The Royal Governor's good judgement was manifested in his desire to maintain friendly relations with the tribe. He was well-respected by the Cherokee, and he was joined by War Chief Chuloch-Culla[35] who told him: "What I now speak the Great King should hear. We are brothers to the people of South Carolina, one house covers all.... We freely surrender a part of our lands to the Great King. These [meaning a bow and arrows he showed to Governor Glen] are all the arms we can make for our defense." The chief then thanked the British for helping defend the Cherokee Nation. Chief Chuloch-Culla formally ceded land that would later form the counties of Edgefield, Abbeville, Laurens, Newberry, Union, Spartanburg, York, Chester, Fairfield, and Richland. This ceded land formed a strict border that the Cherokee were not to cross without permission. This transfer of land was important for establishing the Long Canes settlement.[36]

When the Calhouns and others settled Long Canes, Patrick Calhoun, deputy surveyor for the settlement, set his family property up on the Cherokee side of Long Canes Creek in disregard of Governor Glen's agreement.

A parallel event at that time was the French and Indian War (known to Britain as the Seven Years' War based on the time of Britain's actual declaration of war against France).[37] Many disputes between French and British settlers had occurred in the northern colonies since 1744 that resulted in various pitched battles between the rivals for control of North

America. The French and their northern Indian allies fought with an alliance of the British army, local American militias, and the Cherokee from the South Carolina backcountry.[38]

In 1753, French forces began to build a string of forts in the north, including Fort Duquesne in the Ohio Valley. George Washington, under the flag of Virginia Colony, approached the French and demanded they withdraw from the Ohio Valley and leave Virginia alone. The French refused this demand, and Washington observed that the French were, indeed, planning incursions deeper into the south.

On May 28, 1754, Washington led a militia to defeat a small band of French soldiers in the Ohio Valley. This is considered the first action of the French and Indian War, although it would not be officially declared for another two years. After the defeat, Washington retreated a few miles and built Fort Necessity to face a rebuttal from a much larger French army regiment. He lost Fort Necessity to the French July 3, 1754, and resigned after he was criticized for the loss. He later returned as Commander-in-Chief of the Virginia Militia. Ever since Washington lost Fort Necessity, Virginia Lieutenant Governor Robert Dinwiddie consistently pushed for the British army to force the French from Fort Duquesne.

Braddock's Defeat occurred shortly after a force of 1,500 British and American troops (from Virginia, Maryland, North and South Carolina) finally answered Dinwiddie's call. They marched from Will's Creek in Maryland under General Edward Braddock in late June 1755. On July 9, they forded Monongahela River at the forks with the Allegheny and Ohio Rivers and began the last leg of seven miles to the fort. An enemy force of 500 Indians (Ottawa, Miami, Huron, Delaware, Shawnee and Mingo) and 30 French colonial troops ambushed and routed them. The losses were staggering; 26 officers killed and 37 wounded, while 430 soldiers were killed and 385 wounded. This was enough to cause the Virginians around Staunton to construct Fort Defiance, an action typical of other backcountry communities.

Churchgoers fortified the Old Stone Presbyterian Church, in late July of 1755, and they came to church services heavily armed. They named the fortification Fort Defiance. The worshippers were confident they could defend themselves against the French, and especially against any of the northern Indian allies to the French. This was three and one-half years after the Pickens family left for the Waxhaws.

Britain officially declared war against France on May 18, 1756. On August 8, 1757, the French captured Fort William Henry from the British as depicted in James Fenimore Cooper's *The Last of the Mohicans.*

Britain's Cherokee allies returned home to South Carolina after the surrender of Quebec on September 13, 1759. While passing through Virginia, they stole a number of horses from a group of settlers who then pursued and killed twelve Cherokee. Shortly thereafter, some Cherokee braves declared vengeance for their slain brothers. The Cherokee were already upset with the British because of boundary violations, such as the location of Patrick Calhoun's family plot. Many Cherokee braves went on the warpath and killed fourteen settlers near the Catawba River and three on the upper Broad River.[39]

The primary Cherokee chiefs of the lower villages tried to calm the braves and sent a 24-man delegation to Charles Town to reconcile with South Carolina. Governor William Henry Lyttleton, not as adept at dealing with the Cherokee as was his predecessor, imprudently imprisoned the delegation and began to plan an incursion into the Cherokee Nation. Lyttleton was not nearly as charitable toward the Cherokee as was Governor Glen; he saw no value in befriending the tribe, so the effort to strengthen the British/Cherokee alliance took a reversal. The Cherokee delegation asked that two of their number be allowed to return to the Cherokee Nation while the rest remained as hostages. Governor Lyttleton sent the remaining Cherokee braves to Lieutenant Richard Coytmore, commander of Fort Prince George.

The Cherokee held no reverence for Coytmore, so Chief Oconostota decided to rescue the remaining prisoners. He surrounded the fort and set a trap by sending a Cherokee woman to Coytmore with a message that Oconostota wished a parley. Coytmore, accompanied by Lieutenants Bell and Foster, went to meet Oconostota who signaled some hidden braves. The braves attacked and killed Coytmore and wounded his two companions. At the same time, a scuffle erupted within the fort as the garrison tried to manacle the prisoners. Three of the guards were stabbed. The garrison slew the remaining Cherokee prisoners.[40]

Governor Lyttleton marched his state troops into Ninety Six on November 21, 1759. He stayed at Ninety Six for one week and ordered construction of a fort (a ninety-foot square stockade) to be erected around Gouedy's barn. Though called Fort Ninety Six, it was not at the exact site of the Fort Ninety Six later built at the eponymous village that figured prominently in the American Revolution.[41]

On January 19, 1760, Cherokee braves avenged the deaths of the Fort Prince George prisoners when they brutally slaughtered 24 traders near the Long Canes settlement.

On the 30th, two Indian women from Fort Prince George came to Fort Ninety Six and warned of an impending Cherokee attack. Two traders stopped later that day with the same warning.[42] The infamous Long Canes Massacre occurred on February 1, 1760.[43] The Long Canes settlers, wearied by the Indian threat, decided to vacate their homes and head for Augusta. One hundred-fifty settlers, including the Calhouns, took wagons loaded with families and personal effects and crossed Long Canes Creek near present-day Troy, South Carolina. During the crossing, several wagons became mired. One hundred Cherokee braves suddenly surprised the settlers, and a half-hour battle ensued. Several settlers were killed before survivors were able to scramble away. A number of children had been lost during the escape; some were severely wounded and left for dead by the Cherokee. Eight survived, including some who had been scalped.

(The original practice of scalping was not done to obtain trophies. It amounted to a spiritual practice that was rarely used. When an enemy's scalp was taken, the Cherokee believed he lost control of his soul and became socially and spiritually dead. The Europeans bastardized the practice in prelude to the French and Indian War as the settlers and soldiers of the two countries began to scalp each other, and each other's Indian allies. They eventually offered bounties for enemy scalps. The promise of bounties caused the practice to grow between whites and Indians alike; among the tribes, scalping then became something different than its original spiritualistic practice, and trophies were collected.)

Fourteen-year-old Rebecca Calhoun, daughter of Ezekial, successfully hid herself in some reeds during the massacre, and later in a calico or kalmia bush. From there, she watched the slaughter and saw her Grandmother, Catherine Calhoun, murdered and scalped. A visitor from Ninety Six reported to the *South Carolina Gazette*:

> Yesterday se'nnight the whol [sic] of the *Long-Cane* Settlers, to the Number of 150 souls, moved off with most of their Effects in Waggons; to go towards Augusta in *Georgia*, and in a few Hours after their setting off, were surprized and attacked by about 100 *Cherokees* on Horseback, while they were getting their Waggons out of a boggy Place: They had amongst them 40 Gunmen, who might have made a very good Defence, but unfortunately their Guns were in the Waggons; the few that recovered theirs, fought the *Indians* Half an Hour, and were at last obliged to fly: In the action they lost 7 Waggons, and 40 of their People killed or taken (including Women and Children) the Rest got safe to Augusta.[44]

A few days later, Patrick Calhoun led a group of settlers to bury the dead. The group managed to rescue the surviving children, including Rebecca. Two years after they had departed to settle in Long Canes, the remaining Calhoun family members returned to the Waxhaws where Andrew Pickens met young Rebecca Calhoun.

On February 3, 1760, 30 Cherokee attacked old Fort Ninety Six which was defended by some 45 South Carolina militiamen. After an exchange of gunfire, two braves were killed and the warriors departed. Robert Gouedy's home and outbuildings had been burned, but the fort was not harmed. Thirty of the garrison became afflicted with smallpox shortly after the conflict. By this time, approximately 12 defensive fortifications had been erected throughout the Ninety Six District.

On March 3, 1760, two traders from Fort Prince George warned the Ninety Six garrison of an estimated 300 warriors encamped nearby. Two hundred braves then attacked the fort. The battle lasted for nearly 36 hours. On March 6, soldiers explored the grounds and found six dead warriors. Various bloody conflicts with the Cherokee continued throughout the remainder of the year.[45]

In the Waxhaws, on September 1, 1760, Joseph William Pickens married his first cousin, Eleanor Baskin Pickens. Joseph was 23 years old; Eleanor was three months shy of 14. Andrew Pickens was 21 years old at the time. The brothers had matured into fine young men. They were tall for that era; Andrew having stood shy of six feet and Joseph a bit shorter. They were each lean, sinewy, agile and strong, yet not muscle-bound. Joseph was somewhat stockier than Andrew. Their bodies were toned by years of grueling farm work, and they each had considerable endurance. Andrew usually tied his shoulder-length hair neatly in a queue while Joseph tended to let his hang freely. Each of the brothers was known for honesty, tenacity, and sincerity, and each was held above reproach.

Andrew was blunt and did not mince words. His stern gaze when added to his speech let one know right away his thinking and his intentions. The recipient of such a stare might easily think that Andrew was reading his mind or accessing the depths of his soul. However, terse as Andrew's communications were, he was rarely mean or thoughtless with them; indeed, he rarely raised his voice above his normal speech level. Joseph was not as controlled and could tongue-lash with the best of them.[46]

On October 25, 1760, King George II died and his grandson, King George III, attained the throne. He was the "King George" of the American Revolutionary War era.

In January 1761, the South Carolina General Assembly and acting Governor William Bull decided to establish a new regiment of Royal Provincial Militia under Colonel Thomas Middleton. The organizers were told the militia must be structured before any British regular troops could be dispatched to help in the South Carolina backcountry. Included in this regiment were Lieutenant Colonel Henry Laurens, Major John Moultrie, Captain William Moultrie, Lieutenant Isaac Huger, Lieutenant Francis Marion, and Captain Andrew Pickens.[47] (Bull acted for Thomas Pownall who had been appointed in April of 1760 but did not take office. Governor Thomas Boone would be appointed and take office December 22, 1761.)

Joseph Pickens became a volunteer private. He and Andrew were close and shared the same ideals. They were to fight together several times throughout the Revolutionary War, and Joseph was often subordinate to his younger brother. Since Andrew was single, and Joseph and Eleanor did not have any children at that time, the brothers lacked some of the family distractions that could complicate involvement in the Royal Provincial Militia.

Colonel Middleton's regiment provided the first military action for Andrew and Joseph, and it was not surprising that the Pickens brothers became involved. Their father had set an early example for them when he captained a North Carolina colonial peacekeeping militia.

It was common for males on the frontier to become proficient in the use of firearms and to ably conceal themselves amid their surroundings when hunting or defending themselves from danger. Andrew and Joseph were proud of the freedoms they had acquired since their father had come to the colonies. Their father and uncles had taught them to hunt and fish for the majority of their food. They thrived on venison, squirrel, 'possum, rabbit, duck, geese, and quail. In rare spurts of leisure time, they even made targets and practiced their shooting. They enjoyed competing with one another to see who could accomplish the first kill when hunting.

They were eager to defend the settlements especially since their friends, the Calhouns, had been back in the Waxhaws for almost one year. Andrew and Joseph had received firsthand accounts of the massacre, and the young men desired to avenge their friends and to help ensure the Calhouns could resettle on their Long Canes property.

Andrew's appointment to captain in a state-level Royal militia at 21 years of age is indicative of the respect he had already earned. It bears witness that he had become the responsible and trustworthy individual his father believed him to be, and that he was adept with firearms. It is also further evidence that Andrew was not as bashful as some have written. His quiet demeanor has been mistaken for reticence in some contemporary texts, but is more the result of his seriousness and complete focus on responsibility. He would not have been chosen to lead a company of men at his age if he were extremely bashful; however, his quiet and serious aura would definitely have been a positive asset.

Andrew Pickens wrote to Henry Lee: "During the War with the Cherokees in 1761 and 2, I was young, fond of a gun and an active life and was much out in that war, was entructed [sic] for some time with a small detachment of men on the frontier, where the inhabitants had been driven from their newly settled plantations."[48]

Before Colonel Middleton completed the militia regiment, British Lieutenant Colonel James Grant came to Charles Town with 1200 British regulars. He began to march up the Cherokee Path with the regulars and the partially-filled South Carolina Militia. They slowly added troops and gathered supplies as they went. Lieutenant Colonel Grant arrived at Moncks Corner in late March and dispatched Major John Moultrie to establish a base at Fort Ninety Six, gather more supplies, and reinforce the stockade.[49]

Well into spring, while Andrew and Joseph were off on the expedition, a severe tornado formed near Kings Mountain, moved through the Waxhaws, and caused significant damage. The estate house of Andrew, Sr., was so completely destroyed that hardly a shingle was ever found. The house was torn off its pillars and demolished. Several women were at the house, including Andrew's mother and another elderly woman, though none was badly injured. They had likely taken cover in a root cellar, a common practice during times of danger. The house was located approximately two miles from the home of Robert Pike Pickens.[50]

On May 14, 1761, the Grant Expedition arrived at Fort Ninety Six. The fort had been previously reinforced and was defended by some 400 South Carolina rangers. This brought Lieutenant Colonel Grant's complete force to 3000 men, including British regulars and provincials, South Carolina militiamen and rangers, Indian guides and wagoners. Grant, who began his march toward Fort Prince George on the 18th, left Captain Daniel to lead a fifty-man defensive garrison at Fort Ninety Six.[51]

When Grant marched the expedition into Fort Prince George on May 27, 1761, he found the fort badly deteriorated. He erected a stockade and established a headquarters; then, Grant tried to arrange a peace talk with the Cherokee, but he failed. The Cherokee had begun to work themselves into a frenzy in preparation for war.[52]

On June 7, Grant set out across the Keowee River for the lower villages of the Cherokee. Thus began what was locally known as the Grant Indian War.[53] He found the villages abandoned, marched further into the Cherokee Nation, and on the 10th was ambushed by countless warriors in a narrow valley. The Cherokee had concentrated on the provincial forces that guarded pack animals laden with food and supplies. Lieutenant Francis Marion led 30 riflemen to drive off the Indians. Grant then decided to leave the pack animals under guard of a detachment, so he could rapidly move through the middle villages of the Cherokee. Grant's force burned villages for one month and destroyed whatever crops and stock it could not use. The Cherokee's current foe had previously been their only ally, so the Indians began to despair. In the end, several braves had been killed, and the remainder were driven to the over mountain villages. Grant reported, "All the Indians of the middle, lower, and back settlements are drove into the mountains to starve."[54]

Henry Laurens. Portrait artist: J.S. Copley; sketch artist: W.G. Armstrong; engraver: T.B. Welch, 1862.

Fifty years later Andrew Pickens wrote to General Lee of the experience: "I served as a volunteer in Grant's expedition against the Cherokees in the year 1762 [actually 1761]. There I learned someting [sic] of British cruelty which I always abhorred."[55]

Andrew's first action hadn't amounted to much of a war, but the experience he gained concerning the Indians would be valuable later. Andrew proved in years to come that he was capable of fighting the Cherokee when required to protect the settlements; however, he thought highly of the Cherokee and earned their respect for the fairness he so often exhibited. This is evidenced in Andrew Pickens' letter to General Lee as he described an action covered in a later chapter:

> To endeavor to put a stop to the cruel murder of women and children which had been long practiced both by the white people and the Indians in their war on each other I issued positive orders that no Indian woman, child or old man or any unfit to bear arms should be put to death on pain of death of the perpetrator, giving at the same time the object I hoped to obtain by it. This order was readily obeyed and the Indians soon followed the example.
>
> In two excursions which I made into the Indian country while Genl Green was in the lower part of the state I took a number of prisoners the last which I made into the Cherokee Country was a little before the British evacuated Charlestown. There were a great many desperate white men with the Indians who had taken refuge amongst them and encouraged them on their mur-

derous excursions.... After surprising the town and making [sic] the prisoners in the evening I sent out three of the most active Indian men that we had taken and told them to go tell their people that I was there, that I did not blame the Indians so much as the white men that was amongst them, I would go no further nor destroy any more of their towns and would release all their prisoners on their delivering to me all their prisoners they had of ours including the Negroes they had taken, that I would remain there two days and that if they refused to comply I would proceed and as far as I could I would destroy as many of their towns and as much of their provisions as possible and if they wished to fight they knew where to find me.

The next day they sent in a flag, they said they had heard my talk and would comply with my demands.

Grant's army entrenched at Fort Prince George for the remainder of summer, and then returned to Fort Ninety Six. Grant gave his men ample liberty to rest and recuperate. During that time, Andrew Pickens visited the Long Canes area to plan for his future home. He later returned to the Waxhaws where he was able to renew his friendship with the Calhouns, especially with Rebecca.

It was recently written that the purpose of Andrew's visit to Long Canes was to see the Calhouns. However, the Calhouns had left Long Canes at the time of the massacre one and a half years earlier, and they were not to return from the Waxhaws for another one and a half years.

Andrew was 22 and Rebecca, 15. The two spent much time together in the Waxhaws comparing notes about their experiences with the Cherokee. He spoke of the cruelties he had witnessed on the expedition, and she explained what she had seen during the massacre. They shared a strong religious commitment to Presbyterianism and family. Andrew was doubtlessly impressed with Rebecca's sweetness and beauty. Rebecca, in turn, found Andrew similar in character and demeanor to her Uncle Patrick, to whom she was very close. Before long, their friendship became an "understanding."

Courtship between the two dedicated Scots-Irish Presbyterians did not involve barn dances or the like. Rather they took frequent long walks along the river or through the woods. At 15, Rebecca was hardly a child. Since the tender age of 10, she had regularly performed such tasks as spinning, dying wool, weaving, knitting, mending, candle making, and food preparation and cooking. Rebecca probably enjoyed pointing out various natural herbs and berries and telling Andrew of their practical utility and benefits. Andrew, in turn, may have scoped out paw prints and spores along the way. He may have identified various birdsongs to Rebecca. Each had great regard for the other. They had serious and very proper discussions about their faith; contemplated their future together, discussed marriage and children, and pondered what might lie ahead with the Cherokee (now that Andrew had taken an active role in the defense of the settlers). A formal arrangement of a marriage between the two by their elders would not have occurred, as had been practiced in the not too distant past, but a tacit approval would have been absolutely necessary. In their case such approval was no problem as both families were of like mind regarding religion and politics. Andrew had fully influenced the Calhoun family with his diffidence and responsible behavior. His own uncles were likewise impressed with him since he had been a teenager with the mental and physical strength, as well as the tenacity and maturity, of a proper Presbyterian adult. Indeed, the Calhouns and the Pickens families were so closely knit that they were already bound as if related. Andrew's and Rebecca's "understanding" had a capital "U."

On December 18, 1761, Cherokee Chief Attakulla Kulla signed a treaty with the South Carolina Royal Province and agreed to surrender all British property and captives from the conflict while he allowed the British to erect forts wherever they deemed necessary, even on Cherokee land. No Cherokee would be permitted to enter the settlements more than 40 miles from Keowee without permission or without being under escort. Additionally, it was agreed to reestablish trade between the Cherokee and the British. Apparently, the alliance between the two had been resurrected.

On June 20, 1761, the Cherokee fulfilled their commitment by taking their white captives to Fort Ninety Six where they were exchanged for Cherokee prisoners that had been held in Charles Town.[56]

On June 23, 1762, Charles, Earl Cornwallis died in England. At this time his son, Brevet Lieutenant-Colonel Charles Cornwallis, who had fought in the French and Indian War, became the 2nd Earl Cornwallis. He also was advanced to the House of Lords; he had earlier been elected to the House of Commons and took that seat in January of 1760.

The Treaty of Paris, signed on February 10, 1763, ended the French and Indian War. Cornwallis returned to England and began the settlement of his father's vast estate. This apparently took considerable time. Some of the settlement is mentioned in a 1764 issue of *The London Chronicle* (see Appendix G for the complete text):

> To be sold at Auction by Mr. PRESTAGE,
> On the PREMISES,
> On Wednesday the 28th of November instant,
> Punctually at One o'Clock.
>
> A substantial, large, and well-built Brick House belonging to the Right Hon. EARL CORNWALLIS, deceased, situated in Hill street, Berkeley Square. Containing three large Rooms on a Floor, elegantly fitted up with Statuary and other Marble Chimney Pieces, rich carved Ornaments, exceeding good Offices, Coach Houses for three Carriages, and Stabling for eight Horses, a large Kitchen, Laundry, and Wash-house, at a proper Distance from the House, with several Fixtures thereunto belonging.... Likewise on Thursday the 29th Instant, and the following Day, will be sold all the genuine and rich HOUSEHOLD FURNITURE; consisting of Genoa Damask, Mohair, and other Furniture, French Chairs, Sophas, large Pier, and other Glasses, Variety of Mahogany in Presles, Book Cases, Tables, and Chairs, Marble Tables, Screens, Carpets, and a large Quantity of Kitchen Furniture.[57]

Also in early 1763, since the Cherokee uprising had been quelled, the Calhouns returned to Long Canes and brought many other settlers with them, including some of the Pickens family. Andrew asked Patrick Calhoun to survey a plot for him in Long Canes, and presumably one for Joseph also. The Pickens brothers had business to tend to before they could relocate.[58]

At Mecklenburg County, North Carolina, it is recorded in Deed Book 2, page 213:

> DEED: Andrew and Joseph Pickens, both of Mecklenburg, Co N.C. convey to Robert and Joseph Crawford of the same county and state.... Andrew and Joseph Pickens, heirs of the estate of ANDREW PICKENS, ESQ., deceased ... for 30 pounds ... 551 acres, by virtue of the last will and testament of the above mentioned Andrew Pickens, Esq. beginning at a hickory on north side of Waxhaw Creek, etc. ... with house, orchards, fields, meadows, water and water courses, etc.... Witnesses: Robert McClenachan and John Bogg.
> Signed ANDREW PICKENS
> JOSEPH PICKENS.
> Date: March 4, 1763

On August 18, 1763, Andrew Pickens bought 250 acres on Long Canes Creek 20 miles west of Ninety Six. His brother, Joseph Pickens, and his uncle, Robert Pike Pickens, also purchased land nearby.

There is a gap of almost six months between the sale of the land in the Waxhaws and the purchase in Long Canes. Part of the delay for Joseph's and Andrew's move may be attributed to their mother's ill health. She died no later than the end of 1763.

There is evidence that some Cherokee regularly made it their practice to break the treaty and enter the Long Canes settlement to steal stock. In October 1764, it was recorded in *The London Chronicle* (see Appendix G):

> By letters from Fort Boone at Long-Canes we are informed, that on the 24th past Capt. Calhoun [Patrick], of the Rangers, received information from two Cherokee Indians, that they had discovered some Indians, which they took for Creeks, with two horses, at some distance. Capt. Calhoun immediately dispatched his Lieutenant, with a party, accompanied by one of the Indian Informants as a guide; they soon came up with an Indian camp, round which, as there was nobody in it, they placed themselves in ambush, in order to seize the Indians on their return, which happened soon after, when the Lieutenant took and made prisoner the head of the gang, who, to his great surprise, proved to be a Cherokee from Toogoloo [sic], as were likewise the seven others with him: The Lieutenant took the horses, which he knew to be the property of one of the inhabitants near Long-Canes. We are told a very shameful traffick has been carried on with the Indians for horses, which they are induced to steal in the settlements.[59]

Earlier in 1764, Patrick Calhoun had been made Captain over a company of rangers sent to Long Canes by the Royal South Carolina government specifically to protect the settlers against just such Indian activity.[60]

Andrew and Rebecca continued their courtship and married on March 19, 1765, at the home of Ezekial Calhoun. Rebecca's Uncle, Justice of the Peace William Calhoun, performed the ceremony. (William had lost two daughters who were kidnapped during the Long Canes Massacre.) Theirs was the largest wedding party that had ever been assembled in the backcountry, and the festivities lasted uninterrupted for three days. The entire Pickens clan and their neighbors congregated to share an elegant supper which consisted of roasted venison, turkey, goose, quail, and bear meat, along with corn pudding, succotash, pumpkin, baked breads, and apples, pears and plums. The women also provided berries, peaches and jams they had preserved in summer. Beer and cider were served, as well as brandy made from harvested fruit.

The women baked for days and proudly served their cakes and pies. Adult family members and guests enjoyed singing, dancing, and card playing, while the children exhausted themselves with various games of sport and fun. The celebration was remembered as the event of the decade, and some locals actually marked their calendars for years by that event.[61]

The population in the Ninety Six District was increasing. Dr. John Murray sold 400 acres of his land to John Savage in 1767. Savage later sold ten acres to be divided into lots where the village of Ninety Six would stand, near Gouedy's trading post (the location of the original Fort Ninety Six).[62]

As the population increased, so did the criminal element and the lawlessness. In 1896, the Cowpens Centennial Committee quoted an unidentified writer about Andrew Pickens, "A beautiful and devoted wife; a cheerful fireside; peace and plenty about him — what more could a man crave? All this he was soon called upon to forego, and take the field, fighting for what he conceived to be duty and right."[63] Andrew Pickens, along with his Scots-Irish Presbyterian neighbors, was soon to become directly involved in the affairs of the backcountry.

2

Edging Toward War (1765–1775)

By late 1765, the future appeared promising for the Pickens family. Andrew had recently wed, and Joseph had been married for five years. The Cherokee had signed a peace treaty with South Carolina in 1761. The Seven Years War was over. The Pickenses and Calhouns, among others, had settled comfortably at Long Canes, and the entire backcountry had remained serene for some time. However, changes were coming.

The settlers in the lowcountry had begun to express anti–British sentiment. The lowcountry was primarily made up of plantations that held a large plurality of black slaves. The plantation owners, called "Rice Kings," looked upon themselves as aristocrats on a par with the nobility of England, but the British elite looked upon the Rice Kings simply as lowly colonists.

Produce, especially rice, indigo, beef, lumber, fur, and tobacco from the coast, was conveyed on British ships and sold in England. The coastal residents, in turn, purchased such necessities as apparel, paper, tea, tools for applied trades, silver, and weapons that were transported to the colonies by the same vessels on their return trip. Problems developed when England decided to recoup the cost of the French and Indian War by taxing some of the goods they exported to America. In addition, revenue was needed to further sustain the British army within the colonies. It would have been irrational to reduce the size of the army; many aristocratic officers would have had to return to England without prospects of positions, thus without means of support. The British people would not agree to finance a standing army within England's borders. Therefore, the British decided to maintain an active army within the American colonies (claiming colonial protection obligations) that would primarily be funded by colonial taxation.

Britain first resorted to the Stamp Act on March 22, 1765. The Stamp Act, to take effect in November of 1765, would require that printed materials in the colonies be produced on paper from London papermakers and would bear an embossed revenue stamp. The affected printed materials would include legal documents, magazines, newspapers and many other types of paper used throughout the colonies. This method of taxation was successful within Great Britain as it generated considerable revenue with little collection expense. The system was self-regulating since a legal document without the required stamp would be null and void under the law.

Charles Lord Cornwallis, who was actively involved in the House of Lords, campaigned against the Stamp Act and other import duties under consideration. He deemed enactment of these would cause hardships for the colonists; however, he could not mount a serious effort against the action. His primary stumbling block was King George III. In 18th century Britain, the Monarch held much political authority. Lord Cornwallis and his peers knew that the King eagerly awaited the passage of all taxation bills for Royal Assent. Therefore, service to the British Crown being paramount, passage was assured.[1]

The Colonial elitists, mostly located along the coast of South Carolina, were outraged; hence, they rioted and expounded with fiery rhetoric. The Stamp Act was quickly repealed in the colonies. It had lasted until only March 18, 1766, partially because of pressure applied by British merchants. Their imports to the colonies were greatly affected by colonial economic problems exacerbated by the Stamp Act. However, between June 15 and July 2, 1767, Parliament passed the Townshend Acts that had been under consideration. The best known was the duty on tea; however, duties were also to be placed on glass, paper, painters' colors, and other imports. The Americans continued to object strongly to these new measures, and the lowcountry aristocracy declared, "Taxation without representation is tyranny." The Rice Kings thought themselves powerful enough to be represented in Parliament on such matters.

The backcountry settlers, much to the chagrin of the lowcountry elite, were more sympathetic toward British control and regulation. Andrew Pickens did not believe in taxation without representation; indeed, neither did any of the backcountry Scots-Irish, given the history of their ancestry. However, they were little affected by British levies in this instance. They did not even drink tea. Their ancestors boycotted the drink in Ireland as a defiant gesture against England, and they maintained the boycott throughout the relocation to America. The backcountry settlers also used little of the other imports Britain placed under duty.

English merchants provided the commodities to America under agreement with Parliament and King George III; however, the colonists reacted to the issue by purchasing smuggled goods that were cheaper and tax free. The British wares, though, were of much better quality. Britain relented and repealed all of the duties in 1770, except for tea. The colonists viewed this as a workable compromise until the Tea Act of 1773. (The Tea Act is covered later in this chapter.)

Several backcountry settlers had received Royal land grants and definitely approved of Britain retaining power. Additionally, they were all reliant upon the South Carolina Royal government for law enforcement and general protection against Indians and criminals. The differences between the sentiments of the lowcountry and backcountry colonists defined the original Tory and Whig factions in South Carolina: Whigs in control of the coast and Tories the backcountry.[2]

This led to a huge problem as outlaws began to freely rob, loot, burn and murder in the backcountry. The Royal government had difficulty overcoming this lawlessness because of the distance from Charles Town and lack of sufficient manpower. British priorities were to police the coast around Charles Town, especially to assure that the huge slave population did not rise up against the plantation owners. Convinced that the British offered no real resistance, the backcountry criminal element had a huge incentive to migrate toward the Loyalist cause. This is not to say that all Tories were criminals because many had definite political reasons for loyalty to the British. James Louis Petigru, early 19th century South Carolina lawyer, politician, and jurist, is quoted in 1896 by the Cowpens Centennial Committee: "It is not true that the Tories were a horde of ruffians. They were conservatives, and their error was in carrying to excess the sentiment of loyalty which is founded in virtue. Their constancy embittered the contest, but did not provoke it."[3]

Petigru made a valid point; however, it was rather simplistic. The outlaw element, one of four main groups within the Tory movement, is the primary Tory affiliate in the South Carolina backcountry. The second group, found primarily on the coast but sporadically in the upcountry, was yet hopeful that the British would be able to provide protection from criminals, although the British had failed miserably at that service. This group contained many that would eventually be counted among the Whigs.

The third Tory type held a true loyalty to the King for many reasons. Some had received Royal land grants and feared for the loss of that land. Those sincere Tories, spread throughout the colony, provided leadership for the ruffian majority in the backcountry. The last Tory faction wavered from one side to the other depending upon whom they calculated might finish with the upper hand. This motley bunch did not openly engage in warfare but declared whatever allegiance they believed necessary for survival. A few of them took an active part in the hostilities, mostly out of personal revenge that sprouted from previous dealings with Whigs (see Moses Kirkland and Robert Cunningham later in this chapter.)

Biographer A. L. Pickens described the backcountry Tories very well: "Unfortunately ... a number of plundering banditti, out more for loot than for love of a Royal Master they so ostentatiously clove to. The best and most constructive families on the frontier had joined the Whig movement. Lazy and disgruntled anarchists were ready to join any movement that would pull down those whom they hated for their very industry."[4]

True, the resentment to British control originated along the South Carolina coast. It was born of British tyranny rather than any precise threat by the Loyalists. However, since the criminal element did infiltrate the Tory faction in the backcountry, the Whig sentiment there eventually strengthened; i.e., a self-defense initiative. This was important to local safety issues, but necessary for the final outcome — American independence. It would have been a different story had the increased motivation of backcountry settlers' security not been available. That provided the incentive for many to finally join the effort.

Meanwhile, since protection was a priority issue in the backcountry, mobs of vigilantes, much to the chagrin of Acting Royal Governor William Bull, began to combat the outlaws with violence. The vigilantes, though, were a minority of the populace. The Pickenses and many other backcountry settlers tended to remain neutral. They wanted to give Britain every chance to fulfill its responsibility. The more civic-minded of the backcountry were of a very strong breed (see Chapter 1), and were certainly capable of defending their families themselves — to a point. The Pickenses were not to be drawn into the politics of the situation for another ten years or so, although the Whig initiative would gradually strengthen during those years. Finally, neutrality would prove unsuccessful, and the Pickenses would eventually be forced to actively support the Whigs.[5] (Bull was in his second stint as acting Governor. He succeeded Governor Thomas Boone in May 1764 and served until the arrival of Governor Charles Montagu in June of 1766.)

The backcountry, with a population of 30,000, greatly outnumbered the lowcountry by the late 1760s. The Royal government, to appease the upcountry settlers, rebuilt Fort Prince George in 1765 and completed Fort Charlotte in December of 1766 to protect the Ninety Six District. However, Fort Prince George fell into disrepair and was abandoned by 1768. The British did not actively utilize either fort for the defense against the criminal element they had promised.[6]

Claim jumpers, robbers, counterfeiters, and murderers continued to be a growing problem. Anglican Reverend Charles Woodmason was ordained by Church of England authorities. He was born in the backcountry, trained in England, and then returned to Charles Town in 1761 to begin a South Carolina backcountry ministry. Once he returned to his roots, he discerned the plight of the more civically-constructive settlers and subsequently petitioned the Royal government for stronger laws, courts, and jails. As an Anglican minister, Woodmason was a representative of the Church of England, a state-sponsored religion. He and his church were usually at odds with the backcountry Presbyterians and other denominations; however, the settlers found a sympathizer in Woodmason regarding lawlessness.

Local Whig leaders Moses Kirkland and Thomas Woodward signed Woodmason's petition.[7] Kirkland and Woodward, unsatisfied with Governor Montagu's efforts, formally organized the vigilante bands into a group called "Regulators" in the autumn of 1767. Woodmason actually became a supporter of the Regulators. An excerpt from his journal reads:

> But the people wearied out with being expos'd to the Depredations of Robbers— Set down here just as a Barrier between the Rich Planters and the Indians, to secure the former against the Latter — Without Laws or Government Churches Schools or Ministers— No Police established — and all Property quite insecure — Merchants as fearful to venture their Goods as Ministers their Person.... No Regard had to the numberless petitions and Complaints of the people — Thus neglected and slighted by those in Authority, they rose in Arms— pursued the Rogues, broke up their Gangs ... Whipp'd and drove the Idle, Vicious, and Profligate out of the Province.... For the Mildness of Legislation here is so great ... that when a notorious Robber was with Great Pains catch'd and sent to Town, and there try'd and Condemn'd he always got pardon'd by Dint of Money, and came back 50 times worse than before. The fellows thus pardon'd formed themselves into a large Gang, ranging the province with Impunity.... I wrote to all in Authority — and received for answer, that if they would apply in a Constitutional Way, their Grievances should be redressed. I drew up for them a Remonstrance, which was presented to the House. Many articles of a Civil Nature were granted. But those of a Religious remain the same as they were.... But the Regulators (so the Populace call themselves) will not long be passive — If the next sessions do not relieve them, they are determin'd to surround the Metropolis.[8]

The percentage of those involved with civic defense in the backcountry grew, and by November the Regulators numbered 4,000 men. Their commander in the Ninety Six District was James Mayson, a Scot who had previously been a Justice of the Peace and had fought the Cherokee with Grant. The district leaders made numerous unsuccessful attempts to present the Regulators to the Royal government as a locally-organized militia; however, since the group continually rode roughshod over the region they would not gain Royal sympathy. The Regulators did, however, severely punish criminals which successfully increased the safety of the settlers. Serious crimes often resulted in lynching, while other criminals were punished with flogging, dunking, or expulsion. Many of those sought out for punishment had been British sympathizers. Backcountry criminals lost confidence when law enforcement was usurped from the hands of the Royal government. Royal law enforcement, which had been ineffective in the backcountry, was quite sufficient in the minds of the outlaws. Inevitably, the split between Tory and Whig factions there became critical, and the lowcountry Whigs garnered backcountry allies, albeit for different justifications.[9]

Acting Royal Governor Bull became enraged at the Regulators. The Court of Common Pleas, in early summer of 1768, sent Deputy Sheriff John Woods to the Ninety Six District with writs for appearance by the arrogant leaders, including Moses Kirkland and Thomas Sumter. During his trip, Woods was captured, disarmed and mistreated by Regulators posing as Indians. He finally escaped and reported Moses Kirkland's involvement to the Royal government.[10] (Bull was in his third session as acting Governor having succeeded Governor Montagu in May 1768. He served until the return of Governor Mantagu the following October.)

The government officials responded on July 25, 1768, when they sent out a constable with a posse of a dozen deputies. The group was impeded by a well-armed throng of Regulators. One deputy was killed, and the others were captured and harshly treated. A brother of Regulator leader Gideon Gibson was wounded, and the Regulators threatened to hang the constable. Woodmason referred to this:

> Several days later a new incident was reported. A constable, with warrants of distress to serve on the property of the Regulators, summoned thirteen men to his aid. Near Marr's Bluff, on the Peedee River, this group met a larger party of Regulators. A fight followed and, it was reported, some of the constables party were killed and others afterwards whipped. All that part of the country was said to be the scene of riot and disorder.[11]

Reverend Woodmason, at one point, prepared to leave Charles Town for the backcountry when acting Royal Governor Bull added a packet to his baggage. The packet contained a proclamation ordering the Regulators to cease and desist.[12] It was not unusual for Anglican ministers to carry such packets. Church of England representatives were often required to be messengers for British authority to help put down opposition based on religion. The Regulators fit the bill, as they were almost entirely made up of Presbyterians aided by smaller numbers of Baptists and miscellaneous other denomination members. Woodmason found the packet on the 17th of August as noted in his journal:

> Next day went down to Pine Tree. Here I found a Packet from the Lieutenant [actually "acting"] Governor enclosing some Proclamation lately issued for the Rioters to disperse on Pain of Proscription—with a pardon for all who would remain Quiet for the future. This I am directed to publish thro' the Country, and to accompany it with suitable Exhortations.[13]

The Regulators' leaders were popinjays and defied the orders from the Royal government. Later in August, Provost Marshal Roger Pinckney carried warrants to arrest the leaders that were involved in the July 25th incident, including Gideon Gibson. Colonel G. G. Powell, with his local Royal Militia Regiment, was to support Pinckney. The Colonel gathered 25 men at Lynches Creek and another 35 at Marr's Bluff where he was then told that Gibson had a large guard detail and could rally 300 more men in an hour. Powell ordered three captains and two lieutenants to marshal 25 men apiece and join the 60 he had already amassed. Oddly, the officers returned with 300 men, stopped several yards away from Powell, and waited for him to speak. Pinckney read his orders and the proclamations after which Powell informed the militia they were to arrest Gibson and others of the Regulators. The 300 then refused to take arms, responding they were of like mind with Gibson who had already asked them for assistance. Apparently, these men that Powell's officers had mustered were the same 300 he had been told about at Marr's Bluff.

The 300 men expressed grievances especially regarding the lack of courts and sufficient Royal Provincial law in the backcountry. They finished by refusing to assist Powell who failed at a last attempt to convince the group to participate. Powell, embarrassed, sent his resignation to acting Governor Bull; he included an observation that, had he not been there, the Regulators probably would have treated Pinckney very harshly.[14] (Marr's Bluff was present-day Mars Bluff, South Carolina, located four miles west of Pee Dee, South Carolina. It overlooks the Pee Dee River south of US Highway 76/301 off of Paper Mill Road. Lynches Creek is two miles north of present-day Johnsonville, South Carolina, where State Highway 51 crosses Lynches River.)

Bull then established a new backcountry Royal Militia under Tory Colonel John Schofield. Schofield's militia was to counteract the Regulators, declared an "illegal Whig militia" by the British. The Royal Militia was informally, and derogatorily, referred to as the "schofieldites" (sometimes Scovilites). Captain Richard Pearis was among those Schofield had recruited for his legal Royal Militia from the dregs of the backcountry Tories. The Regulators had originally been formed to bring to order the very criminals who comprised the Royal Militia.

The backcountry was then made up of active Whigs (Regulators), active Tories (Schofieldites), and the rest of the settlers (those that weren't actively involved but leaned one way or the other). Most inactive settlers leaned toward the Tory persuasion.

The Regulators tried to send a formal delegation of 300 men toward Charles Town to vote and gain representation in the General Assembly. However, Pearis advised Schofield to stir up trouble for the Regulators' families. The Regulators could not proceed to Charles Town in time for the election. They had to return home where they gathered some 700 men at Ninety Six to engage the militia. Several of the Tories were killed; thus, the schism between backcountry Whig and Tory factions deepened even further. Despite this distraction, however, Moses Kirkland did get elected as the first backcountry assemblyman in the province. The Pickens family grew increasingly concerned about the lawlessness in the district, yet they continued to prosper and to ably protect their own.[15]

Royal Governor Charles Montagu, who had returned to office in October of 1768, recognized the problem of lawlessness in the backcountry and worked to correct the matter. He organized a group called "Moderators" in 1769 to provide law and order in the backcountry. They were specifically to oppose the Whig and Tory mobs that evolved from the Regulators and the Schofieldites. The Moderators had some confrontations but successfully deactivated the Regulator movement.[16]

The Royal Colonial government seemed finally to have addressed the problem. Governor Montagu signed a bill on July 29, 1769, which provided for circuit courts in seven judicial districts throughout South Carolina, including Ninety Six District. King George III authorized the bill through the Circuit Court Act signed on November 25, 1769. Backcountry districts that were authorized circuit courts under the act were Beaufort, Camden, Cheraw, Georgetown, Orangeburg and Ninety Six. The act provided for the court to meet semiannually in each backcountry district and authorized district sheriffs to serve two-year terms.

The Circuit Court Act could not be implemented in any district until that district had a jail and a courthouse. James Mayson, Robert Gouedy, John Savage, Patrick Calhoun, Andrew Williamson, Thomas Bell, and John Lewis Gervais were appointed to a committee that ensured these buildings were constructed in the new village of Ninety Six by November of 1772. The jail was an imposing 40-foot cubed brick structure.[17]

(The jailhouse and courthouse projects were the last pertinent actions of Robert Gouedy. Gouedy was very prosperous and eventually owned over 1,500 acres of land in Ninety Six. He had been a trader, land speculator, auctioneer, and civic activist for the Ninety Six District. His will is dated July 2, 1775. See Appendix B for the text of Gouedy's will.)

The establishment of the court system was accompanied by an old English tradition — Court Days. This was a forerunner of today's county fairs. Farmers had to depart for Ninety Six many days ahead of Court Days to allow enough time to drive in their livestock. Settlers on horseback herded cattle, sheep, pigs, and mules from long distances. Those nearer to Ninety Six would sometimes walk their livestock to Court Days. Even flocks of geese or turkeys were walked toward Ninety Six, or crated up and hauled by wagon if brought from a distance.

Farmers would show and sell or trade this livestock, and would bring their reaped crops for sale when Court Days occurred in the fall. Horses were especially important to the livelihood of the remote backcountry settlers. What few horses could be spared might be auctioned, traded, or sold. Even hunting dogs were sometimes made available for purchase or swap.

Women brought their freshly-baked specialties: breads, cakes, and fruit pies in season. Their canned produce gleamed in glass jars arranged to tempt Court Days buyers.

Many others arrived besides the district settlers. Drummers and grifters would set up shop from wagons: patent medicine salesmen, minstrels, fortunetellers, carnival side show barkers, knife and gun dealers, and pocket watch hawkers the more prevalent. The Cherokee, during peaceful periods, would bring bead and leather works, blankets and moccasins to trade.

Accommodations were not abundant; however, a few travelers managed to arrange room and board with acquaintances or relatives who lived in or near Ninety Six. Others made arrangements to encamp in the nearby fields owned by John Savage or Robert Gouedy. Each of these men had lobbied for a circuit court system, and they served on the committee to establish and construct the Ninety Six jail and courthouse required by the Circuit Court Act. They were very civic-minded, did all they could to help sponsor Court Days, and they demanded little in return for making their land available.

Savage and Gouedy generally assigned settlers to camp in a specific area laid out in adjacent fields, almost as an extension of the village. This encampment area included proper unimpeded paths between individual camps. The drummers and grifters were usually restricted to setting up their wagons in a particular portion of the nearby field much like the concessionaires at present-day fairs. The Cherokee were provided a separate area to erect teepees and lean-tos. Many people preferred to sleep within their campsites in bedrolls under the stars rather than in tents.

Visitors built containment pens in a portion of the adjacent fields to hold the livestock they brought to sell or trade. The livestock owner had to assure his animals remained penned under penalty of a fine. Those who stayed at nearby farms often opted to make arrangements with the farm owners for use of their existing corrals.

Court Days were also a major social event. Men would compete in foot and horse races, complete with betting. A few of the thrifty (especially the Scots-Irish), however, wouldn't dare risk a valuable horse in a race. Men and boys liked to wrestle, box, play a game similar to quoits that was the forerunner of horseshoes, and pull sticks. Stick pulling was a contest where two opponents sat on the ground, faced each other with the flats of their feet abutting, reached forward to grasp a rod, then pulled to see who could either wrest the stick away from the other or pull the other's butt off the ground. Men gambled on cockfights and poker games if they were so inclined.

Women also competed. They entered pie-tasting, canning and bread-baking contests. Some even set up concessions where they sold helpings of their goods to the hungry. They enjoyed visiting while they quilted, braided rugs, crocheted, or sewed. Sometimes they watched the men's contests or shopped the display stalls to sample others' fare.

Court Days was an important activity for the backcountry settlers and is still practiced on a smaller scale in some parts of the country. The modern activities, however, bear little resemblance to the practices of the original.

Another backcountry delegation headed for the polls at Charles Town in autumn of 1769 and successfully elected Patrick Calhoun to the General Assembly. Since the majority in the backcountry was still Tory, law enforcement remained the top issue for Whigs. Backcountry Georgia militia leaders Elijah Clarke and John Dooley, later to become important Whig militia leaders, represented the Tory leanings in the area. Still inclined to rely on the Royal government for backcountry law, they signed a petition supporting British rule in 1774. The area remained fairly quiet over the next few years. However, Whig fever heated up in the lowcountry, and taxes were pushing the colonies ever closer to rebellion; South Carolina became a driving force as tension increased.[18]

Georgia, South Carolina's neighbor, at 25 years old was the newest province. It was the southern frontier of British colonial America. British colonization had extended only as far south as South Carolina in 1732. The Spanish controlled Florida and constantly prodded the Yamassee Indians to cross the Savannah River and assault the Carolinians. Britain decided to establish another colony as a buffer to protect the Carolinas, and the idea gave birth to Georgia.

General James Oglethorpe, an English businessman and Member of Parliament, was one of the visionaries. He also thought that Georgia would solve another problem for Britain. British prisons were in horrible condition, and a friend of his died in a debtors' prison. He sensed that Georgia could be a haven for inmates and for refugees from Germany and Scotland, and thus free up the overcrowded penal system.

Oglethorpe led 113 colonists to Charles Town aboard the *Anne* on January 13, 1733. South Carolina offered military assistance to settle the colonists on the Savannah River at what is now Savannah, Georgia. They were each given 50-acre farms and were trained to double as an effective militia to protect the colonies from enemies to the south. One year later there were still approximately 90 colonists who had survived malaria and other hardships typically experienced in the New World.

Oglethorpe quickly developed allies. He entered into a treaty with Yamacraw Indian Chief Tomochichi, a local inhabitant. The Chief recommended that Oglethorpe also approach the Creeks for a peace conference. This led to a friendship treaty in May 1733. The General was viewed as a fair-minded man by the Indians who rumored him to be part "Red Man." Oglethorpe declared that he was "an Indian, in my heart, that is I love them." Oglethorpe created local militias and a provincial ranger system over the next few years. He also expanded the settlement throughout the new colony to extend to the coast and near St. Augustine, Florida.

In 1739, after a few years of tolerance, hostilities broke out between the Spanish and the Georgians. Militias and Cherokee Indians from South Carolina aided the Georgians. Interestingly, some of their enemies were a few black militia regiments made up of former Carolina slaves. The Spanish had enticed them to escape their bonds with the promise of free land if they would form militia regiments to offset the British expansion toward Florida. The Spanish invaded St. Simons Island. They captured Fort St. Simons from the British who hastily retook it. Hostilities ended in 1742 when the British successfully defended St. Simons Island and defeated the Spanish who had attacked Gully Hole Creek and Bloody Marsh. There were no more attempts by the Spanish to occupy Georgia, and the threat officially ended with the signing of the Treaty of Aix-la-Chapelle in 1748. Hence, the South Carolina and Georgia militias were continually linked throughout the Revolutionary War era.[19]

On May 10, 1773, the British increased coastal Whig discontent by passing the Tea Act. This act did not provide a new tax on tea; indeed, the tea duty established under the earlier Townshend Acts was still in force. The East India Tea Company had previously been required to sell its entire commodity in London and was levied a heavy duty payable to

Britain. The company was in dire straits due to a number of factors, and its management feared they would have to cease operation. Under this new act, the company sold its surplus tea in the colonies through its own sales agents at a price that undercut even that of smuggled tea. In return, Britain agreed to cover 80 % of the company's shipping cost. On the surface it seemed a good deal for the colonists; however, they looked upon it as a maneuver to bail out the East India Tea Company, shore up the tea duty, and establish a monopoly that left the local merchants out altogether. Thus, the rebellion gained momentum.

British Captain Alexander Curling sailed the ship *London* into Charles Town Harbor on December 1, 1773, with a cargo of tea. This was not long before the historic Boston Tea Party. Colonel G. G. Powell, then with the South Carolina Provincial Whig Militia, met with a committee of Charles Town business leaders on the 3rd that passed a resolution called Non-importation. The committee members agreed not to accept delivery of the tea consigned to them. Curling asked them what he should do with the cargo, and they demanded he return it to England; however, the British stockpiled it in Charles Town.[20]

The Boston Tea Party took place on December 16, 1773, and is the most famous tea boycott action in the colonies. Tea boycotts quickly spread throughout the provinces.

South Carolina Presbyterian minister Reverend William Tennent strongly believed the Tea Act was a primary factor in the rebellion. In an undated anonymous and passionate (to the point of being verbose) letter he tried to convince the lowcountry aristocratic ladies to stop hosting daily tea times with their friends. Excerpts from his statement:

> Instead of abridging I could wish to add to the number of your lawful enjoyments. But I cannot think you so Divested of all love to your Country as to be willing to partake of any trivial pleasure at the Expense of the Liberties if not of the blood of your Husbands & Children. Will not my fair Readers be persuaded to lend their hand to save America from the Dagger of Tyranny?... Be persuaded to inquire & you will find that the grand Struggle at present between Britain & this Country is whether the Revenue on Tea shall be carried into execution here.... It is Tea that has brought Vengeance upon Boston.... It is to cram down that East India poison & make you pay tax on it that Armies & Fleets are sent over to put you to death if you oppose. It is in support of the Tea act that the Chartered Privileges of a great Province are sacrificed & that brave People are put under the harrow of Military law.... It is our resistance to this in which the loss of all our privileges is involved, that brings down the Vengeance of the Throne upon us. Our King himself is an East India Merchant. Tea is their greatest Revenue. In a short time you probably will see these Streets trodden down with Soldiery in favor of this same Tea act.... If the Ladies in America will only agree to use no more East India tea it will have the following good Effects ... 1st It will entirely disarm the Tea Revenue Act ... 2nd It will convince them that American Patriotism extends ever to the fair Sex ... 3rd It will punish the East India Company ... 4th It will discourage any more attempts to import tea into the Colonies, for who will import a thing that must rot when it goes into the warehouses?[21]

Backcountry representatives were to become more active in South Carolina politics. The leaders of the Non-importation resolution organized a formal "General Meeting of Citizenry" that involved citizens of Charles Town in early 1774. A "General Committee" was organized and on March 3, 1774, authorized to enforce Non-importation in Charles Town Harbor. At that time, the British Parliament closed Boston Harbor to imports. Another General Meeting of Citizenry was scheduled for July 6, 1774, and this time the backcountry districts were invited to participate. In an early matter, they decided that more could be done to support the citizens of Boston. One hundred and four delegates attended the meeting. The backcountry representatives were among those who supported a measure on July 7 to send delegates to a Continental Congress session scheduled for September 5. They were empowered to present resolutions and to support actions condemning England. Then on

July 8, the General Meeting of Citizenry enlarged the General Committee to 99 members. The entire affair was reported in *The London Chronicle* (see Appendix G):

> Charles-Town, July 11. In consequence of the advertisements lately published by the General Committee, and other proper means used, to obtain the sense of the whole Colony on the present alarming state of American affairs; on Wednesday last, the 6th inst. The largest body of the most respectable inhabitants that had ever been seen together upon any public occasion here, or perhaps any where in America (for Gentlemen of the greatest property and character, animated with an ardent zeal to relieve their suffering brethren, and to preserve their own freedom, and the birthrights of their posterity, notwithstanding the extreme inconvenience of the season, from even the remotest parts of the country, attended) met at the exchange in this town, in order to "consider of the papers, letters, and resolutions, that had been transmitted to the said Committee from the Northern Colonies; and also of the steps necessary to be pursued, in union with the inhabitants of our Sister Colonies on this continent, to avert the dangers impending over American liberties in general, by the late hostile Act of Parliament against Boston, and other arbitrary measures of the British Ministry;" ...continued in solemn deliberation upon these important matters on that and the two succeeding days, during which several resolves were unanimously entered into....
>
> Thursday, July 7. Resolved, That Henry Middleton, John Rutledge, Thomas Lynch, Christopher Gadsden, and Edward Rutledge, Esqrs. Be and they are hereby nominated and appointed Deputies, on the part and behalf of this colony, to meet the Deputies of the several Colonies of North America, in general congress, the first Monday in September next, at Philadelphia, or at any other time or place that may be generally agreed on ... there to consider ... and of the statutes, parliamentary acts, and royal instructions which make an invidious distinction between his Majesty's subjects in Great Britain and in America — with full power and authority, in behalf of us and our constituants, to concert, agree to, and effectually prosecute, such legal measures (by which we, for ourselves and them, most solemnly engage to abide) as in the opinion of the said Deputies so to be assembled, shall be most likely to obtain a repeal of the said acts, and a redress of those grievances....
>
> Resolved, That while the oppressive acts relative to Boston are enforced, we will cheerfully, from time to time, contribute towards the relief of such poor persons there, whose unfortunate circumstances, occasioned by the operation of those acts, may be thought to stand in need of most assistance....
>
> Resolved, That a Committee of 99 persons be now appointed, to act as a general Committee, to correspond with the committees of the other colonies, and do all matters and things necessary to carry these resolutions into execution; and that any 21 of them meeting together may proceed on business, their power to continue till the next general meeting.[22]

An editorial appeared in *The London Chronicle* on September 17, 1774, that expounded upon British apathy regarding the developments that loomed in America. Apparently, the citizens of England (including the elite) read the news of the colonies with amusement and presumed the colonists to be on a lark that would soon come to an end. The article (see Appendix G) stated:

> SIR,
> THE inconsistencies of the Boston Agents and American Emissaries are beyond example. For this month past they have been bullying and insulting us with the plenty they enjoyed; boasting that their sheep and their flour, their fish and their rice, came in faster than they could use them. That that was the fortieth day of their ports having been shut, and notwithstanding this they want for nothing, they fear nothing, they will pay nothing for the private property they have destroyed, nor make the smallest submission to our government; but set us at open defiance. After all this, stoutness, the next letters hold them out to us as objects of our compassion; represent the miserable condition they are in, as in danger of starving; wish to set forward a subscription for their relief, and call upon particular New England Merchants by name to begin it; and our Coffee-house Politicians read each of these accounts, and implicitly believe them both....
>
> In the beginning of the last war, when the French were attacking the Americans, and threatening, in the phrase of those times, to push the English into the sea, then the Colonists were most importunately calling out to us for help; and so long as we were taxing ourselves to pay the inter-

est of all the millions we were spending in their defence, so long they acknowledge themselves to be fellow-subjects and a part of ourselves, and persuaded us to think that fighting for them was only fighting for ourselves. But no sooner had we by our conquests taken the French from off their backs, and placed them in a state of security, but they instantly fly in the face of their Protectors, and tell us that they are different people from us; that our government has nothing to do with them; and that King, Lords, and Commons, have no authority to lay taxes or make laws for them; for, say they, they live three thousand miles off from us. Was not the distance cross the Atlantic just as great twelve years ago as it is now? And, if the Americans were then a part of ourselves, must they not be so still; and subject to our government just as much as they were then? Yet how contradictory soever [sic] these two propositions may be, the good people of England believe them; and, to save themselves the trouble of thinking, contentedly swallow them both....

Yet under all their insults, the good people of England look on with indifference; and are taught to think of an attempt to dissolve and break up the Empire, as nothing more than an exertion of British liberty, and the rights of Englishmen.

The Rutledges and the other delegates reported to the General Committee on November 8, 1774, that the Continental Congress pledged a boycott of all trade with Great Britain in support of the Colonial businessmen. The General Committee then decided to establish a much larger committee, the "General Provincial Assembly" to spread representation out over more of South Carolina.[23]

The General Provincial Assembly was a Whig committee; its primary effort was to establish the best means of supporting Non-importation. The first meeting was set for January 11, 1775, and nearly 200 delegates declared themselves the "Provincial Congress," and elected Charles Cotesworth Pinckney its President. The backcountry was represented by 46 delegates, ten of whom were from the Ninety Six District and included Andrew Williamson, James Mayson, Patrick Calhoun, and LeRoy Hammond. They pledged to continue the Non-importation agreement for Charles Town Harbor and to generally support the Continental Congress by boycotting all trade with Great Britain in a resolution called "Association." Interestingly, South Carolina refused to sign off on Association unless rice was excluded from the ban of exports. It seems that England was the only purchaser of rice from South Carolina. The Continental Congress, after lengthy negotiations, agreed that Association would include all exports, except rice, and scheduled the new resolution to take effect on September 10, 1775.[24]

The Provincial Congress selected a secret "Action Committee" of five Whigs for the purpose of intercepting British dispatches. The Action Committee seized official mail on April 17, 1775, and the documents clearly expressed that England intended to use force if necessary in the face of growing tendencies toward Whig action. The Action Committee followed up on the 21st by seizing arms and ammunition that had been stored in the Royal government's statehouse.[25]

On June 4, 1775, the new Provincial Congress elected Henry Laurens its President. It also created a 13-member "Council of Safety" to function in times of emergency when the Congress was not in session. President Henry Laurens was also elected to lead the Council of Safety which was to direct defensive measures and act as a war council. The Provincial Congress, at the same time, created an oath for subscribers to swear to uphold independence ideals even by force of arms if necessary. The oath, circulated among the delegates, amounted to a supporting gesture in response to the recent battles at Lexington and Concord. The Congress also took action to store supplies for Whig use throughout the backcountry, including 200 barrels of flour to be placed at Ninety Six.[26]

The split between Tory and Whig factions was soon to become more pronounced and would affect the military. Governor Montagu's Moderators were initially a new 12,000 man

Royal Militia in the backcountry (aside from the Schofieldites) that served primarily to defend the locals against criminals and Cherokee incursions. Colonel John Savage commanded the Ninety Six District Militia Regiment. Major James Mayson and Major Andrew Williamson supported him. The Pickenses finally became actively involved in the law and order effort. Captain Andrew Pickens reported to Williamson, and his older brother Joseph served as a private in his company.[27]

The Tories, members of the backcountry Royal Militia, outnumbered the Whigs two to one, and many Tory militiamen used their authority to exercise unrighteous dominion over their Whig neighbors. This concerned the Provincial Congress, so during the session on the 4th they created the South Carolina Patriot Militia to counter the Royal Militia.

The Provincial Congress formed two regiments of infantry for the lowcountry on June 12, 1775. Colonel Christopher Gadsden was selected to command the 1st Regiment. As he was a member of the Continental Congress, he did not assume active command until February 1776.

Colonel William Moultrie was assigned command of the 2nd Regiment with Francis Marion to serve as Lieutenant Colonel under Moultrie. Two days later, the Provincial Congress also formed the 3rd Regiment of Rangers to patrol the backcountry, and named Lieutenant Colonel William Thomson the Regimental Commander with James Mayson a Regimental Major reporting to Thomson. Moses Kirkland and Robert Cunningham, each under consideration for the ranger regimental major, were chagrined at not having been selected.

Colonel Charles C. Pinckney. Artist: Alonzo Chappel; engraver, 1862.

Kirkland did accept a captain's commission, but Robert Cunningham refused the same. Alienating Cunningham would cause much grief for the Patriot cause in days to come.[28] Andrew Pickens later said regarding these events:

> I was a farmer and had a wife and family of small children at the commencement of the Revolutionary war. At that time I had a company of Militia.... At the commencement of the war it was thought advisable by our Council of Safety to have one or two regiments raised and officered in the upper part of the country.
>
> The candidates for Col. for the four regiments were ROBERT CUNNINGHAM — Mayson, and Tory Kirkland. Mayson got the commission, which so exasperated the others that they immediately took the other side of the question. They both being men of influence, but particularly Cunningham who lived on the east side of Saluda river and having considerabale [sic] connections in that part of the country. If Cunningham had been appointed Colonel at that time, we would not have had so violent and [sic] opposition to our cause in this country, and I have never had a doubt that he would have made the best officer.[29]

Pickens apparently admired Cunningham and was confident in his abilities as an officer. His comments indicate Cunningham would have been the best choice for overall commander of the South Carolina 3rd Provincial Regiment of Rangers; however, that may have been faulty recollection on his part because the three were under consideration for regimental major rather than colonel of all regiments.

Selected for captains, in addition to Kirkland, were Samuel Wise, Ezekial Polk, John Caldwell, Ely Kershaw, Robert Goodwin, Edward Richardson, Thomas Woodward, and John Purves. Andrew Williamson and the Pickens brothers were still members of the Royal Militia up to this time because, except for the ranger regiment, the new South Carolina Patriot Militia had only been established in the lowcountry.

On June 18, 1775, Lord William Campbell arrived in Charles Town and assumed the office of Royal Governor. He and Henry Laurens promptly entered into a period of contentiousness that resulted in continuous friction between the Council of Safety and the Royal government. One result of the pressure from the Council of Safety was the relocation of British Chief Indian Agent, Major John Stuart, from Charles Town to St. Augustine, Florida. Alexander Cameron remained his Chief Indian Agent to the Cherokee and resided with the natives in the lower villages.

The Council of Safety decided, late in June of 1775, to take a shipment of gunpowder from a British ship when it approached Savannah because they were concerned that the Governor of Georgia might ship it to the Cherokee. Likewise, the Council of Safety was afraid that 1,750 pounds of gunpowder stored at Fort Charlotte on the upper Savannah River would find its way to the Cherokee. Therefore, they instructed Major Mayson to seize the fort and munitions. Mayson took two of his companies under the leadership of Captains John Caldwell and Moses Kirkland on the assignment.[30] (Fort Charlotte was a structure of 40 feet by 50 feet located near the present-day Mt. Carmel, South Carolina. The site is submerged under present-day J. Strom Thurmond Reservoir, and a marker is located in Mt. Carmel on highway 81, six and one-half miles northeast of the actual site. Fort Charlotte was within 20 miles of the Long Canes settlement.)

Major Mayson moved to seize Fort Charlotte on July 12, 1775. This has widely been considered the first action of the Revolutionary War to occur in South Carolina. Once the fort was captured, Mayson left Captain Caldwell with most of his company to garrison the post. Mayson himself, with Kirkland and the rest of the rangers, proceeded toward Ninety Six with 500 pounds of lead and 250 pounds of powder.

Captain Kirkland was still agitated at not being Major Kirkland, so it didn't help that he had just taken part in a major action under the man selected for his desired rank. He decided this was the appropriate time for him to make his move, and it would be momentous. He got word to Tory Colonel Thomas Fletchall regarding the action at Fort Charlotte and the movement of the rangers to Ninety Six with the munitions. He recommended that Fletchall's militia might take the munitions, and he declared his intention to defect with his entire company of rangers and join Fletchall.[31]

Fletchall sent Tory Major Joseph Robinson, accompanied by brothers Captain Robert and Captain Patrick Cunningham, to seize Ninety Six. They surrounded the village on July 17, 1775, and demanded the ammunition be turned over to them. Kirkland had already left, disbanded his company of rangers, and headed for Charles Town to acquire a commission for a company of Tory militia. Robinson had no difficulty recapturing the munitions, and he also arrested Mayson and jailed him right there at Ninety Six. Mayson was charged with stealing the munitions from Fort Charlotte.[32]

On July 23, 1775, the Council of Safety sent Provincial Congressman William Henry Drayton and Presbyterian minister Reverend William Tennent on a mission into the backcountry. Their charge was to explain the Whig position regarding the importance of, and to get signatures declaring support for, the resolutions of Non-importation and Association. The signatories were to also pledge not to do business with anyone who did not support the resolutions.

It was a long and arduous trek as is shown by the following excerpts from their letters and journals. It was hard mentally as well as physically, but they did have a modicum of success to show for their efforts. They met with mixed reactions dependent upon whether the audience was primarily of a Tory or Whig nature. The backcountry still predominately leaned toward loyalty to the crown, such that many Whig supporters were not yet ready to take up arms against King George III. Also, many in the backcountry balked at declaring to not do business with their neighbors.

Drayton and Tennent, while at Congaree Store, reported to the Council of Safety on August 7, 1775:

> Upon our arrival at the Congaree Store ... we despatched notices to particular persons of influence among the Dutch, to endeavor to procure a meeting.... To our great mortification not one German appeared, but by one or two of our friends ... we were informed, their countrymen were so much averse to taking up arms, as they imagined, against the king, least they should lose their lands; and were so possessed with an idea ... that they would not by any arguments be induced to come near us.[33]

Drayton wrote another report from Congaree to the Council of Safety on the 9th describing a success:

> Yesterday, being Tuesday, we went over the Congaree River some miles to an election; to which some evil disposed persons purposely went to do what mischief lay in their power. Mr. Tennent and myself spoke a considerable time; and I have the pleasure to inform you, that we gave at once general information and satisfaction; for we had the good fortune to speak so as to be universally understood. In short, those who came with an intent to disturb the meeting, became converts and cheerfully signed the Association. And, the election being finished, the people formed themselves into volunteer companies.[34]

Tennent wrote of the weather and bedbugs in his August 13th journal entry (transcribed from Tennent's original handwriting by the author):

> Rode 10 miles in the Evening through the rain ... if we can stand this we need fear nothing. But the Inclemency of the Skies was not to be compared to the fury of the little inhabitants of the Bed. After a sleepless and wet night I was shocked by the Blood and Slaughter of my Callicoed Shirt and Sheets in the morning.[35]

On August 16, 1775, Drayton wrote of another success, this time from King's Creek near Enoree:

> Here is a settlement in our favor. It begins near about the division line between Orangeburg and Ninety Six, and reaches to Hendrixs' [sic] mill, upon Enoree. Yesterday I had a pretty large gathering as we say here; and I gave a discourse which was generally satisfactory. Having finished and the people expressing their pleasure and readiness to sign, a man stepped in and said Cunningham [speaking of Robert] was at hand, and he hoped the people would stay and hear what he had to say. Immediately all was at a stand. The company now expected to hear the affair argued on both sides, and thus I was to be made a public disputer in spite of my teeth.... We then collected all the people, and he and one Brown, he that was tarred and feathered at Augusta ... took out Dalrymple's address from the people of England to the people of America ... read by Brown from beginning to end.... I applied ridicule where I thought it would have effect, the people laughed heartily and Cunningham and Brown could not but grin—horribly. In short I so answered the whole, that the people rejoiced, and Cunningham had not one word to say in response. The people are perfectly satisfied ... Cunningham is beat out of the field. Sure it is that he was highly mortified; and with his companion, Brown, stole away.[36]

Thomas Brown had been previously tarred and feathered for having made fun of the American cause while toasting at a dinner party in Augusta.[37] He was severely burned by the hot tar, thus he was tagged with the nickname "Burn Foot." He became a bitter and bloody enemy of the Whigs throughout the Revolutionary War.

Tennent and Drayton met with a large group of Tories at Ford's upon Enoree on the 23rd. The group consisted of several of the leaders, including Fletchall, Robinson, Patrick and Robert Cunningham, and even Kirkland. The situation was tense as Drayton and Tennent described:

> We arrived here yesterday and met with Col. Fletchall, Kirkland, the two Cunningham's and Brown.... Kirkland treated the Congress, the Committee, the Council, and ourselves with the highest insolence. Nay, he was on the point of assaulting Mr. Drayton ... Kirkland and the Cunninghams appeared here with arms, sword and pistol.[38]

Drayton found that Kirkland, the Cunninghams, and Colonel Thomas Brown were often at some of the sessions he led throughout the backcountry, and they inspired enough contempt to create danger of a Tory uprising. Drayton described the temperament of the backcountry Tory leaders on the 21st:

> I reached Col. Fletchall's last Thursday ... and there I found Brown, Cunningham, and Robinson, who had arrived the evening before.... Mr. Tennent and myself, after breakfast, engaged Col. Fletchall in a private conversation during near three hours.... All that we could get from him was this. He would never take up arms against the King or his countrymen ... [a promise] to call out his regiment [for the purpose of presenting the Association].... This man's [Fletchall] looks are utterly against him. Much venom appears in Cunningham's countenance and conversation. Neither of these men say much; but Brown is the spokesman, and his bitterness and violence are intolerable.... Upon our return to the house where this Brown, Cunningham, and Robinson were, he mentioned what he had promised. All these at once were open-mouth against the measure and Mr. Tennent and myself had much to do, to keep the Colonel to his promise ... these men manage Fletchall as they please, when they have him to themselves.[39]

Drayton and Tennent split their routes on the 25th. Drayton arrived at Ninety Six very concerned about his experiences with the Tories during this venture, so he ordered Major Andrew Williamson to beef up the sentries at Ninety Six and send 30 troops to reinforce the garrison at Fort Charlotte. His dealings provided Drayton insight regarding the future and which individuals might become major obstructions for the Whigs.

In the meantime, Tennent recorded in his journal on the 25th:

> Met with the greater part of Robt Cunningham's Company & two of his Officers in a large Congregation at the meeting house ... on Little River. Preached to a large & concerned Audience. After a short Intermission spoke for two hours & a half upon the subject of my Mission, to the most

fixed people that I have ever yet seen. This is the Centre of the Opposition in this Regiment. Therefore finding I had catched the attention of the sober & judicious, I spared no pains to convince them.... In short order it would seem that the force of Violence is broke here. Mr Drayton joined us in the evening with Major Terry.[40]

Drayton had considerable success near Ninety Six and Long Canes; he was able to obtain many signatures on the resolutions. He also organized three companies of backcountry South Carolina Provincial Whig Militia under Major Williamson, as described by Tennent in a report to the Council of Safety penned on September 1, 1775: "Three Volunteer companies are formed. One under Major [Champness] Terry, who now seems animated in the cause; another under Capt. [Andrew] Pickens; a third under Capt. James McCall."[41]

Pickens' move from Royal to Whig militia was predictable. He was concerned about the Tory attitude and realized that, as long as the local Royal Militia was primarily of Tory persuasion, his family, and those of his Whig neighbors, would not be safe. Pickens, as the political and military leader in the area, set the example for others to follow with this move.

The New Acquisition Militia Regiment of Colonel Thomas Neil also gave Drayton a positive reception. Neil verified that Kirkland, Brown and the Cunninghams were considering an attack on Fort Charlotte; additionally, he told Drayton that Royal Indian Agents John Stuart and Alexander Cameron were stirring up the Cherokee. He reported all that Neil told him to the Council of Safety on August 30, 1775.[42]

Militia regiments were created in all of the backcountry districts with the regimental commanders reporting militarily to South Carolina 2nd Regimental Colonel William Moultrie. He, in turn, reported to the Council of Safety.

Tennent, still working the vicinity of Long Canes, made the following journal entry on Thursday the 31st:

> Went to a Meeting appointed last week on the Long Cane Creek in Boonsborough at one of Mr Harris's preaching Sheds. Preached, & in the midst of the sermon had the pleasure to see Mr Hart arrive. After Sermon spoke as usual on the subject of my Mission. Was seconded by Mr Harris & Mr Salvador to good Effect.... M^r [Patrick] Calhoun & other Gentlemen returned with me [to Mr. Reed's] & spent the Evening on the subjects fit for the Times.[43]

A few days later, he continued:

> Saturday 2nd Septem^r Studied a Sermon in the morning & went 5 Miles to Bull Town Meeting House about 15 Miles from the Indian Line. The Assembly was the most crowded that I have seen.... The people mostly Opposers ... willing to hear, I gave them a Discourse upon the American Dispute of near 3 hours, I think I was more animated & demonstrative than usual. The Effect was very visible, the people holding a profound Silence for more than a Minute after I was done.... The people seemed satisfied & many of those who had signed Flechalls [sic] Association now subscribed over. This day has it is hoped put an end to the strength of Discord in this Regiment ... to lodge this Night at Patrick Calhoun's Esqr 10 Miles Distant. Accompanied him home, having this Day rode 18 or 20 Miles.[44]

Early in September, Drayton and Tennent visited Augusta to check on the defenses. Drayton ordered Williamson to go to Harden's Ferry on the Savannah with another 300 militiamen to further reinforce Fort Charlotte. He also detached several small militia units around the backcountry to deter Tory militia units from engaging in any such attack, and Tennent filed a report of these actions with the Council of Safety.[45] Tennent recorded in his journal regarding the inspection of Fort Charlotte:

> Sunday 3rd Septem^r Started early in the morning, & by half after 8 was at Fort Charlotte, having missed our way & rode not less than 15 Miles.... Being very wet when I reached the Fort, had a good fire kindled, washed my feet with rum & took every precaution to avoid a Cold. Surveyed

the Fortification, Magazine, Stores, Ordnance & Barracks, & find that the place though much out of repair, is still capable of a good Defence. It is a large Square with good Bastions at each Corner, so constructed as to be able to work 16 Cannon. The Wall is of stone, about ten feet in heighth with Loop Holes to fight musketry.... The Barracks are able to lodge 200 Men, & the Officers Building, the Armory & its Officies are not despicable. It has a good Well within it, & its gate is of strong plank.... Gave orders therefore for completing its repair.[46]

Apparently, Reverend Tennent secured notice about a coming Tory offensive. This information directly pertained to attacks planned for Fort Charlotte and Augusta by Kirkland and some of his henchmen. The intelligence was likely linked to the coming assault on Ninety Six. Tennent recorded:

Monday 4th Septem^r.... Met with one of the *King's Men* as they are absurdly called, from whom I learned that they expected a Meeting on Wednesday of all their Comrades on the Banks of the Savannah about 20 Miles above Augusta, from which & sundry Circumstances it appears that they mean some Stroke ... crossed the River to Captn Hammond's. Found his House forted in & a large body of Militia there ready to move with Mr Drayton.... Consulted with Mr Drayton & found that on a Discovery of the intention of Kirtland [sic] & the others to embody on Wednesday & go upon some Enterprise, he had ordered the Regiment of Horse to march, & the Militia, in all to the amount of 1000 effective Men. We agreed upon the Necessary movements & I consented to make the best of my way to Charlestown, to lay a State of the whole Matter before the Council of Safety.[47]

Tennent ordered Captain Caldwell to erect cannon platforms for defending Fort Charlotte and to mount two four-pounders for field use. He also insisted that the Indian corn around the fort be cut down and that any other cover the enemy might use in an attack be removed.

Drayton returned to Ninety Six on September 8, 1775, accompanied by 120 of Williamson's militiamen; his intention was to arrest several Tory leaders including Kirkland. Drayton was told on the 10th that Colonel Fletchall was on the way with his Royal Militia regiment to attack Ninety Six. Based on this information, plus that which Tennent provided to him on the 4th, he ordered several defensive actions. He had swivel guns placed at the windows of the jail, 100 men detached to Island Ford on the Saluda, and another 100-man detachment situated midway between Ninety Six and Island Ford. However, Fletchall and his troops had not appeared — yet.[48] Although Tennent completed his trip through the backcountry, his return to Charles Town was not uneventful:

Monday 11th Set out early for the Ferry at the Two Sisters: reached Stritchland between 9 & 10 O clock. He advised me that the Waters were high but that I might pass. I since found that his Intention was to convince me by finding it impossible that even in so low a fresh Mr Williamson's Ferry was not good.

He succeeded in the unkind Experiment, for in addition to much Difficulty, I had nearly drowned my best Horse, & was glad to return to the house. He most kindly offered to set me over *gratis*. I accepted ... but in my life I never endured more burning heat of the Sun, I striped [sic] to my shirt and laboured for four hours to gain but one mile. Got to the ferry house much spent & after a little refreshment threw myself on a Bed and slept; awoke in a sweat much relieved by it. My Friends would have smiled to see my repast and the figure I cut in eating it. Fried pork & milk was a Dish to which necessity gave an high relish. It was in the night before I reached the Widow Allisons. It is an easy matter to write Novels if a man travels & describes nothing more than the truth.[49]

Moses Kirkland had heard Drayton was now taking direct charge of the South Carolina Provincial Whig Militia. He also heard that the militia was hot on his trail, so he took his son to Charles Town on the 11th, and the British put the lad in protective custody aboard the *Tamar*, a warship.

The Council of Safety ordered Captain Adam McDonald of the First Regiment of the South Carolina Provincial Whig Militia to gain access to Governor Campbell. McDonald captured a former Kirkland bodyguard and threatened his life if he did not introduce him to the Governor as a Tory militia officer. Campbell told McDonald to keep the backcountry Tory militia organized, but to be patient because he had correspondence indicating that Britain was going to invade South Carolina. Governor Campbell breached normal security ethics by discussing a sensitive subject with someone he had just met. It would haunt him later; however, he knew that the Loyalist militia was very important to the Royal cause, and that it was imperative that the militia remained positive.[50]

The Council of Safety decided action was in order. Representatives approached the Governor and demanded that he turn over all correspondence he had with the backcountry Tory leaders. They also desired the dispatch he had received from General Clinton regarding the planned invasion of the province. Finally, they wanted Moses Kirkland, himself.

The visit by the Council of Safety unnerved the Governor, and on September 14, 1775, he had the British Navy remove 21 cannons from the lower battery of Fort Johnson on James Island. This was completed the next day, and the Navy took the gunpowder with them when they left the Island. On the 15th, the Council of Safety decided to take Fort Johnson; Colonel William Moultrie sent a contingent of South Carolina State Troops to accomplish the task. When the detachment, including Lieutenant Colonel Francis Marion, arrived they found the fort abandoned, the ammo taken, and the cannons removed from their carriages. The cannons, surprisingly, were not destroyed but could be reassembled and used. Campbell fled for protection to the *Tamar* and attempted to run the colony from the harbor.[51]

Concurrently in the backcountry, Drayton had a declaration printed on September 13, 1775, that served as justification for Non-importation and Association. He cited, "Whereas, the liberties of America being treacherously and cruelly violated.... And thus, having, in the name of this Colony, declared the terms upon which peace and safety may be had ... it is my duty also to declare, that I shall march and attack, as public enemies, all and every person in arms, or [thought] to be in arms, in this part of the colony, in opposition to the measures of Congress [meaning the Provincial Congress]." The declaration was posted throughout the Ninety Six District and was read to Fletchall and 127 of his militiamen at the Upper Saluda on the 14th.[52]

Fletchall started for Ninety Six with over 2,000 men, including the militias of "Burn Foot" Brown and the Cunningham brothers. Drayton's militia contained over 1,000 men; they, though outnumbered, were much better trained, armed, and more confident than the Tories. Indeed, their demeanor made them an intimidating sight. Drayton sent an overture of peace to Fletchall who was becoming worried about Drayton's impressive force. Fletchall knew his force was poorly trained and commanded, so he began to consider the offer. Some of Fletchall's company commanders were going to attack Ninety Six anyway but were never able to accomplish the action. On September 16, 1775, Fletchall and a few of his captains agreed to sign the peace offer, which became known as the Treaty of Ninety Six. This irritated the Cunninghams who believed Fletchall was not fit to command.[53]

Drayton sent a report to the Council of Safety on the 17th stating Fletchall signed a peace treaty; then, Drayton left for Charles Town. On the way, he stopped to talk with Tory Captain Richard Pearis who admitted that Indian Agents, Stuart and Cameron, mainly caused the problems with the Cherokee. In the meantime, Governor Campbell sent Kirkland to St. Augustine with an order that Stuart enflame the Cherokee. He wanted the Indians to prepare for a second front against the Whigs in the event the British attacked South

Carolina. Kirkland presented the order to Stuart on September 25, 1775. Subsequent to his visit with Pearis, Drayton wrote Alexander Cameron from Congarees on the 26th stating:

> It gives me great concern, sir, to be under a necessity of telling you, that from your connection with the King's government, and our knowledge of your incapability of betraying your trust, we look upon you as an object dangerous to our welfare; and, therefore, as an object, that we ought to endeavor to remove to a distance from your present residence.... I do, therefore sir, in the name of the Colony request, that you will forthwith remove to such a distance, from the Cherokee Nation, that will satisfy us that you cannot readily exercise the functions of your office among them, and thereby remove our apprehensions.[54]

Kirkland tarried in Florida for two weeks while Stuart developed a plan to initiate Governor Campbell's order to stir the Cherokee against the backcountry Whigs. Stuart then sent Kirkland to Boston on October 3, 1775, to present his plan to General Thomas Gage. The British ship that transported Kirkland was seized en route, and Kirkland was captured. So were his dispatches. Kirkland was jailed, and his papers, that addressed inciting the Cherokee, were printed and widely circulated.[55]

In the meantime, Andrew Pickens and his neighbors began to prepare for the obvious—the coming strife in the backcountry.

3

Pickens Sees Action (1775)

When the backcountry began to heat up in late 1775, the Pickens brothers became heavily involved. The Scots-Irish Presbyterians had sustained oppression from the British — and the Church of England — for generations. Now they had begun to fear they would be haunted by the past in their new land. Andrew Pickens had already gleaned a scent of what lay ahead when he and his older brother, Joseph, were involved in the campaign waged by Grant. The younger Pickenses had probably heard stories about British cruelty through tales handed down from their ancestors. Andrew had seen such cruelty first-hand when he campaigned with Grant; indeed, he expressed his abhorrence for it many times in later years. (One such instance is noted in Pickens' letter to General Lee in Chapter 1.)

Andrew Pickens likely had been expecting the British to turn the backcountry Tories loose to harass the Whigs. The Tories, indeed, had become haughty. They could afford to be confident. With British support, they often displayed harsher brutality than the British. This was not unusual. Regarding a similar setting in the north, *Harper's Weekly, Journal of Civilization*, published in 1877: "When the British occupied the Jerseys, the Tories, feeling strong under their protection, made themselves obnoxious to the Patriots."[1]

The backcountry had become a dangerous place. Serious contentions arose daily between neighbors because of their political differences, a problem worsened by jealousies from supposed past offenses. Captain Robert Cunningham was still chagrined over Thomas Fletchall's signature on the Treaty of Ninety Six. Cunningham believed Fletchall had forsaken the Tory cause and did not deserve to be a militia commander. Robert and his brother, Captain Patrick Cunningham, tried their best to enflame the local Tory faction in the backcountry. They succeeded. The Cunninghams' primary short-term goal was to avenge the exoneration of the Whigs at Ninety Six. Robert and Patrick tried to stir the Loyalists to a new attack on the village.

Provincial Congressman William Henry Drayton had been well informed of Robert Cunningham's activities and was concerned. He wrote to Robert from Ninety Six on September 21, 1775. Drayton stated:

> It was, therefore, with the highest pleasure, that on the 16th instant [the current month], I, together with Colonel Fletchall and other gentlemen, signed an instrument of writing [meaning the Treaty of Ninety Six].... But it is with concern, that I have heard that you do not hold yourself as included in the above ... and that you will not be bound by it. I am sincerely inclined to believe that these are not your sentiments.... I, therefore, sir, entreat that you will, as soon as may be, favor me with an answer to this letter, assuring me that you hold yourself as included in the above instrument of writing.[2]

Drayton did receive a response, but it was hardly what he had hoped for. Cunningham replied on October 5, 1775, from Page's Creek: "I think sir, at this time the question is rather unfair; however ... I do not hold with that peace—at the same time as fond of peace as any man—but upon honorable terms.... It appears to me, sir, you had all the bargan [sic] making to yourself."[3]

On the 16th, Indian Agent Alexander Cameron, from Keowee, responded to Drayton's letter of the previous month (see Chapter 2):

> I received your letter of the 26th ultimo [the previous month], which I have maturely considered ... the concern you express for requesting me to remove to some distance from my present residence.... I cannot find myself at liberty to comply with it ... while I have the honor to serve in my present office, I must implicitly observe the directions and orders of my superiors, and cannot recede from my part without first obtaining their leave.[4]

He then withdrew to the safety of the Cherokee over mountain villages.

Royal Governor Lord William Campbell was informed on the 19th that the British were preparing to sail for the south. He was also told that Indian Agent John Stuart had arranged to activate the Cherokee and thus create havoc against Whigs in the backcountry. Drayton was well aware of the British plans (thanks to an earlier seizure of British mail packets), so he lined the Charles Town waterfront with defensive batteries and made repairs to Fort Johnson. Drayton also ordered Colonel Owen Roberts to construct a small fort on Sullivan's Island. Roberts erected an impressive sand-filled double-wall fort.[5]

Captain Robert Cunningham's threatening actions in the backcountry had the Whigs on edge. Tensions continued to mount, and on October 23, 1775, South Carolina Ranger Captain John Caldwell filed charges of seditious language against Cunningham. The Council of Safety, in turn, issued an arrest warrant against Robert Cunningham and ordered Major Andrew Williamson to proceed with the action. Williamson assigned Captain Benjamin Tutt to apprehend Cunningham, who was captured without difficulty and jailed in Charles Town. Captain Patrick Cunningham had gathered a group of Tories to rescue his brother before Williamson's militia could reach Charles Town. The group, unable to act quickly enough, failed to overtake the captors.

Near the same time, the Continental Congress authorized the colony of Georgia to establish a Provincial Army. This was to become important to the backcountry Whigs of South Carolina as the two provinces, together, progressed toward independence.

On November 1, 1775, the 2nd Provincial Congress opened its session and elected William Henry Drayton to succeed Henry Laurens as its President. One important matter of business involved Robert Cunningham; Captain Tutt reported on Cunningham's arrest and brought him before the Provincial Congress. The Congress ordered his continued incarceration and charged him with "high crimes and misdemeanors against the liberties of this colony." He was not allowed visitors nor incoming and outgoing communications.[6]

Captain Robert Cunningham's arrest did little to relieve the situation for the Whigs around Ninety Six. On October 4, 1775, the Council of Safety, in an attempt to moderate the pressure on the backcountry, agreed to appease the Cherokee with 1,000 pounds of powder and 2,000 pounds of lead. Both Tory and Whig factions were fearful that the other might ally with the tribe, even though the Cherokee were actually forming an alliance with the Royal government.

A contingent of wagons laden with the ammunition left Charles Town for Ninety Six on the 3rd of November. The Tory leaders knew of the shipment and riled the rank and file of their militia; they convinced their men that the powder and lead were Whig presents to align the Cherokee against the Tories in the backcountry. About noon, Captain Patrick Cunningham and approximately 150 Tory militiamen seized the shipment at Mine Creek

18 miles from Ninety Six. Cunningham and the other leaders continued to hint that the Whigs were trying to use the ammunition to buy an alliance with the Cherokee.[7]

The Council of Safety received a report of the seizure and promptly ordered Patrick Cunningham arrested and "others of the King's mad people." Major Andrew Williamson was directed to gather the Ninety Six Militia and generally harass the Tories in the vicinity.[8] On November 6, 1775, Williamson established an encampment near the village of Ninety Six and issued a militia muster call. On the same day, he appealed to Tory leaders north of the Saluda that he feared the Cherokee would take revenge against settlers in that area. He explained the Cherokee would be upset with the seizure of ammunition promised them. He further stated that his intention to retake the ammunition and capture the perpetrators was an intercessory move to calm the young braves. His plea, however, fell on deaf ears.[9]

President Drayton received permission from the Provincial Congress on the 8th to parallel Williamson's action by sending Camden District Militia Colonel Richard Richardson into the backcountry to serve the arrest warrant for Captain Patrick Cunningham and his followers. Richardson went to his plantation to muster a large militia force. (Colonel Richardson's plantation, called Big Home, was located two miles south of present-day Rimini, Clarendon County, South Carolina. His grave marker is on the west side of Old River Road, State Road 14–76. The results of his campaign follow further treatment of Williamson's actions around Ninety Six.)[10]

Tory Captain Richard Pearis effectively countered Williamson's plea to the Tory settlers on the Saluda. He traveled to Ninety Six and signed an affidavit attesting Drayton had met with the Cherokee in September to plan an action against the Tories. Cunningham's army began to swell as New Acquisition Loyalist Militia Major Joseph Robinson and his men joined him at the Saluda. As the Tories moved toward Ninety Six, they imposed an oath of allegiance upon any settlers they encountered; those that would not submit to the oath were disarmed. Patrick Cunningham still had control of the lead and powder he had seized, so things looked bleak for Williamson. He, however, remained optimistic.

By the 17th of November, Williamson had mustered a force of only about 550 men. Not only was he in "Tory country," but the locals were disinclined to ally with the Whig militia because of Cunningham's rumor about the Cherokee ammunition. Williamson's militia amounted to skeleton crews. Captain Alexander Noble, husband of Andrew Pickens' sister-in-law, Catherine Calhoun, had only two officers and two enlisted men. The other companies were not in much better condition. Captain Andrew Pickens had only mustered two officers, three sergeants and 35 privates, while Captain James McCall had merely three officers, three sergeants and 45 privates. Williamson appealed to the Whigs in Georgia who assisted him with 75 militiamen.[11]

On the evening of the 18th, Williamson's scouts informed him that a Loyalist brigade of nearly 2,000 men was crossing the Saluda River at Island Ford. Until then, he had been rather certain that Major Robinson would not sanction a direct attack on the Whig militia, but news of this huge band caused him to reconsider.

Major James Mayson had just arrived with 40 South Carolina Rangers. Williamson was happy to receive them; however, their arrival did little to tilt the balance of forces to the Whig's favor. Additionally, Williamson and Mayson, each a major, disagreed over which of them should have seniority. They finally consented to share command and rely on a council of war of with all officers for major decisions. Williamson would take sole command when engaged with the enemy.

Major Williamson was inclined that, with the enemy only six miles away, he should gather his force and surprise them with a preemptive attack. He hastily called his first council of war and presented his decision. Several of the officers indicated agreement; however, Mayson and Captain Andrew Pickens each spoke and strongly urged the council to reconsider the option. They believed the militia would have no chance against such vastly superior numbers. They convinced the council to accept another alternative. Williamson assented and ordered the militia to break camp at the village and secure a better defensive position.[12]

At daybreak on November 19, 1775, Williamson withdrew the militia across Spring Branch to the property of John Savage. Williamson ordered construction of a stockade that used Savage's barn and other outbuildings as the core. The Ninety Six courthouse and jail were about 600 feet away across the Spring Branch gully. From their position on a high open ridge, the Whigs could spot any enemy approach, and they would be able to utilize artillery as necessary. The militia took two hours to fortify the defenses. The stockade became known as Williamson's Fort. (It was located at the site of a future stockade that would be defended by Tories during an American siege in 1781. See Chapter 12.)[13]

The hasty construction was just completed in time because Major Robinson and Captain Patrick Cunningham arrived at 11:00 A.M. with their imposing force. Captain Richard Pearis was among the Tory militia who immediately took control of the courthouse and jail; then, from a distance, they surrounded Williamson's militia. This position gave the Tories control over Spring Branch, a major drawback to the Whig's choice for their defensive position. It would be difficult to withstand a lengthy siege without water.

Once the Tories settled in, Williamson dispatched a Whig officer to carry a white flag, approach Robinson and Cunningham, and request the Tories' intentions. However, Robinson refused to talk to anyone other than Williamson or Mayson. Major Mayson, accompanied by Captain John Bowie, met for 15 minutes with Robinson, Cunningham, and Captain Evan McLauren about halfway between the two primary positions. Williamson learned from his officers that Major Robinson had issued terms that required the Whigs to surrender all arms, disband the militia, and remain in the stockade for their own safety until negotiations completed. About 3:00 P.M., while Williamson was considering the terms, two of his militiamen ventured outside the stockade and were captured by some of the Tories.

Williamson immediately ordered a rescue attempt, and the Whigs began to fire upon the Tory positions with swivel guns, rifles and muskets. The Tories, armed with rifles and muskets but no artillery, returned fire upon the stockade. The shooting continued for about two and one-half hours until dusk, after which the Whigs fired sporadically to discourage any approach by the Tories.[14]

It was fairly quiet until daybreak Monday, November 20, 1775, when firing recommenced from both sides and lasted throughout the day until dusk. Patrick Cunningham initiated a plan to burn the Whigs out by having Tory Major John Robbins construct a mantelet of sticks and stones. He then ignited the field and some fencing near the stockade to provide a smoke cover for Robbins to approach the fort. However, his moveable shelter caught fire when he made the attempt, so he abandoned the plan. Williamson, realizing that lack of water was his primary strategic weakness, had some Whig militiamen begin to dig for water through heavy clay indigenous to the area.[15]

At dawn on the 21st, both sides recommenced firing with sporadic sniping that continued throughout the day. Williamson's concern mounted regarding the Whigs' position;

the militiamen had not found water, and gunpowder was running low. They did have some food provisions. Finally, just prior to dusk, a joyful shout went up from within the stockade, so loud it concerned Major Robinson inside the Ninety Six jail. The militiamen had struck good water after digging hard to 40 feet. Williamson was buoyed and decided to take aggressive action. He organized six groups of 20 men each, under the command of Captains Andrew Pickens, James McCall, James Middleton, Robert Anderson, Francis (Frank) Sinquefield, and James Colson to go out after nightfall and attack groups of Tories at six separate locations. He believed a successful hit-and-run action would worry the Tories and would also reduce the superior Tory advantage.

Major Robinson, quite upset about the ruckus he heard from Williamson's Fort, was concerned that he had lost his advantage of controlling the Whig's water supply. Additionally, he had probably heard by this time of Colonel Richardson's foray into the backcountry to search for the same Patrick Cunningham that was engaged at Ninety Six. Robinson feared the Whig might meander near enough to Ninety Six to be a problem. Robinson was also aware that his own force was composed of undisciplined and ill-trained ruffians. Consequently, before night fully took hold, he had draped a white flag from a window on the top floor of the jail. He did not want to risk being penned at Ninety Six by Richardson, and he feared he would experience desertions should the siege drag on.

Major Williamson put the nighttime attack plan on hold and received a courier from Robinson with a demand for surrender of all Whig arms and immediate dispersal of the Whig militia. Williamson responded by sending Captain John Bowie to the jail with his reaction as noted in a report to President Drayton written on the 25th, "Major Mayson and myself jointly answered that we were determined never to resign our arms."[16] Bowie was asked to tarry at the jail while Robinson and Cunningham considered their next action.

Williamson continued in his report, "and in about two hours, Mr. Bowie, who carried our answer returned, with a letter making the same demand, and with him Patrick Cunningham, whom I met about 50 yards from the gate."[17] After a brief discussion, the three went inside to continue their talk. They agreed to have a formal peace conference to be held at 8:00 A.M. the next morning at a building within the village. Cunningham then returned to the jail.[18]

Majors Williamson and Mayson, with Captains Pickens and Bowie, went to the village at 8:00 A.M. on the 22nd and met with Major Robinson and Captains Cunningham, McLauren, and Richard Pearis. Williamson was unaware that he could negotiate from strength; he had not yet heard of Colonel Richardson's approach into the backcountry. Robinson, however, was eager to finalize and withdraw, so the negotiations went well. The two factions agreed to immediately end hostilities and deliver their existing disputes to higher authorities for arbitration. The Tories would appeal to Royal Governor Sir William Campbell and the Whigs to the Council of Safety. A truce would be maintained for 20 days to allow the negotiations to transpire in Charles Town and for couriers to return to the backcountry with any decisions or orders.

The Tory militia was to withdraw forthwith beyond the Saluda River at Island Ford until they received orders from the Governor, and the Whigs would promptly march out of the stockade. All prisoners taken by each side since the November 2 would be returned to their own camps. Williamson's Fort was to be destroyed without harm to any of Savage's outbuildings, and the well would be filled in. Some 400 Tory militiamen heard of the pending agreement and gathered near the negotiators' location. The mob demanded that any agreement include surrender of the Whigs' swivel guns. Williamson refused to yield the cannons. He was firm that the Whigs should keep all of their arms; however, Major Robinson convinced him that relinquishment of the swivel guns would be temporary. The agreement, called Articles of Cessation of Ninety Six, was then altered and signed.

In his report of the 25th, Major Williamson stated the Whigs had adequate food and water; however, they were limited in how long they could withstand a siege because of the shortage of powder. He continued,

> after the articles were agreed on and were ready for signing, their people to the number of between three and four hundred surrounded the house where we were and swore if the swivels were not given up they would abide by no such articles, on which the gentlemen of the opposite party declared (to us privately) upon their honor that if we would suffer it to be so inserted in the agreement they would return them.[19]

Robinson actually returned the swivel guns the day Major Williamson wrote the reports, and Williamson sent them to Charles Town.[20] Major James Mayson also wrote in a report:

> We had, at most, not more than 500 men. At first consultation with Major Williamson, we agreed to march and meet the opposite party and give them battle; but, upon consideration, we thought it most prudent to march all our men to Col. Savage's old field, near Ninety Six, as our numbers were small, compared with the other party, and to fortify the same place with rails thereabouts. We arrive there about daybreak, and in about two hours a square of one hundred and eighty-five yards, was fortified in such manner as to keep off the enemy; but before three days had expired, our men began to be outrageous for want of bread and water, and we had not above sixteen pounds of gunpowder left. On Tuesday last, in the afternoon, the enemy held out a flag of truce and sent into our fort a messenger with a letter from Major Robinson to myself.[21]

The skirmish at Ninety Six was recorded as a Tory victory in arguably the first official hostile action of the Revolutionary War within South Carolina. The Tories successfully evicted the Whigs from Ninety Six. However, the Whigs only suffered one killed (James Birmingham) and 12 wounded. The numbers for Tory losses vary, depending on the report used. The Tory leaders claimed that only one (Captain Luper) was killed, and the Tory wounded are reported as anywhere from 12 to 52. Major Mayson recorded the Tory losses as 27 killed and as many wounded. Birmingham is often described as the first South Carolinian to die in the Revolutionary War.[22]

Regarding the fray, Captain Andrew Pickens is likely the only member of the family specifically mentioned because of his participation in the negotiations. However, other kin, including his brother Joseph, were a part of his militia company and involved in the defense of the stockade. His cousin William Pickens recorded in his pension application, "That about the first of August 1776 [actually 1775] he volunteered in the State of South Carolina, Abbeville [actually Ninety Six] District ... commanded by Col. Drayton.... They marched to Ninety Six at which place they were stationed, or near that place, until the 19th of November of the same year at which time the battle of Ninety Six was fought & which battle this applicant was engaged. After which time they were marched to the Long Fork of Saluda River and were engaged in scouting." (See Appendix E.)

Colonel Richard Richardson, who took leave from his Provincial Congressional seat, had set out to arrest Captain Patrick Cunningham and retake the ammunition as Drayton had so ordered. He took several days to assemble the Camden militia at Big Home Plantation on Jack's Creek. Colonel William Thomson of Orangeburg joined him with his militia and rangers. The group then set out across the Wateree for the Congarees. En route, they were joined by more militiamen. Additionally, Richardson sent orders to Ninety Six Militia Colonel John Savage, Spartan Militia Colonel John Thomas, and New Acquisition

Militia Colonel Thomas Neil to join him with their regiments. Richardson wanted to march against the Tories with an imposing force, so he further invited North Carolina Militia Colonel Thomas Polk to participate with his regiment. Richardson and Thomson encamped in the Congarees on November 26, 1775, where they heard of the siege at Ninety Six. They immediately marched toward Ninety Six to relieve Williamson but heard of the agreement and were, therefore, too late to affect the outcome. Richardson held a council of war, and it was decided that his militia was not bound by the Articles of Cessation drawn up at Ninety Six.[23]

Richardson heard on the 30th that a group of Tories was tarrying at Captain Evan McLauren's property on the Dutch Fork, so he abruptly recommenced his march. He arrived at McLauren's on December 2, 1775, and surrounded the property where Colonels Thomas, Neil, Polk and James Lyles soon joined him with their militias. While at McLauren's, they were able to round up numerous Tory militiamen, including several captains, who readily surrendered as they wanted no part of Richardson's imposing 2,500-man force. Tory Colonel Thomas Fletchall was still smarting from embarrassment. He had lost the confidence of his men after he signed the September treaty. Some of Thompson's rangers found Fletchall on Fair Forest Creek in either a cave or a hollow tree.[24] The Whigs also captured Captains Richard Pearis and Daniel Plummer.

Private William Hillhouse, Jr., later a captain of Colonel Neil's New Acquisition Militia Regiment, met his first real action. He stated in his pension application, "I entered the service of the United States, in the month of December in the year 1775, under the command of Brigadier General Richardson [colonel at the time], in the Regiment of Col. Thomas Neil, as a private soldier in the company commanded by Captain Thomas Kirkpatrick and left the service the first of October 1781." (See Appendix E. General Cornwallis' bivouac at the Hillhouse estate during the Battle of Cowpens will be treated in Chapter 9. A result of later associations between the Pickens and Hillhouse families is the marriage of Elijah Boyd Hillhouse, grandson of William Hillhouse's brother, James, to Ann Gibson, great-granddaughter of Captain Joseph William Pickens. See Appendix F.)

Colonel Richardson had arrived at Ninety Six on the December 8. He met with Major Williamson who was not yet ready to join the venture. Williamson was determined to honor his obligation under the Articles of Cessation for a few more days. Richardson issued a proclamation to put the Tory sympathizers on notice:

> Patrick Cunningham ... did raise a dangerous insurrection ... did feloniously take and carry away a quantity of ammunition ... and did attack, besiege, kill and wound a number of good people of this colony. I am now come into these parts, in the name and behalf of the Colonies to demand of the inhabitants, the delivering up of the bodies of the principal offenders herein, together with the said ammunition and full restitution for the ravages committed, and also the arms and ammunition of all the aiders and abettors of those robbers, murderers, and disturbers of the peace.... And in case of neglect or refusal ... I shall be under the necessity of taking such steps as will be found disagreeable; but which I shall certainly put in execution for the public good.[25]

On the 16th, Colonel Richardson dispatched his son, Captain Richard Richardson, Jr. (who had been injured in the foray), to lead a group to Charles Town. The Captain's detachment was ordered to deliver those Tory militia officers captured at McLauren's for incarceration. Colonel Richardson sent a letter of introduction along with his son that named the prisoners, most notably Colonel Fletchall and Captain Pearis. Colonel Richardson stated, "These being all adjudged by the officers and people here to be offenders of such a nature that from the active part they have taken, it would be dangerous for me ... to let either of them go."[26] He went on to say that Pearis, and other Tories, clearly were enflaming the Cherokee against the Whigs.

As Richardson planned to resume his venture into the backcountry, he was ordered by the Council of Safety to present an option to any Tories he might encounter. The Loyalists could, if they chose, lay down their arms and declare neutrality. In return, they would receive mercy and the protection of the Provincial Congress.

In mid–December, North Carolina Militia Colonels Griffith Rutherford and Joseph Graham, and Lieutenant Colonel James Martin, joined Richardson. Colonel Richardson began his second foray with over 3,000 militiamen, and he reached Hollingsworth's Mill December 20, 1775. Beaufort Colonel Stephen Bull, Georgia Captain LeRoy Hammond, and Ninety Six Major Williamson joined Richardson there with their militias. Richardson's force was now an overwhelming 5,000 men. As they marched, they did encounter several Tories who surrendered their arms.

Backcountry Loyalists were awestruck by the size of Richardson's force and several Loyalist captains surrendered, with their militia companies, at Hollingsworth's. Each signed an affidavit vowing to never take up arms against Provincial Congressional forces at risk of forfeiture of property. Those captives were then paroled to return home and were also allowed to retain their arms. Captain Patrick Cunningham and his group had withdrawn to Cherokee country and made camp at a canebrake on the Reedy River (in present-day southern Greenville County, South Carolina), only 25 miles from Richardson's encampment.[27]

Colonel Richardson assigned Colonel William Thomson to lead a force of just over 1,000 men to capture Cunningham's camp. (Most historians don't specifically mention others that were along on the foray with Thomson. A few have expressed doubts that the Ninety Six Militia was involved; however, A. L. Pickens and J. B. O. Landrum specifically mentioned that the subcommand under Thomson was shared by Colonels Neil, Polk, Lyles, Martin and Rutherford and Major Williamson.)[28]

The pension application of William Pickens noted, "Saluda River and were engaged in scouting ___ until they marched to Reedy River & routed the Tories that were encamped there. This was about the last of December in the same year." (See Appendix E.) Clearly, the Ninety Six Militia was involved.

Thomson's command, comprised entirely of volunteers, left on their venture in early morning on December 21, 1775. They reached Cunningham's camp after dark, surrounded it, and waited for morning. The attack began at dawn on the 22nd, and the Tories were taken completely by surprise. Cunningham did not have time to fully clothe himself before he made a drastic bareback ride out of camp and escaped shouting for everyone to, "shift for himself." In all, 130 Tories were captured; six were killed, and much of the powder had been retaken. Thomson took the prisoners back to Hollingsworth's on the 23rd. Upon his return, a harsh winter storm blanketed the camp.[29]

The snow fell for 30 hours and accumulated to a depth of two feet. Richardson began to release his militia units on the 25th, but he retained enough men to handle the prisoners. Major Williamson's militia carried the reacquired ammunition to the Cherokee for whom it had originally been intended.

Richardson's force, along with the prisoners, finally arrived back at the Congarees on January 1, 1776. On the 2nd he wrote the Council of Safety:

> Eight days we never set foot on the earth or had a place to lie down, till we had spaded or grabbled away the snow, from which circumstances, many are frost bitten, some very badly; and on

the third day a heavy cold rain fell, together with sleet; and melted the snow and filled every creek and river with a deluge of water; but with all these difficulties we reached this place yesterday with the prisoners.[30]

Captain Thomas Sumter, Colonel Richardson's Adjutant, took a detachment and escorted the prisoners to Charles Town.

Hence, the Snow Campaign, and the Battle of the Great Cane Brakes (or the Reedy River Fight) ended. The campaign had been very successful, and the Whigs totally controlled the backcountry—for a while.

4

Here Come the Redcoats! Here Come the Cherokee! (1776)

The beginning of 1776 was uneventful in the South Carolina backcountry. Although tentative, peace did abide. John Savage sold the remainder of his Ninety Six property to his wife's (Ann's) brothers, Tacitus and Isaac Gaillard, who would only own it for one year.

The prisoners captured at Great Cane Brakes were received and jailed at Charles Town. Captain Thomas Sumter, Colonel Richardson's Adjutant General, had brought them in from Ninety Six. The Council of Safety, upon jailing the prisoners, offered a substantial reward for the apprehension of Patrick Cunningham who had escaped capture.

Generally the Whigs tried to maintain order with their newly-gained control; however, it was evident that the British and their puppet regime (the Royal Provincial government) were expending considerable energy to incite the Indians against the Whigs.[1]

Moses Kirkland, still a resident of "the Gael of phiadelphia [sic]" on January 11, decided he had made a huge mistake when he took the mantle of a Tory, so he tried to humble himself by writing Henry Laurens (original spelling errors included):

> MAY IT PLEASE YOUR HONOUR: ...Wherefore: I Humbly Beg the fuivor of you to move to the Counsel of Safety to Have me Remove from Hear Before them as I may have the pleshor To have a hearing Before them as I Cant Butt have hopes that when thay Com to Be made acquantd With al my Conduct thay will have pity on me and Grant me Such Release as they in thire Wisdom shall se Best ... and you may depend on my Traviling through the Cuntry of Being al the Servis to the Cause I Can as I am now Convince of the Stranth of America So pray Sir fail not In Grantting my Portion and I shal Be in Duty Bound to Eevr pray for you:
> And am with Dew Respect
> may it plese your Honnor
> Your Honour mosst obedient
> And Verry Humble Serv't
> MOSES KIRKLAND[2]

Council of Safety President Henry Laurens read Moses Kirkland's letter to the Council of Safety on the 20th, and it was decided to present the matter at the upcoming meeting of the Provincial Congress.

The 2nd Provincial Congress opened its session on February 1, 1776, with numerous grave business matters on the agenda. The first item was a decision to write a letter of thanks to Colonel Richardson "for the very important and signal services he has rendered to his country and to the common cause, by putting a stop to the late dangerous and alarming insurrection which the enemies of America had excited in the interior parts of the colony; desiring the Colonel to signify the thanks of this congress also to the officers and men who were under his command upon that expedition."[3] Those actions at McLauren's and

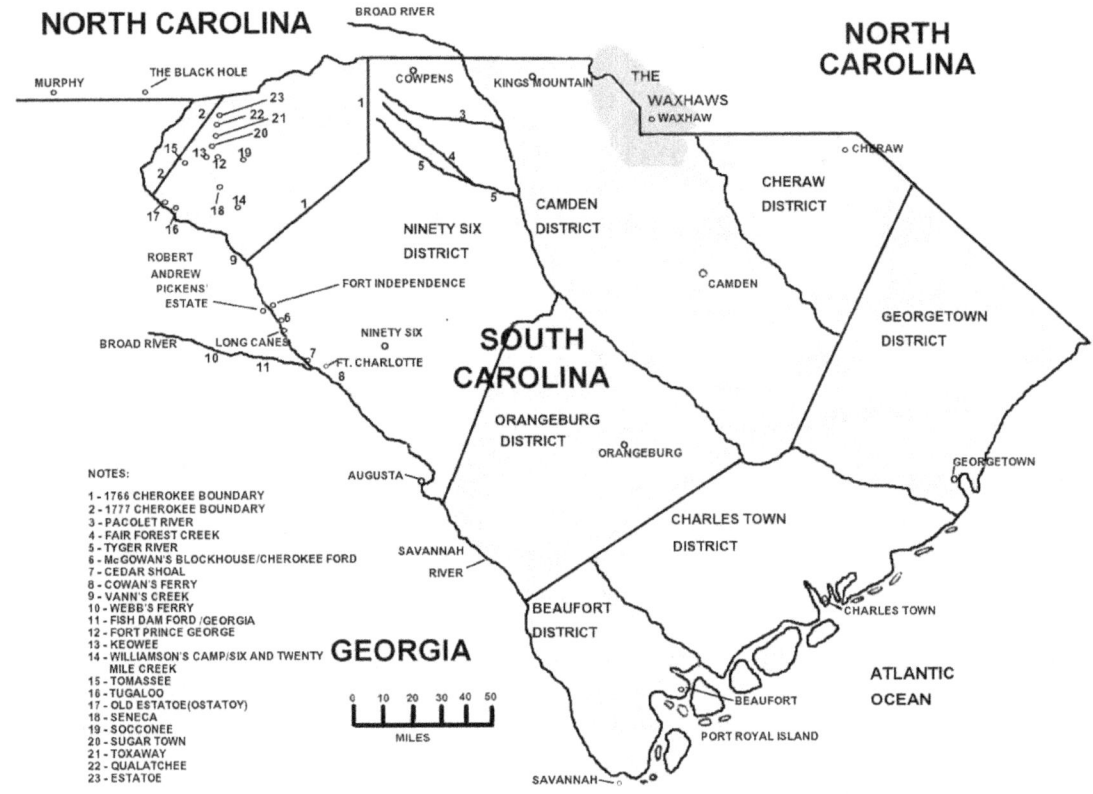

South Carolina points of interest in 1776.

the Great Cane Brakes not only resulted in the capture of Colonel Thomas Fletchall, but also broke up the Tory militia. Therefore, Congress took advantage of the opportunity and created three new military districts from a portion of the original Ninety Six Militia. The new militia districts were Spartan, Little River, and Lower Ninety Six. They would become more localized, which would thus better enable them to maintain control of the backcountry.

When the session continued on the third, Congressional President William Henry Drayton assigned Laurens, Charles Pinckney, and John Rutledge to lead an eleven-member committee that would outline a complete reorganization of the South Carolina Provincial Government. The Continental Congress had requested the change.

Laurens presented Kirkland's letter to Congress along with the British papers confiscated upon Kirkland's capture. Congress decided that Kirkland could not be trusted and should remain a prisoner.

Charles Town's defense was ever on the agenda since previously-captured communications indicated the British planned a future invasion. The Provincial Congress created two rifle regiments to bolster this effort: the 1st Regiment of Riflemen under Colonel Isaac Huger and the 2nd Regiment of Riflemen under Lieutenant Colonel Thomas Sumter. The Congress was effecting inspired decisions while formulating the future. On February 12, Commodore Peter Parker, aboard the flagship *Bristol*, set sail for America with a fleet carrying British soldiers commanded by Lieutenant General Charles Lord Cornwallis.

The Provincial Congress met again on February 27. One important item of business was the presentation of a letter, referenced as dated 25th Instant (meaning February 25, 1776), from militia Major Jonathan Downs. Downs wrote he had captured Patrick Cunningham and was on his way to Charles Town with prisoners who also included William Duggins and Hugh Brown. Then it was "Ordered, That Mr. President do issue his Warrant for the immediate commitment of the said Patrick Cunningham, Hugh Brown, and William Duggins, to the common Jail in Charlestown"[4] where they were incarcerated as Robert Cunningham had been.[5]

On March 2, 1776, The Battle of the Rice Barges ended what little British control was left in Georgia. British troops had boarded these rice-laden barges near Savannah, but a Whig militia had already burned most of the grain.[6]

Laurens' committee, which had acted quickly to outline the reorganization of the South Carolina Provincial government, presented a draft constitution on March 5. The legislature would consist of a General Assembly (comparable to a House of Representatives) of 202 members, 138 from the lowcountry and 64 from the backcountry (ten of which would be from Ninety Six District). Debate lasted the better part of a month and centered primarily on South Carolina's future relationship with Britain. John Rutledge and Henry Laurens, representing a majority of the Provincial Congress, thought it important to maintain ties with Britain while William Henry Drayton and Christopher Gadsden led a minority effort to declare independence. The South Carolina Constitution of 1776 was adopted on March 26, 1776. In the meantime the Continental Congress divided the colonies into two departments: a Northern Department under the command of a major general and two brigadier generals and a Southern Department under the command of a major general and four brigadier generals.

The Southern Department comprised Virginia, North Carolina, South Carolina, and Georgia, and was placed under the command of Major General Charles Lee. Years earlier Lee had coveted the position of Commander of the Army which was given to General George Washington.

General Lee had an extensive military background. He fought with Russian Cossacks, against Turkish fighters, and served Britain during the Seven Years War in the American theater. The Mohawk Indians called him "Boiling Water" due to his unpredictability.[7]

General Lee already had orders, now superseded, to take command in Canada. He was chagrined over the change and wrote to Washington: "As I am the only general officer on the continent who can speak or think in French, I confess I think it would have been more prudent to have sent me to Canada; but I shall obey with alacrity, and I hope with success." Washington expressed some surprise to Lee when he answered:

> I was just about to congratulate you on your appointment to the command in Canada, when I received the account that your destination was altered. As a Virginian, I must rejoice at the change, but as an American, I think you would have done more essential service to the common cause in Canada.

This was the first of several miscalculations by Congress regarding command in the Southern Department. A hint of this was evidenced when General Washington wrote to his brother, Augustine, "He is zealously attached to the cause; honest and well meaning, but rather fickle and violent, I fear, in his temper." However, Washington did think Lee a capable military officer. He continued to his brother, "He is the first in military knowledge and experience in the whole army.... I congratulate my countrymen on his appointment to that department." General Charles Lee headed south on March 7, 1776.[8]

On March 13, the Provincial Congress declared amnesty for all Tory prisoners except for the Cunningham brothers and a few other notorious leaders. Another major event occurred on the 21st when Britain declared by proclamation that all ships, including cargo, would be subject to seizure as long as the colonies remained in rebellion.

William Henry Drayton performed the first order of business for the new General Assembly and swore in, as assemblymen, all members of the now defunct Provincial Congress. The General Assembly created a Legislative Council (similar to a Senate). The legislature then elected John Rutledge as President of South Carolina. Henry Laurens was elected Vice-President and William Henry Drayton, the Provincial Chief Justice.

Governor John Rutledge. Artist: James Herring; engraver: G. F. Storm, 1854.

Major General Sir Henry Clinton was the Commander of the British Army in the South. He reported to Major General Sir William Howe, Commander of the British Army in America. Clinton believed that success in the South would depend upon the Tories who still greatly outnumbered the Whigs. He and Lieutenant General Charles Lord Cornwallis, acting as his second-in-command, left New York aboard the *Bristol* to meet with a group of North Carolina Tories. On May 2, the British fleet, commanded by Commodore Sir Peter Parker, arrived at Cape Fear, North Carolina. The British had planned to launch a southern campaign aided by North Carolina Tory militias. Clinton arrived, but the Tories did not. They had been ambushed and routed by a Whig militia. Discouraged, Clinton and Cornwallis invited the South Carolina Royal Governor, Lord William Campbell (who had been trying to govern in absentia), to meet with them aboard the *Bristol*. Their final determination was the key to victory would be the conquest of Georgia and South Carolina. They would assign control of those colonies to the Tories. The British would work their way into North Carolina, then Virginia, and finally force General Washington to capitulate in the north.[9]

The British decided to concentrate on Sullivan's Island, South Carolina. If they controlled the Island, they could coordinate an invasion of Charles Town from there. The South Carolina Patriots had been busy creating defensive structures on Sullivan's Island (see Chapter 3), but the works were incomplete. American Colonel William Moultrie wanted to continue working on the defenses, but the newly-arrived Southern Department Commander, Major General Charles Lee, thought the island would not stand and overruled him. President Rutledge ordered Moultrie to hold the island at all costs. He then dispatched reinforcements (Colonel William Thomson with his South Carolina Ranger Regiment and Lieutenant Colonel Thomas Sumter with his 2nd Rifle Regiment) to assist with the effort. As a concession to General Lee, Rutledge put him in charge of organizing the defenses at Charles Town proper. Lee inspected Drayton's efforts to construct the works and was dissatisfied with the results. He immediately ordered the batteries to be revamped. Indeed, he had written Washington that Charles Town was "utterly defenceless."[10]

The British fleet anchored off of Sullivan's Island on June 10, 1776. Clinton's first move was to issue a pardon for any Whigs willing to lay down their arms and take up allegiance to King George III. General Lee was elated to see that Clinton initially directed his efforts at Sullivan's Island rather than defenseless Charles Town. He told his staff, "He has lost an opportunity ... of taking the town."[11]

On the 28th, General Clinton ordered Sir Parker to cannonade the island; however, the weather was not conducive to a successful attack. Additionally, the British greatly miscalculated the effort required to bring the island under their control; hence, the bombardment was generally ineffective. The fort was a low-built structure, and the earth-filled double walls were constructed of palmetto wood which is soft and will not splinter under impact. Nevertheless, the British kept up the barrage for 12 uninterrupted hours.

Major General Charles Lee. Artist: Colonel J. Trumbull; engraver: G. B. Hall, 1859.

Colonel Moultrie and Lieutenant Colonel Francis Marion had better luck with their artillery. They returned deadly fire against the *Bristol*. The ship's captain and Governor Campbell were mortally wounded. Commodore Parker was severely injured and also received a concussion. Lord Cornwallis, himself, received lacerations. A British historian recorded in 1779:

> While the continued fire of our ships seemed sufficient to shake the fierceness of the bravest enemy, and daunt the courage of the most veteran soldier, the return made by the fort could not fail calling for the respect, as well as of highly incommoding the brave seamen of Britain. In the midst of that dreadful roar of artillery, they stuck with the greatest constancy and firmness to their guns; fired deliberately, and slowly, and took a cool and effective aim. The ships suffered accordingly, they were torn almost to pieces, and the slaughter was dreadful ... never did our marine in an engagement of the same nature with any foreign enemy experience so rude an encounter.[12]

A British soldier, signing as WILL. FALCONER, had been aboard one of the ships during the attack on Sullivan's Island. He wrote his brother in Scotland from New York one month after the action:

CAMP, LONG ISLAND, 13th July, 1776.
  DEAR BROTHER,
  With great difficulty I have procured this small piece of paper, to inform you of my being very well, notwithstanding the miserable situation we are in. We have been encamped on this island for this month past, and have lived upon nothing but salt pork and peas.... By this sloop-of-war you will have an account of the actions which happened on the 28th June, between the ships and the fort on Sullivan's Island. The cannonade continued for about nine hours, and was, perhaps, one of the briskest known in the annals of war. We had two 50 gun ships, five frigates from 24 to 30 guns playing upon the fort ... without success, for they did the battery no manner of dam-

age; they killed about fifteen, and wounded between forty and fifty. Our ships are in the most miserable, mangled situation you can possible imagine.... Our killed and wounded amounts to betwixt 200 and 300. Numbers die daily of their wounds. The Commodore [Parker] is wounded in two different places; his captain lost his arm and right leg, and was wounded in different parts of his body. He lived but two days after the action. Captain Scott of the Experiment [a ship], died of his wounds, and a number of officers. We are now [he is speaking of the time immediately after the battle] expecting to embark for New York, to join General [Sir William] Howe with the grand army.[13]

Several British ships ran aground while trying to evade the deadly return fire from the Americans. Most were extricated with much difficulty except for the *Acteon* on which Captain Morris was killed. Commodore Parker ordered the *Acteon* to be abandoned and set ablaze, its guns loaded and colors at full staff. The Americans boarded the ship, hauled down the colors, and fired the loaded guns at the fleeing British armada. They gathered abandoned stores from the ship and departed one-half hour before the *Acteon* blew up. The final casualty count: 35 Americans killed and wounded, 175 British killed and nearly that number wounded.

The fleet left the vicinity of Sullivan's Island while Clinton pondered his next move — to put Charles Town under siege. However, Commodore Parker would not cooperate further, and the fleet sailed for New York with Clinton, Cornwallis and their army. Any ground invasion against Charles Town would have to wait. The British would likely not have been repulsed at Sullivan's Island, and Charles Town would have fallen had the Carolinians acceded to the wishes of General Lee and withdrawn from the island fort.[14] Dr. A. L. Pickens recorded a blunt assessment of General Charles Lee and of Congress:

> The generals furnished by the Continental Congress for the operations in the South were a dynasty of tragedies. The first of the number was Charles Lee, eccentric, selfishly ambitious, and perhaps at last, traitorous. Though he lived in Virginia, he was not one of the glorious lion's brood of that state, but was a native-born Briton. Offensively superior, he sought to discourage Moultrie, who in spite of, rather than because of him ... won a glorious victory.[15]

Chief Justice William Henry Drayton was just as severe in a letter dated July 24, 1776:

> Every Idea of his [meaning General Lee] must be right, and, of course, every contrary idea in every other person must be wrong; and, contrary to the saying of the wise man, we now find, that even in a multitude of counsellors [sic] there is no wisdom, when they entertain different ideas from him, even in cases as plain as my hand. However, the General has rather been unlucky in his ideas.[16]

Major General Charles Lee initiated an ill-advised and lackluster offensive toward Florida in August but was recalled to Philadelphia. He pulled his army back and left the Florida initiative in the hands of the South Carolina State Troops under Colonel Moultrie. Lee was ordered to turn command of the Southern Department over to Brigadier General Robert Howe and returned to fight in the Northern Department. He held reduced responsibilities although was not demoted in rank.

The Declaration of Independence (though ratified on July 4, 1776) was officially signed on August 2, an event that provided legality for the Continental Army that had been operating informally for about one year. This would confuse the issue regarding the South Carolina State Troops that were still operating in Florida. The colonies were each required to provide a specified number of soldiers for the Continental Army. One way to accomplish this was to put state troops under orders of the Continental officers. State troops were similar to the local militias; however, they had an enlistment period of up to 18 months while the typical local militia enlistment was three months. The South Carolina General Assembly wanted to support the national army, so it recalled the state troops and put them under the auspices of Brigadier General Howe. Thus, General Lee's Florida campaign came to an end.

Early in May, while the British fleet was still at Cape Fear, North Carolina, General Clinton sent messengers to Indian Agent Alexander Cameron. His orders were to incite the Cherokee to open warfare against the Whigs in the backcountry, beginning July 1, 1776, to coordinate with Clinton's assault on Charles Town. This was the attack that the Whigs had feared since the capture of Kirkland, and indeed, the Cherokee acted with a vengeance. The attacks were horrific.

The Cherokee had four specific tendencies that clarified their approach to battle:

- They preferred to use superior numbers to surprise a small encampment or homestead or to draw a small undermanned detachment into an ambush. This resulted in hand-to-hand combat with tomahawks or knives, and the enemy was defeated in minutes.
- Their next favored option was to surround, or draw into ambush, a larger enemy group. They pinned the enemy down with rifle fire from an elevated position until they obtained a greater advantage through attrition (i.e., the enemy suffered illness, starvation, thirst, individual deaths in the ranks, or depleted ammunition). The Cherokee were courageous and willing to risk the loss of braves, but they would not initiate hand-to-hand combat until certain of victory.
- They were loath to encounter a large body of the enemy on equal footing. The Indians would scatter without incident if they could not secure a definite advantage, such as elevation with plenty of cover.
- The Cherokee became distressed if mounted enemies, no matter the size of the group, initiated an attack immediately upon contact (especially while brandishing sabers). The braves could not perform rapid fire and reload maneuvers with any accuracy or efficiency. They could not defend against such an attack with tomahawks or knives, so dispersed posthaste.

Andrew Williamson, as well as Andrew Pickens, was experienced with the tribal wartime inclinations that dictated their strategy throughout the coming conflict. Even though the Whigs were aware of possible Cherokee attacks, they hoped to placate the tribe. Appeasement appeared to be working; however, the Indians hid their British alliance well, and the situation seemingly changed overnight.

It is often thought that the Cherokee attacked the Whigs because of their proximity to Cherokee lands; however, the Cherokee did not attack Tory property which was just as near. Actually, the Cherokee thought it in their best interest to align with the British. They had previously relied on the redcoats for protection and had allied with them in the French and Indian War despite British encroachment upon their land which opened it to settlement. It was British Lieutenant Colonel James Grant who led the murderous expedition into Cherokee country in 1761. (See Chapter 1.)

The Cherokee would experience a similar fate at the hands of the Whigs; however, the tribe's allegiance to the British led to devastating Indian attacks upon Whig families: hence, a cataclysmic outcome in return.

Late in June, Major Andrew Williamson was falsely encouraged by his dealings with the Cherokee and reported to Chief Justice Drayton:

WHITEHALL, June 27, 1776.
Dear Sir:
...The two Cherokee Indians returned to the nation on Wednesday week, seemingly well satisfied with their journey. I gave them a strong talk, the substance as follows: That I had, agreeable to the desire of the warrior of Sugar Town, accompanied them across the frontier settlements, and told them before I set out, that if they saw, and would show me any bad white warriors, who carried lies and bad talk amongst them from the settlements, that I would take them into custody, and punish; and in return demanded liberty to send some of our people into the nation to secure

York, and other bad white people, who had carried lies and bad talk amongst them, and endeavored, by every method they could devise, to make them quarrel with us. If they complied with this proposal, I should then know they wanted to live in peace with us; but, if they denied us that liberty, I should believe they did not care to continue in friendship with us longer.... I desired them to remember — talk well, and tell it to the warriors, and return an answer soon, which I received yesterday by one Price, a half breed ... and returned an answer as follows: Thanked me for the good talk ... that the warriors of the lower towns would not interfere between the white people in their quarrel, and in future would not prevent me sending men into the nation, to take into custody such white people as went into the nation with bad talk and lies....

I am, dear sir,
Your most humble servant,
A.WM.SON.[17]

Typical Continental soldier. Artist: F.O.C. Darley; Engraver: A. Bollet, 1877.

It seems simplistic that Major Williamson put such high value on the word of the Cherokee representative without having really considered that the Indians might have been putting on a front. However, it soon became apparent to him the good relationship he had hoped for was not to be. Francis Salvador, a backcountry settler and member of the South Carolina Provincial Congress, volunteered and was appointed (likely with a staff-position rank of captain) as aide-de-camp to Williamson. Salvador reported to Drayton by letter on July 19, 1776:

Dear Sir:
...P.S. ...Capt. McCall, with 20 men, was sent by Major Williamson to the Cherokees at Seneca, to make prisoners of some white men, by the encouragement of some Indians, who had been at the Major's. When the detachment got near, the Indians came out to meet them, spoke friendly to them, and invited the captain, lieutenant, and another man, to sup with them ... and, in a few hours after, in the night, the Indians returned, and suddenly attacked the detachment, which fled as fast as possible. They are all returned but the captain and six men.[18]

Williamson may have thought the Cherokee to be too simple-minded to pull off such a ruse, but he learned from this maneuver that they were very smart and, indeed, cunning. Militia Captain James McCall was the one who would suffer because Williamson failed to account for possible betrayal.

McCall and his detachment embarked June 28 or 29, in accordance with Williamson's "agreement," to capture Indian Agent Alexander Cameron and other Tories who lived in the lower villages and were engaged to incite the Cherokee. When they arrived at Seneca, the Cherokee sprung a surprise attack. They captured McCall and six others, and killed four militiamen, including an Ensign Calhoun. Six of the Cherokee were killed. The captives were held at Seneca along with others who had previously been imprisoned in the village.

Private Charles Holland was one of a few fortunate militiamen to have escaped. He provided details of the experience for his pension application in 1832 (see Appendix E):

> He [meaning Holland] volunteered, some time in the month of September (as well as he can recollect) 1776 [actually July], in a company of militia under the command of Captain James McCall, in the District then called Ninety Six, now Abbeville, in the State of South Carolina, that said company was attached to a Regiment, or corpse [sic] of men, under the command of Major Andrew Williamson or Wimson, the Colonel, if any, not recollected; that he continued with Capt. McCall until about the month, July 1777 [actually 1776], when the Capt. was taken prisoner by the Indians & this relator was transferred to a militia company commanded by Capt. Andrew Pickens.... Captain McCall & a part of his company, including this relator were detailed to go into the Indian Nation in the northern part of the State of Georgia, after some Tories who had retreated there, when the Indians made an attack upon said detachment, killed several men & wounded several others and took Captain McCall & another prisoners.

Several times McCall had been taken to a place that the Cherokee set aside to torture and slay prisoners. Indian tribes had been known to use gruesome rituals such as scalping and torture (see Chapter 1). Horrific tortures practiced by the Indians appalled and frightened the settlers (even though these same settlers used some very grotesque means of punishment of their own — hot tar with feathers, for example). It was recently explained regarding the Indians' frightful practices:

> Their treatment of captives ... had more in common with the Pre-Columbian rituals of the Aztec and Maya. Excruciating tortures were inflicted to test the captive's soul... "burning was a common element in torture. The victim was frequently made to walk barefoot over fires, as well as being slowly roasted in other ways.... Hot irons or splinters would be thrust through his limbs.... The whole village — men, women, and children — would usually participate."[19]

The Cherokee wanted to make an impression upon McCall; consequently, he was required to witness a few of these events, some being extremely repulsive. One such presentation was the torture of a 12-year-old boy who was suspended, naked, upside down between two posts such that his head was about three feet off the ground. The braves then prepared splinters about 18 inches long that were pointed on one end and frayed on the other. They lit the frayed end and threw the splinters like lances at the boy, and the Cherokee whooped whenever the pointed end of a splinter stuck into his torso. This activity continued for about two hours until the child succumbed to the agony.

The Cherokee made the captain view a number of heinous actions. Since the Indians thought they had McCall's attention, Agent Cameron sent an Indian woman to arrange a meeting. McCall refused. He then underwent periodic torture at the hands of the braves. One night, when his guard was "preoccupied," he made good his escape and luckily fell in with a Virginia Whig militia unit on its way to Ninety Six to assist Williamson.[20]

Robert Andrew Pickens, one of Andrew and Joseph Pickens' cousins, had a very close brush with the Cherokee about the same time as McCall's frightening expedition. Pickens later told Lyman C. Draper (see Chapter 1) he had been married to his first wife (name unknown) only a few months, and was working his farm on the Georgia side of the Savannah River, due west of the Long Canes settlement. A few Cherokee braves, returning to the lower villages from Fort Charlotte, helped themselves to several settlers' horses, three of which belonged to Pickens.

Old Skiuka, the main chief of the lower villages, knew Robert Andrew Pickens very well. The Chief arranged for a half-breed trader named Hughes to carry a message to Robert Andrew. Pickens was invited to Tugaloo and told to bring two kegs of whiskey to ransom his horses. He complied with the message and, accompanied by a friend named John Welch, left with Hughes. As soon as Hughes reached his home in Tugaloo, he was notified by a young black boy that Chief Skiuka had come, taken all of Hughes' gunpowder, and gone to attack the settlers.

Pickens and Welch were in a critical situation and spent the night at Hughes' home. The next morning Hughes told them to hide under a nearby river bank because Indians were approaching. Two braves rode up to Hughes and asked him why two white men were staying there. He responded that they had come into the Nation to join the Indians in their war against the Americans. The Indians demanded to see the white brothers, so Hughes sent for Pickens and Welch. The Indians, who had apparently been drinking heavily, accepted them as brothers. Hughes then quietly advised Pickens and Welch to take two fresh horses and leave. They did as he suggested, and the Indians asked him where they were going. Hughes said he had sent them to round up his pastured horses, so he could protect them during the coming war. The braves noticed that Pickens and Welch rode two of Hughes' horses, so they were satisfied.

Pickens and Welch had not gone far when they noticed they were being watched from behind a tree. When they saw a brave run toward Tugaloo, the men figured he was suspicious. Welch suggested they speed off, but Robert Andrew decided it would draw attention to them since they were still within sight of Tugaloo. Pickens replied, "Wait till we descend the hill at hand and cross the creek at its base and then push to the utmost." After they had gone several miles, they struck the trail that led to the ford of Seneca River. Interestingly, they found Welch's coat at the ford. He had apparently left it there when coming to Tugaloo.

They crossed the river near the village of Seneca and took the path toward the settlements. They had not gone far when they saw fresh signs that indicated substantial Cherokee activity. They took to the woods to avoid the trail and trekked until night. Welch was in pain and suffering from having traveled in miserable weather. He had required several breathers, so after dark the travelers rested. Welch urged Pickens to go ahead and get help at the settlement, but Robert Andrew would not leave Welch behind.

The two men hobbled their horses and retired. Welch felt better the next morning. Once they struck the trail to the settlements, about half a mile from where they had bedded down, they discovered that an Indian war party had returned from a raid in the settlements while they slept. Had Pickens and Welch proceeded on, made a short rest rather than sleeping through the night, or even built a fire to ease Welch's discomfort, their lives would have been at great risk.

That day, the men reached Fort Independence on Rocky River, the extreme frontier of Abbeville District. On the way, they passed the house of Sam Marrow. Apparently, the same returning Cherokee party they had avoided as they slept had reduced the house to ruins. Sam, who lived alone, had escaped to Fort Independence. Pickens greatly feared for his family and kindred, but his fear eased considerably when his wife ran out from the fort to meet him. The refugees in the fort were relieved to see that Pickens and Welch had not succumbed to a war party. Robert Andrew was then told that some of his wife's relatives had been killed, and that all local families had come to shelter at Fort Independence.

(This Fort Independence is not the well-known fort on the Georgia side of the Savannah. John Pickens, uncle of Andrew and Joseph Pickens and father of Robert Andrew Pickens, built this fort upon his land on Great Rocky Creek near Lowndesville, South Carolina. It was one of many small forts that had sprung up on private estates throughout the backcountry when the Cherokee went to war. The early settlers believed this fort was needed for protection against the Indians, as they were on the then-extreme frontier. The location is now under Lake Secession on Rocky River.)

Many of these smaller fortifications were simply modified houses or outbuildings that were altered with the addition of timbers. These structures were often named after the owners of the property. Fort Independence is mentioned in the pension applications of Robert Andrew Pickens, William Pickens, and William Gabriel Pickens, all cousins of Andrew and Joseph Pickens (see Appendix E). Land grants for 1765 show that several Pickenses had land on Great Rocky Creek.

William Pickens assisted to erect this fort, and William Gabriel Pickens was detached there under the command of his brother, Captain John Pickens. Many families relocated to Fort Independence about July 1, 1776, as the Cherokee War of 1776 began. (Robert Andrew Pickens obtained a grant for the property in 1784, and it adjoined land he inherited from his father in 1770. His farm, mentioned in the experience he related to Draper, was directly across the Savannah River from the fort.)[21]

Skiuka commanded Cherokee who participated in attacks on Whigs in the backcountry as requested by the British. He, himself, led raids down the Georgia side of the Savannah and killed many settlers. When he returned to Tugaloo, he found that Pickens had been there. Skiuka was sorry he had missed Robert Andrew, and he thought he had probably been killed en route to the settlements. He regretted he could not have killed Pickens himself "in an easy death, for he loved him."[22]

Royal Indian Agent Alexander Cameron guided some of the Cherokee on raids into backcountry settlements where they killed without regard to age or sex. Those settlements lay mostly between the Savannah and the Saluda Rivers. Interestingly, only Tory houses escaped the carnage. The Tories had been warned in advance to erect peculiarly-crafted poles in front of their houses. Some Tories may have been attacked if they weren't prepared with the designated protective monument; however, this verifies the bloody contest was not primarily Cherokee versus white settlers but Cherokee versus the enemies of Britian.[23]

Several of the atrocities that took place were recorded; one included in Francis Salvador's report to Chief Justice Drayton on July 18, 1776, from Dewitt's Corner: "You would have been surprised to have seen the change in this country ... one of Capt. Smith's sons [John Smith] came to my house, with two of his fingers shot off.... I immediately galloped to Major Williamson's, to inform him, but found another of Smith's sons there, who made his escape, and alarmed that settlement."[24]

The boys' father, Captain Aaron Smith of Long Canes, Smith's wife, five of their children, and one black servant were all slain. Only the two boys and two of their sisters, who were captured by the Cherokee, survived. The girls were returned after the Cherokee War was settled.[25]

Salvador lived on Coronaca Creek at the outer edge of the backcountry settlements. He spread the alarm of the Cherokee attack through the small settlements on his ride to Williamson's plantation. This earned him the sobriquet of the Jewish Paul Revere.

(Williamson's Plantation, called White Hall, was located six miles south of present-day Greenwood, South Carolina, 1,000 feet north of US Highway 221 on Whitehall Road or State Road 24–156, 12 miles west of Ninety Six. Salvador's estate was near present-day Coronaca, South Carolina.

The distance of Salvador's ride is normally reported as 30 miles; however, the distance from Coronaca to White Hall is closer to 18. Even if an historian allows for an indirect route to warn settlers, Salvador would not have strayed far from the direct line of travel because of the injured John Smith. It is probable he rode from White Hall to sound the alarm at Ninety Six. That would have been a ride of 30 miles from Coronaca via White Hall.)

At the headwaters of the Tyger River, Anthony Hampton, his wife, one son (Preston), and a grandson were slain. The location was a holy place for the Cherokee, and they had been awaiting an opportunity to evict the Hamptons. Coincidentally, Anthony Hampton's married sons (Henry, Wade, Edward and John) who lived nearby, but a little farther toward the settlements, had been trying to arrange talks with the Indians to negotiate a peace treaty. These sons and their families somehow avoided the massacre.

Concurrently, James Reed, who was visiting the Tyger settlement from North Carolina, "was attacked at the old ford on the North Tyger River, a short distance below Snoddy's Bridge." He was wounded through the breast and thigh. When a brave came to scalp him, he fought the Indian for his tomahawk, took it from him, and chased him away.[26]

Another Tyger area settler, a Mr. Miller, had been visiting his neighbors. While he and two other men (a Mr. Leach and a Mr. Orr) were crossing Middle Tyger River, some Cherokee shot him. Leach and Orr tried to escape but were chased to a marsh by the Indians. Leach fell into the marsh and played 'possum while Orr jumped across and kept running. The Indians chased Orr and left Leach where he lay, as they thought him dead. When they caught up with Orr, they killed and scalped him. Leach, meanwhile, escaped. Orr was buried where he fell, and Miller was buried at the fork of the North Tyger and Middle Tyger Rivers.

The Cherokee killed a Mr. Bishop and captured his three children while Mrs. Bishop was away visiting friends. The children were returned after the end of the Cherokee War.

The Hannon family lived on the North Pacolet River. A Cherokee war party killed Mr. Hannon and some of his family members as they planted corn. When he spied the Indians and saw them attack his family, ten-year-old Edwin Hannon grabbed his little brother, John, and ran for the North Pacolet with some of the braves close behind. At the river's edge, Edwin had to drop his brother to escape capture. As he was crossing the river, he heard the blows that ended John's life. His eight-year-old sister, Winnie, had grabbed another little brother, William, and successfully hid in some nearby canebrakes until the Indians rode away.

Cherokee surprised the Kemp family on the Broadmouth River. The Indians rapidly killed them, burned their house and outbuildings, and threw the dead bodies into the flaming structures. One young son was the sole survivor.[27] The slaughter and destruction were widespread and severe. Reverend James Creswell wrote to Chief Justice Drayton from Ninety Six on July 27, 1776:

> Honored Sir: I make no doubt but you are anxious to hear how our affairs stand in this perplexed and unhappy district, since the heathen has broke in on our frontier.... The savages have spread great desolation all along the frontiers, and killed a great number.... Ninety Six is now a frontier. Plantations lie desolate and hopeful crops are going to ruin. In short, dear sir, unless we get some relief, famine will overspread our beautiful country.... Fences are thrown down, and many have already suffered a great loss. Such of us as are in forts have neither suitable guns nor ammunition, for the defence [sic] of our wives and little ones.[28]

Major Williamson began mustering forces right after the initial Cherokee incursion. Robert Andrew Pickens, in his interview with Lyman C. Draper, stated:

> General Williamson assembled his troops July 1, 1776 on a creek, a tributary of the Saluda River in Pendleton District, S.C. They numbered about 8 or 10 hundred me [sic]. There were two regiments. General Williamson was at the head of one and General Andrew Pickens at the head of

the other. In Picken's [sic] regiment it is recollected that Capt. Norwood, Capt. Robert F. Anderson and Captain Joseph Pickens, the latter a brother of Gen. Pickens.[29]

(Williamson was actually a major, Andrew Pickens a captain, and Joseph Pickens a lieutenant at the time. Also, Williamson did not have that many men early in the campaign.)

Many of the militiamen wanted to protect their remaining family members who were holed up in the many makeshift forts that had sprouted on private Whig properties throughout the backcountry. Therefore, Williamson had only mustered about 40 men by July 1, 1776. Larger numbers of settlers had moved into the aforementioned Fort Independence and the village of Ninety Six which had been stockaded.

On July 3, 1776, Major Williamson began to move toward the Cherokee Nation with his small party. He camped near the burned-out dwelling on the Smith property. There he awaited additional militia. On July 4, 40 more militiamen arrived; then, 30 more on July 5, so Williamson, albeit slowly, began his foray toward the lower Cherokee villages. He stopped at Dewitt's Corner on Hogskin Creek on July 8; he had then marshaled 200 men. Williamson's march was concurrent with the atrocities already described as the Cherokee war parties trailed him through the settlements.[30] (DeWitt's Corner was located at present-day Due West, South Carolina.)

On July 14, 1776, several Whig families relocated to Lindley's Fort for protection and were joined by a large militia force under Major Jonathan Downs. (This is the same officer that had captured Captain Patrick Cunningham.) A large force of Cherokee and Tories dressed as Cherokee attacked the fort on the morning of the 15th.[31] The army was still at Dewitt's Corner on July 19, 1776. There, on the same day, Captain Salvador completed a letter to Chief Justice Drayton that he had begun on the 18th. The addition included a description of the attack:

> I rode there [Lindley's Fort on the Saluda River] last Saturday, and found Col. Williams and Liles, and two companies from Col. Richardson's regiment, amounting to 430 men. They were attacked on Monday morning, by Indians and Scopholites [a variation of Schofieldites, the old Tory militia], but repulsed them, taking thirteen white men prisoners. The Indians fled the moment day appeared.... We have just received an account that two of the Cherokees' head warriors were killed in the late skirmish at Lindley's Fort.... P.S.—We, this day, increased to 600, all from the same regiment.... At Lindley's Fort ... the fort was attacked by ... eighty-eight Indians and one hundred and two whites.[32]

Major Williamson wrote a follow-up report of the incident from his camp on Barker's Creek on the 22nd: "exasperated at the behavior of Hugh Brown, and others, who have lately joined the Indians against us, thirteen of which were taken prisoners, a few days ago, and sent to Ninety-Six jail—four of which were found painted as Indians."[33]

Reverend Creswell also mentioned the affair in his letter to Drayton of the 27th and included an estimate of the number of Indians and Tories involved:

> The savages have spread great desolation.... On the 14th they attacked a part of Colonel Williams' regiment at Lindley's Fort, but were repulsed.... This attack was made by ninety Indians and 120 white men. Ten of the white Indians were made prisoners, nine of which were painted. They are now safe at Ninety-Six.[34]

(There are differences between Reverend Creswell's account and those of Salvador and Williamson regarding the date of the action, the numbers of enemy combatants, prisoners, and prisoners dressed as Cherokee. The accounts of Salvador and Williamson are likely the more precise.)

Williamson had amassed only 450 men by July 16 and was still encamped at Hogskin

Creek.³⁵ He had issued several muster requests and continued to wait for additional militiamen to answer the call. While he was biding his time and planning his campaign, he was visited by two old nemeses. Captains Robert Cunningham and Richard Pearis, recently released from prison at Charles Town, had heard of the attacks in the backcountry and offered their services to Williamson. Their release from prison was of great concern to the Whigs in the backcountry; Williamson was no exception. Salvador noted in his aforementioned letter to Drayton:

> Williamson was employed night and day sending expresses to raise the militia ... we were joined by forty more, and have been gradually increasing ever since, though all the men in the country were loathe to turn out, till they had procured some kind of fancied security for their families. However, we had last night [meaning the 17th] 500 men.... On last accounts from town, that Cunningham and his companions were set at liberty, we were very near having a mutiny in camp; and it is really a measure ... very alarming to all ranks of people. Cunningham and Pearis came here last night [meaning the 18th] ... he was treated politely, but with reserve, the Major and myself having advised him to go home, and mind his private business, at which he seemed chagrined. I am clear he had not yet given up the idea of being a man of consequence; but the friends of liberty in this part of the world are determined to have no connection with him.... We have just heard ... that the white people in general had quitted the Indians, after the repulse at Lindley's, and were delivering themselves up to Col. Liles. He has sent all those to Ninety-Six jail.³⁶

Williamson also addressed his muster attempts, his campaign plan, and the visit by Cunningham in his letter of the 22nd written from Barker's Creek:

> I am now encamped here with about 700 effective men from this regiment, which, with 136 who do duty in the different forts, you'll see turned out pretty well.... Capts. Tate and Prince's companies of Riflemen, have just now joined me. They consist of ninety-three effective men; and tomorrow Col. Williams ... will also join me, with about 200 men. Captain Hammond marched with a detachment of 100 picked men, on Friday morning, for Paris' [sic] house, where I am informed a party of the enemy have been skulking about there some days past. I expect hourly to hear from him, and some agreeable news. He has my orders if he can conveniently join Col. Thomas and Niel [sic], to act in concert with them, and proceed directly into the nation by Estatoe, while I penetrate by way of Seneca and the Sugar Town.... Lieut.-Col. Polk, of Niel's [sic] regiment, with 800 men well armed, has joined Thomas; and I am told ... that Polk is eager to join me.... Robert Cunningham and Paris [sic] came to my camp. The former ... declared himself our fast friend, and that he came to stand and fall with us. I was sorry I could not show him the countenance I would have wished, owing to the people being so much exasperated.... I have no doubt of Cunningham proving true to his declaration, but at present it would be improper to confer any public trust on him.³⁷

It is interesting that while Pearis accompanied Cunningham to visit Williamson, several Tories who had attacked Lindley's Fort were sheltered at his property near the eastern boundary of the Cherokee Nation (proximate to the outskirts of what is now Greenville, South Carolina.) Those Tories were the "party of the enemy" Williamson referred to in his letter, and they used Pearis' place as a base camp while they continued to attack Whig settlers around the area.

Chief Justice Drayton was no fan of Pearis, Cunningham, Tories or the Cherokee. In a July 24 letter to Salvador he stated:

> the discharge [release from prison] of Cunningham and his companions.... I must applaud your resolution to consider Cunningham "in future merely as an individual, and not as head of any party. Such is the station he ought ever to hold.... As for the fate of the thirteen white prisoners taken upon the repulse of the Indians— speaking as W.H.D. [William Henry Drayton] in private character, I think the republic would have received an essential piece of service had they all been instantly hanged.... For my part, I shall never give my voice for peace with the Cherokee Nation upon any other terms than their removal beyond the mountains.³⁸

Colonel Ross and his Spartan Militia arrived at Pearis' property shortly before Captain John Hammond. There they captured a large number of Tories and dispersed the remainder. Ross burned the structures, took Pearis' wife and daughters captive, and also took Pearis' cattle, horses and personal effects. Ross' militia headed back to Ninety Six with the prisoners and the loot. When he arrived at Colonel Hight's place, he found a horrific scene of destruction and murder. The Tories had turned the only survivors, Mrs. Hight and her daughters, over to the Indians who had taken them to the Cherokee Nation for their amusement.[39]

Besides Andrew and Joseph, several Pickens cousins and a future in-law took part in support of this campaign. Pension statements of the following show their participation in, or direct support to, the foray (see Appendix E):

> On this 4th day of February 1833 personally appeared ... William G. [Gabriel] Pickens.... As soon as I joined the service, which was to aid in guarding the frontiers and in repelling these Indians, Captain Anderson stationed himself at one of these forts called Independence, situate on the Savannah, where we remained fourteen months in constant service against these Indians—in scouring the country and protecting the inhabitants. In the latter part of the year 1777 [actually 1776] (I think in December) General Williamson made a campaign into the Indian Country and defeated the Indians first at Sinico [sic] and next at Tomassa [sic], or some such name; which gave the frontier inhabitants an interval of peace, as the Indians were driven off.... I was not in this campaign, having been left with others under Captain John Pickens (my brother) to guard the fort. But the most of my company, under Captain Anderson was in this expedition.
>
> On this the 16th day of September, 1833, personally appeared ... William Pickens.... The following year [1776] the Indians committed frequent depredations and this applicant together with many families were compelled to erect a fort for their safety and defence called Fort Independence. They remained stationed in this fort about two or three months during which time this applicant was constantly engaged discharging the duties of a spy.
>
> On this 23rd day of October, 1832, personally appeared ... Andrew Pickens [meaning Robert Andrew the interviewee of Lyman Draper].... That he entered the service on or about the 15th July, 1776, and marched into the Cherokee Nation, in what was called the Cherokee Expedition.
>
> On this third day of February— personally appeared ... William Hillhouse.... My next term of service commenced about the last of July 1776, and continued two months. This tour was performed principally in the then Indian Country, now the Districts of Greenville, Anderson and Pickens, in the State of South Carolina. In this period of service there was skirmishing with the Indians, some of them, and a few of our soldiers were killed.

Williamson's problem with mustering men was due in part to the militiamen who wanted to see to the security of their families; however, there was also a problem with his rank. Several of the militiamen didn't understand why they should begin such a foray under the leadership of a Major. Williamson, though he was selected by Congress to lead the expedition, was to coordinate his plan with other regiments that did have Colonels for their commanders, and military discipline was endangered due to the natural jealousies that emerged.

Francis Salvador, in his letter of the 18th and 19th, stated:

> They grumble at being commanded by a Major; and I fear, if they join us at all (which I doubt), they will be very apt to prejudice the service by altercations about command. I cannot help saying, that if Williamson is fit to conduct such an expedition, he certainly ought to have a much higher rank than any of these classes, who don't object to his person, but his rank. I likewise think it an omission that the colonels on the other side of the river have no written orders to put themselves, or their men, under his command.[40]

Chief Justice Drayton answered on July 24:

> As for my friend, Major Williamson, I long to see him Colonel of the regiment ... he does infinitely more honor to it than any Colonel it ever had; of this rank we must say something hereafter. At

present the title of Commander-in-Chief of the expedition against the Cherokee, with which he is vested, will give him command of any colonel in his army ... they cannot have in the camp or army but what is derived from the Major ... the major may authorize them to command their several detachments under him ... receive their usual pay while in active service. But this may be depended upon , that any conduct that shall clash with Major Williamson's orders will be carefully examined into.[41]

This lack of action regarding Williamson's rank did not do him any favors. Drayton implied that such consideration needed to await a future session of the Provincial Congress. Williamson's responsibility to head an expedition into the heated Cherokee Nation was much more complicated as he was forced to maintain a superior position over higher-ranking officers. Granted, this was a militia and not a "regular army." Militia decorum was often more relaxed than that of the Continental Army. However, the success of such an important mission would have to be top priority, and Williamson's situation endangered his mission.

The coming war with the Cherokee would be handled differently than was Grant's 15 years earlier. Grant was a British officer, and he moved with a full entourage that included wagons with food, artillery, ammunition, and extra clothing. This new incursion into the Cherokee Nation would be entirely a militia action. The militias (Whig or Tory) traditionally traveled light. Each man carried what he could in his saddle pack or on his belt. A militiaman was mounted and relied on a rifle, saber, small caliber pistol, knife and tomahawk. He carried a powder horn, shot bag, and extra flints. He subsisted primarily on water (carried in a canteen or leather flask), jerked beef, and journey cake, which was a mixture of cornmeal and water fried or baked until firm. (Journey cake was later called Johnnycake — the forerunner of hardtack in the old west.) He might also have carried his corn meal as mush boiled to the consistency of heavy bread and wrapped in corn husks or linen for flexibility; either eaten as is or sliced and cooked further into journey cake. Other backcountry travel fare might have been parched corn or dried pumpkin. The troops usually commandeered any other required subsistence, such as grain or fresh beef, from the properties of enemy sympathizers.

Militias primarily pressed an attack on horseback with small arms and rarely dismounted. When they did, they alit with their rifles, quickly staked their horses, fired from cover for a short time (as long as they had a suitable advantage), and then quickly remounted to chase a fleeing enemy or to retreat when necessary.

On July 29, 1776, Williamson established his base camp with 1,150 men on a ridge beyond Six-and-Twenty Mile Creek, about 15 miles across the Cherokee Nation boundary. The time to press the enemy had arrived. On the 31st at 6:00 P.M., after he received intelligence regarding Alexander Cameron's location, Williamson embarked across Eighteen Mile Creek with Captains Andrew Pickens, LeRoy Hammond, James McCall, and a 300-man regiment.

Major Williamson's objective was to move quickly and surround the enemy encampment at Oconee Creek by daybreak, August 1, 1776. The only direct route necessitated crossing the Keowee River at Seneca (near where Clemson University now stands, the village site now beneath present-day Lake Hartwell). Two Tory prisoners told the Whigs where Cameron was and led them toward the encampment. However, the Tories intended to lead Williamson into a trap at Seneca after they had assured him the village was deserted.[42] Major Williamson split his regiment for the march. The Commander took the point with Captain Hammond and a 33-man advance party. Pickens, with his entire company, trailed a bit behind the advance. McCall followed several miles back with the remainder of the force; a common arrangement to avoid exposure of an entire force to possible ambush. Pickens was to quickly support Williamson in the event of surprise, and McCall would join them at Oconee once the enemy had been located and surrounded.

Williamson, from an encampment below Keowee, stated in a letter to Drayton on August 4, 1776:

> I accordingly marched about six o'clock in the evening, with thirty-three men on horseback, (taking two prisoners with me to show me where the enemy were encamped...) intending to surround their camp by day-break ... the river Keowee lying on the route, and only passable at a ford at Seneca, obliged me (though much against my inclination) to take the road; the enemy ... laid themselves in ambush ... had taken possession of the first houses in Seneca, and posted themselves behind a long fence on an eminence close to the road where we were to march, and to prevent being discovered had filled up the openings betwixt the rails ... suffered the guides and advance guard to pass ... poured in a heavy fire upon my men ... which being unexpected, staggered my advanced party.[43]

(Many letters and reports were issued from backcountry bivouacs. Quills made from cane, readily available near marshlands, were substituted for feather quills that were abundant only in the villages. Ink was often a mixture of gunpowder and a small amount of water.)

Williamson's advance party approached Seneca at 2:00 A.M. on August 1, 1776, and intended to pass quietly through the supposed evacuated village. However, they had been watched since they left their base camp. A large group of Tories and Cherokee braves, led by Chief Skiuka, ambushed them at the village. Cameron, himself, was not in the area as he had planned the ambuscade from the relative safety of Oconee. Williamson's army stiffened, and a fierce fight ensued. The combat around the fence where a majority of the concealed party had waited was especially intense, and vision was difficult in the darkness.

Several were wounded early in the battle, and Captain Salvador, dressed in a very bright white uniform, was hit three times. The Cherokee had thought Salvador to be Williamson because of his finery; however, Williamson was plainly dressed in accord with common militia practice. A Cherokee brave approached and scalped Salvador who died less than an hour later. Captain John Smith, one of the two surviving sons of the massacred Aaron Smith family, was near Salvador. The Indian, however, had approached unusually slowly, and Smith thought him to be Salvador's servant.

Williamson's horse was shot out from under him, and he reportedly shouted to a subordinate, "Get me Salvador's horse! Damn you! Get me Salvador's horse!" In Williamson's letter of the 4th he continued:[44]

> Here Mr. Salvador received three wounds, and fell by my side; my horse was shot down under me, but I received no hurt. Lieut. Farar, of Captain Prince's Company, immediately supplied me with his. I desired him to take care of Mr. Salvador, but before he could find him in the dark, the enemy unfortunately got his scalp, which was the only one taken.... He died about half after two o'clock, in the morning, forty-five minutes after he received the wounds, sensible to the last.[45]

Captain LeRoy Hammond forged a critical saber charge at a gathering of Cherokee and Tories who were in a prime firing location. Hammond dispersed them with great effectiveness.

Captain Andrew Pickens' company reached the ford shortly after the initial attack. Having heard noise from the ambush, he urged his men across the creek and approached the fence. The Captain ordered his men to dismount and "hitch if you can! If you can't, let the horses go and rush forward!"[46] The Indians and Tories dispersed, and the braves headed for some nearby trees, firing as they went. Pickens' company had a slight elevation advantage since the fence was on a rise; however, a Tory named Samuel Miller captured William McBride of Pickens' company. A Whig named Moore tried to rescue McBride, but Samuel Miller yelled "Shoot that man!"[47] Samuel Miller's brother William then shot Moore. He died about two hours later after having begged for water throughout the battle.

The Cherokee braves, who had sought refuge from the trees, suffered a heavy loss at the hands of Pickens' company as evidenced by the amount of blood left behind and by a constant mournful howling as they continued to retreat.

McCall, who had expected to overtake Williamson at Oconee, arrived after the fighting had quieted and daylight brightened the village. The entire regiment moved through the abandoned town and began to torch the cabins. The survivors fed on the Indian's crops and destroyed what they couldn't use. They found twenty of their number wounded; six very severely. Militiaman James Noble was detached to take the more-seriously affected, some on litters, back to the settlements for care. Three men, including Salvador and Moore, had been killed outright during the battle. They were quickly buried in a hole that was left by a fallen tree near the village.[48]

Robert Andrew Pickens was one of those severely wounded as described in his pension application (see Appendix E):

> That he entered the service on or about the 15th July, 1776, and marched into the Cherokee Nation, in what was called the Cherokee Expedition — that they marched to the Beaver-dam creek, where they made a short halt for some days — That they then marched to Seneca river, where they were attacked by the Indians & Tories, & had a battle in which he was wounded in the knee, & carried to Fort Independence on a litter between two horses, where he lay under the Doctors for ten months.

Francis Salvador, a man of excellent judgment, had made a poor decision that day to wear such attractive clothing. He likely would not have been killed had he not drawn attention to himself with his attire in the predawn hours. The common practice of the militia of that time was to don normal backwoods raiment, i.e., buckskin or other plain earth-toned clothing so as to melt into the background. Even leaders such as Andrew Pickens, Francis Marion, and Thomas Sumter utilized a bland and functional wardrobe.

Whigs throughout South Carolina mourned Salvador's death. Chief Justice William Henry Drayton declared that Francis Salvador "sacrificed his life in the service of his adopted country."[49] A rule against Jews being able to vote and hold office had been overlooked by all when Salvador was elected to the Provincial Congress. South Carolina Provincial Vice-President Henry Laurens declared that Salvador's death was "universally regretted."[50] Francis Salvador was one of the first real heroes slain in the early days of the war in South Carolina, and he is considered to be the first Jewish revolutionary to be killed in the war.

Quick action by Captains Pickens and Hammond saved their commander and his advance party. Those determined men were experienced Indian fighters. They wielded their knowledge of Cherokee battle tendencies to counter the Indians. Pickens fought with a rifle barrage from an elevated position and Hammond with a direct saber assault.

(Those maneuvers addled the braves who were notoriously poor shots. After all, the British who had trained them were definitely not marksmen themselves. The British trademark was to use muskets in a bayonet attack, and they would fire from the hip while on the move. It was rare that a redcoat stood still and took aim with his musket. When the Cherokee realized they were losing the advantage, they typically withdrew when charged. They simply had no time to constantly reload and fire a rifle when under such an assault.)

R. W. Gibbes in his *Documentary History of the American Revolution* attributes Williamson's letter regarding Seneca as having been written by Col. Thomson to W. H. Drayton on August 4, **1775**. Thomson had nothing to do with the events detailed in the missive. Colonel William Thomson had been selected commander of a South Carolina ranger regiment in early 1775. In August 1775, he supported Drayton during his travels through the backcountry and was not involved in any such action that would necessitate a letter of this nature (see Chapter 2). In November and December 1775, Thomson played a key role in support of Colonel Richard Richardson during an expedition against Tories who were creating havoc in the backcountry (see Chapter 3).

Replacing **1775** in the date of the letter with **1776**, and attributing the authorship to Major Williamson rather than Colonel Thomson, is necessary to fit the action described therein. This letter is obviously written by Williamson and inadvertently attributed to Thomson one year earlier to the day. Thus, it is out of place as compiled in Gibbes' Volume I. Volume III is the appropriate location because it contains other letters from the same period. Williamson's letter provides extremely valuable information for historians. There is a great diversity of detail in contemporary texts regarding this battle, likely due to the letter's misplacement within Gibbes' *History*.

One example of misinformation caused by the nearly hidden letter is the disagreement over the number of men who initially rode into Seneca with Williamson. Another example is that many current references regarding the life of Francis Salvador refer to Colonel Thomson as being the commander who comforted Salvador after he was shot, and cite him as author of the letter in 1775. These same modern references, at the same time, use Salvador's proper death date of August 1, 1776, without addressing that the letter's date as collected in Gibbes' *History* does not agree. Unfortunately, the error has been carried over onto many websites effectively smothering persons interested in Francis Salvador with misinformation. Williamson's description should obviously be considered the most accurate of all period accounts of the battle.

Major Andrew Williamson established a new base camp with his entire 1,500-man regiment at Seneca following the battle before he set out to find Colonels Neil and Thomas. On August 2, 1776, he sent small detachments to various nearby locations to establish satellite camps for flexibility.

Williamson stated in his letter of August 4:

> Knowing that the Indians would carry immediate intelligence of my strength to the place [Oconee] where Cameron lay encamped, who would directly remove from thence, and having ordered the detachment from Col. Neil's and Thomas' Regiment to attack and destroy Estatoe and Taxaway and join me this day in Sugar Town obliged me to march that way, which this day a strong detachment consisting of four hundred men has totally reduced to ashes.[51]

On August 8, Williamson, with a detachment of 640 men, left base camp and proceeded to Oconee to find it deserted as he had expected. Cameron was aware he was outnumbered by four to one. After they destroyed the village, Williamson's militia did the same at Ostatoy and Tugaloo where they bivouacked.

On the 10th, they crossed and proceeded up the Tugaloo River with Captains Andrew Pickens and Robert Anderson who led an advance party. As the vanguard moved, they found that Cherokee braves were tailing them from the other side of the river. As they reached a shoal on the 11th, they observed Cherokee braves cloaked in the brush on the other side. Andrew Pickens said, "Boys, I think here is a place over which we can cross and give the enemy a brush!"

His friend Robert Anderson replied, "But those bushes over there are full of Indians!"

Pickens stated confidently, "Yes, that is just what I want, and if we march to the head of the river, there will be just as many in the bushes opposite to the point we may cross! Come boys, follow me!"[52]

He again displayed the proper counter for familiar Cherokee battle tendencies. The Cherokee were horrible shots when pressed, and the best way to effect a positive outcome was to charge on horseback and slash with sabers. As the militiamen plunged into the river, they were targets of a heavy fusillade that proved ineffective, as Pickens expected. However, Andrew himself had a close call. When he raised his legs out of the stirrups to keep his boots dry, a musket ball passed through the saddle skirt and hit his horse exactly where one of his legs would have been. Robert Anderson secured an abandoned horse for Andrew Pickens. That was the first of several close calls Pickens encountered throughout the war, and the first of several times Captain Anderson rescued his friend. Pickens wrote to Henry Lee, "I served with Genl. Lincoln before and in the battle of Stono, had my horse killed under me in covering the retreat ... I had another horse killed under me in a conflict with the Cherokees."[53] Several braves were killed in the skirmish, but once the advance reached the shore, the Cherokee swiftly dispersed.

After the militia reached Little River, Williamson sent Pickens with 25 of his company militiamen on foot to reconnoiter the vicinity. Their primary arms were rifles, since they were not mounted, but they also carried axes, knives, or pistols (or some combination of the three) in their belts depending on what was comfortable to each individual. Two miles ahead, they reached an old crop field that had grown over with grass nearly five-feet high. Some 200 Cherokee braves watched from a nearby ridge and charged when the militiamen were in the middle of the field. The chief yelled, "Rush in! Rush in! Tomahawk!"[54] according to the guide, a half-breed named Brennan. The chief apparently calculated that the whites were so badly outnumbered, that the braves would not need their rifles.

Andrew Pickens ordered his men to form with an inner and outer ring; one ring was to fire and drop to the ground to reload while the second ring would rise and continue the sequence. "Don't fire until I do! Fire in relays, two at a time, then fall into the grass, reload, rise and fire again!"[55] he shouted. The firing began once the braves were within 25 feet. The devastating and continuous militia fire greatly confused the Cherokee. Brennan was hit and was down. Pickens' gun had jammed, so he picked up Brennan's piece and continued to fire.

The Cherokee were completely baffled. They did not understand how such a small and disadvantaged band of enemies could withstand their onslaught. That was a prime example of their favorite combat situation; however, the militia's speed and efficiency with a rapid fire and reload defense was the antithesis of the Indians' abilities.

The braves retreated to the ridge, retrieved their own rifles, and began to return the militia fire. The militia, however, had located better cover and were better shots, so many braves were killed. The Cherokee also worked to retrieve their fallen comrades. The new battle scene gave the militia even more time to reload and carefully aim its devastating fire.

Lieutenant Joseph Pickens, who had heard the fire from his position with Williamson on the Little River, gathered more of Andrew's company. He rushed them toward the sound of battle using vehement language as he tried to hurry the militiamen along. The arrival of reinforcements was all the Cherokee needed to disperse. Immediately upon the end of the fray, Andrew Pickens gently but pointedly chided his older brother for using such unacceptable language with his men. The militia lost 11 men, and the Cherokee 75, in what has famously become known as the Ring Fight.[56]

Andrew Pickens, just as he had done at Seneca and at Tugaloo River, remarkably kept his cool. He had shown no sign of anxiety; he quickly and rationally sensed exactly what to do, and his troops, as before, exhibited an unequivocal trust in their leader.

Williamson's forces proceeded up the Little River to Tomassee, camped, and found signs that the Cherokee had recently been there. Captain Pickens and his friend, Captain Robert Anderson, detached with some 60 men to reconnoiter the area and look for more Indian signs. They had gone a short distance when Anderson decided to take 25 men and investigate a creek that emptied into Little River. Shortly thereafter, Pickens' force came upon two braves who let out a few war whoops and galloped away. Pickens' men gave chase, apparently not fearful of a common Cherokee tactic for setting a trap. Shortly, they were engaged with nearly 300 Indians, and the fighting was fierce. Major Downs, who had detached to reconnoiter another area with 25 men, heard the commotion. Anderson also heard the fray. He arrived on the Cherokee rear the same time as Downs, and began to engage the enemy. Hand-to-hand combat ensued for the most part. At one point, a stocky militiaman was engaging a brave. They were apparently unable to reload, so were using their rifles as clubs. Once they broke the rifle stocks, they began to grapple, and the militiaman gouged at the brave's eyes forcing the brave to shout, "Canaly! Enough!" The militiaman shouted back, "Damn you! You can never have enough while you are alive!"[57] He used his strength to toss the brave to the ground, plant a foot on his head, and scalp him before he killed him.

Williamson, on a foray with 150 men, was attracted to the battle, fell upon the enemy's rear, and began to encircle the war party. The Cherokee still had the advantage of numbers; however, fighting while surrounded was not their favorite tactic. Hence, they fled, unable to carry away all of their dead. The militiamen found 16 Cherokee bodies; the militia had lost two killed outright and 21 wounded, four mortally so. Captains Neel and Lacy were among those who later died as a result of their wounds.

After burning Tomassee, the militia again broke into detachments and attacked some other lower villages. Jocassee, Tugaloo, Chehohee and Eustash were burned by those troops; Pickens led a detachment to do the same at Estatoe. They burned crops of corn and peas, and slaughtered livestock in each location. Williamson then led the militia back to his base camp at Seneca.

Colonel Ross' Spartan Militia made its way to the town of Estatoe and noticed indications that Pickens had been there. The militiamen looked for the Hight women but found the town deserted and burned. They burned Qualhatchee and Toxaway as they made their way toward Williamson's position. Some of Williamson's detachment joined Colonel Ross and his men at Keowee, and together they moved toward the village of Chatooga. There they captured a Cherokee woman and two black men who informed them the Hight women were being held at a Cherokee camp in the nearby mountains.

Colonel Ross' troops approached the camp and surrounded it. Cherokee defenders began to fire. The Indians successfully held the militia off until darkness fell, and the braves were able to slither away. The next morning Ross, with the combined militia, carefully entered the camp and found it deserted. They checked their personnel and found one soldier injured and one horse killed. They found Mrs. Hight's body one hundred yards out of camp. She had been stripped, murdered and left face-down in the dirt. After they buried her, they met Major Williamson at Seneca. The Commander furloughed Ross' militia, so they could proceed to the settlements for fresh clothing and provisions. They were to rejoin him on August 28.

Williamson's campaign settled into a lull at Seneca where he ordered a crude, but strong, defensive structure built, called Fort Rutledge. Colonel Samuel Jack and his Georgia Militia had attacked villages up to the Tugaloo River. After that, they joined Major Williamson at Seneca as did Colonels Thomas and Neil with their regiments.[58]

Other militia regiments had participated in coordinated attacks in Cherokee country as described by Williamson in a letter to Drayton:

> CAMP AT SENECA, August 22, 1776. DEAR SIR: This is to acknowledge the receipt of your favor of the 10th instant, acquainting me of the independence of the United States of America being declared, which I agree with you is a glorious event.... I have now burnt every town, and destroyed all the corn, from the Cherokee line to the middle settlements.... I have received letters from Gen. Rutherford, wherein he acquaints me that he will be in the middle settlements about the 4th or 5th of next month, with about 2,000 men. I have wrote him the day I am to move from home for the same place ... while Col. Lewis, from Virginia, attacks the Overhills, with about the same number.[59]

(General Griffith Rutherford commanded the North Carolina Militia and was staging a parallel attack on the Cherokee from that province. He, as a Colonel, had joined with South Carolina Colonel Richard Richardson in an action against the backcountry Tories one-year earlier. See Chapter 3.)

After Major Andrew Williamson received word of the Declaration of Independence, he held a council with the other regimental commanders to apprise them of the August 2 signing. Next, he met with his own regimental officers to offer them the same information. Captains Andrew Pickens, James McCall, Robert Anderson and LeRoy Hammond then passed the word of American Independence along to their respective companies. Assuredly there were differing reactions to the news. Some of the men cheered; others sang and danced around. The rest were so touched that they were quiet and pensively regarded their future. They would now fight not only for their defense, but for a new country. The Pickens brothers were among the latter group.

Chief Justice Drayton likely bent President Rutledge's ear regarding Andrew Williamson because he was finally promoted to Colonel. Captain Francis Salvador had exhibited good judgement when he earlier approached Drayton regarding the necessity to promote Williamson. Salvador, himself, may even have had expectations toward the rank of militia major should the day ever come when Williamson would be promoted. However, he had worn that bright white uniform in the early morning hours of that eventful day at Seneca.

The militiamen elected Andrew Pickens to be Ninety Six Militia Major, an easy choice considering the leadership he had already shown during the campaign. The election of company grade officers by the militiamen themselves was a common practice. The provincial authorities would almost always select the colonels; majors, however, were either chosen by the colonel or elected by the militiamen. Captains over companies were mostly militia-elected officers. This process worked very well since militia companies were local units. Militiamen had an incentive to select a man familiar to them. He often was a leader in their community who would be firm but fair, someone they could trust to adequately train them and lead them into battle. This was especially important considering the differences between militia training and that of the Continental Army. The army officers would train soldiers mostly in the European style of fighting, i.e., ordered lines of men with muskets and bayonets fronted the enemy while the cavalry ran flanking maneuvers.

Militias, however, relied on rifles for accuracy rather than cumbersome muskets and bayonets. Most militia actions involved men on horseback charging at an enemy with sabers. That action often developed into hand-to-hand combat with the men using axes or knives. Militiamen dismounted when at a safe distance from the enemy, checked their rifles, took careful aim, and kept their horses at the ready so they could remount and ride when necessary. Therefore, militia training involved almost no organized marching drills but consisted primarily of the men practicing with their weapons and their mounts. They would spend much time training to quickly change from one style of fighting to another because they knew they could rarely plan a battle to be fought in one specific manner. The men had to be ready to change focus immediately upon direction of the leaders while in the midst of a skirmish. Often, battle noise was ear-splitting, so the men were prepared to watch for signs of a shift in the fighting and to react accordingly without specific orders. The militiamen and their leaders had to work together and trust each other enough to be able to function almost entirely from instinct.

Personal relationships were not to interfere with that hierarchy. The men were expected to follow the leadership of an elected officer just as they would an officer selected by the provincial government; and the officer thus elected was expected to lead well. As an example, it is a known fact that Andrew Pickens gave orders to his subordinate brother just as he would to any other subordinate. He addressed Joseph as "Captain or Lieutenant Pickens" and signed his orders as "Andrew Pickens." It was recently written, "Officers were often elected by the men.... General Richard Montgomery complained in 1775 of the militia...' the privates are all generals ... they carry the spirit of freedom into the field and think for themselves.'"[60]

There are some indications that Joseph Pickens was elected as captain at this time: "Alexander Garden, evidently the oldest printed authority ... by Garden's account Joseph appears to have attained a Captaincy about the time of this campaign or before."[61] However, Charles Holland stated in his pension application (see Appendix E):

> On this 13th day of October 1832 personally appeared in open court ... Charles Holland ... [speaking of July 1776] was transferred to a militia company commanded by Capt. Andrew Pickens, in the same Regiment; that soon after this, Williamson was promoted [to colonel] to the command of the Regiment & Capt. Pickens was made the Major & one Thomas Weems became the Captain, who was previously Lieutenant under Pickens— that after the lapse of two years or more, Captain Weems resigned and one Joseph Pickens was promoted to the Captaincy of said Company, under whom the relator served twelve months & more.

Holland's pension application makes it clear that Thomas Weems was promoted to captain and Joseph Pickens remained a lieutenant when Andrew Pickens received his promotion to major. Furthermore, Holland verifies that Joseph Pickens didn't receive a promotion to captain until after at least July 1778. Early writings that listed Joseph Pickens as a captain, such as the above reference by Alexander Garden, led to his rank having been mistakenly identified in some of his military actions.

(Alexander Garden was a Revolutionary army officer in Henry "Light Horse Harry" Lee's Legion, and later an aide-de-camp to General Nathanael Greene. He, however, was known primarily for his collection of Revolutionary War anecdotes and character portraits published in 1822. The subject of Joseph Pickens' captaincy is covered further in Chapter 6, Chapter 7, and Chapter 9.)

Colonel Williamson's next action would be to first attack the remaining lower villages of the Cherokee and then as many middle villages as he could prior to winter. However, he had to await the arrival of Major William Henderson who was en route with his rifle regiment. Colonel Thomas Sumter, who was also on his way with his regiment, had to recruit while on the move; thus, his progress was slower.

Colonel Ross and his regiment made a timely return, and on September 1, 1776, one of his companies made a short foray to scatter some Cherokee that were near the proximity of Fort Rutledge.

Major Henderson had already arrived at the fort by the time Colonel Sumter got there on the 12th. Williamson's force then numbered 2,300 militiamen. He planned to move out the next morning, Friday the 13th, and decided to leave 300 men to garrison the fort.

Williamson organized the entire force into three columns with a colonel at the head of each. Colonel Sumter led the right-flank column and Colonel Hammond, the left. Colonel Neil commanded the center column wherein Williamson marched. They rode out to the beat of drums, and on the 15th they encamped on the Tugaloo River. On the 17th, they reached Coweechee where they had hoped to meet General Rutherford; however, they missed him by at least one week.

The men followed Rutherford's trail. On September 19 they found conflict, and plenty of it, at a place called The Black Hole on the Coweechee Branch of the little Tennessee, nine miles south of present-day Franklin, North Carolina. Some 600 Cherokee braves fired on them from shelter of forest. The enemy was positioned on the flanks atop steep walls, so the militia decided to charge into the middle of the gorge straight ahead. Edward Hampton (a married son of the Anthony Hampton who was murdered with some of his family in July) turned the battle as he and 30 men found the rear of the enemy. The Cherokee, forced to retire, left 13 slain militiamen and 18 wounded. The Indians lost many warriors, but a count had not been taken.

Williamson's force moved upon Timossee on September 25, then on to Tilicho. Each town was destroyed in the same manner as those encountered the previous month. On the 26th, they found that Canusee and Ecochee had already been ruined by Rutherford. They continued to follow Rutherford's trail until they finally caught up with a company of the North Carolinians (near the present-day town of Murphy, North Carolina).[62]

General Rutherford had tired of waiting for Colonel Williamson, so he went on to Cowee and left the above-mentioned company of men to await the Colonel. After he bided some time at Cowee, Rutherford left another company to remain there while he made a foray to destroy villages located in the Hiwassee River valley. He became lost and did not find the valley. Williamson then went to Cowee and arrived two days after the General had left. He encamped with his regiment and detached a company that found Rutherford, who had circled aimlessly and wound up about three miles away. The detachment set General Rutherford straight with directions and reported back to Williamson. Rutherford and his force went on to destroy the Hiwassee River villages. En route, he lost several men in a skirmish with a Cherokee war party.

Williamson's and Rutherford's forces spent a few days together recuperating, and on Sunday, September 29, 1776, they held a religious service. North Carolina Militia Chaplain, Reverend James Hall, preached a touching sermon to some 4,000 militiamen who were seated on the ground.

Following the service, Williamson and his men returned to their homes. Andrew and Joseph Pickens were elated to see their families in Long Canes and relieved to find them safe.

During the Cherokee Campaign, Williamson's forces lost 100 men, and the estimated

Cherokee losses were set at 2,000. It has been noted that Andrew Pickens, in his letter to General Lee, expressed contempt for the viciousness of the Grant Campaign against the Cherokee (see Chapter 1), but the Williamson Campaign was even more brutal. Over 30 villages were destroyed and five battles won against large Cherokee war parties.

Pickens did not express the same ill will for Williamson that he had for Grant at this for two likely reasons:

1. This time the Cherokee incursion was not centered on Indians taking revenge on whites as was the campaign of 1761. Neither was it because of whites settling Indian land. Their purpose was to ally with the British against the Whigs because they thought the British, who by virtue of their "superior force" and previous mutual alliance during the Seven Years War, were better able to see to the needs of the Cherokee Nation. Especially, the Cherokee believed the British would be able to protect them from their enemy tribes that had allied with the French. Thus, the enemy of the British was to be the enemy of the Cherokee.
2. Williamson did not determine how much punishment the Cherokee would receive for having attacked the upcountry settlements; that was the responsibility of the politicians in Charles Town. Probably, Salvador had passed the words of Chief Justice Drayton along to Williamson, received by letter:

    CHARLES TOWN, July 24, 1776. MY DEAR SIR: I am much obliged by your favor of the 19th.... And now a word to the wise. It is expected you make smooth work as you go—that is, you cut up every Indian corn-field, and burn every Indian town—and that every Indian taken shall be the slave and property of the taker; that the nation be extirpated, and the lands become the property of the public. For my part, I shall never give my voice for a peace with the Cherokee Nation upon any other terms than their removal beyond the mountains.[63]

Some justified the Cherokee attacks upon the upcountry Whig settlers by the severity of the Williamson Campaign — that is, maybe the Indians had reason to fear a propensity of coming Whig violence against them. However, the Whigs had tried extremely hard to get along with the Cherokee Nation, i.e., they provided powder to convince them of some camaraderie with the hope that the Indians would stay out of the conflict entirely. There would have been no decision to punish the Cherokee so severely had they not allied with the British and attacked the settlements in the first place.

Additionally, Grant's campaign of 1761 was a British foray resultant from Indian attacks on then–British upcountry settlements. Had the Cherokee allied with the Whigs in 1776, the British might have launched an effort of punishment equally as severe as Williamson's campaign, or at least Grant's. The best choice for the Cherokee would have been to remain neutral; they had originally told Williamson they were going to do just that when he had talked with them late in June (just prior to McCall's capture). Thus, the Cherokee Nation effectively brought the punishment upon themselves by virtue of their decision. They had certainly underestimated the strength of the Whigs, and they had likely expected more help from the British who basically failed to open a western front since they were repulsed at Charles Town.

Cherokee Chief Oconostota, the most formidable and respected Cherokee chief in the lower and middle villages (see Chapter 1), surrendered in October. A treaty was signed on May 20, 1777, with Colonels Williamson and Hammond the signatories for South Carolina. Some have listed Andrew Pickens as a signatory, but they may have confused this event with a later treaty (see the Epilogue). The Cherokee ceded approximately one million acres to South Carolina at the signing.[64]

> In the conquest of 1776–'7, they ceded to South Carolina their lands east of the Unakaye Mountains, reserving to themselves the territory which now comprises, for the most part, the present county of Oconee.

The South Carolina land retained by the tribe amounted to a very narrow strip along the Chattooga River. The Chattooga marks the boundary between northeastern South Carolina and northwestern Georgia before it joins the Tugaloo and heads for the Savannah. Thus the formidable Cherokee threat was effectively neutralized, except for a few minor incidents to be covered later. A tentative peace again spread over the backcountry—but, as before, it was not to last.[65]

5

The Backcountry Heats Up (1777–1778)

The events of July 4 and August 2, 1776, initiated considerable change in the alignment of all parties involved with the future of the American colonies. Prior to the Declaration of Independence, Tories and Whigs were generally regarded by all as Americans. The primary difference, especially on the coast, was the differing political viewpoints; i.e., were the colonies' best collective interests to remain British subjects or to be independent of British control? The discord had become more pronounced in the backcountry where the criminal element, out of its own self-interest, had infiltrated the Tory cause. There, the opposing viewpoints were less philosophical than on the coast, and related more to the quality of life.

General perception of the disputants changed permanently following the formal declaration. The American and British press corps referred openly to the Whigs as Americans and rebels on the one hand, and to the Tories as loyal British sympathizers on the other. The formality of political difference that had existed for some time in the lowcountry had become a social division much as had already been experienced in the backcountry. There had always been some hope among the coastal Tory Americans that their Whig brethren would see the light and reach some agreement with Britain. Even a few Whigs in the South Carolina Provincial Government aspired to such an arrangement. However, the mere existence of the Declaration of Independence forced each individual to decide where his or her loyalty would forever lie. In the colonies, Whigs and Loyalists each viewed the other as traitors, and their rift became irreconcilable.

The already deep schism in the backcountry grew more pronounced with time and led to bloodier confrontations than had previously occurred. The upcountry Whigs and Tories continued to define each other by those same names, but now did so with increased bitterness.

On March 1, 1776, the Continental Congress promoted Robert Howe of North Carolina to Brigadier General and then to Commander of the Southern Department of the Continental Army. (See Chapter 4.) A. L. Pickens was no more enamored with Howe than he had been with Lee. He wrote, "Followed him [meaning Lee] Robert Howe, who accomplished little more."[1]

Early in 1777, the most excitement in all of South Carolina occurred in the South Carolina Provincial Government. The General Assembly decided to develop revisions, fine-tuning requested by the citizenry, for the Provincial Constitution of 1776. The Anglican Church would find itself thrust into forefront of the discussions.

In America, similar to England, the Anglican Church was the official State Religion (the "established church"), and members of other religions were labeled "dissenters." The Royal government heavily supported the established church with public funds, and only the rights performed by Anglican clergy were recognized civil rites, such as marriage.

The British considered the Presbyterians (led by Reverend William Tennent) and the Association of Baptists (led by Reverend Richard Furman) to be the leaders of dissent. The Scots-Irish were reminded of the driving force that compelled their ancestors to migrate throughout Europe, and eventually to America. That they intended to avoid Anglican control would become a major element of the rebellion. The attitude of the Anglican community had been extreme; quite evident to the backcountry settlers. The established clergy did little to hide their contempt for the dissenters.

Reverend Charles Woodmason, the Anglican minister who aided the backcountry settlers in obtaining a judicial system, had recorded an entry in his journal June 13, 1768:

> one John Gaston a Justice of Peace among these Presbyterians ... has also set up to marry People, and has actually married Several Couple.... There is a strict Law against all this—And altho' I have got Depositions against this Wretch, I can find none to serve ... this Part of the province were [sic] I am, has been settled within these 5 Years by Irish Presbyterians from Belfast or Pensylvania ... and got Pastors from Ireland and Scotland ... a Great Number of New Lights and Independents come here from New England, and many Baptists from thence.... Some of these maintain their Teachers. But to keep up their Interests, and preserve their People from falling off to the Church established [meaning the Anglican Church] the Synods of Pensylvania and New England send out a Sett [sic] of Rambling fellows yearly.... 'Tis these roving Teachers that stir up the Minds of the People against the Establish'd Church, and her ministers.... I would sooner starve in England ... than to live here on 200 Guineas, did not the Interests of Religion and the Church absolutely require it.... I find them a Sett [sic] of Rhapsodists—Enthusiasts—Bigots—Pedantic, illiterate, impudent Hypocrites—Straining at Gnats, and swallowing Camels.... They are not tolerated in this Government.... Among this Medley of Religions—True Genuine Christianity is not to be found. And the perverse persecuting Spirit of the Presbyterians, displays it Self much more here than in Scotland.... They have even married People under my Eye in defiance of all Laws and Regulations.[2]

The General Assembly consented to include the matter of the Anglican Church as a related consideration.[3] Presbyterian minister Reverend William Tennent, who had earlier traveled the backcountry with William Henry Drayton, provided an impetus for that inclusion. On January 11, he made an impassioned plea before the General Assembly. He dramatically assailed consideration of the Anglican Church, the American arm of the Church of England, as the proposed State Religion in the Constitution of South Carolina. Excerpts from his oratory:

> Mr Speaker ... I dissent from the Church of England, it is true, but I trust, it is upon the most liberal grounds: when I oppose its establishment, I do not mean to oppose the Church itself.... And now Sir, I beg leave to offer a few of those reasons which induce me to oppose the religious establishment of any one Denomination of Christians in the State, under our new Constitution.... Its chief characteristics are, that it makes a legal distinction between people of different denominations, equally offensive; it taxes all denominations, for the support of the religion of one; it only tolerates those that dissent from it, while it deprives them of Sunday privileges which the people of the establishment enjoy.... The law knows & acknowledges the society of the one, as a Christian Church; the law knows not the other Churches.
>
> The law knows the Clergy of the one, as Ministers of the Gospel; the law knows not the Clergy of the other Churches, nor will it give them a license to marry their own people ... licenses marriage are ... refused ... to any but the established Clergy. The law makes provisions for the support of one Church,—it makes no provision for the other. The law builds superb Churches for the one,—it leaves the others to build their own Churches....
>
> ...The law vests the Officers of the Church of England with power to tax not only her own people, but all other denominations within the bounds of each respective parish, for the support of

the poor: an enormous power! which ought to be vested in no one denomination more than another. ..And why all this inequality? ... the Machiavelian policy of the British government; which ought not any longer to take place in this Country.[4]

The peace treaty at the end of the Cherokee War (see Chapter 4) was affected at Dewitt's Corner on May 20, 1777. Georgia and South Carolina Provincial Governments participated. A new boundary line between the Cherokee Nation and backcountry settlements was established. In return for one million acres ceded by the Cherokee, the provincials assured that trade and peace would be re-established. Cherokee Chief Attakulla Kulla, who had been the primary negotiator with Royal Governor Glen during the peace negotiations in 1753 (see Chapter 1), officially declared an end to the conflict.

The Chief promised the Provincial Government that, should the need arise, he would send 500 warriors to aide them. This was a problem for War Chief Dragging Canoe who declared he would not accept the secession of territory, but would continue to follow the Tories, Captain Richard Pearis and Indian Agent Alexander Cameron, to attack the backcountry and over mountain settlers. He withdrew from the established Cherokee villages 90 miles west with several hundred hostile braves and their families. They settled along Chickamauga Creek near the "The Whirl" of the Tennessee River and became known as the "Chickamauga."[5] (The site of the Chickamauga villages is near present-day Chattanooga, Tennessee. Also see Chapter 7.)

Tsi'yu-gunsini, "Dragging Canoe," Cherokee war chief. Artist: Mike Smith. Used by permission of D. Ray Smith.

Tsi'yu-gunsini (He is Dragging his Canoe or Dragging Canoe), the son of Chief Attakulla Kulla, was born circa 1734 in the over mountain villages. As a child, he had suffered from smallpox that left his face badly scarred, yet he survived the disease and became a stately warrior for the Cherokee. His name was bestowed upon him when young as he attempted to prove his readiness to go on the warpath by carrying a canoe. The braves chided him when they saw he could only drag the vessel. When he persisted, however, the elders chanted of his tenacity.

Dragging Canoe fought in North Carolina during the Cherokee War of 1776. With 700 warriors he attacked two forts during the conflict: Eaton's Station and Fort Watauga. However, he felt no allegiance to the British nor thought of them as the protectors of the Cherokee Nation.

Coincidentally, the date of July 4, 1776, had a powerful meaning to several in the Cherokee Nation. Dragging Canoe and other activist Cherokee, supposedly without the consent of Chief Attakulla Kulla, held a council that day with similarly-minded leaders of the Iroquois, Shawnee, Delaware, Ottawa and other tribes at Muscle Shoals on the Tennessee River.

The Iroquois Confederacy, composed of Mohawk, Seneca, Oneida, Onondaga and Cayuga since the 1500s (joined by the Tuscarora in 1722), included in its basic articles "The Great Law of Peace of the Longhouse People." One essential part of this law affected the Americans after 1776 — the right of conquest. Basically, the tenet stated that the Longhouse

People desired peace with all nations outside of the confederation, and further held the right to declare war upon any that refused, by word or action, the confederacy's overtures to peace.

The council at Muscle Shoals decided the tribes should continue to fight the Americans and especially deter their colonial expansion into Indian land—such incursion being viewed as a threat to their peaceful existence. They neither gave thought to, nor cared about, the meaning of the conflict between the British and the Americans. Their council primarily believed resisting colonial expansion would stave off future attempts at intrusions into their lands. They decided to worry about the Americans "now" and the British "later"— much to the chagrin of Cherokee tribal leaders.[6]

Dragging Canoe was not driven by a desire for conquest or power, but by his need to free the Cherokee hunting grounds. He had previously differed from the majority of Cherokee leaders by his lack of desire to ally himself with the British over the Americans. He really saw no difference between the two white communities and firmly believed it would eventually be necessary to drive away all existing settlers. Therefore, he refused to abide by the peace accord Chief Attakulla Kulla had signed with the Americans and, in agreement with the Muscle Shoals Council, decided immediate assistance to the British would serve the Cherokee during the short term.

Dragging Canoe was known as a fierce warrior, and he labored the remainder of his days to accomplish his goal by attacking every white settlement he found. He is reported to have died on March 17, 1792, in Georgia after a scalp dance that had lasted for several days. The War Chief and his followers performed the scalp dance to give thanks to Yowa (God, Creator) for a recent great victory. He apparently suffered an infection from an untreated flesh wound he received during a battle that the dancers were ritualizing. He seemingly died from exhaustion or a heart attack after the dance. (Dragging Canoe and his warriors failed to help the British overcome the Americans; however, it is unlikely that the future for the Cherokee would have changed had the British held the colonies.)

Early in 1777, Tacitus and Isaac Gaillard sold the old John Savage property to James Holmes who held the property for several more years.[7] The Whigs firmly controlled the politics around Ninety Six even though they remained greatly outnumbered by Tories. Indeed, Tory prisoners charged with such crimes as murder, robbery, rape and seditious acts often filled the Ninety Six jail. Many were tried, found guilty, and taken to Charles Town for execution.[8]

Major Williamson wrote:

> A. WM.SON TO HON. W. H. DRAYTON, ESQ.
> WHITE HALL, April 25, 1777
> Dear Sir:
> I am ordered by his Excellency, the president [meaning Rutledge], to send down to Charlestown immediately, under a strong guard, all the prisoners in Ninety-Six gaol, who are convicted on the Sedition Act, and are under sentence of death, together with the seditious persons lately committed, and the charges against them on oath. As I apprehend before the removal of these last it is necessary to obtain a writ of habeas corpus, I inform your Honor thereof, in order that the needful may be immediately done, as I intend Capt. Hopkins, who escorts them to Charlestown, shall set off on Saturday morning next.
> I am, with great respect, dear sir, your most humble servant,
> A.WM.SON[9]

By mid-1777, South Carolina had settled into a fragile peace regardless of the deepening political divide. The British had been repulsed at Charles Town, but they maintained a token presence within the southern colonies. Britain's failure was devastating to its Cherokee allies who had opened an eastern front against the Whig settlers. The Cherokee effort was a debacle without a British front on the west to occupy the backcountry Whigs. The incompetent Tory militias failed to live up to expectations and were of no lasting help to either the British or the Cherokee. The Loyalists remained eerily quiet and docile. President Rutledge dared to hope that the British would now be willing to cooperate with the Whigs, negotiate a livable presence, and thus reestablish South Carolina as a loyal British colony.

Most coastal citizens seemed to echo Rutledge's feelings; consequently the elections for open lowcountry General Assembly seats in 1777 were not even contested. Most coastal Whigs generally believed that the Carolinians and the British would drift back into the mutually beneficial trade pattern they had formerly enjoyed. The backcountry presented a different story; the Whigs greatly distrusted the British, especially with regard to law and order around Ninety Six. The Tories bided their time and hoped for the British to regain control, so they could regain power under the British umbrella.[10]

The British had withdrawn to New York after their failed attempt at Charles Town, but the war was not going well for them. Major General John Burgoyne was Commander of the British Army of America in the North. He had moved into America from Canada late in 1777 and initially experienced little difficulty as evidenced by the capture of Ticonderoga. However, the Battle of Freeman's Farm (the First Battle of Saratoga) occurred. The results guaranteed the British would renew military efforts within the southern colonies. Several of the American generals involved at Saratoga would even later be assigned to command the Southern Department. (Freeman's Farm was owned, or leased, by Loyalist John Freeman who had been forced from the land earlier in 1777 and temporarily settled in Canada. He and his son, Thomas, returned with Burgoyne and fought at the battle.)

American Major General Horatio Gates, who had been given command of the Northern Department, moved to counter Burgoyne and face off with him at Saratoga in October. Burgoyne and his army were greatly disadvantaged. Gates had Burgoyne severely outnumbered and trapped in a thick forest. Burgoyne was low on rations, and his only hope was for Gates to become impatient; however, that hope was not to be realized.

American Brigadier General Benedict Arnold, who had been passed over for promotion by the Continental Congress, was in camp and formally exhorted his commander to press the British. He wrote Gates:

> I think it my duty (which nothing shall deter me from doing) to acquaint you, the army are clamorous for action. The militia (who compose great part of the army) are already threatening to go home. One fortnight's inaction will, I make no doubt, lessen your army by sickness and desertion, at least four thousand men. In which time the enemy may be reinforced, and make good their retreat.

True, the army was eager for action; however, Arnold was the one who was doing the "clamoring." He was deeply hurt at being passed over for promotion to major general; he was the oldest of all the brigadiers eligible for the rank. General Washington pressed Congress for an explanation and was told that promotions were given on a state-by-state basis; the number of general officers per rank was limited to a ratio of the relative number of soldiers provided by each state. Connecticut already had its allotment of two major generals. This made it clear that past performance did not affect Arnold's pass-over. That, however, did little to console him, as he clearly wanted to redeem himself, though redemption was entirely unnecessary.[11]

Gates observed regarding British General Burgoyne, "Perhaps despair may dictate to him to risk all upon one throw; he is an old gamester, and in his time has seen all chances. I will endeavor to be ready to prevent his good fortune, and, if possible, secure my own." Gates seemed to be correct. On October 7, 1777, Burgoyne began to form his army, under cover of the dense forest, less than one mile from the American encampment. He desired to accommodate the best position to either push through the American lines or to conceal a retreat as advantage might present itself.

This was the opportunity that Gates was anticipating. Once his scouts brought him word of the British movements, he formulated a battle plan and immediately moved units forward to encircle Burgoyne and his army. One of Gates' units became engaged and Arnold, who was still in camp, couldn't resist any longer. The instant of the battle sound, he mounted his horse and raced toward the racket.

Gates, sure that Arnold would take drastic action, sent his aide to corral him, but to no avail. Arnold usurped command of a brigade and led a desperate charge into the center of the British formation on Freeman's Farm. It was a frenzied scene as he galloped hither and thither wildly brandishing his saber and shouting orders. He even, without realizing, struck the head of one of his own officers with the flat of his sword and rendered the man dazed and unfit for battle.

While Arnold held the attention of the British, Colonel Daniel Morgan opened an active engagement on the British right flank. During this skirmish, a sniper mortally wounded British Brigadier General Simon Frazer (sometimes Fraser). Burgoyne realized that his force could not survive the onslaught, so he ordered a retreat to the British encampment for a defensive strategy. Benedict Arnold's horse was shot out from under him during the action, and his leg was pinned beneath the animal. He suffered severe wounds, and his leg bled copiously. Arnold was out of action for the remainder of the battle. (On the grounds of the Saratoga National Historic Park, a monument to Benedict Arnold's leg rests on the exact spot where he fell.)

The Americans had completed the advantage; many British soldiers were killed, wounded or taken prisoner. Burgoyne and the rest of his army remained in control of their primary camp. In the dark of night Burgoyne moved his army one mile north. He then decided his only option was to withdraw to Saratoga. Gates had decided to cover all avenues for further British retreat. He again bided his time and awaited this precise initiative by Burgoyne.

The Americans arrived at Saratoga ahead of Burgoyne and were already entrenched when he arrived on the evening of October 9. On the 13th, after the Americans had assailed the British for several days, General Burgoyne sent a flag bearer with a note requesting that negotiations be opened with General Gates. Gates responded that the British would immediately lay down their arms and surrender — "immediately" was rejected by Burgoyne.

Burgoyne's army was the first British unit to be soundly defeated by the Americans. It was a surety that he and his officers would face disgrace, and he had no idea what was in store for his rank and file. There was no precedence. The British themselves had captured many enlisted men already during the war and had confined them to horrible conditions aboard prison ships. However, it was a common occurrence for officers on either side to be paroled. Burgoyne decided to hold out for the best situation he could arrange for his men.

After much negotiation, Burgoyne offered that he and his entire 5,000-man force would march out of camp under arms with colors flying, lay down their arms at the order of the British officers, and then be paroled by the Americans to return to England. Furthermore, they would agree to not re-enter the current war in America. Gates accepted these terms, and Burgoyne signed the surrender document on October 17, 1777.[12]

The British catastrophe at Saratoga was not entirely the fault of either General Burgoyne or his commander, Major General Sir William Howe. Howe asserted he did not have full control of his command. He thought Lord George Germain (the British Secretary of State for the American Colonies within the cabinet of Prime Minister Lord Frederick North) treated him much the same way the Continental Congress had treated General Washington early in the war. The ministry, which decided Burgoyne's command could take care of itself, redirected possible supporting troops to other theaters but did not consult Howe. Burgoyne was thus left high and dry, and Howe could do nothing to alter the situation.[13]

Despite the victory at Saratoga, General Washington's Northern Department was not in good order. He began to move his troops toward Winter Quarters in Pennsylvania. They were tired, starving, and had been badly treated at the Battle of Brandywine on September 11. The army was wont for food, clothing and military armament, all of which were in short supply because the Continental Congress was under a severe financial strain. (Congress had issued worthless scrip on the promise of future value once the war was won. The Continental scrip was offered beginning in 1775 on a dream. It was printed in odd denominations by today's standard, such as, 1/6th of a dollar, 1/3rd of a dollar, $55, and $80, and had competition as each state also tendered its own scrip. Additionally, the British had been counterfeiting the Continental scrip. So much scrip circulated among the colonies that Continental currency was worth 1/40th of its face value by 1780.)

General Sir William Howe tried to salvage his reputation. He was hot on the trail of Washington, and although his situation was not as dire as Washington's, he too, was running short of provisions. His brother, Admiral Lord Richard Howe, was on his way up the Delaware River with 250 ships that carried food, clothing, armament and ammunition for General William Howe's forces. If that mission had been accomplished, it likely would have marked the end for Washington's army and the beginning of cessation for the rebellion. It was not to be.

In 1771, the British began to construct Fort Mud on Mud Island in the Delaware River. The new fort was to provide additional defense for Philadelphia, then a British-controlled city. They abandoned the nearly completed fort in 1776 because Philadelphia was rapidly developing into the Americans' capital. The Continental Army gained control of the fort, completed the construction, and renamed the facility Fort Mifflin after Major General Thomas Mifflin. They also erected a crude installation called Fort Mercer (named after Brigadier General Hugh Mercer) on the New Jersey side of the river. The Americans fended off General Howe's ground forces and Admiral Sir Richard Howe's armada from October 2 to November 19, 1777. The forts were ultimately lost and destroyed, but the Americans' gallant stand allowed Washington time to get his forces to safety for the winter. This probably saved the rebellion and definitely dealt General Sir William Howe another embarrassment. The battle represented bravery at its finest. Two thousand Hessian troops surrounded Fort Mercer before dawn on October 22 and demanded surrender, as the officer carrying the message recited, "The king of England commands his rebellious subjects to lay down their arms (etc ad nauseam)." The fort commander, Colonel Christopher Greene, delivered a customary refusal of terms, but he used the unique phrasing, "We'll see King George Damned first!" The war for the American colonies would continue on for several years thereafter; however, the end would occur in the southern provinces under a different British commander and at great expense to Britain.[14]

The prevalent viewpoint persisted within the British realm that Sir William Howe had generally neglected his responsibilities throughout his tenure as the commander in America. This was evident in 1780 and 1781 when a series of letters, classified as essays, appeared in *The London Chronicle* over the pseudonym of ARISTIDES. He declared in designated *LETTER IV* (see Appendix G for the entire text of this letter):

> In my former Letters ... I have said, that the great rule, which you laid down to yourself, seems to have been, to gain the confidence of your Sovereign, by repeating declarations of your zeal in his service: by shewing [sic] to him in all your letters, that you perfectly well knew your duty; and what was proper to be done for subduing the rebellion; and thereby leading his Majesty to conclude, that you intended to do it. In all your Letters, previous to the campaign of 1776, both while you was at Boston, and after you was driven out of it, you are perpetually writing, that nothing was more to be desired by you, than to bring the rebels to a decisive action. In words, it is impossible for you to express a more determined resolution to do so: By your actions, Sir, it seems impossible for you to shew [sic] a more fixed and determined resolution not to do it. Five times did the rebels put it in your power to shut them up, and force them to a decisive action: five times did your superior care provide a way for them to escape without any decisive action at all. To this end, I have said, you invariably attacked them on the side opposite to that by which only they could escape.

Aristides goes on to detail instances of Howe's neglect at Bunker's Hill, Long Island, and especially at White Plains. Concluding with the latter he states:

> Had you, Sir, given no reason at all, your friends might have fancied one for you; but it is impossible for us to conceive, that this was your real one. You had performed the longest, and only difficult part of the voyage, by nine o'clock in the morning. But had you gone on the other ten miles to Rochelle, you might have shut up the rebel army, without having given them any warning. And the North River being guarded by your ships, they must have laid down their arms, or have fought you under every possible disadvantage. The most sensible and best informed writers among the rebels acknowledge this, and laugh at you for not having done it. The loyal part of the Americans saw, and mourned it. His Majesty, from all the solemn assurances of your Letters, could not but judge, that you would do your best in his service: But a leader of the party seems to have known you better, when he said of you, He is one of us, and will do the Americans no harm.[15]

The original Aristides (or Aristeides, 530 BC to 468 BC) was an Athenian statesman, nicknamed "The Just." Therefore, it is no accident that Sir William Howe's denouncer chose the sobriquet which was likely well-planned by someone of political import in London who had dealings with Howe during the early days of the war. Aristides may, in reality, have been someone of the stature of Lord Germain or perhaps even Lord North. They each had the incentive to defend the North Ministry against blame for Britain's poor position in the latter years of the war and to cast suspicion upon Howe.

The 18th century Aristides was no stranger to his subject. *LETTER IV* manifests his extraordinary command of facts and figures regarding actions in New England in early years of the conflict. He and General Howe had been exchanging a public and politely heated conversation by letter for some time. Aristides was informally acting as a representative of a large faction that had concluded the American Revolution should have ended in Britain's favor long before it ever was removed from New England to be settled in the southern colonies. He made a strong declaration in blaming Howe as the major cause for losing the war.

Regardless of reality, Howe did receive blame for the lack of British success early in the war. He was, after all, a member of the Whig party in Britain and leaned politically toward relaxation of control over the colonies. He resigned in May of 1778 and sailed for Europe near the end of the month. Lieutenant General Sir Henry Clinton, having been

5. The Backcountry Heats Up (1777–1778)

Howe's second-in-command, replaced him as Commander of the British army in America on May 20, 1778. Earl Cornwallis would eventually replace Clinton as Commander of the British Army in the South.

The situation became so dire for the British that Clinton abandoned control of Philadelphia and the rest of the northeast; however, he maintained firm control of New York City. On June 18, 1778, Clinton allowed the Loyalist citizens of Philadelphia to sail to New York, but he led the British troops on a march as the fleet lacked room for all. General Washington controlled the area outside of New York City, and he arranged for the French fleet to attack the British fleet. He anticipated French success knowing that would allow him to defeat Clinton in New York and win the war. However, though outnumbered by the French, the British fended off the attack. The northeast settled into a standoff as Generals Washington and Clinton closely watched each other, but neither was able to gain an advantage.

Each side in the northern theater was disappointed. England's attempt to end the war with their superior ground forces proved inept, and America's counter failed due to the French fleet debacle.

Lord Germain continued to run the war from England. He and Lord North were convinced the southern colonies were key to Britain's future in America; however, they were no longer confident that the Americans could be beaten. North assumed a negotiation might settle the difficulty. He was positive that the British army needed to control the southern colonies so that he could bargain from a position of strength. Britain could live with giving the Americans the northern provinces as part of an agreement to allow that Britain maintain control of the southern colonies. Most of the American exports the English enjoyed were produced in the south.

In April 1778, Lord North had privately planned compromises he might make to America in the event of negotiations. These possible concessions included not only the repeal of taxes but also:

- An end to a standing British army in America.
- No changes to colonial charters without colonial assent.
- Colonial offices would be elective with preferences to American candidates.
- Colonial American seats would be added in the House of Commons.[16]

Britain immediately acted upon the taxes. They, under the Taxation of the Colonies Act of 1778, repealed the Tea Act and the remainder of the Townshend Acts. Lord North thought the prompt repeal of the Tea Act might appease the colonists and avoid a stiff defense against the British when they later would attempt to regain control of the southern provinces. The exact date of the new act is difficult to ascertain. It is simply identified as "18 Geo. III, c. 12" basically meaning the 18th year of the reign of George III, and "c. 12" meaning the 12th chapter of the annual book. There appear to be 80 chapters for 1778 that lend credence that the Taxation of the Colonies Act occurred early during the year.

Clinton's plans centered on Britain's decision to reinvest efforts on the southern colonies. However, Clinton had a different goal than did Lord North. He believed that, once the south was under control, it could be turned over to the large Tory regiments promised to him by the southern Royal Governors. They assured him the Tories were up to the task. The British army, according to his plan, would then move north, encircle General Washington, and force him into submission.[17]

The backcountry was peaceful once again, and citizens were free to contemplate civilized activities. Andrew Pickens was an early member of the Mt. Zion Society, comprised of a group of Scots-Irish Presbyterians, French Huguenots, and English churchmen from a variety of congregations. This group established a school of higher learning near Camden. The thought behind this effort was, if the coast of South Carolina should ever fall back into the hands of the British, the Whig residents would need a school further inland. Additionally, they had the support of leaders in Charles Town, as Charles Cotesworth Pinckney also became a member (Pinckney later became a Continental Army brigadier general, a delegate to the United States Constitutional Convention in 1787, and the unsuccessful Federalist candidate for President of the United States in 1804 and 1808.)

Major General Sir Henry Clinton. Artist: J. Stuart; Engraver: John Rogers, 1862.

The preamble to the Mt. Zion Society constitution was, "Arise, shine; for thy light is come, and the glory of the Lord is risen upon thee." The predominate attitude held among the Whigs of that time was one of hope, courage, and assurance of the future success in their goal of civil freedom.[18]

The General Assembly began debate over the proposed revisions to the state constitution on March 5, 1778. President John Rutledge thought the proposal was too harsh and would serve to widen the schism between the colony and Britain. Rutledge trusted that South Carolina could resolve differences with Britain and mediate a strong relationship. His was an interesting position for, in 1776, he finally agreed to the need for independence, was a member of the Council of Safety, and helped to write the original constitution for South Carolina. He apparently was leery that South Carolina would lose Britain as a business partner, although the previous partnership overtly favored British interests.

The legislature thought him ineffectual and demanded changes that caused Rutledge to resign in protest. The General Assembly elected Rawlins Lowndes to replace him as president. Lowndes was a lawyer and had been an Associate Justice in South Carolina until the Royal Government removed him from office in 1772 because of his Whig tendencies. Lowndes, as Justice, was the recipient of the formal charge from Reverend Woodmason against John Gaston in 1770, two years after the entry in Woodmason's journal noted earlier in this chapter.[19]

Lowndes was pro Declaration of Independence, and he led the legislature to a more independent state constitution. On March 19, 1778, the Constitution of the State of South Carolina was born. The revisions, however, were not to become effective until later in the year, as noted in the Second Article (see Appendix H):

I. That the style of this country be hereafter the State of South Carolina.
II. That the legislative authority be vested in a general assembly, to consist of two distinct bodies, a senate and house of representatives, but that the legislature of this State, as established by the constitution or form of government passed the twenty-sixth of March, one thousand and seven hundred and seventy-six, shall continue and be in full force until the twenty-ninth day of November ensuing.

Even though the effect of the revised constitution was delayed, Lowndes proactively led the state toward independence. The legislature also disestablished Anglicanism as the officially recognized state religion. Religion was a real sensitive point for each side, as is shown in a letter from Captain Johann Heinrichs of the Hessian Jäger corps written in Philadelphia on January 18, 1778, "Call this war, dearest friend, by whatsoever name you may, only call it not an American Rebellion, it is nothing more nor less than an Irish-Scotch Presbyterian Rebellion."[20]

At the same time, a requirement was initiated that all males within the state boundary must declare allegiance to South Carolina vis-a-vis Britain, or prepare to leave the state within one year.

Additionally, the South Carolina Militia was reorganized into three brigades: the coastal regiment commanded by Brigadier General Stephen Bull; the middle country under Brigadier General Richard Richardson; and the backcountry led by Brigadier General Andrew Williamson (because of his experience with the Cherokee and with the Georgians). Richardson had the additional duty to act as liaison with the Continental Army. Lowndes promoted Andrew Pickens to Colonel to replace the promoted Andrew Williamson (While Williamson and Pickens acted in these functions right away, the promotions were not to become official until the newly-revised constitution was effective later in the year. Correspondence between the officers shown later in this chapter indicates they retained their original ranks until at least November and likely December. In modern military vernacular, Williamson was actually a Brigadier General Select and Pickens a Colonel Select designated by the new rank followed with [S]).

The lowcountry and backcountry Whigs were finally fully united into a brotherhood with a shared goal—to secure an independent South Carolina. The legislation, as well as the required declaration of male citizenry, was worded to indicate allegiance to South Carolina rather than America. America, still an ideal, had not yet held its constitutional convention.[21]

In spring 1778, Loyalist Colonel Thomas Brown raided the backcountry of eastern Florida under British Major General Augustine Prevost. Brown had fled the Carolinas for Florida and raised a company for the British called the King's Florida Rangers (later known as the King's Carolina Rangers). In April 1778, American Major General Robert Howe (he had been promoted from Brigadier General on October 20, 1777) decided it was time to embark on a foray into the south to face the British and Tories who controlled Florida. A. L. Pickens continued his criticism of Howe: "Slow to learn from history, Howe also would have a new expedition toward Florida."[22] Dr. Pickens' allusion to history evoked Major General Charles Lee who had the not-so-bright idea to act against Florida just before his removal as Commander of the Southern Department (see Chapter 4).[23]

President Lowndes wanted to cooperate with the Continental Army, so he ordered the militia to prepare and join the effort. Williamson began to put the militia together before the end of April. On April 19, Colonel Charles Cotesworth Pinckney and Colonel Thomas Sumter led South Carolina regiments to Savannah. In May, the expedition progressed toward the destination, according to Pickens, "straggling and wriggling along thru Georgia like the parts of the mythical joint snake trying to reassemble after a blow."[24]

Howe crossed the Alatamaha River in southern Georgia on April 25, but Continental Army Colonel Samuel Elbert did not march for the Sattilla River in southeastern Georgia until June 5, 1778. General Howe registered complaints with Georgia and South Carolina about the slow progress of their respective militias. On the 12th, Howe arrived at St. Mary's River on the Georgia border with Florida. He had sought Loyalist Colonel Brown; however, he found Fort Tonyn abandoned and burned by the British. Brown had rejoined General Prevost, and they had withdrawn to St. Augustine fully aware they had no reason to face off with Howe. They just needed to bide their time until the American rank and file dried up from the summer heat and exposure to the swampy environment.[25]

Lieutenant General Charles Lord Cornwallis. Artist: Samuel Hollyer; Printer: William Pate, 1859.

Williamson dragged his feet. He apparently was not sold on leaving the defense of the Ninety Six District for an expedition into Florida. On June 20, he tried to arrange a juncture of his regiments just south of Savannah. On July 4, 1778, Georgia Governor John Houston and his state troops joined Major General Howe; however, Houston refused to turn over control of his troops to the General. Andrew Williamson had just crossed Cathead Swamp halfway between Savannah and Fort Tonyn.

On the 5th, Robert Howe complained bitterly to Lowndes about Williamson's dawdling. General Howe eagerly wanted to pass into Florida where he thought Governor Houston would have to relinquish control of the Georgia troops. Howe was chagrined that Williamson had waited so long to join the expedition and expected that, when the South Carolina troops arrived, Williamson would cede command to him. Dr. Pickens continued, "Without judging, let it be said that Howe's talents were not considered above the mediocre, and his generalship was condemned both by his officers and the people at large."[26]

General (S) Williamson arrived at Fort Tonyn on July 8, 1778, and upon his arrival refused, just as Governor Houston had done, to allow his troops to take orders from General Howe. The militias acted independently. Houston's Georgia Militia under Colonel Elijah Clarke trailed Major General Prevost to a place called Alligator Creek near St. Augustine, and Colonel (S) Pickens tracked Thomas Brown to a battery nearby on the same creek. Pickens found Brown had vacated his battery. Clarke's militia became ensnarled with a bastion of downed logs that mingled with underbrush in a swamp at the front of Prevost's entrenchment. Three of Clarke's militiamen were killed while he, himself, received a ball in the hip. The militias each had to withdraw back to the main camp.

That the militias continued to resist taking orders from General Howe certainly contributed to Howe's lack of success. However, early in the war, it would have been a huge adjustment for local militias to become subjected to the direct command of the regular army. It was recently written:

> Within the intricately structured and close-knit societies of colonial America membership in the militia was something more than just an obligation; it was a part of being an acceptable member ... white, male, property-owning [group] — that held the largest stake and stood to benefit most from the self-protection the militia afforded.... Thomas Barrett [Concord Massachusetts militia Colonel] transmitted his orders through a son and son-in-law, both captains, to a second son and a brother, both ensigns, down to yet another son and a nephew, both corporals...
>
> In societies so closely linked by marriage, property ... politics ... business, where everyone pretty much knew everyone else ... lies an explanation why, during the war, the militia were ... disinclined ... to serve under any but their own officers or ... for fighting away from their home base.[27]

This directly explains Williamson's reluctance to leave Ninety Six as described above. It also explains why Williamson and Georgia Governor John Houston may have refused to subject their militias to the direct leadership of General Howe. In addition, it was apparent that the Continental Congress had exhibited poor judgement in the selection of commanders for the Southern Department.

The local militias trained together regularly and were accustomed to their own hierarchy and their own peculiar military regimen. Militia training varied from state to state and even from locality to locality. It was profoundly different than the training for the regular army. Even the weapons used and the style of fighting were dissimilar. A typical militia situation is described as:

> technically every able-bodied man ... was required to turn up armed, for regular training ... the Patriot Committee of Frederick County, Virginia, proclaimed in the spring of 1775: "Every Member of this County between sixteen & sixty years of Age, shall appear once every Month, at least, in the Field under Arms; & it is recommended to all to muster weekly for their Improvement."[28]

The militiamen more readily responded to familiar commanders that they respected than they did to unfamiliar Continental generals who had not earned their trust. (It is obvious in later chapters that militia leaders eventually worked in harmony with Continental Army Commanders, and that was a huge turning point in the war — especially in the southern theater.)

Major General Robert Howe had no choice but to withdraw his army to Savannah. Half of his men were down with malaria and other heat-related illnesses. Most of Howe's horses had died from heat exposure and lack of forage. However, General Howe declared the mission a success as the British were "driven" from Georgia and eastern Florida, and Fort Tonyn had been destroyed (albeit at the hands of the British themselves as they "withdrew" of their own volition).

Many militiamen had also become ill from the intense heat and consequent exhaustion during the long summer foray. All of the Georgia and South Carolina militia units began to return to their homes. The Ninety Six Militia Regiment gathered at Cathead Swamp south of Savannah where Brigadier General (S) Andrew Williamson issued orders to the militia regiments (the promotions were not yet officially enacted):

ORDERS FOR LIEUT.-COL. JONAS BEARD, LIEUT.-COL. ROBERT McRARY
AND MAJOR THOMAS BRANDON,
LIEUT.-COL. JOHN WINN, COL. ROBT. GOODWYN,
AND MAJ. ANDREW PICKENS.
CAMP AT CAT HEAD, JULY 25, 1778

You are to proceed with all expedition by the following rule of march with the different detachments under your command to the State of South Carolina, taking with you under your escort all the waggons belonging to the districts of your respective regiments, letting the men and the horses have the necessary provisions and rest, at such places as you shall find convenient. If any horses belonging to the waggons should tire, so as to render it inconvenient or prejudicial to your detachments to wait for them, such must necessarily be left after getting into the settlements in Georgia or South Carolina, with the driver or owner, until the horses are refreshed. The line of march, after separating the army to be observed so as to make it equally convenient to each detachment, so that if the detachments in front by any kind of delay are passed by the others, they must necessarily fall in the rear. All the provisions in the army will be divided in just and equal proportions to the different detachments according to the number of men in each. The commanding officer will order the proper returns to be made for this purpose and send their Quarter-Masters to receive it. Orders on the Governor of Georgia will be given by the commanding officer for the necessary supplies to the detachments on their march through this State. If any difficulty in getting such should happen within this State, or in South Carolina, the commanding officer of such detachment will impress what may be absolutely necessary upon oath, that a just recompense may be made to the owners.

Col. Williamson having the greatest confidence in the care and diligence of the field officers, their zeal for the service, the honor of the State to which they belong, and the reputation of the troops, that he relies upon them for the preserving of good order and preventing the men from committing any depredations or injuring or insulting any person whatever on their return through this State or South Carolina; and, although the expedition to which they have been called has not been attended with the wished for success, he returns them and the officers and men under them his thanks for their perseverance and alacrity on so trying and difficult a service.

ORDER OF MARCH ON DETACHING THE ARMY.

1st. Col. Winn and his detachment; 2nd. Col. Williamson's detachment; 3rd. Col. Goodwyn's detachment; 4th. Col. Beard's detachment; 5th. Col. McRary and Maj. Brandon's detachment.
A. WM.SON[29]

Note the care that Williamson distinctly ordered for the men and the horses during the return trip — an indication of the exhaustion and illness that had been experienced.[30]

The Ninety Six Militia Regiment had not been home long before they were ready to help Georgia deal with a threat from the Indians. In August of 1778, Andrew Williamson issued orders to Andrew Pickens regarding the matter. Pickens followed up with missives to his captains using this format:

ANDREW PICKENS TO CAPT. JOHN IRVIN. OR IN HIS ABSENCE TO HIS LIEUTENANT.
August 29, 1778
Sir:
By order of Col. Williamson, you are hereby required to embody the State draft from your company, and march with them, well armed and accoutered, with three days' provisions, to the place where the Long Cane road crosses Little River, near the Rev. Mr. John Harris.' You will be at the above place of rendezvous punctually on Friday, the 4th day of September next, as the situation of the distressed people in Georgia, to whose assistance we are to march, will admit of no delay. There will be wagons at the place where we meet, to carry the men's baggage, as the horses must be sent home if the men bring any from home.
I am, sir, your most humble servant,

ANDREW PICKENS
N. B.— Order every man to bring a good hatchet. Since I wrote the above I have got intelligence that a party of Indians are on their way to our frontier. I desire you would, with all possible speed, march up to John Cameron's old place with five or six days' provisions.
A.P.[31]

(Letters and orders of the period variously spell the Captain's name as Irvin, Irvine, or Ervin.) The other captains that mustered their companies at that time were Thomas Weems, Robert Anderson, James McCall, Andrew Hamilton and Levi Casey. Lieutenant Joseph Pickens was assigned to Captain Weems' unit.

On September 25, 1778, the Continental Congress appointed Major General Benjamin

Lincoln to replace Howe as the Commander of the Southern Department; however, Lincoln had business to attend to in Philadelphia and it would be some time before the change of command could be effected. South Carolina and Georgia leaders had campaigned for Lincoln because he was "a more experienced American general than Howe"[32] and had built a sturdy reputation with his record under General Gates against General Burgoyne at Saratoga.

On November 28, 1778, Andrew Williamson wrote to Colonel Robert Goodwyn from White Hall, "DEAR SIR: My having been continually employed in Georgia since the Southern expedition [Howe's expedition to Florida], prevented me being able before this period to attend to and examine and adjust the expense arising from that service."[33] There is no indication the militia engaged in any major action prior to the return home. It is likely Williamson spent the nearly three-month muster patrolling both sides of the Savannah River in support of the Georgians. The Wilkes County Georgia militia was lightly manned at that time but held its own against Tory attacks and Indian incursions.

Shortly thereafter, Williamson received a letter that led to additional action for the Ninety Six Militia:

> W. WARDLAW TO A. WM.SON
> LONG CANE, December 7, 2 o'clock, P.M., 1778.
> Sir:
> I have just received information that the Indians have carried away Thos. Stevenson and his family, and three others that were there, and robbed his house. They were tracked some distance, and seemed to bear up the other side of Barker's Creek. This conduct seems unusual, but from the signs it appears that there are Indians in the company. I am also informed that on yesterday there were several guns heard from the Corner. The alarm is sufficient to direct you how to proceed. Please to forward the other letters as directed.
> I am, your humble servant,
> W. WARDLAW
> P.S.— Our company is met this morning by day at the Corner, to proceed as necessity appears.[34]

The militia was again mustered for up to three months duty (the customary period) to handle the alleged Cherokee incursion, but the handling did not take the full term. At this time the promotions for Brigadier General Andrew Williamson and Colonel Andrew Pickens became official. It was noted earlier in this chapter that the revised constitution for South Carolina was to become effective on November 29th, and thus coincide with this foray.[35]

With regard to Howe's situation after the Florida expedition, the timing could not have been worse for the Southern Department of the Continental Army. As fortune would have it, Major General Sir Henry Clinton was ready to begin his campaign against the southern colonies. Howe was ill prepared. Many of his command still suffered the adverse effects of their recent torturous foray.

Near the end of November, General Clinton dispatched Lieutenant Colonel Sir Archibald Campbell to Georgia with over 2,000 troops aboard a squadron of ships commanded by Commodore Hyde Parker. Earlier in November, Clinton had ordered Major General Augustine Prevost to march from St. Augustine to the Savannah River and prepare for Campbell's campaign. Prevost's forces were to disrupt the settlements in the area so to draw attention away from the coming activity on the coast.[36]

General Prevost sent his brother, British Lieutenant Colonel John Mark Prevost, into southern Georgia. John Mark Prevost arrived on November 19, 1778, at Midway, a community 50 miles southwest of Savannah. He detached Lieutenant Colonel Lewis Fuser to take the last remaining fort in the area (later named Fort Morris) at the Port of Sunbury on St. Catherine's Sound. Lieutenant Colonel Prevost himself, along with Tory renegade Colonels Daniel McGirth and Thomas Brown, raided Whig communities in the vicinity of Midway.

The Whigs mustered a force, and there ensued a formidable skirmish near Midway during which one of Brown's Florida Rangers, Captain Moore, was killed by a rifleman. John Prevost withdrew five miles north and awaited word of Fuser. When he received no word within a reasonable time, he began his withdrawal to St. Augustine. He was certain that he had fulfilled his goal to disrupt the Whig communities.

On November 25, Fuser reached the fort at Sunbury and demanded surrender. Continental Lieutenant Colonel Lachlan McIntosh replied, "We, sir, are fighting the battle of America ... as to surrendering the fort, receive this laconic reply — Come and Take It!"[37] Fuser, aware he did not have a sufficient force to attack the fort, sailed down the coast with his detachment and joined Colonel Prevost at St. John's River 50 miles north of St. Augustine.[38]

Major General Benjamin Lincoln. Unknown engraver, 1861.

Major General Benjamin Lincoln finally arrived at Charles Town December 4, 1778, and he immediately began to lobby South Carolina President Rawlins Lowndes for supplies. He planned to gather forces and link up with Major General Robert Howe. After he would formally take command, he desired to force action against Major General Augustine Prevost; however, Lowndes was not convinced to commit supplies until he knew more about Lincoln's strategy. President Lowndes finally consented to work with Major General Lincoln on the 25th, but it was too late to save Major General Howe.

On December 27, Commodore Parker's squadron anchored at the mouth of the Savannah River. Howe had encamped just east of the Savannah city limit, south of the Savannah River, on the main causeway since "a mortal malady which desolated his camp"[39] forced him to abandon his invasion of Florida the preceding summer. The causeway passed over a wide marsh to Howe's rear which separated him from the east side of town. The south bank of the river was primarily a deep swampy area cut by several creeks and smaller rivers. The only way to traverse toward Savannah was atop one of several causeways with quagmires on either side. A small raised path passed through the swamp at some distance from the American right flank. Howe ignored a suggestion from Colonel George Walton, a Georgia delegate to the 2nd Continental Congress and future Governor, that he should order a detachment to secure the path.

On the 29th, Lieutenant Colonel Sir Archibald Campbell disembarked three miles east of Howe's position with 3,000 experienced provincial Tory and regular troops that included the well-known 71st Regiment of Foot. They began to move toward Savannah. Once he reached the Girardeau Plantation, Sir Campbell began to advance on the main causeway that led into the city, the very same causeway where Howe was encamped. Campbell met one of Howe's forward detachments under the command of Captain John C. Smith, and he dispersed it back to Howe's position.

Once General Howe heard of Campbell's advance, he called a council of war at which he decided he would defend Savannah. His command amounted to no more than 1,500 men, a few of which were green militiamen. He posted Colonel Isaac Huger's South Carolina Militia on the right flank. Colonel Samuel Elbert led a group of Georgian Continentals on the left flank, while the General held the remainder of the Continental Army in the middle. The swampy riverbank was to the Americans' left, a marsh to their right. The causeway in front of them crossed a deep morass.

As Sir Campbell neared Howe's post, Quanimo "Quash" Dolly, a local black resident, informed him of the small remote causeway ignored by Howe by which Campbell could access Howe from behind. Archibald Campbell detached Captain Sir James Baird with a small company of light infantry to quietly work their way along the remote causeway. Campbell maneuvered in front of the Americans with the main British force while Baird worked his way to Howe's back side. Once in position, Baird dispersed a rear guard led by Walton and immediately launched an attack on General Howe's rear. Campbell, upon hearing Baird's firing, initiated a full frontal attack against the Americans. It was over in minutes. The South Carolina militiamen escaped back down the causeway and through Savannah followed by Howe and his Continentals. The Georgia Continentals tried to cover the withdrawal from the left flank but were quickly cut off from the retreat route. They tried to escape through the swamp, but few were actually able to do so. During the rout, the Americans suffered a devastating loss: 83 killed in action, 30 drowned, and 453 captured (38 officers), including wounded.

The British had taken Savannah and regained control of a major portion of populated Georgia (including the entire coastal region). Initially, the British soldiers committed some heinous brutal attacks upon the civilians of Savannah, but Lieutenant Colonel Campbell interceded and protected persons and private property within the city. He would superciliously issue a proclamation that inhabitants would be secure if they declared their allegiance to King George III (see Chapter 6). Tories became active throughout Georgia from the coast to the backcountry, and the Whigs in the area were in trouble.[40]

Georgia demanded that Major General Robert Howe face a court martial. He did face a board of inquiry and was exonerated of blame for the loss of Savannah. His reputation, however, was effectively ruined. General William Moultrie observed, regarding the initial advice and decision to defend Savannah rather than to move northward out of danger and link up with Lincoln's gathered troops: "This was the most ill-advised, rash opinion, that could possibly be given; it was absurd to suppose that six or seven hundred men, and some of them very raw troops, could stand against two or three thousand as good troops as any British had."[41] General Henry Lee pondered why Howe, who had been in command in that country and encamped in the area for four months since the Florida campaign, was not aware of "the by-way passing to his rear, when Lieutenant-Colonel Campbell contrived to discover it in a few hours."[42]

The relationships between the state governments and the Continental Congress were delicate. It would be some time before they could work smoothly together and affect a strong coordinated military action with combined forces and supplies. How different circumstances might have been for Savannah, and especially for Howe's reputation, had Lowndes readily agreed to support Lincoln early in December. The result is anyone's guess. It is reasonable to expect that, had Lincoln relieved Howe earlier as he desired, Campbell may not have had the success he experienced on the 29th.

The conclusion of 1778 would not bring closure to the rebellion. The repeal of the Tea Act was too little, too late to assist the British with appeasement or a strong position for future negotiations. Additionally, the last 15 months had been rough for anyone named General Howe regardless of his command — British or American. It was about to become rough for everybody, beginning in Georgia where Colonel Andrew Pickens would soon lower the boom on a substantial body of Tories.

6

Georgia Explodes! (1779)

On January 4, 1779, British Lieutenant Colonel Sir Archibald Campbell and Commodore Hyde Parker manifested total control of Savannah and arrogantly issued a loyalty oath which read:

> I (name) do solemnly swear that I will bear true and faithful allegiance to his majesty King George the Third, my lawful Sovereign, and that I will, at all risks, stand forth in support of his person and government. And I do solemnly disclaim and renounce that unlawful and iniquitous confederacy called the General Continental Congress, also the claim set up by them to independency, and all obedience to them, and all subordinate jurisdictions assumed by or under their authority. All this I do sincerely promise without equivocation or mental reservation whatever. So help me God.

Initially, this proclamation was to have been signed by the residents of Savannah in return for the protection Campbell promised after the defeat of Major General Robert Howe's troops in December (see Chapter 5).[1]

Major General Benjamin Lincoln finally acquired command of the Southern Department and moved toward the British center of action. He had left Charles Town with only 1,500 men, but by January 7, 1779, he bivouacked at Purysburg (now Purrysburg Landing), South Carolina, with a force of 3,500 men that included the remnants of Howe's army, plus some local militia units. (Purysburg was 15 miles upriver from Savannah.)[2]

Also on January 7, British Major General Augustine Prevost and 2,000 men surrounded Sunbury, Georgia, 15 miles south of Savannah. He had departed Florida immediately after he had learned of Campbell's success at Savannah. On the 9th, Prevost demanded that Major Joseph Lane surrender Fort Morris at Sunbury, but the Major resisted. He declared his duty and intent to defend the fort, whereupon Prevost unleashed his artillery. After a short exchange of cannonade, Lane surrendered. As a result, the British captured 212 Continental soldiers.[3]

South Carolina Patriot Brigadier General Williamson's militia muster of November 1778 was still in force during (and after) the raging battle at Savannah; however, his men were not involved in that action. Williamson had gained control of Augusta and used the site as his headquarters. From there, he detached his militia regiments to patrol the backcountry. Andrew Pickens, in 1811, wrote to General Henry "Light Horse Harry" Lee, "My regiment was mostly small detachments on the frontier from Saluda to Savannah River to guard against incursion of Indians."[4]

Following the action at Fort Morris, Prevost marched to Savannah, where he linked up with the recently-arrived Campbell, and established his headquarters. The General laid out his plan before Campbell. General Prevost would maintain control at Savannah; Lieutenant Colonel Campbell would take Augusta from Williamson, and Campbell would send

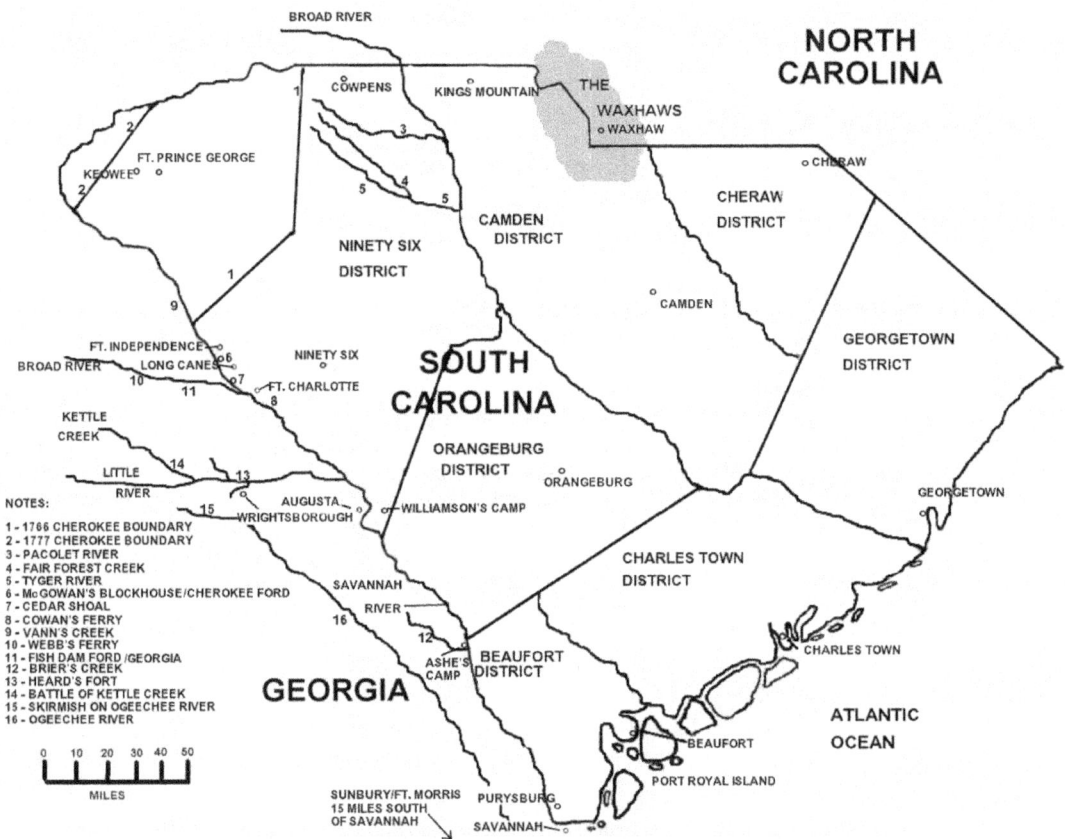

South Carolina points of interest in 1779.

for a large provincial Tory regiment from the North and South Carolina backcountry. Campbell would administer the loyalty oath to the backcountry Georgians and, by so doing, establish an additional provincial regiment of Tories. The huge coordinated force of British regulars and provincials would then move into South Carolina and gain control of that colony as well.[5]

The British Regular Army was undermanned, and reliance on local Tory militia groups was ineffective. The backcountry Tory militiamen were not well-trained, not inclined to follow orders, and their leaders were generally criminals who were truly not focused on "the cause." The British organized local Tories into provincial regiments in an attempt to solve that problem. Those regiments were usually commanded by regular British officers (though sometimes by proven Tory militia officers) responsible to recruit and train in the British mode of warfare. Those were long-term commitments much like the Whigs' South Carolina State Troops, and payment was comparable to that of British regular soldiers. Several successful provincial regiments became well-known: British Lieutenant Colonel Banastre Tarleton's Legion, Tory Major John Hamilton's North Carolinians, and British Major Patrick Ferguson's South Carolinians.[6]

On January 14, General Prevost announced a full pardon for all Georgians willing to take an oath of allegiance to King George III and join Tory militia forces. The next day, Prevost dispatched Lieutenant Colonel Archibald Campbell with 1,000 troops to drive

Williamson's forces from Augusta. Sir Campbell was skittish about his assignment because of the reputation of Andrew Pickens' regiment.[7]

Campbell, prior to leaving Savannah, ordered South Carolina Tory Lieutenant Colonel John (sometimes listed as James) Boyd into the backcountry of northwestern South Carolina and southern North Carolina. He was to recruit a vast body of Loyalists to assist in the Georgia backcountry. Boyd, and North Carolina Provincial Major John Hamilton, had arrived from New York with Colonel Campbell and had commanded the Tory troops that participated in the capture of Savannah.

Lieutenant Colonel Campbell was convinced that colossal numbers of Loyalists awaited the advent of the British and were eager to take control of Georgia and South Carolina. He was sure that Boyd would bring at least 6,000 avid troops to exercise dominion over the backcountry Georgians. Britain could then proceed with its overall plan to move quickly through South Carolina and bring it to submission. Boyd left Savannah for the backcountry on January 24, 1779.[8]

Lieutenant Colonel Boyd was destined for the assignment. He had been one of the Tories north of the Saluda River when Drayton tried to recapture ammunition the Tories had stolen (see Chapter 3). Boyd was not a typical backcountry Tory. He was an ardent believer in the British colonial system and wanted to do more to enhance that cause than exert haphazard action against the Whigs with a group of local Tory militia thugs.

Boyd went to New York and signed on with British Lieutenant Colonel Sir Archibald Campbell who commissioned him "Lieutenant Colonel" Boyd. The relegation was conditional upon Boyd's successful completion of his mustering task, after which he was required to organize his provincial regiment of Tories.

Major Hamilton had previously been assigned to lead a similar provincial regiment of North Carolinians. Normally, a Tory provincial commander had to drum up his own Loyalist force and train his men to emulate British regulars. Boyd would return home to recruit the very criminals he had tried to avoid, convinced they would be eager to join him and follow the orders of their colleague-made-good Lieutenant Colonel.

Boyd knew the Pickens family well; he was married to one of Andrew's cousins (not specifically identified). Like John "The Tory" Pickens (see Chapter 4) the Boyds were ostracized by the rest of the Pickens family for their extreme political leanings. Mrs. Boyd held much contempt for her cousin, Andrew, and thought him haughty.

Lieutenant Colonel Boyd stealthily moved toward his target campsite near Grindal Shoals on the Pacolet River. He arrived by the end of January and immediately began to recruit among Tories familiar to him. His recruiting area consisted entirely of his old haunts from Fair Forest Creek, on the southwest, to northeast of the Broad River into North Carolina. He sent a messenger to North Carolina Militia Colonel John Moore to request Moore gather Loyalists from the northern portion of the muster zone. (Grindal Shoals was located 20 miles southeast of present-day Spartanburg, slightly north of where State Highway 18 crosses the Pacolet River, and near an island.)

Meanwhile, Campbell passed Major General Benjamin Lincoln's encampment on the way to Augusta, albeit from across the Savannah. Major General William Moultrie supported Lincoln on the Savannah and sent word to General Williamson regarding Campbell's movement. Williamson pulled his militia out of Augusta and crossed the Savannah River to encamp. Captain Irvine's company was the only one of Colonel Andrew Pickens' regiment attached directly to the General. Pickens had assigned Irvine as the General's point of contact while he and the remainder of his troops patrolled the backcountry. Andrew

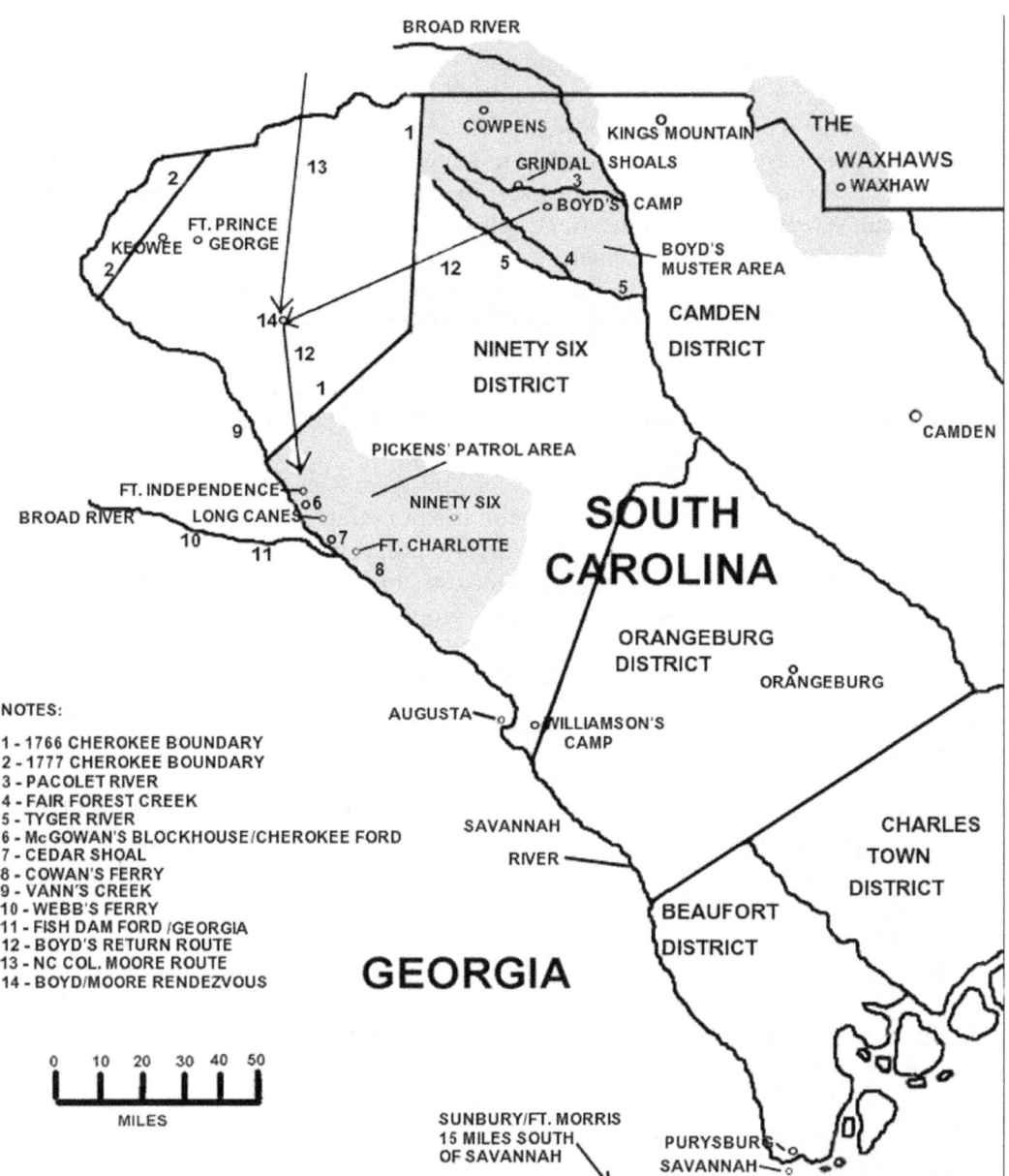

Lieutenant Colonel Boyd enlists Tories in South Carolina.

Pickens wrote Henry Lee, "Genl. Williamson went with the Militia except part of my regiment to oppose Campbell's crossing Savannah river."⁹

Before he reached Augusta, Lieutenant Colonel Campbell dispatched Florida Ranger Provincial Colonel Thomas "Burn Foot" Brown, who had come north with General Prevost, and Georgia Tory Major Daniel McGirth. They led 400 men to the vicinity of the Burke County, Georgia, jail to locate a local Tory militia colonel named Thomas. Patriot Georgia State Militia Colonel John Twiggs had discovered the movement and successfully intervened with fellow Colonels William and Benjamin Few. The Loyalists were turned back after a merciless thrashing, and Brown suffered painful wounds. He had been agonizingly burned near Augusta once before and later faced off with the Whigs around Ninety Six (see Chapter 2).[10]

Tory Major Daniel McGirth had a ravenous desire for revenge against the Whigs. A few years earlier, he had adopted Whig politics and joined the local militia. McGirth had a fine mare. His commanding officer coveted the horse and offered to buy it. Daniel indicated the animal was not for sale, whereupon the officer suggested a trade. McGirth was not receptive and bluntly told the officer so. The officer had him publicly lashed and then jailed with the promise of another whipping if he did not reconsider. McGirth escaped with the mare, vowed vengeance, switched his politics and joined a Tory militia regiment. Not every Whig officer had the spirit of knighthood flowing through his veins; indeed, some individuals had downright ugly dispositions.[11]

Major General William Moultrie. Artist: Col. J. Trumbull; engraver: Edward Scriven, 1865.

Sir Campbell reached Augusta on January 31 and was relieved to see that Williamson had abandoned the area. Campbell wasted no time applying the oath of allegiance and was disappointed to find only 10% (1,400) of the able-bodied men around Augusta would sign on. Extremely agitated (he expected 10,000), Campbell decided to immediately subjugate the Georgia backcountry. He decided Boyd could take over that operation when he returned with his huge group of Loyalists.

Campbell then detached Major McGirth further up the Savannah to build boats. He was planning to eventually cross the river with provincials and attack Williamson from the upriver flank. Additionally, Campbell detached Tory provincial Major John Hamilton 30 miles upriver to Wilkes County, the Georgia backcountry center of Whig militia activity. The Major was ordered to recruit local Tories and administer the oath of allegiance to all citizens he would encounter. Hamilton labeled those who did not submit to the oath treasonous, and he ensured they suffered retribution. Homes were looted and burned. Livestock was slain. Crops were destroyed. A number of citizens endured severe tortures. Men were branded with a hot iron. Women were raped. Countless Georgia Patriots began to cross the river to seek protection within Ninety Six District. Patriot Colonel John Dooley of the Georgia State Militia encamped 30 miles inside South Carolina. From there he made several small recruiting forays into Georgia that netted him 100 men.[12]

Colonel Dooley tried to make a move back into Georgia with his recently-gathered militia, but Hamilton was in position to block the action. Andrew Pickens wrote Lee, "Coln. Campbell detached Coln. Hamilton ... with 200 mounted mostly irregulars up Savannah River on the Georgia Side. The Whigs of Wilkes County fled to the Carolina side of the river and gave me immediate notice."

It was early February when Dooley formally requested assistance from Williamson. Also, at that time, newly-elected South Carolina Governor John Rutledge heard about Boyd's enterprising trek into the backcountry and ordered Williamson to detach Colonel Andrew Pickens' regiment to disrupt the flow of Tories toward Georgia. Williamson, in turn, ordered Pickens to lead his regiment in a coordinated action with Dooley against Boyd and Hamilton to free the Wilkes County Whigs from their desperate situation.[13]

Rutledge and Williamson each knew that Andrew Pickens' reputation had been well-earned. Pickens was definitely the militia officer for the job. In 1896, the Cowpens Centennial Committee quoted an unidentified writer about Andrew Pickens:

> A beautiful and devoted wife; a cheerful fireside; peace and plenty about him — what more could a man crave? All this he was soon called upon to forego, and take the field, fighting for what he conceived to be duty and right. In those peaceful times: "All good men loved the King: not to do so was a crime ... not to drink to his health was treason."[14]

Pickens could see history repeating itself. He was aware of the trials and tribulations his ancestors suffered under the Royal Crown and the Church of England. Britain exposed the colonists to unending burdens, such as the Townshend Acts, and had recently delegated power to the Anglican Church to further subjugate the Presbyterians. The British had gone too far. The anonymous Cowpens Centennial Committee author continued:

> Andrew Pickens had no personal end to serve, no personal grievance ... but the voice of duty called him, and at that critical moment he flung his whole influence into the American cause.
>
> He was widely known all through the Piedmont Section for his piety and fearless bravery, and he turned the tide of public opinion. The moment Andrew Pickens took the field Upper South Carolina declared against George III ... with Indians hostile in his rear, and British troops and Loyalists in front, his family exposed at all times, he went resolutely forward, with an approving conscience — the freedom of the colonies his only aspiration.

Brigadier General Andrew Williamson with 1,300 troops, all militia except for 300 Continentals, had been encamped across the river from Augusta for several weeks and made no move to bear down upon Campbell or to move upriver and pressure Hamilton. He and Campbell each warily eyed the other's forces while Generals Prevost and Lincoln did the same at Savannah. Lincoln waited for North Carolina Militia General John Ashe to join him before he would initiate any action. (The North Carolinians had been directly assigned to the Continental army.) Campbell was still awaiting the return of Boyd with his "horde" of Loyalists. One attempt at action occurred on February 3 when General Prevost sent British Major William Gardner with 200 soldiers 15 miles north to the vicinity of Port Royal Island. That was an intended flanking maneuver against Lincoln to cut off his supply line from Charles Town; however, Lincoln dispatched Moultrie with 300 troops to chase Gardner back to Savannah. It then became a waiting game; the only real activities were those of Hamilton, Pickens, and Dooley in the backcountry. Pickens told Henry Lee, "Campbell soon retreated.... There was not a gun fired between him and Williamson all this time opposite each other at Augusta ... and nothing of consequence happened in separate [meaning Williamson's] command further till after the fall of Charleston [Williamson's command being] almost constantly on duty."[15]

During his detachment to the backcountry, Lieutenant Colonel Boyd successfully recruited 350 Loyalists—a far cry from the 6,000 that Campbell was expecting. Boyd departed for Augusta on February 5, 1779. He initially exercised discretion on the march back when he headed west toward the Cherokee Nation. He then passed over the old 1776 Cherokee Nation boundary line before Colonel John Moore met him with 250 North Carolina Loyalists as previously arranged. The area west of the old boundary was no longer Cherokee land; however, it had not largely been settled except for a few notorious Tories who were trying to avoid dominant South Carolina backcountry Whig regions.

The command structure for the march to Augusta was Boyd with Major William Spurgin (also Spurgeon or Spurgen) of Rowan County, North Carolina, next in authority, followed by Colonel Moore. Command was a challenge because the mustered Loyalists were malefactors as Boyd recalled from his previous experiences. A few others were actually Whig sympathizers who joined the march under the guise of being Loyalists, so their families would not be threatened by the ruffians.

It would have befitted Boyd to avoid detection and continue a furtive return to Augusta. He might have remained west of the old Indian boundary until he could cross the Savannah at Cherokee Ford, but instead he returned to predominately Whig populated country near Long Canes. As he proceeded toward the Savannah River, his troops approached every able-bodied male they came across and immediately administered Campbell's loyalty oath. They also pressed several more into service with threats toward the men's families if they didn't join the excursion. Boyd's ruffians harassed the families of those who refused to submit to the oath, tortured the men, and took several as prisoners. The motley agglomeration captured and burned Fort Independence near Long Canes while en route. Boyd ended up with a total force of 800 not including prisoners. (Andrew Pickens' uncle, John Pickens, had built Fort Independence during the Cherokee War. See Chapter 4.) A. L. Pickens explained the situation, "Unfortunately for the loyal cause, Boyd had taken into his force a number of plundering banditti, out more for loot than for the love of the Royal Master they so ostentatiously clove to. The best and most constructive families on the frontier had joined the Whig movement."[16]

Colonel Andrew Pickens received his orders early in February 1779. At that time, his regiment was still divided into detachments, mainly by company, with some of those separated into smaller groups yet. He quickly moved to the village of Ninety Six and put out a call for his companies to promptly join him for the coming action. Lieutenant Joseph Pickens, of Captain Weems' company, was mindful of the Tories' movement into the vicinity of Long Canes, so he tailed them. He feared the pack might run amok through the Ninety Six District. Andrew Pickens' brother realized reconnaissance was in order, so he did not immediately rejoin the regiment.[17] (Lieutenant Joseph Pickens is invariably reported to be a captain at the time of these events, especially at the coming Battle of Kettle Creek. The facts about his rank are related following the account of that battle.)

Colonel Andrew Pickens and his militia would soon open an intensely aggressive incursion in support of his Georgia colleagues. He had a nonpareil cadre of officers who were ethical, reliable, and totally focused on the task at hand. Two of his most trustworthy company commanders were Captains James McCall and Robert Anderson. His demonstrative brother, Joseph, was markedly conscientious and reliable.

Should Tory Major Daniel McGirth have had any one of these officers in lieu of his original Whig commanding officer, he might have remained a patriot — indeed, a capable Whig officer. However, due to one narcissist, he sought vengeance upon as valiant an assemblage as could be found. Had he really been committed to the idea of independence, no demonic demonstration by any one leader would have altered his track.

The McCall and Anderson families had made the trek over the Great Wagon Road near the same time as the Pickens and Calhoun families. They all tended to stay together through relocations to the Waxhaws, on to Ninety Six and then Long Canes.

In 1775 Captains James McCall, Robert Anderson, and Andrew Pickens helped defend against a Tory siege at Savage's old field near Ninety Six. Each of the three had been among six captains selected to lead portions of a nighttime raid on different gatherings of Tories during the action. When chosen they had each been eager to lead the small hand-picked guerrilla teams. However, those raids became unnecessary when negotiations opened.

McCall had been captured at the onset of the Cherokee War in 1776, before Williamson's campaign began, but had soon escaped and partook of the action. Anderson had commanded Fort Independence before the foray and had aided Pickens at skirmishes on the Tugaloo River and at Tomassee during the campaign. Joseph Pickens had made his presence known when he had come to the aid of his brother during the Ring Fight with a Cherokee war party and "gently prodded" members of Andrew's company to hurry them along. They had all been together when Williamson gathered his companies to announce the ratification of the Declaration of Independence. What a special moment that was to share with such devoted comrades.

These men had developed an unbreakable bond during their experiences. They had grown so close they could sense each other's thoughts during life-threatening actions; verbal communication had become almost unnecessary as they performed their duties for the cause of freedom. Their mutual respect was unparalleled for a militia unit. Each one, though an exceptional leader in his own right, had for years enthusiastically conceded leadership to Andrew Pickens. Additionally, Pickens had discreetly exercised his default role as their group leader. Alexandre Dumas might easily have written a book about their camaraderie which would have rivaled that of Athos, Porthos, Aramis and d'Artagnan.

The war for American Independence was at a new beginning. While there would be problems along the way, control of the southern colonies was in capable hands early in 1779.

On February 7, Andrew Pickens, who had retired to Ninety Six village to call in his companies, gathered about 100 of his regiment and met Georgia Colonel John Dooley and Lieutenant Colonel Elijah Clarke (Dooley's second-in-command) at Cowan's Ferry on the Savannah River. He had left word for the remainder of his regiment to meet him there, which they did, except for Joseph Pickens' detachment. Andrew's manpower then amounted to 150, compared to the Georgians' 100. Pickens, Dooley, and Clarke then spent the evening planning an action against provincial Major John Hamilton. This was the onset of an epic and historic week for the combined Whig militias.[18]

On the morning of the 8th, Hamilton appeared on the Georgia side of the river and apparently desired to cross. He was somewhat surprised to see the Whig militia, so he moved away to seek another crossing. He wasn't sure he had been spotted by Pickens' force. He was. A. L. Pickens wrote, "So, for two days, up and down the river, a distance of ten miles, both parties manouvered [sic], and on the evening of the second day Hamilton disappeared."[19] Andrew Pickens added in his letter to Henry Lee, "we had secured all the flats on the Carolina side. I had enough to ... guard the places which were necessary. We maneuvered opposite each other for two days up and down the river for ten miles ... on the evening of the second day he disappeared — I immediately sent two men to reconnoiter to know whether it was a feint or whether he was gone some distance."[20] Pickens had not yet learned of Boyd's whereabouts, so he was unaware that Hamilton was keeping an eye out for his fellow Tory.

Henry "Light Horse Harry" Lee later stated: "Colonel Pickens, of the South Carolina militia, true to his country, and correctly interpreting the movement under Hamilton, assembled his regiment and drew near to him for the purpose of counteracting his operations."[21]

The scouts were dispatched on the 9th and reported back that night. Hamilton broke camp that very morning on Captain Thomas Water's plantation, near the mouth of the Broad River. He left for Heard's Fort, site of present-day Washington, Georgia, where his forces bivouacked for the night. Stephen Heard built this stockade when he settled the area in 1774. Such small stockades were typically erected on private property and utilized existing outbuildings, sometimes even the owners' houses. Timbered walls were added to these basic edifices to connect the structures. Neighbors were invited to seek protection therein during times of crisis. Pickens continued in his letter:

> They returned and informed me that he had taken the road to a fort about 10 miles from the River where there were some old men with some women and children — I immediately commenced crossing the river and as we had but one ford at the place and all horsemen it was nearly break of day before we got all over — When we all had gotten over, I had the men paraded for as Dooley was a full Colonel in Georgia and I in Carolina he then had command — Clark was then Lieut. Col. under Dooley.[22]

It was the morning of the 10th before they completed the crossing. By that time Pickens had gathered most of his regiment, 200 men, and Dooley, 160. It was customary that when commanding officers of a joint action held the same rank, the officer who resided in the state where the action took place had command authority. Thus, Pickens was in command before crossing the Savannah, and Dooley afterward.[23]

Andrew Pickens was a respecter of military discipline and protocol; however, he and his men were in a special circumstance that required a deviation from the norm. The Ninety Six militia was in superior military disposition. They diligently drilled at their weekly training sessions when not at muster, and Pickens was relentless at working his troops on intricate situational details. They practiced hard to modify an action on the fly to counter an enemy's movement. Andrew and his captains utilized numerous gestures to alert the troops of necessary changes in plans, and the men reacted instantly as if they had read their officers' minds. Such responsiveness was absolutely necessary. Colonel Pickens trusted Dooley and Clarke, but was uncertain to what degree he could rely upon the Georgia militiamen for quick reactions in battle. He decided he must take the lead with his experienced militia, so he asked Dooley to take a supporting, though important, role. Pickens continued in his letter to Henry Lee:

> I then spoke to Dooley and told him that unless he gave up the full Command to me I would not proceed further to which he readily consented and then spoke to the men and told them that I was determined to pursue the enemy and attack him wherever I found him and that if any wished they might return: but further that I was determined to be obeyed to which they all heartily agreed.[24]

Before he moved his militia, the Colonel ordered the men into formation. He made the criticality of the mission clear to them and, as only he could, sternly informed them of his intention to be absolutely obeyed. All inherently agreed they had complete confidence that Pickens should be their leader, and they all pledged to follow him against the enemy. "As soon as it was clear light we proceeded with all the rapidity possible and when we came to the fort where they had stayed that night, they had just left it and said they were going to Kerr's [Carr's] Fort which was bout twelve miles further,"[25] Pickens continued.

Robert Carr's Fort was another of the many outposts that had sprung up on the frontier for protection of backcountry settlers. (Robert Carr's Fort was 12 miles south of present-

Colonel Pickens chases Lieutenant Colonel Hamilton.

day Washington, Georgia, on Beaverdam Creek before it empties into the Little River. Genealogically, Kerr and Carr are derivatives of a common name.)

Hamilton continued to administer the loyalty oath as he slowly moved ahead of Pickens through the backcountry. Colonel Pickens dispatched two scouts to Carr's Fort. He desired for them to arrive ahead of Hamilton. They were to present a message for the inhabitants that expressed the Colonel's wish that the gates be secured. Then, the Whig militia could come upon an exposed Tory force. However, the scouts took a circuitous route to avoid Hamilton. Hamilton thus arrived at Carr's Fort before the planned action could be accomplished. Pickens, himself, got to the fort quickly enough to see Hamilton's rear guard enter the compound. The events happened so swiftly that Hamilton was not able to unload his supply wagons before the gates were closed. Due to the crowded conditions within, the wagons and horses, including saddles and bridles, remained tied outside the stockade.[26]

The Tories immediately commenced sniping from the walls, and a few militiamen were wounded. A small wooden cabin sat alongside a spring that provided water to the fort. Pickens ordered Captain William Freeman to gather a detail of forty men and take the structure. They succeeded even though under fire from the Tories. They were also able to cover the stockade walls' firing platforms.

Colonel Pickens controlled the fort's water source as well as Hamilton's supplies outside the compound. The Whig militiamen pinned the defenders down within the stockade and settled in for a long siege. They were confident they would eventually force Hamilton to surrender.

According to military custom, Andrew Pickens sent a flagged messenger who petitioned Hamilton to avoid bloodshed and relinquish the post. Hamilton, also as was customary, refused the initial request. The Colonel then sent a message that requested Hamilton to release all women, children, and elderly men. Hamilton also refused this petition.

The Whig militia encampment was on a rise that overlooked the main gate. There was a smooth, straight road leading to the entrance. Pickens ordered the militia to prepare a wagon with flammable materials so that he could, after dark, set it ablaze and roll it down the road to smash against the gate. Carr's Fort was old and contained a collection of small, very dry, wooden cabins. Andrew knew it would be a veritable tinderbox. As darkness approached, Andrew held a council of war with his officers. They agreed that setting fire to the complex would put the lives of the civilians therein in extreme jeopardy. The Colonel then decided against burning the fort.[27]

Lieutenant Joseph Pickens ceased tailing Boyd because he feared that the band of ruffians might turn northward toward Long Canes, since Boyd seemed to be in no particular hurry. Joseph determined he would take his detachment and head for Cowan's Ferry. He would there search for his brother and apprise him of the situation. Joseph sent a messenger ahead on a quick horse. (Cowan's Ferry was located near Fort Charlotte. The site, six and one-half miles southwest of present-day Mt. Carmel, South Carolina, is submerged under present-day J. Strom Thurmond Reservoir. A marker designating the location of Fort Charlotte is found in Mt. Carmel at the intersection of modern State Highway 81 and State Road 91.)

It was still the evening of the 10th, about 10:00, when the messenger located Colonel Pickens. Pickens was told of Boyd's advance with a 700-strong force and about the destruction of Fort Independence. He was also notified that, should Boyd not move on Long Canes, he would probably reach the Savannah River before night had ended.

"I ordered the wounded men to be taken off, called the principal officers together and communicated to them the intelligence — It was immediately agreed to cross the Savannah River and try to intercept them if possible — We immediately kindled a long line of fires just over the top of the ridge which ran parallel with the fort about 150 yards from it, so that they could see the light of the fire from the fort,"[28] reported Pickens. He believed that night fires would distract Hamilton, make him think they were campfires, and that

Colonel Pickens chases Lieutenant Colonel Boyd.

the siege was still underway. However, it was a stale ruse and would not fool Hamilton for long. Under cover of darkness, the militia commandeered many of Hamilton's horses, along with saddles and bridles that had been left outside the stockade. Pickens then raised the siege, headed for the Savannah, and arrived there across from Fort Charlotte at daybreak February 11, 1779.

Henry Lee later stated, "Finding this officer [Major John Hamilton] invulnerable, he suddenly turned from him to strike the loyalists advancing toward Augusta."[29]

Andrew Pickens recounted, "We got to the Savannah River early the next morning, got over that day and ten or twelve miles on the Carolina side, but could get no certain account of where Boyd [went] with his party."[30] The Colonel was soon joined by his brother, Joseph, and the remainder of the regiment. Lieutenant Pickens was still unsure whether Boyd had made for the Savannah or tarried around Long Canes, so Andrew Pickens detached Captain Robert Anderson to lead 80 men, including Captains Baskin and Miller, up the river to try and head Boyd off should he attempt a crossing. Lieutenant Joseph Pickens accompanied the detachment because he would be able to recognize any members of Boyd's party. Another militiaman in the detachment was Andrew's and Joseph's cousin, William Pickens, who was a member of Anderson's company. William Pickens' pension application reads: "February 1779 he volunteered in Abbyville District, South Carolina, in the company commanded by Capt. Robert Anderson, Col. Andrew Pickens & Gen. Andrew Williamson were the officers. Marched to Savana [sic] River ... they pursued the Tories to Kettle Creek in Georgia when they overtook the Tories and defeated them." (See Appendix E.)

Once Colonel Pickens became aware of Boyd's direction, he led the militia quickly toward Cedar Shoals on the Savannah and angled toward Boyd's expected crossing point.[31] (Cedar Shoals was located six miles north of Fort Charlotte in the vicinity of present-day R. B. Russell Dam that holds the waters of Russell Lake on the Savannah River.)

Lieutenant Colonel John Boyd was eager to merge with Major John Hamilton in the backcountry but was totally unaware of the Major's close call at Fort Carr. At daybreak on the 11th, about the time Pickens' militia reached the Savannah, Hamilton thought he could venture in safety. He retreated toward Augusta and left no one for Boyd's expected linkup.

Had Boyd continued on and promptly crossed the Savannah while west of the old Cherokee boundary, he likely would have forded unnoticed, could have approached Pickens' militia from the rear, and encircled it as the siege of Fort Carr was taking place. Pickens would have been hugely outnumbered and awkwardly pinched between Boyd and Hamilton. Pickens' experience dictated that he always deployed militiamen as outriders on his back trail and the flanking countryside. Thus, his riders could forewarn him of an approaching force. Boyd at least would have arrived in time to affect a conjuncture with Hamilton at the fort.

Also on the 11th, Boyd and his Tories approached Cherokee Ford at McGowen's blockhouse on the Savannah. The blockhouse sat high on a hill that overlooked the east bank of the ford. Boyd did not know that Anderson had gained control of the blockhouse and had posted Lieutenant Thomas Shanklin there with eight men and two swivel guns while he continued to patrol the river looking for the Tory. The defenders spotted Boyd as he approached, realized they were greatly outnumbered, and decided more armament and reinforcements were required. Four men were ordered to leave the rear of the blockhouse and cross the Savannah while the garrison stalled Boyd's approach. The group was to retrieve a nearby four-pounder and to bring back any of Anderson's detachment they could find.

Meanwhile, Boyd sent one of his more notorious ruffians, William "Bloody Bill" Cuningham (sometimes Cunningham, purported to be a cousin of brothers Robert and Patrick Cunningham covered in earlier chapters), to demand surrender of the blockhouse. The defenders realized that Boyd had no idea of their strength and asked for two hours to consider the demand. Boyd consented.

The four Whigs returned to the blockhouse with the four-pounder, Captain James Little, and 40 reinforcements. They arrived in time for Captain Little to refuse Cuningham's second delivery of the surrender demand. The Tories expected rifle fire at most but were met with clusters of 30-caliber balls that whistled through the air after they were fired from the cannon. Boyd immediately retreated and headed upriver with his band. (McGowan's Blockhouse and Cherokee Ford were located four miles upriver from present-day R. B. Russell Dam and is under the waters of Russell Lake.)

This would not be the last time the Whigs would hear from "Bloody Bill" Cuningham; indeed, he would become one of their more formidable obstacles to peace and would cause personal grief for Andrew Pickens. (See Chapter 13.)

A messenger left the blockhouse to inform Anderson of the skirmish. Anderson immediately took his regiment across the Savannah at Cherokee Ford near McGowen's and headed upriver parallel to Boyd. Anderson got to the ford at Vann's (sometimes Van's) Creek prior to Boyd's arrival and prepared to defend against his crossing attempt. Boyd's throng met a severe fusillade as they began to move into Georgia; however, Anderson's detachment was immensely overwhelmed and had to withdraw. The Tories crossed for a mile up and down the Savannah and eventually gained Anderson's rear. Even though Boyd successfully entered Georgia with his mob, he had lost 100 men killed, wounded, or missing. Anderson lost 16 killed and another 16 captured. Those captured included Captains Baskin and Miller. Captain Robert Anderson, Lieutenant Joseph Pickens, and the detachment immediately set out to find Colonel Pickens.[32] (Vann's Creek Ford was located on the Savannah River at present-day Ruckersville, Georgia, and the site is under Russell Lake.)

On the evening of the 11th, Colonel Pickens received a messenger near Cedar Shoal who informed him of Anderson's *defeat* at Vann's Creek and that Boyd had affected the crossing into Georgia. Pickens described it to Lee:

> I sent two or three active men with good horses to proceed up the River and when they got certain intelligence of the Enemy one to return and in meantime I would proceed up the river as far as possible. About the middle of the day one returned. I had then gone 14 miles up the river.... We then halted, Capt. Baskin and Miller were made prisoners with some men. When Captains Anderson and [actually Lieutenant Joseph] Pickens came in and gave us a full account of this business, numbers who had not turned out at first had joined us, we amounted to about 400 men—officers and men willingly agreed to pursue them, we recrossed the river that evening and sent out spies to discover the rout they had taken who returned in the night but could [not] give us satisfactory intelligence.[33]

Pickens recorded that he crossed the Savannah that night and encamped on the Georgia side of the river. Several contemporary writings attribute his crossing to be on the morning of the 12th after he had camped on the South Carolina side; however, since a shoal usually provides ease of crossing, there would have been no reason for him to wait. Crossing on the evening of the 11th enabled the militia to awaken the next morning for breakfast and set out at daybreak without any delay. This encampment afforded the militia a much needed respite from the chase. They had not experienced a complete sleep since the 8th. One entire night was spent fording the Savannah River into Georgia to track Hamilton. The next night, after having raised the siege at Fort Carr, they marched to the Savannah where they crossed into South Carolina to locate Boyd.

Colonel Pickens dispatched a Captain Neel with a detachment to seek information on Boyd's whereabouts. Pickens continued his account:

> As soon as light sent out again and directed them to proceed up Broad River the Western bank of Savannah River till they found the trail, in the mean time I would proceed up the river until

I heard from them, knowing that they might cross that river to get to the British at Augusta and as it was then above the hostiles could get us information of them until we could find their rout — In the evening (my spies returned) and had seen them recrossing Broad River for 10 miles higher up and had taken a straggler prisoner who could give satisfactory information respecting them.— I then immediately crossed the river to the South side desiring to get between them and Augusta and still keep a few active men ahead to reconnoiter and give intelligence.[34]

Boyd traversed the Broad River near its fork at Webb's Ferry before he bivouacked on the evening of the 12th. Pickens was actually camped north of the Broad River at Fish Dam Ford when his spies brought the news. He followed Boyd by crossing the river the following morning. (Fish Dam Ford was located on the "Georgia" Broad River nine miles upstream from its mouth at the Savannah River. Webb's Ferry was six miles upstream of Fish Dam Ford.)

On the 13th, Lieutenant Colonel Sir Archibald Campbell heard commotion and gunfire from Williamson's camp and assumed the Whigs were celebrating General John Ashe's arrival from North Carolina. Sir Campbell decided not to repeat American Major General Robert Howe's recent misjudgment, so he withdrew to Savannah with his British regulars. He departed Augusta at 2:00 A.M. on the 14th.

Boyd encamped 12 miles west of Heard's Fort on the night of the 13th, and Pickens was four miles northeast. Pickens received exacting reports of Boyd's position; however, Boyd had no inkling of Pickens' whereabouts. Boyd was eager to join Hamilton and expected to have a juncture the next day at Wrightsborough, Georgia. His camp was a cold camp. The weather was damp and frigid; his motley crew, exhausted and starving.[35]

Boyd "beat his drums" (broke camp) early on the 14th. High winds tore through the camp, and the wet and cold weather had intensified. His malcontents were miserable. Boyd knew he had to find something substantial for them to eat. They ventured upon a Whig farm and stole some cattle. The Tories continued on and looked for a good place to prepare breakfast. Boyd marched his troops two more miles and decided on Kettle Creek. His men needed nourishment and a better attitude to successfully work their horses through the swamp and across the flooded and swift tributary.

The regiment set up camp on the lower slope of an incline, presently referred to as War Hill. Normally, the swampy creek bank they found would have been a fairly flat field that offered comfort, but the Tories had to be satisfied with the rising ground at the foot of the hill. There was a saddle behind the camp that joined the two peaks of War Hill. There Boyd placed a few pickets. Those sentries, however, were inclined to seek shelter rather than keep watch in the miserable weather.

The flanks of the encampment were deep with swamp and canebrakes. The Tories had barely enough room on the slope below the steeper ground to rest and warm themselves with campfires. The horses had been turned out into the swampy area along the creek to graze. Boyd assigned a butchering party to slaughter the beeves and prepare the meat for cooking.

Most contemporary writings put the butchering operation between the hill and the creek which is unlikely, given the reduced available room. According to Andrew Pickens, "½ of a mile in their rear was a beef killed and a few men butchering it."[36] This puts the butchers at least behind the hill (on the opposite side from the creek) in the direction from which Pickens would come. However, Andrew's recollection that it was one-half mile behind the camp must be a little long. They were definitely not far from the pickets, so the butchers had to be on the lower slope of the backside of the hill. It is doubtful they were in the

Entrance to Kettle Creek Battlefield.

field behind the hill which, even though higher than Kettle Creek, was extremely muddy and would have made butchering difficult.

While his detail readied the meal, Boyd detached Major William Spurgin with a group of men to explore the swamp and find a decent place to cross Kettle Creek.

Colonel Andrew Pickens also ventured out early on the 14th, and he soon came across Boyd's cold camp from the night before. A little further along, he came across the farm where Boyd had stolen the cattle. The farm belonged to a Georgia militiaman in Colonel John Dooley's regiment. The farmer's wife gave the officers pertinent information regarding Boyd and where he might be found. Pickens dispatched Captain James McCall to reconnoiter. McCall returned with information that Boyd was seemingly unconcerned with regard to his safety and had camped at a farm on Kettle Creek. He further reported that Boyd's men were ill prepared to defend against an attack and seemed lackadaisical.[37]

Colonel Pickens recollected:

> I then halted, examined and had our guns fresh fitted and primed and told my men that if any of them had anything to eat to divide it with their comrades. I then made arrangements for the attack.... Col Dooley had the right division line and Col Clark the left with orders when we come up with their escorts press forward on their flank while I would press forward upon their rear.... We then moved on out with my divisions and I went on with the center on their trail with a small advance with orders when they discovered any of the enemy not to fire first but immediately let me know.... My advance — pretty near before they discovered them being too eager and not attending to their orders they imprudently fired on them which gave the alarm.[38]

It was 10:00 A.M. on February 14, 1779, when Pickens quickly arranged a battle plan and fed his troops. Colonel Pickens' main force consisted of his 200 South Carolinians. Colonel Dooley on the right flank commanded 100 Georgians, and Lieutenant Colonel Elijah Clarke on the left led 60. Captain McCall took the small vanguard ahead of Pickens.

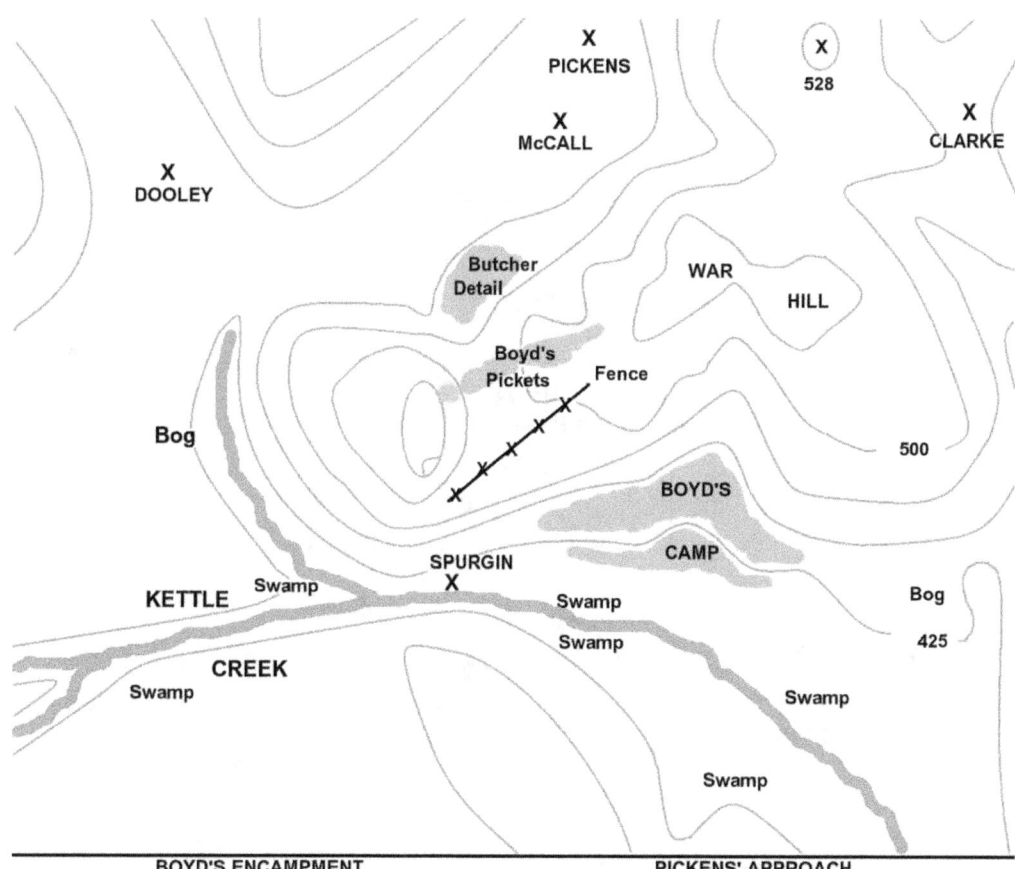

BOYD'S ENCAMPMENT

February 14, 1779, Tory Lieutenant Colonel Boyd encamped.

The weather was cold, windy, and rainy.

Kettle Creek was swollen and rapid with muddy swamps on each side.

Boyd established a line of pickets across the saddle of the hill at his rear and detached troops to butcher cattle for breakfast.

Boyd ordered Major Spurgin to look for a possible location to ford the creek.

PICKENS' APPROACH

Pickens ordered Captain McCall and part of his company to scout Boyd; McCall reported that the Tories were relaxed, confident, and lackadaisical.

Pickens fed his troops and organized them for an attack.

At 10:00 a.m., Pickens' combined militia approached Boyd's camp.

Pickens placed Georgia Colonel Dooley in command of 100 men on his right flank and Lieutenant Colonel Clarke with 60 men on his left.

Pickens commanded 200 men at the center; he dispatched Captain McCall's company 200 yards in advance.

Since they were so close, McCall's advance party engaged with Boyd's pickets at 10:30. Pickens had ordered McCall not to initiate contact because he wanted to maintain the advantage of surprise; however, this early engagement was not entirely McCall's fault. He had moved across an open area and approached the wooded slope where the butchers were hard at work. Once the butchers spotted McCall, they grabbed their weapons, shouted an alarm for the pickets, and scrambled up the hill for better cover. McCall's van, who began to fire on the fleeing Tories, received return fire once the scramblers reached the sentinels' location. The merged group of Tories stopped shooting and retreated a few yards within the saddle to take cover behind a fence and some downed trees.

Once Boyd heard the skirmish, he scaled the hill from camp. He could only rouse 100 men to move up with him and join the watchmen and butchers. The Tories then awaited Pickens' force of 200 Whigs, including McCall's detachment, which had started up the hill.

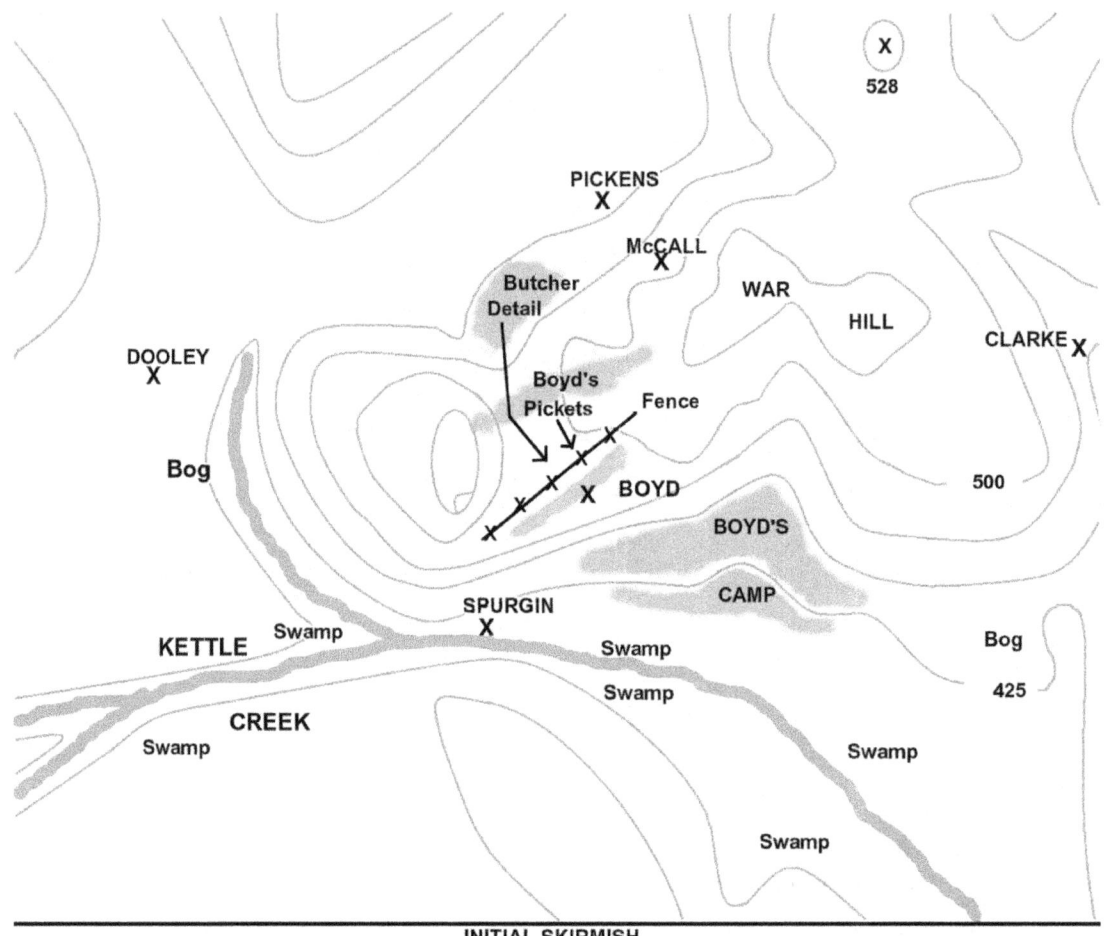

INITIAL SKIRMISH

The butcher's spotted McCall's advance and alerted the pickets who opened fire on the Whigs.

Dooley pressed around the knoll on the Whig right flank and Clarke around the knoll on the left.

McCall fell back to Pickens' main force, and they scaled the hill toward the saddle.

Boyd heard the skirmish, headed up the hill with 100 men, and took cover behind a fence that ran from one knoll to the other.

The pickets and butchers retreated to the fence for cover.

Spurgin found an adequate ford on Kettle Creek.

Andrew was told that Dooley's force was mired in the muddy swamp on the right and that Clarke suffered the same fate on the left, so Colonel Pickens dispatched Captain McCall around the peak on his right to flank the Tories in the pass. Andrew's regiment remained mounted. They picked their way through trees as they ascended the slope.

The Patriots did not receive additional fire from Boyd's well-concealed troops until they had gained the saddle's rim. The opposing sides were 30 yards apart when the Tories opened up. They killed and wounded a few of the Whigs. Once Pickens gained the pass, he spread his forces between the peaks so each of his flanks might gain an elevation advantage over the Loyalists.

At that time, McCall completed his flanking maneuver. It was 11:00 A.M., and Boyd's destiny was unavoidable. The Tories began to retreat back toward camp. Boyd had traveled fewer than 100 yards when he took three balls that mortally wounded him. The Whigs pressed the attack hard. Pickens roared down from the saddle of the hill. McCall thundered

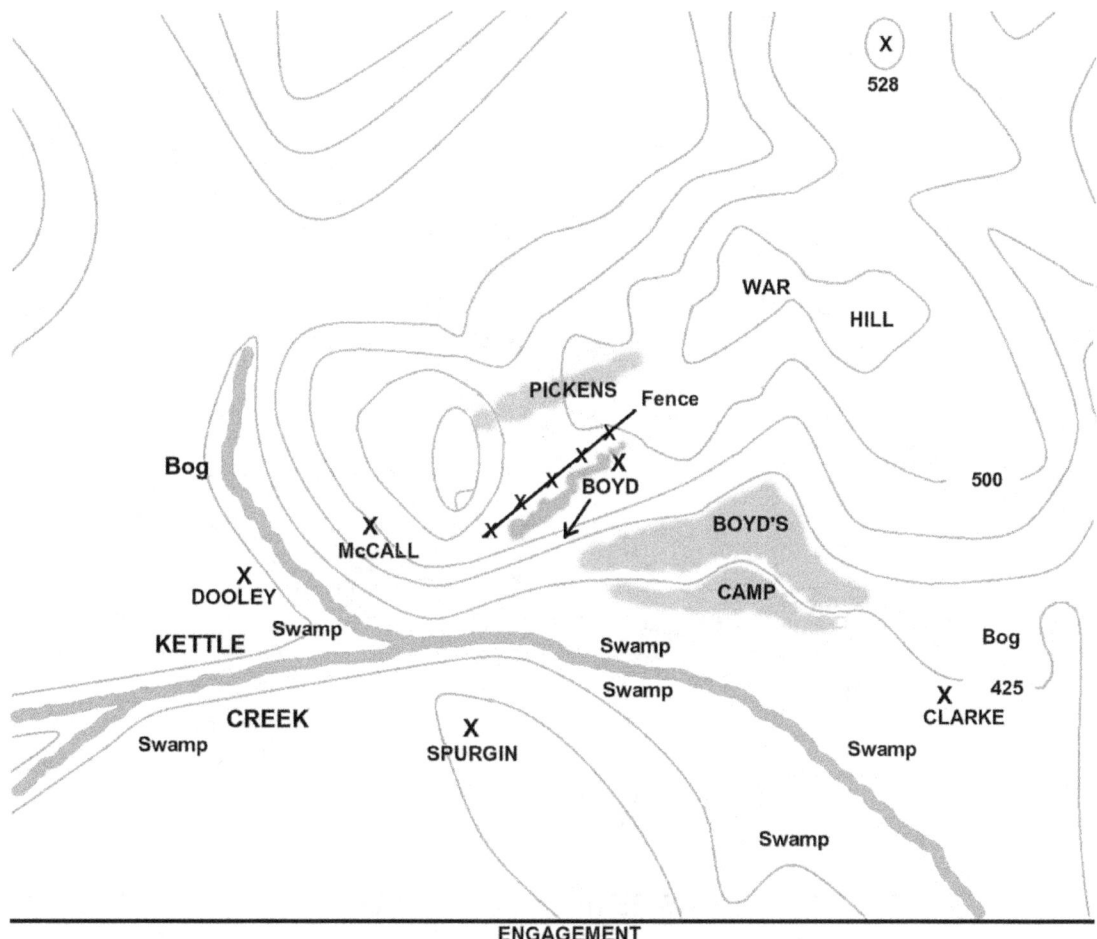

ENGAGEMENT

Dooley became mired in the swamp on Pickens' right; so Pickens sent McCall around the knoll on the right flank.

Pickens pressed the center and took Tory fire when he reached the saddle. He positioned men up the knoll on his right to gain advantage over Boyd at the fence.

Clarke was mired in the swamp on Pickens' left flank.

Spurgin established a rally position on a hill across the creek.

Boyd retreated down the hill because of his disadvantage.

from the Tory camp's left flank. Dooley, finally free from his mire, followed. Clarke moved on the camp from its right.

Panic ensued as the Tories left their grazing horses and scrambled to wade the swollen creek. Major Spurgin, who had witnessed the action from across the creek, attempted to rally the fleeing men on a hillside. Clarke quickly spotted Spurgin, left 35 men near the camp to abort any avenue for the Tories to scatter in his direction, and headed for the Tory Major with the 25 remaining men of his detachment. As he entered the swollen waters, his horse was hit by a rifle ball. Clarke immediately commandeered another mount and continued with his detachment. He charged over the hill, gained Spurgin's rear, and chased him from the Tory rallying point. Spurgin, with what force he could gather, then withdrew toward Wrightsborough.

McCall guarded a few captured Tories, their supplies, weapons, and horses while Pickens and Dooley pressed the main group that had sloshed through the deep cold creek. Lieu-

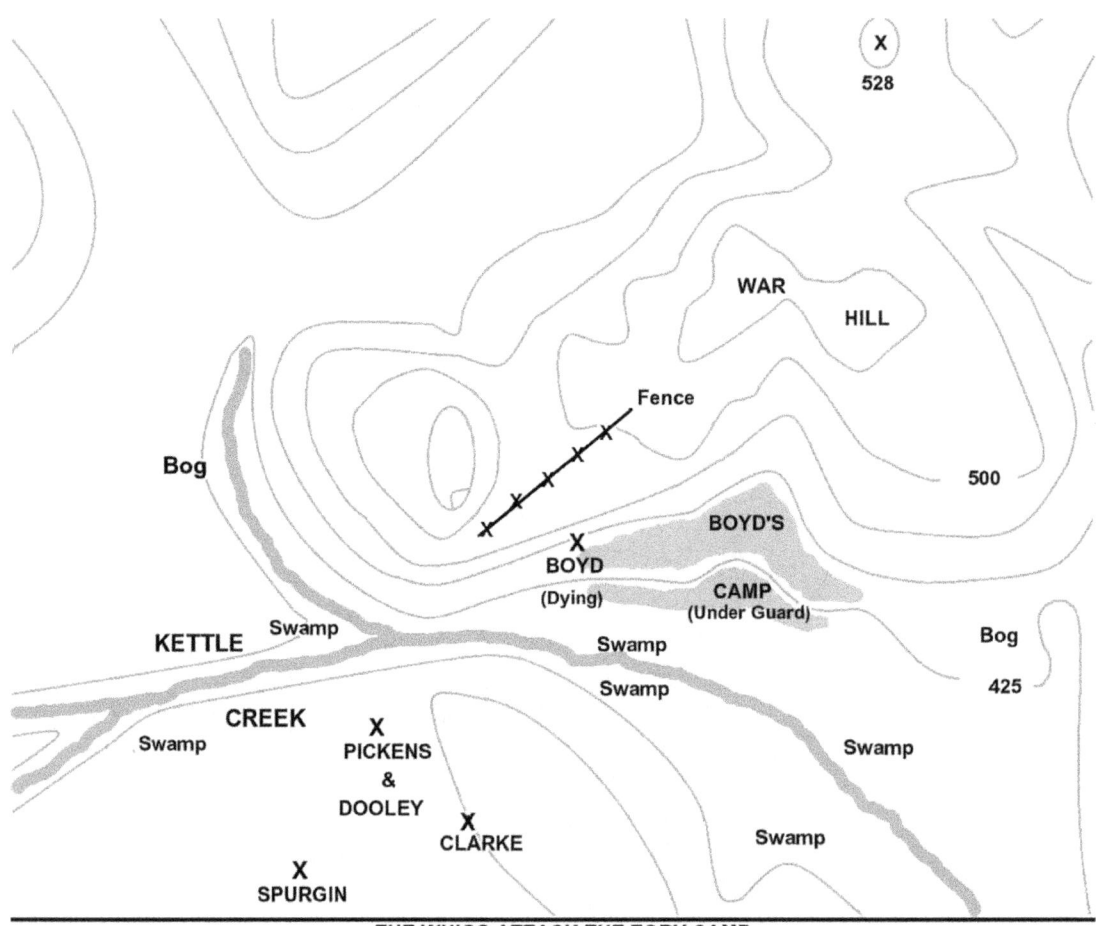

THE WHIGS ATTACK THE TORY CAMP

Boyd was mortally wounded as he retreated down the slope.

The Tories panicked, and 450 men scrambled on foot across Kettle Creek and joined Spurgin.

Dooley joined McCall and attacked the camp's left flank. Clarke attacked from the British right. Pickens attacked from the hill at the camp's rear.

Clarke spotted Spurgin, left 35 men to keep the Tories from escaping the attack. He led 25 men across the creek to attack Spurgin.

tenant Joseph Pickens also had his horse shot out from under him as he crossed. He was also able to confiscate an abandoned Tory pony. Joseph's misfortune would come to provide the indisputable proof of the true rank he held during this action.

By 11:30 A.M. the Loyalists had been demolished by an inferior force (at least as to numbers). Pickens ordered a field hospital for the wounded be set up north of Battle Hill. He then went to check on Lieutenant Colonel Boyd while his militia chased escaping Tories through acres of woods.[39]

Boyd, still alive, was fading and disheartened by his failure. Andrew began to express regret for Boyd's condition, but the Tory interrupted with, "Sir, I glory in the cause; I die for my king and country."[40] He thanked Pickens for his civilities and desired an account of the battle. Boyd then asked the Colonel for favors: that he allow two Tories to remain and serve him water while he lived and to bury him once he died, that he send a messenger to inform Mrs. Boyd of his death, and that he take charge of and deliver a special brooch to Mrs. Boyd. Andrew agreed. The courier reached Mrs. Boyd well ahead of Pickens, who

6. *Georgia Explodes! (1779)*

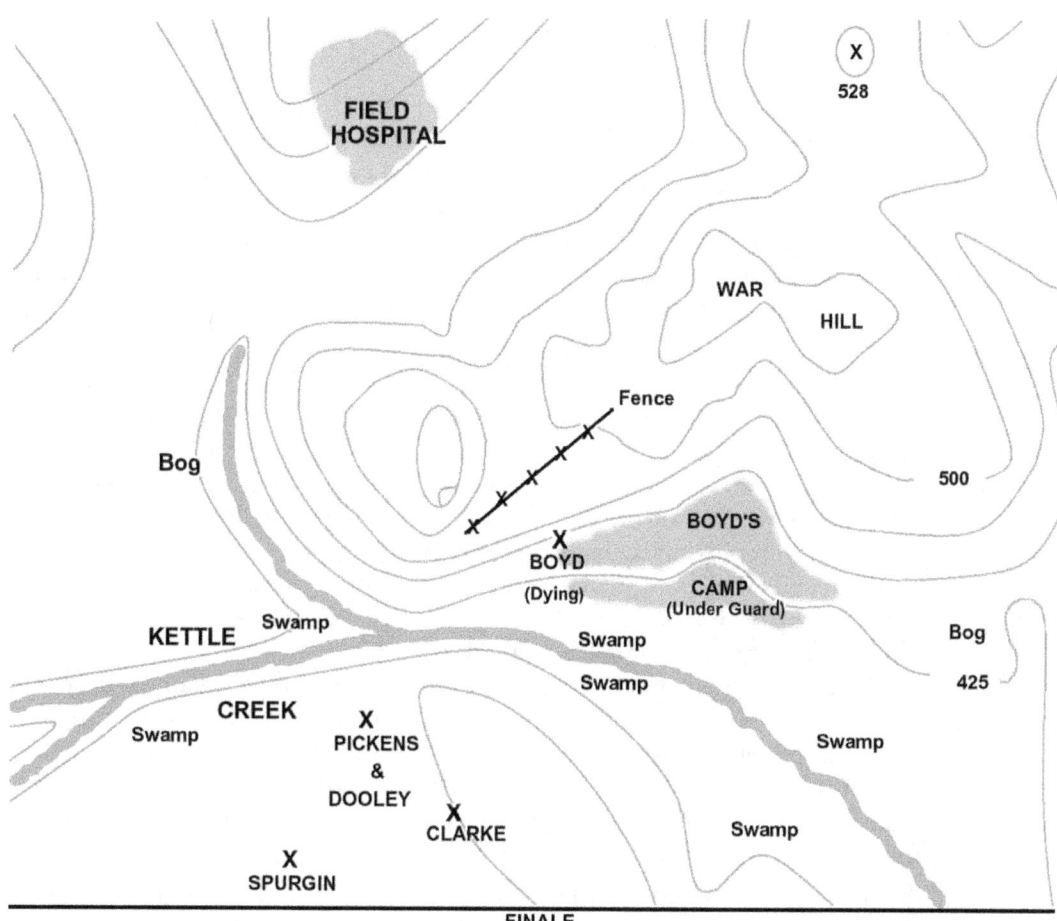

Clarke forced Spurgin from the Tory rally position.

Pickens left a guard detail at the camp and crossed the creek to engage Spurgin.

Spurgin and 350 men escaped and retreated to Wrightsville, Georgia; they had hoped to join British Colonel Campbell who had departed the area.

Seventy Tories were killed, 70 wounded, and 50 captured; 150 dispersed and likely headed for their homes.

Pickens' combined militia lost nine killed and 21 wounded.

At noon, Pickens returned to the hill to tend to the dying Boyd and ordered that a field hospital be established on a nearby hill.

was seeing to prisoners. Mrs. Boyd reacted to the advisement with, "It's a lie! No damned rebel ever killed my husband!"[41]

(Some reports indicate that Colonel Pickens sent the brooch to Mrs. Boyd by messenger while others declare that he delivered it personally. It is certainly plausible that the courier making the notification also delivered the treasure since Pickens was very busy with the war effort. However, Boyd had entrusted the Colonel with the meaningful artifact, and Andrew's sense of duty would require that he present it himself. He had given his word and he likely saw to the accomplishment of the task.)[42]

Andrew Pickens reported about the aftermath:

> Then when about 70 of the enemy killed on the ground and many wounded We took a number of prisoners, nearly all their horses and bridles with a number of good rifles which they had collected in their progress (our losses were inconsiderable) though some brave men fell and some died of their wounds and the [Whig] prisoners which they [the Tories] had were recovered....

> The severest conflict I ever had with the disaffected Tories was in Georgia at Kettle Creek in 1779.[43]

The Whigs suffered nine killed, two missing and 21 wounded, while the Loyalists experienced 70 killed and/or wounded, and 150 taken prisoner. Less than half (275) of the Tories successfully joined the British with Major Spurgin. The remaining 200 apparently had enough and, effecting an escape, returned to their homes.[44]

The Battle of Kettle Creek serves as a microcosm of militia warfare in the backcountry and offers an ideal comparison of Whig versus Tory militia effectiveness, especially their respective leadership capabilities:

- Andrew Pickens was consistently aware of the position of his enemy. In the rare situations when he wasn't informed, he detached scouts to acquire needed information. Boyd was seldom mindful of Pickens' location and was not inclined to worry about that lack of knowledge.
- Colonel Pickens constantly had outriders survey the country for several miles in all directions to eliminate unwanted surprises. Boyd often subjected himself to surprise attacks which completely offset his advantage in manpower.
- The Whig militia was well-trained and adapted smartly to any situation. The men were focused and ready to obey orders without question. The Tories were not only ill-trained, but the men were disinterested in following orders.
- Pickens' militiamen were completely focused on the ultimate goal of obtaining freedom from criminal activity for their families and from the tyranny of the British government as well as the Church of England. Indeed, they worked as a well-organized team to reach their common objective. Boyd's men were a collection of individuals each out to achieve a personal goal, usually either revenge against some Whig or to further idiosyncratic criminal tendencies.

This brief analysis illuminates why Pickens' militia, though outnumbered by twice the manpower, was able to demolish Boyd's force. Similar examples of such disparities occurred throughout the remainder of the war; the few exceptions are noted in later chapters. The British, however, persisted with hope for the fabled "great collection of backcountry Tories" that was enthralled with the Royal government and would march to offset the Whigs and thus control the southern colonies for King George III. (The battle occurred five miles upstream of where the creek enters the Little River.)

When Lieutenant Joseph Pickens lost his horse as he crossed Kettle Creek, he was unable to recover his saddle, horse blanket, or saddle bags from the swollen, swift stream. Joseph mounted a horse that had been abandoned by a Loyalist during the Whig attack. He rode the horse for the remainder of his mission. However, he was not allowed to keep the horse. His brother, the Colonel, was a stickler for military protocol. Colonel Andrew Pickens made sure his men adhered to the proper practice that all captured weapons, stock, and supplies were public property. Such captured assets were turned over to the area's senior commanding Continental Army officer for disposition. This practice is exemplified in a letter, dated March 12, 1779, from Pickens to Captain John Irvine which states:

> Elijah and Samuel Moore, that were with me at the Battle of Kettle Creek, I am well informed have some horses and two rifle guns that were taken at that battle, and as that property belongs to the people in general, you will order them, without loss of time, to bring those effects to me, or they may depend on being prosecuted for the same.
> I am, sir, your humble servant,
> ANDREW PICKENS.[45]

6. Georgia Explodes! (1779)

Kettle Creek Battlefield monument showing a third of the Upper Ninety Six militiamen that participated. Note Lieutenant Joseph Pickens' rank is shown as captain (left column, fifth name).

As a member of the South Carolina militia, Joseph was later allowed to file a claim (called an indent) with the state for restitution for his losses at the battle. The petition, declared on July 21, 1779, five months after the Battle of Kettle Creek, is recorded in his indent file at the South Carolina Department of Archives and History. The document (see Appendix E) states:

> NINETY SIX DISTRICT: Personally came Lieut Joseph Pickens before me and on his oath deposeth that on the eleventh day of February last past [1779] he being called out with part of Capt. Thos. Weems' Company of Militia under the Command of Col. And^w Pickens in the Public Service of this state on Savannah River near a place called the Cherokee Ford where Being Engaged in a fight with a large body of disafected armed men called Col. Boyd's Tories, that in said fight he the Deponent lost a Saddle and Saddle Cloth and a pair of Saddlebags and blanket, appraiseth same to one hundred and twenty pound total.

The document was filed under oath before Justice of the Peace, Patrick Calhoun, and certified by Colonel Andrew Pickens.

Several current reference books mention Joseph Pickens in connection with the Battle of Kettle Creek and its preceding events, and many credit him with the rank of Captain at the time of the action. The indent record clarifies that Joseph was a Lieutenant at least through the date of its declaration. It also explicates that he reported to Company Commander, Captain Weems. This fits in well with the statement of Charles Holland in his pension application that Joseph Pickens became Captain after the retirement of Captain Weems (see Chapter 4 and Appendix E). The indent, as well as the Kettle Creek Battlefield monument, exposes that Captain Weems was not retired. Interestingly, he is listed on the shrine right next to "Captain" Joseph Pickens.

Some of the confusion understandably occurs because of Alexander Garden's reference to "Captain" Joseph Pickens as reported by A. L. Pickens (see Chapter 4). The misunderstanding is promulgated by Andrew Pickens' letter to Henry Lee wherein he states, "He informed me that Boyd with upward of 700 men had crossed the river above the settlement on rafts—Capts. Anderson, Baskins and Miller and my brother, a captain had crossed Savannah River at the Cherokee Ford."[46] However, since Andrew witnessed the indent in 1779, five months after the battle, his signature on that document has more veracity than his signature to General Lee on a letter written 32 years later. When Andrew Pickens authored that letter, he recalled his brother was a captain but was likely speaking generically and disregarding the time frame. (In summary, the author's ancestor, Joseph, was "Lieutenant Pickens" during his actions at the Battle of Kettle Creek rather than "Captain Pickens" as is customarily recorded by historians and labeled on the monument at the battlefield.)

Andrew Pickens spoke of his post-battle actions in his letter to Henry Lee. He stated:

> We took a number of prisoners, nearly all their horses and bridles with a number of good rifles which they had collected in their progress [looting as they moved through Ninety Six District] ...and the prisoners which they had [captured] were recovered—I left a few of the prisoners to bury their dead with a promise that they might [immediately] return to their families if they would [later] return to me which they did—It was dark before we got from the ground. I brought off all my own wounded and recrossed the Savannah River the next morning at Fort Charlotte.[47]

Pickens had left one-half of his least notorious prisoners to take care of the killed and severely-wounded Tories. On the morning of February 15, 1779, Pickens crossed the Savannah and marched the remaining 75 prisoners to White Hall, Brigadier General Andrew Williamson's well-fortified backcountry estate and headquarters. There Pickens rested his troops and kept the prisoners under guard. He, then, sent orders to Captain Irvine:

> TO CAPTAIN JOHN IRVIN[E]
> FEBRUARY 20, 1779
> SIR:—You are hereby desired to be at White Hall on Wednesday next with one third of your Company—they to be horsemen—and one Lieutenant, and one other third of your Company to continue at White Hall until further orders. You will receive further orders on that day.
> I am, sir, your most humble servant,
> ANDREW PICKENS.[48]

Irvine took charge of the prisoners, including the original 75 parolees that had returned as promised after they had visited their families.

On the 28th, General Benjamin Lincoln dispatched North Carolina General John Ashe with 1,500 men to cross the Savannah and give chase to Lieutenant Colonel Archibald Campbell. Ashe camped where Brier's Creek empties into the Savannah River. There he awaited reinforcements. Lincoln had hoped that General Williamson would move to support Ashe en masse, but Williamson assigned his brigade, including Pickens' regiment, to wide-ranging patrol areas in the Georgia and South Carolina backcountry. Their primary assignments were to protect Whig settlements from attack. Williamson did provide Ashe with a company of mounted men under Major Francis Ross.

Major General Augustine Prevost ordered Campbell to return and impede Ashe's progress. Campbell, in turn, dispatched Lieutenant Colonel John Mark Prevost to gain Ashe's rear. At 3:00 P.M. on March 3, Prevost began to drive in Ashe's rear pickets. Campbell opened up on Ashe with an artillery barrage at 4:00 P.M. and followed with a full frontal attack. The Americans were demolished and lost 200 killed, 50 wounded, and 170 captured. The survivors evacuated the Brier's Creek camp and crossed the Savannah River so quickly that the British captured most of Ashe's ammunition, weapons, supplies and horses. The American prisoners were taken to Savannah and boarded onto the infamous British prison ships located there. An excerpt from the pension application (see Appendix E) of South Carolina militiaman, Private John Wallace, testifies:

> On this fifth day of August in the year of our Lord 1833 personally appeared in open court before the Justices of the County Court of Ray County ... Missouri ... John Wallace ... aged eighty seven years.... I was then next engaged under Major Ross of South Carolina Militia by orders of the Government of that state. We traversed some time ... into the state of Georgia in reconnoitering the British forces and as we approached the British camp of Brier Creek we were discovered ... the enemy charged upon us. I was dismounted and escaped by swimming the Savannah River. I made the best of my way on foot to General Williamson's camp where I joined my former commander Ross.

Colonels Andrew Pickens and John Dooley, while on patrol, had planned to link up with Ashe but got to Brier's Creek too late to participate in the battle. They could only assign burial details for the killed Whigs; then, they moved on to Williamson's encampment and learned details of the slaughter.[49]

Andrew Pickens continued to make arrangements for controlling the vast number of Kettle Creek prisoners. The White Hall blockhouse was too small, so the captives were marched to the Ninety Six jail. The jail was also overcrowded but offered additional stockade possibilities. Pickens wrote:

> TO CAPTAIN JOHN IRVINE
> MARCH 12, 1779
> SIR:
> On receipt of this immediately march, with twenty-five of your company, to Ninety-Six, and join Col. Williams, in order to guard the prisoners while on trial. You will receive orders from Col. Williams when you arrive at Ninety-Six. Dinborough is to supply you with provisions while on duty. You will have Lieut. Wardlaw and any others of your company that were prisoners with the Tories, and can be any evidence against any of them...
> I am, sir, your humble servant,
> ANDREW PICKENS.[50]

Shortly thereafter, Colonel Pickens received orders to move his own regiment into Georgia which necessitated a revision to the orders of Captain Irvine's company:

> TO CAPTAIN JOHN IRVINE
> MARCH 14, 1779
> SIR:
> I wrote you a few days ago to reinforce Colonel Williams at Ninety-Six with twenty-five men from your company; but, as I have just got orders from Gen. Williamson to march a strong party of my regiment to Cowan's Ferry on Savannah River, you will, therefore march with two parts of your company to that place, to be there on Wednesday next, the 17th inst., armed and accoutered, with good horses. I have wrote to Col. Williams to let your men come home, though you had better see him yourself. I hope you will be spirited in this matter.
> I am, sir, your humble servant,
> ANDREW PICKENS.[51]

It was not long before the regiment again saw action. While on patrol, Pickens, ever on the alert, had received some important intelligence as he explained to Henry Lee:

> I went again into Georgia as the men were in high spirits to attack a part of British and Tories which I had intelligence of. Brier Creek 35 miles south west of Augusta — We proceeded near to Wrightsborough on Little River where we got intelligence that there were 7 or 8 hundred Creek Indians encamped on Ogeche [sic] River about 25 miles distant with Tate [sic] a British agent at their head on their way to join Col. Campbell at Augusta — I immediately halted and sent a few men to reconnoiter their encampment — they returned the next day and gave me a true account of their situation — I got a small reinforcement, we were then about 500 men, we marched late

in the evening and reached their encampment by daylight — They had ... gone off in small parties — I sent on the different trails, several were overtaken, some killed and one principal chief made prisoner — They were completely dispersed and defeated in their designs — I believe not a man of them reached Col Campbell — Those that escaped the pursuit returned home.[52]

Royal Indian Agent John Stuart had died and was replaced by Colonel Thomas "Burn Foot" Brown (see Chapter 2) who attained authority over the backcountry tribes. Brown's deputy, Agent David Taitt, had organized 800 Creek Indians under Chiefs Alexander McGillivray and Emistisiguo. (McGillivray was the mixed-breed son of Lachlan McGillivray, one of the original settlers of Georgia, and Sehoy Marchand, a mixed-blood Creek woman of the prestigious Wind Clan.) This was another assembly, in addition to Boyd's and Hamilton's supposedly large provincial forces, that would join Lieutenant Colonel Campbell for a combined attack against South Carolina. They were encamped near Folsom's Fort, another backcountry stockade set on the Ogeechee River not far from Wrightsborough.

Colonel Dooley, with 100 Georgians, joined Pickens' force of 200 South Carolinians as he moved through Wilkes County, Georgia. At Wrightsborough, on the 21st of March, they were joined by Georgia Colonel Benjamin Few, South Carolina Colonel Leroy Hammond, and South Carolina Major Francis Ross. The Whig militia then amounted to 500 men. Pickens sent Lieutenants Alexander and Williams to find the Creek camp. He received word back on the 22nd and marched the militia overnight to reach the deserted camp at daybreak on the 23rd.

Tales of Kettle Creek and the reputation of Colonel Andrew Pickens' Whig militia preceded them to the Ogeechee River. The Indians dispersed into several small groups and tried to fade away before the Whigs' arrival. Colonel Pickens followed suit and broke his force into detachments to chase the fleeing Creeks. Three of the militia groups met with action; many of the Creeks were killed, and 211 were captured, including the son of Chief Emistisiguo. The Whig-combined militia lost four men, Major Francis Ross among them. The prisoners were dispatched to Ninety Six to join those from Kettle Creek.

While the action at the Ogeechee River was underway, Georgia Whig Lieutenant Colonel John Twiggs undertook a parallel effort near Beech Island on the Savannah River just southeast of present-day Augusta. There he met Tory Major John Spurgin, brother of Major William Spurgin from the Battle of Kettle Creek. Major John Spurgin commanded some of the Tories that survived the Battle of Kettle Creek. In the ensuing battle 20 Loyalists were killed, including Spurgin.[53]

Andrew Pickens stated, "The defeat of Col. Boyd with the dispersion of the Indians with Tate [sic] completely disappointed the designs of the British at that time."[54]

Henry Lee added:

> seven hundred Loyalists embodied with the determination to force their way to the British camp.... He fell in with them at Kettle Creek, and instantly attacked them. The action was contested with zeal and firmness; when Colonel Boyd, the commander of the loyalists, fell; and his death was soon followed by a rout of his associates.... This single, though partial check, was the only interruption of the British success from the commencement of the invasion [of Georgia].[55]

Indeed, the actions of the Whig militia were astoundingly the only positive occurrences for the Americans in early 1779. The disastrous defeat of General Ashe brought the state of affairs in Georgia back to reality. It became obvious to all that the British could control Savannah and the coastal area but could not compete for dominance in the backcountry. It was also clear to all (except, it seems, for the Royal government) that Tory militia power was nonexistent and that any assistance from either the Creek or the Cherokee would prove inconsequential. That General Williamson kept the British from invading South Carolina from Augusta was not a big factor. He did not provide any specific action to deter that movement except that he was in the way when the enemy required a quick exit to escape from Colonel Pickens. Specifically, Williamson underscored another instance when the state militia and the Continental army acted independently rather than cooperated toward a united conclusion.

General Ashe was court-martialed. The board, presided over by General William Moultrie, consisted of General Griffith Rutherford, Colonels Charles Cotesworth Pinckney and Francis Locke, and Captain Edmund Hyrne. The court gave Ashe a slap on the wrist but acquitted him of any severe wrongdoing. The final statement indicated he had neglected to account for everything he should have, but he was brave enough to stay and fight as long as prudently possible. However, Ashe's military career was effectively over.

The last piece of unfinished Kettle Creek business, the trial of the prisoners at Ninety Six, was finalized on April 9, 1779. After almost three weeks of sessions, the commission appointed by Governor Rutledge found 70 guilty of treasonous acts. Of those, all but seven ended up on parole; only five were actually hanged.

On April 5, Governor Rutledge ordered General Williamson and the entire Ninety Six militia into Georgia. The Loyalists in the area were becoming vigorous after the defeat of General Ashe, and the militia was, again, to provide relief to the backcountry Georgia Whigs.

Major General Benjamin Lincoln, Commander of the Southern Department, was perturbed that Rutledge would consider such a prominent move in the southern campaign without consulting him. General Moultrie interceded and convinced the Governor to hold off on the orders and to coordinate with Lincoln. Rutledge did so but continued to complain about the lack of activity by the Continental Army.

Williamson had already mobilized his militia to prepare for the Georgia invasion. Pickens issued orders as is shown by the following letter to Captain Irvine on April 12, 1779:

> Sir:
> It is the Governor's order that two-thirds of the militia of this State be embodied, and General Williamson's orders to me, to embody the same number of this regiment. You will, therefore order one third part of your company, with yourself, to join me on Friday, the 16th inst., on horseback at Cowan's Ferry, well armed; and, those who neglected going with your lieutenant when ordered, you will bring with you, that they may be dealt with as the law directs. You will bring an exact list of your company, as I am ordered to make a return of the payment.
> I am, sir, your most humble servant,
> ANDREW PICKENS[56]

The movement of the Ninety Six militia put more pressure on Lincoln who held a council of war with his officers on the 20th. It was decided that General Moultrie would hold Purysburg with 1,000 men, while Lincoln would leave that day with the remainder of the Continental force to take possession of Augusta. The entire Ninety Six militia that had gathered at Williamson's camp joined Lincoln's march. His force then totaled 3,600 men. Lincoln was still chagrined and hoped this movement into the Georgia backcountry would get Rutledge off his back. He reached Augusta on the 23rd.

Lieutenant Colonel John Mark Prevost, who had replaced Archibald Campbell as the military authority in the Georgia backcountry, related the American activity to his brother and Commander, Major General Augustine Prevost. General Prevost wasted no time and, on the 25th, decided to take advantage of Lincoln's absence from Purysburg. He crossed the Savannah River and moved on Charles Town with 2,400 men.

Once Brigadier General William Moultrie became aware of Prevost's action, he immediately broke camp at Purysburg and raced toward Charles Town with 1,000 militia and 200 Continental soldiers. He also sent a messenger to apprise Lincoln of the situation.

Moultrie, with a reduced force, arrived at Charles Town on May 9, 1779. Many of the militia had left his service to look after their own families. They were concerned about rumors of Tory and Indian atrocities in the backcountry. General Moultrie did what he could to impede Prevost's progress. He ordered his detachments to burn the bridges and destroy the ferries along the British line of march. Prevost still arrived at, and surrounded Charles Town, on the 11th. He demanded immediate surrender of the city.

Governor Rutledge responded with the willingness that South Carolina would "propose neutrality, during the war between Great Britain and America."[57] This same Governor Rutledge, who had earlier criticized General Lincoln for not having been decisive in dealing with the British, was now ready to withdraw from the war effort.

Several officers, including Lieutenant Colonel John Laurens, refused to advance with the overture. General Prevost declined to hear the offer (once presented to him) and indicated he would only deal with General Moultrie. General Prevost then sent his brother to speak with Moultrie.

Lieutenant Colonel John Mark Prevost declared to Moultrie that he was not there to negotiate political ideology, but only to accept Moultrie's unconditional surrender. Moultrie professed to Rutledge that he absolutely refused to give the Governor and other state officials up to the British. Additionally, Moultrie remained steadfast in his determination to defend Charles Town.

Moultrie did not have to debate long before General Lincoln would arrive with his entire force. General Prevost, outnumbered and in danger of being trapped between Lincoln and Moultrie, withdrew from the vicinity of Charles Town. His primary overland avenue of escape was cut off by Lincoln, so overnight during low tide he moved his troops to swampy James Island and then gradually to the equally saturated Johns Island. That process took until mid–June. There, Prevost set up a rear guard to assure American troops didn't follow the same route. He and his men battled mosquitoes, biting flies, sand fleas, poisonous snakes, and other vermin in the miserable heat and humidity. Still they successfully built boats. Prevost had also sent word for his garrison at Savannah to ferry any available boats to Johns Island. Once he had sufficient seaworthy craft, he could successfully withdraw to Savannah.

Lincoln had received Moultrie's message, regarding Prevost's move, on May 10. He headed for Charles Town and arrived on the 14th. Lincoln knew it was possible to prevent Prevost's evacuation; however, he realized a British guard was stationed at Stono Ferry. The ferry provided a crossing to Johns Island from the mainland, so his first step was to destroy the guard. Colonel John Maitland and Lieutenant Colonel Archibald Campbell, with the 71st Highlanders, controlled the ferry. The troops were supplemented with a force of Hessian soldiers and two regiments of North and South Carolina provincial forces. The British evacuation would continue to be a slow one.

General Lincoln was eager to mount an attack. He camped eight miles west of the ferry with 1,200 men and left the remainder of his force to supplement General Moultrie at Charles Town. Lincoln still had a North Carolina militia force with him, but General Williamson and the Ninety Six militia had left for the backcountry as they were worried about the news of renewed Indian and Tory attacks on Whig settlements. Colonel Andrew Pickens convinced his regiment to remain with Major General Lincoln. Pickens' group was the only South Carolina militia unit available to assist with an attack on Prevost.[58]

6. Georgia Explodes! (1779) 127

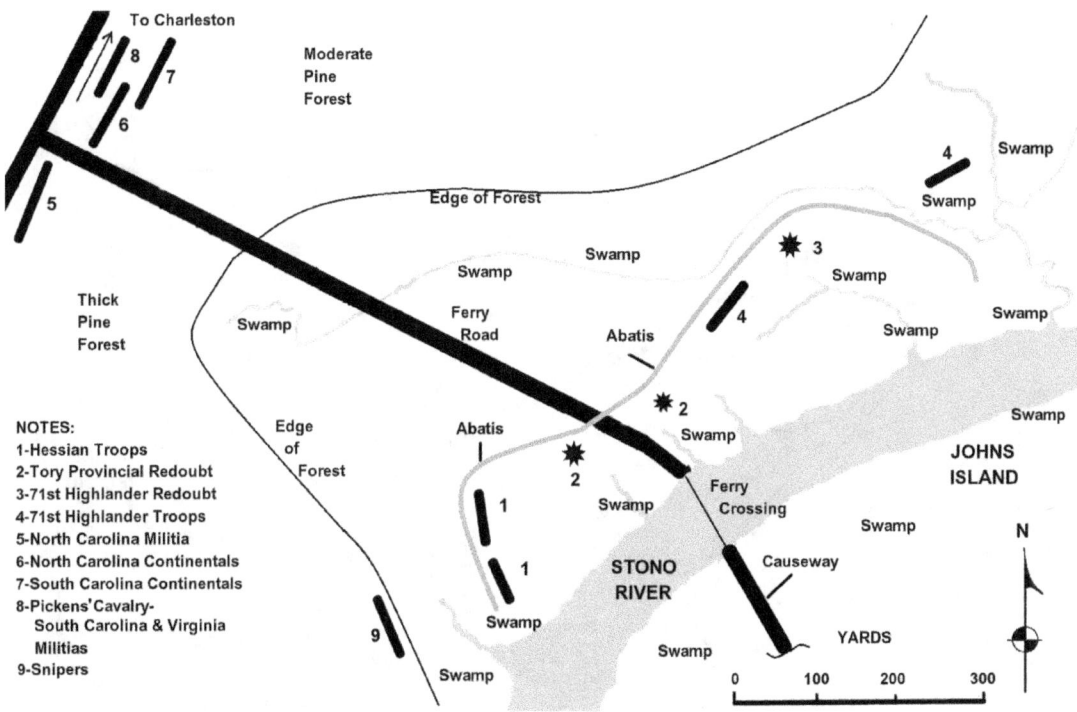

Troops form for battle at Stono Ferry.

Once Lincoln bivouacked his force, he dispatched a troop of light infantry to proceed as far as they could down the Stono Ferry road. There they began sniping actions against the British guard. Lincoln then returned to Charles Town to plan the attack with Moultrie and to gain the approval of Governor Rutledge.

The snipers found that the guard had constructed an abatis of piled logs interwoven with treacherously spiked jutting limbs. This was set on the near side of Stono River. The ferry road leading to the abatis was nearly 30 feet wide and one mile long, measured from the main Charles Town road. A pine thicket bordered each side of the ferry road. The road eventually crossed a creek that was flanked by swamp land.

Three redoubts, armed with large artillery pieces, were behind the abatis. The two redoubts on the British middle and left flank were manned by the provincial Tories. The redoubt on the British right flank was manned by 71st Highlanders. The Hessian troops were to the extreme left flank beyond the last provincial redoubt, and additional troops of the 71st manned the abatis from the center to the British extreme right flank. Other 71st Highlanders were stationed outside the abatis to act as pickets with a small unit of skirmishers to the British right.

General Lincoln had reached a mutual agreement with Moultrie and Rutledge for a plan of action. He returned to the encampment on June 19. The next morning Moultrie would take the combined forces under his command from Charles Town and press the British from James Island. This activity would serve as a cover for Lincoln's main force to storm down the Stono Ferry road and overrun the redoubts.

Major General Lincoln had obtained intelligence, though incomplete, from snipers that had been relieved through rotation with men from camp.

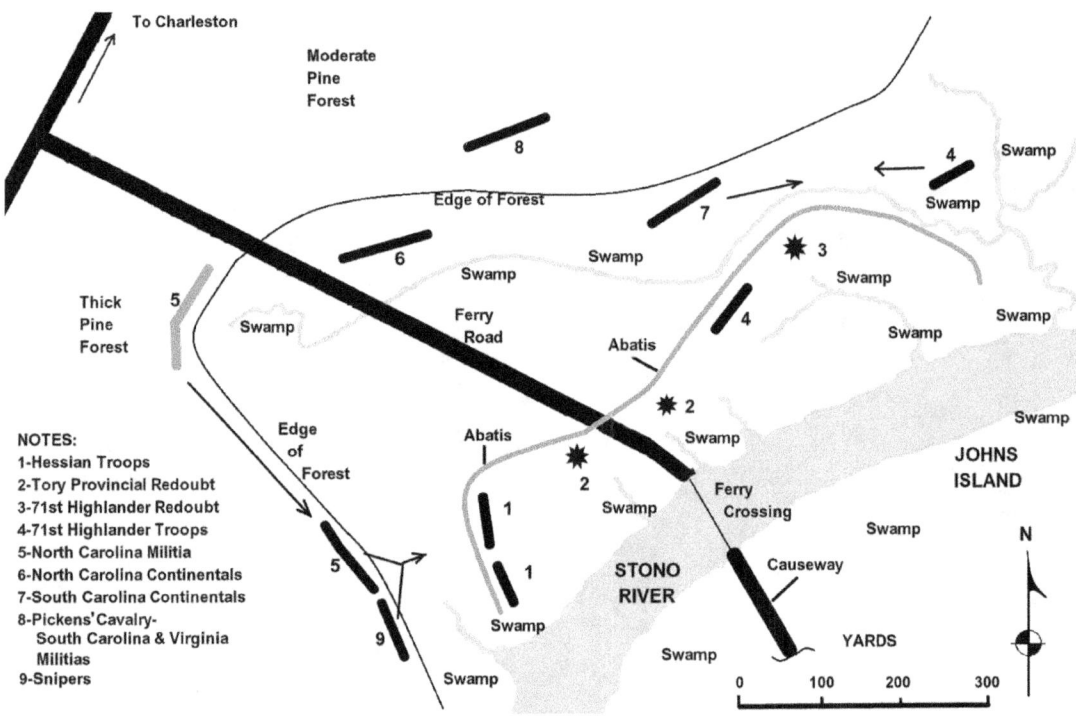

The Americans attack.

Shortly after midnight on the 20th, Lincoln marched his men to the end of the Stono Ferry road and set his formation. He placed the North Carolina Militia units to the American right flank with three or four grasshoppers (three-pounders).[59] They were the only unit to the right of the road. The American center, to the road's left, was made up with men from the North Carolina Continental army units flanked on the left by the South Carolina Continental forces. The Continentals had two grasshoppers. Brigadier General Isaac Huger commanded the South Carolina Continental forces, while Brigadier General Jethro Sumner led the North Carolina Continentals as well as the North Carolina militia (which effectively were attached to the Continental force by North Carolina).

The Virginia and South Carolina mounted militia components, under the command of Colonel Andrew Pickens, were stationed on the extreme left and followed the main units as reserves. Lincoln had not accounted for a creek and severe swampy area, about halfway to the abatis, due apparently to incomplete intelligence garnered from the snipers. He did not realize he would have been better off to first follow the Stono Ferry road with his force in columns and later decide on the battle formation. Lincoln might have then discovered what lay ahead for him. As he reached the edge of the forest, the creek, swamp, and abatis would come into view. Lincoln began the march at 7:00 A.M., the hour he expected Moultrie's diversion from James Island. At first, the right flank moved more slowly because of the thick pine forest. The North Carolina militia eventually joined the snipers who had been operating from the same pine thicket. The middle and left flank then became slowed by the unexpected creek and bog. At that point the pines gave way to a clearing that opened the Americans to exposure from British artillery in the redoubts. The American grasshoppers proved to be too light for success against the redoubt structures.

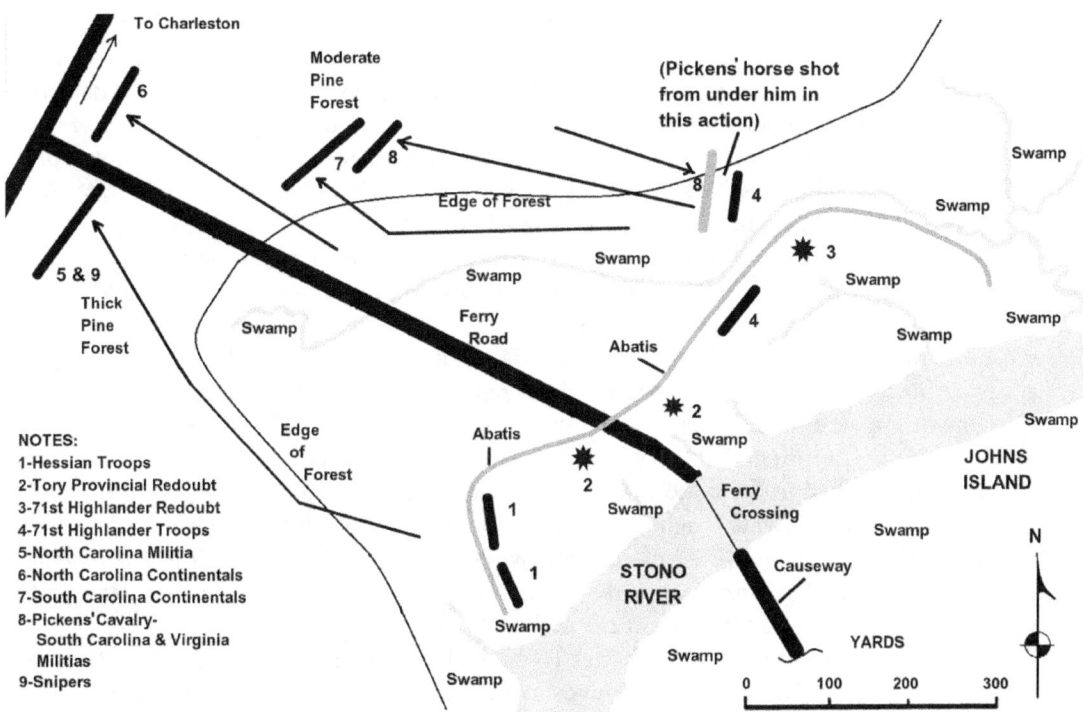

Colonel Pickens covers the American retreat during which his horse is shot from under him.

The North Carolina militia on the American right advanced to within 100 feet of the abatis. They threatened to overrun the Hessians but were driven back by the provincial artillery battery. Continentals on the far left then crossed the creek, engaged British pickets in battle, and killed several of them. Once their own pickets were out of the picture, the 71st Highlander artillery battery opened up on the Americans and drove them back; 71st Highlander troops followed in pursuit.

The American center never did get beyond the creek. Lincoln could see, down the ferry road from the creek to the Stono River, that there were many 71st Highlander skirmishers prepared to advance. Lincoln was painfully aware that his center would be fully exposed to the middle artillery battery, that there was no diversion from Moultrie on the James Island side. Consequently, the British were only concerned with his force. Exasperated, he ordered a retreat.

Moultrie blamed windy conditions for his inability to assist while others have reported that he simply missed the low tide.

The center troops and the North Carolina militia withdrew without difficulty. The wounded on the center and right were carried off and, for the most part, the evacuation of the field was orderly. The Americans on the left, however, were hotly pursued by 71st Highlanders as they approached the creek. Pickens led a cavalry charge into the midst of the pursuing 71st Highlanders. The clash was intense. The mounted militia was using the weapon of choice — the saber. The British were armed with muskets and fixed bayonets. The combat was close-order with bayonets against sabers. There was no time for a redcoat to reload once he fired his musket. New Acquisition Militia Colonel Thomas Neil (see Chapter 3) was shot in the head during this action.

Pickens' cavalry successfully beat back the Highlanders to cover the escape of the American left flank. His force also rescued several wounded officers from the field. The Colonel, himself, was in such close contact with the enemy, and so closely challenged, that his horse was shot from under him for the second time in his military career (see Chapter 4). Luckily, Captain Robert Anderson was able to pick him up, and they escaped doubled on Anderson's horse. This was the second time Pickens' good friend had assisted him after he lost a horse in battle (see the Cherokee War in Chapter 4).

Andrew Pickens wrote to Henry Lee, "I served with Genl. Lincoln before and in the battle of Stono, had my horse killed under me in covering the retreat which I was ordered to do by the General and brought off some wounded officers."[60] General William Moultrie wrote his memoirs in later years and gave this accolade, "and the vigilance of the light troops commanded by Colonel Andrew Pickens rendered it [the British pursuit] fruitless."[61]

One of the wounded officers rescued by Pickens' militia was Major Andrew Davie, a North Carolina Continental cavalry officer. He had been shot off his horse, wounded in the thigh, and picked up by a mounted militiaman. The Americans lost 30 killed including Colonel Neil and Private Hugh Jackson (an older brother of Andrew Jackson) who died of heat exhaustion. One hundred fifteen were wounded, and 155 were missing. The British reportedly lost 150 Highlanders, mostly during combat with the American left flank and with the countercharge by Pickens at the end of the battle.

Lincoln withdrew his force to Charles Town; Pickens and his militia headed for Ninety Six to link up with Williamson, and Prevost completed his evacuation to Savannah. Thus ended the Battle of Stono Ferry.[62]

Colonel Pickens' action, after he rejoined General Williamson during the backcountry threat, is noted by A. L. Pickens who wrote, "from August 10 to October 8, of 1779, Pickens was into Georgia after Cameron [Indian Agent Alexander Cameron], we have the testimony of one of his men given in the Logan manuscript."[63] Cameron had been riling members of the Chickamauga to attack backcountry settlements. However, as a war party of 300 warriors was on the way to the Whig settlements in North Carolina, they were completely surprised by a large group of militia from that area. Thus, the problem never became severe, and most of the Chickamauga braves quietly blended into the mountain villages.

A legend of a ring fight near Tomassee that involves Colonel Pickens and his militia is strangely similar to THE ring fight of the Cherokee war in 1776. The details match: number of men in the advance party (25), number of Indians (250), method of the attack (no firearms in the initial phase by the braves), and the force having been saved by reinforcements driven vehemently by Joseph Pickens. The only detail, significantly altered from the original account, is that Pickens set fire to the canebrakes and the resulting discharge of steam from the joints of the cane issued explosions that duplicated the sound of rifle fire. The noise scared the Indians into an initial retreat.

A. L. Pickens presents the concept that these accounts were not only confused with the original, but that the confusion was likely due to an early account containing a typo for the date, i.e., the "6" being inverted to a "9" showing 1779 when it should have been 1776. Dr. Pickens believed that the time Pickens was supposed to have been in Georgia would not have allowed a foray into the lower villages when this 1779 Indian threat was to have taken place.

Colonel Pickens may have made an effort to quell a Cherokee threat during this time, and it could have easily involved "a" ring fight as that was a common attack method for the Cherokee when they had an enemy outnumbered. The detail about canebrakes being fired adds some credibility to the story; however, it is certainly unlikely that so many details of the original ring fight would have actually been repeated in a separate incident. It is, therefore, important to acknowledge the possibility of such a confrontation, but it is just as important to not designate this ring fight as "the" ring fight and to leave the details of the 1776 action in 1776.[64]

Major General Benjamin Lincoln, stunned by the failure at Stono Ferry, sensed imminent danger should Major General Prevost not be driven from Savannah. Lincoln knew that Charles Town would undoubtedly be the next British target in their effort to take control of the southern colonies. The 2,500-man British garrison could not effectively work outside of Savannah because the Americans had little difficulty harassing them with snipers and skirmishers should they venture beyond the city.

Prevost detached Colonel John Maitland with 900 troops to Beaufort, South Carolina, to keep an eye on Charles Town, which was defended by a combined American force of 5,000 men. He also had stationed Lieutenant Colonel John Harris Cruger with 100 Tory provincials at Sunbury, Georgia, 20 miles to the south. Lieutenant Colonel John Mark Prevost, the General's brother, had there taken Fort Morris one year earlier (see Chapter 5). (Cruger would figure prominently in the later years of the South Carolina fighting. See Chapters 8–12.)

Lincoln would need naval assistance to blockade and shell the city if he were to overrun Savannah. Therefore, he requested aid from French Admiral Comte Jean Baptiste Charles Henri Hector d'Estaing who had battled a British fleet in the Caribbean for the previous year. D'Estaing was a veteran of the Seven Years War and would later lose his head in the French Revolution. French vessels put into port at Charles Town on September 3, 1779, with a message for Lincoln. He was told that Admiral d'Estaing would shortly arrive at Savannah with a 25-ship fleet. Action against Savannah was in motion.

General Lincoln, with 2,000 troops, left Charles Town September 12 to march on Savannah. American Commander General George Washington had dispatched Polish General Kazimierz Pulaski to the Southern Department to assist with cavalry training. Lincoln sent Pulaski to locate Brigadier General Lachlan McIntosh who was at Augusta with 1,000 troops. Pulaski and McIntosh were to jointly march on Savannah and drive in the British pickets. Pulaski actually rushed ahead to link with d'Estaing. Lincoln met McIntosh, and they marched to Savannah together.

Also on the 12th, d'Estaing arrived at Savannah and put 1,200 troops ashore just south of the city. Savannah sat atop a forty-foot high bluff that overlooked the Savannah River on its north. Due to poor weather, the French waited until the 15th to move on the city.

When General Prevost heard of the French arrival, he worked ceaselessly to strengthen the defenses around Savannah. He also sent messengers to Beaufort and Sunbury to order in the detachments.

Benjamin Lincoln arrived late on the 15th with his combined force of 3,000 troops. He was informed of d'Estaing's landing but would not connect with the Admiral until late on the 16th. Included among the Continental troops were members of the 1st and 2nd South Carolina Brigades under Brigadier General Isaac Huger. (These troops had been drawn years earlier from militia to fulfill South Carolina's requirement to attach men to the Continental army.)[65]

In addition to the Continental army units, Lincoln had the support of several Georgia militia units: Colonel Benjamin Few's Upper Richmond Regiment, Colonel John Dooley's Wilkes County Regiment, and Colonel John Twiggs' Burke County Regiment.

On the 16th, with the city surrounded on the mainland and blockaded seaward, d'Estaing issued a demand to Prevost that tersely stated, "Comte d'Estaing summons his Excellency General Prevost to surrender himself to the arms of his Majesty the King of France."[66] Prevost needed to stall and allow the outlying detachments time to arrive, so he politely asked d'Estaing for 12 hours to consider the summons. Admiral d'Estaing consented. Later, the truce was extended to the afternoon of the 17th. Had d'Estaing refused the request, immediately bombarded the city from his ships, and initiated an attack, he would likely have overrun the British: That, however, was not to be.

Lincoln met with d'Estaing who apprised him of the state of affairs. Lincoln tactfully chided d'Estaing for his lack of diplomacy regarding the surrender demand and for not refusing the truce request. When the General returned to his forces and relayed d'Estaing's report to his officers, Lieutenant Colonel Frances Marion reacted vehemently. Major Peter Horry of Marion's 2nd Regiment wrote, "I never beheld Marion in so great a passion. I was actually afraid he would have broken out on General Lincoln. 'My God!' he exclaimed, 'Who ever heard of anything like this before!—First allow an enemy to entrench, and then fight him!! See the destruction brought upon the British at Bunker's Hill! And yet our troops there were only militia! Raw, half-armed clod-hoppers! And not a mortar, nor a carronade, nor even a swivel—but only their ducking guns!'"[67]

On the 17th, the detachments Prevost had awaited sailed, under cover of dense morning fog, along the coastal waterways and arrived in the city. That afternoon, Prevost sent a message to d'Estaing that, if he did not agree to the surrender by the regular firing of the evening cannon at one-hour before sundown, hostilities should begin. In the meantime, Prevost continued to work on the defenses. He had already increased the number of cannons on the city's defensive perimeter and, largely with the help of black laborers, established a dozen redoubts in an arc around the southern outskirts. Once it was clear that there would be no British surrender, the French abandoned any idea for full assault in favor of a siege.

General Lincoln had no other options at that point but to join in the siege which lasted several weeks. Prevost continued to strengthen his defenses. On October 4, the French fleet began to bombard the city. Lincoln wanted d'Estaing to pound the redoubts and defensive perimeter, but the Admiral refused and, instead, hammered the city proper with little effect. Prevost continued to strengthen his defenses.

Lincoln and d'Estaing developed an assault plan while the bombardment was taking place. Pulaski and Marion thought the plan inane, but they were overruled. The attack would begin at precisely 4:00 A.M. on the morning of the 9th. When that time came, the British were not surprised. The plan had been presented to Prevost by spies, so he had plenty of time to reorganize his troops for the onslaught.

The Americans initially attacked at Spring Hill on the right flank. Since the column got lost in the fog, however, it was daylight before the assault was actually underway. The British had an easy time picking off the French soldiers who were decked out in bright-white uniforms ala Francis Salvador (see Chapter 4). Pulaski, who led the charge, was mortally wounded. A second attack, under the leadership of Swedish Count Curt Von Stedingk, met some initial success, but the Americans he was leading were soon overwhelmed. Only 20 survived, and Von Stedingk, himself, was wounded. He later wrote, "I had the pleasure of planting the American flag on the last trench, but the enemy renewed its attack and our people where annihilated by cross-fire.... The moment of retreat with the cries of our dying comrades piercing my heart was the bitterest of my life!"[68]

Finally, d'Estaing and Lincoln ordered a full retreat, but not before the Americans had lost 244 killed, 600 wounded, and 122 captured. The Charles Town militia regimental losses were one captain killed and six privates wounded. The British suffered 40 killed and 63 wounded. About noon on the 9th, d'Estaing requested a cease-fire for the purpose of burying the dead. Prevost consented to a four-hour truce. Major Horry wrote, "We then proceeded to bury our dead which was done by digging large pits, sufficient to retain about a hundred corpses. Then taking off their clothes, with heavy hearts, we threw them into the pits, with very little regard to order, and covered them with earth."[69]

Lincoln dismissed the militia units on the 15th. The men, nearing the end of their enlistments, headed for home. On October 18, 1779, General Lincoln led his beleaguered force back toward Charles Town. D'Estaing had boarded his troops on the fleet by the 19th and quickly set sail for France.[70]

(There are some writings that indicate Brigadier General Williamson was at Savannah with his "1st and 2nd Militia" Brigades. The only South Carolina "militia" in action at Savannah were Charles Town companies. There is some confusion because the South Carolina 1st and 2nd Brigades, though drawn from militia years earlier, were attached to the Continental troops and had been assigned to Continental Brigadier General Isaac Huger of South Carolina just prior to the Siege of Savannah.[71]

Some historians have suggested that the lack of any record regarding backcountry actions with the Cherokee during this period is an indicator that General Andrew Williamson may have already been seduced by the British. Only Colonel Pickens' militia regiment was involved at Stono Ferry when a possible elimination of Prevost's force was at hand. The reason for Williamson's return to Ninety Six with the main force of the militia, i.e., a major Indian threat to the Whig settlements, is not borne out by any specific major actions other than the rumor regarding the possible ring fight mentioned above. Once Pickens rejoined Williamson in Ninety Six District, the Colonel was assigned to patrol in backcountry Georgia for two months while the assault on Savannah took place. It is suspicious that Williamson's active militia didn't take part in the effort, another major action to try and eliminate Prevost's force. Had Williamson and the Ninety Six Militia arrived at Savannah early in September and aligned with d'Estaing, they might have jointly destroyed the Savannah defense before Lincoln arrived. Williamson's inaction in these last few months is a likely major contributor to Prevost's ability to maintain a foothold in the southern colonies.)

Andrew Pickens thought that Williamson may have leaned toward support of the British as early as the Battle of Kettle Creek. He is clear about the period of Williamson's inactivity which included the time frame surrounding the Siege of Savannah as he wrote to Henry Lee, "Col Campbell soon retreated from Augusta and went below Brier Creek— There was not a gun fired between him and Williamson all this time opposite each other at Augusta — there I believe Williamson was corrupted and nothing of consequence happened in separate command further till after the fall of Charleston and his almost constantly on duty."[72]

However, beyond innuendo that stemmed from his inactivity, there is no evidence that Williamson was on the British payroll or that he had even talked with Prevost or his agents regarding any alliance prior to 1780.

Northern Georgia settled again into a chess match of British control of Savannah, and America, the backcountry. Many bitter and bloody skirmishes transpired between the Georgia Whig and Tory militia units, and British attention would soon turn toward South Carolina. The year 1780 had dawned with bad news for the Americans.

7

South Carolina in Jeopardy (1780)

Brigadier General James Patterson commanded the British Garrison at Savannah early in 1780. Britain had just sent 3,000 reinforcements to the Commander in Chief of the American Theater, Major General Sir Henry Clinton. This increased the entire British force in the colonies to 39,000, including active Tories and Hessian allies. General Clinton decided to build on the success of Major General Augustine Prevost who held Savannah and thus maintained the toe-hold the British held in the southern colonies. Clinton left New York on December 26, 1779, with a force of 8,500 men that included his second in command and new Commander of the Southern Army, Lieutenant General Charles Lord Cornwallis. They sailed on a British fleet of nearly 100 ships commanded by Admiral Mariot (sometimes Mariott) Arbuthnot. Destined for Tybee Island at the mouth of the Savannah River, Clinton sculpted his ambitious plans to make a move on Charles Town. He was eager to control Georgia and South Carolina, leave them in the hands of a vast army of Loyalists, and move into North Carolina and Virginia.

At that time, Charles Town, South Carolina, was the largest city in the southern colonies with a population of 12,000 that was evenly split between black and white residents. Three thousand soldiers, including cavalry, disembarked at Tybee Island on February 1, 1780. Then the fleet sailed toward Charles Town. They arrived at Johns Island on the 11th, and Clinton began to debark with the remainder of his troops. He moved his troops to James Island, encamped, and inched closer to Charles Town to await General Patterson's arrival from Savannah. Patterson had left a detachment of troops to defend that city. He marched toward Charles Town with a force of 1,500 that included the crack 71st Regiment of Foot, Fraser's Highlanders, under the command of Major Archibald McArthur (also MacArthur and MacCarthur). (Some writers have labeled him Major Arthur McArthur rather than Archibald; they have likely confused the name with Douglas MacArthur's father, Lieutenant General Arthur MacArthur, Jr.) They were accompanied by Lieutenant Colonel John Hamilton, Commander of the Royal North Carolina Provincial Regiment of Tories.

As soon as the General Assembly heard of the British landing in February, they hastily conferred dictatorial powers on Governor John Rutledge, adopted a resolution to defend Charles Town to the last extremity, and adjourned. Lincoln began the defense with 2,500 troops. On March 3, he received reinforcements of 1,500 Virginia Continentals and 1,000 North Carolina militiamen. General Lincoln believed that the Continental army was subservient to the local authorities. He approached Governor Rutledge with a request to call in all South Carolina militia units. Rutledge immediately issued the muster call.

Major Thomas Pinckney exhibited a high degree of optimism when he wrote his mother on April 10:

7. South Carolina in Jeopardy (1780)

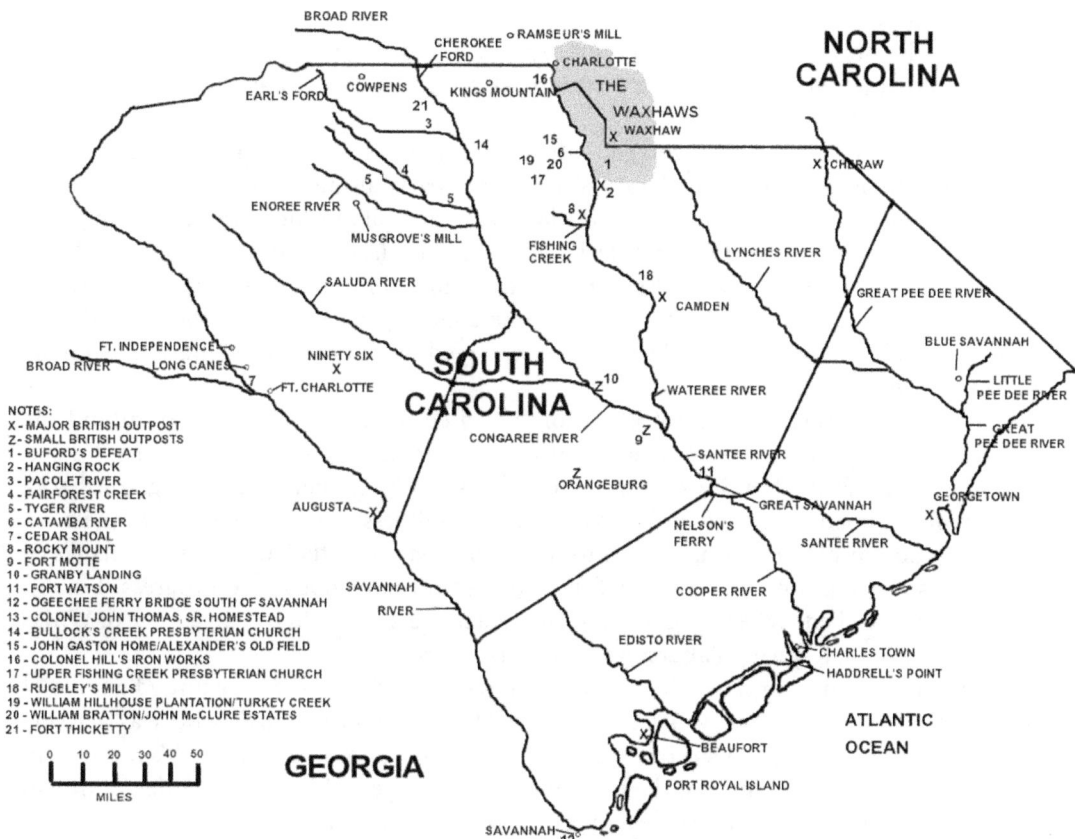

South Carolina points of interest in 1780.

Fort Moultrie, April 10, 1780
  Honored Madam:
    When I went to town [Charles Town] yesterday, I found our works as strong as the high ideas which had been raised of them by report had made me figure them to myself. I likewise saw every part of them thronged with men, and matters in general in the best posture for a vigorous defense. I heard it reported that the Governor is shortly to take the field and draw down as many of our country militia into a camp to be formed somewhere on this side of the country as he can collect, as our militia in general cannot be prevailed on to come into town, and it is hoped this measure will be productive of very good consequence. The enemy continue their approaches but slowly; none of their works are nearer than 600 yards to our lines. Their men-of-war continue opposite to Fort Johnson. Their Admiral's ship was so much damaged as to be obliged to continue on the careen, part of two days, in order to repair.
    The North Carolina and Virginia troops which cannot now be at a very great distance, together with such of our country militia as the Governor may collect, will, it is thought, be sufficient to oblige the enemy to raise the siege, or at all events will much incommode them and in the end render their repulse the more certain.
    I remain, dear mother, sincerely your affectionate and dutiful son,
      THOMAS PINCKNEY[1]

However, the backcountry militia regiments failed to show. They were concerned about a smallpox outbreak in Charles Town. Lieutenant Colonel Francis Marion answered the call with his Second Regiment of state troops. Major General Lincoln was sadly disappointed as he was expecting reinforcements of 9,900 Virginia Continentals and North and

South Carolina militiamen. Matters became even worse when, on the 24th, the muster period for the North Carolina militia units expired, and the men disbanded to return home. The American General was left with 5,500 troops to defend the city against a British force of nearly twice that size.

Francis Marion was only involved in the preparations, not in defense of the siege itself. Late in March, he attended a moderate-sized dinner party at the home of Captain Alexander McQueen, Adjutant General to Brigadier General William Moultrie. Following dinner, McQueen locked the door and declared his guests should drink wine and celebrate toasts to liberty. Marion was a light drinker and abhorred intemperance, so he looked for a way out. He found a second-story window he could open, jumped to the ground, and broke an ankle. Then, unfit for duty, he was removed by litter to his plantation where he sat out the British siege.

Brigadier General Andrew Williamson activated his militia but did not attend the defense of Charles Town. His brigade continually harassed Patterson on his march from Savannah. Colonel Andrew Pickens was able to muster his regiment even though the backcountry militiamen were tired of the coast and feared illness. They had enough of the heat, humidity, and disease-carrying mosquitoes. The militia was sufficient to ride the flanks of Patterson's army and cause some grief, but they could not impede the progress. Finally, Williamson detached Pickens' regiment to Georgia to see if he could recruit a force of Whigs to assault Savannah during Patterson's absence.

Pickens found Georgia Colonel John Twiggs on March 20, and they united a force of 300 men. Their first action was against Tory Major Daniel McGirth who was actively patrolling along the Ogeechee River. The Whigs quietly approached McGirth's location in an attempt to surprise him, but the foray ended in a chase rather than a battle. With two or three of his force dead and three or four captured, McGirth escaped.

Pickens organized a post on the banks of the Ogeechee. There he could launch raids against Tories throughout the backcountry. On March 27, Pickens' troops had a brush with a party of Tories and Indians that left four Tories and six braves dead. The Whigs suffered no losses.

On April 4, British Captain Thomas Conklin (sometimes Conkling) left Savannah with a detachment and reached the Ogeechee River ferry at 10:00 A.M. Shortly after his arrival, some local black men informed Conklin that the Whig force was nearby. After they crossed the river, the Captain detached Ensign James Supple and 15 men to locate the Whigs and try to flank them. Pickens and Twiggs watched the crossing from a ridge. Pickens decided to avoid Supple's flanking maneuver, so he could trap Conklin. He sent one of the Inman brothers (either Captain Shadrick or Captain Joshua) and 20 men into the open to draw Captain Conklin into a chase. Pickens and Twiggs had set an ambush, but Inman entered into an engagement with Conklin, so the ambush was aborted. Pickens and Twiggs joined the scuffle, and Conklin was mortally wounded. Supple avoided the Whigs, returned to the troops, and led them back across the Ogeechee. Two British privates were killed, and six men were wounded. It is reported that Pickens continued to patrol in Georgia throughout the siege of Charles Town.

Lieutenant Colonel Banastre Tarleton, Commander of the British Legion (a mixture of Tory provincials, British light infantry, and British light cavalry) would shortly become infamous. He joined Patterson's march on March 21, took the vanguard for the remainder of the journey, and met General Clinton at Stono Ferry on the 25th. Clinton's total available force for the siege then numbered 9,000.[2]

The British moved on Charles Town, surrounded it, and began the siege. On April 1, 1780, their troops dug trenches and built redoubts for the artillery. Sand fleas and biting gnats plagued the laborers; consequently, they accomplished much of their labor at night. The Americans sent out parties of skirmishers to interrupt the British. On April 6, the Americans were finally able to activate their own artillery, so they began to shell the British workmen. Admiral Arbuthnot sailed into Charles Town Harbor on the 8th and cannonaded Charles Town with the fleet's artillery. "Their fleet, availing themselves of favorable winds and tides, hurried past Fort Moultrie without repeating the error of Sir Peter Parker, in stopping to engage it."[3] (A reference to Commodore Peter Parker and the failed British attempt to take Charles Town in 1776. See Chapter 4.)

On the 10th, Lieutenant Colonel Francis Lord Rawdon and 2,500 troops, including his provincial force of Volunteers of Ireland, united

Major Thomas Pinckney. Artist: Col. J. Trumbull; engraver: W. G. Armstrong, 1865.

with the besiegers. (Lieutenant Colonel was Rawdon's official British officer rank; his rank as commander of the Tory provincial regiment was Colonel.) The siege was off to a good start for the British, and on April 10 Sir Henry Clinton properly offered terms requesting that Lincoln surrender the town or face the resentment of an angry British force.

General Lincoln had watched the British movements for several weeks and knew them to be aggressive. He was well aware that he would soon be greatly outnumbered and that he had plenty of time to evacuate the endangered troops from Charles Town. That move would have saved the force for future actions; however, the General decided his duty was to defend the city and answered with customary words regarding "duty to defend to the last extremity."

Benjamin Lincoln realized what lay ahead, so on the night of the 12th or early morning of the 13th, he ferried Governor Rutledge and several members of the General Assembly across the Cooper River. The evacuees found safety at Monck's Corner, 32 miles north, a site garrisoned by Brigadier General Isaac Huger and Lieutenant Colonel William Washington with 400 troops. Rutledge, aware that the British would be hot on his trail, immediately trekked toward North Carolina where he would govern the free portions of South Carolina in absentia.[4]

On April 14, Clinton sealed the city. He sent Lieutenant Colonel Banastre Tarleton with his Legion, Major Patrick Ferguson and his sharpshooters, and Lieutenant Colonel James Webster with the 33rd and 64th Regiments of Foot to attack the American force at Monck's Corner. Most of the Continentals escaped through a swamp, but 100 were captured, and the British gained 83 prime horses for Tarleton's Legion which was primarily a dragoon force. The British also acquired 102 draft horses and 42 wagons laden with supplies.

The Continental officers at Charles Town, cognizant of that action, realized the yoke of defeat was upon them. As the situation grew increasingly desperate, Lincoln called a

Charles Town, South Carolina, around 1780. Engraving by John Kirk, circa 1860.

council of war. The consensus among his officer corps was to gain such honorable terms of surrender as he could. However, Lieutenant Governor Christopher Gadsden, still in Charles Town, informed Lincoln that the South Carolina State Troops would continue to defend the city with or without the Continental Army. A member of the General Assembly added that, if the Continentals were to prepare for departure, he would immediately allow the British access to the city and aid them in the attack.

At noon on the 21st, passion subsided and General Lincoln asked for six hours to negotiate surrender. General Clinton agreed. Lincoln offered terms of a 10-day free evacuation of Charles Town for all American troops with honors, plus the privilege to remove their arms and equipment. Clinton refused.

On April 25, General Lincoln received word from the Continental Congress that no further reinforcements would come to his aid. Then on May 7, 1780, on the shore of Charles Town Harbor, Fort Moultrie fell to the British. Negotiations reopened on the 8th but went nowhere. On the 10th, the state troops refused to man the defenses, and on the 11th they presented a petition to Lincoln that requested he accept the British terms of surrender. Lieutenant Governor Gadsden backed the request.

General Lincoln finally sent a message to General Clinton which read:

>Charleston, May 11, 1780 –
>Letter, Lincoln to HIS EXCELLENCY SIR H. CLINTON
>   SIR: The same motives of humanity which inclined you to propose articles of capitulation to

this garrison, induced me to offer those I had the honor of sending to you on the 8th instant. They then appeared to me such as I might proffer, and you receive with honor to both parties. Your exceptions to them, as they principally concerned the militia and citizens, I then conceived were such as could not be concurred with; but a recent application from those people, wherein they express a willingness to comply with them, and a wish on my part to lessen, as much as may be, the distresses of war to individuals, lead me now to offer you my acceptance of them.

I have the honor to be, &c.,
B. LINCOLN[5]

General Clinton soon answered:

CAMP BEFORE CHARLESTON, May 11, 1780,
Clinton to MAJOR-GENERAL LINCOLN,
SIR: When you rejected the favorable terms which were dictated by an earnest desire to prevent the effusion of blood, and interposed articles that were wholly inadmissible, both the admiral and myself were of the opinion, that the surrender of the town at discretion was the only condition that should afterward be attended to; but as the motives which then induced them are still prevalent, I now inform you that the terms then offered will still be granted.

A copy of the articles shall be sent for your ratification as soon as they can be prepared; and immediately after they are exchanged, a detachment of grenadiers will be sent to take possession of the hornwork opposite your main gate. Every arrangement which may conduce to good order in occupying the town, shall be settled before noon to-morrow; and at that time your garrison will march out.

I have the honor to be, &c,
H. CLINTON[6]

Article #4 of the negotiated agreement would become a preamble and have a varying effect upon all of the state's militia forces in the coming weeks whether the militiamen were at Charles Town or not. Pertinent articles of surrender read,

ARTICLES OF CAPITUALATION BETWEEN THEIR EXCELLENCIES SIR HENRY CLINTON, MARIOT ARBUTHNOT ESQ., AND MAJOR-GENERAL BENJAMIN LINCOLN.
ART. 1ST.—That all acts of hostility and work shall cease between the besiegers and the besieged, until the articles of capitulation shall be agreed on, signed, and executed, or collectively rejected.
Answer.—All acts of hostility and work shall cease, until the articles of capitulation are finally agreed to or rejected.

─────

ART. 3ᴅ.—The Continental troops and sailors, with their baggage, shall be conducted to a place to be agreed on, where they shall remain prisoners of war until exchanged. While prisoners, they shall be supplied with good and wholesome provisions in such quantity as is served out to the troops of Britannic majesty.
Answer.—Granted.
ART. 4TH.—The militia now in garrison shall be permitted to return to their respective homes, and be secured in their persons and property.
Answer.—The militia now in garrison shall be permitted to return to their respective homes as prisoners on parole; which parole, as long as they observe, shall secure them from being molested in their property by the British troops.

─────

ART. 6TH.—The officers of the army and navy shall keep their horses, swords, pistols, and baggage, which shall not be searched, and retain their servants.
Answer.—Granted, except with respect to the horses, which will not be allowed to go out of the town; but may be disposed of by a person left from each corps for that purpose.
ART. 7TH.—The garrison shall at an hour appointed, march out with shouldered arms, drums beating, and colors flying, to a place to be agreed on, where they will pile their arms.
Answer.—The whole garrison shall, at an hour to be appointed, march out of the town to the ground between the works of the place and the canal, where they will deposit their arms. The drums are not to beat a British march, or colors to be uncased.

─────

ART. 9TH.—That the citizens shall be protected in their persons and properties.

Answer.— All civil officers, and citizens who have born arms during the siege, must be prisoners on parole; and with respect to their property in the city, shall have the same terms as are granted to the militia: and all other persons now in the town, not to be described in this or other article, are, notwithstanding, understood to be prisoners on parole.

ART. 10TH.— That a twelvemonth's time be allowed all such as do not choose to continue under the British government to dispose of their effects real and personal in the State, without any molestation whatever; or to remove such parts thereof as they choose, as well as themselves and families; and that during that time, they or any of them may have it at their option to reside occasionally in town or country.

Answer.— The discussion of this article of course cannot possibly be entered into at present.
————

ART. 12TH.— That a vessel be permitted to go to Philadelphia with the general's dispatches, which are not to be opened.

Answer.— Granted; and a proper vessel with a flag will be provided for that purpose.

All public papers and records must be carefully preserved and faithfully delivered to such persons as shall be appointed to receive them.

Done in Charleston, May 12, 1780.
B. LINCOLN
Done in camp before Charleston, May 12, 1780.
[Signed] H. CLINTON
M. ARBUTHNOT[7]

The British losses amounted to 70 killed and 189 wounded. The Americans suffered 102 killed and 157 wounded. The Americans reportedly lost 4,650 troops of 10 Continental regiments to capture, including seven generals and several other officers. In addition, the British acquired three artillery battalions. While the militiamen were paroled, the Continental prisoners were put on British prison ships at Charles Town. The officers, however, including Brigadier General William Moultrie, were kept comfortably under guard at Haddrell's Point across both the Ashley River from Charles Town and the Stono River from James Island.

The British victory at Charles Town was inevitable; however, it was not as easy as it looked. Hessian Captain Johann Ewald was charged with building some of the British approaches with his Hesse-Hanau Jäger. He later wrote:

> the dangers and difficult work were the least of the annoyance: the intolerable heat, the lack of good water, and the billions of sandflies and mosquitoes made up the worst nuisance ... all our approaches were built in white, sandy soil, one could hardly open his eyes during the south wind because of the thick dust, and could not put a bite of bread in his mouth which was not covered with sand. The few wells we had dug in the trenches for water were mixed with sand and as white as milk.... I tried to protect the workers as much as possible but there were at least one hundred sharpshooters ... whose fire was so superior to mine that the jägers [sic] no longer dared to fire a shot.[8]

The terms of Major General Benjamin Lincoln's parole dictated that he report to the Continental Congress in Philadelphia with a full account of the siege, then retire to New England and refrain from further military action while a prisoner on parole. This was a major embarrassment for the General, and his career was effectively over. Most of Lincoln's military peers believed that, for the good of the country, Lincoln should not have exposed the troops to a siege. The loss of Charles Town to the British was not sufficient justification for the risk. There was no precedent for such action. Even when Philadelphia was threatened, the Continentals evacuated before they were in jeopardy. They lived to fight another, more advantageous, day. Henry "Light Horse Harry" Lee said in later years:

> Indeed, the loss of Charleston was a sad deranging blow for the South; the force of which was aggravated by the injudicious, though faithful, effort to preserve it.... General Lincoln no more

ought to have been influenced by the remonstrances of the citizens of Charleston, when weighing in his mind the propriety of evacuation, than ought to a tender father to regard the crying of his child on his administering a dose of physic to save its life ... the loss of men, stores, &c.... was a severe blow upon the United States, and excited very gloomy sensations throughout America. The error of risking a country to save a town which only can be retained by the reduction of the country, was now perceived with all its pernicious consequences.[9]

News from the south was slow to arrive at Philadelphia. Clinton did not release Lincoln on his parole until early June, and his official report was slow to make its way north. The *Royal Gazette*, a Loyalist publication in New York, reported the fall of Charles Town on June 2, 1780.[10]

Major General Sir Henry Clinton wrote to his superior, Lord George Germain (the British Secretary of State for the American Colonies), on June 4 and his exaggerated account of the citizens' attitudes is recorded in the July 1780 issue of *The Gentleman's Magazine*, a London publication:

> Charles-Town, June 4, 1780
> MY LORD,
> I HAD the honour in my dispatch by the Earl of Lincoln to communicate to your Lordship the surrender of Charlestown. I am now able to give your Lordship a return of the prisoners taken, amounting (exclusive of near a thousand sailors in arms) to 5618 men.... With the greatest pleasure I further report to your Lordship, that the inhabitants from every quarter repair to the detachments of the army, and to this garrison, to declare their allegiance to the King, and to offer their services, in arms, in support of his government. In many instances they have brought prisoners their former oppressors or leaders; and I may venture to assert, that there are few men in South Carolina who are not either our prisoners, or in arms with us.[11]

(See Appendix G. Major General Clinton reported a significantly higher number of American captives than did American sources. The difference may be the number of paroled militiamen; perhaps counted by the British and not the Americans.)

A little-known happening occurred in mid-1780. The Carolinas and Georgia suddenly found themselves at the front of the war for American Independence. The southern colonies were the last to give up on resolving differences with Britain; however, Britain's choice to attack America from the south put them in that precarious position. Now that Clinton had initiated his plan of action, and had developed a foothold in the southern colonies, the British had something of value with which to negotiate. The ten northern colonies, relatively peaceful at that time, were open to British overtures that would allow them to maintain independence.

After the failure at Savannah and the fall of Charles Town, the American level of confidence was extremely low. The Americans sorely wanted independence; however, like the British, many American leaders leaned toward salvaging what they could from the situation.

England had approached France to intercede and arbitrate a settlement that would allow the northern colonies their autonomy while Britain would retain Georgia, North Carolina, and South Carolina as part of the realm. This made sense to many, including the French. England wanted to continue to import valued produce from the southern colonies and would distribute some to France as a part of the settlement.

A. L. Pickens stated: "Arthur Middleton, took down in shorthand ... a speech supporting a resolution which the future president, [James] Madison, introduced in Congress, looking toward independence for all other colonies, the three [the Carolinas and Georgia] ... to be left to Britain. Madison offered both the speech and the resolution." He further stated, "In May, 1780, the belief that South Carolina and Georgia were to be abandoned by Congress from this time pervaded all ranks. And evidently the people were not ill-advised." He added verification with, "John Mathews, a member of Congress, but later governor, bore witness to the effort to sacrifice the three southern colonies for the independence of the other groups."[12]

Colonel William Hill explained in his memoirs that the Continental Congress settled the issue; it passed a resolution to not sacrifice any of the southern states.[13]

The deal was never consummated, but its public knowledge ably quashed any optimism for most of the southern colonists. One effect was a large swing toward the Tory persuasion in the backcountry. After the loss of Charles Town, Loyalists outnumbered the Whigs by four to one.

Once Charles Town fell, the British controlled Georgia and coastal South Carolina. Word had not yet filtered into the backcountry regarding militia paroles, so Sir Henry Clinton still faced rebellion within the state. Additionally, a Whig South Carolina civil government operated in exile.

While convalescing, Lieutenant Colonel Francis Marion learned of Lincoln's defeat. He and Major Peter Horry quickly got their affairs in order and left for North Carolina to try and locate any remnant of the Continental Army.

Sir Henry Clinton knew it was imperative the British secure Georgia and South Carolina, a must if he were to proceed against North Carolina. He ordered the Loyalist militias be armed for that purpose. He further supplemented the existing Tory militias by establishing youth Provincial units within those two British-held southern colonies. The youths' enlistments were for a six-month period, and the young men were paid on a par with British regulars. They also elected their own officers, as did the established militia units.

On May 12, Colonel Abraham Buford (sometimes Beauford) was bivouacked at Lenud's Ferry on the Santee River with 350 men of his 3rd Virginia Detachment (of the 2nd Virginia Continental Brigade). While there, he learned of the fall of Charles Town. His force was a small unit of the much larger Virginia Continental reinforcement that Major General Lincoln had expected. Now that the siege had ended, Brigadier General Huger ordered Buford's force to withdraw to Hillsboro, North Carolina. Governor Rutledge, Francis Marion, Peter Horry, and now Abraham Buford were all on treks northward, as were probably several others.[14]

On the 18th, Lord Cornwallis was ordered north with a force of 2,500 infantry and cavalry. Clinton received intelligence that Buford had connected with Governor Rutledge and was on his way to North Carolina. Buford's force and the Governor needed to be stopped.

While Cornwallis was on the move, General Clinton was busy preparing the first of his famous "three proclamations." On the 22nd, he declared those who would take up arms against Britain, or would try to influence others to do so, would be imprisoned and have their properties confiscated. This, effectively, was an extension of the parole that was offered the militia captured at Charles Town. They were to keep their noses clean and not interfere with the tranquility and order of the colony.

Whig riders were moving ahead of Cornwallis to advance a warning. Colonel Thomas Sumter knew they would be passing his estate, so he headed north toward Camden to catch up to Buford. He left his family at the Sumter estate, a normal practice. The British had customarily been courteous to Whig family members, not a custom honored by Tories. British Lieutenant Charles Campbell broke from custom that day. Cornwallis, just as Sumter expected, dispatched Campbell to Sumter's home. Campbell, who found that Sumter had departed, had Sumter's invalid wife, Mary, carried into the front yard and seated in a kitchen chair. From there, she watched helplessly as the British ransacked her home, gathered valuables, food, clothing, and other supplies. She was then forced to observe as her home burn to the ground. The redcoats rode away to rejoin Cornwallis. (Mary Sumter lived to the age of 94. She died October 24, 1817.)

On the 26th, Buford received word of the British advance and left his camp at Rugeley's Mills north of Camden. (Rugeley's Mills was located on Tory Henry Rugeley's farm about five miles northwest of present-day DeKalb, South Carolina.) Buford began a hasty retreat toward Charlotte, North Carolina. Governor Rutledge also headed for North Carolina by a back road suggested by the men of the General Assembly who traveled with him. Thomas Sumter followed a similar, but separate, path. Cornwallis' force was huge; the logistics to haul wagonloads of supplies, ammunition, artillery, and spare clothing for all of his troops (normal for large regular army units in that day) were mind boggling and would slow him down.

Lieutenant Colonel Banastre Tarleton. Artist: Sir Joshua Reynolds; engraver: J. R. Smith, 1903.

Cornwallis realized he needed to send a light regiment ahead to catch Buford. The task fell upon the British Legion, commanded by Lieutenant Colonel Banastre Tarleton, and he made the most of it. He led a force of 127 Legion dragoons, 40 cavalrymen of the British 17th Dragoon Regiment, and 100 Legion infantry. They arrived in Camden on the evening of the 28th; Loyalist sympathizers told the troops where Buford and his force could be found. On the 29th, Tarleton led his regiment on a quick effort to catch the slow-moving Buford who, like Cornwallis, was encumbered with a burdensome collection of supplies.[15]

It was quite an accomplishment for such a large force to average two miles-per-hour over two days and then prepare to fight at the conclusion of the march. Tarleton drove his force hard and caught up with Buford's army that afternoon. Lieutenant Colonel Tarleton immediately summoned Colonel Abraham Buford to surrender his force. Buford made the customary response of:

> Lt.-Col. Tarleton Comm'ing British Legion
> Sir: I reject your proposal, and shall defend myself to the last extremity.
> I have the honor to be, &c,
> ABM. BUFORD[16]

Tarleton staged the attack quickly, and his dragoons made short work of the battle. Accounts of what transpired vary, and debate has abounded ever since as to whether Buford or Tarleton was to blame for the massacre. The Americans later capitalized on Buford's defeat, and it provided them with propaganda. Buford's men did get off some shots before they were overrun. Popular reports dwell on how the British abominably attacked the Americans with sabers even after the soldiers had grounded their guns, or dropped them completely and raised their arms to surrender. Buford apparently dispatched a messenger with a white flag, but the courier became lost in the confusion.

The American losses were 113 killed, 150 severely wounded, and 53 taken prisoner. Colonel Buford managed to escape with 35 men to North Carolina. Some of the 113 slayings may have been unjustified, even by the most liberal practices of warfare. However, Buford did reject Tarleton's surrender demand and pledged to fight.

Tarleton went down in the heat of battle when his horse was shot. The incident injected some confusion in the minds of the British Legion. They thought he might have been killed, so they became furious. Additionally, Tarleton's men knew they were greatly outnumbered by Buford's force, so it was not unusual for a cavalry operation to begin with a "traditional" saber blitz to overcome the enemy's advantage. This practice was often used by the Whig militias during the war (see Chapter 4 regarding the 1776 Cherokee War), and by Henry "Light Horse Harry" Lee, himself, in command of Lee's Legion (his dragoon force).

On one hand, Henry Lee indicated that responsibility for the massacre should rest upon the head of Colonel Abraham Buford. Lee wrote:

> the American commander, thus advised of the enemy's approach, he could have prepared for his defence. This, it seems, never occurred to the retreating officer; or, if it did occur, was neglected. To this want of precaution Lieutenant-Colonel Buford added evidently much indecision, always fatal in the hour of danger.... If Buford had prepared for battle instead of sending in a flag, or even had so done while the negotiation was going on, Tarleton must have been foiled.[17]

Lee's comment is compounded by Tarleton's penchant for brashness and the knowledge that Buford's force was considerably larger than the British Legion. The fury exhibited by the Legion cavalrymen when Tarleton went down with his horse exemplifies the likelihood that a large number of American casualties was inevitable.[18]

On the other hand, that Tarleton could engineer such a slaughter fits his personality. He later wrote: "Colonel Buford also committed a material error, in ordering the infantry to retain their fire ... which when given had little effect either upon the minds or bodies of the assailants, in comparison with the execution that might be expected from the successive force of platoons ... commenced at the distance of three or four hundred paces."[19]

This seems to add to Henry Lee's indictment of Buford; however, Tarleton's words place the blame on himself. It was well known that if a foot soldier were to fire his long arm at a cavalryman who was 400 yards away, the infantryman would have no time to reload before that horseman would be upon him. Thus, Tarleton words exemplify his awareness that he had complete control of the action. Once Buford's men had fired, the Legion could easily have surrounded the Americans and forced retirement while the rebels grounded their arms.

Lieutenant Colonel Tarleton sent a quick preliminary message to Lieutenant General Cornwallis in which he stated, "I am extremely fatigued with overtaking the enemy beating them — I summoned the Corps— they refused my terms— I have cut 170 off'rs and men to pieces."[20] His statement, and the battlefield littered with killed and wounded, earned Tarleton the nickname "Bloody Ban" and gave rise to the battle cry of "Tarleton's quarter" (take no prisoners), comparable to "Remember the Alamo" of later years.

Another example of Tarleton's usual demeanor is represented in a Horace Walpole quotation. Walpole was a British Whig, a sympathizer for the American cause, and an historian. He wrote to the Anglican Reverend William Mason on February 23, 1782, and quoted Tarleton, "Tarleton boasts of having butchered more men, and lain with more women than anybody in the army."[21] While this would be considered as hearsay in court, if true it does not enhance Tarleton's defense of the Legion's action at the Waxhaws.

A separate episode during the war adds to the likelihood that Tarleton pressed for butchery at Buford's defeat. At the Battle of Cowpens (see Chapter 9), British Captain Robert Duncanson of the 71st Grenadiers surrendered his sword to Lieutenant Colonel John Eager Howard. Howard commanded the Continental Army line for Brigadier General Daniel Morgan at that battle. As he capitulated, Duncanson informed Howard that Tarleton had ordered the British force not to give quarter to surrendering Americans. The Captain feared he would die at the hands of Morgan's men and was surprised to find that Howard immediately instructed his Continentals to grant quarter to all surrendering British soldiers.

The July 1780 issue of *The Gentleman's Magazine* recorded a short formal report from Tarleton to Cornwallis written the day following Buford's defeat (see Appendix G). Tarleton stated:

> I Have the honour to inform you, that yesterday at three o'clock, P. M. after a march of 105 miles in 54 hours, with the corps of cavalry, the infantry of the legion mounted on horses, and a three pounder, at Wacsaw, near the line which divides North from South Carolina, the rebel force, commanded by Colonel Buford, consisting of the 11th Virginia, and detachments of other regiments from the same province, with artillery, and some cavalry, were brought to action.[22]

In the same issue of *The Gentleman's Magazine*, General Clinton continued in his report to Lord Germaine (see Appendix G):

> The troops immediately under his Lordships command have pressed so effectually upon a body of the rebels which remained in the province, that the Earl, by detaching his corps of cavalry, and with them the legion infantry (mounted), has completed the destruction of every-thing in arms against us in this province.
> Lieut.-Col. Tarleton headed this detachment, whose celerity in performing a march of near an hundred miles in two days, was equal to the ardour with which they attacked the enemy. These refusing the terms which were offered them, were charged and defeated, with the loss of one hundred and seventy-two killed, and some taken, together with the remaining field artillery of the southern army, their colours and baggage.

While "Tarleton's quarter" later rallied the Americans, it is recorded that the 150 wounded were paroled on the scene. The British carried them to Waxhaw Presbyterian Church. Tarleton's officers summoned surgeons from Camden and Charlotte to provide care. Indeed, two-thirds of Buford's force survived the attack. Whether tenable or not, Buford had made a practice of being late for action, and he did face a court martial for negligence regarding his decisions (or lack thereof) at Waxhaw. The Colonel was acquitted; however, he was shelved by his superiors to never again take part in a serious action. In December of 1780, he was assigned as Commander of the Continental Army Hospital in Salisbury, North Carolina (about 40 miles NNW of Charlotte).

Lieutenant Anthony Allaire of Ferguson's brigade mentions Tarleton's action in his journal:

> Thursday, June 1st.... By express were informed that Col. Tarleton ... fell in with a body of rebels, forty miles above Camden. He summoned them to surrender — received an insolent answer, charged them, killed one Lieutenant-Colonel, three Captains, eight Subalterns, one Adjutant, one Quartermaster, and ninety-nine Sergeants and rank and file ... three stand of colors taken, two brass six-pounders; two howitzers, two wagons with ammunition, one artillery forge wagon, fifty-five barrels powder, twenty-six wagons loaded with clothing, camp equipage, musket-cartridges, cartridge boxes, flints, etc.[23]

Buford and Tarleton each share responsibility for the slaughter in the Waxhaws; However, Tarleton was new to the southern campaign and eager to establish a reputation. That reputation, the Duncanson event at Cowpens, and the fact that the Legionnaire controlled the field against Buford indicates that the decimation suited Tarleton's desires, so "Bloody Ban" plausibly deserves the lion's share of the responsibility for the carnage.

A parallel event to Buford's defeat occurred on May 26, 1780. Sir Henry Clinton detached Lieutenant Colonel Nisbet Balfour, who commanded a regiment of regulars, and Brevet Lieutenant Colonel Patrick Ferguson with his Tory provincials, to Ninety Six to subdue the Whig militia. Clinton was concerned about General Andrew Williamson's Ninety Six Militia Brigade, especially Colonel Andrew Pickens' regiment. The British were not sure whether Brigadier General Williamson knew of the parole, but they were familiar with the problems that his militia could cause.

Jealousy festered between the two British Lieutenant Colonels. The trip toward Ninety Six was icy as Balfour constantly addressed "Major" Ferguson (his true military rank gained when promoted in 1779 with the 71st Regiment of Foot), and Ferguson showed no respect as he replied with "Captain" Balfour. Cornwallis delegated considerable responsibility to Balfour, but Cornwallis' boss, Major General Sir Henry Clinton, favored Ferguson. (Historians variously refer to Ferguson by his actual rank of major and also his brevet rank of Lieutenant Colonel. Major is the more common usage for his rank in texts.) Major Ferguson would frequently bypass Cornwallis, the Commander of the British Army in the South, and correspond directly to Clinton. Balfour sidestepped Ferguson with firsthand reports to Cornwallis. Ferguson, just to irritate Balfour, would circumvent him and write personal messages to Cornwallis. Lieutenant General Charles Earl Cornwallis was irritated that Major General Sir Henry Clinton communicated directly with Ferguson. Thus, the popinjays danced around each other continuously.

Augusta, Georgia, was garrisoned by British Colonel Thomas "Burn Foot" Brown, his Florida Rangers, and some 500 Creek and Cherokee warriors. He was also accompanied by Moses Kirkland, Richard Pearis, and Evan McLauren (see Chapter 2).[24]

On June 1, Cornwallis established his headquarters at Camden with 2,500 men. He sent several detachments throughout the South Carolina backcountry: Major Archibald McArthur went to Cheraw, Lieutenant Colonel Thomas Pattinson to Hanging Rock, and Lieutenant Colonel George Turnbull to Rocky Mount. Lieutenant Colonel Francis Lord Rawdon took command at Waxhaw, North Carolina. Those assignments supplemented the strongholds at Augusta and Ninety Six. Additional garrisons were created at Georgetown and Beaufort on the coast, as were smaller outposts at Fort Watson, Fort Motte, Orangeburg and Granby Landing to guard the roads between the larger outposts.

Ferguson operated from Ninety Six when he patrolled the Saluda River area to look for Whig militia activity and gather more Tories. Lieutenant Colonel Alexander Innes was assigned to oversee activities at Ninety Six. He arrived apart from Balfour and Ferguson. A Tory Colonel Housman (sometimes Houseman), and Captain Christian Huck, who commanded a troop of Tarleton's Legion dragoons, were to join Turnbull at Rocky Mount.[25]

General Clinton, the same day, proclaimed that all Whigs who returned to their British allegiance would receive a full pardon. This was a caveat to the parole for the Whig militiamen who had served at Charles Town. On the 3rd, Clinton went a step further when he decreed that all paroled civilians sign an oath of allegiance to King George III within 17 days or be deemed still in rebellion. The original parole conditions allowed parolees to remain neutral in the war. This new declaration was momentous: the Whigs were not only required to declare allegiance to King George III, but must also take up arms for Britain against America.

Spartan Militia Regiment Colonel John Thomas, Sr., had been a defender at Charles Town. He was one of the militiamen released upon the fall of the city. His son, Captain John Thomas, Jr., led a company of the regiment that surveilled a large cache of ammunition hidden on the Thomas homestead for four years. When Charles Town was under siege, Captain Patrick Moore and his 150-manTory militia unit decided to capture the stores. When they approached the house, they found it defended by Colonel Thomas' wife, Jane Black Thomas, assisted by three daughters, her youngest son, William, and a son-in-law, Josiah Culbertson. Jane and her family formed a line to keep guns loaded and in the hands of Culbertson who was quickly firing from various rifle portals throughout the house. The group was able to hold off the Tories and cover Captain Thomas and his company as they removed the cache from the property. When Moore decided on an all-out assault to rid the house of "the militia" that had been defending it so hotly, Jane Thomas bravely moved out on the front porch with a saber in her hand and dared Moore to advance further. Captain Moore, embarrassed, withdrew. (The Thomas homestead was located on the north bank of Fair Forest Creek southeast of present-day Croft State Natural Area. Captain Moore is sometimes credited with the rank of Colonel during this period, a likely confusion with his older brother, John Moore.)[26]

On the 5th, Brigadier General Andrew Williamson, who knew Lieutenant Colonel Alexander Innes was coming to Ninety Six, sent a message ahead and asked for terms of surrender. Colonel Thomas Brown at Augusta had offered terms to South Carolina Colonel LeRoy Hammond, who accepted. Brown then dispatched Captain Richard Pearis to Ninety Six to present terms to General Williamson. This action was independent of Innes, Balfour, and Ferguson who had not yet arrived at Ninety Six.

On June 7, 1780, Balfour sent a message to Cornwallis stating, "By the best accounts I can get, Williamson is still in arms, as I mentioned, with a Col. Pickens, but believe they mean, not to continue in a body, but in small partys in the back country."[27]

Pearis moved into Ninety Six on the 7th, and Williamson sent a delegation to meet with him there. Once Williamson received the terms of surrender and parole, he read them to his brigade, sans Pickens and his regiment who were encamped a few miles away. The brigade voted on the terms and decided that Williamson should carry a flag of surrender to Pearis. The terms did not include Clinton's latest proclamation to take up arms for the Crown. Communications in the backcountry were notably slow; the Whigs still assumed they could declare allegiance and sit out the war. Additionally, even though the brigade voted to accept terms, that only served as a vote to disband the brigade. Each individual militiaman had to decide whether he would personally sign the declaration or continue to fight.

Williamson immediately rode to Pickens' camp to speak with the Colonel. The General then read the terms to Pickens' regiment. After Williamson made the presentation, he returned to his brigade. Andrew Pickens' regiment haggled for three days. On June 10, Pickens' regiment, as did Williamson's brigade, overwhelmingly voted to disband and accept the terms of parole. The Colonel sent the results to Williamson. Lieutenant Colonel James McCall was the most notable of only six who voted not to disband; however, an unknown number of militiamen abstained from the ballot.

Also on the 10th, Innes (unaware that the issue had been resolved by Pearis) received Williamson's original message about terms. Innes responded by messenger that the militiamen must surrender their arms, sign paroles, and disband their units. Appropriate punishments for previous actions would be implemented at the conclusion of the war.

Williamson went to Ninety Six that evening and signed the parole. He also agreed to turn his fortified estate at White Hall into a British outpost. Pearis agreed that protection for the parolees would begin on the 12th. On the 13th, Pickens traveled to Ninety Six with 300 of his regiment, and they signed the agreement with Pearis.[28] (A. L. Pickens wrote that as many as 70 had left for North Carolina to reorganize and continue the fight. It is likely that they joined the newly re-formed New Acquisition Militia (see below). He further expressed the likelihood that Joseph Pickens did not have the same pressure to sign the terms as did his high-profile brother, Andrew. Joseph, not a major British target, may have continued the effort with McCall. Captain Robert Anderson apparently did not accept parole. See Chapter 8.)[29]

In the meantime, several actions occurred in the backcountry, some of which concerned General Cornwallis. He was eager to bring South Carolina under control, so he could begin his march northward; however, South Carolina had to be in such a state that the Tory militia and provincial forces could maintain British sovereignty.

On June 5, The New Acquisition Militia of York County, South Carolina, met at Bullock's Creek Presbyterian Church. (Bullock's Creek is located where the Pacolet and Broad Rivers meet.) The regimental commanders, Colonel Samuel Watson and Lieutenant Colonel William Bratton, had been informed about Colonel Abraham Buford's Massacre and that Brigadier General Andrew Williamson and Colonel Andrew Pickens had capitulated to Captain Richard Pearis. Colonel William Hill wrote in his memoirs:

> When these events came to be known ... Watson & Bratton ... did not encourage the men, but much the reverse, by telling them that they had hitherto done their duty. But it appeared to them that any further opposition to the British would not avail & as for their parts could have nothing more to say to them as officers but to advise each of them to do the best they could for themselves.[30]

Also on the 5th, Tory Colonel Housman visited Justice of the Peace, John Gaston, at his home near Cedar Shoals on Fishing Creek. Housman requested Gaston to convince local militiamen to gather the next morning at nearby Alexander's Old Field to relinquish their arms and sign oaths of allegiance. Gaston indignantly refused. After Housman left, the Justice notified his nephews, Captain John McClure and Lieutenant Hugh McClure, about the Tory's visit. The brothers spent the night gathering their militia. (John Gaston's home was about two and one-half miles southwest of present-day Fort Lawn, South Carolina.)

Two hundred militiamen turned up at Alexander's Old Field on the morning of the 6th to listen to Housman's spiel. The McClures and 33 militiamen, attacked, dispersed the crowd, killed four Tories, and wounded several more. The Whigs suffered two wounded. (Alexander's Old Field is now present-day Beckhamville, South Carolina, two miles south of Justice Gaston's home site.)

The same day, the New Acquisition Militia met at Colonel William "Billy" Hill's and Isaac Hayne's Iron Works on Hill's estate. (This is sometimes written as New Era Ironworks. It was advertised as the new AEra Ironworks, new because it was erected in late 1779. Colonel William Hill referred to it in his memoirs as Hill's Iron Works, the designation used in this chapter. It was located at present-day Lake Wylie, South Carolina, southwest of Charlotte, North Carolina.) Lieutenant Colonel Francis Lord Rawdon sent one of his Tory provincials to meet with them and read the terms of surrender. Colonel Hill explained in his memoirs:

> The anxiety of the citizens to know ... this mission was great & ... the person from Lord Rawdon met them & exhibited his commission from under the great seal of Lord Rawdon that he was empowered to take their submissions & give paroles & protections to all that choose to become British Subjects— he, the said commisr [sic], took his stand & proceeded to read a proclamation of his Lordships that begun by asserting that Congress has given up the two Southern states. & would not contend further for them that as Genl. Washington's army was reduced to a small number of men. & that he, with that small army had fled to the mountains.... [Colonel Hill] then stopped the commissr. [sic] from reading more of the proclamation and took the stand himself, & addressed the citizens in the following language ... that both the facts stated in the sd. [said] proclamation was false and that it was in order to intimidate & deceive the citizens ... and that we had all taken an oath to defend & maintain the Independence of the state to the utmost of our power and that if we could not raise a force to meet the foe, we had one open side, we cd. [could] keep in a body, go into No. Ca. meet our friends & return with them to recover our State — After saying this and much more not necessary to relate, there was a visible animation in the countenances of the citizens and their former state of despondency visibly reversed, and the poor commisr. [sic] was obliged to disappear with his proclamation & protections for fear of the resentment of the audience.... And after these things took place the men appeared very anxious to keep in a body but they had no officers— I then advised them to Ballot for two Colonels and they did so and it appeared their choice fell upon a young man by the name of Neel [Andrew Neil] and [William Hill] ... we then proceeded to further arrangements and that was for the men to choose all other of their officers to form into companies &c.[31]

(Colonel Andrew Neil was the son of Colonel Thomas Neil who was killed at the Battle of Stono Ferry. See Chapters 3 and 6.)

Also on the 6th, Major General Clinton embarked for the return trip to New York and left Cornwallis to command the British Army in the South and, especially, to enforce the new surrender terms. Clinton demanded that Cornwallis bring South Carolina into submission before he attempted a move into North Carolina.

On June 8, 1780, Cornwallis placed Rawdon over the affairs of backcountry South Carolina and moved his headquarters back to Charles Town. Rawdon moved his own headquarters to Camden to be more central to the outposts.

Colonel Thomas Brandon, Commander of the 2nd Spartan Militia Regiment, had established a camp on Fair Forest Creek to imprison Loyalist detainees. One man escaped and informed Tory Militia Major William "Bloody Bill" Cuningham, a survivor of the Battle of Kettle Creek, who launched an attack on the 8th. Colonel Brandon and 11 Whigs in camp were eating in the dim light of morning. Colonel Brandon and six of his men escaped down a ravine. Five militiamen were killed.

Lieutenant Colonel Bratton and the McClures had been using the Upper Fishing Creek Presbyterian Church for their headquarters. On the 10th, Lieutenant Colonel George Turnbull's spies reported the location to him at his Rocky Mount headquarters. Turnbull immediately dispatched Captain Christian Huck with his company of Tarleton's Legion dragoons to attack the rebels. Huck was accompanied by Colonel James Ferguson, who had been operating around Lower Fishing Creek, with a company of his provincials.

When Bratton's scouts got word to him that the British were moving in his direction, the Whigs, including Reverend John Simpson and the men in his congregation, quickly vacated the church. Huck arrived on Sunday the 11th to find an empty meeting house. While Huck burned the church and Reverend Simpson's home, Ferguson harassed local residents to wrest information of the Whigs' whereabouts. Ferguson raided the home of Mrs. Janet Strong, sister of Justice of the Peace Gaston, and killed a young Whig named William Strong.

Also on the 11th, a Covenanter (Reformed Presbyterian) minister, the Reverend William Martin, preached a sermon at the Covenanter Church on Rocky Creek. He denounced Tarleton's massacre of Buford's troops, railed against British domination and the Anglican Church, and pressed the men of his congregation to take up arms against the British. They took him at his word. The next day, a company of Covenanters gathered seven miles north of Rocky Mount with Captain Benjamin Land. Before they could act, they were surprised by a company of British dragoons garrisoned at Rocky Mount. One of the dragoons hacked Captain Land to death with a saber. The dragoons attacked another company of Covenanters two miles away. They killed one Whig and dispersed the rest. They next arrested the Reverend William Martin and imprisoned him at Rocky Mount.

On June 14, Colonel Alexander Innes heard that Pearis had taken control at Ninety Six. Innes wrote Cornwallis to suggest that Colonel Brown's Augusta provincials, including Captain Pearis, should stay in force at Augusta. He further recommended that provincial Lieutenant Colonel John Harris Cruger should take command at Ninety Six.

Colonel Henry Rugeley, owner of Rugeley's Mills, was given control of a Tory regiment to garrison Camden. On the same date, Colonel Andrew Neil and his New Acquisition Militia regiment set out for the Broad River to attack Tory settlements. He left 15 men with Colonel William Hill at the ironworks. Colonel Thomas Brandon and Captain Andrew Love took another New Acquisition Militia regiment to attack a company of Tories who had moved in on the plantation owned by John Stallings on Upper Fishing Creek. Mrs. Stallings, sister of Captain Love, was killed by a stray bullet during the melee. The Tory company was demolished.

On the 15th, Colonel Matthew Floyd, from the Broad River area, arrived at Rocky Mount and complained to Colonel George Turnbull about poor treatment from local Whigs. Turnbull also received word that the New Acquisition Militia regiment from Hill's ironworks had attacked Tory settlements along the Broad River. He proposed to Cornwallis that the ironworks be destroyed. He also reported that prominent Whigs had abandoned their plantations around Rocky Mount. He further stated that, although corn was scarce, there were ample provisions at Irish settlements on Turkey Creek and Bullock's Creek. (Turkey Creek is the location of the William Hillhouse estate. See remarks about William Hillhouse, Jr., of Neil's regiment in Chapter 3. This would become important forage information to General Cornwallis at the time of Cowpens in a few months. See Chapter 9.)

Colonel Innes arrived at Ninety Six on the 16th and found the Whigs had already complied with the surrender terms. All was relatively peaceful in that community. The surrender terms only regarded a declaration of allegiance. The British had yet to press General Clinton's new proclamation requirement of military service to the Crown. That would occur later in the year.

The same day, Tory Lieutenant Alexander Chesney from the Pacolet River led a militia company in a skirmish on Bullock's Creek and defeated the Whigs as they attempted a crossing. Also, Captain Christian Huck marched out early that morning from Rocky Mount with his detachment of Tarleton's Legion dragoons. He was accompanied by Captain Floyd and 60 militiamen. They were headed out to destroy William Hill's ironworks and to disperse the New Acquisition Militia.[32]

Captain Huck and 500 Tory provincials reached William Hill's ironworks on the 18th; however, when Hill had received word they were en route, he withdrew his small garrison. Huck destroyed the ironworks, Hill's house, saw mill, grist mill, and slave quarters. He confiscated 90 slaves and captured a Mr. Calhoun, who was related to Andrew Pickens' wife, Rebecca. Huck hanged Calhoun to try and force him to reveal William Hill's location. Calhoun refused to divulge the information, so Huck's militia rode away. One of Hill's slaves was hiding nearby and observed the activity. He quickly cut Calhoun down and managed to revive him.

During this period, one of Andrew Pickens' Loyalist neighbors began to visit regularly at Andrew's home. He bragged about each Loyalist victory as he heard of it. He once declared, "It Ain't no use fer the rebels to keep on fightin' the king. Ef they don't stop they air all a-gwine 'a be kilt!" At that time, Andrew grabbed him, led him to the gate, and booted him hard enough to give him momentum to run down the hill toward the creek. Andrew gave chase and added kicks as he went.[33]

Also on the 18th, General Cornwallis sent a message to General Clinton that the rebellion in South Carolina had been quashed. That was not entirely true, but Cornwallis needed to justify his plan for an invasion into North Carolina.

On June 19, Colonel Thomas Sumter met units from the Spartan, Fair Forest, and New Acquisition Militias at Tuckaseegee Ford on the Catawba River. (Tuckaseegee Ford was located at present-day Charlotte, North Carolina, between where Long Creek enters and Interstate 85 crosses the Catawba. The site is now called Tuckaseegee Ford and Trail, is owned by Mecklenburg County, and the listed address is 5000 Whitewater Center Parkway. It is near the United States National Whitewater Center.) The militiamen decided to unite, declared Sumter their leader, and bestowed upon him the rank of Brigadier General. It was unusual for a militia unit to elect a Brigadier General, but because Governor Rutledge was in exile and unavailable, it was a necessary action. Indeed, Rutledge was on his way to Philadelphia to plead before the Continental Congress, so all active local militia leaders were required to act with full authority in his absence. Since Williamson disbanded the Ninety Six Militia, the "new Brigadier General" Sumter became the ranking militia leader in South Carolina. (Griffith Rutherford, Commander of the Spartan North Carolina Militia, was also a Brigadier General; however, the South Carolina militia units were much larger. Hence, Sumter was selected as the commander of the combined militias—reminiscent of Pickens having taken command in Georgia prior to the Battle of Kettle Creek. See Chapter 6. The method by which Sumter was declared a Brigadier General would become an issue prior to the Battle of Kings Mountain. See Chapter 8.)

William Hillhouse (see Chapter 3 and Appendix E) stated in his pension application:

> In May 1780 I again went into actual service, and continued till October 1781. I entered as orderly Serjeant, in which capacity I served a short time, when I was elected Lieutenant of the Company in which I had hitherto done duty. Brigadier Gen. Thomas Sumpter [sic] now commanded the Brigade, and Col. Andrew Neil the Regiment to which I belonged; and Captain J. Jamison the company.

On June 20 Brigadier General William Lee Davidson and Colonel Francis Locke, with

400 militiamen of the Rowan County North Carolina Militia, attacked and defeated Tory Lieutenant Colonel John Moore and the 1,000 recruits he had gathered at Ramseur's (sometimes Ramsour's) Mill. (Ramseur's Mill is located near present-day Lincolnton, North Carolina, 20 miles northwest of Tuckaseegee Ford.) Seventy were killed, and 200 wounded; casualties were evenly split between the two forces. The remainder of the Tory recruits was dispersed. Sumter was aware of the impending attack, but his force under Brigadier General Rutherford did not arrive until noon, too late for the battle. They helped bury the dead and obtained some of the captured Tory provisions.

Brigadier General Thomas "Gamecock" Sumter. Artist: C.W. Peale; sketcher: W.G. Armstrong; engraver: G. Parker, 1865.

General George Washington had sent Major General Johann de Kalb to assist with the defense of Charles Town. When he learned that Charles Town had fallen, Washington declared de Kalb temporary Commander of the Southern Department of the Continental Army to replace Major General Benjamin Lincoln. General de Kalb was 35 miles northeast of Hillsboro, North Carolina, when he received the news.

British Lieutenant Colonel Nisbet Balfour and Major Patrick Ferguson arrived at Ninety Six on June 22. Balfour camped outside the village. Ferguson bivouacked his force in Savage's Old Field near the site of the stockade used by Williamson's force during the Loyalist siege of 1775 (see Chapter 2). No sooner had they settled in, when Brigadier General Andrew Williamson secretly paid them a visit. Balfour and Ferguson each wrote messages to Clinton; Balfour stated that Williamson pledged to aid the British as a civilian and that he believed the entire backcountry could be brought to British allegiance if they could also win over the support of Pickens and Hammond. Ferguson wrote, "By General Williamson's report ... if he could work without disgusting them [the Ninety Six District Whig militiamen] he hoped to convert the majority of them into good Loyalists."[34]

Colonel William Hill stated in his memoirs:

> Shortly after the fall of Charleston ... the British had advanced above Camden to the Waxsaw & fixed a post at Rocky Mount, and Granby, on the Congarees [sic], Orangeburg & &c. At that time all the upper division of the State was commanded by Genl. Pickens as Genl. Williamson that had the chief command previous to that time, turned a traitor to his country. & went to the enemy then in Savannah, & made his peace with them.[35]

The backcountry Whigs had not counted upon General Williamson's treachery. He was the only one of their officers who had not only signed an allegiance, but actually offered his active service on behalf of the Crown. Indeed, he had promised to try and bring Andrew Pickens into the fold, which was a prime goal for Lieutenant General Cornwallis. The British Commander knew the value of Andrew Pickens in a Loyalist uniform. He was certain that the majority of Whigs would lay down their arms and follow Pickens into a provincial regiment.

Lieutenant Anthony Allaire continued to update his journal and entered a description of Ninety Six when he wrote on Tuesday, June 22, 1780:

> Ninety Six ... is a village or country town ... contains about twelve dwelling houses, a court-house and a jail, in which are confined about forty Rebels, brought in prisoners by the friends of Government, who have just got the opportunity, and gladly embrace it, many of them having been obliged before this to hide in swamps to keep from prisons themselves. Ninety Six is situated on an eminence, the land cleared for a mile around it, in a flourishing part of the country, supplied with very good water [Spring Branch that ran between the village and Ferguson's encampment], enjoys a free, open air, and is esteemed a healthy place.[36]

Ferguson met with Captain Robert Cunningham (see Chapter 2), promoted him to Colonel, and gave him command of the Ninety Six Loyalist Militia Regiment.

Two days later, Lieutenant Allaire moved into the village across from the jail and added in his journal: "I have the constant view of the Rebels peeping through the grates, which affords some satisfaction to see them suffer for their folly. Some of them are magistrates; one the executioner of the five that were hanged here some time in April, 1779."[37]

General de Kalb reached Hillsboro, North Carolina, on June 22, 1780. He proceeded west-southwest to Buffalo Ford on the Deep River where he encamped. (Buffalo Ford was located two miles north of present-day Coleridge, North Carolina.)

On the 23rd, Lieutenant Colonel George Turnbull led Captain Christian Huck and his Legion dragoons to a place called Major Brown's Crossroads (present-day Edgemoor, South Carolina). He was determined to protect the Loyalists subsequent to Moore's defeat at Ramseur's Mill. Soon after his arrival, he was joined by Colonel James Ferguson and his Tory militia.

On the 30th, General Cornwallis sent another message to General Clinton to proudly report Brigadier General Andrew Williamson's submission at Ninety Six. He explained that Williamson offered his assistance to bring Andrew Pickens and others to the British standard. He also related details about the destruction of Hill's ironworks and stated that it "put an end to all resistance in South Carolina." (This must have been a curiosity for General Clinton since he had heard from Cornwallis that South Carolina had been subjugated nearly two weeks earlier.)[38]

On July 8, 1780, Major Patrick Ferguson met with several Tory leaders that had gathered at Ninety Six. Major Ferguson reorganized the backcountry Loyalist militias by regions similarly to those of the Whig militias. Each company then elected captains and lieutenants. Ferguson's most notable selection was Major William "Bloody Bill" Cuningham, assigned to command a unit on the upper Saluda River.

On the 10th, Loyalist Lieutenant Colonel George Turnbull was advised that Whigs Captain John McClure and Lieutenant Colonel William Bratton were in the vicinity of their properties. He dispatched Captain Christian Huck with 105 men to find and arrest them. Likewise, Brigadier General Thomas Sumter received intelligence of Huck's foray. Sumter held a council of war with his officers, and they planned to ambush Huck's force.

Huck, like some of his superiors, was also a popinjay and treated the backcountry Whigs cruelly whether they were active militia or civilians. Major General Clinton had requested that the Tories in the backcountry temper their violence toward civilians, especially women and children, so as not to provide additional incentive for the Whigs to increase their resistance. Still Huck made it his priority to attack Presbyterians. He burned their churches and Bibles, and harassed their clergymen. (Huck was brutal and guilty of horrendous acts; however, there is no record of Huck, Tarleton, or any other well-known

Tory militia or provincial officer having barricaded a congregation inside of a burning church as depicted in some 20th and 21st century movies.)

Several actions were about to take place, and each would be a setback for the British. Spartan Militia Regiment Colonel John Thomas, Sr., had been imprisoned at Ninety Six. Some reports indicate he was jailed for not having taken the loyalty oath, while others argue that, after he took the oath, he became actively involved with the Whig militia. (The former reasoning is probably correct. Had it been the latter, Thomas would likely have already been hanged.)

The brave Mrs. Jane Thomas, who had earlier defended a cache of ammunition for the patriots (see earlier this chapter), was allowed to bring her husband his personal supplies and visit him at the jail. As she strolled the village on the evening of the 11th, she passed a group of Tory wives and heard them discuss a planned raid on a Whig militia unit at Cedar Springs. That Whig unit happened to be Colonel Thomas' regiment, then commanded by his son, Colonel John Thomas, Jr. Mrs. Thomas left Ninety Six early the next morning and rode 50 miles to Cedar Springs to warn her son of the coming attack.

Colonel Thomas and 60 Spartan Regiment militiamen spent the day preparing an ambush for the Tories. A provincial force of 150 Loyalists from Ninety Six approached Cedar Springs at midnight. They found several campfires spread throughout the camp with apparent groups of sleeping men. Believing they had surprised the Whigs, they quickly charged and shot at the baited sleeping bags and blankets. Thomas' regiment had pulled away from the firelight to the rear of the camp. When they saw the Tories silhouetted against the flames, the Whigs opened fire. The Tories were routed and suffered severe losses. The patriots had no casualties. Neither the Loyalist commander nor the number of Loyalists killed and wounded in the action is known.[39] (The Cedar Springs Battlefield was near the present-day South Carolina School for the Deaf and Blind outside of Glendale, South Carolina, not far from Colonel Hill's Iron Works.)

In a second and parallel action on the morning of the 11th, Loyalist Captain Christian Huck arrived at Captain John McClure's plantation with 120 Tory provincials and militia, including his detachment of Tarleton's Legion dragoons. He raided the storehouse and destroyed crops. In the process, he found John McClure's younger brother, James, and their brother-in-law, Edward Martin, casting rifle balls for the militia. Huck arrested them and declared they would hang the following morning. The attackers then set the house ablaze.

When John McClure's wife tried to protest their treatment, a dragoon struck her across the face with the flat of his saber. As the force rode away, Mrs. McClure sent her daughter, Mary, to locate Captain McClure at Brigadier General Sumter's camp on the east side of the Catawba River at Clem's Branch. A combined militia force of 250 men from the areas of York, Chesterfield, and Fairfield eagerly set out to find Huck's force. They were led by militia officers: Colonels Andrew Neil, Edward Lacey, and Richard Winn, Lieutenant Colonels William Bratton and William Hill, and Captain John McClure.

Captain Huck's advance arrived at Lieutenant Colonel William Bratton's home that afternoon, but Bratton was nowhere to be found. One of the men threatened Mrs. Martha Bratton, but Loyalist Lieutenant John Adamson from Camden intervened. Huck appeared with the rest of his force, and he questioned Mrs. Bratton. Huck left her and the estate unharmed; however, he did arrest three older gentlemen including William Bratton's older brother Robert. The prisoners were told they would hang the next morning along with the two who had already been sentenced to the same fate. Huck then rode on and camped for the night at a nearby plantation, that of James Williamson, Bratton's elderly Whig neighbor.

The Whigs were hot on the trail of their quarry. They captured Major John Owens, a member of Colonel James Ferguson's regiment, who informed them that Huck and his entire force were asleep at Williamson's plantation. They rode to Williamson's, quietly surrounded the dark encampment, and launched a surprise attack at dawn on the 12th. The British and Tories were completely surprised and unable to muster a successful counterattack. Huck jumped on his horse and tried to rally the dragoons, but Whig Private John Carroll saw him, took aim with a double-ball load in his rifle, and fired. One of the balls hit Huck in the head.

In addition to Captain Huck, Loyalist militia Colonel James Ferguson was killed. The enemy loss amounted to 35 killed and 30 wounded. Twenty-nine were taken prisoner. Huck's five condemned prisoners were elated to have been rescued; William Bratton and John McClure thrilled to have rescued their kinfolk.

British Lieutenant Colonel Banastre Tarleton later wrote that "only 24" Loyalists had escaped. Late that morning, twelve dragoons and twelve militiamen reported to Lieutenant Colonel George Turnbull at Rocky Mount. Turnbull sent a preliminary report of Huck's defeat to Lieutenant Colonel Francis Lord Rawdon at Camden. Turnbull understated, "This is a very unfortunate affair." Shortly thereafter, 10 more arrived at Rocky Mount. (This total of 34 survivors differed from Tarleton's account. Tarleton may have only been told of the first group to return to Rocky Mount.) Turnbull then offered a more detailed report to Rawdon that included numbers of the lost.[40]

Colonel Hill wrote of the character of Captain Huck in his memoirs: "Capt. Hook [sic] the same that had a few weeks before destroyed the Iron works ... and he far exceeded the Assyrian Genls [sic] ... in blasphemy by saying that God almighty had become a Rebel, but if there were 20 Gods on that side, they would all be conquered, was his expression."[41]

William Hillhouse testified of the event in his pension application (see Appendix E):

> Thomas Sumpter [sic] now commanded the Brigade, and Col. Andrew Neil the Regiment to which I belonged; and Captain J. Jamison the company.
>
> During this campaign I marched through the greater part of the middle and lower sections of S. Carolina, and through a considerable portion of North Carolina. As well as I can recollect, I was, during this term of duty, in the following Battles, viz., at Williamson's plantation in the District of York S. Carolina I was in a battle in which the British and Tories were commanded by the British officers, Captains Huck and Adams, and most gloriously defeated by a few Militia Boys, my Companions in arms, commanded by Col. Neil.

Although Major Patrick Ferguson's brigade was not involved in that action, his Lieutenant Anthony Allaire wrote of it in his journal:

> Thursday, 13th. Lieut. Hunt of the Legion Cavalry ... was one of the party defeated the twelfth inst ... gave an imperfect account ... Capt. Huck commanded the party consisting of one subaltern and seventeen dragoons of the Legion, three subalterns and eighteen New York Volunteers, twenty-five militiamen.... They were sent in pursuit of a rebel party, and arrived at ... Col. Bratton's ... very much fatigued. Unfortunately a rebel party ... came upon them at four o'clock in the morning of the twelfth.... Captain Huck, with four dragoons, attempted to make off. Huck got shot through the neck, of which he died.[42]

Also on the 11th, the Georgia militiamen were on the move to assist in South Carolina. Colonel Elijah Clarke had crossed the Savannah to locate North Carolina militia Colonel Charles McDowell of Quaker Meadows. McDowell had moved into South Carolina to disrupt the movement of British and Loyalist soldiers toward North Carolina. (McDowell's home, Quaker Meadows, was northwest of present-day Morganton, North Carolina, on route 181 at St. Mary's Church Road.)

Clarke had replaced Colonel John Dooley who took British parole just as Andrew Pickens had done. Clarke decided there were too many Tory militia units in the vicinity, so he returned to Georgia. Colonel John Jones took command and continued on with 35 volunteers. He found a route to circumvent the Tory patrols.

On the 12th, McDowell encamped on the Pacolet River at Earl's Ford (located at Earlsville, now present-day Landrum, South Carolina), and the Georgians bivouacked not far away on the Broad River. Jones found McDowell on the 13th, and they were joined by Colonel John Thomas, Jr., of the Spartan Regiment. This union brought the total militia force at Earl's Ford to 400 men.

Colonel Alexander Innes had set up an outpost at Fort Prince. (Fort Prince, also known as John Prince's Fort, was located on the west side of present-day Spartanburg, South Carolina, on Fair Forest Creek before it meets the Tyger River.) On July 14, Innes ordered Loyalists provincial Major James Dunlap and militia Colonel Ambrose Mills with 75 men to find and assail McDowell. Dunlap arrived at Earl's Ford during the night and found Jones' encampment first. Not realizing how many Whigs were nearby, he launched an attack upon the Georgians. McDowell was aroused by the racket, and he with his force came to Jones' aid. Dunlap then realized he was at a great disadvantage and ordered a retreat. The Georgians lost two killed and six wounded in the initial skirmish; one of the wounded was Colonel Jones who suffered eight saber cuts to his head. McDowell lost six killed and eighteen wounded.

After daybreak on the 15th, McDowell directed Captain Edward Hampton to take 50 of his men to chase Dunlap. Hampton caught Dunlap at present-day Inman, South Carolina. They skirmished, and eight Tories were killed. Hampton and Dunlap maintained a running battle all the way to the fort before Hampton returned to McDowell. Colonel Innes feared that Hampton would bring McDowell with his entire Whig militia against Fort Prince, so he evacuated and returned to Ninety Six.

Continental Major General Johann de Kalb arrived at Hillsboro, North Carolina, with 2,000 men, including North Carolina State Troops under Major General Richard Caswell. He had also been joined by South Carolina Lieutenant Colonel Francis Marion and Major Peter Horry.[43]

Brigadier General Thomas Sumter dispatched Major William R. Davie to take a position near Hanging Rock. He was to interrupt British supplies from Camden, harass the Tories as they foraged near the Waxhaws, and protect Whigs in the area from attacks by Loyalist militias. Davie was joined on the north side of Waxhaw Creek by Whig Major Robert Crawford of the one-month-old Kershaw Militia Regiment, Catawba Indian Chief General Newriver, and Mecklenburg North Carolina militia Colonel Robert Irwin. (The Cherokee had lobbied hard for the Catawba Indian tribe to unite with them and the British; however, the Catawba, allied with the Americans. The Catawba Indians were a small tribe that numbered fewer than 1,000 braves at that time. Their villages were located along the banks of the Catawba River near present-day Charlotte, North Carolina.)

On July 20, Major Davie took a detachment of his force to attack a caravan of provisions en route from Camden to Hanging Rock. That night, one of the Whigs strayed too far and was captured. On the morning of the 21st, Davie set an ambush at Flat Rock on the main Camden Road. He commandeered the British supply wagons with little trouble, took the escorts prisoners, and destroyed the wagons and provisions.

The Major and his men headed for their camp at dusk with their prisoners; however, they took a remote route to avoid the enemy. They feared the straggler from the previous night might have been seized and divulged information about the foray. The Whig cluster reached Beaver Creek Ford at 2:00 A.M. on the 22nd. As they entered a plantation to bivouac, they were hailed by Tories concealed under a fence and in a cornfield. After they were challenged a second time, they faced musket fire, upon which they withdrew to a nearby hill that overlooked the plantation. (Beaver Creek Ford was located three miles northeast of present-day Liberty Hill, South Carolina, just east of where State Highway 522 jogs north.)

Most of the prisoners from the convoy were killed outright or were mortally wounded by the Tory fire. Only four survived. The Whig losses were light; one killed, and two wounded. Davie returned to camp on Waxhaw Creek with no further difficulty.[44]

The British would next experience the advent of the "over mountain" men (also called "backwater" men): the militias of Colonels Isaac Shelby, John Sevier (sometimes John Xavier), and Andrew Hampton. (Sevier didn't immediately come because of Indian difficulties, but he had sent a detachment under the command of Major Charles Robertson.) The militiamen were from southwestern Virginia (within present-day eastern Tennessee), and they were hardened, experienced backwoods fighters, thought of as wild frontier riflemen.

These over mountain families resided in the midst of Indian country. They were very rough and independent settlers who sought the opportunity to be away from British control. However, the settlers had encroached deeper into Cherokee lands. Many tribal members were not happy.

A great council had been held at Sycamore Shoals, on the Watauga River at present-day Elizabethton, Tennessee, between March 14 and 17, 1775. The council was organized after frontiersman Daniel Boone had heard the Cherokee wanted to sell a large tract of land on the frontier. Attendees at the council were Boone, a speculator named Richard Henderson, and representatives of the eventual settlers in the Watauga, Nolichucky, and Holston valleys.

The Indians were represented by Chiefs Attakulla Kulla, Oconostota, Willanawaw, Doublehead and Dragging Canoe. Attakulla Kulla was the primary negotiator. He was interested in allowing more white settlement. He felt the white men would settle regardless of Cherokee efforts to resist, so the tribe should sell a portion of the land and get something in return. Oconostota had been more hawkish, but was getting older and gave way to Attakulla Kulla.

Chief Dragging Canoe (Tsi'yu-gunsini) had sat through the primary negotiations and spoke against them. He was very wise and realized that, once the settlers got a toe-hold in the over mountain region, they would usurp more of the Cherokee land. He was aware of a similar situation that the Shawnee had faced just five months earlier. A Virginia militia battalion of 1,100 men, commanded by Colonel Andrew Lewis, made a foray to the Ohio River. The purpose of his foray was to force the Shawnee to abide by a treaty Virginia had negotiated with the Iroquois. Lewis had camped where the Kanawha River meets the Ohio River near present-day Point Pleasant, West Virginia.

On October 10, 1774, Shawnee Chief Cornstalk attacked the militia with between 800 and 1,000 braves. The battle lasted for hours and was devastating for each side. The Virginians had lost 75 killed and 150 wounded. The surviving militiamen found 33 dead braves, but the Shawnee had removed many more, as was their custom. One of the dead was Pucksinwah, father of Tecumseh. This was originally called the Battle of Kanawha, but it became better known as the Battle of Point Pleasant.

Dragging Canoe did not want to delay action to stop encroachment into Cherokee land. As soon as agreement had been reached at Sycamore Shoals, Henderson asked for additional land (as predicted by Chief Dragging Canoe). Henderson desired to own a road through the Cherokee Nation to the new settlement areas, much like a present-day easement. That so angered Tsi'yu-gunsini that he walked out of negotiations and declared:

> Ani-Yunwiya, THE REAL PEOPLE, once so great and formidable, will be compelled to seek refuge in some distant wilderness.... Should we not therefore run all risks, and incur all consequences, rather than submit to further loss of our country? Such treaties may be alright for men who are too old to hunt or fight. As for me, I have my young warriors about me. We will have our lands. A-WANINSKI, I have spoken.... There is no more game left between the Watauga and the Cumberland. There is a cloud hanging over it. You will find its settlement DARK and BLOODY.

The Treaty of Sycamore Shoals was signed on March 17, 1775, and the land opened for the over mountain settlers. It was shortly after this that Chief Dragging Canoe withdrew from the over mountain Cherokee villages and created the Chickamauga tribe. (See Chapter 5.)[45]

The over mountain militiamen had been engaged with the braves of Cherokee War Chief Dragging Canoe for the past five years. The backwater men were often referred to as the "Yellin' Boys" or the "Screamin' Boys." Their battle cry so perfectly emulated that of the Indians that it created fear and dread among their enemies.

On July 25, the over mountain militiamen joined North Carolina Colonel Charles McDowell at his new camp and headquarters located at Cherokee Ford on the Broad River. They were also met by Georgia Colonel Elijah Clarke and South Carolina Lieutenant Colonel James McCall. (Cherokee Ford is located south of where today's US Highway 29 crosses the Broad River east of present-day Gaffney, South Carolina.) McDowell welcomed the newly-arrived militias and explained that his goal was to prevent the British from invading North Carolina. Clarke and McCall, more concerned about reclaiming Georgia and South Carolina, desired action against the Tories who were centered at Ninety Six. They set out to locate General Sumter. The over mountain militias remained with McDowell.[46]

Major General Horatio Gates. Engraver: H. B. Hall, 1862.

Major General Horatio Gates, another "hero" at Saratoga, caught up with Major General Johann de Kalb in North Carolina July 25, 1780. The Continental Congress had appointed Gates on June 13 to replace Major General Benjamin Lincoln as Commander of the Southern Department. General George Washington had given General de Kalb interim command until Gates could arrive. Washington was not consulted on the selection of Gates; he had prepared to recommend Major General Nathanael Greene for the position. Before Gates left his Virginia estate, Major General Charles Lee, who previously had the dubious honor of being Commander of the Southern Department (see Chapter 4), warned Gates, "Beware that your Northern laurels do not change to Southern willows!"[47]

Gates relieved de Kalb from his temporary command and planned to march upon Camden, South Carolina, with the remnants of the army. He moved out on the 27th. However, Whigs in the vicinity of present-day Williamsburg County, South Carolina, made a request before the march could begin. They desired that Lieutenant Colonel Francis Marion be detached from the army to lead their newly-formed militia. Marion and Major Peter Horry met with Major General Horatio Gates and Governor John Rutledge. It was agreed this was a worthwhile opportunity, and Governor Rutledge immediately conferred the rank of Brigadier General of the South Carolina State Troops 2nd Regiment upon Francis Marion, and that of Colonel upon Peter Horry.

In the meantime, Brigadier General Thomas Sumter planned to keep the backcountry British outposts busy, so the garrisons could not assist the British at Camden. On the 30th, Sumter launched an attack with 500 militiamen on the small British outpost at Rocky Mount. He summoned Loyalist provincial Lieutenant Colonel George Turnbull to surrender the fort with his 150-man garrison, but Turnbull refused.

Sumter had thought the large-framed house on the outpost contained only originally-constructed thin clapboard walls; however, it had been fortified with a second wall of logs one foot inside the original walls. The space between had been filled with heavy clay. Sumter ordered an attack as he thought his rifle balls would penetrate, but they did not. The garrison had also installed firing ports and, during the initial action, Colonel Andrew Neil and seven privates of the New Acquisition Militia were killed. Sumter made a few more attempts and then withdrew. Lieutenant William Hillhouse stated in his pension application (see Appendix E):

> Some time in the same month I was called to face my Country's enemy at Rock [sic] Mount, where my brave and beloved Col. Neil was slain. Eight days after, I was in the battle of the Hanging Rock, in which my Captain was severely wounded, and rendered unfit for service. In the heat of the battle I took command of the Company, which command I held until sometime in the April following when I resigned.

Also on the 30th, Colonel Elijah Clarke, Colonel Isaac Shelby, Captain Andrew Hamilton, along with Major Charles Robertson, were dispatched to attack a Tory garrison at Thicketty Fort, also called Anderson's Fort, on Thicketty Creek. The fort was commanded by Captain Patrick Moore. Moore gave up the post without a fight. He and his 93 men were paroled by the Whigs who captured a large supply of arms and ammunition. (Fort Thicketty, also called Fort Anderson, was located southwest of present-day Gaffney, South Carolina, ten miles southwest on State Highway 150. Thicketty Creek must be crossed and a stop made at the bridge over Goucher Creek. Thicketty Fort was three miles west near the north bank of Goucher Creek.)

On August 1, Sumter proceeded to Hanging Rock and put the Loyalist garrison of 500 men commanded by North Carolina Colonel Samuel Bryan under siege. There was considerable exchange of gunfire over the next few days, and on the 6th, Sumter made a successful all-out assault. Many British and Tories were killed and wounded, and 200 were captured. Captain James Jamison of the New Acquisition Militia was wounded. (Much of the ammunition Sumter used at Rocky Mount and Hanging Rock was from the cache defended earlier in the year by Mrs. Jane Black Thomas. A member of Sumter's militia was a 13-year old courier named Andrew Jackson who was captured by the British along with his brother, Robert. They nearly starved to death. When Andrew refused to clean the boots of a British officer, the officer hit him with the dull side of his saber and left a scar that remained for the rest of his life. Andrew and Robert each contracted smallpox while imprisoned, and Robert died shortly after their release. Andrew's other brother, Hugh, had already died at the Battle of Stono Ferry. See Chapter 6.)[48]

British Lieutenant Colonel Nisbet Balfour was reassigned to Charles Town August 1, 1780, and Tory Lieutenant Colonel John Harris Cruger was assigned to take command of the Ninety Six garrison. He did so with 150 Loyalists of DeLancey's Brigade of New York Volunteers, 200 of the 2nd Battalion of New Jersey Volunteers, and 200 South Carolina Tory militiamen.

Shortly after Cruger took command of Ninety Six, Andrew Pickens and Andrew Hamilton (a captain in Pickens' regiment who was also under parole) were arrested and kept in the Ninety Six jail for about one month under guard of Lieutenant Colonel Isaac Allen of the New Jersey Volunteers. The record is clear that Colonel Pickens had accepted and was abiding by parole, but the conditions surrounding the arrest rendered a suspicion that he may have broken parole terms. Therefore, he and Andrew Hamilton joined Colonel John Thomas, Sr., behind bars pending an investigation and/or trial. They were at the mercy of Cruger and Allen because many who had broken parole were hanged immediately upon arrest. However, Cruger was well aware that Cornwallis had a keen interest in coaxing Colonel Andrew Pickens into the British cause. His assistance would be more valuable than Andrew Williamson's in drawing others to serve the Crown. Therefore, he and Hamilton were eventually released.[49] (Colonel Thomas was later transferred to prison in Charles Town until the end of the war. He and his wife, Jane, each died in 1811.) Hamilton stated in his pension application (see Appendix E):

> The deponent further says that he omitted heretofore to mention that Colonel or General Pickens & himself went unaccompanied by others to confer with a Colonel Few from Georgia who had a few troops in the District of Ninety Six, all true Whigs, that when Colonel Pickens & himself (the deponent) were on their road to see Colonel Few, a private [unintelligible] of the Tory stamp directed them to a Camp of British soldiers & Tories by whom Pickens & himself were made prisoners & sent to the Village of Cambridge or Ninety Six, where they remained prisoners one month, under a British officer by the name of Allen, by some means Colonel Pickens obtained his & my release, from imprisonment, while prisoners we were treated with great attention & kindness by the British attributable I believe to the popularity & influence of General Pickens.

The arrest likely occurred after August 1, 1780, when Cruger and Allen moved into Ninety Six. It just as likely occurred prior to August 18 when the Georgians returned home since Hamilton stated he and Andrew had spoken with Colonel Few. Reference Chapter 8 for the following — Andrew Pickens was likely released from jail prior to September 14. He had a conversation with James McCall on that day regarding Pickens rejoining the active militia. Andrew could not have tried to locate Colonel Few after that date. On the 15th the Georgians and McCall put Augusta under siege. There was not a full month following that to coordinate one month of inactivity for Andrew Pickens. The Georgians didn't return to South Carolina until the end of September, and Cruger sent Pickens on an errand of mercy on October 15. The British actively tried to enlist Pickens' services after that date, which left no other period available for a month of imprisonment.

Lieutenant Colonel Francis Lord Rawdon's detachments were spread throughout the backcountry. Rawdon summoned them to Camden to prepare for the advancement of Major General Gates from North Carolina.

Gates encamped 12 miles north of Camden on August 11, 1780. He ordered Sumter to control any crossings on the Catawba River should the British try to withdraw from the ensuing battle in that direction. He ordered Brigadier General Francis Marion and Colonel Peter Horry to do the same with the Santee River and to especially destroy any boats or skiffs that the British might use.

Cornwallis arrived at Camden the next day. The two sides remained encamped for two days as they each prepared for the coming fight. As if they had been coordinated, each army marched toward the other at dusk on the 15th. Cornwallis with 2,000 troops gave Gates with his 3,000 an apparent advantage.

At 2:00 A.M. on the 16th, the vans of each army found one another five miles north of Camden. Each vanguard withdrew to its army without engaging the enemy beyond a slight skirmish from the surprise. The two armies marched on the main Camden to Charlotte road. They met at dawn on the north side of Saunders Creek near where the advance units had met the night before. The battlefield stretched for one mile across the road; contained between two swamps.

If Major General Horatio Gates had any advantage, by virtue of commanding the greater number of men, he proved to be a master at losing it when he poorly set his battle line to face the British. It was a British army tactic to place their most formidable fighting unit on their own right flank; therefore, most opponents customarily placed their best units on their own left flank to offset the British position. Gates, however, set his most poorly trained and least experienced unit, the Virginia militia, opposite the very capable British 23rd Regiment of Foot. In reality, he should not have committed his inexperienced force to that situation. His larger army, especially the militias, was unpracticed in close-order battle.

Each army van had taken a few prisoners during the skirmish the previous evening. Lieutenant Colonel Otho Williams interviewed a few British prisoners and learned that Lieutenant General Charles Lord Cornwallis was leading 2,000 crack troops and was 600 yards in front of the Americans. Williams informed Major General Johann de Kalb of his intelligence before he approached General Gates. General de Kalb told Lieutenant Colonel Williams that the American army should definitely withdraw and await a better opportunity.

Gates seemed stunned and called a council of war. General Gates communicated his news. His officers remained silent. Gates asked, "What is best to be done?"[50] Brigadier General Edward Stevens, who commanded the inexperienced Virginia militia, imprudently replied, "Gentlemen, is it not too late now to do anything but fight?"[51] No other officer challenged the Brigadier and General Williams later reported, "No other advice was offered, and the general desired the gentlemen would repair to their respective commands" to prepare for battle.[52]

Gates' line was anchored by the North Carolina militia posted on the road. On their left, the Virginia militia made up the American left flank which stretched to the swamp 600 yards from the road. Gates posted the Delaware Continentals to the right of the North Carolinians, followed by the Maryland Continentals on the right flank whose extreme reached the swamp 1,200 yards from the road. These Continental regiments, commanded by Major General de Kalb, were crack troops with plenty of experience. However, they were facing the weaker units in the British line. The Americans were further depleted by Gates because he had sent an entire company of the Maryland Continentals to assist Sumter. He also had detached Major William Davie and his fine militia regiment to oversee the evacuation of wounded troops from Hanging Rock and Rocky Mount.

The British posted the 23rd Regiment of Foot to the British right of the road, with a unit of light infantry on their flank. The 33rd Regiment of Foot was set to the British left of the road. Rawdon and his Volunteers of Ireland provincials were left of the 33rd. Next was Lieutenant Colonel Banastre Tarleton's Legion Infantry, with a North Carolina Tory militia unit placed on the left flank. The 71st Regiment of Foot was in reserve to the rear, and Tarleton's Legion dragoons floated as needed.

The 23rd gave three cheers, their custom, and mounted a fearful bayonet charge at the Virginians. The inexperienced Virginia militia immediately turned tail and ran. Most dropped their rifles without firing a shot. That withdrawal left the North Carolina militia to cover the American left flank. They fought hard at first but, when they noticed they were to be overrun, they too withdrew. The Continentals continued to fight, and with the loss of the left flank, the remaining American force was soon completely engulfed.

General Horatio Gates, the hero of Saratoga, got caught up in the retreat of the Virginia militia which he tried to turn for a while. He was on a fast horse and didn't stop until he reached Charlotte, North Carolina, at midnight. After less than two months in the position, and one month on the job, as Commander of the Southern Department, Major General Horatio Gates was done. Major General Charles Lee proved prophetic; General Gates' laurels had indeed turned quickly to willows. General de Kalb fought diligently at Camden in the face of impending defeat and suffered 11 saber gashes that rendered him mortally wounded. Some of the Continentals were able to retreat to Hanging Rock. Tarleton and his Legion were hot on their trail.

The American Continentals, crushed once more, lost 700 killed or wounded and 170 captured. The North Carolina militia lost 100 killed and wounded. Three hundred militiamen were captured. The Virginia militia left the field of battle so quickly, they suffered no casualties. The next day, Major General Gates left Charlotte and made his way to Hillsboro, North Carolina. The British had lost 80 killed and 240 wounded.

Colonel Otho Williams, Adjutant General of the Continental Army, later remarked that two-thirds of the entire American force fled the field without having fired a single shot.[53]

A. L. Pickens, not a professed fan of any of the Commanders of the Southern Department since its inception, and a staunch critic of the lack of wisdom exhibited by the Continental Congress in making the selections, stated: "General Gates superseded DeKalb in the southern department. Came Gates. Came Cornwallis! And then came the disaster of Camden! Oh long-suffering Liberty! Lee! Howe! Lincoln! Now Gates! With what sadness could the mounted militiamen of the Up-country call that roll!"[54]

Colonel William R. Davie remained between North Carolina and Camden with his cavalry. He recovered supply wagons that the Americans had abandoned during their haphazard retreat. Davie reconnoitered the British army and sent messengers to locate General Gates and deliver intelligence.

Davie later wrote of Gates' command decisions at Camden. He specifically noted that the militia, unaccustomed and unable to withstand a severe bayonet charge such as that which opened the battle, were misplaced. He remarked:

> He ought to have pushed forward his light troops with 2 or 3 pieces of artillery and taken possession of that pass ... at this place There is a wide boggy morass passable only by the causeway, and the ground rises considerably on the Northern side — Had the light troops been in possession of this post, their patroles must have given early notice of the Enemys advancing in force The cause way might have been disputed & the light troops supported or withdrawn at pleasure and arrangements made for attack, keeping the Enemy in check, or avoiding a general action could have been easily made
>
> As the recovery of the two Southern States and the security of the remainder depended upon the army then collected it was the grossest folly to stake the whole blindly upon a single throw

of the die; the whole army were necessarily brought into action, the Enemys force was unknown, he might succeed but there was no certain data to calculate this success upon, the want of success was inevitably followed by a total defeat — nothing but the most desperate circumstances could warrant a General to stake so much upon a singel Hazard.

Three fourths of this army were militia, these alone might have been a match for the royal army if properly fought under such advantages as a country covered with woods morasses and broken grounds almost every where affords. There never was a necessity to attack the British army at any particular point or place and the militia always behaved well when served up by detachment, and under the impulse of attack.

The center and left of the front line were composed of militia, these could not be expected to wait the shock of a charge made by regular troops, otherwise discipline would be useless and military tacticks a farce. The consequence was this flank was immediately turned, the whole reserve could [not] have been brought up in time.... DeKalbs Division on the right was of course instantly overwhelmed, and the reserves soon involved in their fate.[55]

Gates tried to keep the remnants of the Southern Department together. He garrisoned 1,000 Continentals at Hillsboro, insufficient numbers for any action against the British. He mustered enough nerve to write to General Washington on August 30, and completed the letter on September 6. He stated: "I shall continue my unwearied endeavors to stop the progress of the enemy ... and recover all our losses in the Southern States. But if being unfortunate is solely a reason sufficient for removing me from command, I shall most cheerfully submit to the orders of Congress."

Washington replied that he was shocked by the affair, but credited the bravery of the Continentals. He was also magnanimous in telling Gates that he was wise to not attempt any action until he would once again be in a position of strength. Meanwhile, Washington began anew to lobby for the general that he had for years wanted to command the Southern Department, Major General Nathanael Greene.[56]

Following his victory at Camden, Cornwallis became keen to work his way north. Granted, he had demolished the Southern Department. He still, however, talked of leaving the colony in the hands of the Loyalists because of the formidable combined Whig militia force that operated throughout South Carolina. He painted rosy pictures whenever he wrote General Clinton. Clinton wanted his subordinate to take his time and gain firm control of the colony before he moved on. That meant the rebels had to be either appeased or deftly handled, but they were not yet at either stage. In fact, the British and the Loyalists consistently continued to rile the Whig militia forces.

British Major James Wemyss had been a particular problem. He often used excessive force against civilians. He declared that the Presbyterian congregations were seditious and assumed all Presbyterians were, if not militiamen, at least active supporters of rebellion against the Anglican Church. He proceeded to burn Presbyterian buildings as he encountered them.

On August 18, 1780, Lieutenant General Charles Lord Cornwallis issued an order to Lieutenant Colonel John Harris Cruger at Ninety Six to make sure he understood in no uncertain terms that he was expected to bring the backcountry under control. The order read in part:

> I have given orders that all the inhabitants of this Province, who had submitted, and who have taken part in this revolt should be punished with the greatest rigor ... they should be imprisoned, and their whole property taken from them ... that every militiaman who had borne arms with us, and had afterwards joined the enemy, should be immediately hanged ... you will take the most vigorous measures to extinguish the rebellion, in the district in which you command ... you will obey, in the strictest manner, the directions I have given in this letter.[57]

Also on the 18th, Lieutenant Colonel Banastre Tarleton and his Legion stopped chasing the surviving Continentals from Camden and turned his attention to a more serious matter—Brigadier General Thomas Sumter and his huge militia force. Sumter had withdrawn to Fishing Creek (near and north of present-day Great Falls, South Carolina) once he heard that Gates had been badly beaten.

Tarleton intercepted Sumter's baggage train and gained intelligence on his location. The Legion infantry numbered 60 and was ordered to ride double with some of the 100 Legion dragoons to hurry the march toward Sumter. Tarleton attacked the Whig band at dawn. First, he managed to capture Sumter's pickets, and then he launched a surprise attack on the Whigs who were just rousing from sleep. The battle was short and one-sided. Sumter lost 150 killed and 300 captured. Tarleton suffered a total of 16 killed and wounded. Sumter escaped and withdrew to Charlotte, North Carolina. Tarleton was able to rescue 150 Tory prisoners that the Whigs had captured in previous encounters. He also garnered 800 horses for his dragoons, 1,000 rifles and muskets, two grasshopper cannons, and 46 wagons.

South Carolina's exiled Governor, John Rutledge, joined General Gates at Hillsboro and tried to communicate with the active militias from there. He wanted to divide the state under the auspices of the militias: Francis Marion on the coast, Thomas Sumter in the middle, and Andrew Pickens in the backcountry. That would have to wait. Pickens was still honoring his parole, and Sumter was now in exile in North Carolina with a reduced force.[58]

Colonel Charles McDowell relocated his militia force from Cherokee Ford, about ten miles downstream on the Broad River, to Smith's Ford. They needed a new area for forage as they had been stationed at Cherokee Ford for some time. The over mountain militiamen were nearing the end of their musters, and the leaders, Colonels Isaac Shelby and John Sevier, wanted a last foray before they returned to their own settlements.

McDowell had learned that Major Patrick Ferguson and his provincial force were operating around Fair Forest, and that 200 Tories were encamped at Musgrove's Mill (near present-day Cross Anchor, South Carolina) on the Enoree River. The Tory camp was on the south bank overlooking a rocky shoal.

McDowell dispatched 200 militiamen led by Colonel James Williams with a company of South Carolinians. Williams was accompanied by Colonel Elijah Clarke with his Georgia men, and Colonel Isaac Shelby with a contingent of the wild riflemen from the over mountain communities. (It was customary when officers of identical rank were involved in the same action that command fell upon the officer from the state and the vicinity of the action.)

Early on the morning of August 18, a scouting party ran into a Tory patrol near the mill. A skirmish ensued, and two Tories escaped back to their camp to warn the officers. In the meantime, some local Whig sympathizers told the patriots that Lieutenant Colonel Alexander Innes had ridden into the camp on the 17th with 200 provincials and 100 Tory militiamen. They were on their way to meet up with Ferguson and would rest at camp for the night.

When Williams and the other Colonels heard of Innes' arrival, and that the Tory camp had been apprised of the Whigs' coming, they decided to prepare a defense. The Americans quickly built a berm of dirt, logs, and brush in a semicircle near the top of a rise just out of view of the enemy. Georgia Captain Shadrick (sometimes Shadrack) Inman led a 25-man patrol near the enemy camp to feign confusion. Once they were spotted by Innes and his troops, they wheeled around and ran as if trying to escape.

Inman successfully led Innes into the semicircle entrapment and a furious battle ensued. At first, the over mountain militiamen under Shelby stationed on the right had to give way under a severe bayonet charge. While in retreat, one of the wild riflemen turned, fired, and knocked Innes from his saddle. William Smith, a private under Shelby, yelled, "I have killed their commander!"[59] Shelby rallied the men; they raised their horrendous Indian yell and charged the enemy with hatchets, knives, and sabers and forced them back in a successful counterattack. The Tories withdrew and were constantly pressed by the Whigs. Captain Shadrick Inman was killed in the skirmish.

Colonel James Williams strongly held the center of defense during several attacks that allowed the over mountain men to counterattack from the flanks until the enemy was overcome. The yells and screams of the retreating provincials and Tory militiamen, intermingled with the yells and screams of the pursuing over mountain militiamen, and the groans of the wounded and dying, were "terrific and heartrending in the extreme."[60]

The British lost 63 killed (including Innes), 90 wounded, and 70 captured; the Americans lost four killed (including Inman) and fewer than 10 wounded. Shelby and Clarke considered moving on to an attack at Ninety Six, but after a messenger brought news of Gates' defeat at Camden and of Cornwallis' move into the area, they decided to return home. They realized that Major Ferguson would soon try to cut them off with an angled route from Fair Forest, and that Lieutenant Colonel John Harris Cruger would join in a chase from Ninety Six as soon as he heard the news.

Colonel Elijah Clarke returned to Georgia to gain a new muster of militiamen. He did not expect to fail once he reported the success at Musgrove's Mill. Colonels Shelby and Sevier hurriedly retreated over the mountains to their home communities with the same outcome in mind as Clarke. They, in fact, met Colonel Charles McDowell and his militia near Gilbert Town (present-day Rutherfordton), North Carolina. Colonel Shelby recommended, and the others agreed, that they assemble a large army from both sides of the mountain, large enough to deal with Ferguson. Colonel McDowell consented to keep an eye on Ferguson while the musters were being developed. The day after the battle, Major Ferguson dispatched Tory Captain Abraham De Peyster with a company of men to catch the over mountain men, but his effort was too late. Colonel Shelby and the others were gone.

South Carolina Colonel James Williams marched the prisoners from the battle to Hillsboro, North Carolina, where he turned them over to General Gates. Governor Rutledge met with Williams and immediately promoted him to Brigadier General in the South Carolina State Troops as a result of his sterling performance as commander of the battle.

After Gates was crushed at Camden on August 16, 1780, and Sumter's forces were handed a similar fate at Fishing Creek by Lieutenant Colonel Banastre Tarleton's Legion dragoons on the 18th, Colonel McDowell disbanded his gathering of militias and retreated over the mountains to his home at Quaker Meadows.[61]

Once Brigadier General Francis Marion and Colonel Peter Horry left Gates for their new assignment, Marion organized a brigade on August 16. The next day, he sent Colonel Peter Horry to march on Georgetown while Marion, himself, went to the upper Santee to implement Gates' plan. On the 19th, Marion heard of the defeat at Camden. He then received a message that a company of 90 British soldiers was marching prisoners captured at Camden to Charles Town, and that they were taking the route toward Nelson's Ferry on the Santee. He was advised that the force was encamped on the east side of the river at Sumter's abandoned plantation on the Great Savannah of the Santee. The road from there to the ferry crossed a large swamp at a pass over Horse Creek.

Before daylight on the 20th, Marion positioned Colonel Hugh Horry and 16 militiamen beyond the pass. Once the enemy was on the pass, Marion, with 12 men, attacked the rear. It was an easy victory for the Americans. Marion wrote Peter Horry on the 27th: "On the 20th inst. I attacked a guard of the 63rd and Prince of Wales Regiments, with a number of Tories, at the Great Savannah, near Nelson's Ferry; killed and took twenty-two regulars, and two Tories prisoners, and retook [meaning released] one hundred and fifty Continentals of the Maryland line ... our loss was one killed."[62]

He also informed Horry of Gates' defeat at Camden. (Nelson's Ferry was located under present-day Lake Marion north of present-day Eutawville, South Carolina. The Prince of Wales American Regiment was a provincial force. The 63rd Regiment of Foot was a regiment from Ireland known as the Bloodsuckers.)

On the 23rd, Major Patrick Ferguson went to Camden and conferred with General Cornwallis. The Commander explained that he was ready to invade North Carolina and would expect Ferguson and his provincials to move north on his left flank. Ferguson would protect Cornwallis from any Whig action on that side and would raid Whig estates to supply the main army with provisions during the march. Ferguson slowly moved his brigade northward on September 2 to be in position to support the main army as requested.

On September 4, Marion heard that a force of 200 Tories was marching down the Little Pee Dee River in an attempt to capture him. He, with 50 men, decided to initiate the action, so they surprised the Tory vanguard with an attack. The van fell back to the main Tory regiment. Marion led his militia to an open sandy plot called Blue Savannah. It was west of the Little Pee Dee and was surrounded by scrub pines. He secured his men in the trees and awaited the Tory charge. When the Tories entered the open area, the Whigs opened fire from their impenetrable position and inflicted a heavy loss upon them. Marion's force suffered no losses in the exchange.[63]

In spite of a few setbacks, General Cornwallis was confident that the situation had generally gone his way. He busily prepared his foray unaware that everything would soon drastically change.

8

It Comes Apart for Britain (1780)

Lieutenant General Charles Lord Cornwallis was eager to move into North Carolina after the British victories over Major General Horatio Gates at Camden and Brigadier General Thomas Sumter at Fishing Creek. Cornwallis had met with Major Patrick Ferguson on August 23, 1780, to explain that the fall campaign would begin with the army's march to Charlotte, North Carolina. He had also determined that Ferguson would disjoin from the army and take his detachment into North Carolina to the west of Charlotte. There Ferguson would guard Cornwallis' left flank, harass and punish active local Whigs, raid Whig farms for supplies, and deliver the supplies to the army. He would also recruit Tories to comprise local militia regiments and also to supplement his own provincial force.

Ferguson left Fair Forest Creek on September 2, and on September 8, General Cornwallis marched his army out of Camden. The General enthusiastically headed for Charlotte, North Carolina; however, his force was weakened as several men were down with malaria. He also missed Lieutenant Colonel Banastre Tarleton who was ill with yellow fever. Cornwallis ordered Tarleton's Legion to remain with their leader and protect him from Whig capture. Cornwallis wrote two separate messages to Lieutenant Colonel Nisbet Balfour about Tarleton's illness and how it inconvenienced the General. He lost Tarleton's services; the British Legion was useless because it had to protect Tarleton from Whig attacks, and they were unable to demolish Thomas Sumter's militia while it was yet being organized.

Illnesses were a huge concern for the British. Summer in the southern campaign had been devastating since the fall of Charles Town. The humidity, heavy rains and mud, bugs, and reptiles, and other vermin had taken their toll on the forces. Moreover, the two mosquito-borne ailments had depleted the roster, and the ever-reliable Lieutenant Colonel Banastre Tarleton was suffering.

Historians typically confuse the two diseases and often use them interchangeably. There are, however, considerable differences.

Yellow fever is caused by a virus that is spread by mosquitoes. This severe disease results in death for 20 to 50 percent of those who develop it in the present-day and usually occurs within two weeks from the start of infection. Complications during the toxic phase of a yellow fever infection include kidney and liver failure, jaundice, abdominal pain with vomiting (sometimes of blood), heart arrhythmia, bleeding from the eyes and nose, and brain abnormalities including delirium, seizures, and coma. Survivors recover gradually over a period of several weeks to months, and they sometimes experience secondary bacterial infections, such as pneumonia or blood infections.

Malaria is caused by a parasite transmitted by mosquitoes. A malaria infection is generally characterized by recurrent attacks of chills and fever, profuse sweating with dropping body temperature, headache, nausea, vomiting, and diarrhea. The signs and symptoms of malaria typically last for several weeks; however, some malaria parasites can lie dormant in the body for months, or even years.

Given the difference in the quality of medical care, the fatality rate and duration of illness for these two diseases was likely far worse in 1780 than noted above.

Major Patrick Ferguson arrived at Gilbert Town (present-day Rutherfordton), North Carolina, on September 7. He camped on a hill that overlooked Gilbert Town from the west, later referred to as Ferguson's Hill (present-day Ferguson's Ridge). Ferguson was an experienced British military officer with an excellent service record. He had been assigned to several command positions and was eager to embark upon his new assignment. He was aware of the over mountain (or backwater) settlements and knew they could pose a threat to Cornwallis' flank. On the 10th, the Major tried to secure that flank as ordered by the General. He paroled prisoner Samuel Phillips, cousin to Isaac Shelby, with a message for the over mountain men. Ferguson told them to stay on their side of the mountain and "desist from their opposition to the British arms, and take protection under his standard." If they did not, he threatened to "march over the mountains, hang their leaders, and lay their country waste with fire and sword."[1]

On the 12th, Ferguson took a detachment to try and locate Colonel Charles McDowell; however, McDowell had evacuated the area and crossed over the mountains to locate Colonels Isaac Shelby and John Sevier. Samuel Phillips found Colonel Shelby at his home in the Holston settlements and reported Ferguson's warning. Shelby then located Colonel Sevier in the Nolichucky settlements, and together they decided they could not allow Ferguson to get away with his threat. Sevier began to look for McDowell whom he knew to be in the vicinity. Shelby agreed to contact Washington County, Virginia, Colonel William Campbell. Shelby and Sevier were laying plans to set up a massive rendezvous to take place in the near future.

Colonel Shelby's home was at Shelby's Fort (located on the South Fork Holston River near present-day Bristol, Tennessee, then a part of Virginia) near Samuel Phillips' home. Colonel Sevier's abode was on the banks of the Nolichucky River (10 miles south of present-day Jonesborough, Tennessee, then also claimed by Virginia). Colonel Campbell lived near a salt lick 60 miles further up the South Fork Holston River from Shelby (near present-day Marion, Virginia).

It was likely that Andrew Pickens and Andrew Hamilton were released from the Ninety Six jail (see Chapter 7) during the same time period. Lieutenant Colonel James McCall thought that Pickens' imprisonment might sway him, so he tried to convince the Colonel to forego his parole and take command of the militia. That discussion occurred before McCall departed for Georgia to aid Colonel Elijah Clarke with an attack on Augusta that would begin on the 14th. McCall had wanted to raise 500 men, including Colonel Andrew Pickens, for the action, but he only mustered 80 — and no Pickens. Andrew explained that he had given his word to abide by parole, and that as long as the British kept their end of the agreement, he was honor bound to do the same.

Lieutenant Colonel Thomas Brown still commanded the British outpost at Augusta, Georgia, and Colonel Clarke wanted to oust him. The outpost was heavily involved in Indian trade which further endangered the safety of Whig settlements in backcountry Georgia. Clarke, McCall, and Major Samuel Taylor of Thomas Sumter's South Carolina militia

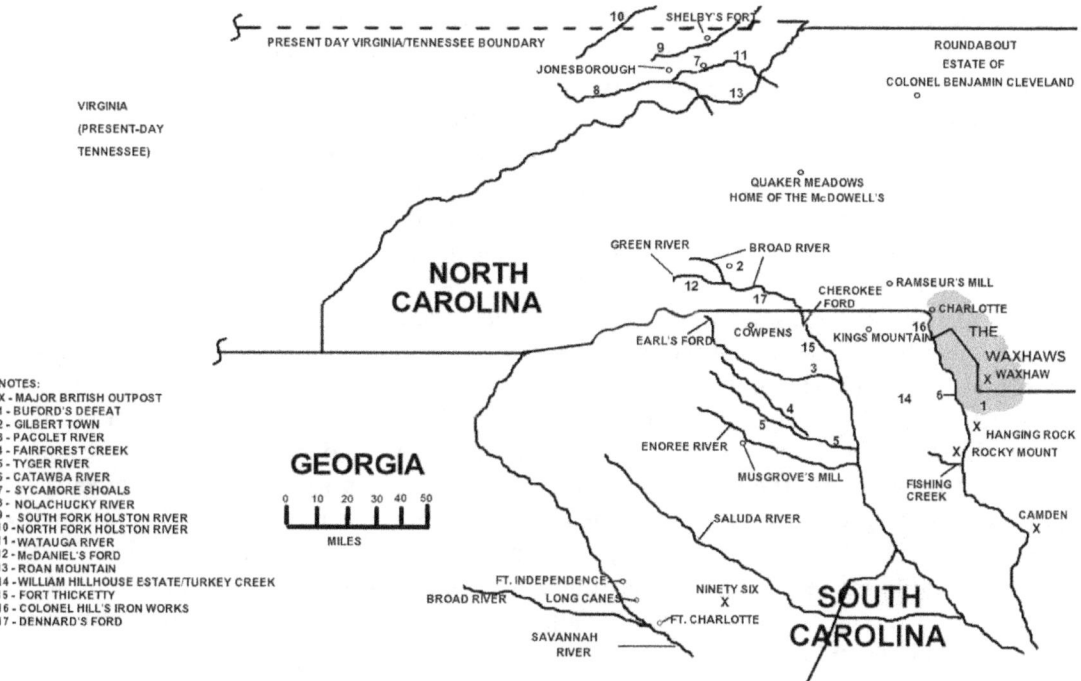

Battle of Kings Mountain points of interest.

brigade put Augusta under siege with 500 militiamen on the 14th. Clarke, counting on greater success from McCall, had hoped for a force twice that size.

Brown was in a severe position. As Clarke approached, he moved quickly to The White House, a fortified trading post on the primary Savannah road. Brown's 150 King's Carolina Rangers, a provincial force, were supplemented by 200 Cherokee braves. Brown requested reinforcements in a message to Lieutenant Colonel John Harris Cruger at Ninety Six. Cruger and a company of provincials reached the Savannah River on the 18th and prepared to cross. Clarke quickly raised the siege and withdrew to avoid being trapped. The fighting had been intensive. Brown had been severely wounded and was confined to his bed. Several wounded Whig militiamen left behind were captured after Clarke withdrew.

Brown had already captured 26 men, and before Cruger could cross the river to stop him, he had 13 of them brought to The White House, including Captain Anthony Ashby of Pickens' old regiment. Brown had ordered his bed be moved into a foyer, and he watched as Ashby and the other 12 men were hanged from the stairwell. Brown was running out of time, so he turned the remaining 13 captives over to the Indians to be taken away, tortured, and killed by tomahawk. Cruger then chased after the fleeing Whig militiamen and captured 21. He held them as prisoners at Ninety Six for five months; then, he issued paroles.[2]

Cruger detached provincials to Ferguson. They would enhance his effort against the active Whigs as described in a September 1780 diary entry of Lieutenant Anthony Allaire, Ferguson's Adjutant, "Wednesday, 20th. Got in motion at six o'clock in the morning, and marched a mile and a half to one White's plantation, where we joined Maj. Ferguson again. This day three officers belonging to Cruger and Allen's regiments, joined us from Ninety Six, with fifty militia men."[3]

On the 22nd, Cornwallis received a report that Tarleton felt better and expected to take the field in short order. He ordered Major Archibald McArthur and his 71st Regiment of Foot to protect Tarleton until he fully recovered. Meanwhile, Colonel Elijah Clarke realized that the Georgia backcountry Tories were in complete control. He knew that Whig families were not safe, especially those of the militia leaders. Clarke gathered 700 Whigs, 300 of them militiamen and the rest family members, and left Georgia for the safety of the over mountain settlements. He was aware that backcountry South Carolina contained many dangers. A large party of Whigs would stand out and invite an attack by the Tory militias. Clarke decided to take a high country route through the mountains near the 1777 Cherokee boundary.

Allaire then continued in his journal, "Sunday, 24th. Five hundred subjects came in, also a number of ladies. Received intelligence from Col. Cruger, that he had marched from Ninety Six to Augusta, to the assistance of Col. Browne, who was besieged by six hundred Rebels, under the command of Col. Clarke."[4] The 500 that Allaire said came into camp consisted of 250 North Carolina Tory militiamen; the remainder were family members.

After he heard of the action at Augusta, Lieutenant William Stevenson of Major Patrick Ferguson's brigade wrote regarding the aftermath, "Several of whom they immediately hanged, and have a great many more yet to hang. We have now got a method that will soon put an end to the rebellion in a short time, by hanging every man that has taken protection, and is found acting against us."[5] Clinton's orders to bring the Whigs under control were seemingly in full force.

Cruger's note independently complimented Cornwallis' orders to Ferguson. The General instructed Ferguson to capture Clarke should the Georgian avoid Cruger's troops as they passed through Ninety Six. Ferguson began to patrol the area near Gilbert Town where he actively recruited militiamen while keeping a keen eye peeled for Clarke and company. Shortly thereafter, Ferguson heard that Clarke was moving into North Carolina further to the west, so he decided to set an ambush at McDaniel's Ford on Greene River. The movement was described by Allaire:

> Wednesday, 27th. Got in motion at five o'clock in the morning, and marched three miles to Rucker's Mill, and halted.... Thursday, 28th. Got in motion at five o'clock in the morning; marched seven miles to Mountain creek, forded it, although very difficult, continued on about a mile farther to Twitty's Ford of Broad river, and took up our ground on its banks. At six o'clock in the evening got in motion, forded the river; marched two miles to McDaniel's Ford of Green river; forded it, and marched two miles farther; halted on the road; lay on our arms till four o'clock the next morning.... Friday, 29th. We then, at that early hour, moved on three miles to one James Step's plantation, and halted. This man has been very unfortunate in his family; his wife, who is a very decent woman, was caught by the Indians about a twelvemonth past. They scalped and tomahawked her several times in the head, treated the infant she had in her arms in a most inhuman and savage manner. They mashed its head in such a manner that its recovery is truly astonishing; but what this poor, unhappy woman seems most to regret is the loss of her oldest son, whom the savages took, and she now remains in a state of uncertainty, not having heard from him since.... Saturday, 30th. Lay at James Step's with an expectation of intercepting Col. Clarke on his return to the mountains; but he was prudent enough to take another route.[6]

Ferguson, after he found that Clarke was even further west, also learned that the over mountain militias had gathered again, en masse, and were headed in his direction. He then decided to forget about Colonel Elijah Clarke and return to fulfill his original orders to cover Cornwallis' flank. On the 30th, he headed for a juncture with the General at Charlotte. Cornwallis had arrived and established his headquarters there on September 26.[7]

Brigadier General Francis Marion saw action at Black Mingo Creek. The British had decided to create a small garrison near their major outpost at Georgetown. British Colonel John Coming Ball of that garrison, with a detachment of 200 men, encamped in a field at Dollard's Tavern (called Red House) outside of Willtown, South Carolina (near present-day Rhems, 20 miles northwest of Georgetown). Shortly before midnight, Marion's van crossed the wooden bridge over Black Mingo Creek. The sound of their crossing alerted Colonel Ball's sentries, and they began to fire warning shots.

Marion, with 150 men, decided to immediately press the attack. The British were confused, and within 15 minutes were beaten and had dispersed through the nearby swamp. Marion lost 71 killed, and the British lost 74 killed, including Colonel Ball. Brigadier General Marion buried his dead militiamen 500 yards south of Shepherd's Ferry. He also buried the dead British soldiers at the Red House where they had camped. (Some sources record this event as being on the 28th and others the 29th, because the short battle spanned from just before midnight to just after. The South Carolina historical marker, as well as other sources, states the action occurred on the 14th.)[8]

When Samuel Phillips delivered Ferguson's message to his brother-in-law, Isaac Shelby, at Shelby's Fort, he also provided intelligence regarding the strength and make-up of Ferguson's force. He added that one of Ferguson's Loyalist troops had been caught, tarred, and feathered by some of Captain Robert Sevier's light-horse militia in the Nolichucky settlements (Robert was Colonel John Sevier's brother). The Tory offered to guide Ferguson and his force through the passes to the over mountain settlements.

This was too much of a threat to the backwater communities. It was time to muster the large over mountain militia to deal with Major Patrick Ferguson as Shelby had recommended six weeks earlier when they had retreated to their homes following the Battle of Musgrove's Mill (see Chapter 7).

The Whig militia planned the rendezvous for September 25 at Sycamore Shoals on the Watauga River (site of the great council and Treaty between the settlers and the Cherokee in 1775—see Chapter 7). Colonel Shelby sent his brother, Captain Moses Shelby, with an invitation for Colonel William Campbell of the Washington County, Virginia, militia to participate in the gathering. Campbell was not receptive at first. He was busy vying with Tories and Indians around his home. They had been roiled by Cornwallis to harass the Whigs of the area prior to Cornwallis' planned invasion.

Colonel Campbell called a council of war with his officers. They agreed to assist with the proactive effort to attack the British while still in South Carolina. Campbell then decided he would split his force and leave one-half of the militia to defend their home area. He next sent a message to Wilkes County North Carolina Regiment Colonel Benjamin Cleveland that invited his participation and advised him to meet at Quaker Meadows, the home of Colonel Charles McDowell. Colonel Cleveland owned an estate called Roundabout in Wilkes County, North Carolina (at present-day Ronda less than 10 miles northeast of North Wilkesboro, North Carolina).

On September 25, 1780, Colonels Isaac Shelby and John Sevier arrived at Sycamore Shoals with 200 militiamen each. They were greeted by North Carolina Colonels Charles McDowell and Andrew Hampton who had been camped at the shoals for several days with 450 men between them. Early the next day, Colonel William Campbell appeared with 200 more men to total 1,050. The Colonels had assembled a magnificent throng. A militiaman dressed for service in his customary home-made hunting attire of cotton breeches, buckskin or flannel shirt and broad-brimmed leather or 'coonskin hat. He carried his rifle (squirreling gun), and toted a hunting knife and tomahawk as well. He packed his saddle bags with coffee, journey cakes, jerky, parched corn, dried pumpkin, and a tin cup and tied a blanket roll behind his saddle. The British military, and likely the Continental Army, would have laughed at the sight. What could an army of rag-a-muffins do without a wagon caravan of supplies?

Colonel Sevier's troops included John Crockett, father of frontiersman Davy Crockett. (John Crockett lived on the Nolichucky River at the present-day site of Davy Crockett Birthplace State Park near present-day Limestone, Tennessee, five miles southwest of Jonesborough. Davy Crockett, born in 1786, was named after his paternal grandfather. The elder Crockett was killed by Cherokee braves in 1777 at his home on the lower Holston River near present-day Rogersville, Tennessee, 30 miles west of Jonesborough. The Indians were led by War Chief Dragging Canoe as he made good on his threat made at Sycamore Shoals.)

Shortly after Campbell's arrival on the 26th, the group prepared to march. Local missionary Reverend L. Samuel Doak invoked God to protect the settlements, and those within, while the men were away. A day of reckoning was coming.

The militiamen marched 20 miles the first day to Roan Mountain (located in present-day eastern Tennessee). Colonel McDowell quickly formed an advance party and crossed the mountains ahead of the march to gain intelligence. He also contacted Colonel Cleveland and suggested he quicken his pace to Quaker Meadows.

While on Roan Mountain, James Crawford and Samuel Chambers of Colonel Sevier's force deserted during the night and headed for Ferguson's known camp at Gilbert Town, North Carolina.

On the 27th, the main force tarried to slaughter some beeves and jerk more meat for the journey. They continued the march on the 28th, but decided to alter the route because of the deserters and even split into two segments for a time. They arrived at Quaker Meadows on the 30th. Colonel Charles and Major Joe McDowell allowed the throng to rest. Shortly thereafter Colonel Benjamin Cleveland arrived with Surry County North Carolina Militia Colonel Joseph Winston and 350 men. Manpower then totaled 1,400. (Winston was a first cousin of Virginia statesman Patrick Henry.)

Colonel Cleveland was known as the "Terror of the Tories," a well-earned sobriquet. Two Tories once looted the home of his Patriot friend, George Wilfong. The Tories had used Wilfong's clothesline to spook his horses. When Cleveland captured the Tories, he hanged them with the same clothesline. Captain William Riddle, a Tory company leader, kidnapped Cleveland in revenge. Cleveland managed to escape. He gathered his men, captured Riddle and two others, and hanged all three from the same tree, which became known as the "Tory Oak."

The additional force of men who had arrived with Colonels Cleveland and Winston camped just 16 miles from Gilbert Town on October 2, 1780. They remained for the day to take shelter from heavy rains. The large group of top-ranking officers held a council of war and decided, since action was imminent, they needed an overall commander to take charge during battle. They selected Colonel William Campbell to take overall command of the force, and they agreed that any major decisions when not under duress would be made by the council.

On the 3rd, the troops prepared to march from their camp and engage Major Patrick Ferguson at Gilbert Town. Colonel Benjamin Cleveland addressed the rank and file. During his address he stated:

> The enemy is at hand, and we must [be] up and at them. Now is the time for every man of you to do his country a priceless service — such as shall lead your children to exult ... their fathers

were the conquerors of Ferguson. When the pinch comes, I shall be with you. But if any of you shrink from sharing in the battle and the glory, you can now have the opportunity of backing out, and leaving; and you may have a few minutes for considering the matter. You who wish to back out will, when the word is given, march three steps to the rear and stand.[9]

A smiling Major Joseph McDowell added, "Well, my good fellows, what kind of story will you, who back out, have to relate when you get home, leaving your braver comrades to fight the battle and gain the victory?"[10]

Colonel Shelby then added to Colonel Cleveland's instructions, "You have all been informed of the offer. You who desire to decline it, will, when the word is given, march three steps to the rear, and stand, prior to which a few more minutes will be granted you for consideration."[11] Following a period of silence, the commanders of each unit gave the order. None of the 1,400 crawfished.

Crawford and Chambers, who had deserted from Colonel Sevier's company, arrived at Gilbert Town on September 30 and reported to Tory Captain James Dunlap. Dunlap sent a message to Ferguson at McDaniel's Ford on Greene River. The message reported the intelligence Dunlap had received from the turncoats, "McDowell and Shelby were collecting men to return over the mountains ... their large partys will not fall short of 1,000."[12] Major Ferguson read the message and left McDaniel's Ford on Greene River immediately after he wrote to Cornwallis and asked for help from Tarleton's Legion dragoons. Ferguson was weary and eager to join General Cornwallis. He spent October 4 and 5 camped 35 miles from Charlotte, in the area south of present-day Shelby, North Carolina.

On the 4th, Major Ferguson was visited by a mysterious local man described as "elderly" who represented himself as a die-hard Loyalist. The Major, camped within a Tory stronghold, was impressed by the man's demeanor and explained that he had sent a message to Cornwallis asking for reinforcements. He further told the man that he had, "selected my ground [speaking of Kings Mountain] and I defy God Almighty, and all the rebels out of hell to overcome me."[13] Ferguson had decided to stand his ground against the over mountain men at Kings Mountain until the reinforcements arrived. There on the 5th, he penned a desperate letter to Cornwallis which read in part, "I am on my march toward you by a road from Cherokee Ford north of King's [sic] Mountain. 3 or 400 good soldiers part dragoons would finish the business. Something must be done soon.... If your Lordship should be pleased not to supersede me by sending a superior officer, it will be an addition to the obligations I owe you."[14]

Major Patrick Ferguson was an anguished man. Only 35 miles from Charlotte and the safety of Cornwallis' headquarters, he received a return dispatch from Cornwallis that ordered him to rejoin the main army posthaste. Ferguson despaired as he believed his movement to Charlotte would conflict with his responsibility to guard Cornwallis' left flank from the Whigs. Allaire recorded, "Friday, 6th. Got in motion at four o'clock in the morning, and marched sixteen miles to Little King's [sic] Mountain, where we took up our ground."[15]

As he trekked northward, Colonel Elijah Clarke encountered a militia unit on its way to join Shelby's force. The militiamen informed him of a decent pass to the Watauga settlements. In return Clarke detached 30 of his men under Major William Candler to join the foray against Ferguson.[16]

The over mountain militiamen were disappointed they had not caught Ferguson at Gilbert Town. Colonel Charles McDowell was selected to head northeast to locate the Continental Army and invite them to participate. He left his brother, Major Joe McDowell, to lead the Burke County Regiment.

The Whigs were convinced that Ferguson, given the direction of his travel, was headed for Ninety Six. The troops resumed their march early on October 4; they hoped to catch Ferguson before he reached that stronghold. When they approached Dennard's Ford on the Broad River (southeast of present-day Forest City, North Carolina), they lost his trail. Ferguson had spread the rumor around Gilbert Town that he was en route to Ninety Six because he wanted the over mountain men to remain confused about his direction. Shelby's men picked up the Major's trail downstream of Dennard's Ford and observed that Ferguson continued to follow the Broad which runs nearly west to east at that location, an obvious sign he was not headed for Ninety Six.

Many of the men had become footsore, and their horses were beginning to wear down. The colonels held council in the vicinity of Dennard's Ford and decided to leave those men and horses that were in poor shape. Colonel Cleveland, who remained with the stragglers, was ordered to follow as quickly as possible. Colonel Campbell, with the healthier half of the force, 700 mounted men, continued the march from Dennard's Ford early on October 6. Before Campbell and his force departed, Clarke's 30-man Georgia detachment (under Major Candler and Captain Stephen Johnson) joined the group. The main throng rode twenty miles and arrived at Cowpens, South Carolina, that afternoon. They camped where a great battle would take place three months later.

(This is not the present-day town of Cowpens, but the location of Cowpens National Battlefield.) Colonel Cleveland arrived later in the day with the rest of the force. Cowpens was a sparse forest of oak, hickory, chestnut and maple trees owned by a wealthy man named Saunders. Drovers used that area, one of many backcountry tracts named Cowpens, to hold, brand, and feed cattle in the spring. Once the cattle were fattened, the drovers herded them to East Coast markets. That particular spot was often referred to as Hannah's Cowpens, named for an earlier settler who had either owned or used the pasture.

Saunders, a Tory, had heard of the over mountain men's approach and took to his bed. The Whig militia rousted Saunders from his feigned sickbed and questioned him. He truthfully replied that Ferguson had not passed through Cowpens, a further indication to the backwater men that Ferguson was not on his way to Ninety Six. The group bivouacked and feasted on Saunders' cattle and corn.[17]

Meanwhile, another group was on its way to the same area. Governor Rutledge promoted James Williams to Brigadier General when Williams delivered the prisoners from the Battle of Musgrove's Mill to Major General Gates at Hillsboro, North Carolina (see Chapter 7.) Though a South Carolina militia officer, Williams approached North Carolina Governor Abner Nash for 100 men to be the core of his militia. Nash agreed.

Williams also recruited Colonel Thomas Brandon who fought with him at Musgrove's Mill. He later added Major Samuel Hammond who had been trained by Andrew Pickens in the Ninety Six militia. Williams' militia located a detachment of Sumter's men camped on the South Fork Catawba River northeast of Charlotte. Colonels Edward Lacey and William Hill commanded Sumter's militiamen.

There was notable animosity between Williams and Sumter, seemingly derived from jealousies over their respective ranks. That animus carried over to their subordinates. Sumter's men would not cooperate with Williams. From the beginning, the new Brigadier General tried to demand his rights as a general to lead the group southward to face Ferguson. Lacey and Hill intended to find Brigadier General William Davidson. Davidson led a North Carolina militia effort to harass British soldiers and Tories north of Charlotte and disrupt Cornwallis' march northward.

On October 5, the "elderly" man that had visited Ferguson rode into Williams,' Lacey's, and Hill's camp with intelligence about Ferguson and Kings Mountain. Once Lacey and Hill received the message regarding the backwater men and their effort to confront Ferguson, they decided to travel toward Cowpens. They traveled separately from Brigadier General Williams and camped several hundred yards away from his force. They were joined by another group, a North Carolina militia unit from the west (near present-day Tryon), commanded by Colonel Frederick Hambright. Additional South Carolina militia, led by Major William Chronicle, joined them as well. The only way they could continue their march would be if the North Carolinians, Sumter's detachment, and William's militia each were responsible to their own leader.

Brigadier General Williams dispatched a spy, Joseph Kerr who was described as crippled from birth, to gather more intelligence. Kerr found Ferguson's camp in a Tory stronghold a few miles from Kings Mountain. Kerr had no problem passing himself off as a local Tory, especially with his handicap (likely a malformed leg).

Williams' and Hill's differences continued until they arrived at Cowpens on October 6, 1780, with a combined force of 400 men. The over mountain militiamen could not assign comprehensive command to the higher-ranking Williams without a major in-house rebellion. The decision was made to reconfirm Colonel William Campbell as the overall leader. Joseph Kerr, the "crippled" man who had visited Ferguson's camp, rode into Cowpens and informed the Colonels of the intelligence he had obtained. The Colonels, under the leadership of Campbell, began to make their plans. The Georgia detachment was assigned to James Williams' militia.

(Colonel William Hill, in his memoirs, spent several pages leveling indictments against the honor of James Williams. He charged that Williams misrepresented his responsibilities at Musgrove's Mill to Rutledge to gain the promotion, that Williams challenged the promotion given to Thomas Sumter by his men when Governor Rutledge was unavailable, and that he misrepresented his efforts regarding the march against Ferguson. The latter charge stated that Williams allegedly made the rounds of all the Colonels in an attempt to convince them that Ferguson was headed for Ninety Six. This was supposedly an effort to free his homeland from Cruger. This will be further discussed after the account of the battle.)[18]

On the evening of October 6, 1780, Major Patrick Ferguson organized his force on Kings Mountain. He prepared to make a stand against the combined patriot militias led by the over mountain men under Colonel William Campbell. He walked among the exhausted men in his camp and repeated his declaration to inspire them by firmly stating that he was "on Kings Mountain, that I am king of that mountain and God Almighty and all the Rebels of hell can not drive me from it."[19]

Ferguson was a brave soldier and quite an intelligent engineer. He developed the Ferguson breech-loading ball and powder rifle around 1770 and received English patent number 1139 for design details in December of 1776. However, he was unable to devote the required time to develop it. (Breech-loading firearms did not become practical for nearly another century.) The Major also designed all of the defensive improvements that Cruger was to install at Ninety Six. His designs for that installation impressed not only Cruger, but Cornwallis and Clinton.

Ferguson's shortcomings were his relative inexperience and a desire for greatness. While Ferguson was no coward, he tarried unnecessarily for two days to decide whether to tuck his tail or make a stand. On the 4th, he was 25 miles ahead of his pursuers and was only 35 miles away from the safety of General Cornwallis' headquarters at Charlotte. A Tory stronghold between him and headquarters would have assured his safety had he continued that direction. However, just as American Southern Department Major Generals Howe and Lincoln had done, he made an imprudent move and subjected his huge force to unnecessary risk. This provincial force would have been a valuable asset for Cornwallis if he had to defend against General Gates who was said to be advancing toward Charlotte. Instead, Ferguson's faux pas became a major factor to the undoing of Lieutenant General Charles Lord Cornwallis. Perhaps the hardest lesson many American Revolution leaders had to learn was garnered from Cherokee war practices: to realize the value in withdrawing from a known hazardous situation to fight later when the odds became favorable.

Major Patrick Ferguson was impressed with Kings Mountain when he first spotted it from miles away. The monolith is a rocky and forested hill, in the upper Piedmont of South Carolina, nearly due west of Charlotte, North Carolina. It is shaped like a footprint running from the "heel" on the southwest to the "ball" on the northeast. The summit of Kings Mountain is 600 yards long, 70 yards wide at the heel and 120 yards wide at the ball. The highest point at the heel is a plateau 40 yards wide by 150 yards long and 160 feet above the surrounding terrain. It has a steep drop-off, and then slopes gradually to the ball where Ferguson set up his camp 60 feet above the countryside.

Ferguson believed the mountain's height and steepness made it impenetrable. He suspected the only possible mode of attack would be to scale the sides and try to overrun the camp. He was confident he could repel such an attempt with bayonets. He was wrong. The mountain was indefensible given the British fighting style versus the backcountry militia approach to battle. The Tories camped at the top of the ridge which was sparsely treed. The walls, however, were so densely timbered that logs and rocks could provide the Americans with additional protection. The Whig militiamen had rifles, and with cover they would not need to expose themselves by overrunning the camp. They could make controlled attacks and withdrawals as Ferguson's forces counterattacked.

Surprisingly, Ferguson ordered no defensive preparations be made. He neither felled trees nor removed them or existing logs from the hillside approach to eliminate cover for an enemy attack force. He also did not construct an abatis from the abundance of already downed trees nor a defensive wall of earth and rock around the camp to provide a shielded firing position for his troops.

Ferguson was the only actual British soldier involved. The American Volunteers, 120 experienced provincials, formed the core of his force. Half of those were men from the New Jersey Volunteers 4th Battalion; the balance having been detachments from New York and Connecticut. Those troops were well-trained in the British style of bayonet warfare. If they were aggressive enough to move at least toward the edge of Kings Mountain and shoot at the protected patriot militiamen, they would leave themselves exposed to accurate rifle fire.

One-thousand newly-recruited Tory militiamen comprised the rest of Ferguson's brigade. He had trained them in the bayonet style of warfare, but they were not as adept as the provincials. The militiamen provided their own weapons, primarily a variety of muskets and rifles. Some equipped themselves with plug-bayonets, a long knife with a handle carved to jam into the barrel of a long arm. Others with rifles, but no bayonet, were to take available cover near the camp and fire at Whigs as they appeared from the mountain's rim. (All of Ferguson's force will generally be referred to as Tories or Loyalists in the battle description.) They normally loaded their 75-caliber muskets with a 69-caliber ball and three or four 30-caliber balls for close-quarter battle. However, they could not safely attempt a bayonet charge far down a steep hillside into the face of deadly rifle fire, especially while dodging trees, rocks, and logs. The British had practiced bayonet charges for action in an open field with no obstructions. Additionally, the British, not trained marksmen, consistently overshot their targets throughout the war. Shooting downhill compounded that problem for them. Muskets were accurate at up to 80 yards. Beyond that distance, a shooter had to guess at the adjustment. Without allowance for wind or changes in elevation, the aim required at 150 yards would be five feet above the target. The British were not inclined to hold target practice with their troops. Their main objective consisted of well-practiced, close-order bayonet charges, with muskets fired only from point-blank range to precede the assault.

The backcountry American militiamen were armed with 43-caliber to 54-caliber hunting rifles accurate to 300 yards. Those shooters were marksmen regularly trained at firing from a variety of positions, angles, distances, and windy conditions. The trees and logs that obstructed a bayonet charge allowed the riflemen to move from cover to cover as they loaded their single-shot rifles and fired as they moved.

General Henry "Light Horse Harry" Lee later wrote about Ferguson's position, "a position thickly set with trees, and more assailable by the rifle than defensible with the bayonet."[20] He was describing the approach up the sides of the mountain. J. B. O. Landrum wrote, "the crest of the mountain was bare, and the British, when in column, were unprotected."[21] Major Patrick Ferguson gave the backwater men from North Carolina no credit at all. He often referred to them as curs or mongrels. Ferguson had cast his die and sealed his fate.[22]

At Cowpens, Colonel Campbell held a council of war with the other colonels and decided on a specific plan of action. They would again leave the infirm and poorly-mounted militiamen in camp and proceed with the healthiest riflemen and horses. They began their march at 9:00 P.M. on the 6th with 940 mounted men. They were chosen from each regiment, brigade, or company by its commanding officer: 200 by Colonel Campbell, 120 by Colonel Shelby, 120 by Colonel Sevier, 110 by Colonel Cleveland, 90 by Major McDowell, 60 by Colonel Winston, 100 by Colonels Lacey and Hill, 50 by Colonel Hambright and Major Chronicle, and 90 by Brigadier General Williams, including Major Candler's 30 Georgians.

Progress was slow throughout the night because of the dense forest and added inconvenience of a cold and steady rainfall. Some of the guides became turned around and were lost. At dawn, Colonel Campbell's men had not even moved ten miles from the camp at Cowpens. The other colonels sent runners to locate them and guide them to the main corps. Before long, the confused Virginians had all been gathered, and the march continued.

Soon, the soggy troops reached the Broad River near where Ferguson had camped the day before. They did not want to risk discovery in case Ferguson had posted a detachment to watch his back trail, so they went two and one-half miles downriver to Cherokee Ford. Still leery, Major Chronicle directed Enoch Gilmer to reconnoiter the crossing. After a few minutes, the force heard Gilmer sing a well-known song called "Barney Linn" that indicated all-clear. By that time they had covered half of the 30 miles from Cowpens to Kings Mountain.

The backwater men stopped for lunch at noon. It was still raining hard, and Colonel Campbell wanted to halt the march. He conferred with Colonels Sevier and Cleveland, and they considered a delay to give some of the horses and men a much-needed rest. The decision required a unanimous council vote. When they broached the matter to Colonel Shelby, Shelby let them know he preferred not to take a chance that Ferguson could escape them.

He stated, "I will not stop until night if I have to follow Ferguson to Cornwallis' lines."[23] They continued on.

The rain finally ceased, and the force approached a homestead owned by Solomon Benson. He was one of many in the backcountry with divided loyalties, depending upon circumstance. He informed on Ferguson and turned two Tory soldiers over to the militiamen. The over mountain colonels made sure the Tories understood their lives were in jeopardy, so they led the force toward the Kings Mountain ridge where Ferguson camped.

The over mountain militias approached two more homesteads as they made their way along the main road to the mountain. At the first, a woman told them that she had just sold some chickens to Ferguson on the ridge. The second property apparently belonged to a Tory sympathizer who gave no information. When the man re-entered his house, his daughter, seemingly favorable toward Whigs, quietly asked Captain Robert Sevier, "How many are there of you?" Sevier's answer was that they had plenty to whip Ferguson, whereupon she responded, "He is up there on that mountain."[24]

Enoch Gilmer, on the prowl for information, came to Colonel Campbell with the precise number of men in Ferguson's command and exactly how they were encamped upon the ridge. Major Chronicle stated that he was familiar with the exact spot.

After the Patriots rode two more miles, they came across a teenager named James Ponder. Colonel Hambright was familiar with Ponder's family, and he knew some of the members were Tory recruits in Ferguson's force. The Colonel suggested Ponder be searched. A dispatch from Major Ferguson addressed to General Cornwallis was discovered. It read:

> My Lord,
> I arrived today at Kings Mountain and ... I do not think I can be forced by a stronger enemy than that against us.... Good soldiers as reserves ... and a few real Dragoons to ... support upon the enemies flanks would enable us to act decisively and vigorously....
> I have the honor to be with greatest respect,
> Pat Ferguson
> Major of 71st Regt.[25]

Ponder, after further questioning, responded that Ferguson was wearing a fine red uniform coat, but had a checked shirt draped over it. Colonel Hambright joyfully shouted, "Poys, hear dot, shoot for the man wit da pig shirt."[26]

When they reached a point one mile from Kings Mountain, they dismounted and prepared the battle plan. They received additional information when George Watkins rode up. He explained Ferguson had just paroled him; then he verified the position of the Loyalist troops.[27]

The officers outlined the initial battle plan to their men; they would surround the Tories on top of the hill, keep them there, and fight from cover with their longer-range weapons. They would shoot uphill to enable them to overshoot their own forces on the other side.

Some accounts state that, after the Whigs had marched an unspecified distance, they left their horses with 20 men and marched the remainder of the way on foot. The commanding officers retained their horses to more easily communicate with their men. Draper indicated, however, that the entire force rode to the base of the mountain while only the officers remained on horseback for the battle. Private Thomas Young, a 16-year-old Patriot, verifies that in his memoir 63 years later: "Major Ferguson had taken a very strong position upon the summit of the mountain, and it appeared like an impossibility to

Colonel Isaac Shelby's approach up Kings Mountain.

dislodge him, but we had come there to do it, and we were determined, one and all, to do it, or die trying.... When our division came up to the northern base of the mountain, we dismounted."[28]

Whether they dismounted away from the mountain or when they arrived at its base, it makes sense that they did so prior to circling the mountain. It is much easier to be silent when parading afoot than when mounted, and a major concept of the battle plan was stealthy movement to maintain surprise.

Colonel Hambright, described as elderly at 53, was prepared to fight, but he turned command of his unit over to Major Chronicle whom he believed was better acquainted with the terrain. Colonel Campbell split the force, and they marched in two columns: Colonel Campbell, himself, led the right column; Colonel Cleveland, the left. The men were ordered to march in silence.

When the units arrived at the southwest base of the mountain at 3:00 P.M., the men received their final instructions. There would be a specific order of engagement only at the beginning to draw the Tories out; then every element would be on its own to participate as its commander felt was best. The last instruction was, "Fresh prime your guns, and every man go into battle firmly resolved to fight till he dies."[29]

The two columns silently marched; the right column quietly crossed over the heel of the ridge far enough from camp to be unseen. The left column marched along the north side of the ridge.

On the right, Colonel William Campbell positioned his unit first just inside the "instep" of the "foot" near the "heel." His unit spanned left to cover the heel against the tall precipice at that end. That group faced Ferguson's camp. Colonel John Sevier positioned his unit to Campbell's right. He was followed by Major Joseph McDowell and Colonel Joseph Winston with their units. Both reported to Sevier.

Colonel Isaac Shelby positioned his unit first on the left opposite Colonel William Campbell. Brigadier General James Williams, Colonel Thomas Brandon, and Majors Samuel Hammond and William Candler respectively, each under the overall command of Williams, established their forces on Shelby's left. (Lieutenant Colonel Robert Anderson led two companies of the Upper Ninety Six District Militia regiment as a unit under Colonel Brandon. This is an indication that Colonel Pickens' good friend either did not take parole or excused himself prior to the Battle of Kings Mountain.)[30]

They were followed by Colonel Edward Lacey's unit, and lastly, by the forces of Colonel Benjamin Cleveland, Major William Chronicle, and Colonel Frederick Hambright, respectively, under command of Colonel Cleveland. Colonel Hambright's squad on the left formed adjacent to Colonel Winston's on the right. Thus Ferguson's command was silently surrounded except for a 200-man foraging party that Ferguson had dispatched earlier in the day under a Tory Colonel named Moore. (This is generally assumed to be John Moore, the North Carolina Colonel who assisted John Boyd with his muster of Tories prior to the Battle of Kettle Creek. See Chapter 6. However, it is also possible that Colonel Patrick Moore led the foraging party.)

The Whigs were to withhold fire until the entire Whig army was stationed. When the most extreme regiment had reached its position, the men were to shout the "over mountain scream." The terrifying battle yell would notify all that they were ready for action. However, before the entire left column reached its assigned position, Colonel Campbell led his unit up the mountain as he yelled, "Here they are, my brave boys; shout like hell, and fight like devils!"[31] The rest of the militias thought that was the awaited signal and took up the horrendous mountaineers' scream. Captain Abraham De Peyster, Ferguson's second in command, had been at Musgrove's Mill and remembered the sound well. He nervously told Ferguson, "These things are ominous—these are the damned yelling boys!"[32]

On the way to his position, Colonel Cleveland and his men encountered some of Ferguson's pickets. He moved among his men telling them, "I will show you by my example.... I can undertake no more. Every man must ... act from his own judgement.... Fire ... and stand your ground.... When you can do no better, get behind trees, or retreat; but I beg you not to run quite off ... make a point of returning, and renewing the fight,"[33] and they forced the pickets up the hill.

Colonel Campbell's group faced a very rough climb over a rocky surface, though not on the steepest side of the mountain. When they reached the top of the ridge, they leveled an exacting and successful fusillade at Ferguson's regiment. Ferguson formed a company of his Tories, and they made a bayonet charge across the top of the mountain at Campbell's force and drove them back down. The Tories followed but were exposed to crossfire from Shelby's force on their right flank. The Loyalists moved back up the mountain.

Campbell's men had retreated to the next ridge before he could stop them. They reformed and repeated the charge. Again, they were forced back down by the Loyalists. While the Tory company was busy with Campbell, Shelby led his men toward the top. Shelby's militiamen fired at the enemy attackers who were on the side of the hill chasing Campbell; then when Shelby reached the top, his troops fired on the main camp. The Tories climbed back to the top of the ridge and, with another bayonet charge, turned their attention on Shelby's force. Shelby's unit retreated down the hill and fired back at the provincials from cover. The over mountain men found it easier to scale the hill and retreat than did the provincials because of their dress. The mountaineers wore the suitable hunting attire described earlier in the chapter.

Ferguson's provincial soldiers' raiment consisted of short, red wool overcoats with blue facing. The red coats covered white waist coats and were worn with white breeches. Brown full-length leggings called gaiters covered the pants and were kept in place by leather garters worn just above the knee. They sported leather caps rather than the traditional British tricorn hats. Two belts crossed the abdomen of each man; one supported a cartridge box on the right hip, the other a scabbard for the bayonet on the left.

Most of Ferguson's militiamen wore handmade flannel hunting shirts and cotton breeches.

When Shelby's men regrouped from retreat, the Colonel yelled, "Now, boys, quickly re-load your rifles, and let's advance upon them, and give them another hell of a fire!"[34] Shelby and Campbell engaged Major Patrick Ferguson's force for ten minutes before the remainder of the units arrived at their assigned positions. They then pressed up the mountain and engaged the Major's provincials. Ferguson ordered more companies fixed with bayonets to face these new threats, but he was overwhelmed from the beginning. Over and over again, trees on the side of the hill offered the charging riflemen requisite cover to fire at the exposed redcoats, yet obstructed the bayonet parties as they charged into the fire.

Thomas Young provided a description of the typical Whig attack at Kings Mountain in his memoir:

> The orders were at the firing of the first gun, for every man to raise a whoop, rush forward, and fight his way as he best could ... I well remember how I behaved. Ben Hollingsworth and I took right up the side of the mountain, and fought our way, from tree to tree, up to the summit. I recollect I stood behind one tree and fired til the bark was nearly all knocked off, and my eyes pretty well filled with It. One fellow shaved me pretty close, for his bullet took a piece out of my gunstock. Before I was aware of it, I found myself apparently between my own regiment and the enemy, as I judged, from seeing the paper which the Whigs wore in their hats, and the pine knots the Tories wore in theirs, these being the badges of distinction.[35]

An over mountain militiaman named Bailey Peyton described the action in person at a session of Congress on January 16, 1834. He said, "When the conflict began, the mountain appeared volcanic; there flashed along its summit, and around its base, and up its sides, one long sulphurous blaze."[36]

Early in the conflict, Major Chronicle and Colonel Hambright began a charge up the steep northeast end of the hill. Chronicle was shot and killed as, from the base of the hill, he implored his men to charge. Colonel Hambright then retook command of his own unit and Chronicle's as well. The troops reached the top where Captain De Peyster led a bayonet unit as they fired their muskets and then charged. Although De Peyster's action drove the militia back down the hill, many Tories lost their lives to the accurate fire of the retreating riflemen who were able to move from cover to cover.

(Similar stories abound regarding each of the units that surrounded the Tories that day. They are covered very well in Draper's book which is listed in the bibliography and is recommended for readers who have an interest in the American Revolution, especially in the southern campaign.)

Colonel Sevier's unit gained the top of the hill and drove the enemy's outer skirmishers back toward the center of their camp. Ferguson's bayonet companies were already busy, so Sevier was not subjected to a countercharge. His unit was the first to gain the hilltop and hold position. The Colonel's brother, Robert Sevier, was killed in the initial charge.

Colonel Williams, initially offended for not having been recognized for his rank of Brigadier General, had first thought about boycotting the battle, but he was too much of a patriot to let that deter him. As his units came into action, he yelled, "Come on, my boys—the old wagoner never yet backed out."[37]

Monument where Major Patrick Ferguson fell on Kings Mountain.

The battle continued for one hour with constant charges and countercharges as the Whigs consistently gained position and advantage during the progress. Ferguson's area of control increasingly waned, and his men began to grow weary from the continuous ineffective countercharges down the hill, followed by retreats back to the top. Colonels Campbell, Shelby, and Sevier steadily drove the Tories from the southeast toward the camp. Colonel Hambright was leading his final charge up the northwest end when he was shot through the thigh. The ball nicked an artery, and blood poured down his leg and filled his boot. He was still mounted and refused assistance. He continued to lead his men and shouted, "Huzza, my prave poys, fight on a few minutes more, and te battle will be over!"[38]

The battle was drawing to a close, but the over mountain men continued to fight furiously. Several white flags started to rise among the Loyalists, but others kept fighting, so the Whigs paid no attention. Ferguson, himself, wouldn't stand for surrender, and he used his saber to slash two of the tokens out of the hands of the hoisters. He declared he "would never surrender to such banditti."[39] As more of his men fell, including members of his small Legion cavalry, the Major decided to attempt an escape. Accompanied by two Loyalist Colonels, he assailed what he thought was the weakest of the enemy line. Ferguson and the two Colonels were shot from their saddles. Ferguson had earlier survived having two horses shot from under him in the action, but this battle ended in tragedy. He reportedly received six to eight balls, one of which hit him in the head. Almost immediately, Captain De Peyster hoisted his handkerchief on a ramrod. One of his officers, emulating Ferguson, tried to cut it out of his hand, but failed.

White flags began appearing throughout the campsite. Many of the Whigs continued to fire at the Loyalists. Colonel Shelby later stated, "Our men, who had been scattered in the battle, were continually coming up, and continued to fire, without comprehending, in the heat of the moment, what had happened."[40] As earlier noted, the majority of these rebels were over mountain men (present-day referenced frontiersmen), a wild back-woods group, as near to uncivilized as could be found in 1780. They were accustomed to fighting the

Cherokee, and they fought just as the Cherokee fought. White flags were a conundrum to most of them.

American commanders rode through the ranks to convince their militiamen to cease firing. Colonel Shelby finally rode to within 15 yards of the Tories and yelled, "Damn you, if you want quarters, throw down your arms!"[41] Still, some of the fired-up Whigs screamed the battle cry of "Tarleton's Quarter" or "Buford's Play" that recalled how Abraham Buford's regiment had been cut down by Lieutenant Colonel Banastre Tarleton in the Waxhaws.

One of those still shooting at the Tories was a young militiaman named Joseph Sevier. He was distraught because he'd been told that his father, Colonel John Sevier, had been killed. He swore he'd keep reloading and shooting until he'd killed every one of the Loyalists. He didn't stop until his father rode up and notified him of his Uncle Robert's death.

Ferguson's remaining force had been corralled into a 60 by 40 yard area. Colonel Shelby demanded they separate themselves by officers; then by rank and file. They were further ordered to remove their hats and be seated. The Americans were then told to close rank as they could around the enemy to prevent escape attempts. Colonel Campbell led the American force in a round of three cheers.

Brigadier General James Williams was shot as he rode toward the prisoners. He turned his horse and told Captain William Moore of Colonel Campbell's unit, "I'm a gone man!"[42] He was mortally wounded but did not die that day. The shot may have originated from men in Ferguson's returning foraging party who had fired shots toward the Whigs, then rode away.

Colonel Campbell saw Williams as he slumped in the saddle. He was unsure whether the shots had come from the foragers or from the midst of the prisoners. Because he chose not to chance an uprising, he ordered Williams' troops to fire upon the captured men. Several were killed before firing was again halted.[43]

Lieutenant Anthony Allaire of Ferguson's regiment thought Williams had been in command of the American force. He stated in his journal, "About two o'clock in the afternoon twenty-five hundred Rebels, under the command of Brig.-Gen. Williams, and ten Colonels, attacked us."[44] The exaggerated number of attackers is likely a result of the haunting battle yell the over mountain men wielded so successfully.

Thomas Young wrote that he witnessed William's fall:

> in the thickest of the fight, I saw colonel Williams fall, and a braver or a better man never died upon the field of battle.... The moment I heard the cry that Col. Williams was shot, I ran to his assistance, for I loved him as a father, he had ever been so kind to me, and almost always carried carrying cake in his pocket for me and his little son Joseph. They carried him into a tent, and sprinkled some water in his face. He revived, and his first words were, "For God's sake boys, don't give up the hill!" I remember it as well as if it had occurred yesterday. I left him in the arms of his son Daniel, and returned to the field to avenge his fall.[45]

Major Patrick Ferguson may have been more effective had he saved his regiment and not faced the aggressive over mountain militia without reinforcements. However, he handled himself very well during the battle. Even though he was harried, he hastened from one quadrant of his camp to another to keep his bayonetted companies on the move, but he did not overreact. He persistently signaled his men with a shrill, silver whistle that could be heard even among the roar of gunfire.

While mounted, he twice lost horses to enemy rifle balls only to quickly secure another steed and resume command. He bitterly resisted surrender as evidenced by his removal of white flags hoisted by his men. His attempt to escape with other officers came after he ultimately realized that all was lost. He was severely wounded by the first few balls that hit him. His right arm was shattered. Still, he wielded his saber with his left hand until he took a ball to the head. When he was finally shot from the saddle, he caught one foot in his stirrup and was dragged for a short distance.

A number of curious Whigs wandered past Ferguson's body throughout the evening. Writers have reported that the major had been mutilated before he was buried in a ravine, wrapped in an uncured beef hide.

Captain De Peyster was often accused, especially by the British press, of having been battle-shy and for surrendering to the "heathens" too quickly. Others who were at the battle insisted he was an admirable leader. Lieutenant Anthony Allaire recorded, "Capt. DePeyster, on whom the command devolved, saw it impossible to form six men together; thought it necessary to surrender to save the lives of the brave men who were left."[46]

The night following the battle was a horrific time. The Whigs were anxious that Lieutenant Colonel Banastre Tarleton or Lieutenant General Charles Lord Cornwallis might arrive with reinforcements. However, the men were exhausted, so they encamped on the mountain amid the dead, dying, and wounded. They took shifts to guard the prisoners. Sleep for the weary did not come easily. David Witherspoon, one of the American militiamen, was later paraphrased by his son who said, "My father used to describe the scenes of the battle-ground the night after the contest as heart-rending in the extreme — the groans of the dying, and the constant cry of 'water! water!'"[47]

Most accounts agree that the battle lasted one hour and five minutes. There are considerable variations in accounts of Tory losses. Two hundred were off on a foraging dispatch, and some 900 fought with Ferguson. The probable combined loss for Ferguson's Legion provincials and his Tory militiamen amounted to 157 killed, including 30 mortally wounded. Prisoners taken numbered 763, including 123 wounded who could be moved. Only the 200-man foraging party escaped.

The Americans lost 28 killed, including 15 officers. Of the 940 militiamen, 62 were wounded. Ferguson's surgeon, Dr. Uzal Johnson, was the only physician on the scene to attend the many wounded. He admirably treated men from each side of the conflict.[48]

Earlier in this chapter it was noted that prior to the Battle of Kings Mountain, Colonel William Hill had leveled several severe indictments in his memoirs that targeted Brigadier General James Williams. One specific assumption Hill made was that Williams was likely killed by friendly fire — on purpose. His exact words were, "It is generally supposed & believed that it was done by some of the Americans, as many of them had been heard to promise on oath that they would do it when they had an opportunity which promises were made at the time the dispute took place before mentioned."[49]

For something "generally supposed & believed," there is no written verification from the people involved in the actions leading up to, during, or after the battle. Any period writing that would back Colonel Hill's remarks would be interesting to view.

One hundred years following the action, noted historian Lyman C. Draper reported the pre-battle incidents as actual events; however, his entire citation for those events relied on Colonel Hill's memoirs. Draper substantially depended on eye-witness accounts to preserve history. Colonel Hill's memoirs fit that criteria, and by 1881 no other independent writing came to Draper's attention to either verify or deny Hill's charges. Much to Draper's credit, he stated regarding Hill's opinion of Williams' death: "The suggestion made by Colonel Hill, in his manuscript narrative, that Colonel Williams was shot by some of Lacey's men, who were inimical to him, and had sworn to take his life, is hardly credible; and, for the honor of humanity, we are constrained to discard so improbable and unpatriotic a supposition."[50] He added that when James Williams died during the post-battle march, "His death was a matter of sincere grief to the whole army."[51]

His further reports of the battle related Williams' shooting as having been discharged by the returning foragers.[52]

Robert D. Bass, a respected historian, also cited Colonel Hill's memoirs regarding problems with James Williams. However, to Bass' credit, he did not dwell on specific indictments that had no verification. He especially made no mention of Colonel Hill's remarks regarding the shooting of Brigadier General Williams. He did state that Williams and Sumter had a disagreement over Sumter's rank, that Sumter's men refused to honor Williams' new rank, and that the colonels at the Cowpens bivouac could not recognize William's authority due to the animosity between the two camps. Bass relied on facts as evidenced by his citation from a Cornwallis letter to Major Patrick Ferguson where the General stated, "Sumter has had a quarrel with Williams about command and has gone to Hillsboro to refer it to Gates."[53] There are other writings that have delineated the identical charges leveled against Williams as fact; however, they each trace to Hill's memoirs as the only source of the information.

An historian takes a risk to rely on Colonel Hill's memoirs as a stand-alone source for the more grievous charges leveled against Brigadier General Williams: that Williams was dishonest when he appeared before Governor Rutledge and received his commission, in his dealings with Sumter's command, and with the over mountain colonels regarding where to find Major Patrick Ferguson. The most grievous account was that any of Sumter's men would intentionally shoot Williams, and that was addressed very well by Draper.

The actual facts of the situation are the animosity between Sumter and Williams, and the bitterness between their two camps. These originated when Williams, given an actual commission of Brigadier General by Governor Rutledge, not so tactfully tried to commandeer Sumter's militia with the true pronouncement that Sumter's commission was not official. Williams was guilty of not having realized his lack of tact would cause hard feelings.

Two examples are compared. First, that Williams was able to quickly overcome his disappointment and participate strongly in the Battle of King's Mountain lends much to his credibility. Second, that the bitterness exemplified by Colonel Hill never eased, and its appearance in his memoirs, written years later, could be viewed as an indictment of Colonel Hill, himself. One could easily question his motives, i.e., subordination of Williams' reputation.

Additionally, Colonel Hill wrote his manuscript in 1815, 35 years after the events surrounding the indictments took place. He then turned the writing over to General Thomas Sumter who maintained it for several years until his death in 1832. In present-day legal vernacular, chain of custody regarding evidence is to assure the believability of said evidence at a later time. Since Sumter had major differences with Williams, the manuscript cannot be said to have been handled in a fashion that eliminates all doubt of its purity.

The above remarks of Thomas Young regarding the shooting of Williams also enhances his credibility, as Thomas Young has often been used as a primary source regarding much of the late American Revolution. It is likely that his statement, though personal, represented a general feeling throughout the army regarding Williams' sincerity.

Unless some hidden facts emerge that truly prove otherwise, an historian should simply remember both Colonel William Hill and Brigadier General James Williams as great patriots who fought bravely for America's Independence.

The exhausted victors of the Battle of Kings Mountain readied the camp for departure February 8, 1780, the morning after battle. They constructed litters to transport the wounded, including the dying Brigadier General James Williams, and they assigned a company to bury the dead. Curious visitors from the countryside milled about to gawk at the dead and the prisoners. They reported a rumor that Lieutenant Colonel Banastre Tarleton was moving quickly and would shortly arrive to rescue the Tory prisoners and exact vengeance upon the over mountain men. Colonel Shelby cautiously readied his men to march by 10:00 A.M. Colonel William Campbell was assigned to remain with the company charged with burying the dead. Before the Whigs departed, Campbell gave orders to his mounted men that, should the militia be attacked, they were to immediately fire into the ranks of the prisoners.

After the force had moved three miles, they stopped at a farm owned by Jacob Randall. There, the suffering General Williams died. Men wrapped his body securely on the litter and proceeded on. The company camped for the night on some acreage owned by a Loyalist and abandoned atop the banks of the Broad River at Buffalo Creek. The men had traveled 12 miles from Kings Mountain and were weary. They found several wooden rails to use for firewood and a yam patch large enough to feed the army.

Shortly thereafter, Colonel Campbell and the burial party rode in. Militiamen traveling afoot followed with a few live beeves; thus, a fine dinner was soon readied for the starving militia.

On the morning of the 9th, Brigadier General Williams was buried with full military honors. That afternoon, the men fired a volley of salute over Williams' grave and resumed their march. The exhausted militiamen only proceeded two and one-half miles by nightfall.

On the 11th, the army camped five miles northeast of Gilbert Town (present-day Rutherfordton, North Carolina) at the estate of Colonel John Walker, a prominent Whig. A Tory prisoner, who had hauled two captured muskets, hid nearby in a hollow sycamore. Unfortunately for him, Colonel Thomas Brandon saw him, dragged him out, and hacked him to death. Several acts of brutality against the Tories caused Colonel Campbell to issue a general order: "I must request the officers of all ranks in the army to endeavor to restrain the disorderly manner of slaughtering and disturbing the prisoners. If it cannot be prevented by moderate measures, such effectual punishment shall be executed upon delinquents as will put a stop to it."[54]

The over mountain army remained at Gilbert Town until the 13th. They required time to recover from the long, tedious march to Kings Mountain, the strenuous battle, care of the wounded, guard duty, and foraging. Additionally, the march from the battlefield was rapid because British reinforcements had been rumored to be on the way. Colonel Shelby described their condition when he later wrote, "Owing to the number of wounded, and the destitution of the army of all conveyances, they traveled slowly, and in one week had only marched about forty miles."[55] The rest at Gilbert Town was necessary, but because Ferguson's corps and others had recently stripped the area of provisions, it was imperative the troops continue to move.

On Friday the 13th, troops and prisoners marched to Bickerstaff's Old Fields on Robertson's Creek nine miles northeast of Gilbert Town. On the 14th, several subordinate officers from both Carolinas apprehensively approached the commanding officers. There had been several escapes, and attempts at the same, among the prisoners. As Lieutenant Allaire wrote on the 15th, "About one hundred prisoners made their escape on this march."[56] The officers were concerned about some Tory prisoners who were well known for having committed severe atrocities upon Whig families in both states. The officers feared those Tories would plan an escape and go unpunished for their iniquities.

This was a serious matter for consideration. Colonel Shelby stated later: When we "reached Gilbert Town ... were informed by a paroled officer, that he had seen eleven patriots hung [hanged] at Ninety Six a few days before, for [just] being Rebels. Similar cruel and unjustifiable acts had been committed before. In the opinion of the patriots, it required retaliatory measures to put a stop to these atrocities."[57]

The colonels obtained a copy of North Carolina criminal laws and determined two magistrates could empanel twelve jurors to consider the cases of the subject Tories. Capital punishment would be considered in such cases as murder, arson, house-breaking, riots, and other acts of violence. (This may seem harsh, but as noted in earlier chapters, the lack of British control against condemnable activities in the South Carolina backcountry was designated as the primary reason those Whig settlers became involved in the fight for American Independence at all. They had been subjected to many atrocities by harsh criminal elements that endeared themselves to King George III just to assure there would be no proper civil authority to control their activities.)

Lyman C. Draper stated it well:

> It has been before observed that, in the ranks of Colonel Ferguson, there were individuals notorious as habitual plunderers and murderers.... There were no [active] courts of justice to punish their offences; and, to detain them as prisoners of war, was to make them objects of exchange ... again enlarged, and suffered to renew their outrages? Capture in arms does not exempt the deserter from the gallows; why should it the cold-blooded murderer?[58]

Many of the North Carolina officers were magistrates, so they seated a jury of colonels, majors, and captains to consider the charges. The number of prisoners condemned to be executed has been variously reported as anywhere from 30 to 40. Nine were hanged that same night, three at a time, from a large tree near the road that became known as the "Gallows Oak."

The nine are listed as: Colonel Ambrose Mills, Captain James Chitwood, Captain Wilson, Captain Walter Gilkey, Captain Grimes, Lieutenant Lafferty, John McFall, John Bibby, and Augustine Hobbs. After those executions, there seemed to be a softening on the part of the commanding officers. Perhaps the severest of those found guilty had already been hanged, or the officers decided enough of an example had been set. Regardless of the reason, the remaining men were pardoned.

The militia marched off at 5:00 A.M. on the 15th and left the nine hanging from the oak. The desired effect had been reached. Word was spread, and following the executions, similar actions by Tories against Whigs became rare.

The Whigs remained concerned that Tarleton was on their trail, so they marched 32 miles in a torrent to arrive in the middle of the night at Quaker Meadows, home of the McDowell family. Major Joseph McDowell rode through the lines and told the troops to avail themselves of fence rails for firewood. The captured Tory officers were permitted to lodge comfortably within the home of Colonel Charles McDowell. The McDowells' mother recognized these officers. She had put up with these same men the previous month when they had invaded the home under Major Ferguson's command. The Tories had threatened Mrs. McDowell with what they would do to her sons once they were captured and had ransacked the house. Now, with the tables turned, the McDowell family was sympathetic toward the condition of the same Tories. The McDowell brothers had some talking to do because their mother was a strong-willed Irish lady with a definite sense of right and wrong; the Tory officers had definitely dishonored her weeks earlier. She had made some comments regarding the "thieving vagabond Tories!"[59] Mrs. McDowell, calmed by her sons, was softened, and saw to it that the Loyalist officers were well fed, dressed in dry clothes, and warmed by the fire.

There was a parting of the ways at the McDowells. The South Carolina troops returned to their own state; Shelby's and Sevier's over mountain men returned to their own valleys, and Colonel Campbell, with Colonels Cleveland and Winston, took charge of the prisoners. On the way to Hillsboro, where they would be turned over to the Continental Army, the prisoner force continued to dwindle. Some escaped; others were transferred to various North Carolina civil authorities who had exhibited some claim upon them. Of those designated for North Carolina, some were bound over for trial, some paroled, some enlisted in local Whig militias, and some in the Continental Army. Only 130 prisoners arrived at Hillsboro and were turned over to Major General Horatio Gates, Commander of the Southern Department. Some of those were paroled.[60]

Colonel Henry "Light Horse Harry" Lee wrote to General Wayne on January 7, 1781, "The North Carolina government has in a great degree baffled the fruits of that victory ... sixty in jail, and ... intelligence from the enemy declares that two hundred of them were actually in arms against us."[61]

Regardless of the small number of prisoners delivered to Hillsboro, the Battle of Kings Mountain had devastating repercussions for the British. Many are discussed in Chapter 9; however, the most obvious blow for the King's forces was the loss of such a large regiment of men. While Tories and not British regular forces, these were the men relied upon to cover General Cornwallis' left flank as he marched on North Carolina. Additionally, they had been counted on, along with Lieutenant Colonel John Harris Cruger's Tory force at Ninety Six, to muster additional Tory militiamen and control the Carolinas' backcountry so Cornwallis could march on Virginia with his full contingent of regulars.

The most obvious result of the battle was the blow to the psyche of potential Tory recruits throughout South Carolina. Except for a few militants, such as William "Bloody Bill" Cuningham's and Thomas "Burn Foot" Brown's forces, the active Tory influence in the state suffered a severe decline.

The year 1780 had shown great promise for the British southern campaign with the fall of Charles Town. However, as the year passed, the British were left seriously disquieted. The remainder of the year, and the onset of 1781, would confirm their concerns. Andrew Pickens would assist to effectuate them.

9

Cowpens! (1781)

By early October 1780, while at Hillsboro, North Carolina, Major General Horatio Gates had gathered what he could of his scattered and tattered army. He was able to do so unmolested. Buoyed by the success at Kings Mountain, Thomas "Gamecock" Sumter (newly commissioned as Brigadier General by Governor John Rutledge on October 6) and Brigadier General Francis Marion kept the British occupied with their militias.

General Gates' Southern Department now merely numbered 1,400 Continental troops. He described the meager force as "rather a shadow than a substance."[1] Gates' soldiers were downtrodden, almost to the point of despair, following the embarrassment at Camden. They lived in lean-tos hastily constructed of limbs, broken fence rails, and cornstalks.

Gates was no longer the egocentric officer he had been; he no longer deemed himself indestructible. The glory of Saratoga had faded. His marvelous achievements in the Northern Department had now been overshadowed. Indeed, he no longer held the trust of his officers, and his army maintained no discipline. The area around Hillsboro had already been stripped of forage, so many of his soldiers terrorized the neighborhood and took what food and supplies they could from local settlers. During this already agonizing time, Gates received word that his son, Robert, had been killed in action in the northern theater.

The Continental Congress determined that General Gates should be replaced as Commander of the Southern Department. The Congress ordered General George Washington to make the selection rather than force one upon him as they had done before. On October 5, 1780, Washington selected the man he had wanted all along—Major General Nathanael Greene.

General Greene, from a Quaker family, was excommunicated from the church when he joined the militia in 1774. He became a Continental Army Major General in August of 1776 and took a command role in every major northern battle between 1776 and 1779. He also was assigned as General Washington's quartermaster general and had the Commander's complete admiration and trust thereafter.

General Gates soon received the official order regarding his coming replacement. A personal letter from General Washington accompanied the order. The Commander offered sincere sympathies for the death of Gates' son, diplomatically referred to Gates' "misfortune" at Camden, and assured him of a command position in the Northern Department. Gates was at first agitated with the orders but became consoled and at peace because of Washington's personal message.[2]

The British suffered a further setback on October 7, the day of Major Patrick Ferguson's defeat at Kings Mountain. Lieutenant General Charles Lord Cornwallis had been planning his next move through North Carolina when he was struck with the same malady that had attacked many of his troops—malaria! (Some references state he was afflicted with yellow fever; however, his recovery was too quick. Also, he wasn't as seriously ill as Tarleton had been, so it is likely the references to malaria are correct.) He had to take to his bed, so he ordered Lieutenant Colonel Francis Lord Rawdon to assume direct command of the forces.

Shortly thereafter, messengers brought word of the defeat at Kings Mountain. Rawdon decided, and Cornwallis concurred, that the army was in no position to march through North Carolina. Too many were ill, and Cornwallis, himself, was in no condition for any such action. Additionally, the General knew that the loss of Ferguson's entire corps meant that the left flank would be open to attack from the over mountain men and other militias. Rawdon ordered Lieutenant Colonel Banastre Tarleton to find a suitable location within South Carolina where the force might withdraw.

The news of Ferguson's defeat was a bitter pill for the British army. British Brigadier General Charles O'Hara, Commander of the First Regiment of Foot Guards, wrote to the Duke of Grafton on November 1, 1780:

> every day confirms me more ... that England has not only lost this Country for ever, but must for ever consider the People of this Continent as the most inveterate of her enemies.... As for the Rebels ... it is a fact beyond a doubt that their own Numbers are not materially reduced, for in all our Victories, where we are said to have cut them to pieces, they very wisely never staid long enough to expose themselves to those desperate extremities ... how impossible must it prove to conquer a Country, where repeated successes cannot ensure permanent advantages, and the most trifling check to our Arms act like Electric Fire, by rousing at the same moment every Man upon the vast Continent to persevere upon the most distant dawn of hope.[3]

Major General Nathanael Greene. Artist: Alonzo Chappel; unknown engraver, 1862.

The British army had been quite comfortable at Charlotte. Many of the senior officers had confiscated the luxurious homes of wealthy Whigs, and much of the army had been housed on a campus of Mount Zion Academy. The Academy was one of the schools built by the Mount Zion Society that Andrew Pickens helped to establish in 1778 (see Chapter 5). The British army was living royally, but would soon become uncomfortable.

Tarleton organized a secure headquarters at Winnsboro, South Carolina, 25 miles northwest of Camden. Cornwallis could finally be moved October 14, so Rawdon organized the army to march. William McCafferty, a local resident, was hired to guide the army through the backcountry. The trek was a debacle. Many men still suffered from illnesses, and McCafferty, who did not want to anger the local Whig militias, piloted the British force in the dark through marshes, across swollen creeks, and through woods. He even veered from the main trail, so Rawdon and his soldiers became completely lost. McCafferty then abandoned the British to themselves in the dark and made his way to the safety of a local Whig militia camp. It was midday on the 15th before Rawdon could gather the entire force and head in the right direction.

Drumming out a Tory. Artist: C. S. Reinhart; unknown engraver, 1877.

Once he resumed his march, Rawdon became concerned for the safety of Ninety Six and Lieutenant Colonel John Harris Cruger's Loyalist garrison. Rawdon ordered Loyalist Lieutenant Colonel George Turnbull to detach Major James Wemyss and the mounted infantry company of the 63rd Regiment of Foot, New York Volunteers, to supplement Cruger's force. The 63rd would be a welcome unit for Cruger; they had served with Lieutenant Colonel Archibald Campbell when he took Savannah in 1778, served at the defense of Savannah in 1779, and at the fall of Charles Town earlier in 1780.

Turnbull was reluctant to comply, but Rawdon ensured the Loyalist officer understood the order was not negotiable. The regiment was under the auspices of Turnbull and had fought with him to defend Rocky Mount from Sumter earlier in the year (see Chapter 7). However the 63rd had remained at Camden where they served to help defeat Gates. They detached to Ninety Six on the 21st.

Rawdon was forced to encamp on the Catawba River for several days due to heavy rains, thick muck, no tents, and few supplies. The troops had abandoned several wagonloads of much-needed provisions and even valuable printing equipment in the marshes. Whig militiamen often rode within gunshot of the army, fired their rifles, and rode away. The British were in no position to pursue them. The Whigs frequently captured mired wagons abandoned by the British. Additionally, General Cornwallis remained ill and needed to be sheltered from the elements; a challenge, considering that available cover was much as that described for General Gates' army at Hillsboro.

The British were finally ready to resume their march on the 25th. By then Lord Cornwallis was feeling well. His Southern Army numbered approximately 4,000 regulars, some of whom were still stationed in the backcountry outposts. Rawdon finally arrived at Winnsboro on the 29th.[4]

Andrew Pickens had honorably kept his parole throughout the events of Gates' defeat at Camden and Ferguson's at Kings Mountain. The latter caused concern for Lieutenant Colonel John Harris Cruger. One week after the Battle of Kings Mountain, Cruger asked

Colonel Pickens to find the over mountain militia and check on the prisoners' welfare. Many of the Loyalists' families were neighbors of Pickens, so he consented to locate them. He departed with Captain John Bowie and local resident John Hamilton as travel companions.

The over mountain militia had left Bickerstaff's Old Fields and the Gallows Oak on their way to the McDowell brothers' place at Quaker Meadows (see Chapter 8). Pickens and his colleagues located Colonel William Campbell on the 15th. Colonel Campbell eyed them with suspicion and put them under guard. He held them at Quaker Meadows for two days, rebuked them for taking parole, again for not carrying arms even while under parole, and then allowed them to view the prisoners. He also informed them about the escapees, those who were hanged, and that 678 prisoners remained under guard.

On October 21, Colonel Pickens reported to Cruger regarding the condition of the prisoners. He also reported that the backwater men were returning to their homes and were not preparing to march on Ninety Six. Cruger repeated the report in a message to Cornwallis and stated that Pickens had exhibited cooperation. The Ninety Six Garrison Commander also suggested that it might be an appropriate time to offer Colonel Pickens a commission at the head of a Loyalist militia unit.[5]

On the 25th, a group of Tories was camped along the Tearcoat River (or Tarcoat as the British called it) with their backs to Tearcoat Swamp. Brigadier General Francis Marion heard of the encampment and rushed his militia to the vicinity. He waited until midnight and launched a three-pronged attack. The Tories were annihilated. Three Loyalists were killed, 14 wounded, and 23 captured. The Whigs seized 80 horses with saddles, bridles, and blankets, 80 muskets, and supplies including food, baggage, and ammunition. A company of the New Acquisition District Regiment led by Captain William Hillhouse was involved in the action.[6]

On October 26, Lieutenant Colonel Nisbet Balfour sent a message to Lieutenant Colonel Francis Lord Rawdon. The message detailed that Cruger had strengthened the Ninety Six defenses. He had rebuilt the stockade with strong fresh timbers which protected a smaller portion of the community than did the original structure of 1776 (see Chapter 4). The plan Cruger used was based on an original design by Major Patrick Ferguson, one of his many engineering accomplishments.

The jail was impenetrable in itself, so it was left outside of the stockade. The garrison constructed two redoubts to the west. The primary was a rebuilt stockade at Williamson's Fort, the old hastily-constructed defense at Savage's Old Field where the Whigs defended against a Tory siege in 1775 (see Chapter 3). This was located across the gulley where Spring Branch ran, and it was within view of the village.

The second redoubt was a V-shaped bunker that ran for 70 feet and began at the southwest corner of the jail toward Spring Branch. Both of these redoubts were positioned to protect the water supply.

Cruger's troops also dug ditches called communication trenches for protected movement of troops and supplies. These were three feet wide by three feet deep with the dirt piled on the side to give additional protection. Portions were covered with timbers to further remove them from view. One ran from the stockade village downslope to Spring Branch and another from the stockade fort to the same area of the creek.[7]

General Cornwallis was well enough to resume full command of his army on November 1, 1780. Denying past experiences, he informed Moses Kirkland on the 2nd that he still envisioned a strong militia force in control of the backcountry. Also on the 2nd, based on the strengthened defenses at Ninety Six and the report from Cruger regarding the over mountain militia, Cornwallis recalled Major Wemyss to Winnsboro.

On the 3rd, the General dispatched Lieutenant Colonel Rawdon to Camden to counter activities by Brigadier General Francis Marion in the lowcountry. Then on the 4th Cornwallis turned his attention back toward Ninety Six. He was confident with the defense of the outpost; however, he had offense on his mind. If he were to eventually march north, he had to gain control of the entire Ninety Six District — and that required an increased militia effort in the area. He sent a message to Balfour that spoke positively of Robert Cunningham. Cornwallis pointed out that local Tories held Cunningham in high regard. The General suggested that the Tory be promoted to Brigadier General in the Ninety Six Militia Regiment. Lord Cornwallis then promoted Tory Captain James Dunlap to Major and put him in charge of a provincial dragoon brigade to operate in that same area.

Also on the 4th, Cornwallis wrote Lieutenant Colonel Tarleton that he was eager for the Legion to do something definite about Francis Marion. On the evening of the 7th, Tarleton received intelligence regarding the Brigadier. Tarleton and his Legion happened on General Marion and his militia November 8 and gave chase for seven hours over 26 miles of marsh, forests, and rivers, but Marion and his militia disappeared into the swamp. Tarleton reported to Cornwallis that Marion was well mounted, and he added that the countryside was so difficult that the Whig could not be brought to action. Tarleton then called off his dragoons with a reference that the devil couldn't even catch Marion. Frustrated, the Legion Commander indignantly exclaimed: "Since the fox avoids me, I will seek the Old Cock [Thomas 'Gamecock' Sumter]. He, I know, will fight, and shall pay the penalty for all the vexations I have suffered from his wily rival."[8]

Tarleton made Sumter his priority, and participants on each side of the war saw the humor. Brigadier General Francis Marion was forever after known as the "Swamp Fox."

On November 8, 1780, Lieutenant General Charles Lord Cornwallis stepped up the pressure on the prominent Whigs as he issued a proclamation to seize their properties. He appointed John Cruden, Esq. to be commissioner to execute the purposes of that proclamation. A copy of Cruden's announcement appeared in the November 8, 1780, issue of the *Royal South Carolina Gazette*, a Loyalist newspaper printed in Charles Town. The announcement was reprinted in the January 11, 1781, issue of *The London Chronicle* (see Appendix G):

> In consequence of the powers to me vested by the Right Honourable Lord Cornwallis, and warrants received from his Lordship and the Commandant of Charlestown; I do hereby make public to all whom it may concern, that I have given orders for the seizure of the estates, both real and personal, of those persons whose names are under mentioned, excepting such property in Charlestown, as is secured to those who were in the town at the time of capitulation. And I do hereby strictly prohibit all and every person or persons from attempting to conceal, remove, or in any way injure the said property, on pain of being punished, as aiding and abetting rebellion.
> JOHN CRUDEN

>> John Rutledge
>> Henry Laurens
>> Thomas Ferguson
>> Christopher Gadsden
>> William Moultrie
>> Pierce Butler
>> Ralph Izard
>> Arthur Middleton
>> Charles Cotesworth Pinckney
>> Francis Marion
>> John Harleston, jun.
>> Isaac Harleston
>> Isaac Motte
>> Nicholas Eveleigh
>> John Lewis Gervais
>> Stephen Bull
>> Peter Horry
>> Hugh Horry
>> Thomas Heyward
>> William Clay Snipes

Georgia Colonels Elijah Clarke, John Twiggs, and Benjamin Few moved back into South Carolina, along with South Carolina Lieutenant Colonel James McCall. They joined with Brigadier General Thomas Sumter who, with a force that now numbered upwards of 1,000 men, camped at a place called Fish Dam Ford on the Broad River. The British had intelligence of Sumter, so Cornwallis allowed Major Wemyss with 100 infantrymen and 50 cavalrymen to find and attack the "Gamecock." They happened upon the huge encampment at 1:00 A.M. November 9, and the result was disastrous for the Tories. Colonel Thomas Taylor commanded the Whig pickets that night. He had huge fires built in front of the camp so the Patriots could easily spot the approach of any enemy troops. That paid off. In the ensuing skirmish, the Loyalists were repulsed. They suffered 14 killed and 27 taken prisoner, including those wounded. Major Wemyss, who had been shot in both thighs, was among the latter. The Americans suffered a total of 14 wounded and killed.[9]

Brigadier General Francis "Swamp Fox" Marion. Artist: Alonzo Chappel; unknown engraver, 1862.

An exaggerated report of the affair at Fish Dam Ford appeared in the November 17, 1780, issue of the *Royal South Carolina Gazette*, a Loyalist newspaper printed in Charles Town. The British military had a flair for reorganizing the facts to make any defeat palatable for their English politicians and citizens. The report (see Appendix G) was reprinted in the January 11, 1781, issue of *The London Chronicle* which stated:

> By late advices from the back country we are informed, that Major Wemyss, with 160 men in the sixty third regiment, on the 9th inst. Came up with a Mr. Sumpter who had about 400 men with him, near Fish Dam Ford: The rebels were surprised and put to the route, and several of them who fled towards the Ford were pushed into the river; but it unfortunately happened, that, at the very beginning of the action, Major Wemyss was so badly wounded, that he was obliged to be carried to the rear. By this time the rebels had fled on all sides, and the King's troops formed upon the ground; but it being thought disadvantageous, it was resolved to quit it, and Major Wemyss's situation not admitting of his removal, he was left at a farm house in the neighborhood. The next morning the rebels, not finding themselves pursued, began to collect themselves, and with great caution appeared on their old ground. Mr. Sumpter having received information where Major Wemyss had been left, came to him about twelve o'clock and gave him a parole. We are happy to inform the Public, that the wound Major Wemyss has received is not dangerous, and he hath arrived at the camp at Wemyss-borough. Our loss upon this occasion, was 1 serjeant and 5 rank and file killed; and, besides the Major, 1 serjeant and 15 rank and file wounded. The rebels say they had near 20 killed, and fifty-two wounded.

November 12, 1780, had been a day for British officer-written missives. General Cornwallis wrote Lieutenant Colonel Balfour that the Tories must establish a formidable offense against the backcountry Whigs; otherwise they would risk losing mastery of the area. Cornwallis continually pressed the Tory militia to step up and take responsibility. If the Tories were in control, the British army could move northward without concern that South Carolina would remain loyal to King George III.

Balfour was already working the issue. He wrote Cornwallis on the same day that he had spoken with Robert Cunningham about command of the Tory militia. Balfour informed the General that Cunningham was excited about the concept, and he also mentioned he would soon meet with Williamson and Cruger. That indicated the officers had already been coordinating on Cornwallis' plan for a strong militia in the Ninety Six District. It also illustrated that Andrew Williamson was working closely with the British under his parole. Indeed, Balfour had sought advice from Williamson which demonstrated the former Whig General exhibited no neutrality at that time.

On the 14th, Lieutenant Colonel Cruger wrote to Cornwallis and verified Balfour's letter regarding the visit. Cruger further stated that Williamson and Pickens were of a mind to accompany him to visit Balfour. Williamson and Cruger heavily courted Colonel Pickens per Cornwallis' desires. They still believed that, if Pickens should don the cloak of a Tory militia colonel, British control of Ninety Six would be a given.

On the 16th, Cornwallis emphasized to Cruger that Kirkland had no ability to lead a militia, and he iterated his previous remarks to Balfour for Cruger's benefit that Robert Cunningham was the best fit for Brigadier General of the Ninety Six Militia.

General Sumter saw some action with Lieutenant Colonel Tarleton on November 20. Sumter and over 1,000 militiamen were moving away from Fish Dam Ford when they heard that Tarleton was approaching with 270 troops (some Legion dragoons, others Legion infantry) and a detachment of mounted infantry from the 63rd Regiment. Sumter conferred with his colonels to determine where they should make a stand. Colonel Thomas Brandon suggested Captain William Blackstock's farm. Blackstock was in action elsewhere with the Spartan Battalion of Lieutenant Colonel Benjamin Roebuck.

Blackstock's estate on the Tyger River was ideal. The structures, and other portions of the farm, were on hills that backed up to the river. Such location would give defenders an elevation advantage over attackers. Additionally, the barn was a well-built structure with many firing ports. The lane that ran through the farm toward the ford on the river was lined on both sides by sturdy fencing constructed of small downed trees that had been notched and tied together. This fencing would allow additional cover for defensive positions.

Sumter arrived at Blackstock's at 4:00 P.M. At 3:00 Tarleton had surmised that, at his own rate of travel, Sumter would reach the Tyger River and be across before he could catch up. Tarleton then ordered his infantry to follow at a normal marching pace while he, the Legion dragoons, and the mounted infantry of the 63rd advanced quickly to try and cut Sumter off. Tarleton arrived at Blackstock's in time to see the last of Sumter's force take refuge.

Sumter had assumed that Tarleton had his full force with him. He planned to defend his position with the superior force and move across the Tyger after dark. He noticed that Tarleton was establishing positions and, uncharacteristically, was not in any hurry to attack. Mrs. Mary Dillard, who lived six miles from Blackstock's, galloped in and avoided Tarleton's position. Mrs. Dillard informed Sumter that she had seen Tarleton rushing past her place without his infantry and artillery. Sumter then knew why Tarleton was settling in — to await his remaining force. Therefore, Sumter decided the best course of action was to initiate conflict before British reinforcements could arrive. He ordered flanking maneuvers, and the Georgia militiamen crept up on the 63rd.

The Georgians fired their rifles before they were within adequate range, and the now dismounted 63rd Regiment infantrymen initiated a bayonet charge before the Whigs could reload. The Georgians fell back, and the British gave chase; however, the British had not ended the pursuit before they neared the barn where more Whigs remained. Whig Colonel Henry Hampton's riflemen opened fire and concentrated on the British officers. Several were hit, including Major John Money, Commander of the 63rd detachment.

Tarleton's dragoons had not yet seen action. While they were intently watching the skirmish involving the infantrymen, South Carolina Colonel Edward Lacey's regiment crept to within 75 yards, opened up on the dragoons, fired buckshot and hit 20 of them. The horsemen were able to repulse the Whigs; then, Tarleton ordered the cavalrymen to extricate the surviving 63rd infantrymen from their predicament.

Sumter, who had been near Lacey's position, retreated toward his original station. He passed too near some members of the 63rd who were retreating in the other direction. Several of the infantrymen still had loaded muskets. They badly wounded Sumter with buckshot. Sumter turned command over to Georgia Colonel John Twiggs and called for a surgeon. Dr. Robert Brownfield immediately realized that Sumter was bleeding dangerously so, without any anesthetic, the doctor removed the buckshot, cauterized the wounds, and applied a dressing with poultice. Dr. Brownfield marshaled a group of militiamen to construct a litter to accommodate Sumter. The men stretched an uncured bull hide over two poles that were tautly bound between two horses.

As darkness enveloped the battlefield, Tarleton withdrew his force and bivouacked two miles away. He hoped to resume action the next morning. Meanwhile, Colonel Twiggs collected the wounded from both sides and ensured they all received medical treatment. The Whigs lit huge fires to convince the British they were still encamped; however, they quietly forded the river during the night. Colonel Twiggs ordered the other colonels to disband their regiments and allow their men to return home. They would be mustered again in the future as required. Georgia Colonels Elijah Clarke and Benjamin Few, rather than disbanding, returned with Lieutenant Colonel James McCall to Long Canes. They still entertained ideas about attacking Cruger at Ninety Six.

Colonel Charles Starkey Myddleton, of the South Carolina 2nd Regiment of State Dragoons prepared the battle report and accounted the British loss as 92 killed and 100 wounded. American losses were three killed and four wounded including General Sumter.[10] British Lieutenant Roderick Mackenzie wrote of the courtesies the Americans showed to the wounded British soldiers. He stated, "It is but doing bare justice to General Sumter to declare that the strictest humanity took place upon the present occasion. They [the prisoners] were supplied with every comfort in his power."[11]

An exaggerated account of the confrontation, likely initiated by Tarleton, appeared in the November 17, 1780, issue of the *Royal South Carolina Gazette*. It was reprinted in the January 11, 1781, issue of *The London Chronicle* (see Appendix G):

> That the Earl Cornwallis having dispatched Lieutenant Colonel Tarleton with part of the legion, and 63d Regiment, in quest of Sumpter, that active and enterprising officer, on the 20th inst came up with Mr. Sumpter's rear guard on the Enoree; they were immediately attacked, and cut up to a man. Colonel Tarleton having discovered Sumter's tract, immediately pursued him with a great rapidity, and came up with him at Black Stolks [sic] on Tyger River. The force of the rebels consisted of about 1000 men, headed by Sumpter, Clarke, Lacy, and Brennan, who were posted on advantageous ground. All the force Colonel Tarleton could bring up, was, 190 cavalry, and 90 infantry. The attack commenced, and notwithstanding the superior numbers of the rebels, and the advantage of the ground, they could not withstand the ardent bravery of the King's troops,

but after some resistance were totally defeated and dispersed; and their horses, waggons, &c all taken.— The slaughter amongst them, which was very great, would have been much more so, if the night had not favoured their escape. Sumpter is dangerously wounded, and it is thought must long before this have fallen into Colonel Tarleton's hands. Our loss consists of fifty killed and wounded.

On November 22, 1780, General Cornwallis gave Robert Cunningham a commission of Brigadier General of the Ninety Six Militia Regiment. Cornwallis was convinced that Cunningham had the ability to take charge and keep the Ninety Six District under control. Cunningham was popular among local Tories, so Cornwallis hoped he would be a successful recruiter for the militia.

Meanwhile, Cornwallis decided to strengthen efforts to convert Colonel Andrew Pickens to the British cause. Colonel Cruger wrote Cornwallis on the 27th and hinted that someone from Long Canes would almost assuredly accept command of a Tory regiment. He further stated that, once the commission of Tory colonel was finalized for that anonymous individual, every backcountry fighter would flock to the Tory unit. Obviously, Cruger did not hide the identity of Colonel Andrew Pickens very well.

The very next day Cruger sent another missive to Cornwallis stating that Andrew Williamson had expressed the same sentiments to Cruger that Cruger expressed to Cornwallis about Andrew Pickens being ready to convert. He added that Williamson was becoming more and more the asset they had hoped he would be. On the 30th, Cornwallis responded to Cruger that he would be grateful when the Long Canes individual would take command.

British Lieutenant Henry Haldane then spoke with Andrew Pickens. Haldane promised Pickens that, if he would muster his old regiment in favor of the British, Cornwallis would assure him of a promotion and of protection for him and his family. Cruger, also at the meeting, assured Pickens that his acceptance would bring peace to the backcountry. Pickens was noncommittal, but agreed to go with Cruger and Williamson to discuss the matter with Balfour at Charles Town.

Major General Gates moved the Southern Department to Charlotte once the British had vacated. Major General Nathanael Greene arrived at Charlotte on December 2, and the official Change of Command was accomplished on the 4th. (Some writings indicate the command changed on the 3rd; however, biographer William Johnson stated it occurred on the 4th.)[12] Greene knew that Congress had ordered a court of inquiry be held regarding General Horatio Gates and his conduct at Camden. Greene determined that it would be in the best interest of all to approach Congress regarding a postponement in deference to the personal tragedy of Robert Gates' death. Greene thought Gates' grief would be hardship enough and would hamper his presentation of a proper defense. Gates pushed for an immediate inquiry, but the postponement request was forwarded. Gates indicated he would await the inquiry at his home. General Greene then wrote General Washington on the 7th, "General Gates sets out to-morrow for the northward. Many officers think very favorably of his conduct, and that, whenever an inquiry takes place, he will honorably acquit himself."[13]

Meanwhile, General Greene was unimpressed with his Southern Department. He found that not only were there a mere 1,500 Continental soldiers, but those were ill-equipped and poorly-disciplined. He also found supplies short with only three days' subsistence in the storehouse. He had predicted such and, while on his way south, arranged for food and clothing to be sent from Virginia to the army in Charlotte.

Neither was the General overly impressed with the situation in the Carolinas. He wrote:

> the powers of government [are] so weak, that every body does as he pleases. The inhabitants are

much divided in their political sentiments, and the whigs and tories pursue each other with little less than savage fury. The back country people are bold and daring; but the people upon the sea shore are sickly, and but indifferent militia.

War here is upon a very different scale to what it is at the Northward. It is a plain business there [in the North]. The geography ... there reduces its operations to two or three points. But here it is everywhere; and the country is so full of deep rivers and impassible creeks and swamps, that you are always liable to misfortune.... The whigs and tories are continually out in small parties, and all the middle country is so disaffected that you cannot lay in the most trifling magazine, or send a wagon through the country with the least article of stores without a guard.[14]

That letter delineated the reason previous Southern Department commanders lacked success, and why the British could not expand on, nor even hold on to, the success they gained. The Continental Army and British forces were not accustomed to the type of guerrilla warfare that enveloped the backcountry, so they would never understand it. The Whig militias were focused and well trained; the British provincial forces were moderately centered on the task at hand, but the Tory militias were not interested in training or subjugation to officers. Therefore, the American reliance on local militias in the latter stages of the southern campaign was successful, but British attempts at similar efforts were failures.

Greene had arranged for Brigadier General Daniel Morgan to meet him at Charlotte. Morgan (a first cousin of Daniel Boone whose mother was a Morgan) had agreed to come out of retirement for the promotion. He agreed despite his suffering from severe arthritis, sciatica, and hemorrhoids. Regardless of his ailments, he was invaluable to General Greene. Brigadier General Isaac Huger also joined Greene. Huger and Morgan would lead two divisions in the reorganized Southern Department. Morgan took command of 400 Continentals (including 80 light dragoons) and 200 militiamen, and Huger led the main force of 650 Continental soldiers (soon to be joined by 1,000 recruits from Virginia). Morgan's wing was designed to be a light, quick-moving force and was called the "Flying Army."

One month earlier, a rumor had made the rounds at Camden that Brigadier General Morgan was prepared to invest that city. It was reported in the January 11, 1781, issue of *The London Chronicle* (see Appendix G):

Charlestown, Nov. 13, [1780]
   Extract of a Letter from Camden, dated the 13th instant
   On the evening of the 9th instant, came in a deserter from the rebels. He informs, that General Morgan having received intelligence that our troops had evacuated this town, marched from North Carolina with 300 foot, and 75 horse, in order to take possession; but on his approaches, as far as the Waxaws [sic], distant 35 miles from this, he was informed, that we still kept possession, and meant to defend the place, let the consequence be what it would, which induced him to retreat with precipitation to his former station.—We have thrown up works all round the town, and at several places about a mile distant.—We are under no apprehensions of having a visit paid us by the Americans. They have nothing, for miles round, to subsist on; and their only incitement for coming into the country is plunder. Lord Cornwallis is perfectly recovered, and his army in high spirits.

General Greene also made contact with various militia leaders. He wrote letters to Brigadier General Francis Marion and Colonel Elijah Clarke. He urged the "Swamp Fox" to continue his current actions with his militia and suggested that Clarke speed up his efforts to harass Ninety Six. He asked Thomas Sumter to write Andrew Pickens and urge him to forsake his parole, rejoin the Patriot cause, and bring his militia to Charlotte.

Greene knew the Whigs in South Carolina would be buoyed by the new Southern Department activities. J. B. O. Landrum wrote:

The Whigs became convinced by the oppression and arbitrary conduct of the enemy that the promised protection ... already disregarded would not be longer afforded. There was a general inclination to resume arms once more. A leader was all that was necessary to arouse them to action. That person proved to be Gen. Andrew Pickens, who, among the rest of the Whigs in South Carolina, had been compelled to submit.[15]

Greene would need help to make this happen, and he would get it from an unlikely source; the British.

Georgia Militia Colonels Elijah Clarke, Benjamin Few, and John Twiggs were still encamped at Long Canes with Lieutenant Colonel James McCall. McCall had learned that Pickens and Williamson were considering a visit with the British. This was of great concern because McCall knew that Williamson had already become sympathetic to Britain. He did not want Pickens to make the same move, so he discussed the situation with Colonel Few. Few called a council, and the group, eagerly agreed to persuade Pickens he should break parole. McCall devised a plan to stage a kidnapping and thus provide cover to protect Colonel Pickens from the British. Andrew Pickens could have been hanged if he were caught meeting with active Whigs while on parole.

Brigadier General Daniel Morgan in battle attire. Artist: Alonzo Chappel; unknown engraver, 1862.

Once he was taken to the Whig camp on the 4th, Andrew Pickens admitted that he and Williamson were to meet with the British. However, he added that he was still honor bound by his parole and must remain neutral. He stated, "My honor is pledged. I am bound by the solemnity of an oath not to take up arms, unless the conditions of protection are violated by the British themselves, or by somebody acting under Royal authority."[16]

Andrew on one hand was thankful for the parole he had been under for the past six months. That had been a rare opportunity for him to spend considerable uninterrupted time with his wife, children, and estate. They had been living in peace and had not been threatened. The neighborhood Tories respected him nearly as much as did the Whigs. He allowed several temporary paroles to Tories after the Battle of Kettle Creek, so the Loyalists could see to their families. He had made a strong impression. Everyone trusted him to be an honorable man. On the other hand, Pickens likely regretted having taken Williamson's advice about parole. Whig fervor was low after Charles Town fell, and Britain controlled South Carolina, so parole seemed necessary for the security of his family. Pickens, loyal to his Whig friends, remained neutral throughout his parole. Williamson, however, actively lobbied against the Whigs. When the Patriot militia became active, the Colonel may have thought he was shirking duty to his country by remaining on parole. There was no alternative for him. No matter how torn he may have been, he was honor bound.

Cruger wrote Cornwallis on the 5th that he had a plan for the Ninety Six District. He would convince Pickens, when commissioned a colonel, to lead a Tory militia regiment. Then Cruger and Balfour would prepare a declaration (yet another declaration) and would demand that the local citizenry sign. Men in the district would be required to pledge their loyalty to King George III and to bear arms for the British.

Major Samuel Hammond led his command to White Hall on the 6th, kidnapped Williamson, and took him before Colonel Benjamin Few and the others at Long Canes. They insisted that Williamson explain his actions in support of the British. He was inimical and refused to cooperate. The Whigs held him in camp for several days. Initially they begged him to change his loyalties and rejoin the effort. Then, since they considered him a traitor, they threatened his life if he didn't. They paroled him to White Hall and suggested he take a few days to reconsider his position. Adding further insult, they accompanied him to his estate and proceeded to eat food that Williamson had stored for the Tory regiments within the Ninety Six District. They commandeered the remainder and took it to Long Canes.

Williamson reported the affair to Lieutenant Colonel Cruger who had already written Cornwallis on the 9th that he had organized the Tories to drive Colonels Clarke and Twiggs with their militias back to Georgia. Cruger had further informed Cornwallis that Williamson was detained by the Whigs.

On December 12, 1780, Lieutenant Colonel Cruger dispatched provincial Lieutenant Colonel Isaac Allen with his New Jersey Volunteers to engage the Whig militia. Allen had a total force of 400 men that included Major James Dunlap and his Tory dragoons. The Loyalists made camp en route to Long Canes and were unaware that 100 Whig militiamen, on their way to harass Ninety Six, were bivouacked nearby. A Whig foraging party stumbled upon Allen's men. The Tories chased the retreating foragers back to the Whig encampment. The Whigs were surprised and routed.

The Loyalists followed the Whigs for two miles, but they could not keep up with the smaller party and so returned to their position. Shortly, Colonel John Twiggs rode into the Tory cantonment under a truce flag and met with Lieutenant Colonel Allen. They discussed the short battle, and Twiggs inquired about the condition of the wounded and captured Whigs. Twiggs then informed Allen that Lieutenant Colonel James McCall had been slightly wounded, but Colonel Elijah Clarke had taken a ball in the shoulder.

Following the narrow escape, Colonels Twiggs, Few, and Clarke departed for Georgia with their militiamen. McCall led his militia toward Charlotte to locate General Greene.[17]

Lieutenant Colonel Allen was content that the Georgia Whigs had withdrawn toward their homes; hence, he returned with his force to Ninety Six. Dunlap, however, did not believe that Clarke was healthy enough for the trip, so he began an intense search with his dragoons. First Dunlap went to James McCall's home to make sure that McCall and Clarke were not there to convalesce. Dunlap did not find them. In a rage, he burned the home, terrorized Mrs. McCall and her children, stripped the family of all their food and clothing, confiscated what cattle he and his men could take with them, and killed the remaining stock. When McCall and Clarke learned of Dunlap's violence, they each were so enraged that they each declared they would not ever forget Major James Dunlap.

Dunlap next made a grievous misjudgment, an error so severe that he would never be able to endear himself to either Cruger or Cornwallis again. Dunlap knew that Colonels Clarke, Pickens, and Lieutenant Colonel McCall had made history together (Kettle Creek), so he presumed that Clarke might recuperate at Pickens' estate. Dunlap attacked the estate!

Pickens was away, and Dunlap did not find Clarke. This was just another Whig plantation to the Major, so he destroyed many of the structures, horrified Becky and the children, and rode away. Andrew Pickens' children were young; they ranged in age from one to twelve years old.

Dunlap, a New Jersey Tory Provincial officer, seemingly had no concept of what he had done. Blindly, he assumed that a Whig is a Whig is a Whig, and he had no inkling of the esteem with which local Tories held the Pickenses. He may have been aware that Cruger was heavily recruiting Pickens, but he just could not comprehend how important the Whig officer could be to the British cause.[18]

The British effort to make a Tory colonel out of Pickens, which had little chance to succeed, was definitely thwarted by Major Dunlap's aggressiveness. Pickens returned to his estate to find dead cattle, empty grain silos, and widespread destruction. His family, though frightened, had not been harmed. Beckie was strong, but the children cried as they told Andrew how rough the Tories handled them, and how the Loyalists verbally abused them with vile language and threats. Andrew understood that his parole would not provide future assurance of protection for his family.

Colonel Pickens was not yet ready to take up arms; something else had to be accomplished first. He would inform the British authorities that he was no longer obligated by the conditions of parole, and that he would no longer remain neutral. He would do so the honorable way — in person.

He deliberated his target, which British authorities he would notify. He first reflected upon the primary authority in the Ninety Six District, Lieutenant Colonel John Harris Cruger. Cruger had dealt with him fairly; however, Cruger's name had been associated with the hangings of those who violated parole. Cruger had a fierce temper and might regard the mere mention of abandoning parole as cause for execution. Pickens decided it would be senseless to go directly to the Commander of the Ninety Six District, so he considered Cruger's subordinates.

There would be some risk no matter to whom he directed his declaration, but the danger could be diminished depending upon the wisdom of his choice. He decided. General Andrew Williamson, though not judged entirely trustworthy, had a small British outpost at White Hall commanded by Captain George Ker (sometimes Kerr) who reported directly to Cruger. The Colonel knew that Williamson was at the post and would likely act as a buffer should Pickens need him to do so.

When Andrew Pickens arrived at White Hall, he was greeted by Williamson who hoped his old friend and subordinate had come to join the cause. However, Pickens simply asked to meet with Ker and requested Williamson to attend. The Captain was available and invited the pair in. Lieutenant Henry Haldane, who had previously spoken with Pickens about conversion to the British cause, was in the room. Andrew invited Haldane to stay as he thought the Lieutenant might be another (though likely unnecessary) ingredient to help deter an irrational, spur of the moment, response by Ker.

Colonel Pickens calmly chronicled James Dunlap's actions. Andrew described how Dunlap had searched for Clarke, harassed his family, and destroyed his property. He told the gathering that he was saddened that they had not fulfilled their promise to protect his family during Andrew's parole. The room was quiet, and the British officers paled. They saw a "Tory Colonel Pickens" slip from their grasp. Williamson hung his head and fidgeted.

Then Pickens arrived at the crux of his visit. He flatly declared that, because the British had violated their oath, he no longer felt bound by his. He would no longer remain neutral.

The officers tried to convince him that to abandon his parole was folly. Haldane told Pickens about the coming proclamation to be signed by all in the district. He stated that Cruger would only promise protection if the Colonel would join his friend, General Williamson, in adopting the British cause. Unruffled, Andrew answered that he had already tried to rely upon the word of the British and suffered indignities because of it. He further declared that he absolutely could not sign such a declaration as Haldane had described.

Captain Ker made one last attempt to dissuade Pickens from his announced action. He said, "You will literally fight with a halter around your neck! Though our countries are at war, you have given proof of personal friendship and I hope you may never fall into the hands of the British government."[19]

Andrew Pickens, in reply, repeated his logic, "I have honorably and conscientiously adhered to the rules laid down in the protection I took, but now I consider myself completely absolved by the wanton plunder and waste, and the indignities that have been offered to my family.... Will you communicate this message to Colonel Cruger at Ninety Six, and thank him for his civilities while I was under British protection?"[20]

Pickens gave a sigh of relief as he left White Hall. He had fulfilled his goal. His honor was secure, and he was not hanged because of it.[21]

Meanwhile, Major General Nathanael Greene contemplated his next move. Charlotte did not offer any long-term possibility for his headquarters. The British had already stripped the area of forage during Lieutenant General Charles Lord Cornwallis' recent headquarters there. The army must move to be fed. Additionally, Cornwallis' army, sans outpost garrisons, outnumbered Greene's 3,500 men to 2,000. Cornwallis was located at Winnsboro, South Carolina, just 50 miles south of Charlotte, which put Greene at a strategic disadvantage. He had to leave Charlotte as he expected Cornwallis might return. Cornwallis' strategy would likely be to attack Green while the Southern Department was in such meager condition. No matter where Greene might try to move, his foe could easily move in the same direction, cut Greene off, and force a fight for which the Southern Department was ill prepared.

Greene solved the problem in a unique way. He split his force, a rare decision for a commander so severely outnumbered. One half of the army could more easily find sufficient forage, so he planned to set the two divisions in different regions. Once each wing arrived at its region, it could spread out over several smaller encampments, far enough from the others to further improve foraging possibilities, yet near enough to quickly conjoin when required.

General Greene marched with General Huger's primary wing to Cheraw Hill (present-day Cheraw), South Carolina. The group departed December 20, 1780. Travel was slow due to rains, mud, and swollen streams. The force arrived at Cheraw Hill on the 26th.

General Morgan left Charlotte on the 21st. Lieutenant Colonel John Eager Howard from Maryland was Morgan's second and had direct command of the Continental Army units. They crossed the Catawba at Biggin's Ferry on the 22nd, generally followed Cane Creek, forded the Broad River on the 24th, and established their main camp at Grindal Shoals on the Pacolet River December 25, Christmas Day. (Grindal Shoals is east of present-day Pacolet Mills, South Carolina, near State Highway 18.)

Another effect of the army's split was that Lieutenant General Cornwallis was blocked from attacking General Greene's position with his entire force. Should Cornwallis depart

Winnsboro with the majority of his army, General Morgan could attack Cruger at Ninety Six with little difficulty. Conversely, a Cornwallis move on Morgan would provide Greene an opportunity to attack the large British detachment at Camden. General Greene's historic decision to split his army in the face of a superior-sized enemy force, and to organize Morgan's wing into the "Flying Army" would prove invaluable. Cornwallis could not expect such an unusual, albeit wise, move.

Militiaman called to arms. Artist: Felix Darley; engraver: A. Bobbett, 1877.

The timing was perfect. "Buckling on the sword, General Pickens resolved to lead the way in exciting the well affected to the American cause to hazard all and rally once more in defense of Liberty."[22] Colonel Andrew Pickens met several confidantes while Morgan made his way to the Pacolet. It was a grand council: Colonel Pickens, brothers John and Lieutenant Joseph Pickens, cousins and Captains Robert and John Pickens, in-laws Majors John Bowie and Alexander Noble, several members of the Calhoun family, and comrade Lieutenant Colonel Robert Anderson. They discussed Cruger's forthcoming declaration. Once Cruger had posted the order throughout Ninety Six, neutrality would no longer be an option for any of the group. Their only option was to reactivate the Ninety Six Regiment under Colonel Andrew Pickens, align with the South Carolina State Troops, and support the Continental Army under General Morgan. Lieutenant Joseph Pickens would be promoted to Captain in the state militia. (Some historians have written that Andrew Pickens talked with his brothers John and Robert at his council. However, Andrew did not have a brother named Robert. Captain Robert Pickens was his cousin, so the writings should have shown the name "Joseph" rather than "Robert." The mistake may have originated with a statement by A. L. Pickens that "Joseph and Robert were soon with him again." However, Dr. Pickens' comment did not pertain to the council, but to formation of the militia. The Colonel had fought for many years with his brother, Joseph, and his friend, Lieutenant Colonel Robert Anderson. These are the Joseph and Robert to whom Dr. Pickens referred.)[23]

Immediately after he settled at Grindal Shoals, General Morgan sent messages to local Whig militia commanders. He sent aides to Colonel Pickens to implore the Colonel to gather his militia and join him. Pickens explained that it would be a problem to recruit and gather his force, and to then march the 80 miles to Grindal Shoals. Pickens was concerned about the large Tory militias that constantly patrolled the area. Colonel Thomas Waters operated out of Fair Forest which lay between Grindal Shoals and Long Canes, and Brigadier General Robert Cunningham was stationed at Williams' Fort (on Williams' plantation located east of present-day Cross Hill, South Carolina, where State Highway 560 crosses Mud Lick Creek).

Morgan decided he could resolve the problem. On December 29, he dispatched Continental Army Lieutenant Colonel William Washington with 80 Continental dragoons and

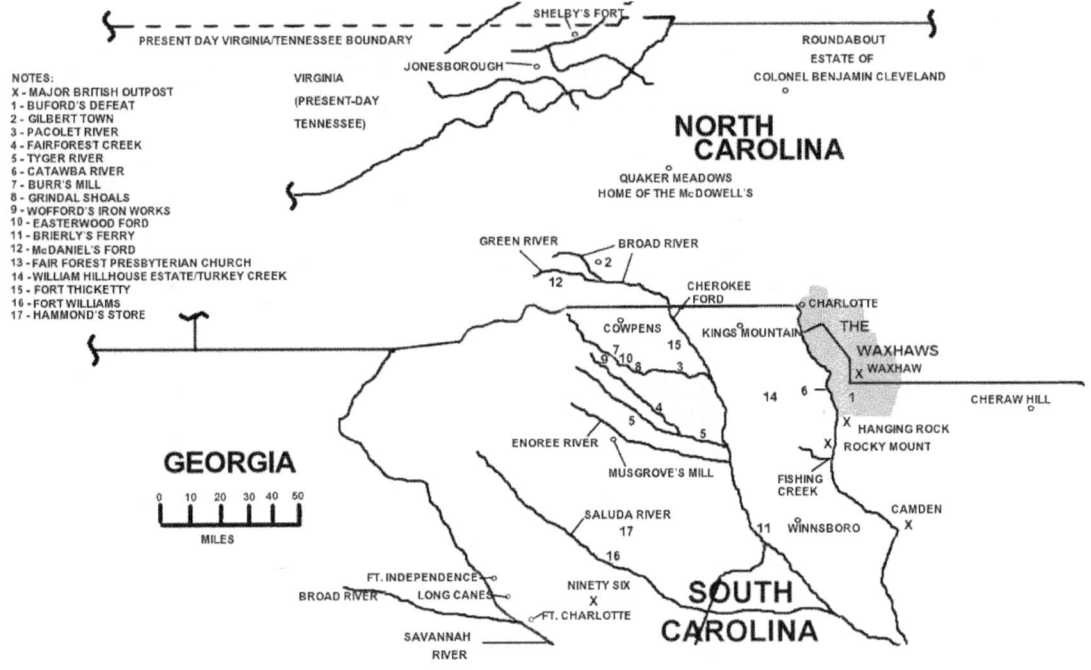

Battle of Cowpens points of interest.

militia Lieutenant Colonel James McCall with 200 of his mounted militiamen to keep the Tories busy.

Colonel Waters had 250 Georgia militiamen. Reminiscent of Major James Dunlap, they were actively engaged in nefarious attacks on Whig-owned estates. They antagonized women and children at their homes, and threatened men who had settled into some semblance of neutrality. Washington and McCall pushed their force hard in country heavily controlled by the Tory provincials and militias, but it was noon on the 30th before the Americans caught up to Waters' throng. The Tories were comfortably camped around Hammond's store and had no warning until the pickets reported the arrival of the cavalry. Waters had just enough time to form a line on top of a prominence. Washington stopped his troops on top of an adjacent rise when he saw the long line of Tories. After just a few seconds, Washington let out a long whoop, waved his saber, and led his force in a charge. (Hammond's store was located on the Bush River due south of Clinton, South Carolina.)

Private Thomas Young of McCall's mounted militia described the action in his journal: "When we came in sight we perceived that the Tories had formed in a line on the brow of the hill opposite to us. We had a long hill to descend and another to rise. Lt. Col. Washington and his dragoons gave a shout, drew swords, and charged down the hill like madmen. The Tories flew in every direction without firing a gun. We took a great many prisoners and killed a few."[24] The skirmish was actually a chase. The Tories lost 100 men either killed or severely wounded. Forty Tories, 50 horses, and over 200 rifles were captured. The Tories reportedly did not get off a shot, thus the mortality might be deemed unwarranted. The South Carolina militia had heard enough of the indignities Waters' militia had forced upon Whig families, and vengeance was unavoidable. Waters escaped through the forest with 100 survivors.

(Some record that Thomas Waters was a Lieutenant Colonel at the time; however, Thomas Brown of the Augusta garrison wrote him in February 1779 and addressed the letter to Col. Thomas Waters. The date of the original citation in the source was only readable to "Feby. 177_;" however, February 1779 fits with Brown's appearance in Augusta. Waters' home was on the Savannah River north of Augusta, and he had apparently been an original member of the Georgia Rangers since 1773.)[25]

The next day, a detachment approached Fort Williams to take care of Brigadier General Robert Cunningham and his 150 Tories. Cunningham, however, had heard of Waters' embarrassment and evacuated toward Ninety Six just as the Americans arrived. The attackers were led by South Carolina militia Lieutenant Colonel Joseph Hayes with 40 militiamen supported by Continental Cornet James Simons and 10 of Washington's dragoons. This amounted to another embarrassment for the British. Cornwallis had sustained high hopes for Cunningham to take forceful control of the Tory militia in Ninety Six and to keep the Whigs in check. However, with a superior force by four-to-one, he was chased out of his fortress and did not even attempt a skirmish. (Cornet was the lowest-ranking commissioned officer in the Continental Cavalry.)

Lieutenant Colonel William Washington. Engraver: G. R. Hall, 1860.

Cruger reported to Cornwallis: "General Cuningham, on hearing of Water's [sic] defeat ... had just marched out with the last of his garrison, as a party, consisting of about forty militia horsemen under Colonel Hayes, and ten dragoons under Mr. Simmonds, arrived."[26]

Cunningham's brigade was, in fact, so large that Hayes did not attempt to give chase but chose instead to raze Fort Williams. Cruger exhibited great control with his report when he did not criticize Cunningham for his timidity; Cornwallis could figure that out for himself.[27]

Many backcountry Whigs knew about the declaration Cruger had printed, so they flocked to Ninety Six prepared to declare their oaths upon his return. Several had been with McCall and the Georgians at Long Canes when they were routed by Lieutenant Colonel Allen and Major Dunlap. With morale at a low, they may have decided discretion made more sense than to continue a battle against the British government.

Things changed drastically in the rollercoaster world of backcountry South Carolina. Word was widespread, not only of Pickens and his old regiment reawakening, but of Lieutenant Colonel Washington and Colonel Hayes respectively forcing Colonel Waters and Brigadier General Cunningham to back down. Additionally, the Americans did so just a few miles from a Tory stronghold; the village of Ninety Six.

On the morning of the 29th, well-coordinated with Washington's foray, Colonel Andrew Pickens, Majors John Bowie and Alexander Noble, Lieutenant Colonel Robert

Anderson and Captain Joseph Pickens mustered 100 of their old regiment around Long Canes and began the trek toward Grindal Shoals. Theirs was not a timid group. The men epitomized courage, especially since each was aware he would be hanged if captured by the British. When they arrived at the Saluda, they deemed it safe enough to rest. Soon Washington, McCall, and Hayes, who were also returning to General Morgan, joined them for the final leg of the journey. Pickens and McCall reunited with a combined force of 260 militiamen.

Pickens and his officers met with Brigadier General Daniel Morgan and then set up camp. The South Carolina militia followed the example that Morgan had set. Morgan split his forces into small detachments that camped separately from each other. This structure aided all to forage as each group had to find food in a smaller area for its own troops. Also fewer soldiers were exposed to danger in the event of a surprise attack. The groupings were still near enough to the main camp that Morgan could quickly get word to each, should the need arise for a quick march. As a light army unit, it was devoid of artillery, with fewer than the customary number of wagons for baggage and supplies. They needed to be able to move quickly; more like a militia force than a Continental Army brigade.

Pickens stationed the South Carolina State Troops, his former regiment including Lieutenant Colonel McCall, on the grounds of the Fair Forest Presbyterian Church Meeting House (located on Dinning Creek two miles east of Union, South Carolina). The three other regiments were spread around the area just as the Continentals were around Grindal Shoals.

Lieutenant Colonel Isaac Allen was the interim Commander of Ninety Six while Cruger was in Charles Town. Allen reluctantly apprised Cornwallis of the repercussions from Major James Dunlap's ill-advised actions: Colonel Pickens left Long Canes and joined General Morgan; one hundred men went with Pickens; Pickens' influence would undoubtedly strengthen the Whig militia; Ninety Six would be in danger.

Allen followed up with a letter to Cornwallis' aide, Lieutenant Henry Haldane, and informed him of Pickens' action. He described Pickens as a good soldier and added that his old Ninety Six militia regiment was the best among the Whigs. He further stated that General Williamson was still at White Hall, and that the general was heartbroken over Pickens "perfidious" deportment.

Indeed, General Andrew Williamson could now foresee the future. He had backed the wrong pony in this race, and he decided to abandon White Hall and head for the safety of Charles Town; the coast remained under firm control of the British.[28]

Lieutenant Colonel Allen authored another letter to Haldane on the 31st. This time he notified the aide that Cunningham had arrived at Ninety Six with only 60 men. The remainder had deserted as Tory militiamen had a habit of doing when faced with difficulties.

General Charles Lord Cornwallis was worried. The last thing he wanted to hear was that his highly regarded and formidable Tory force at Ninety Six was in jeopardy. Consequently, he had to counter Major General Nathanael Greene's move and split his own forces. He still possessed the burning desire to invade North Carolina sooner rather than later. Cornwallis had to carefully plan his future actions after he had received such devastating news from the backcountry. He ultimately decided not to leave South Carolina in the hands of Loyalist militiamen. He would instead rely on the provincial Tory forces to retain control of the colony if he were to follow through with a northward invasion. (Provincial forces were the British version of Whig South Carolina State troops. They were trained as well as British regulars and were more reliable than local militia units.)

On January 1, 1781, Cornwallis sent Lieutenant Haldane to Brierly's Ferry with a message for Lieutenant Colonel Banastre Tarleton. Tarleton was ordered to Ninety Six to protect the outpost against any attack Morgan might launch. (Brierly's Ferry was located on the Broad River, halfway between present-day Richtex and Jenkinsville, South Carolina, and 15 miles northwest of present-day Columbia, South Carolina. Tarleton, when at Brierly's Ferry, was 15 miles southwest of Cornwallis' headquarters at Winnsboro, and 60 miles southeast of Morgan's Continental encampment.)

Haldane would arrive at Brierly's Ferry at 5:00 A.M. January 2. He would then confer with Tarleton and write Major Archibald McArthur, of the 71st Regiment of Foot, to tell him that Tarleton was on his way to join him.

Also on the 1st, Cornwallis wrote to Lieutenant Colonel Francis Lord Rawdon to explain some of his plans. The General had decided that the small 7th Regiment of Foot, Royal Fusiliers, would detach to Ninety Six. The 230 men of that regiment would leave when Cornwallis began his march northward. Several of the troops were still recovering from malaria, but Cornwallis imagined they would be ready to offset the effects of "Mr. Pickens" joining the enemy. He was sure the 7th Regiment would set the locals' minds at ease.

The reference to "Mr. Pickens" exhibited Cornwallis' considerable distress over Colonel Pickens' move to Morgan's camp. The British General further expounded on Pickens' move when he wrote to Lieutenant Colonel Nisbet Balfour that the 7th Regiment had been ordered to Ninety Six to offset any actions that Pickens might initiate. Cornwallis had likely lost a bit of sleep over Andrew Pickens' rejection.

Cornwallis knew he and his 3,500 troops could rely on Tarleton to cover their left flank on the march north, should the over mountain men return to attack the main British army. Cornwallis planned additional action to offset the threat from Nathanael Green at Cheraw Hill. Major General Alexander Leslie, who had recently returned to Charles Town from action on the Virginia coast, was to join the Commander with 1,500 battle-hardened troops.

Lord Cornwallis ordered Major General Leslie to march up the east bank of the Wateree River to Camden. Such a march would be difficult in the winter. Leslie would be forced to navigate marshes and swollen creeks, and the last leg of the march would require him to cross the Wateree to join Cornwallis. The selected route may have been intended to confuse Greene. Cornwallis possibly wanted Greene to think Leslie was marching to Cheraw Hill, or at least that Leslie would provide right-flank cover for Cornwallis once Greene became aware of the British movements.

Meanwhile, Tarleton was resting his troops for a foray against General Morgan's position. He was also waiting for winter uniforms to arrive with the 7th Regiment. Tarleton wrote Cornwallis on the 4th: "when I advance, I must either destroy Morgan's Corps, or push it before me over the Broad river, towards king's [sic] mountain. The advance of the army should commence (when your lordship orders this corps to move) onwards for king's mountain."[29]

The 7th Regiment left Winnsboro on January 5, 1781. In addition to the clothing, the regiment delivered a message from Cornwallis that advised Tarleton of January 9, the target day for the march northward. Tarleton, while covering Cornwallis' left, was to move on Morgan with his force (then numbered at 1,100 men).

General Cornwallis' reply to Tarleton revealed that the two held the same thoughts, and that Cornwallis would march northwest from Winnsboro to cut off Morgan's retreat. The British General left Winnsboro on the 8th; however, the route was a quagmire. He made eight miles before he was forced to stop. It wasn't in his favor that his huge army required a colossal train of wagons for baggage, artillery, clothing, food, ammunition, whiskey for the officers, and myriad other supplies. The route was in such poor condition that Cornwallis expected to remain camped throughout the 9th. He further decided to remain another two days because he had not heard from Tarleton. The weather and the swollen rivers impeded messengers' travels. Cornwallis preferred not to march ahead of his flankers for fear of exposing his immense army to attack by any militias. (The large over mountain militia that previously attacked Major Ferguson at Kings Mountain numbered 940 men. Even if they were to attack the British army of 3,500 troops, it would likely be with a force one-fourth the size.)

Major General Leslie had reached Camden but could not cross the Wateree. He moved north to look for a fordable spot. On the 12th, Cornwallis wrote Leslie that he thought Tarleton and his Legion were likely in the same fix. Lord Cornwallis decided to sit tight and wait for Leslie to come to him. He also decided that conditions did not provide him with the opportunity to cut Morgan's line of travel; however, he could not communicate this change of plans to Banastre Tarleton. The Legion Commander was still under the impression that Cornwallis was moving just as Tarleton was and would be waiting on the other side of the Broad River to entrap Morgan.

Lieutenant Colonel Tarleton had not experienced the same degree of difficulty with travel as did the other two officers. He had waited until the 12th to depart the area near Ninety Six when the stream levels had lowered. In addition, since Tarleton's unit was as light as Morgan's, he was able to more easily travel in the wet conditions.

Colonel Andrew Pickens had organized his state troops much like he had once organized his militia regiment. A critical element in his corps was the assignment of men to reconnoiter and watch for the enemy. It was important to the Colonel to always know the location of his foe. On the 12th, Pickens' scouts informed him that Tarleton was on the move—advancing rapidly. Andrew informed General Morgan who quickly organized his men for action. Pickens and his militiamen commenced a delaying action a few miles south of Grindal Shoals to give Daniel Morgan time to devise an operation.

Tarleton approached Pickens' force on the 14th and gradually drove it back toward Morgan. The British Legion was only slightly slowed. In the meantime, Morgan organized his Continentals for a retreat up the Green River Road, but left some companies of the local Fair Forest Militia at Pacolet River to block the fords and shoals as long as they could. "Bloody Ban" Tarleton kept coming, but his Legion moved so quickly they had no time to forage away from the main route of travel. That track had been stripped by Pickens' forces the previous several days. It was difficult to feed the Legion because their quick movement put them well ahead of their own supply wagons.

Tarleton had ordered that some of his Legion dragoons advance on wide flanks to assure Morgan would only have one way to retreat. The General headed for the Broad River; his only choice. The Legion needed to move fast and keep pushing Morgan. Banastre Tarleton wanted to arrive and trap Morgan against the Broad before Morgan could affect a crossing, which Tarleton was sure he would try to do.

On the 15th, Morgan set up camp at Burr's Mill near Thicketty Creek. His force ate of the grain, packed what they could, and destroyed the rest, so the Legion would have none when they arrived. Morgan sent foragers not only around the vicinity of Burr's Mill, but ahead of his force on the same route to gather as they traveled. Little, if any, forage would be available for Tarleton's force as it covered the same trail.

(The location of Burr's Mill is a mystery. It is normally referenced as having been on Thicketty Creek north of Cowpens Creek. However, Daniel Morgan is the only one to mention a "Burr's Mill." It is likely Byce's Mill—sometimes Byas, Boise's, or Bise's Mill—said to have been located on an old stream called Safford's Creek that emptied into Cowpens Creek .38 miles west of where Little Thicketty Creek enters Cowpens. That would put the mill two to three miles east of the present-day town of Cowpens—not the battlefield by the same name.[30])

General Greene wrote of the foraging problem: "This country is very extensive and thinly inhabited, which renders it exceedingly difficult to getting supplies ... but the loss of ... Charleston and the defeat of General Gates, alarmed North Carolina to such a degree, that they have kept ... such hosts of militia as have ravaged the country from one end to the other."[31] Morgan was in agony; his sciatica was painful as were his hemorrhoids and arthritis. He was perturbed about a dispute over forage areas with Colonel William Hill of Sumter's militia. Morgan contemplated retirement. He penned a letter to Major General Greene dated the 15th. He wrote:

> I have left no means in my power ... to effect this business [foraging]. I dispatched Captain Chitty (...commissary of purchases...), with orders to collect and store ... provisions ... I gave him directions to call on Colonel Hill, who commands a regiment of militia in that quarter, to furnish him with ... men to assist him in the execution of this commission, but he, to my great surprise, has just returned without effecting anything. He tells me ... Colonel Hill ... assured him that General Sumpter [sic] directed him to obey no orders from me, unless they came through him.... Could the militia be persuaded to change their fatal mode of going to war, much provision might be saved, but the custom has taken such deep root that it cannot be abolished ... reasons induce me to request that I may be recalled with my detachment, and that General Davidson [author note: North Carolina militia Brigadier General William Davidson also held a commission in the Continental Army of Lieutenant Colonel of the North Carolina Line] and Colonel Pickens may be left with the militia of North and South Carolina and Georgia. They will not be so much the object of the enemy's attention, and will be capable of being a check on the disaffected, which is all I can effect.... Colonel Pickens is a valuable, discreet, and attentive officer, and has the confidence of the militia.[32]

Tarleton arrived at the still swollen Pacolet River on the 15th and realized he was shadowed from across the river by Whig militiamen. He marched north along the west bank and scrutinized every ford and shoal for a good spot to cross with his Legion. Each place he considered was covered by the militiamen that had been tailing him. He knew the militia would fire into his regiment once he began to cross, so he decided to encamp for the night near Wofford's Iron Works, or so it seemed. The Whig militiamen, assured Tarleton and his men had settled in, also retired for the evening with plans for an early morning rout. After nightfall, the cunning Tarleton quietly led his army south to the unwatched Easterwood Ford and completed the crossing just before dawn. (Wofford's Iron Works was located at Lawson's Fork near the present-day Spartanburg suburb of Glendale. Easterwood Ford was three miles north of Grindal Shoals.)

Once the militiamen discovered the ruse on the morning of the 16th, they quickly informed Morgan that Tarleton was six miles south and moving quickly. Morgan exhibited his division's sobriquet of "Flying Army" as he expeditiously roused his men from their half-cooked breakfast, and headed his troops north. Some of the troopers carried breakfast with them while others abandoned theirs in place over burning breakfast fires. Several of Colonel Pickens' small detachments continually eyed the British force as it moved and kept the main army well aware of Tarleton's location. The militiamen initiated skirmishes with "Bloody Ban's" vanguard, and a few Legion dragoons were captured.

Tarleton promptly reached Morgan's deserted camp and settled in for the day. His troops readily availed themselves of the half-cooked breakfast left by the Americans; then, most napped as they were exhausted from 30 consecutive hours on the move. Tarleton was certain of several things: Cornwallis was near Kings Mountain ready to cut off Morgan; Morgan would continue to run and not fight; Morgan would try to cross the Broad River at Cherokee Ford. He was wrong on all accounts.

On the 16th, Cornwallis arrived at William Hillhouse's abandoned estate on Turkey Creek. William Hillhouse, Jr., addressed that in his pension application: "I would also state to the War Department, that the British Commander in Chief Lord Cornwallis on his march to Virginia in Jan. 1781 made my plantation his place of rendezvous from Tuesday till Friday, stripping me of all my possessions except the land which he could not destroy." (See Appendix E.)

Cornwallis still had Colonel Pickens on his mind. He issued an order for Lieutenant Colonel John Harris Cruger at Ninety Six: "If Colonel Pickens has any Negroes, cattle, or other property that may be useful ... to the supply of the troops, I would have it seized accordingly, and I desire that his house may be burned and his plantations as far as lies in your power totally destroyed and himself if ever taken instantly hanged."[33]

Pickens' old nemesis, Major James Dunlap, was assigned the task; one he relished. He burned Pickens' house (clothing, furniture and all) and outbuildings, commandeered the stored food and what cattle his force could handle, and killed the rest. Beckie watched in horror as Dunlap and his men ravaged her property, tormented her Negroes, and terrified her children. The Pickens children sobbed as they clung to their mother's skirt. Becky, trembly, comforted them as best she could and promised them everything would be alright. The Colonel's personal servant, Dick, consoled the other servants, then organized them into groups. They took the Pickens family into their quarters, fed them, and made sure they were comfortable until such time as Andrew could return. Once Dick had them arranged, he rode off to search for Colonel Pickens to inform him of Dunlap's rampage. (Dick would find the Colonel the night of the 16th at Cowpens. He often accompanied Andrew Pickens during military forays.)

Cornwallis decided he would wait at Turkey Creek for Major General Alexander Leslie. Cornwallis seemed not to have anything on his mind except plans to launch his attack into North Carolina. He had already forsaken the idea of assisting Lieutenant Colonel Banastre Tarleton. (The General would definitely not be on a hill overlooking Cowpens during the battle as has been depicted in some present-day movies.) Cornwallis thought that Tarleton's main objective should be to cover the army's left flank into North Carolina, and if Tarleton were to eliminate Morgan on the way, so be it. If not, Morgan would probably retreat northward and avoid conflict. (The Hillhouse estate on Turkey Creek (Nathan's Branch of Bullock's Creek) was near present-day Bullock Creek, South Carolina, at the junction of South Carolina State Highways 97 and 322. Actions of William Hillhouse, Jr., of the New Acquisition Militia Regiment have been discussed throughout the book, beginning with Chapter 3. His pension application has also been a source of reference throughout. Years later, Elijah Hillhouse, grandson of William's brother, James Hillhouse, would wed Ann Gibson, great-granddaughter of Andrew Pickens' brother, Joseph. Elijah and Ann Hillhouse are the author's 4th great-grandparents.)

On the 16th, Brigadier General Daniel Morgan put another twist on Tarleton's predictions. Rather than cross the Broad River at Cherokee Ford, Morgan decided to advance toward Island Ford. He had heard of Cowpens, a favorite gathering place for militiamen (see Chapter 8) and he knew that would be a good location for the South Carolina and North Carolina militias to join him. They were all familiar with the area.

General Morgan rode ahead of his army to reconnoiter Cowpens himself. Captain

Dennis Tramell, who lived two miles from Cowpens, guided the General over the field. During the tour Morgan told Tramell, "Captain here is Morgan's grave or victory."[34] He decided that Cowpens was the ideal place to camp for the night. Though he still had thoughts of crossing the Broad River the next day, Morgan knew Cowpens offered strong possibilities to his advantage, should he be forced to make a stand. He eagerly awaited his force as it moved toward Cowpens![35]

Morgan's Continentals and the Virginia militia attached to his army joined him at Cowpens later that day. The General had not yet determined he would defend that ground, but deep down he knew the battle was coming. He especially knew, from Tarleton's history, that the Britain would come in hard to disallow the Americans time to cross the Broad River.

It was an extraordinary event! Militia detachments arrived throughout the day and night: militia units from Georgia, Virginia, and North Carolina. Even individuals that had not been mustered entered camp and wanted to participate.

While Morgan expected a fight at Cowpens, he would rather retreat and join General Greene. His desire was not evidence of cowardice, but a realistic view of the situation. He was unsure about the quality of militia assistance, and his health had rapidly deteriorated. He did not want to make the same mistake as had Howe, Lincoln, and others who unwarrantedly exposed their troops to a superior force and suffered severe casualties as a result.

The battlefield was ideal for the Americans. The physical arrangement of the ground would accommodate Tarleton's style — a head-on charge with bayonets and sabers with no time for the enemy to reload as his troops approached. Morgan decided he could use that habit to the Americans' advantage.

The British would advance uphill, such as it was. The rise from the lower right (as Tarleton approached) to the upper left was barely perceptible — 50 feet over a distance of 500 yards. The few hilltops were just enough to provide cover for a line of soldiers standing a few feet behind the edge, although they stood in a rather flat area, not in a deep swale.

A rivulet, one-third of the way up the rise, ran from a spring in the middle of the field to what would be the British left, and emptied into a branch of Island Creek that the Americans called the right ravine. The rivulet had eroded the hill along its path, such that it was a quagmire in winter.

The right ravine began at Maple Swamp, ran down the hill, and bordered the battlefield on the British left. It, too, was as much a bog in the winter as was Maple Swamp, itself.

More water and mire lay on the British right. Three small draws sloped away from the battlefield and provided the separate heads of Suck Creek branches, each of which emanated from springs. The Americans called this the left ravine.

The left and right ravines, as well as Maple Swamp, were covered with canebrakes that warned of swampy ground in the Revolutionary era.[36]

Morgan was often criticized in later years for having chosen this type of ground for battle. Those critics might rather have hailed his victory and realized his back was to the wall; the wall was the Broad River, five miles away.

Those who judged his actions faulted him for having been trapped by the river; however, since Tarleton was coming hard and fast, Morgan would have, at some location, faced a river he would have had no time to cross.

An additional criticism was that General Morgan exposed his flanks to the 250 notorious Legion dragoons because the field was so "wide open." The critics ignored the above description of the ravines, canebrakes, bogs, and swamps. (Present-day Cowpens, it should be noted, does not appear as it did during the battle in 1781. The land had dried considerably, so that only a vestige of the creeks and canebrakes existed after the 19th century.)

Tarleton was not able to employ his 250 dragoons to make a wide flanking maneuver to either side, so he did not attempt one. His flanking operations ran on a much smaller scale because he was hemmed in by the ravines: "A Confederate veteran pointed out [in 1898] that the springs made 'a flank of cavalry or artillery impossible.' Morgan's men were difficult to outflank because of these bogs and springs, especially since it had been raining intermittently for several days before the battle."[37]

Interestingly Daniel Morgan, in defending his decision, either forgot the lay of the land or misunderstood his critics. He wrote: "I would not have had a swamp in the view of my militia on any consideration; they would have made for it, and nothing could have detained them from it.... I would have thanked Tarleton had he surrounded me with his cavalry. It would have been better than placing my own men in the rear to shoot down those who broke from the ranks."[38]

Those comments were made by the man who, prior to Cowpens, made a flowery recommendation to General Greene regarding Colonel Andrew Pickens, the same Colonel Pickens in whom Morgan placed his trust to not only command the militia, but to be overall second in command to the General, himself, during the battle. (The militias were there to the end, and Morgan likely would not have won the battle without them. He needed no help from Tarleton to contain them in the field. Indeed, Colonel Joseph McDowell and his North Carolina militiamen, after having been driven into Maple Swamp, would do much damage to Tarleton's force.)

Militiamen came into camp from all backcountry regiments except for General Sumter's force. They arrived throughout the afternoon of January 16 and into the early morning of the 17th. The South Carolina militiamen were especially eager to face off with the British Legion, and they were well-represented at the battlefield. General Sumter's absence was likely resultant from his anger over General Morgan's letter to General Greene about the foraging incident. The South Carolinians that were present, however, had enough of running away to fight some other time. Thomas Young of Major Jolly's regiment stated in his memoirs: "We arrived at the field of the Cowpens about sundown, and were then told that there we should meet the enemy. The news was received with great joy by the army. We were very anxious for battle, and many a hearty curse had been vented against Gen. Morgan during that day's march, for retreating, as we thought, to avoid a fight."[39]

Had Morgan decided to cross the Broad River, the South Carolinians would have taken it as abandonment. They still feared the trade rumors of an independent America consisting of the northern states, with the Carolinas and Georgia left to the British.

Colonel Pickens arrived late in the evening. Lieutenant Colonel John Eager Howard remarked, "Morgan did not decide on action until he was joined in the night by Pickens."[40] Pickens learned that the decision to fight had not been finalized. He approached General Morgan and stated, "I will fight with my command alone, if for nothing else, to show the people that we do not give up the state!"[41]

General Morgan still seemed leery of fighting with a force that was militia by majority. He was concerned the militia would not fight, while Colonel Pickens was concerned they would not stop fighting at the end of the battle. Morgan called a council of war with his officers. Colonel Andrew Pickens pled his case: "Let's not cross the river. My men will suppose that we are retreating and will be discouraged. They know nothing of [Continental Army] discipline; they have come to fight."[42]

Colonel Andrew Pickens, the taciturn Presbyterian who rarely smiled and never laughed, always spoke with exacting consideration. His speech habits often exasperated impatient listeners. It was once said that he "would first take the words out of his mouth, between his fingers, and examine them before he uttered them."[43]

There was solemn concurrence and the General made his final decision: Fight! During the night he devised a spectacular plan: one that would turn Tarleton's aggressiveness against himself. He reviewed the plan with his officers: Lieutenant Colonel John Eager Howard in command of the Continental line; Colonel Andrew Pickens, the combined militias; Lieutenant Colonel William Washington, the cavalry. The basic plan of battle was set in stone. It was an excellent plan. Howard and Pickens fine-tuned details when they could improve a maneuver. They were required to obtain General Morgan's concurrence, and they did. Morgan had become the confident leader he was known to be, and he again exhibited trust in his subordinate commanders. Washington would use his own judgement about where and how to utilize his cavalry to its best advantage during the battle.

Major General Daniel Morgan and Colonel Andrew Pickens then made the rounds of the militia camps. The militias were divided into small companies. General Morgan exhibited light-hearted banter to relax the soldiers.

Private Thomas Young wrote:

> It was upon this occasion I was more perfectly convinced of Gen. Morgan's qualifications to command militia, than I had ever before been. He went among the volunteers, helped them fix their swords, joked with them about their sweet-hearts, told them to keep in good spirits, and the day would be ours. And long after I laid down, he was going about among the soldiers encouraging them, and telling them that the old Wagoner would crack his whip over Ben [Tarleton] in the morning, as sure as they lived. "Just hold up your heads, boys, three fires, he would say, and you are free, and then when you return to your homes, how the old folks will bless you, and the girls kiss you, for your gallant conduct!" I don't believe he slept a wink that night![44]

Pickens was more dour than the General as he fed his men instructions. He was familiar with militiamen and knew how to talk to them about battle. He was also well acquainted with 150 of these men who were from his old regiment. He said: "We are going to fight, tomorrow. Stand fire as long as you can. Don't shoot until the men are within thirty paces of you. You can dodge behind trees and stand it; but when you can't stand it any more, don't run. Quickly retreat, then form again. Mark the epauletted men and shoot at them."[45]

American placard at Cowpens National Battlefield entrance.

The men prepared their breakfasts ahead of time and settled in for a snooze. The commanding officers conferred with subordinate officers and further refined plans from the original.[46] Tarleton's force was encamped at Burr's Mill, Morgan's previous campsite, on the night of the 16th. The Legion Commander was an experienced officer, so had posted scouts in all directions. He had received advisements that Morgan was at Cowpens. At midnight "Bloody Ban" garnered a scouting report that a mountaineer militia was rapidly approaching from the Green River. He was convinced that the over mountain men, who had been the bane of Major Patrick Ferguson, were on their way to assist General Morgan. Banastre Tarleton was aware that Lieutenant Colonel William Davidson had left Morgan to recruit more militiamen, and Davidson knew Shelby and Sevier well. The pressure was on.

Banastre Tarleton mulled the situation over. He needed to attack Morgan not only before reinforcements arrived, but also before Morgan crossed the Broad River. Tarleton was sure that Morgan would be off to an early start. The British force had to trap the Americans against the river. The Broad was still running swiftly; thus, it would take considerable time to cross with a large brigade.

Lieutenant Colonel Banastre Tarleton roused his men from sleep at 2:00 A.M. on the 17th. He hurried them along as they made preparations to move out. At 3:00, Tarleton called in his pickets and formed a column. The vanguard was comprised of the Legion infantry and three companies of light infantry. The men were instructed to follow a road that paralleled the main road. Each road had been damaged by American wagons and horses; however, the main road was devastated.

The center of Tarleton's column consisted of the 7th and 71st Regiments of Foot. The rear guard was composed of the Legion and 17th Regiment cavalries.

The artillery moved with the center of the column. Wagoners hauling supplies and sundries were ordered to leave camp at daybreak and follow the trail. Tarleton had formed a true light brigade for the hurried trek toward Cowpens.

Tarleton's march was uncomfortable for his men. It was a harsh, frigid, and dark early morning. The men's discomfort was compounded as they waded knee-to-waste deep across icy, swift-running creeks and slogged through the mire of a heavily-damaged road. The only meal the force had consumed in the last 24 hours was the small, abandoned American breakfast when they established camp at Burr's Mill. Additionally, they were fatigued from the forced march and had too little rest because of their Commander's burning desire to catch Morgan — a typical "Bloody Ban" chase.

When Morgan's men completed the same march, they did so in the afternoon and had since been stationed by campfires where they were warmed and rested. They had eaten a satisfying supper the night before, had premade breakfast for the morning of the 17th, and were waiting in as comfortable conditions as the situation allowed.

Colonel Pickens, as his experience dictated, had dispatched scouts to reconnoiter the back trail. Word arrived at Cowpens early the morning of the 17th that Tarleton had broken camp and was coming up the left-hand road. Outriders continued to watch the British force as they traveled. Some of the militiamen felled trees across the road ahead of the redcoats' march. Others set huge fires along the road. The Whigs succeeded in slowing the British column.

Tarleton then placed the 17th Light Dragoons at the point of the march. Cavalry could move more quickly at the head of the column than infantry, so as they patrolled the fore trail they thwarted the practices of the Whig militia. Tarleton's repositioning allowed the British force to move more quickly.

From the first report Morgan had figured that Tarleton would arrive near 6:30 A.M. The General decided to not rouse his men until 5:30. He had estimated well. At 5:30 A.M. a scout brought news that Tarleton was five miles away. Daylight occurred at 6:30, with full sunrise at 7:36 A.M. on January 17, 1781.

Morgan woke his soldiers and had them eat breakfast. He then ordered the supply wagons to head toward the Broad River. He formed his army into battle array, and all was accomplished by daybreak.

His Continentals, the core line, were the key. They were formed at the top of the rise. Thomas Young described, "The regulars, under the command of Col. Howard, a brave man, were formed in two ranks, their right flank resting upon the head of the ravine on the right."[47]

The American right flank consisted of Captain Henry Connelly's North Carolina State Troops at the extreme. Captain Andrew Wallace's Virginia Light Infantry was next, followed by Captain John Lawson's Virginia State Troops. The last unit on the American right, nearer the center of Howard's Continental line, was Captain Patrick Buchanan's Virginia Riflemen. Captain Edmund Tate of the Virginia militia was designated overall commander of the right flank. Those militias had been attached to the Continental Army by their respective state authorities. The extreme right was not exactly at the right ravine, but rather behind a knoll and near the head of Buck's Creek. Thus, a militia unit could have room to fill in later between the right flank and Maple Swamp. The left end of the right flank extended to within 100 yards of the road.

The center of the Continental line was formed with Maryland and Delaware Continental forces directly commanded by Lieutenant Colonel John Eager Howard, overall line commander. They stretched from the right-flank units to the road.

The American left flank began with Major Francis (Frank) Triplett's Virginia militia on the left of the road. The extreme left was manned by Captain Joseph McDowell's Burke County North Carolina Militia. (Captain Joseph McDowell was a nephew of Colonel Joseph McDowell.) The American left end of the Continental line stopped 50 yards from the first head of Suck Creek near General Morgan's campsite. That arrangement provided sufficient room for a militia unit to shore up later in the battle.

The Continental line was ordered to be patient and wait. When the British arrived at the battlefield, the line would be out of view. The intermittent rises and increasing density of the sparse forest near the top provided abundant cover. When the British neared the Continental line, they would have already faced two lines of militia. The Continentals were to finish the redcoats off.

Lieutenant Colonel Washington's 82 dragoons were stationed behind a knoll 100 yards to the rear of the Continental extreme left flank. His force was supplemented by Lieutenant Colonel James McCall and Major Benjamin Jolly with 45 mounted militiamen. This was where 17-year old Thomas Young served. (Young, born January 17, 1764, turned 17 on the day of the battle.) Young later wrote: "It was all important to strengthen the cavalry.... Two companies of volunteers were called for. One was raised by Major Jolly of Union District, and the other, I think, by Major McCall. I attached myself to Major Jolly's company. We drew swords that night, and were informed we had authority to press any horse not belonging to a dragoon or an officer, into our service for the day."[48]

The primary militia line commanded by Colonel Andrew Pickens was formed 150 yards to the front of the Continental line. His would be the first formal line that the British would face. Unlike the perfectly-straight Continental line, this one would be irregular. The riflemen would utilize the cover of trees when they could. This was a typical formation for a militia. Earlier chapters explained that militia riflemen did not subject themselves to bayonet charges, not because of cowardice, but practicality.

Here, Morgan and Pickens instructed the militiamen to wait until the British, with fixed bayonets, came within 50 yards before they were to fire. They would have time to shoot, reload, and maybe fire as many as three times before the bayonet charge would be in their faces. Rifles of that era were not equipped to handle a bayonet insertion. The militiamen used their rifles because the accuracy was necessary for the job they were to do. These men were marksmen and could do much damage to the officer corps of the attackers with one or two shots. The British, accustomed to storming the foe with bayonets, relied on a quick charge to give the enemy less chance to reload. In hand-to-hand combat, the man with the longest knife had the advantage, and a militiaman with his knife and tomahawk could not compete with a bayonet extending four feet in front of a British soldier. Therefore, once the militiaman had no time to reload, he was useless in the face of attack and would necessarily retreat to safety or risk annihilation.

Washington Light Infantry Monument at Cowpens National Battlefield.

The Continental line had an opposite responsibility. The men were outfitted with bayonet-fixed muskets. Less accurate than rifles, the firing power was not so much needed. As the enemy charged on the run, a soldier could fire once and then rely on his bayonet. The Continentals were expected, once they had fired their muskets, to parry the British bayonet charge with their own bayonets. The soldiers of the Continental line were on par with the British infantry as the Continental infantrymen had been trained by men that once were officers fighting for the British (most recently in the French and Indian War). Their training was exactly the same as that of the Legion infantry and the Regiments of Foot.

The militia line extended from the right ravine to the second head of Suck Creek on its left, a distance of 300 yards. Due to the slope of the hill, it, like the Continental line, could not be seen from where the British would appear except for the extreme American left. The American right flank was assigned to Colonel Benjamin Roebuck with his Spartanburg South Carolina Militia regiment. His right end rested at the right ravine. The position from Roebuck's left end to the road was covered by Colonel John Thomas, Jr., also with a regiment of Spartanburg militiamen.

Lieutenant Colonel Joseph Hayes with the Little River South Carolina Militia Regiment was stationed next to Thomas, just left of the road. The Fair Forest South Carolina Militia Regiment of Colonel Thomas Brandon stretched from Hayes' line to Suck Creek on the American's extreme left. Some militiamen were detached another 150 yards forward to form a skirmish squad. Theirs was not a formal line at all; the riflemen located themselves wherever they could each find cover. Trees were sparse at this location and gradually became more dense up the incline.

The American right-flank skirmishers were Colonel Joseph McDowell's North Carolina Militia regimental militiamen. His troops were on a rise just above the rivulet that ran from the right ravine to near the road. On his left, extending from the road 300 yards, but not quite to the left ravine, was Major John Cunningham's Georgia Militia Regiment.

Colonel Pickens tweaked Morgan's original plan to add the South Carolina State Troops to the left of Cunningham's

Washington Light Infantry Monument at Cowpens in 1909 when it was 53 years old.

force. This allowed the skirmishers to cover the area clear to the left ravine. Lieutenant Colonel James McCall had been assigned to the cavalry position, so Major Samuel Hammond took command of the infantry portion. Hammond was then given command of the entire left side of the skirmishers, including the Georgians. Captain Joseph Pickens was assigned direct command over the South Carolina State Troops infantry, the extreme left-flank skirmishers.

As the militia was positioning, Lieutenant Colonel Hayes advanced his regiment about halfway to the skirmishers. There are contradictions as to whether this was a mistake, or another adjustment by Colonel Pickens. Regardless, it provided a retreat target for some of the skirmishers after they had harassed the British with rifle fire as the redcoats formed. The movement forward also brought Hayes' regiment into full view of the British.[49]

Pickens was riding back and forth behind the militiamen shouting reminders: "If the cavalry advances, every third man must fire, while the other two hold their loaded rifles in reserve. Take careful aim and fire low" so as not to overshoot as the British tended to do. "At the first shot pick out the officers. Mark the epauletted men!"[50]

The British began to appear at 7:30 A.M. First to emerge from the woods were the light infantry and the 17th Light Dragoons. They were about 400 yards in front of the skirmishers. Tarleton wanted to gather information regarding the American deployment. He was not able to see the Continental line and assumed Morgan was racing for the Broad River. It was a customary Continental practice to utilize militia to cover a Continental retreat. Tarleton's view of the hillside renewed his confidence that, once he overran the militia, he would be able to run Morgan down from the rear.

The Legion Commander sent the 17th Light Dragoons uphill to force the skirmishers back into the militia line. In so doing, the cavalry was to reconnoiter the Americans and report the details of their defensive arrangement. The light infantry moved to the right of the road, removed knapsacks and other gear to lighten their loads, and began to form.

The dragoons headed for Colonel McDowell's North Carolina skirmishers. McDowell's troops and Major Cunningham's Georgians opened fire. The cavalry troops were sur-

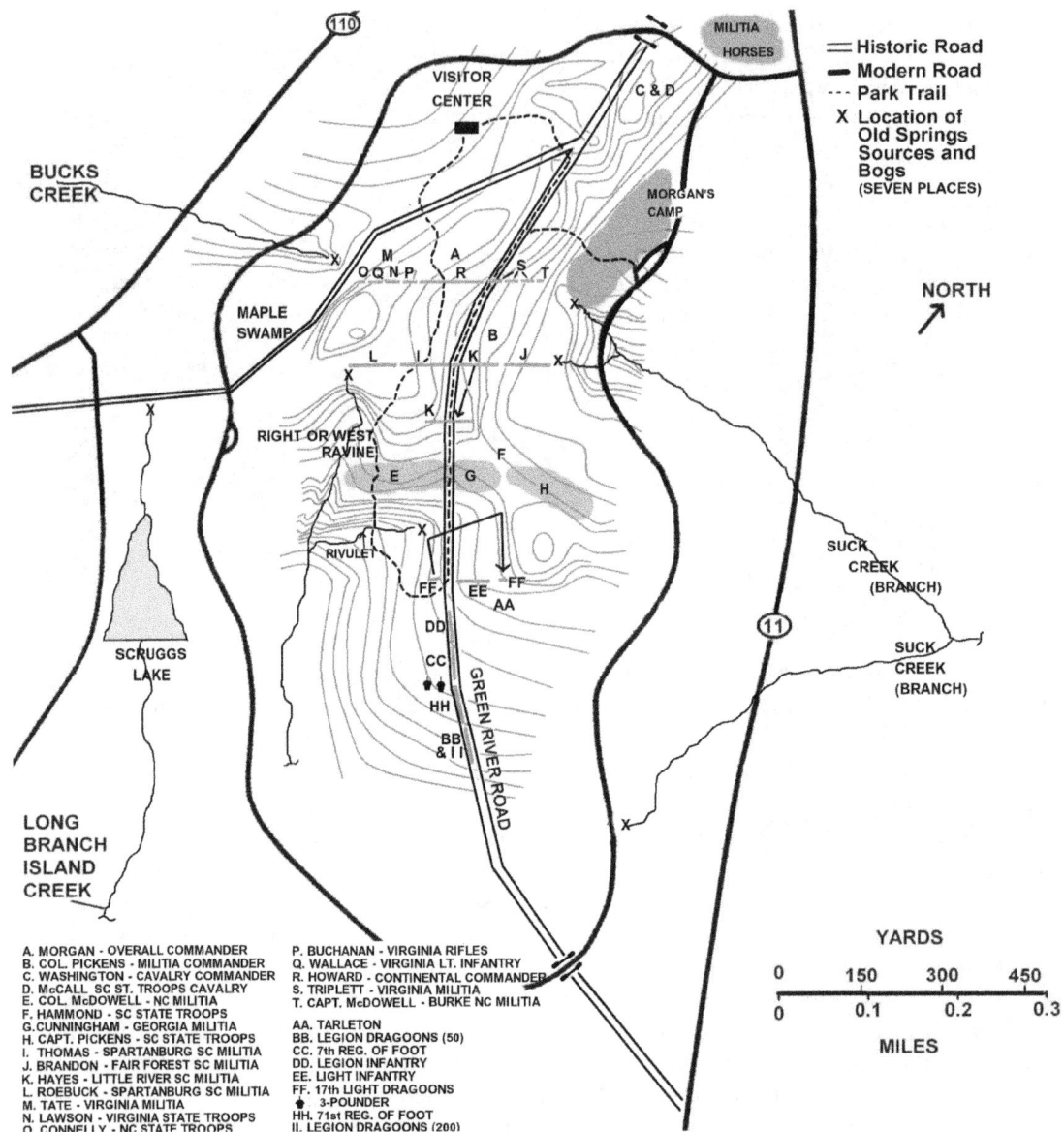

Cowpens initial troop positions and action.

prised that the skirmishers did not give way. Once the riders came to the rivulet, they made an abrupt right turn and rode across the fore of Captain Joseph Pickens' South Carolina State troops, and Major John Cunningham's Georgians. Major Samuel Hammond's left-flank militia force opened up with a devastating fire just as McDowell's had done on the right. The dragoons retreated to the forming British line, but not before 15 of the riders had been shot out of the saddle.

Tarleton did not want Morgan to extend the lead he had in his supposed retreat, so the British Commander ordered a charge. His Legion infantry was set up to the British right of the road, and the light infantry was on the Legion's right flank. The men dragged a three-

Skirmishers' view of the British approach at Cowpens.

pounder up the road and fired canisters of 30-caliber balls as they went. The canisters effectively turned the cannons into a huge shotgun, what in present-day might be called an anti-personnel device. However, the cannon had little effect. The militia and the skirmishers were too well protected. The artillerymen had to adjust their aim to avoid hitting advancing British troops, and they often aimed high and overshot the American lines. In fact, the shot dropped near Lieutenant Colonel William Washington's cavalry, to the rear and left of the Continental line. Washington had to move his force to the safety of another hill to his nearby right.

Hammond's South Carolina and Georgia skirmishers on the American left flank fired two rounds each at the advancing British. The hastening British were directly in front of them, so they retreated to the main militia line as ordered. It was a fighting retreat. They had time to stop, load, and fire from behind trees as they went. Captain Joseph Pickens' regiment stopped when they reached the militia line's left flank. They extended the militia line to their own left and forward to the front of Suck Creek's second head.

While the left flank was retreating, McDowell's force on the right had not yet been pressed, so they began to fire and kept firing at the oncoming British until they were within 100 yards. The 7th Regiment of Foot then set up to the left of the Legion infantry, with another three-pounder. Fifty troopers of the Legion dragoons set up on the British extreme left flank. The 17th Light Dragoons set up on the British extreme right flank. Although the infantries had not received orders to fire, some men of the 7th did so prematurely. The infantries fixed bayonets and moved up the hill. McDowell withdrew to the American mili-

Approaching British view of skirmishers at Cowpens.

tia's right flank. His position was from Colonel Benjamin Roebuck's regiment forward and to the right in front of the knoll at the head of the west (right) ravine.

When the British formed, it was intended the 71st Regiment of Foot be on the left of the 7th; however, there was not enough room as they were forming around the rivulet, so the two regiments became entangled. Tarleton ordered the 71st to drop back 150 yards to the rear. They then joined the remaining 200 troopers of the Legion dragoons in reserve to move as needed.

The British, still with bayonets fixed, continued their march toward Pickens' waiting militia. The militia had been ordered to fire up to two rounds and then retreat to the Continental line before they were overrun by the bayonet charge.

There was some sporadic militia shooting as the British were still not to within 50 yards. Select marksmen from each regiment were allowed to move forward a few paces and fire carefully-aimed shots at British officers. Thomas Young wrote of one such marksman, John Savage from Ninety Six. Young stated in his memoir: "I have heard old Col. Fair say often, that he believed John Savage fired the first gun in this battle. He was riding to and fro, along the lines, When he saw Savage fix his eye upon a British officer; he stepped out of the ranks, raised his gun — fired, and he saw the officer fall."[51]

The 7th had not caught up to the rest of the infantry because of the entanglement; therefore, the left flank of Pickens' militia opened the actual volley firing once the British got within the 50-yard killing range. The volley fire was by regiment. Brandon's force fired first, followed by Thomas' regiment, then Hayes' troops, and finally Roebuck's militiamen. Brandon's soldiers got off another volley before the British, who were coming quickly, forced

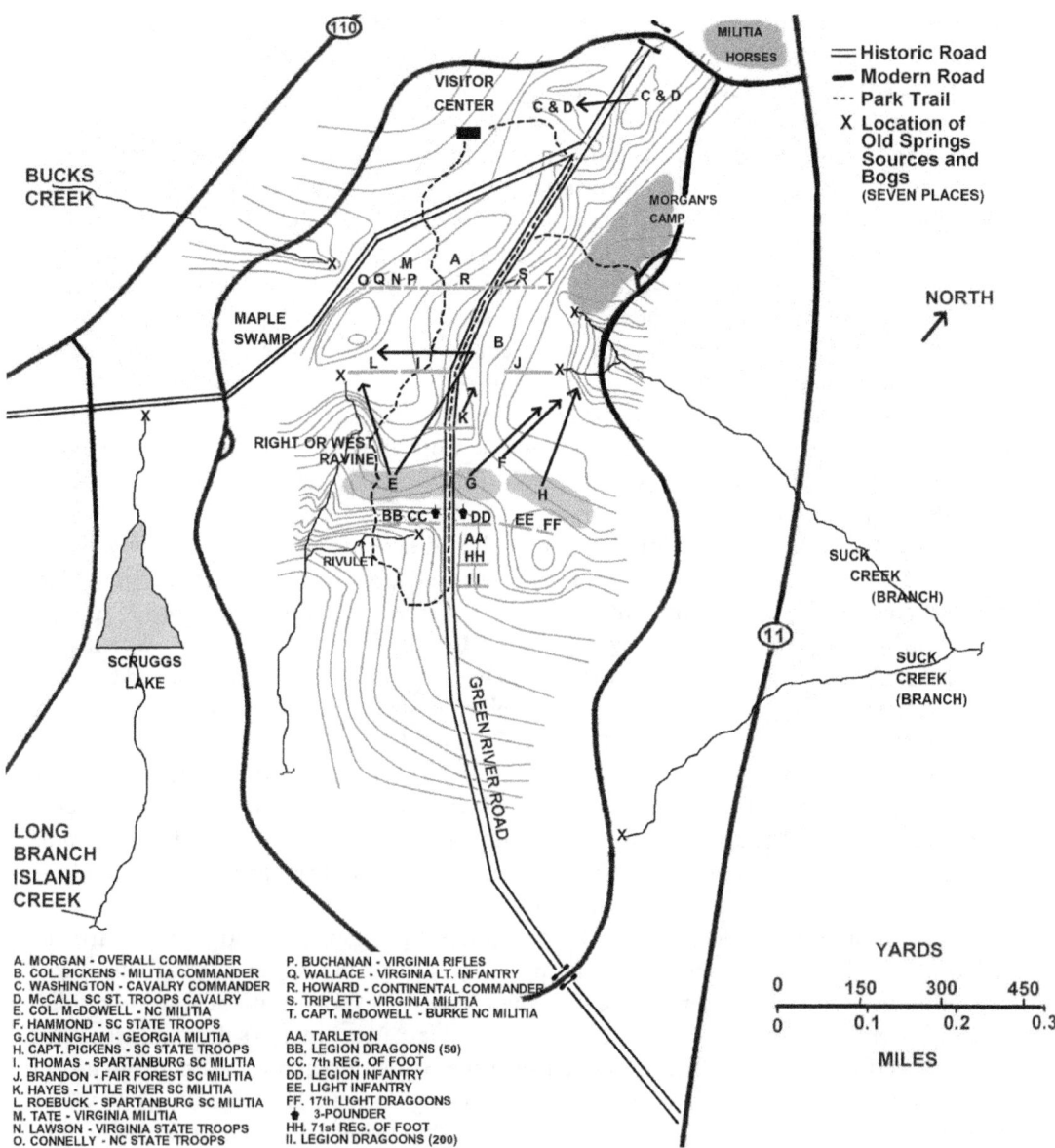

The skirmisher line in action.

them to retreat. The British fired one volley and increased their pace to quickstep with bayonets at the ready. Their shots, as usual, mostly went high.

During the volley fire, Captain Joseph Pickens' South Carolina State Troops and Colonel Joseph McDowell's North Carolinians fired at will from the flanks. The militia barrage was devastating for Tarleton. He lost two-thirds of his infantry officer corps and 90% of the soldiers in four companies of infantry. This was the point where Colonel Pickens, along with Lieutenant Colonel Howard, made another tweak to General Morgan's original plan. Originally, the militia was to do a left face and withdraw in a line around the left flank of the American Continental line. They were to regroup behind the American left flank and prepare for further action. This was an impossible task. In the first place, it would not have given the British any idea that the Americans were in a panicked retreat, which was the goal. A helter-skelter retreat does not employ a controlled march around the end of the entire force.

Secondly, since firing began with the British infantry 50 yards out, they would cover that distance at quickstep within one minute. By the time Brandon's force got off his final volley, the militiamen had to be in full retreat. Colonel Roebuck's regiment, the furthest to the right flank of the core militia regiments (not counting McDowell's force) would have had to march 200 yards to traverse the field and move around the Continental right flank. They would not have even made the Green River Road before the redcoats arrived with their bayonets. Again, because they did not have the equipment to fix bayonets, the militia would have been massacred.

Pickens and Howard developed a plan for Captains Buchanan and Lawson on the Continental line to peel their regiments back a few yards and allow Colonel Roebuck's regiment to retreat straight to the rear. The Continentals then closed the gap, while Roebuck's force made its way to the militia rallying point.

Similarly, Major Triplett's force peeled back and away from the road a few yards to allow Colonel Thomas, Colonel Brandon, and Lieutenant Colonel Hayes to retreat to the rear and escape through the Continental line. Major Hammond's force also retreated straight to the rear and set up as the new extreme left flank of the Continental line which now extended to the left ravine. Most of Colonel McDowell's North Carolinians moved 50 yards rearward to the top of the knoll and set up a delaying action for the American right flank. The remainder of his regiment retreated with Colonel Roebuck.

The retreat was completed three minutes after the beginning of the militia action. The British infantry thought the American militia was panic-stricken; then, the red-coated officers lost control. The attacking lines broke down, gave a loud whoop, and each became an individual rather than a part of a force. They ran after the militia as hard as they could — until they came face-to-face with the Continental line.

In the meantime, Tarleton ordered the 17th Light Dragoons to charge the Continental left flank. The cavalry overran Major Hammond's force and began to attack the forming militiamen who had gathered following their retreat. Several militiamen were injured, and a few were so scared they found their horses and left. Washington's dragoons then had their first action. William Washington had seen the British dragoons break through over Captain Joseph Pickens' state troops, so he immediately charged. He routed the 17th which retreated toward its own lines. A detachment of Washington's horsemen under a Lieutenant Bell gave chase. Washington moved to a rise near General Morgan behind the center of the Continental line where Bell rejoined the unit.

A little known fact involves Captain Henry Connelly's North Carolina State Troops which were set up on the extreme right flank of the Continental line. Major references that describe the Battle of Cowpens omit his company after the British and the Continentals face off. Captain Andrew Wallace's Virginia Light Infantry is discussed as the extreme right flank unit of the Continental line from that time until the fighting ended without discussion of Connelly's departure or further activities.

Captain Connelly's unit is not identified as an infantry company but rather as a cavalry force. The North Carolina State Troops pulled off of the Continental line when Pickens' militiamen retreated. Connelly's men then moved to the rally point and were headed for the militia horse cluster.

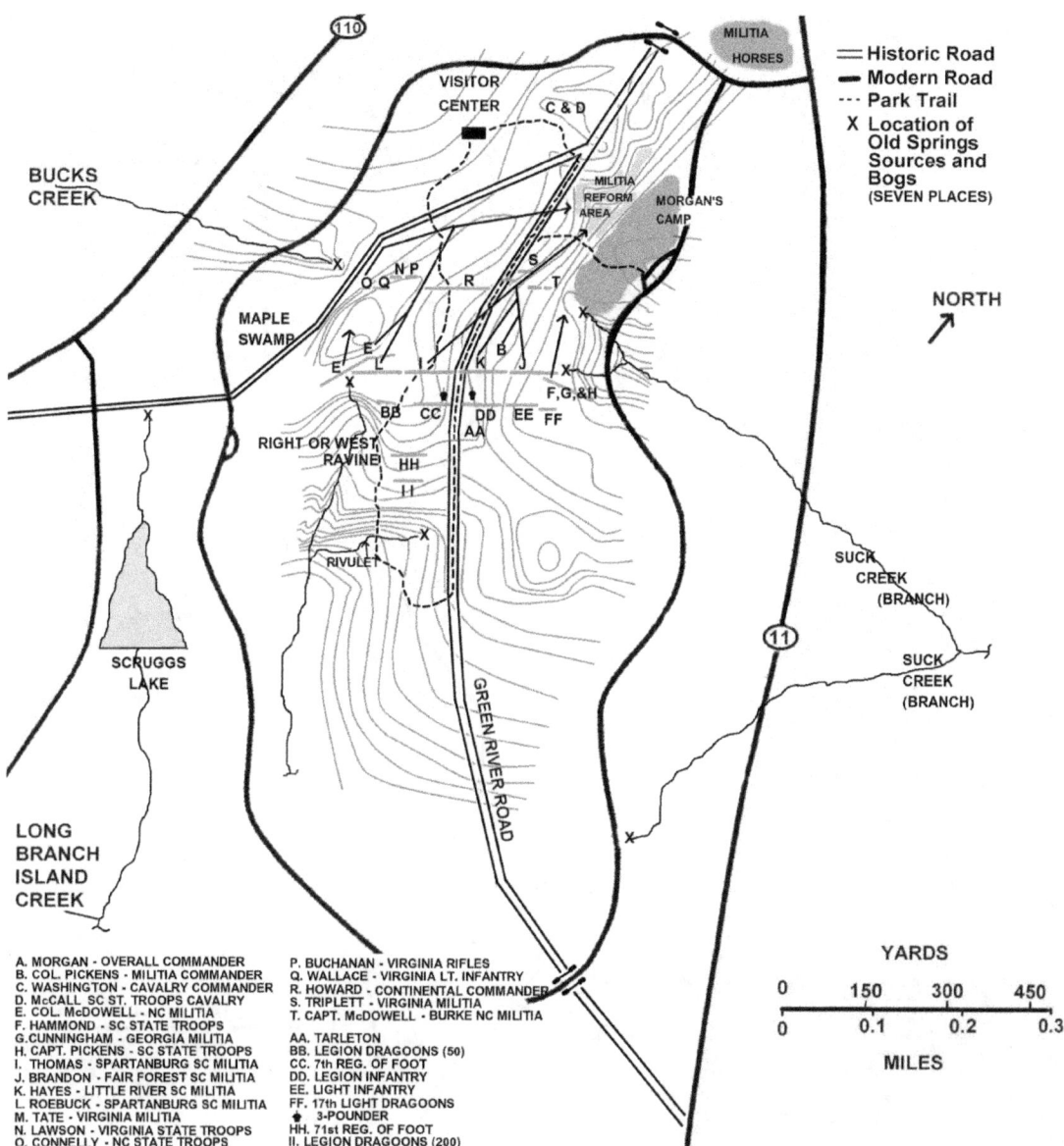

The militia line in action.

Captain Henry Connelly stated in his pension application (see Appendix E):

> This applicant's company was a horse Company.... We were all now under Genl Morgan, and a terrible conflict ensued at the "Cow Pens" between Tarleton's men and the army under Genl Morgan.... This was in January 1781. It was cold weather but inclined to be raining during this battle. The company which belonged to this applicant was placed under Col Howard, on the extreme right of the division.... Our company, when just about to catch up our horses which were hid about four hundred paces in the rear of the line of battle, fell upon us with great fury, but we were fortunately relieved by Washington's Legion that hastened to our assistance.

It is likely that this move was another tweak prearranged between Colonel Pickens and Lieutenant Colonel Howard. General Morgan had issued orders to keep the militia line

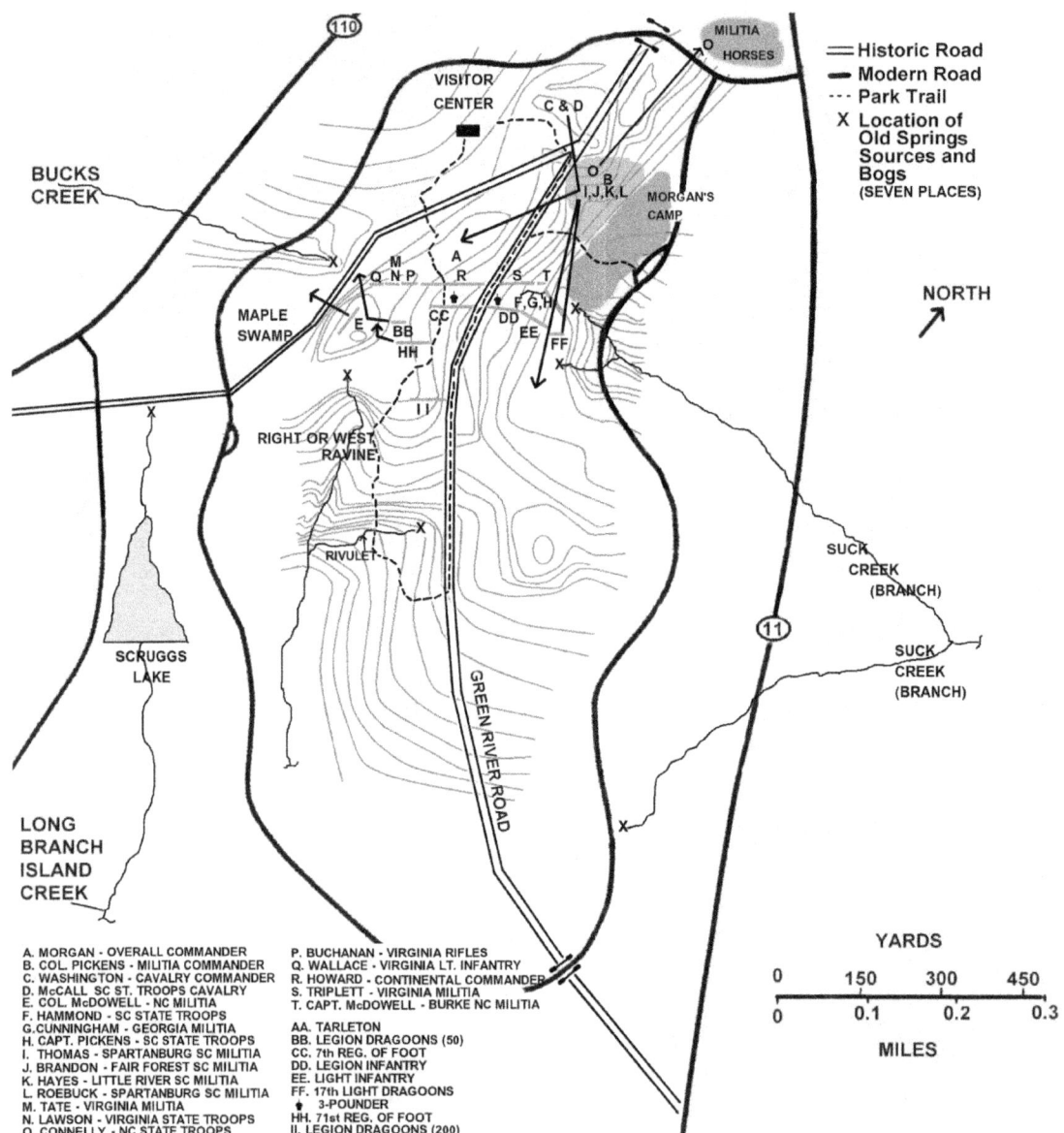

The militia retreats under attack.

away from the horses at this stage of the battle so that none was tempted to ride away. Pickens needed for his main militia to form and be ready to fight, yet he also required someone to take charge of the horses and be ready to bring as many as possible to the militia at the appropriate time. A cavalry-oriented unit that had supposedly not yet seen the action of the enemy in this battle would be the fitting solution. John Eager Howard really did not need a small militia cavalry to anchor the right flank of his line once it was attacked by the enemy. It is unlikely that Connelly's men could handle a musket and bayonet which would have been a necessity.

Note in the citation that Connelly speaks of moving for the horses as if it were an expected occurrence. It is unlikely he would have casually mentioned the event in his application had he been trying to lead his company to an escape from the battle.

General Morgan and Colonel Pickens were able to bring the confused militiamen under control, and the reformation began anew. Morgan displayed his saber in a suave manner and yelled, "Form, form, my brave fellows! Give them one more fire and the day is ours."[52]

Colonel Andrew Pickens then spoke to a few men who were trying to ease away from the group: "Don't act the coward! Are you going to leave your mothers, sisters, sweethearts, and wives to such unmerciful scoundrels, such a horde of thieves? Be Brave, have courage. Return to the fight. If you must lose your life, let it be said you gave it for the protection of your loved ones."[53]

The militia, after they had reloaded their weapons, moved behind the Continental line toward the right flank. Captain Robert Pickens, a cousin of Colonel Andrew Pickens, was a romantic and humorously spoke in later years of having seen a peach tree in bloom as he dodged dragoons during the confusion.

The British infantry stopped when they were suddenly shocked by the appearance of the American Continentals. Then they were overwhelmed by an abrupt volley fire. They fell back, loaded their muskets, and exchanged shots for a few minutes with the Continentals.

(The British infantryman carried a 75-caliber Brown Bess musket usually loaded with a prepared paper cartridge containing one 70-caliber ball and three or four 30-caliber shot. The American lineman was supplied with a French Charleville 69-caliber musket that fired a 63-caliber ball. This was also loaded with a prepared cartridge loaded with the ball and some buckshot.)

The British infantry was in an agonizing situation. They had not eaten since the previous night, had received little sleep, had marched five hours before dawn, and were cold and wet. They had already been repelled by the militia, had to regroup, had moved up an incline, had suffered severe losses, especially from their officer corps, and generally were physically and mentally fatigued. They had to regroup yet again, a seemingly impossible task.

The Legion dragoons on the left flank of the British line and the 71st Regiment of Foot were ordered to outflank the American right. The dragoons and a detachment of the 71st had to drive Colonel McDowell's militia off of the knoll to accommodate the maneuver. McDowell moved rearward off of the knoll to that portion of Maple Swamp at the head of Buck's Creek, and the delay he had caused the Legion dragoons and 71st infantry was invaluable.

Washington returned to Morgan's Hill after having repelled the 17th Light Dragoons. He arrived in time to see the flanking maneuver and immediately hurled his force at the Legion dragoons that were moving behind the American right flank. Lieutenant Bell returned from chasing the 17th and joined in.

The 71st was then moving against the extreme right of the Continentals. At that time, Captain Andrew Wallace's company misunderstood an order. They were told to peel back 90 degrees and protect the right flank against the 71st. Rather, they did an about-face and marched to the rear. In turn, each regiment along the Continental line followed suit and lagged the previous regiment a bit. The Continental rearward march was orderly; however, the British infantry, including the 71st, again lost all control as they thought the American

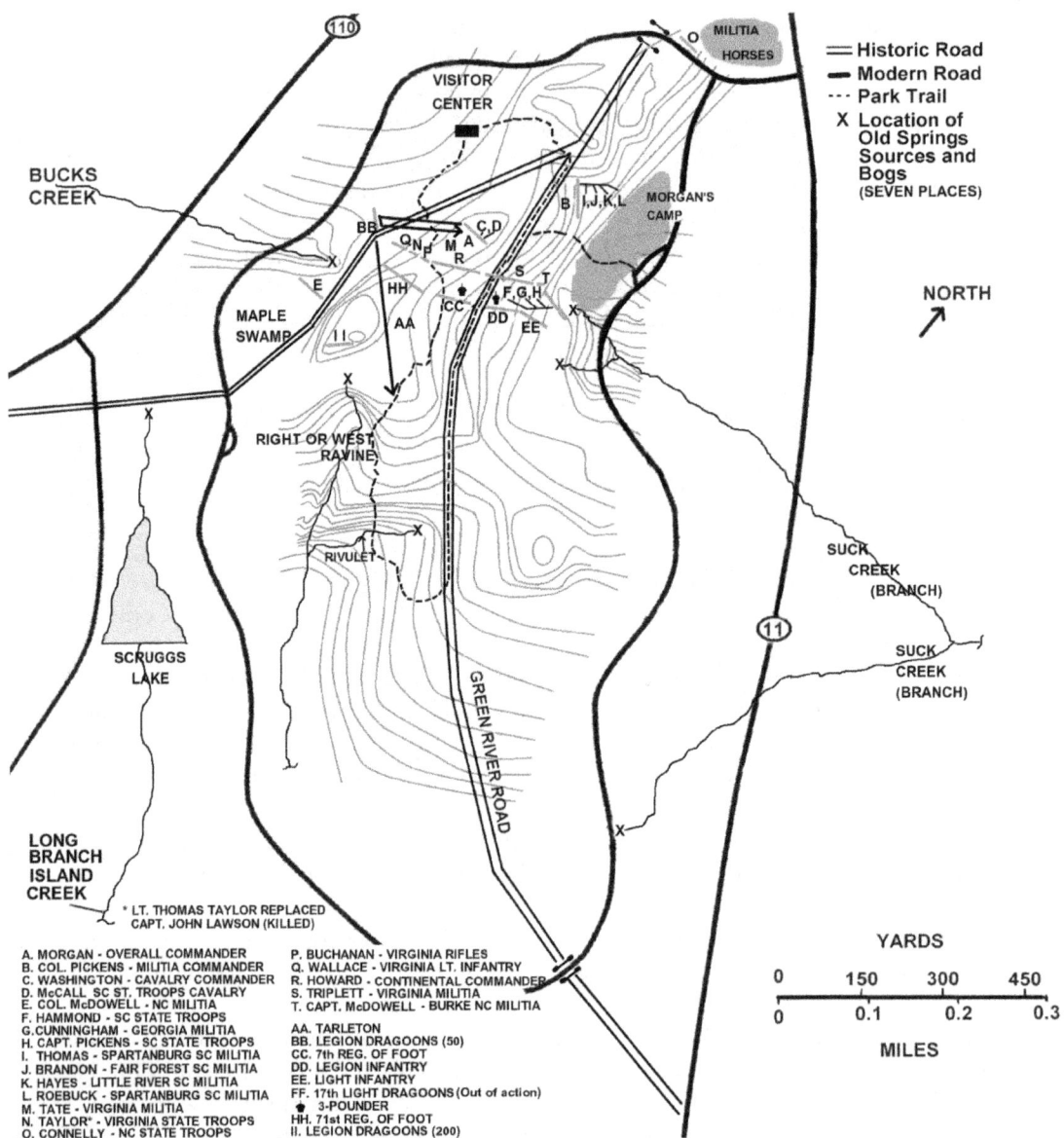

The continental line in action; the militia reforms.

Continentals were in full retreat. The exhausted British line had been buoyed by the participation of the 71st. Each British infantryman, as an individual, quickened his pace, hollered, and chased the American line. Just as before, the officers were unable to reform the British line into a cohesive unit for an orderly charge. The misunderstood American order would benefit Continentals as the British wildly charged.

Washington's riders slashed their way through the Legion dragoons on the American right flank. The American cavalry then returned through the British horsemen on their way to the rear of the Continental line. The 200 Legion dragoon reserves had worked their way to the knoll where McDowell had earlier delayed the British movement against the right flank. The British horsemen saw the American cavalry hack their way through the small Legion detachment just 150 yards away. The reserves, timidly, refused to rescue their comrades.

As Washington returned, he saw the British infantry as they chased the Continentals. He sent a messenger to General Morgan and Lieutenant Colonel Howard stating, "They are coming on like a mob. Give them one fire and I'll charge them."[54]

Morgan got the line turned around, and Howard ordered them to fire. They opened up point blank at the surprised 71st Regiment of Foot, Fraser's Highlanders. The Continental line at that time had still been a fairly straight line, but it was now at an angle. Its juncture with the left flank remained in its original location and acted much like a pivot. The entire right flank had been heavily engaged with the British infantry. Howard ordered the entire line to charge with bayonets. The British attack was crushed.

Washington hurled his cavalry around the American right flank and whacked his way through the 71st Regiment of Foot. Colonel Andrew Pickens and his militia had arrived at the right flank by that time. The militia opened up with their rifles on the reserve British Legion dragoons atop the knoll and caused some damage, but, more importantly, they added to the apprehension of the Legion cavalrymen and drove them away from the action. Once Washington's force had passed through the 71st, the militia poured a devastating barrage upon the Highlanders. McDowell's militia, still in Maple Swamp, also fired on the 71st. Some of the militiamen, then on the American right flank, had mounted horses and advanced rapidly on the 71st Highlanders.

Washington moved through the British 7th Regiment of Foot which surrendered en masse. Many of the British infantrymen dropped to their knees and begged for quarter. The last regiment to continue the fight was the Fraser's Highlanders of the 71st. They had re-formed down the slope from the main line of battle, but became surrounded by Pickens' militia, McDowell's force, and Captain Tate's Continental company. Major Archibald McArthur of the 71st Regiment of Foot had enough. He presented his sword to Colonel Pickens. Pickens wrote Henry Lee:

> We know the particulars of the battle of the Cowpens—That part of the 71st which was there surrendered to me and I believe every officer of that Regiment delivered his sword into my hand.... Major McCarthur of the 71st surrendered to me some distance from the battleground and delivered his sword to me—Jackson acted with me at that time and as Major—I sent back to Genl. Morgan, by Major Jackson, Major McCarthur with the sword.[55]

British Captain Robert Duncanson of the 71st Grenadiers surrendered his sword to Lieutenant Colonel John Eager Howard. Duncanson hung onto Howard's saddle and would not release his hold. Howard challenged him over his action, and Duncanson responded that they were ordered by Tarleton to give no quarter to Morgan's force. The Captain feared he would receive none at the hands of Morgan's men, so he hung onto Howard for protection. Howard then noticed that some of the American troops were screaming "Tarleton's quarter! Tarleton's quarter!" so he rode through his Continental regiments and ordered the men to give quarter to surrendering British soldiers—a sharp contrast to Tarleton's instructions to his men.

Lieutenant Colonel Washington then gave chase to the remaining members of the Legion dragoons. Some of the Americans went after the cannons that the artillery force continued to fire. Maryland Captain Richard Anderson approached one particular cannon and found it was leveled at him and his comrades. The gunner was about to light it off when

Anderson, who carried a spontoon (actually an American pike about six-feet and nine-inches long), used it much like a present-day vaulting pole and landed astraddle the gun. He leveled his short spear at the gunner who then dropped his match.

Tarleton tried to rally his infantrymen to no avail. He even attempted to coerce the men into action by striking some of them with his saber. He also attempted to turn the retreating Legion dragoons so they would face off with Washington's advancing cavalry. Pickens' militia again poured rifle shots into the dragoons, so the British Commander had no better luck in his attempt to spur the dragoons than he did with the infantry. Tarleton's horse was shot from under him, and Assistant Surgeon Robert Jackson of the 71st gave his mount to the commander. Banastre Tarleton desperately wanted to save the cannons, but he retreated with Washington on his tail.

Tarleton turned and saw that Washington was well ahead of his own cavalry. The British Legion Commander and some of his officers stopped, turned, and dueled with the American. Washington whacked and parried with two of the officers until his saber broke at the hilt. Twice he was nearly hit with the full force of enemy swords, but he was saved by some of his men who had finally arrived on scene. Then Tarleton, himself, aimed his pistol at Washington but hit his horse. Washington was given another by one of his horsemen, but by then Tarleton had disappeared.

When "Bloody Ban" led his remaining 50 dragoons toward his wagons, he found them being plundered. He, at first, thought it was American militiamen doing the looting, but when he found out it was his Tory guides, he ordered the cavalry to attack. They then destroyed as many of the wagons as they could, so the Americans would not capture everything.

A small party of Whigs, however, did gain access to a portion of the wagons. Thomas Young explained:

> After this Major Jolly and seven or eight of us, resolved upon an excursion to capture some of the baggage. We went about twelve miles, and captured two British soldiers, two Negroes, and two horses laden with portmanteaus. One of the portmanteaus belonged to a paymaster in the British service, and contained gold. Jolly Insisted upon my returning with the prize to camp, while he pursued a little farther. I did so ... I rode along for some miles at my leisure, on my fine gray charger, talking to my prisoners, when, all at once I saw, coming in advance, a party, which I soon discovered to be British.... I wheeled abruptly to the right into a cross road, but a party of three or four dashed through the woods and intercepted me.... My pistol was empty, so I drew my sword and made battle. I never fought so hard In my life. I knew it was death anyhow, and I resolved to sell my life as dearly as possible. In a few minutes one finger on my left hand was split open; then I received a cut on my sword arm by a parry which disabled It. In the next instant a cut from a sabre across my forehead, (the scar of which I shall carry to my grave,) the skin slipped down over my eyes, and the blood blinded me so that I could see nothing. Then came a thrust in the right shoulder blade, then a cut upon the left shoulder, and a last cut ... on the back of my head—and I fell upon my horse's neck. They took me down, bound up my wounds, and placed me again on my horse a prisoner of war.[56]

The Battle of Cowpens had ended. It was a major embarrassment to Lieutenant Colonel Banastre "Bloody Ban" Tarleton. It was also a devastating loss for Lieutenant General Charles Lord Cornwallis, especially since it followed the Battle of Kings Mountain just three months earlier.

The engagement lasted about one hour. Accounts of the losses vary by report. The Americans lost 2 killed and 61 wounded (militia losses were not reported). The British lost 110 killed of which 37 were officers (one major, 13 captains, 14 lieutenants, and nine ensigns); 830 were taken prisoner, including 27 officers and 200 wounded soldiers. Ten of the officers

Lieutenant Colonels Washington and Tarleton duel at Cowpens. Artist: Alonzo Chappel; unknown engraver, 1858.

killed and several of the epauletted wounded fell in the engagement with Pickens' militia, especially in front of the militia's left flank (South Carolina State Troops and Georgia militia) because the British left flank infantry lagged behind their own right flank units. Many of the rank and file also went down at that point of the battle. Tarleton had sacrificed 90 percent of his force which was 25 percent of Cornwallis' army. The Americans also captured the two three-pounders, 800 muskets, 35 wagons, 60 slaves, 100 dragoon horses, a forge, and ammunition.

A quotation was included in a short biography of Andrew Pickens in *Cowpens Centennial*, 1781–1881, published in 1896. It stated: "The historical writers of the country have been negligent of General Pickens' services to the country ... in connection with the Centennial of Cowpens ... it is in order to show how great were his services in preparation for and in that decisive battle."[57]

Indeed, in later years (as discussed earlier), General Morgan had not given Colonel Pickens and his militia their due when he defended his choice of field for the battle. He generally censured the militia as a unit that would try to escape a fight. However, he had thought well enough of Pickens to make him second in command at the battle, and he wrote a glowing report of the Colonel's capabilities to Major General Greene prior to the battle. Then, immediately following the action he stated the battle was "to a great extent a victory of militia over regulars.... Pickens and all the officers in his corps behaved well.... The volunteers of North Carolina, South Carolina, and Georgia, under the command of the brave and valuable Colonel Pickens."[58]

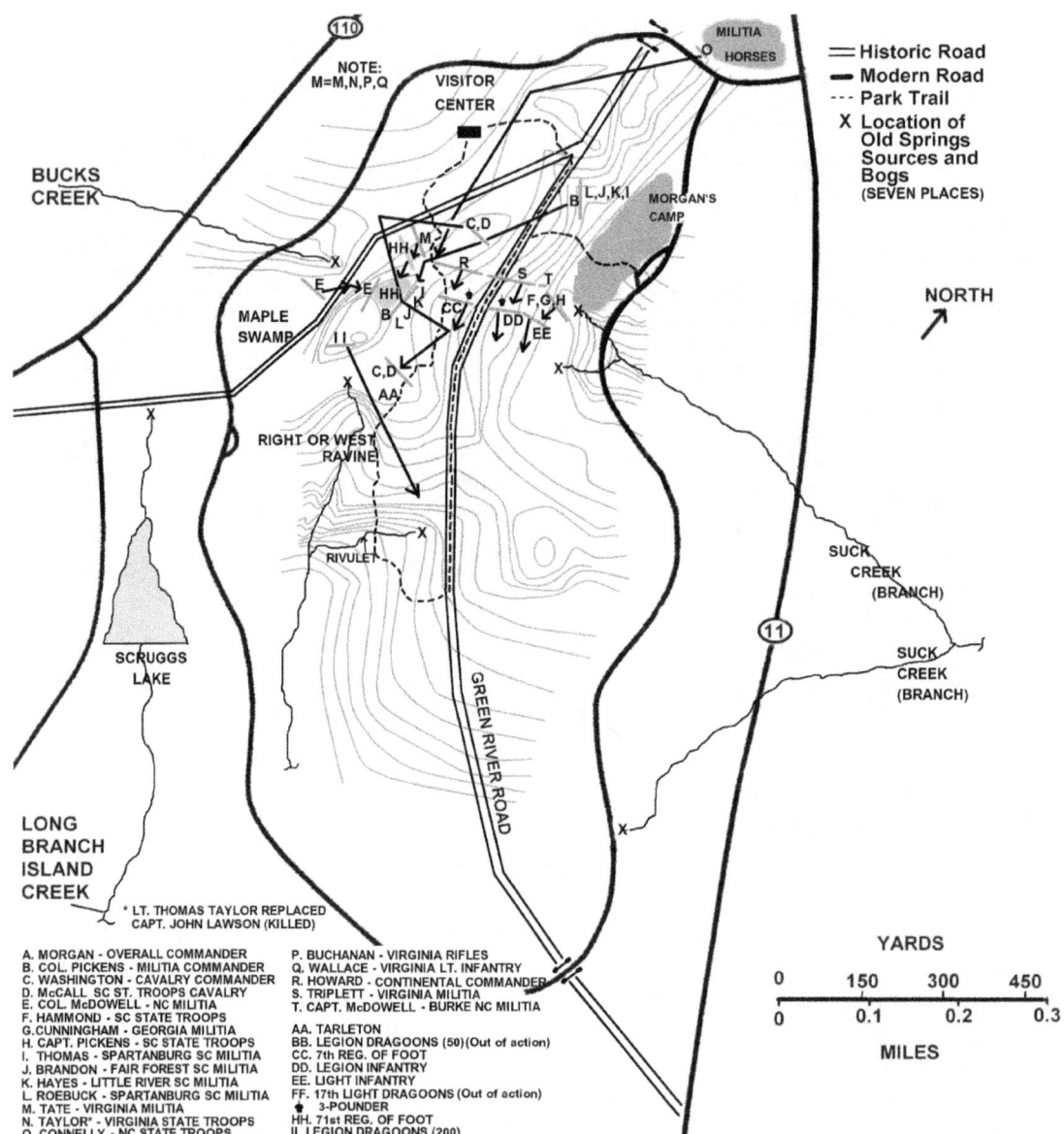

Victory at Cowpens.

Governor John Rutledge added later, "Colonel Pickens' behavior justifies the opinion I have always had of that excellent officer. Inclosed is a brigadier's commission of which I desire his acceptance."[59]

An unidentified officer of the Maryland Continentals said of the militia action, "Here the battle was gained!"[60]

General Henry "Light Horse Harry" Lee stated in his memoirs, "Morgan derived a very great aid from Pickens and his militia."[61]

Lieutenant General Charles Lord Cornwallis, himself, rendered a back-handed compliment when he said, "I will not say much in praise of the militia of the Southern Colonies, but the list of British officers and soldiers killed and wounded by them ... proves but too fatally they are not wholly contemptible."[62]

Lieutenant Colonel Banastre Tarleton later added that the most murderous fire he ever encountered was this, from militiamen under Colonel Pickens.[63]

Several remarks by others are quoted by A. L. Pickens. He wrote:

> The Carolina riflemen, led by Pickens, played the chief part in winning that glorious field. (George White).... The distinguishing feature of the battle of Cowpens upon the American side was undoubtedly the effective work of Pickens' marksmen. (Edward McCrady).... He and his men were the real heroes of Cowpens. (David McKissick).... Animated by the spirit and courage of their commander in this important battle, the militia fairly won an equal share of glory with the regulars. (Anonymous).[64]

An "equal share of the glory" sounds fair. It was a great victory for all, militia and Continentals alike. Brigadier General Daniel Morgan exceedingly out-commanded Lieutenant Colonel Banastre Tarleton.

Indeed, for the victory at Cowpens, "The Congress of the United States voted public thanks to General Morgan and presented him with a medal of gold. Colonels Washington and Howard received medals of silver, and Colonel Pickens a sword." (Pickens' sword was described as highly ornamented, with a silver hilt, and a leather scabbard. The blade was inscribed in Spanish with "Draw me not without cause and sheathe me not without honor.")[65]

The official action of Congress occurred on March 9, 1781, stating: "Ordered****That a sword be presented to Colonel Pickens of the militia, in testimony of his spirited decisive and magnanimous conduct in the action before mentioned."[66]

One exceptional honorific that Colonel Andrew Pickens received was from Lyman C. Draper. In the introduction of his excellent book about Kings Mountain, he wrote of his plans to write other "similar volumes" as a series. One was to be called Pickens and the Battle of Cowpens[67] (as opposed to heroes of Cowpens or other similar titles). This thought was a great tribute to Andrew Pickens.

Lieutenant General Charles Lord Cornwallis wrote a very embarrassing (for him) report about Cowpens to Major General Sir Henry Clinton. Cornwallis, in order to justify his move northward, had continually related to Clinton that South Carolina was well under Tory control. Matters became worse for Cornwallis as stated in an extract of the report (with a short cover note to the Secretary of State Lord George Germaine) printed in the April 3, 1781, issue of *The London Chronicle* (see Appendix G):

> Camp on Turkey Creek, Broad River
> January 18
> My Lord,
> I THINK it necessary to transmit to your Lordship a Copy of my Letter to Sir Henry Clinton, lest the exaggerated Accounts from the Rebels should reach Europe before your Lordship could hear from New York. I shall only say, in Addition to what I have said to Sir Henry Clinton, that this Event was extremely unexpected, for the greatest Part of the Troops that were engaged, had, upon all former Occasions, behaved with the most distinguished Gallantry.
> Extract of a Letter from Earl Cornwallis to Sir Henry Clinton, dated, Camp on Turkey Creek, Broad River, January 18, 1781.
> IN my Letter of the 6th of this Month I had the Honor to inform your Excellency, that I was ready to begin my March for North Carolina; having been delayed for some Days by a diversion made by the Enemy towards Ninety Six. General Morgan still remained on the Pacolet; his Corps, by the best Accounts I could get, consisted of about 500 men, Continental and Virginia State Troops, and 100 Cavalry under Colonel Washington, and Six or Seven Hundred Militia.... Lieu-

tenant Colonel Tarleton, with the Legion and Corps annexed to it, consisting of about 300 Cavalry and as many Infantry, and the 1st Battalion of the 71st Regiment, and 1 Three Pounder, had already passed the Broad River for the Relief of Ninety Six. I therefore directed Lieutenant Colonel Tarleton to march on the West of Broad River to endeavor to strike a Blow at General Morgan, and, at all Events, to oblige him to pass the Broad River. I likewise ordered that he should take with him the 7th Regiment, and 1 Three Pounder.... The Remainder of the Army [Cornwallis] marched between the Broad River and the Catawba. As General Green [sic] had quitted Mecklenburgh [sic] County, and crossed the Peedee, I made not the least Doubt that General Morgan would retire on our advancing.

The Progress of the Army was greatly impeded by heavy Rains which swelled the River and Creeks; yet Lieutenant Colonel Tarleton conducted his March so well, and got so near to General Morgan, who was retreating before him, as to make it dangerous for him to pass Broad River; and came up with him at Eight o'Clock A. M. on the 17th Instant. Every Thing now bore the most promising Aspect; the Enemy were drawn up in an open Wood, and, having been lately joined by some Militia, were more numerous; but the different Quality of the Corps under Lieutenant Colonel Tarleton's Command, and his great Superiority in Cavalry, left him no Room to Doubt of the most brilliant Success. The Attack was begun by the First Line of Infantry, consisting of the 7th Regiment, the Infantry of the Legion, and Corps of Light Infantry annexed to it; a Troop of Cavalry was placed on each Flank; the 1st Battalion of the 71st, and the Remainder of the Cavalry, formed the Reserve. The Enemy's Line soon gave Way, and their Militia quitted the Field; but our Troops having been thrown into some Disorder by the Pursuit, General Morgan's Corps faced about, and gave them a heavy Fire: This unexpected Event occasioned the utmost Confusion in the First Line....

...Lieutenant Colonel Tarleton assembled Fifty of his Cavalry, and, being animated by the Bravery of the Officer who had so often led them to Victory, charged and repulsed Colonel Washington's Horse, retook the Baggage of the Corps, and cut to Pieces the Detachment of the Enemy that had taken Possession of it, and, after destroying what they could not conveniently bring off, retired with the Remainder unmolested to Hamilton's Ford, near the Mouth of Bullock's Creek.

The Loss of our Cavalry is inconsiderable, but I fear about 400 of the Infantry are either killed, wounded or taken. I will transmit the particular Account of the Loss as soon as it can be ascertained.

I shall direct Lieutenant Colonel Balfour to transmit a Copy of this Letter, by the first Opportunity, to the Secretary of State.

The Battle of Cowpens provided the onset of Britain's darkest days of the American Revolution. Except for a few skirmishes, the British army was finished in South Carolina. They had utterly failed. The only hope that Cornwallis held was for success in Virginia. That would be a wasted effort since he had not maintained control of the Carolinas and Georgia as Major General Sir Henry Clinton had desired.

However, the backcountry strife between Whigs and Tories was not at an end. Indeed, it would yet be bloody.[68]

10

Taking Control of South Carolina (1781)

Cowpens battlefield was quiet at 9:00 A.M. on January 17, 1781. The action had ceased. Colonel Andrew Pickens rode to where Lieutenant Colonel William Washington was gathering his cavalry. The two conferred and united their forces to pursue Lieutenant Colonel Banastre Tarleton who had escaped with 50 dragoons. Pickens ordered Georgia Major James Jackson to gather some militia and follow them. It is likely that several militiamen were mounted by that time.

Colonel Pickens wrote to Henry Lee:

> When I met Col Washington with his cavalry in pursuit of Tarlton I ordered Jackson, who was mounted to return as quickly as possible with as many of the mounted militia as he could get — We pursued with Col. Washington 22 miles and [captured] a brigade of prisoners of several in Tarlton's rear but could not bring him to an action. We did not get back to the battleground till the next morning and overtook General Morgan with the prisoners in the night at Gilbert's Town.[1]

Tarleton had a good lead by the time the Americans found his trail. He had retraced his march and arrived at Burr's Mill where he pressed Whig Adam Goudelock into service as a guide. Goudelock feared for his family's safety, so he led Tarleton to Hamilton's Ford on the Broad River where the British Legion Commander intended to spend the night. (Hamilton's Ford was five miles west of Lieutenant General Charles Lord Cornwallis' headquarters on Turkey Creek.)

Thomas Young recorded some information in his memoir about his experiences as a prisoner during Tarleton's trek:

> They took me down, bound up my wounds, and placed me again on my horse a prisoner of war.... Col. Tarleton sent for me, and I rode by his side for several miles. He was a very fine looking man, with rather a proud bearing, but very gentlemanly in his manners. He asked me a great many questions, and I told him one lie, which I have often thought of since. In reply to his query whether Morgan was reinforced before the battle? I told him "he was not, but that he expected a reinforcement every minute." "He asked me how many dragoons Washington had." I replied that "he had seventy, and two volunteer companies of mounted militia, but you know they won't fight." "By G-d!" he quickly replied, "they did today, though!" I begged him to parole me, but he said, "If he did, I should go right off and turn to fighting again." I then told him he could get three men in exchange for me, and he replied "Very well, when we get to Cornwallis's army, you shall be paroled or exchanged; and mean while, I'll see that your wounds are taken care of." ...We got to Hamilton Ford, on Broad River, about dark. Just before we came to the river, a British dragoon came up at full speed, and told Col. Tarleton that Washington was close behind in pursuit. It was now very dark, and the river was said to be swimming. The British were not willing to take water. Col. Tarleton flew into a terrible passion, and drawing his sword, swore he would cut down the first man who hesitated. They knew him too well to hesitate longer. During the confusion, a young Virginian by the name of Deshaser (also a prisoner) and myself, managed to

get into the woods.... We slipped away one at a time up the river, Deshaser first, then myself.... It was now very dark and raining when we came to the Pacolet. I could not find the ford, and it was well, for the river was swimming.[2]

The report of Washington's proximity to Hamilton's Ford was erroneous. It is likely that Tarleton's force spent the remainder of the night on the bank after crossing the rain-swollen stream. Brigadier General Daniel Morgan was aware that Cornwallis would soon be after him, not only to demolish his force but especially to rescue his prisoners. Seventy-five of the prisoners were severely wounded and would be left at the battlefield. Most of Pickens' militiamen were still there, and General Morgan detailed them to remain at the battlefield, bury the dead, and care for the wounded.

Colonel Pickens' servant, Dick, who often traveled with the Colonel, was strolling through the battlefield when he came across a gravely-injured British officer. Dick retrieved some water from a nearby creek and carried it in his hat to the officer. The servant then gently grabbed one of the officer's ankles and lifted it from the ground. Dick asked the officer if he could remove his boots. The officer replied, "Surely boy, you will not take them before I die!"[3]

Dick responded, "Him [the boot] mighty fine." The servant explained that Colonel Pickens' well-worn footwear sorely needed to be replaced right away. He gently removed the officer's boots, likely with consent.

When Pickens departed to find Washington, he left British Major Archibald McArthur, of the 71st Regiment of Foot, in the hands of Lieutenant Colonel John Eager Howard. Howard commented to McArthur about the reckless British charge up the incline. McArthur, speaking of Tarleton, responded, "rash and foolish boy!"[4]

Brigadier General Daniel Morgan had departed the scene by noon on the 17th with his wing of the Southern Department, including the militia units that had accompanied him into South Carolina. Washington and his dragoons had not yet returned from tracking Tarleton and would have to find the General later. It would be a slow march for the Continentals. Because his was considered a "light" army, Morgan had not carried a huge supply train with him. Now, however, he hauled many captured arms with ammunition and had to prod many of the prisoners as they sluggishly moved. They reached the Broad River that night. (They likely crossed at Dennard's Ford and then camped until the next day. See Chapter 8 for the Ford's location.)[5]

The 18th was a busy day for many. Tarleton's pursuers gave up the chase at midnight and returned to the battlefield. They had captured several prisoners on the trek, but none was "Bloody Ban." Washington headed north to rejoin Morgan.

Pickens ordered his militia to set white flags around the battlefield lest a British force arrive while the casualties were under care. The militiamen took tents and some provisions from Tarleton's abandoned wagons to make the wounded, Americans and British, as comfortable as possible. They quickly buried the dead, then Pickens' force marched from the field with the prisoners captured the night before. Colonel Pickens caught up with Morgan and the Continentals at Gilbert Town, North Carolina, that night. (See Chapter 8 for the location of Gilbert Town.)

Tarleton reached the Hillhouse estate on Turkey Creek early on the 18th. He found General Cornwallis standing in front of his tent, leaning forward on his sword as one might do when resting with a walking staff. When Tarleton approached and dismounted, he began to issue an oral report of the battle. Cornwallis tightened up, and his sword snapped. He let out with a loud curse, then allowed Tarleton to continue.

10. Taking Control of South Carolina (1781)

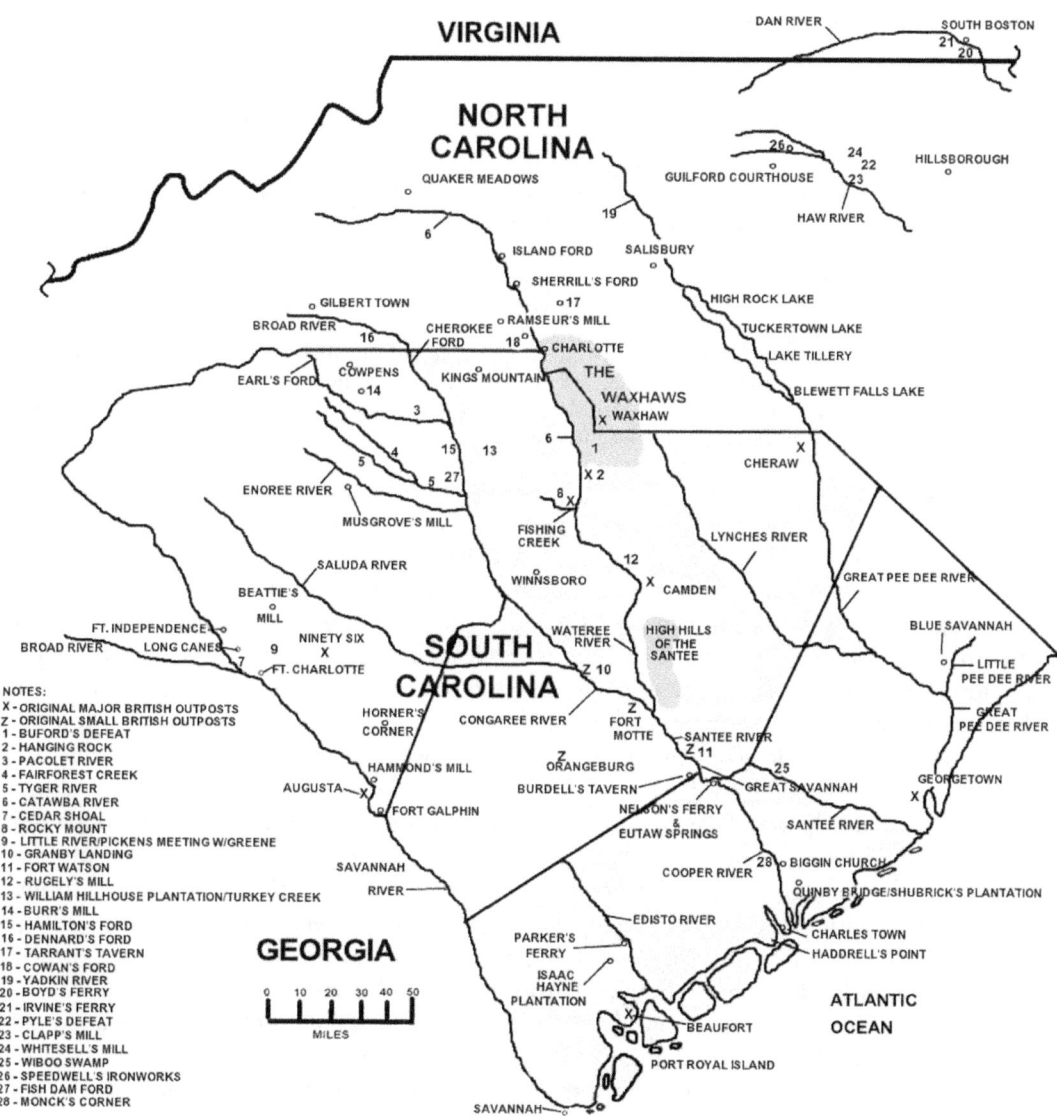

South Carolina points of interest 1781.

The General was furious by the time Tarleton's report ended. Cornwallis had twice told Major General Sir Henry Clinton that South Carolina was under control. However, his supposed Tory solution, Brigadier General Robert Cunningham, had been cowed by the Whigs and abandoned his post. In addition, his most trusted and aggressive officer had just lost one-third of the British Southern Army, and Daniel Morgan was moving freely about the backcountry. Cornwallis wrote a report of the battle for Major General Sir Henry Clinton and forwarded a copy to Lord George Germain, Secretary of State for the American Colonies in the cabinet of Prime Minister Lord Frederick North. The letter was posted in an April 3, 1781, issue of *The London Chronicle* (see Appendix G for a transcription of the letter).

The outcome at Cowpens forced Cornwallis to give up all hope that Loyalists could control South Carolina with little British protection. This should have been apparent to him for at least two years; ever since the Battle of Kettle Creek. William Johnson, Major General Nathanael Greene's biographer, later commented that Cornwallis made serious strategic errors that led to Tarleton's defeat.

> Had Tarleton, instead of being ordered to push his adversary ... been simply instructed to hang upon his rear ... whilst Cornwallis advanced up the east side of the Broad River far enough to cut off his retreat.... Or had he advanced up the east side of the Broad River as was originally projected, whilst Leslie continued his march up the east side of the Catawba: even after the victory obtained over Tarleton (at Cowpens), it would have been impossible for ... Morgan to have effected their retreat.... [Cornwallis'] uncertainty relative to the military force [Greene] collecting in his front ... asserted by his own officers, that with having all the loyalists of Tryon county in his front to furnish him intelligence, he could [not think to] remain in such a state of ignorance on that subject ... though ... a moderate distance from each other, and engaged in joint operations against Morgan, yet from the 14th to the 17th, he left Tarleton entirely without intelligence of his own [Cornwallis'] movements or further intentions.[6]

While Cornwallis seethed, the long-awaited Major General Alexander Leslie and his troops arrived. Cornwallis prepared his huge force to move after Morgan. This took several hours due to the size of his entourage. The British army always hauled an extraordinary number of wagons loaded with not only arms, ammunition, and food, but also clothing, spirited drink, and many other superfluous items. Additionally, Cornwallis assumed that Morgan would not be so quick to leave South Carolina now that Tarleton's Legion had been decimated. He was wrong. He thought Morgan would target Ninety Six before he retreated, so Cornwallis wasted the better part of two days moving west toward his prey, but Daniel Morgan was halfway to the Catawba River from Gilbert Town before Cornwallis got turned around.

Pickens had joined Morgan at Gilbert Town on the night of the 18th. The following morning, General Morgan turned his prisoners over to Colonel Pickens and the militia. They were to take a northern, mountainous, and circuitous route through North Carolina to allow the Continentals faster movement along the much easier southern trails. It is likely that Pickens took a trail toward Quaker Meadows (home of the McDowells), but turned off at the Catawba River and followed it around to Island Ford.

Colonel Pickens wrote Henry Lee about the trek, "Next day Genl Morgan ordered me to take charge of the prisoners and take the upper rout, while he with the Infantry under Col. Howard and Col. Washington's Calvary took a lower rout to draw Lord Cornwallis after him — We got safe over the Catawba River and joined again at Sherral's Ford after a fatiguing march of four days with the prisoners."[7]

He could have crossed the Catawba at Island Ford and moved downriver along the east bank to Sherrill's Ford (sometimes Sherral's Ford and Sherrald's Ford) to ensure he would avoid the coming high water. According to his statement, Andrew Pickens likely arrived at Sherrill's Ford on the 22nd, one day ahead of Morgan.

General Morgan apparently moved from Gilbert Town via Ramseur's Mill and reached Sherrill's Ford on the Catawba River January 23. He crossed before camping for the night. He had developed a routine for his force for the trek. The men arose at 4:00 A.M., had breakfast, and marched by dawn. Other repasts were taken on the move. They made a long day of it and encamped well after dark. When they approached a major river, they crossed before camping if possible. (Sherrill's Ford was located near the present-day North Carolina town of the same name. Island Ford was located near present-day Catawba, North Carolina, ten miles upriver from Sherrill's Ford.)

Morgan was wise to cross the Catawba when he did. Shortly thereafter, the river rose considerably and remained high, swift, and treacherous for days. Since Cornwallis could not cross the river, General Morgan tarried and awaited orders from General Greene. He believed Greene might consider an aggressive move back into South Carolina and even Georgia.

Colonel Pickens was relieved of his captives who were then marched to the Prisoners' Camp at Charlottesville, Virginia. It is reported that Brigadier General Edward Stevens' force assumed the guard duty.[8] General Stevens led a Virginia State Militia Troop that was assigned to General Greene. (This was the same Virginia General Stevens that commanded the Virginia militia under General Gates at Camden.) Some have suggested that the prisoners were removed by Major Edmund M. Hyrne, Deputy Commissary General of Prisoners in the Southern Department; however, General Greene was clear that Stevens had command.

Daniel Morgan continued to agonize with his arthritis, sciatica, and hemorrhoids. He knew he needed to retire his commission, so he penned two letters to Nathanael Greene on the 24th that stated he must retire from the field. He added, "Pickens is an enterprising man, and a very judicious one; perhaps he may answer the purpose.... General Davidson, Colonel Pickens and General Sumter.... Can manage the militia better than I can, and will supply my place."[9]

Apparently Morgan tried to get along with Sumter following their earlier dispute over forage. That disagreement had so angered Sumter that he would not even provide forces for Morgan at Cowpens.

General Cornwallis did not arrive at Ramseur's Mill until January 25, at least two days behind General Morgan. The British Commander realized that, if he were to catch the Continentals, he would have to convert his force to a light army. He staged a huge bonfire at Ramseur's and destroyed many of his wagons and supplies. This demolition reportedly took two days. He started marching again on the 28th, but found the Catawba River too high to cross. Morgan had not yet decamped to march for Salisbury, so was still on the east bank of the river at Sherrill's Ford when Cornwallis was at the west bank of the Catawba River, 15 miles south.

Major General Nathanael Greene had received word of the victory at Cowpens on January 24, 1781. He exulted, ordered in his detachments, and prepared his force to march and reunite with Morgan's wing. Greene left Cheraw Hill on January 25 and planned to meet General Morgan at Sherrill's Ford, North Carolina, on January 30.[10]

On the 25th, South Carolina Governor John Rutledge issued the Brigadier General commission for Andrew Pickens. Rutledge wrote to General Morgan:

> This total defeat of chosen Veteran British Troops by a number far inferior to theirs will for ever distinguish the gallant men by whom the Glorious Victory was obtained, and endear them to their country. Colonel Pickens' behavior justifies the opinion I have always had of that excellent officer. Inclosed is a Brigadier's commission, of which I desire his acceptance. The officers commanding these regiments (those of Colonels LeRoy Hammond, William Harden and Benjamin Gates) are, therefore, to obey his orders as their Brigadier General (this in addition to his own regiment).[11]

After Pickens received the commission, he promoted Robert Anderson to Regimental Colonel.

It is likely that Brigadier General Pickens did not cross the border into South Carolina until after he received his commission. He also acquired orders as to his responsibilities.

He, Brigadier Generals Thomas "Gamecock" Sumter, and Francis "Swamp Fox" Marion comprised a triumvirate to counter the Loyalists and British that remained in South Carolina.

General Marion had command of the lowcountry militia effort. He was to break communication and supply channels between Charles Town and the backcountry outposts. He also planned to harass the Tories in the area.

General Sumter had a similar duty in the mid-state region from Camden northward. General Pickens managed the upcountry that ranged from Ninety Six on the east to the Cherokee Nation on the west, and from Georgia on the southwest to the North Carolina border.

Brigadier General Francis Marion had been busy. He and Lieutenant Colonel Henry "Light Horse Harry" Lee attempted to capture the British garrison at Georgetown, South Carolina, on January 25. Lee was Commander of Lee's Legion, a Continental Army dragoon force equivalent to Lieutenant Colonel Tarleton's British Legion. (This is the same retired General Henry Lee to whom retired General Andrew Pickens wrote on August 28, 1811. That missive, cited in several chapters of this book, offers valuable information for historians.)

The Americans successfully entered Georgetown and captured Garrison Commander, British Lieutenant Colonel George Campbell. The British seemed disinclined to act. Indeed, when Lee attacked the outskirts of the city, the British troops vanished as a turtle withdrawn inside its impenetrable shell. The garrison soldiers had boarded themselves up inside their strong defensive structures. Marion and Lee retreated. They had decided not to risk loss of American lives in order to capture the Georgetown garrison.

General Greene, on the move to Sherrill's Ford, wrote to Henry Lee on the 26th. He suggested that, because of the victory at Cowpens, it might be timely to move back into South Carolina and attack Ninety Six. He further stated that he would discuss the idea with Generals Morgan, Davidson, Sumter, and Pickens after he joined them at Salisbury, North Carolina.

When Greene arrived at Sherrill's Ford on January 30, he held a council of war with his officers. The Commander considered a battle with Cornwallis, but the other officers convinced him to move toward the Dan River and cross into Virginia. Such a long march might further deplete Cornwallis' force. Additionally, the Americans were not prepared for a confrontation.

The officers further decided they would send detachments to aggressively defend the Catawba River crossings and attempt to delay Cornwallis' army. This would allow Greene and the Continental Army time to expand their lead on the British. A small squad of Morgan's Flying Army would defend the upper fords of the Catawba; North Carolina Brigadier General William Davidson would safeguard all of the lower fords. When Cornwallis did complete a crossing, the American defenders were to retreat and catch the Continentals at Salisbury, 20 miles east. Greene sent Morgan with the army to Salisbury while the Southern Department Commander remained near the Catawba to gather Davidson's militia as they retreated from the fords.

Andrew Pickens must have moved into his new assignment prior to January 30, 1781, because he did not sit in on General Greene's council of war and was not involved in defending the Catawba against Cornwallis' crossing.[12]

General Cornwallis had arrived at the Catawba on the 28th. Here he had to wait for the waters to recede. They had done so by the 31st, but heavy rains erupted again. The General, therefore, decided he should ford the river before the water level rose to an impassable level. He chose to cross over that night at Cowan's Ford (sometimes McCowan's Ford). As the troops approached the ford at 1:00 A.M., the officers noticed many campfires that extended for miles along the east bank. Cornwallis knew the Americans intended to defend against his attempt to traverse the river. He dispatched Lieutenant Colonel James Webster with the baggage to create a distraction at Beattie's Ford two miles north.

Webster met little resistance at Beattie's as the Americans had concentrated on the fords further south. Cornwallis began his attempt in the predawn darkness. A local Tory, named Frederick Hager, guided the British through the area.

The Catawba River was 500 yards wide at Cowan's Ford. Although the waters had receded, they were still turbulent and cold. An island lay 150 yards from where the British entered the water. There the ford split. A two-to-four foot deep horse ford angled southeast, and a wagon ford ran straight east. Although shorter than the horse ford, the wagon ford was deeper.

Brigadier General Daniel Morgan. Artist: J. Herring from a sketch by Col. J. Trumbull, Engraver: J.F.E. Prod'homme, circa 1865.

General Davidson had been headquartered at Beattie's Ford but was certain Cornwallis would come to Cowan's Ford. Davidson camped at the east end of the horse ford with 250 men, including a North Carolina militia cavalry unit led by Captain Joseph Graham.

The British crossing was quiet and went well at the beginning; however, Hager had missed the horse ford, and the army headed into the wagon ford. Soon, the horses were unexpectedly in over their heads, and several riders were thrown into the swiftly flowing river. The commotion attracted the attention of Whig pickets, and they began to notice the British as they appeared in the reflection of the campfires.

Davidson heard the pickets firing at the British and sent Graham to reinforce them. The General then followed along with the remainder of his force.

Hager abandoned the British at the first sign of trouble. One of the pickets shot Cornwallis' horse out from under him. The British were confounded by the darkness, swift waters, and Hager's abandonment. They missed the normal exit to the east bank, and the lead units left the river several yards away from the American action. The redcoats loaded their weapons and fired at Davidson's troops that were highlighted by the pickets' campfires.

Because Davidson knew he would soon be outmanned by Cornwallis, he ordered a retreat. As the North Carolinian headed for his horse, he was shot through the heart. Brigadier General William Lee Davidson was dead. The remaining Americans withdrew, and Cornwallis' army completed its crossing of the Catawba River before noon.

The Americans experienced four killed and 26 wounded while the British lost 31 killed and 35 wounded.[13] (Cowan's Ford was located near present-day Cowan's Ford Dam on Lake Norman north of Charlotte, North Carolina. Beattie's Ford was situated two miles north; the original site is now submerged by the lake. General Greene referred to Cowan's Ford as McGowan's Ford. A. L. Pickens also made reference to McGowan's. Likely, the General had misheard someone pronouncing McCowan's, and Dr. Pickens simply repeated what had been written.)

After he passed the river, General Cornwallis dispatched Lieutenant Colonel Tarleton and his British Legion dragoons to chase Davidson's retreating militia. Tarleton captured a few stragglers and learned that the militia was to gather at Tarrant's Tavern. Once assembled, the militiamen were to find General Greene who awaited them seven miles up the road toward Salisbury.

Many refugee Whig families from the Catawba River fords had departed their homes with wagonloads of personal effects. They had amassed at the tavern to seek Whig militia protection from the British. When the militia arrived at noon, the men believed they were safe from Cornwallis' slow-moving army. The militiamen ate lunch and many of them also enjoyed a mug of rum.

Militia vedettes were on watch to warn of Tarleton's arrival. As the British Legion approached, its Commander yelled for the Legionnaires to remember the Cowpens. They attacked. Many militiamen had already saddled up and were riding away. Some fired on the British and claimed casualties. (Tarrant's Tavern was located on present-day State Highway 115, slightly south of Lake Norman Regional Medical Center at Mount Mourne, North Carolina. It was also called Torrence's Tavern as indicated on the highway marker near the site.)

Tarleton gave chase, but as the militiamen had scattered, he returned to the tavern and there burned many of the Whig wagons. He was unaware that a big prize, Major General Nathanael Greene, was less than 10 miles away. Reports vary considerably, but Captain Joseph Graham indicated the militia lost 10 killed. Captain Salathiel Martin of the Surry County Militia Regiment was the only American captured.

While Lieutenant Colonel Tarleton led the British Legion back to the main army, Major General Greene waited for Davidson and his militia until midnight. At that time he learned that Davidson had been killed, that his militia had dispersed, and most of the men had returned to their homes. The Commander then quietly rode to Salisbury.[14]

In an April 3, 1781, issue of *The London Chronicle*, Lieutenant Colonel Nisbet Balfour sent the following report to London regarding both the crossing of the Catawba and the affair at Tarrant's Tavern (see Appendix G). He also casually mentioned Cowpens.

> Extract of a Letter from Lieutenant Colonel Balfour to Lord George Germain, dated CharlesTown, February 18, 1781.
> ...Notwithstanding the unexpected and untoward Event of the 17th ultimo [the Battle of Cowpens], Lord Cornwallis still continued his forward movements, and pressed hard on General Morgan, without being able to come up with him, who, with his Prisoners, pushed for the Catawba, and by crossing that River high up, there is Cause to believe, accomplished his Junction with General Green [Greene's] Army. It was not till the 1st instant that Lord Cornwallis could pass it; this he then did at a private Ford, four miles below Bratty's [Beattie's], though strongly opposed by a Body of Militia, who were routed, and General Davidson, who commanded them, killed. On this Occasion, his Lordship observes, "The Guards behaved gallantly, crossing the River under a heavy Fire, without returning a Shot, until they were over and formed.
> On the same Day Colonel Tarleton had the good Fortune to defeat another Corps of the Enemy's Militia, that had assembled under Colonel Pickings [Pickens], killing and taking many, and entirely dispersing the rest.

Tarleton exaggerated the skirmish at Tarrant's Tavern; there were few killed, and one captured. He also tried to pass Davidson's militia off as being a regiment of Andrew Pickens' brigade.

General Greene, aware that Cornwallis was gaining, headed for the Yadkin River, five miles northeast, on February 2, 1781. The Yadkin was indeed swollen and running swiftly. Greene began to cross his army that night and completed the venture the next day. Greene had originally instructed Polish Colonel Thaddeus Kosciuszko to build flat-bottomed boats which would be hauled with the wagons. Biographer Monica Mary Gardner wrote:

> Often invited to Greene's table, where the general entertained his officers with a kindliness and cordiality that atoned for the poor fare which was all that he could offer them, Kosciuszko was regarded with strong affection and admiration by a man who was himself worthy of the highest esteem. Kosciuszko's office, after the survey of the river, was to build boats for the perilous transport of the army over the treacherous and turbulent streams of the district. Greene writes: "Kosciuszko is employed in building flat-bottomed boats to be transported with the army if ever I shall be able to command the means of transporting them."[15]

Greene indicated in his note that he expected difficulties transporting a fleet of boats on the long trek. Besides adding to the load of his wagons, he would still need to ford the same number of wagons and use the flat-bottomed boats for troops. Thaddeus Kosciuszko overcame the problem and designed special wagons to shorten the time required for the army to ford swollen rivers. The Kosciuszko design offered quickly-removable wheels and axles to convert half of the wagons into flat-bottomed boats. The joints of the boards were sealed with pine tar to render the wagon bottoms and sides waterproof. Much of the ammunition and arms were carried in these unique vessels, and most of the infantry was also able to board at the crossings. The horses and the rest of the wagons were able to ford in half the time it would take had Kosciuszko not completed the conversions of the other wagons.[16] Gardner continued, "The boats of Kosciuszko's devising contributed to the saving of Greene's army in that wonderful retreat from Cornwallis, which is among the finest exploits of the War of Independence."[17]

General Cornwallis' vanguard arrived at the Yadkin, and they spotted General Greene's rear guard with three wagonloads of supplies. The Americans lost the three wagons and their cargo during a brief skirmish; however, the Continental rear guard was able to complete the crossing with the last of the boats. Just as the Americans arrived on the far bank, the heavy rains began anew. By the time the British army arrived at the Yadkin River, the crossing was impassible. General Greene's Army had again been saved by the weather.

When Cornwallis arrived with his main force on the 3rd, he was disheartened by what he saw. He had expected the swollen river, but he also expected the Continentals to be trapped against it. Yet, there they were resting safely on the far bank. Cornwallis ordered a cannonade, but it had little effect.

He then contemplated his next move. His first choice was to move downriver, cross when he could, and cut off the Continental reinforcements led by Brigadier General Isaac Huger. His second consideration was to move upstream, cross the river earlier, and arrive at the Dan River in time to entrap General Greene. His advisers suggested that the Continental Army could not prepare enough boats to cross the Dan before the British force would arrive. He decided the latter choice was the smart one. He headed north on the 4th.

General Greene had watched Cornwallis from across the river, and he knew what his counterpart was planning. The Continental Army headed for Guilford Courthouse (located at present-day Guilford Courthouse National Military Park on the north side of Greensboro, North Carolina). Greene had a 40-mile march ahead of him.

On February 5, General Greene wrote General Huger and ordered him to rendezvous at Guilford Courthouse, rather than at Salisbury. (Courthouse, in some parts of the country, was not only the name of the building itself, but also part of the name of the village that surrounded it; a distinction that exists to the present-day in some instances.) Major General Greene and Brigadier General Morgan arrived at the destination on the 8th, and Brigadier General Huger arrived with Lieutenant Colonel Henry Lee on the 9th.

On the 9th, Greene gave General Morgan his leave as was requested, and the Brigadier headed for his home in Virginia. Greene then penned orders to Brigadier General Andrew Pickens. He asked the militia leader to harass Cornwallis' rear guard and cut off his supply and communications lines from South Carolina. The Continental Army headed for the Dan River later that day.

General Davidson's North Carolina militia regiment had been urging General Greene to assign General Morgan to replace General Davidson as their leader. (North Carolina militia Brigadier General Davidson also held a commission as Colonel in the Continental Army.) Since Morgan had been granted his leave, General Greene recommended that the North Carolinians turn to Brigadier General Andrew Pickens. The North Carolina Salisbury Brigade approached Pickens, and he accepted the assignment to be their Brigadier. Andrew Pickens was then the General of militia brigades from two states at the same time; South Carolina, and North Carolina. He also had a company of Georgia militia attached to his command. Pickens' various brigades totaled 700 militiamen, a worthy force to divide into detachments and harass Cornwallis. His officer corps was the most experienced and focused group of leaders in the south: Colonel James McCall, Colonel Robert Anderson, Major Samuel Hammond, Captain Joseph Pickens, and Major James Jackson.[18]

Polish Colonel Thaddeus Kosciuszko. From an 1829 print by A. Oleszezynski; engraver: W. Holl, circa 1830.

Cornwallis' army crossed the Yadkin River at an upper ford on the 9th. The British were moving fast. Cornwallis was certain that the Continentals would attempt to cross the Dan River at the upper fords because the river was high and swift downstream. Consequently, the British tried to hang a little left of Greene's actual route — to their own detriment. Cornwallis rested his men at Salem, North Carolina, and continued his chase on the 10th.

Greene countered the British scheme with several moves. He detached Colonel Otho Williams to lead a force that would interrupt Cornwallis' front and draw him to the northwest, while Greene would take the main army northeast toward the lower fords of the Dan.

Williams' force was a light cavalry unit, accompanied by Lieutenant Colonel Henry Lee with his Legion of cavalry and infantry, Lieutenant Colonel John Eager Howard with 280 infantrymen, and 60 riflemen of the Virginia Militia regiment assigned to the Continental Army. This body totaled 700 men: 240 cavalry, 400 infantry, and 60 mounted Virginia riflemen. Both wings of the army departed Guilford Courthouse on the 10th.

Colonel Edward Carrington, Quartermaster of the Southern Department, joined Greene at Guilford Courthouse. Carrington was there to assure the commander that he had arranged for sufficient boats to ferry the main army across the Dan River at Boyd's Ferry and Irvine's Ferry. Cornwallis had not accounted for this caveat.

Williams ensured his detachment got to the fore of the British. They then slowed to make sure Cornwallis came near enough to spot them. He did. Cornwallis had the impression Williams' force was the main Continental Army. He slowed his own army because he did not want to force an action until he could catch Greene as he attempted to cross the river.

The game of cat and its prey continued for three days. The Continentals stopped at 9:00 P.M. each night and arose by 3:00 A.M. each morning for a quick breakfast and departure. They took no time in the evening to set up a campsite. When they stopped, half of the army dropped to the ground and slept for six hours while the other half pulled guard duty. The next night they would switch assignments. Williams needed to assure that the British neither got to the fore nor between his detachment and General Greene.

A company of Tarleton's Legion dragoons comprised the vanguard on the British march. The rear guard of the American detachment was Henry Lee's Legion dragoons. Lee's force tried to slow the British as much as it could, until on February 13, Cornwallis' van caught up to Lee's force, and a skirmish ensued. The British lost 18 dragoons in the action; the Americans lost two.

The two forces were near enough that Cornwallis noticed that the detachment was not the rear of Greene's Continental force. The irate British General hurried his army back toward Greene's trail. Then the race was on between Williams' detachment and Cornwallis' army. The Americans, a much lighter force, had the advantage. Each group was always within sight of the other. At times, the two Legion cavalries got near enough to each other to fire a few rounds.

On the 14th, Greene crossed the Dan River at the two ferries. He sent a messenger to inform Williams of the army's passage. On the night of the 14th, as on previous nights, each of the enemies could see the other's fires. Williams left his fire burning and marched his detachment toward the fords prior to midnight. Cornwallis appeared at the south bank of the Dan River just as Lee and his Legion climbed out of the last boats on the north shore. There were no more boats to be had; Colonel Carrington had made sure of that. Cornwallis had been frustrated again. The two armies watched each other across the river as they both rested. (Boyd's Ferry was located on the Dan River at south side of South Boston, Virginia, and Irvine's Ferry was four miles upstream of Boyd's Ferry.)

Greene received word that the river level was dropping, so he had Carrington work on an escape route further to the north. However, the water would no sooner drop than rise again, and so it went all day. Cornwallis waited for it to drop enough that he could spread along the shore and cross at more points than Greene could defend; Greene waited for it to rise so he could continue to rest his troops.

Finally, help was on the way. Brigadier General Pickens was approaching the British rear-left flank with his 700 militiamen. Additionally, militia General Caswell of North Carolina had mustered a force and was nearing Cornwallis' rear-right flank. The British Commander did not want his force penned against the river, so he made a quick retreat to Tory stronghold, Hillsborough, North Carolina. The race to the Dan had ended.[19]

After Cornwallis departed, General Nathanael Greene remained on the north bank of the Dan River. It was February and still cold. Warm clothing was not available. Neither were shoes, desperately needed by many of the soldiers after their long, grueling marches.

Greene anxiously awaited the over mountain men commanded by Colonels Isaac Shelby and William Campbell. Reinforcements were sorely needed as so many men recuperated from illnesses and physical infirmities caused by the march. Two hundred and seventy-four of 1,134 Maryland Continentals, Greene's key Regiment, were hospitalized. In addition, many local militiamen had returned home because their muster periods were expired:

> with the exception only of the gallant little band under Pickens, who alone, in the worst of times, never abandoned the retreating army.... Their numbers were reduced to about 150 [speaking of the race to the Dan], consisting altogether of volunteers from South Carolina and Georgia—the former under Colonel McCall—the latter under ... [James] Jackson of Georgia, at that time a captain [actually a major] of militia. Most of the officers and men from the two southern states who had fought at the Cowpens, had been previously detached under the orders issued to Pickens, to disperse themselves through the interior of those two states, in order to keep alive opposition in that quarter.[20]

(Major James Jackson was with Pickens at, and following, the Battle of Cowpens. See earlier in this chapter.)

On the 16th, Brigadier General Andrew Pickens patrolled the vicinity near Hillsborough, North Carolina, with 350 men to keep track of Cornwallis' activities. Pickens' commanders included Colonel Francis Locke and Captain Joseph Graham of his North Carolina Brigade and Colonel James McCall and Major Samuel Hammond of his South Carolina Brigade.

Hammond dispatched men to reconnoiter different areas around Hillsborough. Captain Graham led one detachment of 25 North Carolina militia cavalry and 20 Georgia militia riflemen. Toward evening, they spotted a small British unit of 27 men camped at Hart's Mill on the Eno River one and one-half miles northwest of Hillsborough. Graham waited until dawn and launched a surprise attack on the British as they awakened. It was a short skirmish with 18 captured (two Loyalists, 16 British regulars) and nine killed or severely wounded. The Americans suffered no losses.

Pickens dispatched Major Hammond to Virginia with the prisoners who were then turned over to General Greene. On February 18, Lieutenant Colonel Henry "Light Horse Harry" Lee and his Legion rode into Graham's camp. Graham's militiamen were startled because Lee's Legion wore green uniform jackets very similar to those worn by Tarleton's British Legion. Greene had ordered Lee to attack Harts Mill, but he was too late.

Lee and Pickens maneuvered around Hillsborough together until General Greene arrived at their camp the night of February 21. The three commanders visited in Pickens' tent, and Greene was pleased to see the camaraderie that had developed between Pickens and Lee. He ordered them to continue to work together under General Pickens' command, and cautioned them to let nothing disrupt their harmony. He informed them that, in a few days, he would re-cross the Dan River and stick to the backcountry. He asked them to increase their efforts to obtain intelligence and to disrupt the movement of Tories who were trying to join Cornwallis' army. General Greene then borrowed Pickens' blanket, napped, and left before dawn on the 22nd.

Before General Greene departed, one of Pickens' scouts returned with information that Tarleton and his Legion had passed on the road from Hillsborough to the Haw River the previous day. Pickens and Lee marched their combined force all day. They stopped late in the afternoon and asked some local Whigs about Tarleton's movements. They learned the direction the British Legion would travel; then, they simply followed the path of destruction.

General Pickens was informed that Tarleton was supping with a local Tory family. Andrew formed his force into columns and approached the farmhouse; however, the British had departed save for two officers left behind with recompense for their hosts. The Americans captured the two officers.

Pickens and Lee discovered that Tarleton planned to travel six miles, then stop for the night. Pickens left the Tory family unharmed and reorganized his force to march after the British. He had the perfect opportunity to put an end to Tarleton and his Legion; Pickens was between the Legion and General Cornwallis, and Tarleton knew nothing of the American unit's nearby location. The Patriots camped for the night and planned to resume their march at dawn.

Lieutenant Colonel Henry "Light Horse Harry" Lee. Artist: James Herring, from J. Stuart; engraver: J.F.E. Prud'homme, 1862.

Coincidentally, local Tory Colonel John Pyle intended to join Cornwallis. He had mustered 300 Tories and, as he moved toward Hillsborough, he learned that Tarleton was in the vicinity. Pyle, like Pickens, was searching the area for Tarleton but for a completely different reason. Pyle wanted a Provincial commission and thought he could obtain one by joining with the British Legion.

On the morning of the 23rd, while two of Pyle's scouts searched for Tarleton, they happened upon Lee's Legion. The Legion was the vanguard for Pickens' brigade. Lee wanted to bypass a confrontation with Pyle for the richer prize of Tarleton, so he devised a plan to capture Pyle's force without a skirmish. The scouts mistook Lee for Tarleton because the two units dressed similarly, and Pyle's militiamen had never seen the British Commander. Lee sent the scouts back to Pyle with the regards of "Lieutenant Colonel Tarleton." Lee then asked that Pyle post his force to the right of the road so that he, posing as Tarleton, could inspect the troops as he passed. He also requested that Pyle be at the end of the line so he could congratulate him after passing.

There was not time for Lee to confer with Pickens. Lee expected his Legion would be in front of Pyle's entire regiment when Lee approached Pyle. Apparently Pyle's line was too long, and Pickens' militia arrived at its extremity before Lee reached Pyle.

The popular account is that just as Lee was opposite Pyle, he reached out appearing to shake the Colonel's hand. He was just about to grab Pyle's weapon and demand surrender when a shot rang out in the rear, supposedly from a Tory who recognized the Patriot militiamen.

However, according to North Carolina Captain Joseph Graham, North Carolina Major Joseph Dickson (commanding the right hand column of militia) had led his men out of their line of march, when they encountered some fences and a creek. They ended up in the woods behind Pyle's line. When Captain Graham's left column of militia approached Pyle's Tories, they mistook the Loyalists for Dickson's column that had somehow circumvented the road and gotten ahead. Graham supposed "Dickson's men" were waiting for Lee's Legion to pass, so they could take their normal position as the right hand column.

As Graham's column neared, he saw that these men were dressed differently than Dickson's militiamen, and that each man had a strip of red cloth on his hat that indicated he was a Tory. Graham, who rode alongside of Captain Joseph Eggleston (commander of the Legion's rear company), informed Eggleston of the situation.

Eggleston then approached an apparent officer of the line and asked him to whom he belonged. When the man replied that he was a friend of his Majesty, Eggleston struck him over the head with his saber. The militiamen, including Dickson's company from the woods, saw the action and mounted a charge with sabers slashing. The reaction extended all the way up the line to Lee. Lee's Legion faced right and charged along the entire front of Pyle's Tories. It took less than one minute for the entire force to be engaged. Pyle screamed at Lee, still thinking he was Tarleton, that he was attacking friendlies.

Ninety of Pyle's troops were killed. Many were severely wounded, including Pyle who was badly disfigured. A few escaped through the woods. (That battle, February 23, 1781, was called by many names: Pyle's defeat and Pyle's massacre among others. A marker for the battle is located just south of present-day Interstates 40 and 85 where they pass through Burlington, North Carolina. It is on State Highway 49 at the junction of Anthony Road.)[21]

Shortly after the battle, some of the survivors located Tarleton's camp and registered a complaint about the treatment they had just received from "his men." Tarleton quickly withdrew his force to Hillsborough. Lieutenant Colonel Lee said of the affair, "Fortune, which sways so imperiously the affairs of war, demonstrated throughout the operation its supreme control. Nothing was omitted on the part of the Americans to give the expedition the desired termination; but the very bright prospects which for a time presented themselves were suddenly overcast — the capricious goddess gave us Pyle and saved Tarleton."[22]

General Greene was happy with the outcome. He believed the victory over Pyle was immensely more valuable than a victory over Tarleton. He wrote a letter to Brigadier General Pickens:

> General Greene to General Pickens,
> CAMP AT DOBBINS, FEBRUARY 26TH, 1781.
> I have now to acknowledge the receipt of your two letters of the 23^d, wherein you acquaint me with the surprise of a British picket, by Colonel M'Call, and another of the 26th, with intelligence of the defeat of a body of tories under Colonel Piles [sic], by the detachment under your command. It gives me infinite pleasure whenever I have an opportunity of expressing my thanks to officers and soldiers, who can embrace opportunities of ornamenting their fame by serving their country. The affair of Colonel M'Call was executed with firmness and address, and discovered a spirit of enterprise and genius, which I shall be ever happy to cherish.
> The defeat of the tories was so happily timed, and in all probability will be productive of such happy consequences, that I cannot help congratulating you on your success. My warmest thanks are due to you, Colonel Lee, and all the officers and soldiers under your command, and for the exertions which were made to bring about so happy an event.[23]

Greene's biographer, William Johnson, believed that many did not give Brigadier General Pickens credit for his accomplishments and abilities, so he added, "The reader must not be misled by the diminished figure given to his commander on the colonel's canvas;

for Pickens was never a mere nominal commander; although the most unaffected and unassuming of men, he was an able and energetic officer; and, although the suavity of his manner might disguise his character, he had a firmness about him that would be obeyed."[24]

General Greene had moved across the Dan River on February 23, 1781. He relied upon Colonel Otho Williams and Brigadier General Andrew Pickens to protect him from possible British or Tory action from his left flank. This was frustrating for Cornwallis. Williams and Pickens constantly attacked the British army pickets who were still in the vicinity of Hillsborough. Cornwallis was reluctant to send detachments to engage them because Lieutenant Colonel Henry Lee also separately harassed him. The General did not want to weaken his main army to pursue American detachments.

Greene wrote to Virginia Colonel William Preston on the 24th and suggested that Brigadier General Pickens would be a good fit for his regiment and would likely be agreeable to lead the Virginians. Preston joined Pickens' army. Andrew Pickens was now leading brigades from South Carolina and North Carolina as well as a regiment from Virginia and a company from Georgia. This brought Andrew Pickens' and Otho Williams' combined force to 1,300 men.

Pickens had become a real danger because of his devilish skirmishes with the pickets, so on February 26 Cornwallis ordered Banastre Tarleton to press Pickens hard. That evening, Pickens wrote to Lee that he desired the Legion to join him the next morning. He explained that his outriders had some small skirmishes with Cornwallis' pickets but had managed to stay one step ahead. Greene, then, was still biding his time near the Dan as he awaited promised reinforcements from Virginia and North Carolina.

Brigadier General Thomas Sumter, who had been ordered to disrupt Tories in the Camden vicinity, attacked several small British posts along the Congaree River in late February. His confidence was high, so on February 24, he decided to attack a British garrison at Fort Watson. The fort was heavily constructed and garrisoned by 400 men. Sumter had no artillery with which to pound the walls, but he attacked despite his poor chances. Eighteen men were killed, to no avail.

During his retreat, Sumter engaged a British supply convoy and captured the cargo. A detachment of men from Fort Watson caught up with Sumter and engaged him in a skirmish. After the engagement, his militia dispersed. Sumter was again on the run and headed north toward Charlotte. (Fort Watson was located on a small isthmus on present-day Lake Marion across from Santee River State Park.)

A 200-man detachment of Colonel Otho Williams' command was in a scuffle at Clapp's Mill with some of Lieutenant Colonel Banastre Tarleton's Legionnaires on March 2, 1781. Captain Joseph Graham, with 40 of Pickens' militia, assisted Williams. Tarleton's Legion force numbered 150. The British force suffered seven killed and 18 wounded while the Americans lost 12 killed and wounded. (The Battle of Clapp's Mill was located five miles southwest of present-day Burlington, North Carolina, on State Highway 62.)

On March 6, Pickens received a message from Major General Nathanael Greene and Governor John Rutledge. Greene wanted to see Pickens at headquarters which was near present-day Burlington, North Carolina. Greene was moving daily, sometimes hourly, to keep Cornwallis guessing about the American Army's strength and location. The two main forces were 20 miles apart as the Williams/Pickens/Lee coalition and Tarleton's Legion operated in-between.

Pickens prepared to depart that day, and his militia officers pleaded with him not to leave them alone with Williams. They were at Whitesell's Mill on Reedy Branch. However,

Pickens was not one to ignore orders from superiors. He left Virginia Colonel William Preston and South Carolina Colonel James McCall to command the militia during his absence. (Whitesell's Mill was owned by Henry Whitesell, a North Carolina militiaman. It was located on present-day State Highway 61 five miles northwest of today's Burlington, North Carolina. It has been variously referred to as Whitesell's Mill, Weitzall's Mill, Weitzell's Mill, Wetzall's Mill, and Wetzell's Mill.)

On the 6th, after Brigadier General Andrew Pickens left, Tarleton attacked with his Legion. When the Americans were alerted of his coming, the Continentals removed to a defensive position across the stream. Preston and the militia covered the rear as the soldiers crossed. The skirmish between the militia and the British Legion was brief, but intense. The Legionnaires drove the militia across the creek, and Williams ordered a retreat. The British were supported by artillery mounted atop a nearby hill. The British lost 30 killed and wounded; the American casualties amounted to eight killed and 12 wounded. Most of the American losses occurred within the militia force as it covered the Continentals' move across Reedy Branch.

Andrew Pickens returned to find angry Carolina, Georgia, and Virginia militiamen packing their duffels. They complained to Pickens that they were improperly exposed as they covered the Continentals' retreat at the creek crossing. The General tried to appease their anger, but to no avail. He extracted a promise that the men would not leave until Andrew could explain to General Greene and return with some advice.

Pickens wrote Lee of the incident:

> You desire to know the cause of my leaving Genl. Green [sic] before the battle of Guilford. A few days before the affair at Whitsell's Mill, Governor Rutledge had arrived from the northward at Genl. Green's [sic] camp & wished to see me. Genl. Green [sic] wrote to me to come to his camp; I went, though much against the wish of the militia officers. While gone the affair at Whitsell's Mill happened. The militia who were under my command, particularly those from South Carolina & Georgia, with those from Rowan & Mecklenburg Counties, & some regiments west of the mountains, were much displeased with the orders of conduct in that affair. They thought they were not treated fairly & were improperly exposed, being ordered to cover the retreat of the regulars. When I joined them, which was on the same evening, they told me they were determined to stay no longer. I tryed to obviate their objections but found it vain. The next day I informed Genl. Green [sic] of the dissatisfaction which had taken place among the militia, that they had determined to go away, but had promised not to go until they knew whether I would go with them. The Genl. with Govr. Rutledge thought it most advisable that I should return with them. The Genl. told me at parting I hope to break this fellow's leg, meaning Cornwallis, & return to S. Carolina. After receiving some general orders I left the army. When I returned to S. Carolina the scenes were awful. When parties in opposition met, quarters were seldom given.[25]

The general orders mentioned by Pickens were from Governor John Rutledge who suggested that Pickens should return to the backcountry with his South Carolina brigade. Rutledge indicated that, while they attended to their families and property, they should remain active and police the Tories in the Ninety Six District.

On March 8, Rutledge wrote to Brigadier Generals Thomas "Gamecock" Sumter, Francis "Swamp Fox" Marion, and Andrew Pickens. The Governor once again divided the state into triads: Marion to operate in the lowcountry, Sumter the midlands, and Pickens the backcountry, including the Piedmont. Rutledge expected them to cooperate and made Sumter the senior Brigadier. Marion did not wish to work with Sumter at all, but Pickens acquiesced to the orders.[26]

William Johnson addressed Pickens and his militia's departure from the service of the Continental Army:

> From the time that General Pickens joined General Morgan, it has been seen, that he had never rested a day. Most of the officers and men under him, had been engaged in the most active service ever since the fall of Charleston ... but their condition now was scarcely to be tolerated; they had not the clothing necessary to common decency. Yet no one deserted, no one murmured ... and never winced from their duty, even in the midst of retreat, privation and suffering ... the obvious necessity of their return at this time, could not be resisted — The enemy were embodying the negroes in South Carolina into regiments, and appearances on the frontier threatened a serious invasion from the Indians: not only their apprehensions, but those of the commanding general were seriously awakened for the fate of their families.... General Pickens was ordered to repair with his followers to the back parts of South Carolina, to protect the Whigs, suppress the loyalists.... This was the only militia force whose services he [Greene] could venture to calculate from day to day.[27]

Brigadier General Francis Marion had been busy operating on his own. On March 6, British Lieutenant Colonel John W. T. Watson and British Lieutenant Colonel Welbore Doyle dispatched to trap Marion in the Wiboo (sometimes Wyboo) Swamp. They split their columns; however, Marion knew the swamp well, so he was able to constantly maneuver and outflank the British with small detachments of his men. The British were limited to the primary causeways through the swamp. The American militia used guerrilla tactics and finally wore the British down. However, before the British withdrew, Doyle found Marion's camp in the swamp on Snow's Island and attacked. His force killed seven and wounded 15 who had remained to guard the position. Doyle also regained several British prisoners kept at the island, seized arms and ammunition, and burned several shelters. The game of chase and hide with Marion lasted for several weeks. (The Wiboo Swamp is submerged by present-day Lake Marion and was located near the present-day Santee National Wildlife Refuge off of State Highway 260.)

On the 10th, General Greene dissolved Colonel Otho Williams' light corps and reorganized the army. Over the next three days, he planned how to confront Cornwallis at Guilford Courthouse. Greene moved into the town on the 14th. Guilford Courthouse had a population of 100 at the time, and Greene encamped on the outskirts with 4,400 men (1,700 Continentals and 2,700 militiamen).

The next morning, Greene set his force in battle array to await Cornwallis. The British Commander had long been eager to confront his American counterpart. General Greene knew the redcoats would come.

Greene wanted an arrangement similar to Morgan's at Cowpens. The General's position, on several hills southwest of town, allowed him to place his line across the road from Salisbury. The British would be coming uphill.

Cornwallis attacked with a force of 2,000 shortly before noon. The American militia skirmishers fired a volley and retreated to the next line. The British suffered heavy casualties from the rifle balls.

The militia line then fought the British for one hour before the redcoats could break through. The two armies faced off with their regulars, bayonet to bayonet. This action went on for an interminable time. When Cornwallis saw a wing of his army surrounded he, over the objections of British Brigadier General Charles O'Hara, loaded his cannons with 30-caliber round balls and fired into the fray. Soldiers from both sides were hit, and several British were killed by the shot. Greene ordered a retreat and left Guilford Courthouse to Cornwallis.

While Cornwallis gained the field of battle, he suffered horribly for the victory. The British lost 93 killed, 413 wounded, and 26 captured by the Americans: over 25 percent of his total force. The American losses amounted to 79 killed, 185 wounded, and 75 captured.

Cornwallis was left with 1,400 men to march into Virginia. Cornwallis should have seen that success was slipping away for Britain. The substantial personnel loss experienced at Kings Mountain, Cowpens, Augusta, and Guilford Courthouse enforced the decline.[28]

Cornwallis' force was beaten up so badly that he was unable to muster a pursuit of the Americans. Greene crossed the Reedy Branch and rested until his straggling troops arrived. Then he retreated to his old camp at Speedwell's Ironworks on Troublesome Creek. He thought to send a surgeon under a white flag to take care of those Americans wounded at the battlefield. (Speedwell's Ironworks was sometimes referred to as Speedwill Ironworks and was located off of present-day U.S. Highway 158 halfway between today's Reidsville and Midway at the northwest tip of Lake Reidsville. Later it was known as Troublesome Iron Works and Buffington's Iron Works.)

General Cornwallis marched his bedraggled army to Wilmington, North Carolina, on the southern coast of the state. He regrouped there and let his troops heal while he prepared for a foray into Virginia. He named Lieutenant Colonel Nisbet Balfour the British Commander in Charles Town, and dispatched Lieutenant Colonel Francis Lord Rawdon to Camden to lead the local Tory militias in backcountry South Carolina.

General Greene was aware that Cornwallis would soon leave the vicinity, so he planned to re-enter South Carolina and capture all British garrisons within the state.

General Pickens united several militia units when he returned to Ninety Six District. Even Colonel Clarke and a regiment of Georgia militiamen joined his force. Eleven colonels reported to Pickens: Robert Anderson, Thomas Brandon, Elijah Clarke, Leroy Hammond, Samuel Hammond, William Hardin, Joseph Hayes, James McCall, Benjamin Roebuck, John Thomas Jr., and a Colonel Wilkinson (possibly Colonel Morton Wilkinson[29]). Pickens was able to intimidate the Tories in the vicinity, so they had to take protection at Ninety Six.

Pickens had intelligence that his old nemesis, Major James Dunlap, was patrolling the Little River area with a force of 90 Tories. The General dispatched Colonels Clarke and McCall with 180 militiamen to deal with the ruffian. The militia caught up with Dunlap at Beattie's Mill on March 23, 1781. Clarke detached McCall to get behind Dunlap's force and control a bridge to cut off any retreat possibilities. Then Clarke charged. The battle lasted for a few hours, and 34 Tories were killed before Dunlap surrendered. The Americans, who suffered no losses, then captured 42 men. (Beattie's Mill was located on present-day State Highway 184, halfway between State Highways 20 and 201, two miles southwest of present-day Due West, South Carolina.)

Clarke personally reported the battle to Pickens on the 25th, and explained that he had dispatched Dunlap and his men to a prison camp in the Watauga settlements. Pickens later learned that a small group of over mountain militiamen, including one named Cobb, overpowered Clarke's men and killed Dunlap. Pickens was furious and wrote General Greene saying that he (Pickens) had issued a proclamation to reward $10,000 for Cobb's apprehension. (Other reports state the reward was for $1,000.) Andrew Pickens, who had no use for vigilante justice, wrote another letter. This one was an apology to Lieutenant Colonel John Harris Cruger at Ninety Six. Pickens offered regrets for the cruel treatment of Dunlap, a magnanimous gesture for a man whose family had been horribly treated by the Major just three months earlier. Cobb was never captured. Most backcountry Whigs knew about Dunlap's reputation. They likely thought Cobb deserved a reward for having slain him.

On March 30, General Greene sent a message to General Sumter and requested "The Gamecock" issue orders for Generals Pickens and Marion. Greene was readying his army for the return to South Carolina and would need assistance from the militias. Andrew Pickens was to gather his militia and establish a base camp at Fish Dam Ford on the Broad River.

On the 31st, Pickens encountered a battalion commanded by Lieutenant Colonel Cruger. The Tories were attempting to garrison a post at Harrison's store, but Pickens' militia chased them back to nearby Ninety Six.

Colonel Elijah Clarke had returned to Georgia after Major Dunlap's capture, and Colonel McCall accompanied him. Before they could take action against the Tories in Georgia, each of the Colonels was afflicted with smallpox. In time, Colonel Clarke recovered, but Colonel McCall returned to South Carolina and died approximately May 1, 1781. Pickens was heartsick over the death of his long-time companion. He was unaware that McCall's passing was the first of three major heartbreaks Andrew Pickens would experience in 1781.

Lieutenant Colonel Cruger, concerned about Pickens' activities, called the Tory detachments back to Ninety Six in early April. Sumter sent four of his own regiments to reinforce Pickens' aggressive activities, while Andrew continued to gather his own militia.

Pickens was engaged in marshaling Whigs near Augusta. On the 3rd, a detachment, commanded by Captain Thomas Key of Colonel LeRoy Hammond's regiment, encountered a company of Loyalists led by Captain John Clark. A confrontation transpired at Clark's Horner's Corner home site. Several Loyalists, including Clark, were killed. Others were captured and paroled by Key. (The action has not only been called Horner's Corner, but also Horner's Creek and Horn Creek, located 25 miles north of present-day Augusta, Georgia, and five miles west of present-day Trenton, South Carolina.)

Captain Key, also on the 3rd, led his company to Colonel LeRoy Hammond's Mill on the Savannah River. The mill had been taken by a Tory force and converted into a British fort. A few Loyalists were killed, and the remaining were captured. Key's men burned the mill, so Tories could not use it in the future. That action, very near to Augusta, Georgia, showed how brazen Pickens' militiamen had become as they patrolled the backcountry. (Hammond's Mill was located at present-day North Augusta, South Carolina, across the Savannah River from Augusta.)

Brigadier General Andrew Pickens ordered his regiments be aggressive with the Tories in preparation for General Greene's arrival. On the 4th, Lieutenant Colonel Henry Lee was ordered to join General Marion and prepare an attack on Fort Watson. Then, on the 7th, General Greene began to march his army toward South Carolina. He issued orders for the triumvirate militia brigadiers to continue attacks upon the smaller British outposts while the Continentals concentrated on Camden and Ninety Six. The militias were to also interrupt British communication and supply lines, and to repeatedly harass Tory militia patrols.[30]

On April 12, 1781, General Sumter wrote Greene that Pickens had mustered several regiments of his own brigade and other units from Georgia. Greene wrote Sumter on the 15th and summarized the details of his plans to advance on Camden. The Commander expected Sumter to order Lee and Pickens to eliminate any forthcoming reinforcements for Lieutenant Colonel Francis Lord Rawdon and his 1,200 Camden troops, especially from Cruger at Ninety Six. Greene mostly received excuses from "The Gamecock." On the 15th, Lee and Marion operated independently of Sumter and split their forces. Lee operated around Camden to prepare for Greene's arrival. Marion led 80 militiamen, along with 300 of Lee's light infantry regiment, toward Fort Watson.

Provincial Lieutenant Colonel John Watson had been called to Camden with 300 troops to assist Rawdon with his defense against Greene. Watson left Lieutenant James McKay at the fort to command 120 troops: 80 British regulars, and 40 Tory provincials. (Watson and his troops were but a portion of Rawdon's 1,200.)

Lee returned to Marion by the 19th. It would not be easy for Marion and Lee to take the fort. Sumter had failed in his attempt six weeks earlier. Though Sumter had faced a larger garrison, the fort was still thought impenetrable. Marion immediately placed the fort under siege. He positioned sharpshooters to cover the nearby lake, so that McKay could not access it for drinking water.

McKay ordered some of his men to begin digging, and by the 18th they successfully established a well. It looked like the Americans were in for a lengthy stay; however, Legion Major Hezekiah Maham approached Lee with an idea he had been pondering. He had sketched plans for a wooden tower that could be easily erected. It would be higher than the walls of the fort, could be moved easily into position, and would give cover to the riflemen who would be stationed on the upper platform. Marion agreed to the effort, and construction was completed on the 22nd. On the 23rd, the garrison awoke to see the tower and they received a rifle barrage from its parapet that would deter them from manning the fort's walls. Marion's troops forcefully attacked. McKay could not defend, so he surrendered the fort. All 180 troops were captured. The Americans lost two killed and six wounded. The "Maham Tower" became famous, and its use was attempted several times before the end of the war.

Greene reached the vicinity of Camden on the 19th and scouted the outskirts of the city. Rawdon was nervous as he had dispatched Watson with 500 men to chase and engage Marion. Rawdon sent messengers to several outposts and requested reinforcements to help defend the city.

On the 21st, Major Thomas Fraser arrived from Ninety Six with 200 dragoons. This brought Rawdon's force to 900 men to defend against Greene and his 1,550. Rawdon sent a messenger to recall Watson, but he did not arrive in time.

Greene withdrew to Hobkirk's Hill. (Hobkirk's Hill stretched across the main road to Waxhaw, North Carolina, as well as to Charlotte. It was located one mile north of Camden.) The General was quite perturbed, not only with the enemy's strong defensive measures around Camden, but with Major Fraser's arrival. Greene wrote to Sumter on the 23rd: "Since I wrote you I have critically examined the fortifications of this place and find them superior to what I expected.... I have had the mortification to hear yesterday that the South Carolina royalists had the day before thrown themselves into the place from Ninety Six.... I must depend entirely upon you to secure us on the quarter from Ninety Six."[31]

Sumter was apologetic, but offered no assurance of assistance before Greene would be engaged at Camden.

A drummer from Greene's corps is reported to have deserted. The turncoat approached Lord Rawdon early the next day and provided valuable information to the garrison commander regarding the strength and location of Greene's force. Rawdon knew he needed the element of surprise on his side, so he marched at 9:00 A.M. on April 25, 1781, intending to attack Greene at Hobkirk's Hill. Rawdon advanced with a very narrow front along the swamp east of the road. The attack began at 11:00 and continued until Greene retreated from the hill. Greene had attempted to set an array similar to that which Morgan had used at Cowpens; however, the hillside was unusually wide, rather than deep. Also, the British attackers were tightly controlled under Rawdon's leadership. Tarleton's attack at Cowpens was haphazard and reckless.

The British withdrew from Hobkirk's Hill and re-established the garrison at Camden.

They had taken Hobkirk's Hill but, once again, suffered greatly for their "victory." British losses are accounted as 39 killed, 210 wounded, and 12 missing; one third of Rawdon's force. The Americans lost 19 killed, 113 wounded, 89 captured, and 50 missing. It has been reported that young Andrew Jackson was a prisoner of war at Camden where he witnessed the battle on a distant rise.[32]

Brigadier General Andrew Pickens and Lieutenant Colonel Henry Lee operated overtly throughout the Ninety Six District. They recruited to replenish Pickens' militia, and they pressured Tory militia companies who unsuccessfully tried to counter them.

Lieutenant Colonel Francis Lord Rawdon was quite concerned about Ninety Six. Pickens did not give an inch, and Rawdon thought that Lieutenant Colonel John Harris Cruger and his provincials were in danger. Lord Rawdon sent several messages to Cruger with orders to abandon Ninety Six and withdraw to the safety of Augusta. However, Pickens' militia intercepted each message; they had Ninety Six completely under control. Since Greene had decided to attack the garrison at Ninety Six, and had already directed Pickens and Lee to invest Augusta at the same time, it might seem at first that Pickens should let one message through, allow Cruger to evacuate, and the Americans could have Ninety Six. However, Pickens knew that if Cruger were to reinforce Augusta with his provincials, Augusta would be much harder to conquer.

On the 26th, General Greene moved his headquarters to Rugley's Mill where he planned his approach to Ninety Six. He continued to track both General Cornwallis and Lieutenant Colonel Rawdon. Cornwallis had already decided he could not re-enter South Carolina, so would move into Virginia. Greene, however, had to prepare as if the British army would return. General Greene meant to control Ninety Six and Augusta before that might happen. Additionally, he knew Rawdon had accumulated reinforcements, and had pursued the American Army and sought an opportunity to attack. Greene avoided him.

On May 10, Lord Rawdon decided to abandon Camden and withdraw to the safety of Charles Town. He sent two more messages to Cruger that requested he retreat to Augusta, but Cruger, as before, received neither of them. Rawdon destroyed much of Camden as he departed.

On the 11th, General Greene sent a detachment to garrison what was left of Camden, while Greene, himself, led the army to Fort Motte on his way to Ninety Six.

It was on May 8, 1781, that General Marion, with 150 militiamen, and Lieutenant Colonel Lee, with 300 Legion infantrymen, besieged the British outpost at Fort Motte. Fort Motte was the large mansion of Mrs. Rebecca B. Motte. Her husband Jacob Motte, a Whig politician, died of illness in 1780. The British removed Mrs. Motte from her home and fortified the mansion with a palisade, a ditch, and an abatis. The British garrison of 150 infantry was commanded by Lieutenant Colonel Donald McPherson. His battalion was reinforced with a small detachment of dragoons that had carried messages between Fort Motte and Camden.

The Americans had the fortress surrounded. Lee and Marion established their headquarters in a nearby overseer's house where the widow Motte took refuge. On the 10th, the co-commanders sent a surrender demand to McPherson. McPherson summarily refused. Early on the morning of the 11th, and again that night, the attackers and defenders spotted Lord Rawdon's campfires in the Santee Hills. He had diverted from his route to Charles Town to relieve the garrison, but had changed his mind. Meanwhile, the sight of the fires was enough to force American action and to buoy the hopes of the British.

Marion's militia had trenched near the mansion. Lee and Marion discussed the possibilities of striking the roof of the house with flaming arrows or tossing a ball of flaming pitch to fire the house and force the garrison out. Mrs. Motte, whose brother was an importer, handed the Americans an East Indian bow and some arrows to use, a gesture of her consent.

The attempt was made on the 12th after McPherson refused another surrender demand. Some have reported the roof was fired by the arrows, while others have declared that one of Marion's men, Private Nathan Savage, accomplished the task by tossing a flaming ball of rosin and brimstone to the roof. Regardless of the method, the task was accomplished and the garrison immediately surrendered. The action transpired so quickly, the fire was extinguished with little damage to the structure. (Lord Rawdon wrote Cornwallis on the 24th and added credence to the flaming arrow version of the tale as he explained the incentive for surrender.)

Mrs. Motte was so happy to be back in her house that she invited both the American and British officers to dine with her.

The entire garrison was captured, and Marion lost two militiamen. General Greene arrived at Fort Motte on the 13th and split Marion's and Lee's forces. He sent Lee to Fort Granby, which General Sumter had under siege, and Marion went to Monck's Corner to try and engage Rawdon who was on his way to Charles Town.

Sumter and 400 men had been occupied at Fort Granby since May 2, 1781. On the 10th, Sumter departed for the British outpost at Orangeburg with his main force. He left a company to continue the action at Fort Granby, while he, on the morning of the 11th, attacked the small stronghold at Orangeburg. That garrison was commanded by Tory Colonel John Fisher who surrendered with 89 Loyalists.

Colonel Thomas Taylor commanded the small unit that Sumter left at Granby. Fort Granby was defended by 292 Tories and 60 Hessian dragoons led by Major Andrew Maxwell. Lieutenant Colonel Lee arrived on the 14th and took command of the operation. On the morning of the 15th, Lee opened up with an artillery barrage on the fort, which was quickly surrendered. The entire garrison was paroled to march to Charles Town and remained there until they were officially exchanged. General Greene arrived at Fort Granby and ordered Lieutenant Colonel Henry "Light Horse Harry" Lee to report to Brigadier General Andrew Pickens and assist with the operation against Augusta. He dispatched Brigadier General Francis Marion to patrol near Georgetown.

Lee's usurpation of command at Fort Granby so angered Sumter that he offered his resignation to Greene several times over the next month. Continental Army Major General Greene refused to accept it each time because the commission had been conferred by South Carolina Governor John Rutledge. He returned the letters and suggested that Sumter reconsider.

The Americans gradually assumed control of the backcountry with a reduced British presence and a meek Tory representation. There were only two outposts remaining: Ninety Six, Greene's destination; and Augusta, Pickens' and Lee's target.[33]

11

The Siege of Augusta (1781)

Major General Nathanael Greene ordered that Lieutenant Colonel John Harris Cruger be penned up inside Ninety Six. Brigadier General Andrew Pickens accomplished that duty. His militia had intercepted several missives from Lieutenant Colonel Francis Lord Rawdon that required Cruger to abandon Ninety Six and reinforce Augusta, but Cruger did not receive any of the messages.

Greene intended to put both British garrisons, Ninety Six and Augusta, under siege, and he thought it best to keep the two separated and the troops unable to assist each other. (Cruger had assisted Lieutenant Colonel Thomas "Burn Foot" Brown once before when he was under siege. See Chapter 8.) General Greene had dispatched Brigadier General Francis Marion to attack a smaller British post at Georgetown, South Carolina. He had also sent Lieutenant Colonel Henry Lee to support Pickens with the action against Lieutenant Colonel Brown at Augusta.

The Siege of Augusta actually involved three separate British posts. Fort Galphin (also called Fort Dreadnought and Fort Gilpin), a fortified plantation house owned by Indian trader George Galphin, was located on the Savannah River 10 miles south of Augusta. Fort Grierson, on the property of Tory Lieutenant Colonel James Grierson, was located on the Savannah River at present-day Augusta on the corner of today's 11th and Reynolds Streets. Thomas Brown's primary location was at Fort Cornwallis (also called Mackay's Trading Post and Brown's Fort), located one-half mile down river from Fort Grierson in Augusta on the corner of present-day Reynolds and Washington Streets.

On April 16, 1781, Lieutenant Colonel Micajah Williamson of the Wilkes County Georgia Militia, attempted to place Fort Galphin under siege but was heavily outmanned. Early in May, Colonel Elijah Clarke reinforced Williamson's army with another 100 men. The militia kept watch on a British flotilla that was laden with gifts destined for the Indians. The ships were anchored at Fort Galphin. The shipment included gunpowder, muskets, lead balls, salt, and whiskey. Clarke's militia had the fort covered from a ridge, so the barges could not be safely unloaded by the Tories. The Whigs did not want such a rich haul to fall into the hands of the Indians, the primary threat against backcountry Georgia Whigs.

When General Pickens arrived, he planned engagements at Forts Grierson and Cornwallis. That left Williamson's force and Colonel LeRoy Hammond's regiment from Pickens' brigade to continue the siege on Fort Galphin.

Fort Galphin was commanded by Captain Samuel Rowarth (also Roworth) who led 70 of Thomas Brown's brigade of King's Rangers. Lieutenant Colonel Brown had recently dispatched them to protect the shipment of supplies for the Indians. There were also 42 local Tory militiamen and 61 local black residents.

Lieutenant Colonel Henry "Light Horse Harry" Lee arrived in the area on May 19, 1781, and ordered his Legion infantry, commanded by Captain Michael Rudolph, to gain possession of Fort Galphin. On the 21st, Captain Rudolph had Williamson's militia make a half-hearted, but realistic, appearance of attacking the gates. They allowed the Tories to drive them away. As they slowly retreated they drew the major portion of the garrison after them. Once the Tories poured out after the Whigs, and before the gates were closed, Rudolph and his infantry gained the fort. Lee led his Legion dragoons to intercept the Tories before they could catch up to the militia bait. The Tories had not realized that the Continental forces had arrived. Lee had hidden them nearby in a grove of trees. The Tories had no choice but to surrender, and the Americans captured 173 men with arms, plus the shipment intended for the Indians. The only American loss was one man from Lee's Legion infantry who died from the heat.[1]

After the fall of Galphin, Pickens asked General Greene for permission to resupply the militia with some of the spoils. Greene agreed and said that Pickens could "divide the whole spoils according to his sense of justice and the good of the service."[2] Pickens loaded 13 wagons with food to send to Greene's Continental forces. He divided the remainder of the food and the clothing equally among the South Carolina militia, the Georgia militia, and Lee's Legion. He distributed the small arms and ammunition among the militias for use in future actions.

Following the disagreement with Brigadier General Thomas "Gamecock" Sumter over the siege at Fort Granby (see Chapter 10), Lee wrote that he was "very happy to be with General Pickens."[3] Lee was especially grateful that his Legion was allowed to command the operation at Fort Galphin. (Lee and most historians have reported that he was commanding at Galphin during the siege of that fort, yet others declared that Lee left the detachment under Rudolph to take the fort while Lee rushed to meet Pickens.)

Lee joined Pickens and Clarke. They held a council of war at Pickens' headquarters camp near Augusta. They planned to attack Fort Grierson first and next place "Burn Foot" Brown under siege at Fort Cornwallis. (It was recently written that Andrew Pickens was eager to attack at Augusta to avenge the death of his brother who supposedly had been tortured and killed by Indians in the vicinity. The brother in question is John who was still very much alive at the time of the Siege of Augusta. See Chapter 13 for an account of John Pickens' death.)

When Lieutenant Colonel Brown heard of the actions at Fort Galphin, he sent a request for aid from the Creek Indians. Approximately 300 braves answered his call and joined him at Fort Cornwallis.

The attack on Fort Grierson began the morning of May 22. General Pickens maneuvered downriver from the north and west while Georgia Colonel Clarke and North Carolina Major Pinkertham Eaton attacked from the south (the side opposite from the river which ran nearly west to east at that point). Lieutenant Colonel Lee took a position near a gulley on the east to cut off the retreat route to Fort Cornwallis. Major Joseph Eggleston of Lee's Legion was to keep an eye on Fort Cornwallis.

The Americans attacked fiercely, and Lieutenant Colonel Grierson was forced to abandon the post through a secret passage on the river side. He and most of his force were able to hide along the bank and gradually creep toward Fort Cornwallis. "Burn Foot" Brown launched a rescue effort with his King's Rangers, but Lieutenant Colonel Henry Lee forced them back to Fort Cornwallis.

Clarke and North Carolina Captain Robert Smith detected Grierson's troop movement, and a sharp skirmish ensued. Grierson and five Tories successfully retreated to Fort

Cornwallis, but by then had lost 30 killed and 45 captured during the battle. The American lost 40 killed and/or wounded. One of those killed was Major Eaton who was replaced by Captain Smith as the North Carolina militia leader. It has been reported that Eaton was wounded in the thigh and then killed by an escaping Tory who used Eaton's own sword.

Captain Tarleton Brown from Colonel William Hardin's regiment of Pickens' brigade noted in his memoirs: "The next fort we attacked was that commanded by the wretched Grason [sic], at the upper end of the town. This we stormed and took — Capt. Alexander shooting Grason for his villainous conduct in the country. Some made their escape by fleeing to Brown's fort near the river."[4]

Note that Captain Brown incorrectly stated Grierson was killed in the skirmish and did not make it to Fort Cornwallis.

Pickens gathered the other commanders that night at camp to prepare for an engagement of Fort Cornwallis. Tarleton Brown described an event of the following morning:

> Before we laid siege to Brown's fort, a fellow by the name of Rutherford (a villain withal) took a company and slipped out in the night down the river opposite Beech Island, and just at the break of day, surprised our horse-guard. It being in the bend of the river, the British and Tories got round them, and [the enemy] having a superior force, our men took to the river, but they killed several of our brave fellows while they were swimming, some making their escape — my brother, Bartlett Brown, was among that number.[5]

The siege began on the 23rd. After one week, Lieutenant Colonel Lee suggested to Brigadier General Pickens that they employ a Maham tower such as Marion's forces used at Fort Watson (see Chapter 10). Pickens consented, and on the 30th the American troops started to construct a 30-foot tall structure.

Though General Greene had ordered that Lee would be second to Pickens, Andrew Pickens treated Lee as a co-commander. On the 31st, the Commanders sent a message to the garrison commander:

> Brigadier Pickens and Lieutenant-Col. Lee to Lieutenant-Col. Browne
> AUGUSTA, May 31st, 1781
> SIR, — The usage of war renders it necessary that we present you with an opportunity of avoiding the destruction which impends your garrison.
> We have deferred our summons to this late date, to preclude the necessity of much correspondence on the occasion. You see the strength of the investing forces; the progress of our works; and you may inform yourself of the situation of the two armies, by inquiries from Captain Armstrong, of the Legion, who has the honor to bear this.
> Lieutenant-Colonel Browne, in answer, to Pickens and Lee
> GENTLEMEN, — What progress you have made in your works I am no stranger to. It is my duty and inclination to defend this place to the last extremity.[6]

On June 1, the Maham tower was high enough to cover the walls of Fort Cornwallis. Captain William Martin, of Pickens' brigade (from Edgeville, South Carolina), was trying to attach an artillery piece to the tower's parapet when he was killed by a Tory sniper. A Tory militiaman knew of the incident and rode out of his way to brag about it to Captain Martin's mother. Their exchange:

"Have you a son in the army at Augusta?"

"Yes."

"Then I saw his brains blown out!"

"He could not have died in a nobler cause."[7]

Lieutenant Colonel Brown attempted a ploy when he sent a sergeant out to feign desertion. The sergeant gained Lee's trust and explained that the Maham tower had not been effective. Lee asked how the tower might be improved upon, and the spy suggested some alterations. Lee ordered the man be taken to the Maham tower to begin work. After Lee had retired for the night, his suspicions became aroused. He sent a body of guards to incarcerate the so-called deserter. The guards found him preparing to set the tower ablaze, but caught him before he succeeded.

On the 3rd, Pickens and Lee essayed another summons:

> PICKENS AND LEE TO LIEUTENANT-COLONEL BROWNE
> AUGUSTA, June 3d, 1781
> SIR, — It is not our disposition to press the unfortunate. To prevent the effusion of blood, which must follow perseverance of your fruitless resistance, we inform you, that we are willing, though in the grasp of victory, to grant such terms as a comparative view of our respective situations can warrant.
> Your determination will be considered as conclusive, and will regulate our conduct.

> LIEUTENANT-COLONEL BROWNE TO PICKENS AND LEE
> FORT CORNWALLIS, June 3d, 1781
> GENTLEMEN, — I have the honor to acknowledge the receipt of your summons of this day, and to assure you, that it is my duty, it is likewise my inclination, to defend the post to the last extremity.[8]

When Augusta first came under siege, Thomas Brown ordered men to tunnel from the fort to an outbuilding. They then mined the structure and hoped for an opportunity to surprise some Whigs should they enter.

On the night of the third, Pickens sent a team of riflemen to investigate the structure for possible use as a sniper stronghold. It was near enough to the fort that Brown's men heard them enter. However, by the time someone could crawl through the tunnel and light the fuse, Pickens men had already withdrawn to deliver their report to the General.

The structure was not only demolished in the blast, but pieces of the building were blown thirty feet skyward.

Tired of fooling around, the co-commanders of the siege tried once more:

> PICKENS AND LEE TO LIEUTENANT-COLONEL BROWNE
> HEAD-QUARTERS, June 4th, 1781
> SIR, — We beg leave to propose, that the prisoners in your possession may be sent out of the fort; and that they may be considered yours or ours, as the siege may terminate.
> Confident that you cannot oppose the dictate of humanity and custom of war, we have only to say, that any request from you of a similar nature, will meet our assent.

> LIEUTENANT-COLONEL BROWNE TO PICKENS AND LEE
> GENTLEMEN, — Though motives of humanity, and a feeling for the distress of individuals, incline me to accede to what you have proposed concerning the prisoners with us; yet many reasons, to which you cannot be strangers, forbid my complying with this requisition. Such attention as I can show, consistently with good policy and my duty, shall be shown to them.[9]

Finally, it seemed "Burn Foot" Brown understood the folly of his answer and realized he was not in a bargaining position. He decided to propose as favorable surrender terms as he could. His new response on the 5th initiated a series of missives that ended in Brown's surrender:

> LIEUTENANT-COLONEL BROWNE TO PICKENS AND LEE
> June 5th, 1781
> GENTLEMEN, — Your proposition relative to the officers of the king's troops and militia being admitted to their paroles, and the exclusion of the men, is a matter I cannot accede to.
> The conditions I have to propose to you are, that such of the different classes of men who compose this garrison be permitted to march to Savannah, or continue in the country, as to them may be most eligible, until exchanged.

PICKENS AND LEE TO LIEUTENANT-COLONEL BROWNE
June 5th, 1781

SIR, — In our answer of this morning, we granted the most generous terms in our power to give, which we beg leave to refer to as final on our part.

LIEUTENANT-COLONEL BROWNE TO PICKENS AND LEE

GENTLEMEN, — As some of the articles proposed by you are generally expressed, I have taken the liberty of deputing three gentlemen to wait upon you, for a particular explanation of the respective articles.

ARTICLES OF CAPITULATION PROPOSED BY LIEUTENANT-COLONEL BROWNE AND ANSWERED BY GENERAL PICKENS AND LIEUTENANT-COLONEL LEE

ARTICLE 1ST. — That all acts of hostilities and works shall cease between the besiegers and the besieged, until the articles of capitulation shall be agreed on, signed, and executed, or collectively rejected.

Answer. — Hostilities shall cease for one hour; other operations to continue.

ART. 2^D. — That the fort shall be surrendered to the commanding officer of the American troops, such as it now stands. That the king's troops, three days after signing the articles of capitulation, shall be conducted to Savannah, with their baggage; where they will remain prisoners of war until they are exchanged. That proper conveyances shall be provided by the commanding officer of the American troops for that purpose, together with a sufficient quantity of good and wholesome provisions till their arrival at Savannah.

Answer. — Inadmissable. The prisoners to surrender field prisoners of war; the officers to be indulged with their paroles; the soldiers to be conducted to such places as the commander-in-chief shall direct.

ART. 3^D. — The militia now in garrison shall be permitted to return to their respective homes and be secured in their persons and properties.

Answer. — Answered by the second article, the militia making part of the garrison.

ART. 4TH. — The sick and wounded shall be under the care of their own surgeons, and be supplied with such medicines and necessaries as are allowed to the British hospitals.

Answer. — Agreed.

ART. 5TH. — The officers of the garrison, and the citizens who have born arms during the siege, shall keep their side-arms, pistols, and baggage, which shall not be searched, and retain their servants.

Answer. — The officers and civilians who have borne arms during the siege, shall be permitted their side-arms, private baggage, and servants; their side-arms not to be worn, and the baggage to be searched by a person appointed for that purpose.

ART. 6TH. — The garrison, at an hour appointed, shall march out with shouldered arms and drums beating, to a place agreed on, where they will pile their arms.

Answer. — Agreed. The judicious and gallant defence made by the garrison, entitles them to every mark of military respect. The fort to be delivered up to Captain Rudolph at twelve o'clock, who will take possession with a detachment of the Legion infantry.

ART. 7TH. — That the citizens shall be protected in their persons and properties.

Answer. — Inadmissable.

ART. 8TH. — That twelve months shall be allowed to all such as do not choose to reside in this country to dispose of their effects, real and personal, in this province, without any molestation whatever; or to remove to any part thereof as they may choose, as well as themselves as families.

Answer. — Inadmissable.

ART. 9TH. — That the Indian families, now in garrison, shall accompany the king's troops to Savannah, where they will remain prisoners of war, until exchanged for an equal number of prisoners in the Creek or Cherokee nations.

Answer. — Answered in the second article.

ART. 10TH. — That an express be permitted to go to Savannah with the commanding officer's dispatches, which are not to be opened.

Answer. — Agreed.

ART. 11TH. (Additional.) — The particular attention of Colonel Browne is expected toward the just delivery of all public stores, moneys, &c; and that no loans be permitted to defeat the spirit of this article.

Signed at Head-Quarters, Augusta, June 5th, 1781, by

> Andrew Pickens, Brig. Militia
> Henry Lee, Jr., Lt.-Col. Commandant, V. L.
> Thomas Browne, Lt.-Col. Commanding the
> King's troops at Augusta[10]

The garrison marched out of Fort Cornwallis at noon on June 5, 1781. The Tories lost 52 killed and 334 wounded and captured. Three of the most notorious captives were Colonel James Grierson, Lieutenant Colonel Thomas Brown, and Captain Richard Pearis. (Some have recently written that the captive was Colonel Benjamin Grierson, apparently confusing him with the United States Army Civil War officer by that name.)

Many, especially the Georgians, were upset that these notorious officers would be paroled. Thomas "Burn Foot" Brown and James Grierson especially had treated innocent Whig families severely in the past. Many wanted to kill Lieutenant Colonel Brown on the spot. Captain Tarleton Brown noted in his memoirs: "Brown had been such a desperate fellow, there existed great anxiety to kill him; but as he came under the capitulation; we had no chance to do so at this time, but I determined to do so on his way down the river. I took a few brave fellows, and slipped down the river to carry into execution my determination, but he made his escape, through the shades of night, in a small canoe."[11] When the garrison marched out Captain Michael Rudolph of Lee's Legion possessed the fort.

Grierson had been under guard in a nearby house; on the 6th someone slipped by the sentry and killed the prisoner. According to Tarleton Brown, the "someone" was Captain James Alexander of Georgia. Apparently, Grierson had severely abused Alexander's father in the past, and revenge was in order although Captain Brown cited a different time for the action. Since he wrote his memoirs at a much later date, Tarleton Brown may have experienced some confusion regarding the details.

General Pickens feared for the safety of Lieutenant Colonel Thomas Brown and Captain Richard Pearis. Pickens assigned Colonel LeRoy Hammond to guard Pearis while Lee assigned a Captain Maxwell to guard Thomas Brown until they could be paroled.

General Pickens sent a missive to General Greene on the 7th:

> Letter from Pickens to Greene
> Augusta, 7 Jun 1781
> Dear Sir: A very disagreeable and melancholy affair which happened yesterday in the afternoon, occasions my writing to you at this time. I had ridden down to Browne's Fort where I had been but a few minutes, when information was brought to me that a man had ridden up to the door of a room here, where Col. Grierson was confined, and, without dismounting, shot him so that he expired soon after, and instantly rode off; and though he was instantly pursued by some men on horseback, he effected his escape. Major Williams who was in the same room, immediately ran into a cellar, among the other prisoners; but standing in view, was soon after shot at, and wounded in the shoulder. I have given orders for burying Col. Grierson this afternoon with military honors, but as Col. Browne was also insulted yesterday, (though the man was for some time confined for it,) and the people are so much exasperated against some individuals, I have found it necessary to give orders to cross the River with the prisoners, under the care of Col. Hammond's regiment, and Capt. Smith's detachment of North Carolinians, and march them to Ninety-Six, or till I meet your orders respecting them; being fully persuaded that were they to march for Savannah, they would be beset on the road, but think they might go to Charleston by way of Ninety-Six, if you should so order.
> With respect, your obedient servant, A. PICKENS[12]

General Pickens offered a reward for the capture of Grierson's killer.

Lieutenant Colonel Lee left immediately for Ninety Six to assist Greene with the siege of that fortress. Brigadier General Pickens remained at Augusta to assure the forts were left in proper Georgia Whig militia hands. He also determined to appropriately handle the captured goods and prisoners. Most writers have recorded that Pickens marched the prisoners to Ninety Six; however, there are conflicting reports that Lee had accidentally marched the prisoners in front of the Ninety Six garrison (see Chapter 12). It is likely that Lee had control of the prisoners since he apparently traveled more slowly than did Pickens. Pickens left Augusta somewhat later than did Lee, yet they each arrived at Ninety Six on the 8th. (Lee, himself, stated that one of his officers had the Augusta garrison with him when he arrived at Ninety Six.[13])

The siege of Augusta was over. The only major British outpost remaining was at Ninety Six; the American Army held it under siege concurrently with Augusta.[14]

Lieutenant Colonel Henry Lee with horse. Artist: Alonzo Chappel; unknown engraver, 1865.

12

The Siege of Ninety Six (1781)

The Siege of Augusta has customarily been considered concurrent to the Siege of Ninety Six. Although the Georgia militia surrounded Fort Galphin on April 16, 1781, it was not fully invested until May 19 (see Chapter 11). Augusta was surrendered on June 5, 1781; the Siege of Ninety Six began on May 22, 1781. Therefore, the two campaigns effectively overlapped by two weeks.

Major General Nathanael Greene dispatched Lieutenant Colonel Henry "Light Horse Harry" Lee to work with Brigadier General Andrew Pickens at Augusta on May 15. The Commander also ordered Brigadier General Francis "Swamp Fox" Marion to engage the British at Georgetown, South Carolina. Hence, three major actions were alive at the same time. The exploit at Georgetown, however, would be the shortest of the three.

General Marion and 400 militiamen arrived at Georgetown on May 28. He ordered his men to dig a series of siege trenches. The trenches, however, were not needed. British Captain Robert Gray had previously been ordered by Lieutenant Colonel Francis Lord Rawdon to abandon Georgetown, should it be jeopardized. Gray commanded a garrison of 80 regulars and 20 Loyalists.

On the morning of the 29th, Marion's forces observed that the garrison had departed on a galley, two gunboats, and an armed schooner. The Americans watched the British vessels, which were anchored in Winyah Bay until June 8, when the ships sailed the coastal waterways to Charles Town.[1] Late in 1780, Lieutenant Colonel John Harris Cruger, Commander at Ninety Six, had installed a number of defensive measures designed by Major Patrick Ferguson (see Chapter 9). Since the beginning of 1781, Cruger had labored to further improve the security of the outpost. He had become motivated after Lieutenant Colonel Banastre Tarleton was defeated at Cowpens.

Williamson's Fort, now the stockade fort to the west of the village, was already palisaded. Cruger decided he also needed a fortress to defend his right flank, so he built an earthen redoubt, shaped like an eight–pointed star, two hundred feet across. His men dug a ditch and used the excavated material to construct the wall of the fort. They added material from the floor of the redoubt to make the parapet higher. Its elevation was 14 feet from the bottom of the ditch to the top of the parapet. The builders placed an abatis around the redoubt at the outside edge of the trench.

Star forts were not a new development by that time; they had often been used to provide crossfire against an attacking force. An enemy could not scale one wall without there being another wall at his back; therefore, an attacker would always have defenders at his front and his rear when he approached the redoubt wall. However, at Ninety Six it was not just "a star fort." It was special; indeed, legendary as the scene of a memorable event. Therefore it is "Star Fort."

Cruger had his men embed fraises into the earthwork of the parapet between the ditch and the top. (Fraises were sharpened limbs, point exposed outward, to hinder an enemy from scaling the wall.) The ditch averaged 20 feet wide with a maximum of 30 feet on the north side. The wall of one point of the star located to the southwest was left open. That was then connected to the stockaded village by a communication trench (the same as described for the stockade fort in Chapter 9; except this trench was three and one-half feet deep, five feet wide at the top, and two feet wide at the bottom).

On May 21, Lieutenant Colonel Nisbet Balfour wrote Lieutenant General Cornwallis that he and Rawdon had tried to get messages to Cruger at Ninety Six for two months. He added that he was concerned for Cruger's safety and was trying to order the garrison to withdraw from Ninety Six and reinforce Augusta.

Balfour was wise to have worried, because on the 22nd General Greene had crossed the Saluda River at Island Ford and was already scouting Ninety Six. The American Southern Department Commander was eager to approach the village, so he could pen Cruger and his forces there. Greene intended to not allow the Ninety Six garrison to relieve Lieutenant Colonel Thomas Brown at Augusta. From the letters that Pickens' militia had intercepted, the General knew that Rawdon intended Cruger to reinforce Augusta. Should that occur, Brigadier General Andrew Pickens and Lieutenant Colonel Harry Lee would likely be unsuccessful with their siege of that outpost.

The Continental Army moved through the Ninety Six District and surprised several Tory militia patrols. Numerous captives from those encounters were deserters from the American forces. They were summarily put to death. The army encountered the last of such patrols within sight of the stronghold. More deserters were executed, an ominous site for those Tories who defended the fortress.

It has been reported that the American headquarters camp was probably located 500 yards directly north of the village's north stockade wall. However, that position is unlikely as it would put the site only 300 yards from Star Fort, within rifle range of the defenders. It was more plausibly located northwest along Island Ford Road about 700 yards from the village. This setting would have been around the corner from the nearest growth of trees, and would not have afforded a view from Star Fort.

Greene stationed pickets to surround Ninety Six. They positioned themselves on all access roads several hundred yards away from the fortification to react should anyone try to approach or vacate the fort. Small groups of Tories were scattered throughout the nearby forests and awaited opportunities to snipe at the Americans.

The garrison at Ninety Six totaled 550 men comprised of 350 provincials who came from the northern campaign with Cruger, and 200 local Tories led by Brigadier General Robert Cunningham. Star Fort was staffed by 150 of the provincials and 50 local militiamen. The remainder of the garrison divided their time and attention among the stockade fort, the palisaded village, and the jail (an impenetrable structure that was outside the stockades).

The besiegers numbered 1,000 Continental Army regulars and attached Virginia militiamen, plus nearly 500 South Carolina militiamen. Included was Brigadier General Andrew Pickens' older brother, Captain Joseph Pickens, who commanded a company of South Carolina State Troops. Colonel Robert Anderson, aided by Major Alexander Noble, led the entire South Carolina militia regiment.[2]

Several other family members were at the Siege of Ninety Six. General Pickens' cousin, William Gabriel Pickens, stated in his pension application (see Appendix E):

until the arrival of Genl. Green [sic] from the North. This gave encouragement to the Whigs, and they began again to take up arms under their several leaders, in defense of their country. If I am not mistaken, Green [sic] arrived late in 1780 or first of 1781. Early in the spring of 1781 (I think in April) I with many others, volunteered under Capt. Caruthers, Major Alexander Noble, and Col. Robt. Anderson (the same who was formerly my Captain) and joined General Green [sic] in May, then before Ninety Six. We continued here with Green [sic], during the siege of this place, and until he was repulsed. Our regiment was actively employed during this siege, the particulars of which I could relate if necessary, but will only mention, that it was Green's [sic] first object to approach cautiously, and take the place by a regular siege, of which he had no doubt if time was allowed him.

Another cousin, William Pickens, attested in his pension application: "In the spring or early in the summer of 1780 as well as he now recollects this applicant again volunteered under Capt. Robert Anderson and joined Genl. Green [sic] at Ninety Six, remained untill the siege was raised and Green marched to Charleston." (See Appendix E.)

In addition to Robert Anderson, some others of General Pickens' old friends took part in the siege. Captain Andrew Hamilton declared: "The Applicant also states that he commanded a Company at the siege of Ninety Six, in the year 1781, and remained there under General Green [sic, Nathanael Greene] in the active performance of Military duty until General Greene raised the siege and marched his troops across Saluda River towards North Carolina." (See Appendix E.)

On the night of May 22, General Greene met with his engineer, Polish Colonel Thaddeus Kosciuszko. The Colonel laid out plans for a siege operation that would use trenches and gun batteries. Kosciuszko had a small cadre of men for the work, supplemented by local militiamen. He made a curious decision to begin constructing a gun battery only 70 yards from Star Fort. Even though he started building that night, it was a dangerous proposition to be so near an enemy's position without cover of a siege trench. Virginia Lieutenant Colonel Richard Campbell provided a small detail to protect those who worked on the site.

The men were still toiling as dawn broke on the 23rd. Cruger noticed the operation and dispatched a small group led by Tory Lieutenant John Roney to disperse the crew. Several Virginia guards were killed as they retreated, and the Tory militiamen broke up the nearly-completed battery works. Cruger lost Roney in the action.

On the night of the 23rd, Kosciuszko began anew with two gun batteries about 400 yards north of the star fort. He apparently had learned a lesson from the previous night.

On the 24th, the Americans cannonaded Star Fort with the new gun batteries. That night the militiamen started to fabricate the primary approach trench and a new battery position. They were each about 275 yards north of Star Fort; the gun battery was 200 yards due east and across a shallow ravine from the trench. The militiamen built a 20-foot high hill for the cannon.

General Greene wrote a letter to General Sumter on the 26th that requested the brigadier verify a rumor that a fleet had arrived at Charles Town Harbor. Work on the approach trench and the elevated gun battery was completed on the 27th. Labor commenced the next day on the first parallel trench. The idea of trenching is to zigzag toward the enemy so the attackers always have a trench wall to protect them from rifle fire.

Greene again wrote Thomas Sumter on the 28th. Greene had awaited assistance from Sumter for several weeks, but received little help. The "Gamecock" informed Greene that he had pressed several members of the local militia into service, troops Sumter was supposed to have already provided. Sumter was ordered to take the lead with General Marion

Stockade Fort viewed from Ninety Six village site.

when the Commander required assistance from the militias. Additional militiamen arrived daily and brought food and supplies with them.

The trenching had slowed, so Greene ordered the Continentals to take turns with the tools. The first parallel was completed on June 1; the second parallel on the 3rd. The first parallel ran from Island Ford Road eastward 60 yards and was 175 yards north of Star Fort. The second parallel was 25 yards long, only 75 yards from the Star Fort, and its west end was 100 yards east of Island Ford Road. Kosciuszko also constructed another gun battery. This one was just east of the approach trench that led to the second parallel. The Americans started to use that trench immediately.

Greene decided that Cruger had enough time to see that the Americans were earnest about the siege. He ordered Colonel Otho Williams to author a summons and deliver it to Cruger under a flag:

> Sir,
>
> The very distant situation of the British Army commanded by Lord Cornwallis— Lord Rawdons [sic] retreat — The reduction of all the British posts upon Wateree, Congaree and Santee rivers: and your present circumstances (which are not more truly known to yourself than to your adversary) Leave you no hope but in the generosity of the American Army. The Honorable Major Gl Greene has therefore commanded me to demand an immediate Surrender of your Garrison. A moral certainty of success, without which the previous measures wo^d. not have been taken, induces the General to expect a compliance with this Summons, which I am authorized to assure you, most Seriously will not be repeated. You will therefore consider yourself answerable for the consequences of a vain resistance or destruction of stores.
>
> I have the Honor to be
> Sir
> Your most Obed^t
> Hble Servant
> O. H. Williams[3]

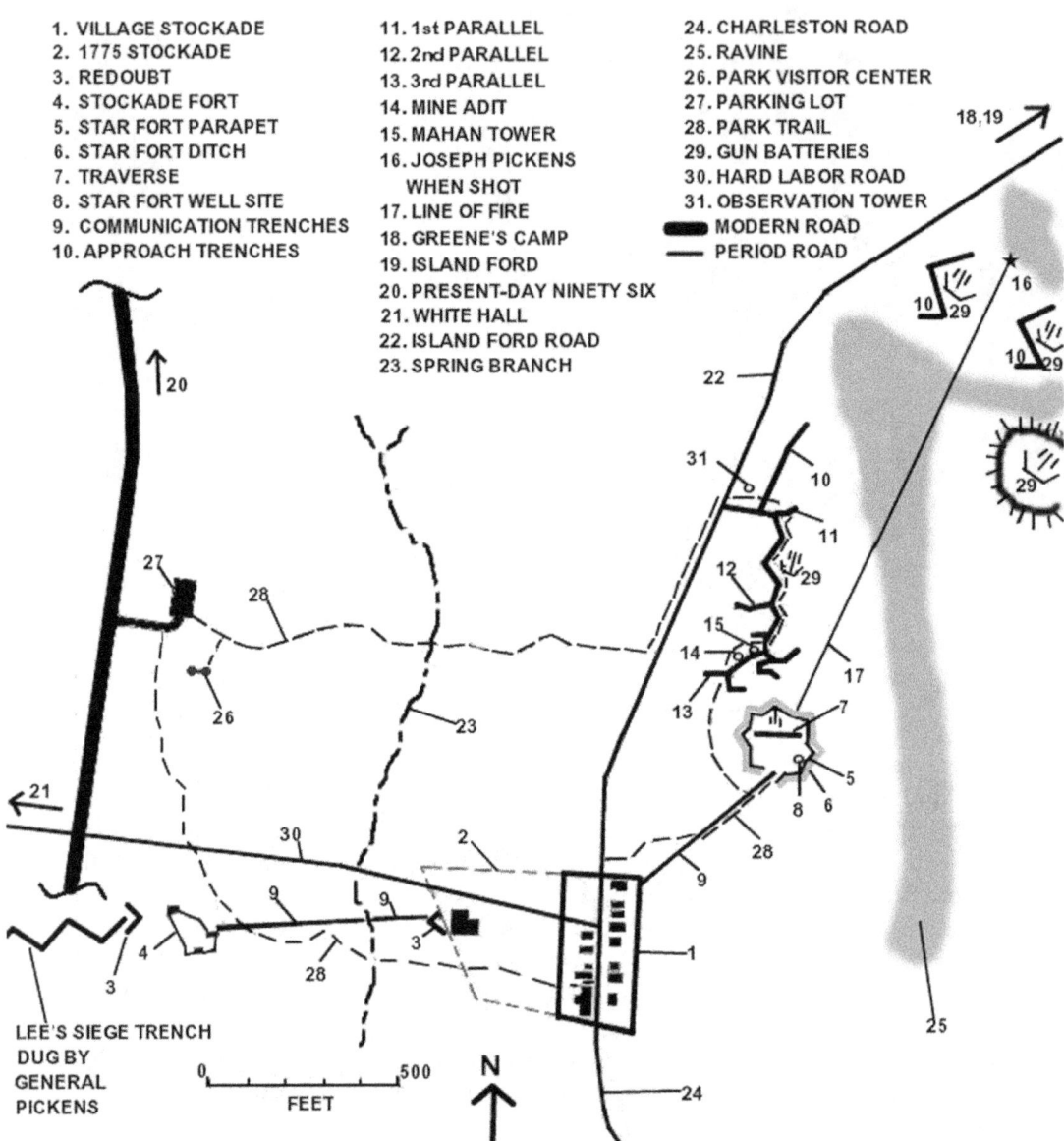

The Siege of Ninety Six.

Cruger, confident he could hold out until reinforcements arrived, politely refused the summons.[4]

On June 4, the Americans shot flaming arrows from their muskets. The idea was to ignite the wooden roof tiles on the buildings within the village. Cruger countered by having his men remove the flammable shingles.

The next day, General Greene issued an order that required any man who did not have a work assignment within the trenches to stay out of the way. He also received a messenger who informed him of the American victory at the Siege of Augusta. He made an entry in his log for June 5, 1781, stating in part, "The indefatigable and Gallant exertions of Gen-

Star Fort at Ninety Six viewed from first siege trench.

eral Pickens and Lieut. Colonel Lee and their brave Officers and men engaged in the Siege merit the highest approbation."[5] Greene added that the success should buoy his troops at Ninety Six and inspire them to a similar outcome.

Also on the 5th, three other incidents occurred. The first two seemed rather innocuous. The first exemplified how magnanimous the American commanders could be. Cruger sent a message to Greene that stated a Lieutenant William Chew was quite ill. The Garrison Commander begged permission to evacuate Chew to Charles Town. Colonel Otho Williams provided approval and stated that Chew, plus his litter bearers, should consider themselves as parolees dependent upon the outcome of the siege.

Additionally, Lieutenant Colonel Francis Lord Rawdon wrote from Charles Town to Major General Charles Lord Cornwallis and advised the Commander that Rawdon would leave for Ninety Six on the 7th with 2,000 troops to relieve Cruger. Rawdon further reported his intent to withdraw the Tory garrison because Ninety Six had become valueless value.

The third event would develop into a major issue. It was not directly involved with the siege but did affect a former militia officer from Ninety Six — Andrew Williamson. Lieutenant Colonel Isaac Hayne made a foray into the suburbs of Charles Town and captured the former Whig Brigadier. (Lieutenant Colonel Hayne had taken parole after the fall of Charles Town. He signed the declaration pledging his allegiance to King George III. In April, Brigadier General Francis Marion convinced Hayne to accept a commission in the militia and to muster a regiment. The new militia force was ready to take up partisan warfare in May. Hayne was a daring officer, thus the movement into the Charles Town suburbs. His fate is described following the account of the siege of Ninety Six.)[6]

On the 6th, General Greene received a copy of *The Royal Gazette*, a Loyalist newspaper, published June 2, 1781, in Charles Town. An article informed him of the arrival of 3,000 British reinforcements commanded by Colonel Paston Gould from Cork, Ireland. It also mentioned Rawdon's planned march to Ninety Six with 2,000 of those troops to relieve the garrison. Greene decided he must press the siege even harder.

Also on the 6th, Francis Marion learned about the reinforcements and Rawdon's planned foray. He forwarded the information to Greene. Greene heard nothing of it from Sumter, the brigadier he assigned to investigate the matter.

Additionally, Kosciuszko decided to order the gun battery near the second parallel be raised 20 feet, a seemingly monumental task considering it was only 100 yards from Star Fort.[7]

June 7, 1781, was a bitter day for the Pickens family. Captain Joseph Pickens, the General's older brother, was shot in the abdomen. At first the wound was not considered serious, so the Captain was taken to camp to rest. However, he suffered from internal bleeding, and an infection developed that resulted in his death on the 17th.

He possibly could have survived because a surgeon served with Greene's army. The doctor likely was not overwhelmed since no direct combat was active that would cause many soldiers to suffer wounds. One reason for possible inattention may have been that Joseph was in the South Carolina State Troops rather than the Continental Army. That difference had been manifested at times. For example, Continental Army regulars were immunized against smallpox while the militiamen were rarely inoculated.

It is curious that Captain Pickens' initial wound was not considered serious because many men so inflicted during the war suffered similar infections. It was recently written, "A man hit in the stomach ... almost invariably died. (Belly wounds, if not immediately fatal, usually led to peritonitis when food in the punctured intestine was released.)"[8] There conceivably could have been more accomplished to relieve Captain Pickens' duress. Continental Army medics had experienced an alarming shortage of medical supplies from the beginning of the war; another likely factor at the Siege of Ninety Six.

General Greene experienced severe problems when he served in the Northern Department. He wrote in 1776: "[There was] no reason either from policy or humanity, that the stores from the General Hospital should be preserved for contingencies which may never happen and the present regimental sick left to perish for want of proper necessities."[9]

(The General Hospital system was a bureaucratic nightmare created by Congress. The lack of supplies caused an excessive number of field amputations, and It also forced the transfer of many wounded soldiers to regional military hospitals known for their filthy conditions. Those patients experienced infections and premature death in crowded and understaffed medical centers.)

There are several conflicting accounts regarding Joseph Pickens' shooting. One description in John A. Chapman's *History of Edgefield County, South Carolina from the Earliest Settlements to 1897* stated: "Joseph Pickens a brother of the General fought at the siege of ninety Six, was shot from within the Star Redoubt while he was at the entrance of the mine that was digging."[10]

Another version was provided by Robert Andrew Pickens in his interview with Lyman C. Draper:

> General Williamson assembled his troops July 1, 1776.... There were two regiments ... and General Andrew Pickens at the head of the other. In Picken's regiment it is recollected that Capt. Norwood, Capt. Robert F. Anderson and Captain Joseph Pickens, the latter a brother of Gen. Pickens, and who was subsequeltly [sic] mortally wounded at the siege of Cambridge (or Ninety Six). Cap-

tain Joseph Pickens when in a small wood, 400 yards beyond the reach of small arms, was recognized by McGuire, a Tory neighbor who had joined Cruger, got an unusually large rifle and wounded Pickens (when ever he shot it is recalled that he said, "Younder stands Capt. Pickens and by God I aim to kill Him"). At first it was not thought to be serious, but bleeding internally, he survived but ten days.[11]

(Robert Andrew Pickens intended to relate that the shot's distance was "400 yards which was beyond the distance of small arms," rather than "400 yards beyond the capability of small arms.")

Except for the misstatement regarding the shot's distance, Robert Andrew Pickens' scenario is more apt than Chapman's. Kosciuszko had not yet begun the mine (which is discussed later). Additionally, the mine adit was only about 100 feet from Star Fort, and it would not have been likely that an experienced captain such as Joseph Pickens would expose himself to a sure sniper attack at such close range. McGuire certainly would not have required an oversized rifle for a 30-yard shot.

The Draper account puts the Captain 400 yards north of Star Fort. He would have been standing near the first gun batteries installed on May 23. This would have been where Island Ford Road emerged from the trees that obscured the American camp from view of the defenders. Captain Pickens may have stepped out of camp and stopped at the tree line to determine the trenchers' progress. He may even have had militiamen working the trenches that day. This scenario fits well with Robert Andrew Pickens' account to Lyman C. Draper. (That location would be on the east side of Island Ford Road, 300 yards northwest of the present-day observation tower which is near the first parallel trench.)

Another discrepancy is whether the Pickens who was shot that day was Captain Joseph. One present-day researcher has indicated that Joseph Pickens was killed by a Tory neighbor while riding along a forested trail near his home.

Another historian has stated, "JOHN PICKENS, son of the old pioneer Andrew Pickens, from the best information obtainable, was lost at the siege of Ninety Six during the Revolutionary war."[12] This is the same John, brother of the General, whose death was supposedly Andrew Pickens' inspiration for the Siege of Augusta. However, John was still very much alive during the Siege of Ninety Six. (John's death is covered in Chapter 13.)

There is plenty of evidence that Joseph Pickens was shot at Ninety Six. The comments by Robert Andrew Pickens to Lyman C. Draper are verified by William Gabriel Pickens. He declared in his pension application (see Appendix E):

> and Genl. Green [sic] called off his troops. The next day he raised the siege, crossed the Saluda and encamped on Little River. In this siege, my brother in law; Captain Joseph Pickens (who was also a cousin) was killed ... and there joined Genl. Pickens (an own cousin to myself, being brother's children, and with whom I had been raised.)... I came to the determination of quiting the service for a while, as the support of an aged mother and a widowed sister (the wife of Capt. Joseph Pickens, Killed at Ninety-Six) now devolved on me, and required my attention.

One other source stated: "JOSEPH PICKENS, a son of the pioneer Andrew Pickens ... was in the Revolutionary War and was a captain of a company of militia in the American army under General Andrew Pickens, and rendered valuable service in this capacity.... He was killed at the siege of Ninety Six, in June 1781."[13]

On the morning of June 8, Lieutenant Colonel Henry Lee arrived at Ninety Six. He had traveled the better part of three days with the prisoners from Augusta. His officer, whose company had charge of the captives, took a wrong road that brought him near the stockade of the village instead of directly to the American campsite. Cruger assumed the action purposeful, so he opened fire on the group whereby he subjected his own allies to danger. No one was injured. Lee reprimanded the officer in charge for jeopardizing his company.

Lee met with Greene and suggested that Kosciuszko had erred by not attacking the weakest point of the enemy defenses; the stockade fort on the enemy's left. They began to make plans for engaging the men in that structure.

Lee wrote, "The enemy's left had been entirely neglected, although in that quarter was procured the chief supply of water."[14] He continued, "His [Kosciuszko's] blunders lost us Ninety-six; and General Greene, much as he was beloved and respected, did not escape criticism, for permitting his engineer to direct the manner of approach ... the general ought certainly to have listened to his opinion, but never ought to have permitted the pursuit of error, although supported by professional authority."[15]

Brigadier General Andrew Pickens arrived later that day and joined the discussion. He agreed with Lee. Pickens assisted the effort by supervising his and Lee's brigades as they excavated a series of siege trenches that began 250 yards west of the objective. Lee used the time to plan with his officers to besiege the stockade fort. General Pickens completed the effort on the 9th with a redoubt sufficient to mount a six-pounder, 40 yards west of the little fort. The cannon would cover any action that Lee might take against the stockade fort.

The Tories had problems obtaining water from Spring Branch in spite of their preparations. They had the creek covered from the jail and from the stockade fort. Additionally, the access trenches that had been dug from both locations gave shelter to those who would venture to retrieve water. Thomas Young gave an account in his memoir:

> Col. Brandon, Major,[sic] Jolly and myself, resolved to make an excursion to 96 where the siege were then going on. Here I remained during the siege. As we every day got our parallels nearer the garrison, we could see them very plain when they went out to a brook or spring for water ... an idea struck old Squire Kennedy, (who was an excellent marksman) that he could pick off a man now and then as they went to the spring. He and I took our rifles and went into the woods to practice at 200 yards. We were arrested and taken before an officer, to whom we gave our excuse and design. He laughed, and told us to practice no more, but to try our luck from the battery if we wanted to, so we took our position, and as a fellow came down to the spring, Kennedy fired and he fell; several ran out and gathered round him, and among them I noticed a man raise his head, and look round as if he wondered where that shot could have come from. I touched my trigger and he fell, and we made off, for fear it might be our time to fall next.[16]

Thomas Young and his companions worried Cruger enough that he changed his operations for getting water. He ordered the slaves within the fortifications to strip all their clothing and move quietly down the trenches to the rivulet at midnight where they filled the canteens and buckets. Additionally, he required the men in Star Fort to dig a well in the southeast section of the redoubt.

Enough of the third parallel had been dug by the 9th to allow Kosciuszko to begin work on his burning desire; a mine. The plan was to tunnel under Star Fort after dark and place explosives beneath the parapet. The mine adit was 100 feet from Star Fort. Although the workers tried to excavate quietly, the noise from the site alerted Cruger, so he sent a dozen men into the third parallel to investigate. They encountered the workers, forced them from the trench, and discovered the entrance to the mine. The Americans retreated hastily, and Kosciuszko was bayoneted in the buttocks. The story of his wound provided a good laugh for both the Patriots and the Loyalists throughout the war.

On the 10th, Greene wrote to Brigadier Generals Francis Marion and Thomas Sumter. In the missive to Sumter, Greene wrote, "By a Charles Town paper of the 2[d], I find a fleet has recently arrived at that place; and it is said with a large reinforcement. As you do not mention anything of it ... I imagine you had not received an account of it. Please to make particular inquiry into the matter."[17] He continued by telling Sumter to work with Marion and attain Rawdon's front and delay his progress.

Greene's letter to Marion stated:

> Gen. Greene to Gen. Marion.
> CAMP BEFORE 96, June 10th, 1781.
> Dear Sir:
> Yours of the 6th I have received with the enclosures. I had information of the arrival of a reinforcement at Charles Town, before your letter came to hand; accounts are various respecting their numbers. By private information, the enemy intend to attempt raising the siege of this place, which I hope, will terminate in our favour. Should the enemy attempt to penetrate the country, I beg you to collect all the force you can and join Gen. Sumter, without loss of time, and give the enemy all the opposition you can, until we form a junction with our collective force, it being my intention to fight them, and I wish them to be crippled as much as possible before we have a general action. Send me all the information you can get. With esteem and regard,
> I am, dear, sir, your most obedient humble servant,
> NATH GREENE.[18]

On the 11th, Greene received verification from Sumter regarding Rawdon's movements. Sumter also informed Greene that he was unable to function effectively because of the injuries he had received at Blackstock's estate. Greene was concerned; he had been counting on Sumter and Marion to thwart Rawdon's movements. Greene immediately dispatched Lieutenant Colonel William Washington and his cavalry to assist Sumter. He also wrote to Marion and ordered him to join Sumter as soon as he could.

General Sumter then wrote a series of letters that befuddled General Marion. On the 13th, he told Marion that the enemy was advancing toward Ninety Six and that Marion needed to disencumber himself of heavy baggage and supplies, then move quickly in that direction. He followed up on the 14th with a missive in which he stated that the enemy was not moving on Ninety Six and that a regiment of local Tories had confused the scouts. He further specified that Marion should halt and obtain as much intelligence as he could to discern Rawdon's activities. Sumter wrote another letter on the 15th wherein he said, "I wrote you since the letter of mine, which you mention having received, that the enemy were not advancing. It again appears probable they are, and from the accounts you have of their reinforcements, there is every reason to think they mean to repossess themselves of this country again." He wrote two more letters to Marion regarding troop movements; each was dated the 16th. In the latter letters Sumter pinpointed Rawdon's movements and directed Marion accordingly. [19]

Lieutenant Colonel Lee sought Major General Greene's attention. On the 11th, he recommended using a Maham tower against the star fort. Pickens volunteered his men to build the structure, and Greene consented. The tower was built just forward of the second parallel.

The action at Ninety Six had aroused considerable curiosity among backcountry men. Often a local would ride up and talk with the Americans on duty about the situation. When there was no immediate exchange of fire, curious residents even approached the fortification to talk with the Tories and further quench their hunger for information.

On the 12th Hugh Aiken, a local Loyalist, casually rode up to the American forces. Although the Continentals were unacquainted with Aiken, they chatted about the siege. Aiken lazily sat astride his horse which eased toward the fort as it grazed. Aiken took the

Americans by surprise as he spurred the horse and galloped to the gate of the village stockade while wildly waving a large envelope. Cruger ordered the gate opened and welcomed the courier who gave him a handwritten message from Lieutenant Colonel Francis Lord Rawdon. Rawdon informed Cruger that he was on his way to Ninety Six with a relief force of 2,000 men. The entire Tory garrison was buoyed and raised a cheer. Cruger's confidence was boosted. He knew he could hold the fort until Rawdon arrived. Also on the 12th, Lee, after much pleading, finally received permission from Greene to mount an attack on the stockade fort. Lee's artillery had been hammering the fort since the battery's installation, and at 11:00 A.M. he dispatched a Sergeant Whaling and nine men to make the attempt.

> a sergeant with nine privates of the Legion infantry, furnished with combustible matter, was directed to approach the stockade in the most concealed direction, under cover of the storm, while the batteries in every quarter opened upon the enemy, and demonstrations of striking at the star redoubt were made, with the expectation of diverting his attention from the intrepid party.... The sergeant conducted his gallant band in the best manner; concealing it whenever the ground permitted, and when exposed to view crawling along upon the belly. At length he reached the ditch [around the stockade fort] with three others; the whole close behind. Here unluckily he was discovered, while in the act of applying his fire. Himself and five were killed; the remaining four escaped unhurt.[20]

Brigadier General Pickens' crew completed the 30-foot high Maham tower on the 14th. Cruger had, of course, witnessed the obvious construction progress, so he installed countermeasures. He stacked sandbags an additional four feet high atop Star Fort's walls and left small spaces between the stacks for firing portals. He also had an earthen berm, called a transverse, built within Star Fort. It was located near the center of the star, was 10 yards long, and the top was level with the parapet. This provided extra cover against enemy fire from the Maham tower, as well as a block against cannon balls.

Shortly after the tower was completed, General Greene, still concerned about Sumter's ability to successfully retard Rawdon's advance, dispatched General Pickens to assist.[21]

On the 16th, Sumter wrote Greene and gave him a detailed description of Rawdon's force that included total numbers and specifications of artillery and the number of cavalrymen Rawdon had with him. General Sumter concluded the missive with, "there is scarce a doubt but 96 is the place of their destination.... I have Great hope your business will be completed before they arrive."[22] That was all General Greene needed to hear. Sumter was not in a position to fulfill his mission to impede Lord Rawdon. The Commander then knew he would need to finalize the effort at Ninety Six before the reinforcements arrived.

Washington and Pickens each arrived at their destination too late to assist. They had trouble locating Sumter who had withdrawn to Granby, and neither of them was lucky enough to have been on the correct line of Rawdon's march. Therefore, Lieutenant Colonel Francis Lord Rawdon was totally unhindered as he moved toward Ninety Six.

Many of Sumter's militiamen had left his service, some from expired musters and others by desertion. He did not succeed in his attempt to unite with Marion. Sumter's cavalry engaged Lord Rawdon's dragoons, but they were soundly defeated. Sumter waited at Granby to ambush Rawdon's force; however, Rawdon's route did not turn toward that direction. Sumter's force, Marion's militia, and now Washington's and Pickens' troops (since the latter two were dispatched on an unsuccessful attempt to locate Sumter) were out of the action.

General Andrew Pickens would later learn that Captain Joseph Pickens had perished of internal bleeding and an infection from his wound on the 17th. His brother's death was the second heartbreak for the General in 1781; it followed that of his good friend, Colonel James McCall, who succumbed to smallpox just one month earlier.

After he planned his withdrawal, Greene launched a last-ditch effort to overrun the garrison. At dawn on the 18th, those ill or wounded were loaded into the regimental wagons, along with the baggage. The caravan moved toward the Island Ford of the Saluda River.

At 11:00 A.M. Greene positioned his marksmen on the platforms of the Maham tower. At noon, all of the artillery batteries opened a barrage upon Star Fort. The snipers in the tower fired to keep the defenders pinned down while the American infantry launched an attack. Lee ordered Captain Michael Rudolph to lead an assault on the stockade fort, which, however, had been abandoned. The stockade fort garrison had safely relocated to the Ninety Six jail via their communication trenches. That move emphasized Lee's point that the army should have attacked the weakest enemy position first. It was too late for his successful effort to be of value for the overall siege.

Lieutenant Colonel Richard Campbell led his 1st Virginia Regiment to clear the way to the ditch around Star Fort. His men ensured the abatis was sufficiently cut open in enough places to allow the attackers access.

Campbell's detachments, led by Lieutenant William Duval of Maryland and Lieutenant Samuel Seldon (also Selden) of Virginia, rushed in with hooked poles to pull the sandbags from atop the parapet into the ditch. They did not succeed.

Tory Major Green dispatched two 30-man clusters to enter the trench from the rear of Star Fort (where the communication trench terminated). New Jersey Loyalist Captain Peter Campbell's group went right; Captain Thomas French of DeLancey's Loyalist Brigade led his men left. They hemmed in the Americans while Tories atop the parapet fired into the enemy ranks.

Action ended at 1:00 P.M. when Major General Nathanael Greene assessed the carnage at Star Fort's ditch and ordered the bugler to issue the recall. Lee ignored the bugler and sought permission to attack the jail; however, Greene had enough and told Lee to hold the stockade fort until dark and then retire to camp. Those who survived the slaughter at the star redoubt withdrew to the siege trenches and slowly made their way to the American camp.

American losses during the siege are reported as 58 killed, 76 wounded, and 20 missing. That accounting, however, does not include militia, except for the Virginia units assigned to General Greene's army. Lieutenant Colonel Henry Lee stated the total American loss was 185 killed and wounded which included a total of 51 militiamen killed and wounded. Thirty-one of the Americans who entered into Star Fort's trench for the final attack were killed, and many were wounded.

The Loyalist garrison lost 28 killed and 58 wounded during the siege. Later that day, Cruger sent a message to Greene to offer a prisoner exchange. Greene immediately responded that he would prefer an exchange of equal numbers. He also expressed concern about the prisoners' treatment as Cruger's original messenger indicated that the Americans were thirsty.

On the 19th, Cruger agreed to the exchange terms and assured Greene that the American prisoners had been given water. Greene than suggested that each force be permitted to retrieve its dead from the trenches. Cruger responded that he would send out those Americans killed within the abatis. It is likely that Greene's killed were buried in a mass grave near to, and probably north of, the American camp. Captain Joseph Pickens may have been buried in the same area, perhaps two days prior.

Greene decamped just past midnight the morning of June 20, 1781. He traveled 14 miles and bivouacked at the Little River; he was en route to Charlotte, North Carolina.

Greene had consigned messengers to find Sumter and order him to meet the army on its line of march. He sent Washington and his dragoons, who had rejoined the General, to observe Rawdon's force and to report back regarding the British movements. Pickens met with Greene that evening at Little River. Greene delegated Pickens to work in the Ninety Six District and reassure the local Whigs that the army would soon return to finish the job. Many Whigs were concerned that the defeat at Ninety Six meant abandonment, so they had packed their belongings and had begun to follow the army. Pickens would discourage that effort and convince the residents that the British would soon be gone.

During their meeting, General Greene expressed his displeasure with Sumter's and Marion's militias for not having united and moved to the front of Rawdon's march. Pickens was dismayed as he listened. He wrote of the event: "I believe not the least attempt was made by them [Sumter and Marion]. The night the siege was raised at Ninety Six, I asked General Greene if he knew the reason of their not harassing the enemy or their not joining the army. He was much irritated, and expressed himself in a manner I had not heard from him before or since."[23]

Some writings state that Sumter's failure to act decisively was due to his poor health. Regardless, the future of the new nation could have hung on the results of such actions. Brigadier General Daniel Morgan's behavior at Cowpens, by comparison, exemplified integrity and grit. Neither his failing health nor excessive pain deterred him from leading his brigade in arguably the most important battle of the American Revolution. Sumter had previously performed wonders for his country, but he seemed unable to excuse the foraging issue with Morgan or forgive Greene for backing Morgan in the process. Sumter may have suffered some mental anguish over the past that hampered his ability to overcome his infirmities. However, his actions early in the war were important contributions to the defeat of British imperialism in America.

The siege resulted in a loss for the Southern Department; yet Major General Nathanael Greene's actions put Lieutenant Colonel Francis Lord Rawdon on notice that such outposts as Cruger's in the backcountry would definitely not be tolerated. Greene obstructed Ninety Six for a good month. He kept Cruger's garrison so occupied in late May that Pickens and Lee could fully invest at Augusta without worry of reinforcements from Ninety Six.[24]

On June 20, 1781, Greene wrote a report to General George Washington of the siege. It was printed in the September 11, 1781, issue of *The London Chronicle* (see Appendix G):

> *Extract of a Letter from Major General Green [sic], dated Camp at Little River, near Ninety-six, June 20, 1781, to Gen. Washington.*
> ...We had pushed on our approaches very near to the enemy's works, our third parallel was formed round their abbatis [sic], a mine and two approaches were within a few feet of the ditch. These approaches were directed against the Star Fort, which stand upon the left of the town, as we approached it from the Saluda. On the right, our approaches were very near the enemy's redoubt; this was a strong stockade fort, with two blockhouses in it. These two works flanked the town, which is picketed in with strong pickets, a ditch around the whole, and a banked [sic] raised near the height of a common parapet.... For the last ten days not a man could shew his head but he was immediately shot down, and the firing was almost incessant day and night. In this stage of the approaches I found the enemy so near us that it would be impossible to reduce the place without hazarding a storm.... The disposition was formed, and the attack made; Lieut. Col. Lee, with his legion infantry, and Captain Kirkwood's light infantry, made the attack on the right; and Lieut. Col. Campbell with the first Maryland and the fifth Virginia regiments, was to have stormed the Star redoubt, which is their principal work, and stands upon the left: The parapet of this work is near 12 feet high, and raised with sand bags near three feet more.... On the right, the enemy

were driven out of their works, and our people took possession of them; on the left never was greater bravery exhibited then by the parties led on by Duvall and Selden; but they were not to be successful....

The behavior of the troops on this occasion deserves the highest commendations; both the Officers that entered the ditch were wounded, and the greater part of their men were either killed or wounded. I have only to lament, that such brave men fell in an unsuccessful attempt.

...The troops have undergone incredible hardships during the siege; and though the issue was not successful, I hope their exertions will merit the approbation of Congress.

We continued the siege until the enemy [meaning Rawdon's force from Charles town] got within a few miles of us, having previously sent off all our sick and wounded, and spare stores.

Return of the Killed, Wounded, and missing, during the Siege of Ninety Six, in South Carolina.

Total. Killed 57; wounded 70; missing 20.

Capt. Armstrong of the Maryland Line, killed; Capt. Benson, and Lieut. Duvall, wounded; Capt. Bentley, of the Virginia Line, prisoner; Lieutenants Evans, Miller, and Selden, wounded. Colonel Koscuitzko [sic], Chief Engineer, was slightly wounded.

O. H. WILLIAMS, D. A. G.
Published by order of Congress
CHARLES THOMPSON, SECRETARY.

Lord Rawdon arrived at Ninety Six on the morning of the 21st; he'd come from the south via the Charles Town Road. Cruger reported to him about the siege and its finale. Rawdon also learned that Greene was only 14 miles away and that the Continental Army was in poor shape. Rawdon's force was badly in need of respite. The British had lost 50 men to heat exhaustion and sunstroke during the forced march from headquarters.

Lieutenant Colonel Rawdon wanted to catch Greene's force and crush the entire American Southern Department. Rawdon quickly organized his men and led them in another forced march to pursue Greene.

Once Greene was aware of the British designs, he ordered his aide, Major William Pierce, to write Brigadier General Sumter (with prescribed military decorum) to express the Commander's expectations. He impressed upon the Brigadier that it was important that Sumter's brigade meet the army at Fish Dam Ford on the Broad River and furnish assistance required against the British. Greene was too livid to sign the message himself.

Greene was not only furious with Thomas Sumter; he was quite indignant with Virginia Governor Thomas Jefferson. He had asked the leaders of Virginia's militia regiments to assist the Southern Department at the siege. When they were on the way to do so, Jefferson stepped in and countermanded the movement. Greene wrote to Congress on the 22nd, and later to others, and bitterly complained that Jefferson left him in the lurch with too few soldiers for the task. He wrote directly to Jefferson on the 27th:

> the countermanding the militia ordered to join this army has been attended with the most mortifying and disagreeable consequences. Had they taken the field in time and in force we should have compleated the reduction of all the enemies outposts ... we have been obliged to raise the siege of 96.... For want of the militia the approaches went on slow and the siege rendered bloody and tedious.[25]

On June 24, Greene crossed the Enoree River and moved to establish his camp at Fish Dam Ford by nightfall. Lieutenant Colonels Henry Lee and William Washington made up the rear guard and had just crossed the Enoree two hours prior to Rawdon's arrival.

The British leader arrived far in advance of his supply wagons, and he needed to rest his men. They were exhausted from the heat and slept, although they were hungry to a man. Rawdon decided he could not push the regiment any further, so he returned to Ninety Six. Greene had Washington and Lee keep an eye on Rawdon's movements.

On the 25th, Greene continued to relieve his frustration with missives. He wrote to Brigadier General Francis Marion and hammered him regarding his lack of support for the army. Greene stated:

> The enemy have obliged us to raise the siege of Ninety-Six, when it was upon the eve of surrendering. It was my wish to have fought Lord Rawdon before he got to Ninety-Six, and could I have collected your force and that of Gen. Sumter and Pickens, I would have done it, and am persuaded we should have defeated him, but being left alone, I was obliged to retire. I am surprised the people should be so averse to joining in some general plan of operations. It will be impossible to carry on the war to advantage, or even attempt to hold the country, unless your force can be directed to a point ... if the people will not be more united in their views, they must abide the consequences, for I will not calculate upon them at all, unless they will agree to act conformably.... Gen. Sumter is preparing for a manoeuver ... and he will require your aid to bring it into effect. You will therefore call out all the force you can, and co-operate with him in any manner he may direct.[26]

(Greene included Pickens' name because the Commander had to dispatch Pickens,' as well as Washington's, force in an attempt to find General Sumter. Except when the combined militias left Greene during the race to the Dan River, the Ninety Six area brigades had been quite supportive of the Continental Army at Pickens' direction.)

Once the British stopped trailing the Continental Army, Greene changed directions. On the 28th, while camped north of Winnsboro, South Carolina, Greene wrote to Pickens that evening: "It is not certain what the enemy means to do with Ninety Six. If they leave a garrison there, we are in a situation to invest it.... I think they cannot if you are active on your quarter ... nor do I believe they dare attempt it."[27]

After General Pickens had met with Greene on the 20th, he returned to his brigade and suggested they take a few days to look after their properties and families. They were to convene later and act resolutely against the Tories in the backcountry.

The militiamen had assembled as instructed by the time Pickens received Greene's letter of the 28th. Detachments watched Rawdon's and Cruger's forces while the main body moved against organized local Tory militias. William Gabriel Pickens noted in his pension application (see Appendix E):

> On the retreat of Genl. Green [sic], the most of the militia dispersed for a few days, but reassembled about fifteen miles above Ninety-Six, and there joined Genl. Pickens (an own cousin to myself, being brother's children, and with whom I had been raised.) After joining Genl. Pickens, we marched toward North Carolina—crossed Broad River at Hamilton's Ford, and proceeded down towards the Congaree. Here I, with others were sent out as spies to ascertain the situation of the enemy then on their march toward Charleston. We (the spy company) came up with the enemy's rear guard, and attacked it; in which we killed five. But we could do no more than harass the rear and flanks, and embarrass their march as much as possible, which we continued to do for ten miles. We were on horse, as were all now under the command of Genl. Pickens. After this we marched up towards the Dutch Fork, into a settlement almost entirely Tories, and who had embodyed in considerable numbers near the line.

Lieutenant Colonel Francis Lord Rawdon planned his departure for Charles Town, and he offered to take as many of the local Loyalists as wanted to go. Some chose to remain in the area despite fears of punishment by Pickens and his militia.

Brigadier General Robert Cunningham, his brother Colonel Patrick Cunningham and their cousin, Major William "Bloody Bill" Cuningham, accompanied Rawdon. "Bloody Bill" would later return with a vengeance. On June 29, after he left 1,400 men to assist Cruger, Lord Rawdon retired from Ninety Six with a force of 800. He ordered a detachment from Charles Town to meet his force at Granby and escort his troops safely to headquarters. That detachment was to be led by Lieutenant Colonel Alexander Stewart.

Many Tories who had remained behind soon realized that Cruger also would leave. Rawdon had ordered Cruger to go to Georgetown, so many Tory settlers planned to follow the provincial force there. Cruger's first objective was to destroy everything. There would be no structure to the village of Ninety Six and no armament left for the rebels to use. That was a time-consuming task, but Lieutenant Colonel Rawdon's detachment helped Cruger to accelerate the razing of Ninety Six.

Greene had intelligence from Henry Lee regarding Rawdon's wing of the British force. Since the General knew the British were on the way to meet Stewart at Granby, he made plans to intercept one or both British forces. General Greene ordered Lieutenant Colonel William Washington to move out quickly with his dragoons, patrol the east bank of the Santee River, and await Rawdon's arrival. The Commander also ordered Lieutenant Colonel Henry Lee to trail Rawdon and harass the British rear guard as they traveled.

Greene left his camp and moved toward Winnsboro where he hoped to find Rawdon trapped between the two cavalries. On July 2, 1781, the Southern Department encamped at Cornwallis' old headquarters at Mt. Zion College in Winnsboro. (Mt. Zion College was created in 1777 by the Mt. Zion Society established by Andrew Pickens and others. See Chapter 5.) Cornwallis had last bivouacked in the area prior to the Battle of Kings Mountain nine months earlier. His troops had depleted the available forage there by the time they left for Charlotte; however, when Greene arrived he found that food and clothing had become available. He eagerly resupplied his army with the necessities.

Lord Rawdon arrived at Granby at 11:00 P.M. on the 2nd. He ordered a detachment to reconnoiter the Santee. Scouts reported that the crossings were covered by Washington's dragoons, so Rawdon maintained a camp in Granby. He had no word of Stewart's location, and the morning of the 3rd, Rawdon marched his force toward Orangeburg.

Also on the 3rd, General Greene arrived at Mrs. Rebecca Motte's house (previously used by the British as an outpost called Fort Motte. See Chapter 10). He bided his time as he watched Rawdon and waited for Lee, Marion, Pickens, and Sumter to join him. Greene had written to Sumter and Pickens on the 7th to request they help with an attack on Rawdon and/or Stewart.

As Andrew Pickens marched his brigade through Ninety Six on the 7th, he displayed Whig power for the Tories to see. On the 8th, en route to join Greene, he moved to the New Acquisition District to resupply his men. Once he camped, he received intelligence that Cruger had paraded a large detachment of Tories through Ninety Six following Pickens' obvious display and departure. Andrew sent word to General Greene and suggested the Pickens' brigade return to Ninety Six and regain control. Greene responded with orders that allowed Pickens to do just that.

On the 9th, Pickens and his 3rd Brigade of South Carolina State Troops moved into Andrew Williamson's old headquarters at White Hall. There they sat and watched while Cruger completed his assignment to destroy anything of military value at Ninety Six. Pickens' force was too small to stop that effort. On the 10th, Cruger and his force, including the large detachment of Rawdon's soldiers, left Ninety Six and headed for Orangeburg. They torched all of the buildings in the village as they left, including the small Presbyterian Church and the roof of the jail. Many Tories with their families followed Cruger as they feared reprisals by Pickens' brigade. Cruger, his garrison, and a multitude of Tory families made such a sight with their huge caravan as they departed. (Some historians wrote that Cruger departed on the 8th. Since the Loyalists raided the Whig estates prior to abandoning Ninety Six, it is unlikely they would risk doing so while Pickens remained in the vicinity. The more plausible scenario, therefore, is that Pickens left on the 8th as reported, and Cruger vacated the 10th.)

Pickens' brigade followed and considered some action against Cruger's force, but the militiamen and their horses were too exhausted from recent actions to harass local Loyalists and obtain intelligence to be forwarded to General Greene. The militia finally stopped on a hilltop and watched as Cruger's force marched away. Brigadier General Andrew Pickens, in a rare attempt at humor, later stated, "[We were] on horses so exhausted by service, that they could neither get up with the enemy nor get away from him."[28]

While Andrew Pickens sent a small detachment to follow the provincials, and to harass Cruger's rear guard when possible, he gave orders not to pester the civilian Tories in tow. The Brigadier then returned to Ninety Six where he received orders from General Greene to gather food and clothing and feed the starving people left in the vicinity. The necessities were not only available from abandoned estates, but also from Whig donors in Ninety Six and nearby districts. Pickens, in an action similar to present-day martial law, followed Greene's orders and took care of not only the famished Whig families, but also the Tories that remained behind.

On the 12th, General Greene received important intelligence. Rawdon had established a well-defended camp at Orangeburg, Cruger was approaching with a large force, and Stewart was also nearing the community. (That Cruger had not yet arrived at Orangeburg on the 12th is another indication that he left Ninety Six on the 10th rather than the 8th.)

General Greene held a council of war, and a majority of the officers decided to stop the search for Rawdon since the British were leaving the outposts. Greene established a headquarters in the High Hills of the Santee where he allowed his men to recuperate for several weeks. During that time Andrew Pickens acted as Greene's representative and governed the area around Ninety Six.[29]

Of the Tories, it was written:

> they gathered in great numbers in the suburbs of the City of Charleston, and lodged in tents and formed a settlement, which ... took the name of Rawdon Town. Here many perished miserably.... Others resolved to return to their native homes. In Colonel [actually General] Pickens, who commanded that section of the country, they found a friend and protector, a man of kindness and benevolence.[30]

Brigadier General Thomas Sumter had been given responsibility for the lowcountry all the way to the backcountry where Brigadier General Andrew Pickens held command. Many of Sumter's 1st Brigade of South Carolina State Troops returned to their homes, so General Greene assigned Lieutenant Colonel Henry Lee and Brigadier General Francis Marion with their forces to assist Sumter. Thus Sumter's 225 men were supplemented with Lee's 300 Legionnaires and Marion's 180-man 2nd Brigade of South Carolina State Troops.

On July 14, Sumter decided to drive British Lieutenant Colonel John Coates from his garrison at the Monck's Corner outpost. Coates commanded 600 men of the 19th Regiment of Foot and was assisted by Major Thomas Fraser with his 150 South Carolina Loyalist Rangers. Coates had been apprised of Sumter's approach, so he withdrew two miles across the West Branch Cooper River and took up a defensive position at Biggin Church. Sumter's force followed and camped nearby on the 15th. (Biggin Church was located across West Fork Cooper River from Monck's Corner and one-half mile south of present-day US Highway 52 on South Carolina Highway 402. It was originally built for an unofficial Huguenot parish that generously shared the structure with an Anglican missionary named Robert Maude. Eventually, the Anglican Church usurped the location and built its own church.)

On the 16th, Sumter planned his action against Coates' position; however, at 5:00 P.M. Major Fraser and his rangers launched a surprise attack on Sumter's camp. Colonel Edward Lacey's riflemen, excellent marksmen, repulsed the Loyalists. However, Fraser's action delayed Sumter and allowed Coates to leave Biggin Church that night. At 3:00 A.M. on the 17th, Coates set fire to the church that was loaded with stores, baggage, and ammunition. He then withdrew his force of the 19th Foot 18 miles south to Quinby Bridge, and Fraser's Loyalist Ranger Regiment retreated to Charles Town. (Quinby Bridge was located 18 miles south of Biggin Church and just below West Branch Cooper River.)

Lee's Legion caught up to Coates' rear guard of 100 men, led by Captain Colin Campbell. Those men possessed the remaining regimental baggage. They were new recruits and immediately surrendered to Lee.

Coates had crossed Quinby Bridge and ordered his men to loosen the planks. He awaited Campbell's arrival, after which he would remove the planks. However, since Campbell's force had surrendered, the first arrivals were Lee's and Marion's cavalrymen. Lee's Captain James Armstrong led his company over the bridge at full gallop; several planks were dislodged in the process. Legion Lieutenant George Carrington and his company followed, also at full speed. As their horses hurdled the growing gap in the middle of the bridge, more planks became dislodged.

Lieutenant Colonel Hezekiah Maham then led two companies of Marion's cavalry across the bridge. Maham's horse was shot from under him. Lee rode up and the two led a small group of men to repair the bridge.

The Americans who had crossed the bridge engaged in hand-to-hand combat before they took shelter in a forest. Coates withdrew his forces to nearby Shubrick's Plantation where he was able to settle into a well-fortified defensive position.

Lee was unable to adequately repair the bridge to handle the remaining cavalry. Consequently, he and Marion took the remaining units upstream to a ford, crossed, and returned through the forest where the first troops had settled. Lee noted, and Marion agreed, that Coates' position was much too strong to attack without artillery, so they awaited General Sumter.

Sumter arrived with his militia on the afternoon of the 17th, well ahead of the artillery unit. He surveyed the situation and immediately ordered an all-out attack over objections from both Henry Lee and Francis Marion.

Sumter decided to keep the cavalry units in reserve and attack with the infantry. Marion took his and Lee's infantries to the left flank while Sumter took most of his to the right. They each covered Camden District Regimental Colonel Thomas Taylor who led 45 infantrymen into the frontal attack ordered by Sumter. Enemy fire devastated the detachment which was then further repelled by a British bayonet charge. Marion rushed in from the left to cover Taylor's withdrawal but suffered heavy losses within his own ranks in so doing. Finally, as night fell, Marion and Taylor were able to withdraw to secure positions.

As the Americans made camp that night, Sumter announced he would renew the attack the following morning once the artillery arrived. He was met with enormous dissention and was verbally abused for having needlessly exposed Taylor's and Marion's men to danger. Marion was so irritated that he left that night with his depleted militia. Henry Lee left the next morning with his Legion. Neither said a word to Sumter before they departed. Colonel Taylor informed Sumter he would never serve under the Brigadier again. Sumter had no choice but to retreat from Shubrick's Plantation. The Americans had suffered a total loss of 60 killed and wounded. The British lost six killed and 38 wounded in addition to the 100 captured with the rear guard. Sumter, who suffered from old wounds and much criticism, retired from active duty under Greene. His brigade was taken over by Brigadier General Francis Marion who assumed the responsibility that Sumter had held as overall militia commander in the lowcountry.[31] (Shubrick's Plantation was owned by Captain Thomas Shubrick who had been captured at the fall of Charles Town, so the plantation was empty during the action.)

On August 2, 1781, Lieutenant Colonel Francis Lord Rawdon wrote to Lieutenant General Charles Lord Cornwallis and stated: "the total failure of my health obliges me now with regret to make use of the leave of absence which the Commander in Chief had the goodness to grant me at the beginning of the year."[32]

Rawdon wrote the letter two days before Lieutenant Colonel Isaac Hayne was hanged. Hayne had captured Andrew Williamson on the outskirts of Charles Town on June 5. Lieutenant Colonel Nisbet Balfour dispatched Major Thomas Fraser with 90 of the Loyalist Dragoon Regiment to intercept the retreating party and save Williamson. Fraser saved Williamson, and he also captured Isaac Hayne.

Hayne sat in the military prison at Charles Town for several weeks as he awaited his fate. Rawdon would play a major role in Hayne's disposition before he officially retired and sailed for England.

A series of letters written by Major Charles Fraser, Town-Major of Charles Town, are exhibited in the October 11, 1781, issue of *The Connecticut Journal* published in New Haven. The letters very well described the events leading to Hayne's execution stating:

26th July, 1781.
SIR,
I AM directed by the Commandant to inform you, that a Board of Field officers will assemble to-morrow at ten o'clock, at the State-House, for your trial.
I am, Sir,
Your most obedient servant,
Mr. Hayne.
C. FRASER, Town-Major

Thursday evening 26th, July, 1781.
SIR,
I AM directed by the Commandant to acquaint you, that instead of a Board of Field-Officers, as mentioned in my letter of this morning, a Court of inquiry, consisting of four Field-Officers and five Captains, will assemble to-morrow at ten o'clock, at the State-House, for the purpose of ascertaining in what point of view you are to be looked upon: paper, pen and ink, will be allowed you immediately, and any person you name will be permitted to attend as your counsel, at the above mentioned hour and place.
I am, Sir, Your most obedient servant,
C. FRASER, Town-Major
Mr. Hayne, in the Provost.

Memorandum, Sunday, 29th of July
THE Town-Adjutant will be so good as to wait upon Col. Hayne, in the Provost, and acquaint him, that in consequence of the Court of Inquiry held on him yesterday and the preceeding day, Lord Rawdon and the Commandant have come to a resolution that he shall be executed on Tuesday the 31st inst. At six o'clock in the morning, for being found in arms and levying a regiment to oppose the British government, notwithstanding he had become a subject of and taken protection under that government, after the reduction of Charlestown.
C. FRASER, Town-Major

The Commandant referred to within the letters is Lieutenant Colonel Nisbet Balfour. Several sources indicate that Lieutenant Colonel Francis Lord Rawdon left for England July 20, 1781; however, the above letters indicate that he was heavily involved in the decision to execute Hayne. Additionally, as noted above, Rawdon wrote to Cornwallis on August 2 regarding his leave.

The last letter indicated that Hayne was to be hanged on Tuesday, July 31, 1781; however, the execution wasn't carried out until Saturday, August 4, 1781.

A few historians have indicated that Hayne had no counsel; however, he was clearly offered counsel in the second letter of the 26th. He did receive advice from John Colcock, an eminent lawyer from Charles Town. Per Colcock's advice, Hayne wrote a letter to protest the basis for the trial; however, British Major Charles Fraser responded that it was not a trial, but a military decision by the Commander resultant from the findings of a Court of Inquiry.[33]

Lieutenant Colonel Francis Lord Rawdon sailed for England shortly after the execution; however, his ship was captured by French privateers who turned him over to French Admiral De Grasse (François-Joseph Paul, marquis de Grasse Tilly) who was an American ally. De Grasse considered Rawdon to be under his protection and would not turn him over to the Americans even though the Continental Congress demanded that he do so.

Rawdon was replaced by Lieutenant Colonel Alexander Stewart who immediately took his force and encamped south of the Santee opposite Major General Greene. Each side's forces approximated 2,000 men, including army regulars and militiamen. The two commanders reconnoitered each other for a few weeks without any real action except for some skirmishes between the scouting parties.[34]

The Tories around Charles Town were beginning to gather as they were buoyed by the hanging of Lieutenant Colonel Isaac Hayne. Colonel William Harden of the local Whig militia near Charles Town was very concerned. He wrote to both Major General Greene and Brigadier General Francis Marion and requested help.

As soon as General Greene heard of Isaac Hayne's execution, his officers delivered a written request that urged the Commander to allow retaliation. They concluded it with: "while we lament the necessity of such ... and commiserate the sufferings to which individuals will be necessarily exposed ... such a measure may ... involve our own lives in additional danger. But we had rather forego temporary distinctions, and commit our lives to the most desperate situation, than prosecute ... war on terms so unequal and dishonorable."[35]

Major General Greene then demanded an explanation from Lieutenant Colonel Balfour. When he wrote to Balfour, he referred to the hanging as a "daring outrage."

Balfour did not respond until September 3 when he explained:

> I come now to that part which has respect to the execution of Colonel Hayne; on which head I am to inform you it took place by the joint order of Lord Rawdon and myself, in consequence of the most express directions from Lord Cornwallis to us, in regard to all those who should be found in arms, after being at their request as subjects, since the capitulation of Charleston and the clear conquest of the province in the summer of 1780 ... on the subjection of any territory, the inhabitants of it owe allegiance to the conquering power (in the present case a voluntary acknowledgement was given, and consequent protection received); and that, on any account to recede from it, is punishable with death, by whatever law, either civil or military, is then present.[36]

The Southern Department of the Continental Army decamped from the High Hills of the Santee on the 21st (some sources say on the 22nd, and others designate the 28th, as the day of decampment). Greene intended to force an action with Lieutenant Colonel Alexander Stewart who had settled his army 16 miles south and across the Santee River from Greene's encampment. However, General Greene would not have a direct line of march. Much flooded and swampy terrain lay between the two commanders, so the Americans would have to travel well out of the way to reach the British army. On the 22nd, General Greene dispatched orders to all detachments, including Brigadier General Andrew Pickens, to join him on his route. He temporarily excluded Brigadier General Francis Marion and Colonel William Harden.

On the 26th, General Greene issued his proclamation of retaliation and ordered it to be distributed throughout the state. The Commander declared that he would "make reprisals for all such inhuman insults, and to select for the objects of retaliation officers of the regular [British] forces, and not the deluded Americans [Tories] who had joined the royal army."[37] Greene believed that, since the Americans had reconquered the area where Hayne lived and fought, Hayne owed allegiance to the Continental Congress.

Apparently General Greene had expressed his intention to issue the proclamation in his aforementioned letter to Commandant Balfour. In Balfour's letter of September 3, he made reference to Greene's proclamation:

> but as the threat in your letter is of a nature which may extend its consequences to the most disagreeable and serious lengths ... referring for the particular justification to the opinion and decision of Lord Cornwallis, immediately under whom I have the honor to act.... To justify retaliation, I am convinced you will agree, a parity of circumstances in all respects is required; without such, every shadow of justice is removed, and vengeance only points to indiscriminate horrors.[38]

In the meantime, General Greene wrote Marion on August 10 and suggested that he aid Colonel Harden. Greene knew that Marion was distraught over the execution of Isaac Hayne because the "Swamp Fox" had been the officer to coax Hayne to reactivate in the militia even though Hayne was under parole. General Greene told Marion he did not want Marion to inflict revenge against Tories, but to exact his fury upon British officers.

Marion gathered 200 of his militia over the next few days and made plans to head south. On the 13th, he crossed the Edisto River and united with Colonel Harden. Their combined force numbered 450 men.

A few days later, they heard that Hessian Lieutenant Colonel Ernst Leopold von Borck was returning from a foray into the backcountry. He led a total of nearly 700 men that included 180 Hessians, 150 infantrymen from the 30th Regiment of Foot, 150 provincials under Major Thomas Fraser, Major William "Bloody Bill" Cuningham with 100 Loyalist Militia Dragoons, and various smaller units.

Marion detached scouts to watch the British force; he received intelligence on the 29th that they had camped nearby at Isaac Hayne's plantation. The enemy would have to cross the Edisto at Parker's Ferry to continue their march to Charles Town 30 miles to the east. A narrow causeway through a bog would be their only access to the ferry.

On the 30th, Marion lined the causeway with 140 of his men concealed in the trees and brush that grew in the bog 40 to 50 yards off the road. He ordered Colonel Harden to organize his 250 troops another 50 yards behind Marion's men to act as a reserve and to cover a retreat if necessary. Then Marion had Major Samuel Cooper mount the remaining 60 men of his force and prepare to draw the British into the trap. Cooper's detachment would be armed only with sabers.

The British left Hayne's plantation in mid-afternoon and arrived at the ambuscade at dusk. When Lieutenant Colonel von Borck saw the mounted militiamen in the middle of the road, he ordered Major Fraser to drive them off. Fraser moved forward and lined three of his companies across the causeway. He sent Lieutenant Stephen Jarvis ahead with a fourth company of light dragoons to shoo Cooper and his small force away. Rather than retreat, Cooper ordered a charge as his men waved sabers. Jarvis' troops turned and raced back to safety with Fraser and the remaining companies.

Fraser did not know that Marion was in the vicinity, so he thought he was dealing only with a small detachment of Colonel Harden's militia. Fraser mounted a charge with all of his companies and chased Cooper's detachment right into the ambush. Marion's men opened fire, and dragoons fell out of their saddles. Confusion abounded within the British force, and Fraser rallied his troops only to face another volley from the militiamen's reloaded rifles. The scene was repeated once more as the militia had time to reload yet again when the dragoons and their horses ran amok. Fraser's horse was killed and the Major was overrun by the horses of his addled troops. Captain Archibald Campbell, Jarvis' immediate superior, was wounded. Fraser's troops were finally able to withdraw, and von Borck moved forward with his infantry and artillery. However, Marion's men were running low on ammunition, and it was getting late. As Marion's and Harden's militias disappeared through the wispy swamp, the British remained to ponder when it might be safe for them to advance.

The British lost 125 killed and 80 wounded while the Americans suffered one killed and three wounded.[39]

(Parker's Ferry was 30 miles west of Charles Town, on the Edisto River halfway between present-day US Highway 17 and US Alternate Highway 17.)

Meanwhile, Brigadier General Andrew Pickens wasted no time joining Major General Greene; Lieutenant Colonel Henry Lee was already with the Commander.

Lieutenant Colonel Alexander Stewart began a slow withdrawal southward as Greene neared. Pickens and Lee moved ahead as a vanguard to reconnoiter Stewart's movements and actions. Greene stayed well to their rear with the main army as he awaited reports from the scouts. Several messengers made round trips between the advance and General Greene. Stewart finally stopped at Eutaw Springs and set up a defense at Patrick Roche's plantation. Apparently Stewart, seemingly unaware of Lee's and Pickens' detachments, did not dispatch outriders to reconnoiter his back trail. The British Commander was confident that Greene would not continue to follow him; however, the Roche estate was well-suited for a strong defense should he need it. (The site of the battle was approximately two miles east of present-day Eutawville, South Carolina, where State Highway 6 takes a short jog to the north on the southern shore of Lake Marion.)

On September 4, Greene finally sent for Brigadier General Francis Marion who united with the Commander on the 7th at Henry Laurens' plantation. Greene had encamped at Laurens' estate on the 6th, just 17 miles from the British army.

Henry Laurens had been a past Continental Congressman and President of the Congress for a time. In 1781, he was Ambassador to Holland at the behest of Congress. He was captured at sea by the British and was imprisoned in the Tower of London at the time of the Battle of Eutaw Springs. Laurens would later be exchanged for prisoner Francis Lord Rawdon. Laurens' estate became known as Mepkin Plantation and was located at Monck's Corner, South Carolina. In later years it was owned by Henry R. and Clare Boothe Luce who eventually donated the property to the Roman Catholic Church to be used by the Trappist Order's Gethsemani Abbey. Twenty-nine monks of the Order of Cistercians of the Strict Observance (Trappists) came from Gethsemani, Kentucky to found the Abbey. Today it is known as Mepkin Abbey.

On the 5th and 6th, Lee and Pickens continued to scout ahead. They had orders from

Greene to not be covert as Greene wanted to see if Stewart would retreat further. Lee received one enemy dragoon under a flag on each of the two days. Each was carrying dispatches for General Greene. When questioned by Lee, each dragoon indicated that, when he left camp at Eutaw Springs, he was told that the American Army was at Fort Motte, 40 miles away. Lee was dumbfounded that Stewart was not aware of the Americans' nearness. He sent the flag bearers to the rear so they could deliver their packets to Greene.

On the 7th, once Greene had made his battle plan, he marched to Burdell's Tavern where he established his headquarters just seven miles from Eutaw Springs. Here he gathered his officers and assigned the battle formation.

The American army formed two columns and marched out at 4:00 A.M. on the 8th. The vanguard was led by Lieutenant Colonel Henry Lee and Colonel William Henderson with their cavalries. Lee had sent Captain James Armstrong several hundred yards ahead with a scouting detachment.

At 8:00 A.M., Lieutenant Colonel Stewart sent 400 unarmed men to dig yams in the direction from which the Americans were approaching. He detached Major John Coffin with his cavalry to patrol in the vicinity of the yam diggers. While the cavalry scouted, it also watched over the unarmed men. Captain Armstrong happened upon the yam diggers. He thought they were skirmishers and charged. The workers successfully fled in all directions and found cover in the forest. Coffin believed Armstrong's detachment was a full vanguard and countercharged. Armstrong retreated back to Lee and reported the incident. Coffin's force galloped down the road. Lee thought they were the vanguard of a full British force, so he ordered another charge. Major Coffin retreated back to the British camp and sounded the alarm, but he had lost five killed and 40 captured including a captain.

An aroused Stewart sent artillery up the road to greet the Americans. Greene countered by sending his own artillery forward. While cannons raged, the two armies formed for battle.

Greene's first line consisted of Brigadier General Andrew Pickens' 307 dismounted militiamen of the South Carolina 3rd Brigade of State Troops on the left, and Brigadier General Francis Marion led 325 dismounted militiamen of the combined South Carolina 1st and 2nd Brigades of State Troops on the right. The middle consisted of 150 North Carolina militiamen commanded by French Colonel Francis Malmedy (sometimes Malmady or Malmody). Lee moved off to the right flank with his 100 Legion infantry and 60 Legion horsemen. Colonel William Henderson, recently promoted to replace the retired Thomas Sumter, moved off to the left flank with 73 militia dragoons of the 1st Brigade of State Troops.

A.L. Pickens stated, "Pickens came into command of all the state troops, being ably assisted by Marion in commanding a worthy body of mounted troops."[40] Years after the event, Colonel Otho Williams stated as quoted by Dr. Pickens, "the South Carolina state troops and Lee's Legion formed the advance and ... the militia of the two Carolinas moved next under Marion."[41]

Apparently Williams' remarks described the columnar march toward Eutaw Springs that morning, while Dr. Pickens' statement regarded the battle. He continued his statement with, "The seeming conflict is probably to be explained by a halt and rearrangement of forces just before the attack."[42]

Regardless, it is apparent from the action that each of the three militias, Pickens brigade, Marion's brigade, and the North Carolina brigades fought independently within Greene's battle plan.

The second line, the Continental line, was commanded by Brigadier General Jethro Sumner and consisted of three North Carolina battalions (355 men) on the right commanded by Sumner, himself. The middle two battalions were Virginians (250 men) commanded by Lieutenant Colonel Richard Campbell. The left was formed by two Maryland battalions (250 men) under command of Colonel Otho Williams.

The artillerymen with two three-pounders were led by Captain William Gaines and moved with the North Carolina militia in the first line. They were followed by a unit with two six-pounders who moved with the Virginia Continentals in the second line.

Lieutenant Colonel William Washington's 80 cavalrymen made up the primary reserves. Captain Robert Kirkwood's second reserve unit of 70 Delaware Continentals moved in parallel, but through the woods rather than along the road.

Lieutenant Colonel Wade Hampton, second in command to Colonel Henderson, and 72 dragoons of the South Carolina 1st Regiment of State Militia were held back as a reserve to Henderson's position.

Greene's total force amounted to 2,100 men including artillerymen.

(Brigadier General Andrew Pickens' brigade consisted of six regiments commanded by Colonel Robert Anderson, Colonel Joseph Hayes, Colonel Edward Lacey, Colonel David Glynn, Lieutenant Colonel Hugh Middleton, and Lieutenant Colonel Samuel Hammond.)

Stewart countered. He initially arranged his defense in one long line. The right flank consisted of the 3rd Regiment of Foot led by Major Thomas Dawson (418 men). Major Henry Sheridan commanding the New York Volunteers (97 men) was stationed next. Lieutenant Colonel John Harris Cruger with the First Battalion of DeLancey's New York Provincial Brigade (73 men) followed Sheridan. He, in turn, was followed by Lieutenant Colonel Isaac Allen's New Jersey Volunteers (106 men). Captain Hayes St. Ledger stood on the New Jersey left with the 63rd Regiment of Foot (125 men). Finally, the 64th Regiment of Foot led by Captain Dennis Kelly (243 men) comprised the left flank.[43]

Major John Marjoribanks, who led a mixed battalion of 343 light infantrymen and grenadiers, covered the line from the far right. The same function was provided on the left by Major John Coffin and his 70 Loyalist cavalrymen.

Stewart's force totaled 1,650, including artillerymen and those detached from several regiments who had been foraging for yams. The British advanced skirmishers from various infantry units 400 yards ahead to delay the Americans while Stewart continued to set his defense. (The size of the British army is variously reported by historians. Stewart has been credited with up to 2,400 men.)

The battle began as the American militia line resolutely moved forward and drove the British skirmishers back to their regiments. Pickens, Marion, and Malmedy continued to advance, and the fighting grew fierce as they neared the main British line. Several soldiers from each side fell during the opening salvos.

The North Carolina militia began to falter in the middle. Colonel Malmedy had a dubious reputation for not following through under fire. Additionally, the militiamen were totally unfamiliar with him and did not know how to react. Not so with Marion's and Pickens' militiamen. They were all experienced veterans and totally trusted their respective commanders.

As the North Carolinians began to lag, the two South Carolina militias moved forward into the teeth of the British line. They yelled as they moved; each man fired, then reloaded and moved a few yards to repeat the effort.

The British had noticed the lagging center of the American first line, so the 64th Regiment of Foot mounted a bayonet charge directly at the North Carolina militia. Some of Lieutenant Colonel Cruger's New York Brigade from the middle of the British line joined the charge.

The South Carolina militias on the flanks continued to fight but could no longer advance. They not only had British soldiers to their fore, but the bayonetted troops were moving between Marion and Pickens. The South Carolinians began to take musket fire from the 64th, and Brigadier General Andrew Pickens was hit and knocked from his horse. His men thought he was dead, but Colonel Robert Anderson was able to remove him while the brigade continued to fight. They, as well as Marion's brigade, fought until they had each used their allotted 17 rounds of ammunition. (Andrew Pickens' friend, Robert Anderson, had come to his aid before: when Pickens' horse was shot from under him in the Cherokee War of 1776, and when he again lost his horse at the Battle of Stono Ferry in 1779. See Chapters 4 and 6.)

The militias retired from the engagement; however, they had done their job and accomplished even more than Major General Nathanael Greene had hoped they would. Brigadier General Jethro Sumner moved into the middle with his North Carolina Continental brigades. He was flanked by Lieutenant Colonel Henry Lee and his Legion on the right with Colonel William Henderson and his cavalry moving forward on the left.

The Americans pushed the British 64th Regiment back to its line and then began to slowly move the British main line of defense toward its rear. Henderson moved forward against the 3rd Regiment, but that drew him even with Major Marjoribanks who opened a devastating volley upon the dragoons from the 1st Regiment of South Carolina State Troops. Henderson was badly wounded, and when he fell his troops began to falter. However, Lieutenant Colonel Wade Hampton moved forward with his reserve dragoons and took command of the entire detachment. They again moved forward against the British with Hampton leading the way.

The British left flank then mounted another bayonet charge. The 64th and 63rd Regiments forced Sumner's Continentals back. The reserves were all called in: the Virginia and Maryland Continentals with fixed bayonets, Lieutenant Colonel William Washington and his dragoons waving sabers, and Captain Robert Kirkwood's Delaware Continentals, also with fixed bayonets.

The Continentals stopped 40 yards from the British and fired a volley after which they charged, and a battle of bayonets ensued. Additionally, Henry Lee was able to charge the enemy from the British left flank. Finally, the redcoats began a harried withdrawal, except for Major Henry F. Sheridan who took his New York Volunteers into the two-story brick plantation house. There they were well fortified. Major Marjoribanks and his mixed brigade retained their position in the woods along the creek north of the battlefield (what had been the British right flank) and covered the British retreat.

The American Continentals thought the British were on the run, so they looted the British camp near the plantation house. They found food and rum and began to celebrate. The Continental commanders tried desperately to get the soldiers back into action to no avail. From the woods, Marjoribanks had his men fire upon the Americans at the British camp. Greene knew he had to do something to disrupt that effort. He ordered Washington to drive Marjoribanks from the vicinity. Washington's effort was a disaster as he and several of his cavalrymen were wounded. Washington, himself, was captured. His dragoons were joined by the Delaware Continentals and Hampton's detachment of dragoons from the 1st Regiment of South Carolina State Troops. Together they succeeded in driving Mar-

12. *The Siege of Ninety Six (1781)* 287

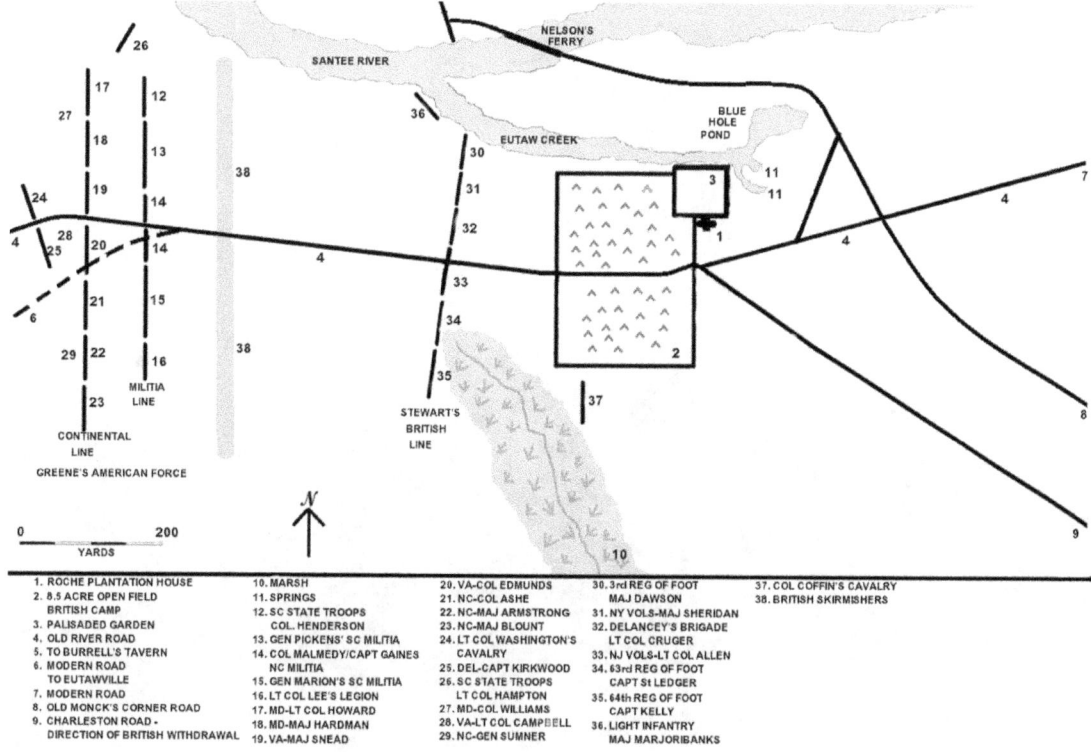

Eutaw Springs initial troop movements.

joribanks from the woods. However, the British Major did not go far. He took a new position behind the palisaded garden in back of the plantation house. There he was supported by Sheridan's men from inside the brick structure.

Lieutenant Colonel Alexander Stewart re-formed the British line by anchoring it off of Major Marjoribanks' new position. Major John Coffin, who had yet to see any action, was on the British left flank.

The American situation was bleak; the militia had withdrawn after doing their job. The Continentals, except for the Delaware brigade, were partying, and Washington's dragoons were at a loss without their leader. Only Lee's Legion on the American right and the Delaware brigade with Hampton's detachment of dragoons on the left were still engaged.

Major Marjoribanks launched an attack on the American left flank, and Major Coffin did the same on the right. Greene then ordered a retreat, which the Americans followed in good order. At that time, Coffin overran Lee's force and drove it from the field, then attacked the Americans within the British camp as they began to withdraw. Lieutenant Colonel Hampton countercharged Coffin but strayed too far while he gave chase. The South Carolinians came under intense fire from Marjoribanks' men and from Sheridan's force still fortified within the house. Several of the troopers were felled by the flurry of musket balls, and Hampton pulled his survivors back to cover the American retreat. The battle ended before noon. The soldiers from each side were exhausted as the scorching summer sun had added to their suffering.

As Greene returned to Burdell's Tavern, he took time to gather his wounded, except for those too near the fortified house. Stewart, too badly beaten up to give chase, held the

Battle of Eutaw Springs. General Greene is prominent on his horse. Artist: Alonzo Chappel; unknown engraver, 1858.

field. The two commanders had communicated that Stewart should bury the dead, but the British were not even able to accomplish that.

When the American troops gathered at Burdell's, they were surprised and happy to find that Anderson had retrieved Brigadier General Andrew Pickens from the field. His militiamen were elated to find that their commander was still alive. Although the musket ball had hit him square in the sternum, it struck the large buckle on his saber belt which lessened its impact. He experienced discomfort from the injury for the rest of his life.

Had Anderson not removed him from the scene, Pickens would have fallen into Lieutenant Colonel Stewart's hands. Pickens might have been captured, imprisoned, and he likely would have been executed for his roles at Cowpens, Augusta, Ninety Six, and Eutaw Springs. Lieutenant Colonel Balfour would like to have made Pickens an example as he had done with Isaac Hayne. Indeed, Pickens' notoriety as a rebel leader, and as a parolee that had rejoined the rebel cause, would have made him an even more valuable prize than was Hayne.

Greene had expected to return the next day and re-engage Stewart, but the British Commander had suffered enough and left for Charles Town on the 9th. Stewart not only left the burial duty for Greene, but also did not remove his own wounded. He left them under a white flag for Greene to capture.

The British suffered 85 killed, 352 wounded, and 430 taken prisoner. The Americans lost 119 killed, 382 wounded, and 78 taken prisoner. The losses amounted to one-third of each army.

Lee and Marion tailed Stewart toward Charles Town and continually harassed the British rearguard. After Stewart arrived at Charles Town, the British were unable to venture outside of the city. The backcountry was well controlled by the Southern Department of the Continental Army and the Patriot militias.

General Greene wrote the next day that Lee and Marion had captured prisoners almost hourly as the British retreated ahead of them. Major Edward Hyrne, Commissary of Prisoners, kept a running total, and Greene indicated that 537 prisoners were then in custody.

The militias had distinguished themselves as they had done at the Battle of Cowpens. On the 9th, General Greene issued General Orders in which he thanked his men for their gallantry. Regarding the militias he wrote, "The militia, commanded by Brigadier Marion and Pickens, and Colonel Malmedy, answered his most sanguine expectations."[44]

On the 11th, Greene sent a report of the battle to the President of the Continental Congress. Regarding the militia he stated, "The militia were ordered to keep advancing as they fired.... General Marion, Col. Malmady [sic] Gen. Pickens conducted the troops with great gallantry and good conduct, and the militia fought with a degree of spirit and firmness that reflects the highest honor on this class of soldiers."[45] (In this report to Congress, Greene clarified that Brigadier General Marion had overall command of the militia line at the battle. However, the "Swamp Fox" was much too busy with his own brigade to spend any time directing the other militias.)

South Carolina Governor John Rutledge wrote of the militia at Eutaw Springs, "That distrust of their own immediate commanders which militia are too apt to be affected with never produced an emotion where Marion and Pickens commanded."[46]

Once the British were settled into Charles Town, General Greene retired with his men to the High Hills of the Santee. Many of his men had become ill with malaria. The entire army needed a resupply of clothing, and they were nearly starved. A respite was necessary. Except for Marion's brigade, the militias were relieved of duty, so they could return home and see to their families and property. Andrew Pickens needed time to recuperate from his injury.

The British would never provide a threat to South Carolina again; however, the Tories and the Cherokee would present another story, indeed.[47]

13

Cleaning Up the Backcountry (1781 and Later)

South Carolina Governor John Rutledge consulted Brigadier General Andrew Pickens about treatment of the soon-to-be defeated Tories. Pickens had been retained in the lowcountry to confer on the matter. Rutledge was impressed by the excellent example the General had set in the Ninety Six District when Major General Nathanael Greene placed the area under martial law in Pickens' hands. Andrew ordered his militia to distribute food, clothing, and necessities to those Tory families that remained in the area after Lieutenant Colonel John Harris Cruger left for Charles Town (see Chapter 12).

Rutledge had also wanted Brigadier General Francis "Swamp Fox" Marion involved in the discussion, but the lowcountry General was busy with skirmishes in the swampy coastal region.

The Governor wrote Marion that Pickens had suggested a free pardon so wives and children of Tories could return to their homes. He requested an immediate response from Marion because General Pickens eagerly anticipated a return to the affairs of the backcountry. Governor Rutledge's letter stated:

Gov. Rutledge to Gen. Marion
Congaree, Sept. 15, 1781
Dear Sir:
I think after the glorious victory at Eutaw, it would be expedient to issue a proclamation offering to all who have joined and are now with the enemy, excepting such as signed the congratulatory addresses to Clinton and Cornwallis, or who have held, or hold commissions under the British government, a free pardon and permission for their wives and families to return and reoccupy their possessions, on condition that such men appearing at our headquarters, or before a Brigade or Colonel of any Regiment, and there subscribing an engagement to serve the State faithfully as a militia force for six months, and declaring in case of deserting in that time, their wives and families shall be sent into Charles Town or the enemy's lines. I apprehend such a measure would be well-timed at this juncture, and might induce some, perhaps many, to return to their allegiance and behave well, which would not only deprive the British of their services, but turn those services to our advantage. However, this is a nice point, and I don't know how it will be relished by our friends. You know mankind generally judge of the propriety of measures from events. These we cannot foresee, but it is our duty to consider what they probably will be, and to take such steps as are most likely to produce the best effects. I now request that you will favor me by bearer, with your opinion on these several points. 1st. Whether you think it advisable to issue any proclamation or offer of pardon. 2nd. Would it be best to make any condition at all of a pardon; if condition is made should it be the person entering into the Continental service for a certain time, (that I am afraid they would not like) or would it be sufficient to require them to serve as militia for a certain time after the expiration of which they would be liable to do duty as the other inhabitants? Is six months service long enough? I think a time ought to be limited for their coming in. Suppose twenty days; — Is that long enough? Would it not be best that they should appear and subscribe the agreement at one certain place, say the headquarters of the army,

13. Cleaning Up the Backcountry (1781 and Later)

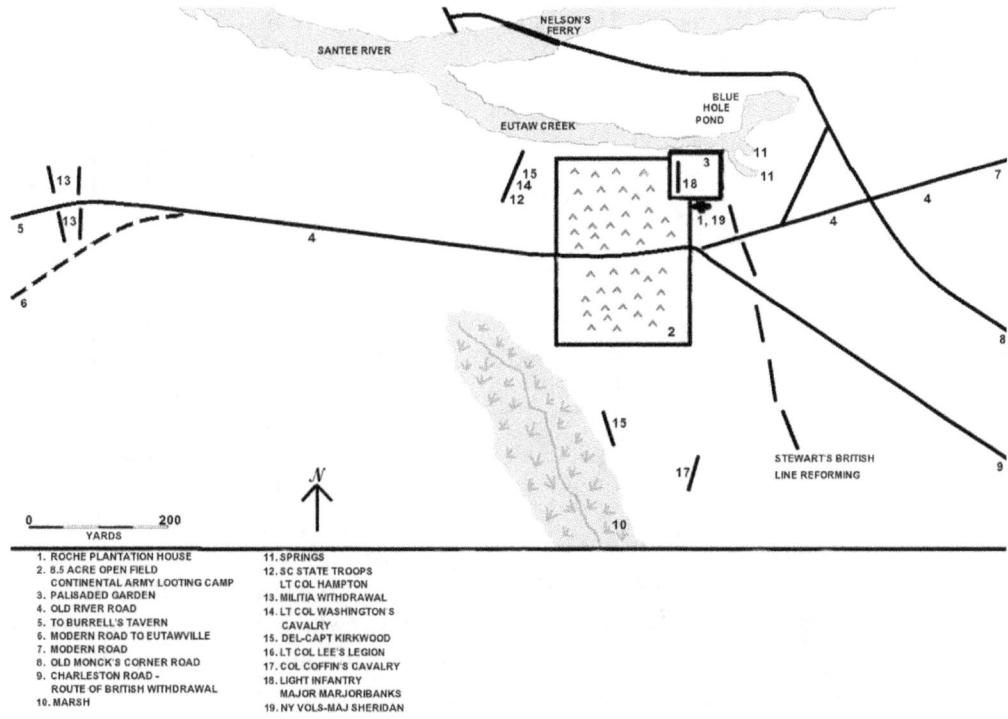

Eutaw Springs troop positions before withdrawal.

or should it be there or before any Brigadier or Colonel, or before a Brigadier only? Pray give me your sentiments fully and freely on this matter, also with respect to the allotment of Brigades, about which I wrote you yesterday, by return of the bearer, and despatch him as soon as you can, for I keep Gen. Pickens only till I hear from you on these points, and he is very anxious to get away. I am, Sir,

Your most obedient servant,
J. RUTLEDGE[1]

After Governor Rutledge received an acknowledgement from Marion, he approved of Pickens' departure. Andrew returned to Ninety Six and began reconstruction within the district. It was not an easy task. Even though the British were no longer a consideration of daily life in the backcountry, several active Tories and many Cherokee braves were. Tory leaders from "Rawdon Town" (the Tory camp established on the outskirts of Charles Town) returned to exact vengeance upon the Whigs. Pickens' militia was worked hard trying to establish peace.

One of the most notorious of those Tory leaders was Major William "Bloody Bill" Cuningham (sometimes Cunningham). He led a regiment of Loyalist dragoons, in the Ninety Six Brigade of Loyalist Militia, commanded by his cousin Brigadier General Robert Cunningham.

William Cuningham had once been of the Whig persuasion. He was jovial, outgoing, and generally courteous. In 1775, he was a member of Captain John Caldwell's company of the South Carolina 3rd Regiment of Rangers. The company had participated in Williamson's foray into Cherokee country in 1776. When assigned to duty in Charles Town, William tried to resign. He claimed he had been promised that option rather than see action in the lowcountry. He then supposedly agreed to fulfill the assignment in return for promotion to the rank of lieutenant. He was not promoted, so he deserted, was court martialed, but was later acquitted.

Surrender at Yorktown. Artist: H. A. Ogden; unknown lithographer, 1897.

All citizens had been expected to fulfill a militia responsibility since the early days of colonization. It became difficult in the late 18th century when two opposing sides were competing for the individuals' membership. Threats and impressment were common. It is reported that Captain William Ritchie of the Ninety Six Militia Regiment had drafted John Cuningham, William's brother, to serve. John, described as epileptic and crippled, refused to report for duty. Ritchie and militiaman Samuel Moore tried to force John into his "commitment." John Cuningham objected, then verbally abused Ritchie and Moore The two whipped him fiercely, and continued zealously until John Cuningham died.

William Cuningham learned of his brother's death and, not having access to a horse, walked from Charles Town to Ninety Six. Supposedly, during his attempt to locate John Cuningham, Captain Ritchie dragged the Cuninghams' elderly father from his sick bed and treated him harshly.

When William Cuningham found Captain Ritchie at the Ritchie home, he shot and killed him in the presence of other Whig militiamen. Thus began "Bloody Bill's" long trail of vengeance at the age of 20.

Lieutenant General Charles Lord Cornwallis surrendered at Yorktown, Virginia, on October 19, 1781. That event was the first formality in the coming end to the American Revolution. Without Cornwallis' knowledge, Major General Sir Henry Clinton had dispatched reinforcements to give Cornwallis aid; however, it was not likely British ships could have broken the French blockade in the Chesapeake.

Following Cornwallis' capitulation, General George Washington was able to send additional Continental troops to assist General Greene in South Carolina and Georgia. Brigadier General Anthony Wayne commanded the reinforcements.[2]

Major Cuningham left Rawdon Town and moved toward his home in the Ninety Six District. He settled there by mid–November of 1781. His first action was to attack the estate of Captain Edward Hampton. Hampton was murdered.

On the 16th, Cuningham, who had amassed a regiment of 300 men, dispatched a foraging party to obtain some beeves. The group, led by Colonel Hezekiah Williams, managed to rustle a small herd of cattle owned by Captain James Butler. Williams' group drove the herd toward Cuningham's camp. While they rested at Tarrar's Spring, they were surprised by 30 Whig militiamen commanded by Captain Butler and Captain Sterling Turner. The two groups engaged in a brief skirmish which ended when the Tories agreed to return the stolen cattle. Butler and Turner allowed Williams' force to leave the area unharmed. (Butler had actually retired and ceded command of his militia company to Turner. Butler specifically gathered the men for this event to regain his herd.)

Williams reported the incident to "Bloody Bill" who decided he could not allow the Whigs to interfere with his efforts to gain control in the backcountry. Following the affair at Tarrar's Spring, the Patriots camped at Cloud's Creek. A heavy rain developed and continued throughout the night. Turner ordered his sodden troops to break camp on the morning of the 17th. They slogged through the mud and stopped at a nearby log farmhouse that belonged to a man named Carter. Captain Turner, over the objections of Captain Butler, asked Carter if the party could come in, eat breakfast, and prime their wet guns with dry powder.

Cuningham knew where the militiamen were, and he surrounded the cabin with his 300 men. After a short exchange of gunfire, Captain Butler sent a messenger to ask Cuningham for surrender terms. The Major had some long-standing difference with the Captain's son, James Butler, Jr., and refused any terms that would include the young man. Captain Butler was aged and offered to exchange his own life for that of his son. While the offer was discussed, the younger Butler shot and killed a Loyalist. James Butler, Jr., was killed by return fire.

The Patriots then pled for mercy, but Cuningham refused. He set fire to a shed that abutted the house and told the Whigs that, if they would surrender, he would deliver them to the nearest British post as prisoners of war. Captains Turner and Butler emerged first. Major Cuningham yelled, "These fellows had better be paroled, and I'll show you what kind of a parole they are to have."[3] He then pulled his saber and swung it at Captain Butler, but he missed him. Butler returned the favor as he smacked a Loyalist with the butt of his rifle. Another Tory struck Butler dead with a saber blow. The Whig militiamen were then slain one by one. Only two survived: Benjamin Hughes, who managed an escape into the creek as Carter's cattle became agitated, and a man named Bledsoe who was reportedly spared at the request of a relative who rode with Cuningham.

"Bloody Bill" Cuningham rode a short distance to Towles' Blacksmith Shop and demanded Oliver Towles, a local Whig, to re-shoe all of his men's horses. Once Towles completed the job, Major Cuningham ordered him, his son, and a slave boy killed. He burned all of the buildings on the property and rode away.

Cuningham's next target was a regiment of Pickens' brigade at Hayes' Station. Colonel Joseph Hayes commanded the Little River Regiment headquartered at his tavern near the Edgehill Plantation. Eighteen-year old Captain Daniel Williams and fourteen-year old Joseph Williams were among 31 members of the regiment present that day. They were the sons of Brigadier General James Williams who died of wounds received at the Battle of Kings Mountain. (Thomas Young referred to the two in his account of the Brigadier's fall. See Chapter 8.)

Hayes was aware of Cuningham's presence but dismissed warnings that he was approaching. When Cuningham and his Tories arrived at Hayes Station, the regiment climbed a nearby hill to the safety of an old Cherokee War blockhouse. Cuningham warned Hayes that if any shots were fired everyone would be killed, and he then promised that the Whigs would be spared upon surrender.

Hayes refused to surrender as he expected additional members of Pickens' brigade to arrive shortly. Someone (reportedly Daniel Williams) from within the fort fired a shot that killed one of the Tories. The resultant battle continued for several hours until Cuningham's men shot flaming ramrods from their rifles which set the roof afire. (The ramrods had been wrapped with pitch-soaked rags, thus Hayes and his regiment were severely overcome by the heavy black smoke.) They surrendered on the condition they be treated as prisoners of war.

"Bloody Bill," accustomed as was Thomas "Burn Foot" Brown to Whig "necktie" parties, marched the prisoners to the tavern and proceeded to hang them. He first placed Colonel Hayes and Captain Daniel Williams on a fodder stack, hung nooses from the support pole, and tightened the nooses about their necks. Young Joseph Williams cried out, "Oh, brother Daniel, what will I tell mother?"[4]

Cuningham replied, "You will tell her nothing, you d__d rebel suckling!" He then slashed the boy to death with his saber. The pole that supported Hayes' and Williams' nooses broke, and "Bloody Bill" killed each of them with his sword. Cuningham swung his blade at another man until the Major collapsed from exhaustion. The man was hacked to death. Major Cuningham turned the remaining prisoners over to his men and suggested they kill any they desired. A Loyalist named Love was selected to scour the field and assure those that had been hacked were actually dead. Four of the Patriots were killed during the initial battle, and 14 were murdered afterward. Six were captured. Seven escaped, likely prior to the battle when they were forewarned of Cuningham's nearness.

(Tarrar's Spring was one mile east of present-day Lexington, South Carolina. The Battle of Cloud's Creek, also known as the Battle of Lick Creek, Carter's House, and Carter's Old Field, and also as the Turner House Massacre, occurred 12 miles due east of present-day Saluda, South Carolina, and two miles south of modern US Highway 378.

Hayes' Station was located 1-1/4 miles north of the Little River, 1-1/2 miles west of present-day State Highway 56 on State Road 30–46 (Old Milton Road), then north 3/4 miles on Williams Road.)[5]

On November 19, 1781, "Bloody Bill" visited the home of his old commander, retired Major John Caldwell. Caldwell was warned of Cuningham's approach, but did not heed the alarm. Cuningham called Caldwell out of his house and, as the retired major approached, the ruthless Loyalist pulled a pistol and shot him. It is reported that the Tories then decapitated Caldwell's body and lopped off his arms. Mrs. Caldwell fainted when her husband was shot; hence, she did not witness the desecration of his corpse.

On December 7, 1781, Cuningham's Tories encountered Brigadier General Andrew Pickens' youngest brother, John. John Pickens was leading a wagon convoy from the canebrakes where the militiamen had gathered corn for the brigade. All of the Whigs with the wagon train were captured.

"Bloody Bill" knew he was the focus of a huge manhunt, so he split his forces. He and 50 of his closest aides returned to "Rawdon Town," while the larger group of 250 men sought protection in the lower Cherokee villages. John Pickens and the other prisoners were in custody of the latter group. When they reached the villages, the Whigs were turned over to the Cherokee.

A. L. Pickens reported, "By one account Colonel Robert Anderson pursued [the larger group], but on the way fell into a creek, and considering it a bad omen gave up the chase."[6] It is probable that Anderson knew John Pickens had been captured and, as close as he was to the Pickens family, it is doubtful that he would give up the chase simply because he fell into a stream. William Gabriel Pickens, cousin of Brigadier General Andrew Pickens, cleared the confusion when he wrote in his pension application (see Appendix E):

> There is another circumstance which I omitted to mention in its right place: While I served under Colonel Anderson in 1781, we made an expedition to the frontier of Georgia in search of the celebrated Bill Cunningham who commanded a party of Tories and Indians, and also had done much mischief after arriving towards the frontier, Capt. Robt. Maxwell and myself were sent forward to spy out the position, strength of the party. We discovered them encamped on Cane Creek on Tugulo [sic] River. We immediately returned to our main body and gave the information. Colonel Anderson immediately planned the attack by dividing his force into three divisions, the right, left and centre. The right and left were committed to the command of Maxwell and myself, and the centre he commanded himself. In this form we advanced, with the sanguine hope of surprising them; but unfortunately, just before reaching their camp, one of the divisions accidentally met a party driving some cattle to the river, and fired upon them. This gave the alarm to the camp, and they instantly fled. Thus our project was defeated, after we supposed they were within our power.

The Cherokee scalped John Pickens and then burned him to death on a pile of lightwood while Cuningham's Tories watched with pleasure. A. L. Pickens wrote of the often-described stoic Andrew Pickens, "General Pickens on learning of his brother's death was said to have wept like a child."[7]

This is the John Pickens sometimes reported as having been killed near Augusta in 1780 prior to General Pickens' siege of that place. (See Chapter 11.) He is also the John Pickens often reported as being killed at the Siege of Ninety Six rather than Joseph Pickens. (See Chapter 12.)

John's widow, who later remarried, filed several claims with South Carolina regarding her husband's death. Two excerpts from those claims (see Appendix E) read:

> SERVICE AND CLAIMS OF JOHN PICKENS STATE OF SOUTH CAROLINA
> Debtor to JOHN PICKENS, deceased for duty as private [in] Col. Anderson's company. Mr. John Pickens, his account for Militia Duty as Private done since the reduction of Charleston, also for a mare lost in service in 1781 ... which was due to him for sundry militia services of this State as a private, serving mostly as a Horse-man, both before the reduction of Charleston and afterwards, until he was taken prisoner by the enemy and given into the hands of Indians, who in a most barbarous manner put him and others to death. Col. Robert Anderson, Commissioner saith that he returned the accounts of said former husband JOHN PICKENS militia duty or services to the auditor's office. Given under my hand this 3-rd day of February 1790.

> NOVEMBER 19, 1819.
> To the Honorable the President and Members of the Senate:
> Your petitioner humbly sheweth that her former husband JOHN PICKENS was killed in service of this state on the 16-th day of December 1781, and left your petitioner with a family of small and very helpless childen.

These excerpts are clear that John Pickens was serving in 1781 until his death on December 16.

Colonel Samuel Hammond and his regiment chased Cuningham toward Charles Town. Hammond neared Cuningham's camp on the Little Saluda River, but since he disliked the odds, he refused to allow his men to attack. Cuningham escaped. General Pickens and his brigade caught up with Hammond and renewed the pursuit. However, "Bloody Bill" had too much of a lead, so Pickens ended the chase at Orangeburg.

In early January 1782, Georgia Major John Cunningham joined General Pickens in an effort to put an end to Tory and Cherokee raids in the backcountry. (Major John Cunningham was likely not closely related to Robert and Patrick Cunningham nor William Cuningham.)

On the 18th, Governor John Rutledge gave a report to the South Carolina legislature that praised "the cool and determined bravery repeatedly displayed by Brigadier Pickens."[8]

The Governor could have added the name "Rebecca Pickens" to his report. Lawless raids continued, and General Pickens attributed them to the Tories who had left Ninety Six to live in the lower Cherokee villages. Beckie had to live with danger for most of their marriage. Dr. Pickens wrote:

> Mrs. Pickens was often obliged to abandon her residence near where Abbeville court-house later stood and flee to the woods or cane-brakes with her children, all sustained and supported by the faithful African servants. During one of Pickens' many absences the old blockhouse was burned. Again the family sought the woods, and one son, supposedly James, died of small-pox.... Rebecca endured all with fortitude never forgetting she was a soldiers wife.[9]

One episode that involved a Tory attack upon General Pickens' cousin, Captain Robert Pickens, was reported during the ebb of Tory activities in the backcountry. A party of Loyalists rushed the Captain's house but was stalled at the door by his wife, Mrs. Dorcus Pickens. Meanwhile, Robert climbed the inside of the chimney to escape. The intruders forced their way into the house, looked out a window and spotted Robert sprinting for the woods. The sparse underbrush gave Robert no place to hide. Some of the younger Loyalists gained on him, and he began to tire. As he clambered over a huge pine log, a weathered piece of bark gave way beneath his foot and fell to the ground. Robert quickly lay down and turned the bark trough-side down over his prone body. There he remained well hidden. The Captain heard the Tories climb over the same log from which he took the bark. They were puzzled by his disappearance and watched the treetops as they expected he had climbed to escape detection. They finally decided he had somehow escaped over the next hill, so they left. Robert Pickens emerged from under the bark and returned home where he lived until his death in 1830.

There continued to be skirmishes between Tories and Whigs. Tory Lieutenant Colonel Benjamin Thompson had two such actions with Brigadier General Francis Marion in February, 1782, and got the better of the "Swamp Fox" in both. One was at Wambaw Bridge on the 14th and the other at Tydiman's Plantation on the 25th.

The actions of the regular British army were drawing to a close. Britain had announced cessation of hostilities with the colonies on February 4.

In March 1782, General Pickens and Major John Cunningham jointly made a foray into the Cherokee towns near Augusta. Their dual purpose was to put an end to Cherokee incursions, and to find and punish those tribal members who were known to have tortured and killed John Pickens. The combined force killed 40 braves and also captured 40 before they returned to Augusta.[10]

Before Pickens left on the venture, the General wrote a letter to Colonel Samuel Hammond who was still watching for Major William Cuningham on the roads from Charles Town. Hammond attached the letter to his pension application in 1832. (See Appendix E.)

> Lt. Col. Samuel Hammond
>   Long Cane 8th Feby 1782
>   Dear Sir
>   I received yours of the 6th Inst. respecting the Enemy — tho it was night before the man from Capt. Towls got her, I immediately wrote Cols. Casey and Roebuck. Col. Anderson sets off this Morning with what men he can collect to Norward's [sic] Mill on Saludy [sic] — and he will wait there for further intelligence. If you can get intelligence as which way the enemy is gone, you will do Every thing in your power to come up with them and send to the Col of Militia between Saludy [sic] and Broad Rivers — advising them of the movement of the Enemy if in your power.

Likewise to Col. Anderson at Norward's [sic] Mill, as I am of opinion they intend for the Cherokee Country—If Cunningham ["Bloody Bill" Cuningham] is along and can make their way through—I wait to hear from you as soon as convenient—wishing you success—and am Dr Sir
Your most humble Serv't
Andrew Pickens

Major General Sir Guy Carleton had replaced Sir Henry Clinton as Commander in Chief of the British Army in America on February 22, 1782. On May 23, Carleton issued an order from New York to evacuate Savannah and all of Georgia. The Royal Council sent a message to British Major General Alexander Leslie that expressed their displeasure. They knew they should also leave as their lives and property would be in jeopardy once the British left. Savannah Garrison Commander, Brigadier General Alured Clarke, ordered his troops to prepare for embarkation.

On the 20th, British and German troops transported all regimental and personal baggage to the waterfront from where it was ferried to transport ships off of Tybee Island. General Clarke led the British garrison from Savannah on July 11 as they embarked on 60 ships for the trip to Charles Town.

A month earlier, in June, 1782, Major William Cuningham made one more foray into Ninety Six. He did not get far, and he was chased so closely by Captain William Butler (a son of Captain James Butler who was killed at Cloud's Creek) that he dropped his saber. Captain Butler recovered the sword and carried it throughout the remaining hostilities.

General Pickens developed a close relationship with Butler, the recipient of a letter from the General dated August 21, 1782. Some historians have declared this letter a model of prudence, wisdom, and force.

ANDREW PICKENS TO CAPTAIN WILLIAM BUTLER
Long Cane, August 21, 1782.
Sir:
As the situation of this country makes it still necessary that a part of the people should constantly be on duty for the purpose of suppressing such parties of men, as lost to every sense of justice, or principle of honesty or humanity, make it their sole study to ruin or distress by every means in their power, every man who shows the least attachment to honesty, regular order and civil government; and as this service will be better performed by men engaged for a certain determinate time, than by the militia called out from time to time as exigencies may require, I desire that you will, with all possible expedition, engage and embody twenty-five good men for your own and Captain John Mitchell's companies, exclusive of one Lieutenant, one Quarter Master and two Segeants, to serve for six months from the day the whole are engaged and reported to me.

They will serve on horse-back, each man furnishing his own horse, saddle, and other accoutrements if he can, but where that is not in his power, you will have horses, saddles, &c., provided for such as are in want by virtue of the warrant to impress such articles herewith given to you; you will be particularly careful to have an exact amount kept by the Quarter Master of all such horses, saddles, &c., as may be impressed by you, specifying the person's name for whom they are got, the time when, and the sums to which they are appraised; all which as well as the people's own horses, you will have the greatest care taken of, that you may always be in a condition fit for service, and that there may be no unnecessary waste of property, you will also take care to make the Quarter-Master give receipts for all provisions and forage you receive, and keep a book in which he is to rate regularly all articles, either horses, saddles, provisions, or forage, the two last articles need not be appraised, but the quantity and quality exactly ascertained that the Legislature may with the more ease fix the prices.

You will be particularly careful not to distress any of the good citizens of this State under any pretence, as the interest of this company is to protect, not to injure; you will, therefore, effectually stop all plundering of every kind, as no property is to be meddled with on any pretense whatever, unless such as may be taken in the field from men in arms against the State, which is to be the property of the captors, except what may be proved to belong to good citizens, doing or always ready to do their duty when called on, who are to have their property delivered to them when proved, without any reward or deduction.

All those who may claim property retaken from the enemy, and who have not themselves done their duty when called on, or who have refused or neglected the same, or moved into other States, will pay one-third part of the value of all such property, to be ascertained by three indifferent men, sworn to appraise the same.

Your company will be governed by the rules and articles for the Government of the troops of this State, and entitled to such pay as is allowed by the present militia law, and they will not be called out of this District, unless on some particular emergency, and by my particular order.

I am, sir, your most obedient servant,
Andrew Pickens[11]

Pickens had been given command of Brigadier General Thomas Sumter's brigade in addition to his own. He had been working with Major General Greene to tighten the noose on Charles Town and assure that the British and Tories would not stray beyond the city.[12]

Tory Colonel Thomas Waters had taken a clan and settled in the Cherokee country of northern Georgia. General Pickens had put together a campaign to find him. He received the authority of South Carolina Governor John Matthews on September 5, 1782. On the 6th, he wrote Captain Butler about supplies:

"ANDREW PICKENS TO CAPTAIN WILLIAM BUTLER
Long Cane, September 6, 1782.
Sir:
Your favor with the cattle by Mr. DeLoach came safe, for which I am much obliged to you. I am glad to hear you have got your company, and are quiet with respect to the out layers, though I would recommend to you to be on your guard, least they should return, at a time when you do not expect them, and come on you unawares. As it is determined to go against the Cherokees, I would be much obliged to you, if you can possibly do it, to collect on Edisto twenty-five or thirty good beeves and send them up so as to be at Cherokee Ford on Savannah River, on Monday, the sixteenth inst. I would not put you to this trouble, but expect beeves will be scarce. As I do not mean to take the men you have engaged to the nation, if any of them should come with the cattle, I will send them immediately back. I would recommend to you to send spies down Edisto, and if possible find out where Cunningham [meaning William "Bloody Bill" Cuningham] keeps, and what his intention is, and if possible drive him from those parts; though I would much rather you could destroy him and his party. I send you six swords you will have care taken of, and when you have done with them, you will have them returned.

I have likewise sent you a few sheets of paper to make your returns. You have my best wishes, and am, sir,
your most humble servant,
Andrew Pickens[13]

The 1782 Cherokee campaign did not last long. On September 5, General Pickens wrote Georgia Colonel Elijah Clarke to enlist his aid. The General took four companies of his own brigade under Captains Robert Carruthers, Robert Maxwell, John Norwood, and Thomas Shankland. Colonel Robert Anderson was regimental commander under Pickens. A regiment of North Carolina militia, led by a Colonel White, joined the foray.

Andrew Pickens and 316 Carolina militiamen crossed the Savannah River at Cherokee Ford on September 10. They united with 98 Georgians who had answered Pickens' request. The combined militia headed west, toward the Chattahoochee River on the 19th and crossed it on the 24th. The militiamen carried rifles in their saddle scabbards, sabers at their sides, and tomahawks and knives on their belts. They rode on seldom-traveled trails to avoid Indian and Tory patrols.

Brigadier General Andrew Pickens issued an order regarding the treatment of noncombative Indians. He later wrote Henry Lee:

13. Cleaning Up the Backcountry (1781 and Later)

To endeavor to put a stop to the cruel murder of women and children which had been long practiced both by the white people and the Indians in their war on each other I issued positive orders that no Indian woman, child or old man or any unfit to bear arms should be put to death or pain of death on the perpetrator, giving at the same time the object I hoped to obtain by it. This order was readily obeyed and the Indians soon followed the example.[14]

He also wrote Lee about the action:

When they evacuated that [Ninety Six] some of the worst tories went to the Cherokees and were almost contiually [sic] harassing and murdering the frontier inhabitants and made no distinction of sexes.... You know the scarcity of ammunition which prevailed after being reduced to Four rounds per man. I met Clark at the place appointed. We proceeded with about 500 men all mounted and nearly one third with swords. I had not more than five or six rounds of ammunition for each man. It may be thought rash to have gone with so little ammunition against a powerful tribe of Indians, aided by a banditti of desperadoes. We went the whole way through the woods unexplored by any of us before. We intirely evaded their spies and completely surprised one of their towns and made prisoners of more than 50 women and children with a few men. We had marched the whole night before, guided by two Indians who we accidentally met with the day before and made prisoners of. They faithfully performed the task allotted them. After surprising the town and making the prisoners in the evening I sent out three of the most active Indian men that we had taken and told them to go tell their people that I was there, that I did not blame the Indians so much as the white men that was amongst them, I would go no further nor destroy any more of their towns and would release all their prisoners on their delivering to me all their prisoners they had of ours including the negroes they had taken, that I would [remain there] two days and that if they refused to comply I would proceed and as far as I could I would destroy as many of their towns and as much of their provisions as possible and if they wished to fight they knew where to find me. The next day they sent in a flag, they said they had heard my talk and would comply with my demands as far as in their power but asked for a few days longer time. I gave them three days longer. On the evening of the last day I had given them their principal chief, with 8 or 10 warriors came in with six white men tied who had been very active with them. We remained in their nation till we had collected a number of their chiefs and warriors and had matters so settled with them that the depredations of the Cherokees on the frontiers of Georgia and South Carolina ceased from that time.[15]

Their plan was to use the rifles only when they scouted the Cherokee positions. When it came time to fight they would immediately charge on horseback while flashing sabers and tomahawks. This technique usually awed the braves. They could not cope with a quick blitz by men on horses. The shortage of ammunition did not affect Pickens' plan of action. He had the utmost confidence in the use of sabers, tomahawks, and knives as cavalry weapons when fighting.

During the campaign, the militia skirmished with some braves at a village called Sauta. One Indian headed for a deep ravine as he carried his rifle. General Pickens gave chase, but the ravine was inaccessible by horse. The General and others fired a few rounds into the ravine to no avail.

A militiaman, identified only as Parata, jumped into the ravine with his rifle and sword. He and the brave came to within 30 yards of each other and fired as they dodged from tree to tree. The warrior charged and swung his rifle at Parata who parried with his saber and yelled, "Now — damn ye, it's my turn!"[16]

They continued to swing their weapons at each other. Finally, Parata sliced the brave's throat with his saber, and the Indian went down. Parata cursed with each blow as he decapitated the warrior. General Pickens said loudly, "Parata acts like a fool!"[17]

Parata climbed out of the ravine with his own weapons and the brave's rifle and shot pouch. He haughtily said, "General you 'lacked' [liked] to have lost the best soldier you have!"[18]

Andrew Pickens gave Parata a stern glare and turned away with a "Huh!"[19]

In another instance, David Pickens, a cousin of the General (see Appendix F), had been living with the Tories and braves in the same lower villages. John "The Tory" Pickens, David's brother, had lured him to join the group in the Cherokee Nation.

David Pickens had just saddled his horse for a race with a Cherokee brave when they were surprised by the arrival of the Whigs. David jumped astride his horse and dashed away from the village. A detachment of the General's force gave chase. When they caught Andrew's cousin, some of the militiamen wanted to kill him, but Captain Maxwell interceded.

Maxwell found the General and said, "Here is someone you know...."

Andrew replied, "Why did you bring him to me?"

Maxwell explained, "Thinking that you might have something to say to him."

Andrew turned his horse, rode away, and firmly stated, "I have nothing to say!" David repented that he had followed his brother to the Tories, and he later rejoined the Whig cause.[20]

The militiamen were dismissed to return to their homes when peace was obtained on October 22. No Patriots were killed, but two were wounded in the Cherokee campaign. Five Tories were captured, and one was hanged. Clarke took the others to Augusta for trial. Forty braves had been killed, and thirteen villages destroyed. The Tory, Waters, escaped the action. The Georgians and Cherokee signed the Treaty of Augusta on May 31, 1783.

On December 14, 1782, the British embarked 500 ships with 2,000 British soldiers, 2,000 Hessian soldiers, 4,000 Loyalists, and 5,000 slaves that had been friendly to the British. The Loyalists included: Ninety-Six Brigade of Loyalist Militia led by Brigadier General Robert Cunningham, Colonel Hezekiah Williams' Regiment, Lieutenant Colonel Moses Kirkland's Regiment, Major William "Bloody Bill" Cuningham's Troop of Dragoons, and Ninety-Six District refugees Colonel Thomas Fletchall, Lieutenant Colonel Andrew Cunningham, and Lieutenant Colonel Patrick Cunningham. South Carolina had seen the last of the Tory Cun(n)ingham's no matter how they spelled the name.[21]

Following the British departure, the citizenry began widespread usage of "Charleston" more than the old form of "Charles Town." Charleston seemed to sound less British; Charles Town more a tribute to King Charles II.

The Cherokee campaign was the last major action in the Georgia and South Carolina backcountries. Andrew Pickens was involved in the first major action of the war to occur in South Carolina at Savage's Old Field in 1775, and he commanded the final action to occur in the backcountry of the southern states in 1782. Thus, Brigadier General Andrew Pickens ended a magnificent military career.

The Treaty of Paris was signed with Britain on September 3, 1783. It was over![22]

Epilogue[1]

The war was over. Brigadier General Andrew Pickens was eager to quietly raise his family and work his plantation in Long Canes. His service, however, had not concluded.

Pickens was elected Justice of the Peace and assisted with the post-war recovery. There were 1,400 orphans and widows in Ninety Six District, including some of his relatives and in-laws. The Brigadier ably represented South Carolina as an extension of Greene's initial martial law appointment. He was aware that the state coffers were bare, so he, unlike others, did not request any recompense for his service.

On August 20, 1783, the Presbyterian Church appointed the General as commissioner to establish boundaries among four local congregations. He settled the matter in a meeting at his estate that same day.

Pickens was appointed to a committee to establish new districts that would replace the initial colonial judicial districts, and he also served as a judge in Ninety Six and Abbeville Districts. The first county court session held in Abbeville in 1785 was called to order in the blockhouse of the Pickens plantation. It is reported that his son, five-year old Andrew Pickens, Jr. (the future governor of South Carolina), drew the lots that impaneled the first jury.

Andrew Pickens was elected to several important political offices, and while he served in those positions for many years, he always felt out of place and preferred to remain at home with his family and work in local community affairs. Some of his elected positions were:

1. South Carolina State Congressman (House of Representatives) from Ninety Six District—1781 to 1784 and 1786 to 1789.
2. South Carolina State Senator from Pendleton District—1789 to 1793.
3. United States Congressman—March 1793 to March 1795
4. South Carolina State Congressman from Pendleton District—1798 to 1800.

People watched for him along the road when he left the backcountry for the United States Congress. He was a stately sight. A. L. Pickens recorded, and in 1896, the Cowpens Centennial Committee verified in *Cowpens Centennial, 1781–1881*:

> approaching his three-score years, of martial figure and dignified demeanor, mounted on a spirited milk white Andalusian steed, whip in hand, and holsters filled with a brace of pistols, the silver mountings of which glittered in the sunlight; under a tri-cornered hat, his hair, now showing a silver that was graying in darker strands, was pushed smoothly back, and tied in a queue, a ruffled shirt he wore with an undress military coat, fair top boots, with handsome silver spurs.... Paint this in your mind's eye, and you have before you a gentleman of the Eighteenth Century ... on his way to Congress; such was General Andrew Pickens, as he passed through to Philadelphia in 1794.[2]

He was petitioned to run for Governor of South Carolina in 1812 but refused the nomination.

Andrew Pickens had a magnificent history with Indians and their affairs in his later years. The Indians held their old foe in high regard. The Cherokee called him Skyagunsta. A. L. Pickens wrote a worthy treatise regarding the origin of the sobriquet that may be found in his book, *Skyagunsta, the Border Wizard Owl*.[3] In summary, many historians believe it to be a combined form of "asgoya" (man) and "gosta" (denotation of importance); therefore, Skyagunsta would mean "Principal Man."

Others declare that rather than "asgoya," the primary word actually came from "atskili" (wizard) and again the suffix "gosta" (but denoting "clear sky" and "chosen"). Thus, the meaning would be "Chosen Clear-Sky Wizard."

"Atskili" (also meaning great horned owl), renders Skyagunsta to be "Principal Owl."

Dr. Pickens thus settled on "Border Wizard Owl," a combination of the two meanings for "atskili." Another variation allotted to Pickens was "Wizard of Tomassee."

For many years after the General died, "his children and grand-children traveling in the Indian country would find free hospitality urged upon them." The Cherokee would say, "Children of Skyagunsta, the Red Man's friend, they more than welcome!"[4]

Pickens included a citation of Presbyterian Historian George Howe who wrote, "He was a man of few words, rather stern in his manner, but of great integrity, wisdom, and courage, and was highly respected by his Indian neighbors."[5]

Had the Cherokee been white men, they possibly would have held a grudge. However, Pickens had convinced the red man that he was not merely his equal, but his superior in the game the red man fancied most, the game of war! For this alone they would have held him in exaltation.... An Indian could admire his foe.... As a Chosen or Principal Wizard the warrior might add the element of the supernatural. Pickens had been sweeping down on the Indians year after year, never with defeat and usually with victory; he had not been so much as wounded [in conflicts with the Cherokee] even though he at times engaged overwhelming forces of red men. They might thus attribute to him the charmed life of a wizard.[6]

Many find it interesting that Andrew Pickens devoted so much of his later life to secure fair treatment for the Cherokee, especially considering his youngest brother, John, was tortured, scalped, and burned at the stake in 1781. However, the General did not hold his heartache against the Cherokee tribe, but against the specific instigator of the action, Major William "Bloody Bill" Cuningham, and the small sect of the tribe that worked diligently with the Tories around Augusta.

In 1785, he relocated from Long Canes to his new estate which he called "Hopewell." (Hopewell was located on the property of present-day Clemson University near the original old village of Seneca.) Gathered there on November 18, 1785, to negotiate an agreement, were 918 Cherokee including chiefs representing 37 villages. The First Treaty of Hopewell was signed 10 days later. The signatories included (in order):

The Commissioners: Andrew Pickens; Benjamin Hawkins; Joseph Martin; Lachlan McIntosh.

The Chiefs: Koatohee or Corn Tassel of Toquo; Scholauetta or Hanging Man of Chota; Tuskegatahu or Long Fellow of Chistohoe; Ooskwha or Abraham of Chilkowa; Kolakusta or Prince of Noth; Newota or the Gritzs of Chicamaga; Konatota or the Rising Fawn of Highwassay; Tuckasee or Young Terrapin of Allajoy; Toostaka or the Waker of Oostanawa; Untoola or Gun Rod of Seteco; Unsuokanail Buffalo White Calf of New Cussee; Kostayeak or Sharp Fellow of Wataga; Chonosta of Cowe; Chescoonwho or Bird in Close of Tomotlug; Tuckasee or Terrapin of Hightowa; Chesetoa or the Rabbit of Tlacoa; Chesecotetona or Yellow Bird of the Pine Log; Sketaloska or Second Man of Tillico; Chokasatahe or Chickasaw Killer of Tasonta; Onanoota of Koosoate; Ookoseta or Sower Mush of Kooloque; Umatooetha or the Water Hunter of Choikamawga; Wyuka of Lookout Mountain; Tulco or Tom of Chatuga; Will of Akoha; Necatee of Sawta; Amokontakona of Kutcloa; Kowetatahee of Frog Town; Keukuck of Talcoa; Tulatiska of Chaway, Wooaluka or the Waylayer of Chota; Tatliusta or Porpoise of Tilassi; John of Little Tallico; Skelelak; Akonoluchta or the Cabin; Cheanoka of Kawetakac; Yellow Bird.

(Each Chief's name was followed by "his X mark." Yellow Bird of the Pine Log and Yellow Bird were different men.)

The Second and Third Treaties of Hopewell were signed on Pickens' estate January 3, 1786, with the Choctaw, and January 10, 1786, with the Chickasaw respectively.

General Pickens continued as South Carolina's de facto Indian agent for several years. In 1787, Chief Hanging Maw sent Joseph Martin to speak with Pickens and protest that white men were not abiding by the treaty and had settled on Cherokee lands. The message stated, "We have been told by people a great way off that the Americans only meant to deceive us.... They [the Northward tribes and the Creeks] want us to join them also [to strike the Americans]. But, I remember your talks and will hold them fast."[7]

On July 11, 1788, Pickens gathered his fellow justices of peace to file official protests with the South Carolina and United States governments over mistreatment of the Cherokee.

In April 1789, President George Washington sent Colonel Marinus Willett to Andrew Pickens to enlist his help with an elusive agreement with the Creek Indians. On June 1, after considerable debate, Pickens, Willett, Creek Chief McGillivray, several other chiefs on horseback, and 26 warriors in three wagons set out to discuss a peace treaty with President Washington, himself.

The President allowed magnanimous terms for the Creeks that included commerce agreements and $100,000 annually for the chiefs of each group. Washington ceremoniously appointed Chief McGillivray a Brigadier General with an annual salary of $1,200.

On December 28, 1791, Andrew Pickens sent a party of six Cherokee to Philadelphia with a letter personally signed by the General. He included a missive signed by South Carolina Governor Charles Cotesworth Pinckney. The letters expressed dissatisfaction to President Washington with the way the Cherokee continued to be treated. President Washington sent the Indians to confer with other government representatives. After several days' conference, Washington agreed that the Cherokee had apt demands. Consequently, he influenced the Senate to correct the matter.

General Andrew Pickens remained dedicated to Indian affairs and championed the cause of the South Carolina backcountry tribes for the rest of his life.

Andrew Pickens was also involved in many other civic efforts. On March 11, 1786, Andrew Pickens, Thomas Sumter, and Robert Anderson sat on a committee to establish the site for South Carolina's capital.

On April 24, 1787, General Pickens, Charles Cotesworth Pinckney, and Pierce Butler met in Beaufort, South Carolina, with Georgia representatives John Houston, John Habersham, and Lachlan McIntosh. After a lengthy negotiation, they settled a boundary dispute that had existed for several months between the two states.

In 1789, Pickens served as a commissioner to locate a court house for the Pendleton District.

Andrew Pickens was promoted to Major General of the Upper South Carolina State Militia Brigade in 1794 by South Carolina congressional action. When he returned from the United States Congress in 1795, he declared he was too old for the military. He stated that conflicts should be left to younger men and recommended William Butler to replace him. The legislature named Butler, who had served as a captain under Pickens, to succeed the General in 1796. The Butlers' son, Andrew Pickens Butler, proudly honored his name and became a United States Senator from South Carolina.

Several of Andrew's progeny followed his example and were active in civil service. His son, Ezekiel, was valedictorian of his Harvard class in 1790 and served as Lieutenant Governor of South Carolina from 1802 to 1804.

Another son, Andrew Pickens, Jr., served as a Lieutenant Colonel in the War of 1812 and Governor of South Carolina from 1816 to 1818.

Andrew Pickens' grandson, Francis Wilkinson Pickens, was elected Governor of South Carolina in 1860 and was in office when the state seceded from the United States. He was a leader of the South Carolina secessionist movement. President Abraham Lincoln, well aware that secession would begin with that state, had no desire to negotiate truce with either Jefferson Davis or Robert E. Lee. The President chose not to meet with representatives of the Confederate States of America (CSA), a move that might have given credence to its authority. Rather, he approached Governor Pickens to try and negotiate a truce, deter an attack on Fort Sumter, and discuss their differences. The President tried to negotiate from a position of strength, thus he declared that American ships were on the way to land troops if the fort were fired upon. Governor Pickens would not take the bluff. He was determined to gain control of Fort Sumter with State Troops.[8]

Governor Francis Wilkinson Pickens and General Robert E. Lee, son of General Andrew Pickens' close friend, General Henry "Light Horse Harry" Lee, would remain leaders of secession.

Andrew and Rebecca Pickens found that the Hopewell area was becoming too crowded. Andrew desired to move closer to his Cherokee friends and settle among his memories. They relocated to Tomassee (sometimes Tamassee) and built a house popularly referred to as the "Red House." This was less than one mile from where his famous Ring Fight had occurred in 1776. (See Chapter 4.) Their son, Andrew Pickens, Jr., retained Hopewell.

Their son, Ezekiel, died in 1813. Then Andrew's beloved wife, Beckie, passed away on December 9, 1814.

Andrew lived almost three more years and quietly passed away on August 11, 1817, while sitting in his yard pondering his memories. He had lived well, and had lost many relatives and friends over the years: Ezekiel, Beckie, brothers Joseph and John, and friend James McCall.

Andrew and Rebecca Pickens are buried in the Old Presbyterian Church graveyard at Hopewell.

Nathanael Greene's biographer, William Johnson, described General Andrew Pickens:

> He was one of the most unambitious and unostentatious of men; public applause he never sought nor regarded, and an opportunity to serve his country he seized on as a gift from heaven. The service rendered, he scarcely seemed to think of it more. His simple unassuming, rather diffident, and even taciturn habits suggested no idea of energy of his character. It was only in the hour of strong opposition or of battle, that his mind animated his figure and exhibited its latent vigor and resource. In times of repose such a man easily passes away from public recollection, especially since Pickens rather shunned than courted public attention. His family, their care and education; his country's independence; a living rather than a formal religion, such summed up

the fruition of his desires. Nevertheless, — sometimes it seems in spite of himself, — he was often called into public service in the councils of his country. There, by nature, he did not shine, an overwhelming humility led him somewhat into the background. But, here as on the battlefield important matters would bring him from his obscurity to the floor, where, not by oratory, but by strong good sense, great weight of character, and full clear conceptions, he usually won success over opposition.

Such a man may merit public expressions of gratitude, but they will be oftener heaped upon the noisy demagogue or assiduous intriguer.[9]

This volume is intended to stand as a testament to the memory of Andrew Pickens. May we remember that he, Henry Lee, Francis Marion, Thomas Sumter, and other heroes kept the dream of independence alive until the American Revolution successfully concluded!

"Down these mean streets a man must go who is not himself mean, who is neither tarnished nor afraid."— Raymond Chandler

Rest well, General; we will not forget!

Appendices

A: *South Carolina Legislature Bill of 2007*

South Carolina General Assembly
117th Session, 2007–2008

S. 461
STATUS INFORMATION

Concurrent Resolution
Sponsors: Senator Verdin
Document Path: l:\s-res\dbv\002pick.kmm.doc
Introduced in the Senate on February 20, 2007
Introduced in the House on February 21, 2007
Adopted by the General Assembly on February 21, 2007
Summary: General Andrew Pickens

HISTORY OF LEGISLATIVE ACTIONS

Date	Body	Action Description with journal page number
2/20/2007	Senate	Introduced, adopted, sent to House SJ-5
2/21/2007	House	Introduced, adopted, returned with concurrence HJ-7

A CONCURRENT RESOLUTION

TO COMMEND AND HONOR GENERAL ANDREW PICKENS, OF PENDLETON DISTRICT, FOR HIS MANY YEARS OF OUTSTANDING AND DEDICATED SERVICE TO THE STATE OF SOUTH CAROLINA AS A PIONEER, PATRIOT, AND STATESMAN WHOSE DEDICATION TO LIBERTY HELPED ACHIEVE AMERICAN INDEPENDENCE AND WHOSE DEDICATION TO SOUTH CAROLINA ENSURED HER STABILITY AND PROSPERITY DURING HER EARLY HISTORY.

Whereas, Andrew Pickens was a successful farmer and was serving as a justice of the peace as the war for American independence began; and

Whereas, in 1775, Pickens became a Captain of Patriot militia, and then participated in the Snow Campaign in the winter of 1775, and then in the Fall of 1776, as a major of the militia, Pickens joined Williamson's expedition against the Cherokee Indians who had allied themselves with the Loyalists; and

Whereas, in July 1776, Pickens and a force of 25 militiamen were surrounded by over 150 Cherokees, but achieved victory in the "Ring Fight;" and

Whereas, on February 14, 1779, Pickens defeated Colonel Boyd at Kettle Creek, Georgia which destroyed Tory morale in South Carolina, while bolstering the numbers of Patriot militia; and

Whereas, at the Battle of Cowpens, Brigadier General Daniel Morgan gave Pickens command of the militia whose tactics proved decisive in the defeat of Banastre Tarleton; and

Whereas, following the Battle of Cowpens, South Carolina, Governor John Rutledge promoted Pickens to Brigadier General and he was also awarded a sword by Congress; and

Whereas, Pickens participated in the Siege of Augusta, Siege of Ninety-Six and Battle of Eutaw Springs; and

Whereas, Pickens was elected in 1782 by the Ninety Six District to the House of Representatives in the Fourth General Assembly at Jacksonborough and continued to serve in the House of Representatives through 1794; and

Whereas, Pickens was one of the commissioners named to settle the boundary line between South Carolina and Georgia in 1787; and

Whereas, in 1787, Pickens moved to his plantation at Hopewell in Seneca. Later in 1802, he moved to the site of the former Cherokee Village Tomassee where he lived until 1817; and

Whereas, Pickens was a member of the state constitutional convention in 1790; and

Whereas, he was the first United States congressman from Pendleton District serving from 1793–1795; and

Whereas, Pickens was appointed Major General of militia in 1795; and

Whereas, Pickens was a member of the State House of Representatives from 1800–1812, and declined the nomination for Governor in 1812; and

Whereas, Pickens was known by the Cherokee as Skyagunsta, or the Wizard Owl, as a tribute to his skill as a warrior; and

Whereas, Pickens remained an elder in the Presbyterian Church until his death in 1817 in Pendleton District whereupon he was interred at the Old Stone Churchyard. Now, therefore,

Be it resolved by the Senate, the House of Representatives concurring:

That the members of the General Assembly of the State of South Carolina, by this resolution, commend and honor General Andrew Pickens, of Pendleton District, for his many years of outstanding and dedicated service to the State of South Carolina as a pioneer, patriot, and statesman whose dedication to liberty helped achieve American independence and whose dedication to South Carolina ensured her stability and prosperity during her early history.

B: Civil Records

Will of Andrew Pickens, Sr.
North Carolina Wills, Volume XXIV, page 42

In the name of God. Amen. The last will and dying testament of ANDREW PICKENS, being weak in body but of perfect memory and calling to mind it is appointed for all men once to die..., First I commend my spirit to God who gave it and my body to be interred, at the discretion of my Extr. and all my lawful debts paid and I do hereby constitute and appoint WILLIAM DAVIS and my dearly beloved wife NANCY to be my lawful and sole executors.

And I do give and bequeath the plantation I now live upon containing five hundred and fifty one acres in ye manner following: that is to say, three hundred acres to my son ANDREW PICKENS to be surveyed off ye upper end of the plantation, and ye remainder to my son JOSEPH PICKENS. But allow my son Andrew to procure two hundred acres of good land for my son JOHN PICKENS at ye first and best opportunity or in five years after date to pay him Ten Pound piece: also I give to my son John a meare called Cathline and her colt and to my beloved wife I give and bequeath a bay meare called Bonney with all ye benefits of ye plantation and all ye movables thereon during her life: and after her departure to be ye property of my son Andrew. And to my daughter JENA [JEAN], a black meare called Bonney and a saddle and bridle with all the other tinge called her property; allowing this to be my last will and testament, disannulling any other ever made by me. Witness my hand and seal. This 5th day of November 1756.

Signed ANDREW PICKENS
Witnessed: Robert McClenachan
John Pickens

Estate Inventory of Andrew Pickens, Sr.
The Register of Deeds Office in Wadesboro, Anson County, North Carolina
Book B No. 1, page 294
ENTERED BY Nancy Ann Pickens and William Davis in 1757

...Horses and mares and colts in all 12–10 cows and calves—and ten head of other dry cattle—about twenty or fifteen head of hogs—and a still and vessels and a cart and a plow and tacklin and pair of plow irons—3 weeding hoes—2 mattocks—mail rings—and wedges,—2 axes—2 pair of chanes—three iron forks—one loom and tacklin with quid wheel—one flax and bi wheel—augus—3 beds and furniture and bed steads—two chists and a trunk and a dresser with pewter and wooden ware—four pots and kettle—one pair of stilliards—three sickles and 2 sithes—a small quantity of books and of notes ten pounds ten shillings and eight pence and a book of account eighty nine pounds seven shillings and three pence....

Abstracts of Augusta County, Virginia, Records, 1745–1751
Relating to Andrew Pickens, Sr., and His Brother John Pickens

1745—February 11, Andrew Pickens deeded land to William McPheeters
February 11, Andrew Pickens signed bond of James Knox as guardian for Jenny Usher
December 9, County Court formed with Andrew Pickens and John Pickens appointed to be Justices of the Peace
1745–1746—Andrew Pickens appointed to act as County Coroner
1746—March 10, John Pickens appointed Sheriff
August 20, Andrew Pickens on committee to report on a road from top of North Mountain
1749—March 22, Andrew Pickens appraiser of land of Andrew Martin
1749–1750—Andrew Pickens served on Committee of the Court.
1751—**August**—Andrew Pickens to William McPheeters, power of attorney
1751—**November 2**—Andrew Pickens deeded to John McPheeters from 400 acres in Beverly Manor—The dower was signed by Ann Pickens

Will of Robert Gouedy (Goudy)
Charleston County Will Transcripts Vol. 17 (1774–1779) pages 413–414
July 2, 1775

In the name of God Amen I Robert Goudy of Ninety Six in the Province of South Carolina being weak in Body, but of Sound and perfect mind and Memory thanks be to Allmighty God for the same do make and publish this my last will and Testament in manner and form following that is to say first of all my will is that all my just debts be paid out of my estate, and also that my funeral expenses be ordered according to the discretion of my Executors whom I shall hereafter nominate and appoint—Item. I will and bequeath unto my well beloved Wife Mary Goudy the equal One third part of all my real and personal estate and the other two thirds of all my real and personal estate to be equally divided between my two Children James Goudy and my daughter Sarah Goudy Share and share alike, and also my will and desire is that my wife One third part shall be after her decease divided between my said two Children James and Sarah Goudy and their Heirs for ever—And also my will and desire that all my whole both real and personal be sold to the best advantage as soon as possible after my Decease, and the Money arising therefrom to be put to Interest for the uses before Mentioned—Item. I will and bequeath unto my three Indian Daughters Namely Peggy Goudy, Kiunagree Goudy and Nancy Goudy One hundred and fifty pounds or two hundred pounds Currency to Each and every one of these My three Daughters before Mentioned to be paid out of my Estate in twelve Months after my decease—And Lastly I do hereby Nominate and Appoint my Well beloved Wife Mary Goudy, Robert Waring, and Robert Dickie to be my true and Lawful Executors to this my last Will and Testament, Hereby revoking all former will or wills by me made heretofore. In Witness whereof I have hereunto Set my Hand and Seal this Second day of July, in the year of our Lord One thousand seven hundred and seventy five.
Robert Goudy (LS)
Signed Sealed published and declared by the above Named Robert Goudy to be his last Will and Tes-

tament in the presence of us, who have hereunto Subscribed our Names as Witnesses in the presence of the Testator and of each other.
William Moore
Hector Dickie
Susanna Dickie

C: 1755 Anson County, North Carolina, Militia

ROSTER OF ANDREW PICKENS' COMPANY OF THE ANSON COUNTY MILITIA
Original spelling errors retained.

Volume 22, page 381
A List of the Millatery Company Commanded by Capten Andrew Pickens in Anson County.

Leftanant, Robert Ramsy.
Ensign, John Crockett.
Sargant, Thomas Wright.
Sargant, William Beard.
Sargant, William King.
Alexander Crockett, Corporal.
*John Hagans, Corporal.
*John Galahen, Corporal.
John Martin Clime, Corporal.
William Hood, Corporal.

Arche Crockett	1
Andrew Nutt	2
Andrew Pickens	3
*Andrew Curswell	4
Andrew McCoune	5
Benjamin Tomson	6
*David Miller	7
Phalex Canady	8
*George Davies	9
*George Walker	10
*George Dougless	11
Hugh McCain	12
Hugh Coffey	13
*John Davies	14
*John Nutt	15
*John Pickens	16

PAGE 382

John Linn	17
John Arnel Pender	18
*John Cannady	19
John Hood	20
*John Tailer	21
*John Wall	22
*John Mount Gomrey	23

John Lockart	24
John Taggart	25
John Bartley	26
James McCorkall	27
*James Walker	28
James Moore	29
*Joseph Pickens	30
*Jeremiah Colens	31
*Joseph Baxter	32
*Moses Davies	33
*Patrick Coin	34
Philip Walker	35
Nethanel Walker	36
Edward Williams	37
Robert Davies	38
*Robert Crockett	39
*Robert Nutt	40
*Roger Smith	41
*Robert McClelland	42
Robert Galt	43
Robert Caldwell	44
*Robert Maheney	45
Robert McCorkall	46
Robert Mount Gomrey	47
*Robert Woods	48
Robert Day	49
Samuel Rogers	50
Samul Burnet	51
William Davies	52
William Nutt	53
*William Nutt, Junier	54
*William Pickens	55
William Ardeng	56
William McKee	57
William King	58
*William Smith	59
William Martain	60

*William Linn	61	Single men Mark'd thus *	34
(Endorsement.)		In All	61
No. of Married men	27		

Research Regarding William Pickens

Family references indicate Andrew Pickens, Sr., may have had two sons, James and William, who were older than Joseph (see Chapter 1). Not much is known about these possible sons except that James was probably born about 1731 and William about 1733. This would make them younger than Catherine Pickens and older than Joseph William Pickens. The estimated birth date for William is an acceptable fit to the timing of the roster.

The best verifications for Andrew Pickens, Sr., having sons named William and James are from the writings of Dr. A. L. Pickens and from the genealogical collection of Thomas Mason Monroe Pickens (better known as "Cousin Monroe"). Dr. Pickens, when writing of a later event on page 27 of *Skyagunsta, The Border Wizard Owl*, stated:

It is even possible that the Battle of Little River, which has been recorded in what seemed to be the proper sequence, belongs to this period rather than to the earlier August campaign. Alexander Garden, evidently the oldest printed authority for the account apparently places it in September, and makes Andrew Pickens a major at the time. This is possibly correct as later we find Pickens a senior officer, which meant that he succeeded to the offices from which Williamson would have been promoted. **Three brothers of the partisan [meaning Andrew Pickens] aided in the Revolution. They were John, Joseph and William**, and by Garden's account Joseph appears to have attained a captaincy about the time of this campaign or before.

Furthermore, on page 2 he stated, "Colonel Andrew [meaning Andrew Pickens, Sr.] called his wife by a pet name of Nancy, though she signed as Anne. Her sons were John, William, Joseph and Andrew."

"Cousin" Monroe included James Pickens in a list of the children of Andrew Pickens, Sr., recorded by Kate Pickens Day in *Cousin Monroe's History of the Pickens Family*, Chapter 4.1, page 39. Furthermore, in Chapter 4.5, page 80, they stated, "James Pickens, a son of the pioneer Andrew Pickens, it is claimed was lost early in the Revolutionary war, or just before it commenced."

We can discount the **known** cousins of Andrew and Joseph that were named William and fought in the Revolution. The first is Revolutionary War Private William Pickens, the son of Gabriel Pickens. He fought with his cousins Captain Robert Pickens and Colonel Andrew Pickens (see his pension application in Appendix E); however, he was born in October 1748 so was only seven years old in 1755.

Another cousin we can eliminate is William Gabriel Pickens, son of John Pickens, Sr., who fought with his brother, Captain John Pickens, and his cousins, Andrew and Joseph Pickens (see Appendix E). William Gabriel, however, wasn't born until 1760.

A reasonable consideration for the William on the roster is a William Pickens who appears in some rosters of the First North Carolina Continental Regiment. William Davis, Catherine Pickens' husband, was a major in the First North Carolina Continental Regiment. Interestingly, William Davis is the son of Ann Pickens, a sister of Andrew Pickens, Sr. Davis is, therefore, a first cousin to Catherine (his wife), Andrew, Joseph, and their possible brother William. It is likely if any Pickens was in the same regiment with Davis, he is related to this Pickens family.

It is a strong possibility the William on the roster is a son of Andrew Pickens, Sr. However, that has not been determined for certain. It has not been disproved either, so more effort will be expended on that consideration at a later time. The existence of a William Pickens in the regiment with Major Davis will also require further investigation. The mystery of William will be set aside for now by relating the following pros and cons.

The positives:
1. The family references to Andrew Pickens, Sr., having an older son "William."
2. A possible William Pickens in the regiment with Major William Davis.
3. The other known William Pickenses of the family were eliminated.
4. The age difference between Catherine and Joseph is seven years, and except for the youngest two, Jean and John, there are no more than two years between any of Andrew's known successive children. There logically could be two more children for Andrew Pickens, Sr., within that seven-year window.

The negatives:
1. William does not show up in **all** Pickens family references.

2. Robert Andrew Pickens does not mention William in his interview with Lyman C. Draper. Negative 1 is not an adequate indictment because:

a. Dr. Pickens' mention that Andrew, Joseph and John Pickens had a brother named William that fought in the Revolution is likely well-founded.

b. William was probably married and independent by 1750 as was Catherine Pickens Davis.

c. Cousin Monroe mentioned a son named James. While not a direct verification of William, this does strengthen the case for the existence of older sons.

Negative 2 is also not a proper indictment of William regarding a position in the family because:

a. We have already seen that Robert Andrew Pickens was obviously mistaken about the relative ages of his cousins, Joseph and Andrew. His confusion during the interview regarding several matters, including the age issue, is probably the result of faulty memory considering that the interview was in 1833. This was about 95 years after the birth of Andrew and Joseph, about 100 years after the birth of William, 80 years after his own birth, and about 50 years following the Revolutionary War.

b. Robert Andrew was only about two years old at the time the militia was represented by the roster, and he was only about 10 years old when the Pickenses later relocated to Long Canes. It is doubtful that William, being much older and probably on his own, ever relocated to Long Canes. Therefore, it is reasonable that Robert Andrew Pickens may not have even been on familiar terms with an older cousin named William.

In summary, there is more work to do on the mystery of William Pickens. However, it seems likely that William and Joseph Pickens are the only sons of Andrew Pickens, Sr., to appear on the roster. This opinion is based upon confidence in A. L. Pickens' research.

D: 1778 Constitution of South Carolina

Constitution of South Carolina
March 19, 1778
An Act for establishing the constitution of the State of South Carolina.

Whereas the constitution or form of government agreed to and resolved upon by the freemen of this country, met in congress, the twenty-sixth day of March, one thousand seven hundred and: seventy-six, was temporary only, and suited to the situation of their public affairs at that period, looking forward to an accommodation with Great Britain, an event then desired; and whereas the United Colonies of America have been since constituted independent States, and the political connection heretofore subsisting between them and Great Britain entirely dissolved by the declaration of the honorable the Continental Congress, dated the fourth day of July, one thousand seven hundred and seventy-six, for the many great and weighty reasons therein particularly set forth: It therefore becomes absolutely necessary to frame a constitution suitable to that great event.

Be it therefore constituted and enacted, by his excellency Rawlins Lowndes, esq., president and commander-in-chief in and over the State of South Carolina, by the honorable the legislative council and general assembly, and by the authority of the same:

That the following articles, agreed upon by the freemen of this State, now met in general assembly, be deemed and held the constitution and form of government of the said State, unless altered by the legislative authority thereof, which constitution or form of government shall immediately take place and be in force from the passing of this act, excepting such parts as are hereafter mentioned and specified.

I. That the style of this country be hereafter the State of South Carolina.

II. That the legislative authority be vested in a general assembly, to consist of two distinct bodies, a senate and house of representatives, but that the legislature of this State, as established by the constitution or form of government passed the twenty-sixth of March, one thousand and seven hundred and seventy-six, shall continue and be in full force until the twenty-ninth day of November ensuing.

III. That as soon as may be after the first meeting of the senate and house of representatives, and at every first meeting of the senate and house of representatives thereafter, to be elected by virtue of this constitution, they shall jointly in the house of representatives choose by ballot from among themselves or from the people at large a governor and commander-in-chief, a lieutenant-governor, both to continue for two years, and a privy council, all of the Protestant religion, and till such choice shall be made the former president or governor and commander-in-chief, and vice-president or lieutenant-governor, as the case may be, and privy council, shall continue to act as such.

IV. That a member of the senate or house of representatives, being chosen and acting as governor and commander-in-chief or lieutenant-governor, shall vacate his seat, and another person shall be elected in his room.

V. That every person who shall be elected governor and commander-in-chief of the State, or lieutenant-governor, or a member of the privy council, shall be qualified as forthwith; that is to say, tile governor and lieutenant-governor shall have been residents id tills State for ten years, and the members of the privy council five years, preceding their said election, and shall have in this State a settled plantation or freehold in their and each of their own right of the value of at least ten thousand pounds currency, clear of debt, and on being elected they shall respectively take an oath of qualification in the house of representatives.

VI. That no future governor and commander-in-chief who shall serve for two years shall be eligible to serve in the said office after the expiration of the said term until the full end and term of four Years.

VII. That no person in this State shall hold the office of governor thereof, or lieutenant-governor, and any other office or commission, civil or military, (except in the militia,) either in this or any other State, or under the authority of the Continental Congress, at one and the same time.

VIII. That in case of the impeachment of the governor and commander-in-chief, or his removal from office, death, resignation, or absence from the State, the lieutenant-governor shall succeed to his office, and the privy council shall choose out of their own body a lieutenant-governor of the State. And in case of the impeachment of the lieutenant-governor, or his removal from office death, resignation, or absence from the State, one of the privy council to be chosen by themselves, shall succeed to his office until a nomination to those offices respectively, by the senate and house of representatives, for the remainder of the time for which the officer so impeached, removed from office, dying, resigning, or being absent was appointed.

IX. That the privy council shall consist of the lieutenant-governor for the time being, and eight other members, five of whom shall be a quorum to be chosen as before directed; four to serve for two years, and four for one year, and at the expiration of one year four others shall be chosen in the room of the last four, to serve for two years, and all future members of the privy council shall thenceforward be elected to serve two years, whereby there will be a new election every Year for half the privy council, and a constant rotation established; but no member of the privy council who shall serve for two years shall be eligible to serve therein after the expiration of the said term until the full end and term of four years: Provided always, That no officer of the army or navy in the service of the continent or this State, nor judge of any of the courts of law, shall be eligible, nor shall the father, son, or brother to the governor for the time being be elected in the privy council during his administration. A member of the senate and house of representatives being chosen of the privy council, shall not thereby lose his seat in the senate or house of representatives, unless he be elected lieutenant-governor, in which case he shall, and another person shall be chosen in his stead. The privy council is to advise tile governor and commander-in-chief when required, but he shall not be bound to consult them unless directed by law. If a member of tile privy council shall die or depart this State during the recess of the general assembly, the privy council shall choose another to act in his room, until a nomination by the senate and house of representatives shall take place. The clerk of the privy council shall keep a regular journal of all their proceedings, in which shall be entered the yeas and nays on every question, and the opinion, with the reasons at large, of anv member who desires it; which journal shall be laid before the legislature when required by either house.

X. That in case of the absence from the seat of government or sickness of the governor and lieutenant-governor, any one of the privy council may be empowered by the governor, under his hand and seal, to act in his room, but such appointment shall not vacate his seat in the senate, house of representatives, or privy council.

XI. That the executive authority be vested in the governor and commander-in-chief, in manner herein mentioned

XII. That each parish and district throughout this State shall on the last Monday in November next and the day followings and on the same days of every succeeding year thereafter, elect by ballot one member of the senate, except the district of Saint Philip and Saint Michael's parishes, Charleston, which shall elect two members; and except also the district between Broad and Saluda Rivers, in three divisions, viz: the Lower district, the Little River district, and the Upper or Spartan district, each of which said divisions shall elect one member; and except the parishes of Saint Matthew and Orange, which shall elect one member; and also except the parishes of Prince George and All Saints, which shall elect one member; and the election of senators for such parishes, respectively, shall, until otherwise altered by the legislature, be at the parish of Prince George for the said parish and the parish of All Saints, and at the parish of Saint Matthew for that parish and the parish of Orange; to meet on the first Monday in January then next, at the seat of government, unless the casualties of war or contagious disorders should render it unsafe to meet there, in which case the governor and commander-in-chief for the time being may, by proclamation, with the advice and consent of the privy council, appoint a more secure and convenient place of meeting; and to continue for two years from the said last Monday in November; and that no person shall be eligible to a seat in the said senate unless he be of the Protestant religion, and bath attained the age of thirty years, and bath been a resident in this State at least five years. Not less than thirteen members shall be a quorum to do business but the president or any three members may adjourn from day to day. No person who resides in the parish or district for which he is elected shall take his seat in the senate, unless he possess a settled estate and freehold in his own right in the said parish or district of the value of two thousand pounds currency at least, clear of debt; and no non-resident shall be eligible to a seat in the said senate unless he is owner of a settled estate and freehold in his own right, in the parish or district where he is elected, of the value of seven thousand pounds currency at least, also clear of debt.

XIII. That on the last Monday in November next and the day following, and on the same days of every second year thereafter, members of the house of representatives shall be chosen, to meet on the first Monday in January then next, at the seat of Government, unless the casualties of war or contagious disorders should render it unsafe to meet there, in which case the governor and commander-in-chief for the time being may, by proclamation, with the advice and consent of the privy council, appoint a more secure-and convenient place of meeting, and to continue for two years from the said last Monday in November. Each parish and district within this State shall send members to the general assembly in the following proportions; that is to say, the parish of Saint Philip and Saint Michael's, Charleston, thirty members; the parish of Christ Church, six members; the parish of Saint John's, in Berkely County, six members; the parish of Saint Andrew, six members; the parish of Saint George, Dorchester, six members; the parish of Saint James, Goose Creek, six members; the parish of Saint Thomas and Saint Dennis, six members; the parish of Saint Paul, six members; the parish of Saint Bartholomew, six members; the parish of Saint Helena, six members; the parish of Saint James, Santee, six members; the parish of Prince George, Winyaw, four members; the parish of All Saints, two members; the parish of Prince Frederick, six members; the parish of Saint John, in Colleton County, six members; the parish of Saint Peter, six members; the parish of Prince William, six members; the parish of Saint Stephen, six members; the district to the eastward of Wateree River, ten members; the district of Ninety-six, ten members; the district of Saxe Gotha, six members; the district between Broad and Saluda Rivers, in three divisions, viz: the lower district, four members; the Little River district, four members; the IJpper or Spartan district, four members; the district between Broad and Catawba Rivers, ten members; the district called the New Acquisition, ten members; the parish of Saint Matthew, three members; the parish of Orange, three members; the parish of Saint David, six members; the district between the Savannah River and the North Fork of Edisto, six members. And the election of the said members shall be conducted as near as may be agreeable to the directions of the present or any future election act or acts, and where there are no churches or church-wardens in a district or parish, the house of representatives, at some convenient time before their expiration, shall appoint places of election and persons to receive votes and make returns. The qualification of electors shall be that every free white man, and no other person, who acknowledges the being of a God, and believes in a future state of rewards and punishments, and who has attained to the age of one and twenty years, and bath been a resident and an inhabitant in this State for the space of one whole year before the day appointed for the election he offers to give his vote at, and hath a freehold at least of fifty acres of land, or a town lot, and hath been legally seized and possessed of the same at least six months previous to such election, or bath paid a tax the preceding year, or was taxable the present year, at least six months previous to the said election, in a sum equal to the tax on fifty acres of land, to the support of this government, shall be deemed a person qualified to vote for, and shall be capable of electing, a representative or representatives to serve as a member or members in the senate and house of representatives, for the parish or district where he actually is a resident, or in any other parish or district in this State where he bath the like freehold. Electors shall take an oath or affirmation of qualification, if required by the returning officer. No person shall be eligible to sit in the house of representatives unless he be of the Protestant religion, and bath been a resident in this State for three years previous to his election. The qualification of the elected, if residents in the parish or district for which they shall be returned, shall be the same as mentioned in the election act, and construed to mean clear of debt. But no non-resident shall be eligible to a seat in the house of representatives unless he is owner of a settled estate and freehold in his own right of the value of three thousand and five hundred pounds currency at least, clear of debt, in the parish or district for which he is elected.

XIV. That if any parish or district neglects or refuses to elect members, or if the members chosen do not meet in general assembly, those who do meet shall have the powers of the general assembly. Not less than sixty-nine members shall make a house of representatives to do business, but the speaker or any seven members may adjourn from day to day.

XV. That at the expiration of seven Years after the passing of this constitution, and at the end of every fourteen years thereafter, the representation of the whole State shall be proportioned in the most equal and just manner according to the particular and comparative strength and taxable property of the different parts of the same regard being always had to the number of white inhabitants and such taxable property.

XVI. That all money bills for the support of government shall originate in the house of representatives, and shall not be altered or amended by the senate, but may be rejected by them, and that no money be drawn out of the public treasury but by the legislative authority of the State. All other bills and ordinances may take rise in the senate or house of representatives, and be altered, amended, or rejected by either. Acts and ordinances having passed the general assembly shall have the great seal affixed to them by a joint committee of both houses, who shall wait upon the governor to receive and return the seal, and shall then be signed by the president of the senate and speaker of the house of representatives, in the senate-house, and shall thenceforth have all the force and validity of a law, and be lodged in the secretary's office. And the senate and house of representatives, respectively, shall enjoy all other privileges Which have at any time been claimed or exercised by the commons house of assembly.

XVII. That neither the senate nor house of representatives shall have power to adjourn themselves for any longer time than three days, without the mutual consent of both. The governor and commanderin-chief shall have no power to adjourn, prorogue, or dissolve them, but may, if necessary, by and with the advice and consent of the privy council, convene them before the time to which they shall stand adjourned. And where a bill hath been rejected by either house, it shall not be brought in again that session, without leave of the house, and a notice of six days being previously given.

XVIII. That the senate and house of representatives shall each choose their respective officers by ballot, without control, and that during a recess the president of the senate and speaker of the house of representatives shall issue writs for filling up vacancies occasioned by death in their respective houses, giving at least three weeks and not more than thirty-five days' previous notice of the time appointed for the election.

XIX. That if any parish or district shall neglect to elect a member or members on the day of election, or in case any person chosen a member of either house shall refuse to qualify and take his seat as such, or die, or depart the State, the senate or house of representatives, as the case may be, shall appoint proper days for electing a member or members in such cases respectively.

XX. That if any member of the senate or house of representatives shall accept any place of emolument, or any commission, (except in the militia or commission of the peace, and except as is excepted in the tenth article,) he shall vacate his seat, and there shall thereupon be a new election; but he shall not be disqualified from serving upon being reelected, unless he is appointed secretary of the State, a commissioner of the treasury, an officer of the customs, register of mesne conveyances, a clerk of either of the courts of justice, sheriff, powder reviewer, clerk of the senate, house of representatives, or privy council, surveyor-general, or commissary of military stores, which officers are hereby declared disqualified from being members either of the senate or house of representatives.

XXI. And whereas the ministers of the gospel are by their profession dedicated to the service of God and the cure of souls, and ought not to be diverted from the great duties of their function, therefore no minister of the gospel or public preacher of any religious persuasion, while he continues in the exercise of his pastoral function, and for two years after, shall be eligible either as governor, lieutenant-governor, a member of the senate, house of representatives, or privy council in this State.

XXII. That the delegates to represent this State in the Congress of the United States be chosen annually by the senate and house of representatives jointly, by ballot, in the house of representatives, and nothing contained in this constitution shall be construed to extend to vacate the seat of any member who is or may be a delegate from this State to Congress as such.

XXIII. That the form of impeaching all officers of the State for mal and corrupt conduct in their respective offices, not amenable to any other jurisdiction, be vested in the house of representatives. But that it shah always be necessary that two-third parts of the members present do consent to and agree in such impeachment. That the senators and such of the judges of this State as are not members of the house of representatives, be a court for the trial of impeachments, under such regulations as the legislature shall establish, and that previous to the trial of every impeachment, the members of the said court shall respectively be sworn truly and impartially to try and determine the charge in question according to evidence, and no judgment of the said court, except judgment of acquittal, shall be valid, unless it shall be assented to by two-third parts of the members then present, and on every trial, as well on impeachments as others, the party accused shall be allowed counsel.

XXIV. That the lieutenant-governor of the State and a majority of the privy council for the time being shall, until otherwise altered by the legislature, exercise the powers of a court of chancery, and there shall be ordinaries appointed in the several districts of this State, to be chosen by the senate and house of representatives jointly by ballot, in the house of representatives, who shall, within their respective districts, exercise the powers heretofore exercised by the ordinary, and until such appointment is made the present ordinary in Charleston shall continue to exercise that office as heretofore.

XXV. That the jurisdiction of the court of admiralty be confined to maritime causes.

XXVI. That justices of the peace shall be nominated by the senate and house of representatives jointly, and commissioned by the governor and commander-in-chief during pleasure. They shall be entitled to receive the fees heretofore established by law; and not acting in the magistracy, they shall not be entitled to the privileges allowed them by law.

XXVII. That all other judicial officers shall be chosen by ballot jointly by the senate and house of representatives, and, except the judges of the court of chancery, commissioned by the governor and commander-in-chief during good behavior, but shall be removed on address of the senate and house of representatives.

XXVIII. That the sheriffs, qualified as by law directed, shall be chosen in like manner by the senate and house of representatives, when the governor, lieutenant-governor, and privy council are chosen, and commissioned by the governor and commander-in-chief, for two years, and shall give security as required by law, before they enter on the execution of their office. No sheriff who shall have served for two years shall be eligible to serve in the said office after the expiration of the said term, until the full end and term of four years, but shall continue in office until such choice be made; nor shall any person be eligible as sheriff in any district unless he shall have resided therein for two years previous to the election.

XXIX. That two commissioners of the treasury, the secretary of the State, the register of mesne conveyances in each district, attorney-general, surveyor-general, powder-receiver, collectors and comptrollers of the customs and waiters, be chosen in like manner by the senate and house of representatives jointly, by ballot, in the house of representatives, and commissioned by the governor and commander-in-chief, for two years; that none of the said officers, respectively, who shall have served for four years, shall be eligible to serve in the said offices after the expiration of the said term, until the full end and term of four years, but shall continue in office until a new choice be made: Provided, That nothing herein contained shall extend to the several persons appointed to the above offices respectively, under the late constitution; and that the present and all future commissioners of the treasury, and powder-receivers, shall each give bond with approved security agreeable to law.

XXX. That all the officers in the army and navy of this State, of and above the rank of captain, shall be chosen by the senate and house of representatives jointly, by ballot in the house of representatives, and commissioned by the governor and commander-in-chief, and that all other officers in the army and navy of this State shall be commissioned by the governor and commander-in-chief.

XXXI. That in case of vacancy in any of the offices above directed to be filled by the senate and house of representatives, the governor and commander-in-chief, with the advice and consent of the privy council, may appoint others in their stead, until there shall be an election by the senate and house of representatives to fill those vacancies respectively

XXXII. That the governor and commander-in-chief, with the advice and consent of the privy council, may appoint during pleasure, until otherwise directed by law, all other necessary officers, except such as are now by law directed to be otherwise chosen.

XXXIII. That the governor and commander-in-chief shall have no power to commence war, or conclude peace, or enter into any final treaty without the consent of the senate and house of representatives.

XXXIV. That the resolutions of the late congress of this State, and all laws now of force here, (and not hereby altered,) shall so continue until altered or repealed by the legislature of this State, unless where they are temporary, in which case they shall expire at the times respectively limited for their duration.

XXXV. That the governor and commander-in-chief for the time being, by and with the advice and consent of the privy council, may lay embargoes or prohibit the exportation of any commodity, for any time not exceeding thirty days, in the recess of the general assembly.

XXXVI. That all persons who shall be chosen and appointed to any office or to any place of trust, civil or military, before entering upon the execution of office, shall take the following oath: " I, A. B., do acknowledge the State of South Carolina to be as free, sovereign, and independent State, and that the people thereof owe no allegiance or obedience to George the Third, King of Great Britain, and I do renounce, refuse, and abjure any allegiance or obedience to him. And I do swear [or affirm, as the case may be] that I will, to the utmost of my power, support, maintain, and defend the said State against the said King George the Third, and his heirs and successors, and his or their abettors, assistants, and adherents, and will serve the said State, in the office of , with fidelity and honor, and according to the best of my skill and understanding: So help me God."—

XXXVII. That adequate yearly salaries be allowed to the public officers of this State, and be fixed by law.

XXXVIII. That all persons and religious societies who acknowledge that there is one God, and a future state of rewards and punishments, and that God is publicly to be worshipped, shall be freely tolerated. The Christian Protestant religion shall be deemed, and is hereby constituted and declared to be, the established religion of this State. That all denominations of Christian Protestants in this State, demeaning themselves peaceably and faithfully, shall enjoy equal religious and civil privileges. To accomplish this desirable purpose without injury to the religious property of those societies of Christians which are by law already incorporated for the purpose of religious worship, and to put it fully into the power of every other society of Christian Protestants, either already formed or hereafter to be formed, to obtain the like incorporation, it is hereby constituted, appointed, and declared that the respective societies of the Church of England that are already formed in this State for the purpose of religious worship shall still continue incorporate and hold the religious property now in their possession. And that whenever fifteen or more male persons, not under twenty-one years of age, professing the Christian Protestant religion, and agreeing to unite themselves In a society for the purposes of religious worship, they shall, (on complying with the terms hereinafter mentioned,) be, and be constituted a church, and be esteemed and regarded in law as of the established religion of the State, and on a petition to the legislature shall be entitled to be incorporated and to enjoy equal privileges. That every society of Christians so formed shall give themselves a name or denomination by which they shall be called and known in law, and all that associate with them for the purposes of worship shall be esteemed as belonging to the society so called. But that previous to the establishment and incorporation of the respective societies of every denomination as aforesaid, and in order to entitle them thereto, each society so petitioning shall have agreed to and subscribed in a book the following five articles, without which no agreement fir union of men upon presence of religion shall entitle them to be incorporated and esteemed as a church of the established religion of this State:

1st. That there is one eternal God, and a future state of rewards and punishments.

2d. That God is publicly to be worshipped.

3d. That the Christian religion is the true religion

4th. That the holy scriptures of the Old and New Testaments are of divine inspiration, and are the rule of faith and practice.

5th. That it is lawful and the duty of every man being thereunto called by those that govern, to bear witness to the truth.

And that every inhabitant of this State, when called to make an appeal to God as a witness to truth, shall be permitted to do it in that way which is most agreeable to the dictates of his own conscience. And that the people of this State may forever enjoy the right of electing their own pastors or clergy, and at the same time that the State may have sufficient security for the due discharge of the pastoral office, by those who shall be admitted to be clergymen, no person shall officiate as minister of any established church who shall not have been chosen by a majority of the society to which he shall minister, or by persons appointed by the said majority, to choose and procure a minister for them; nor until the minister so chosen and appointed shall have made and subscribed to the following declaration, over and above the aforesaid five articles, viz: "That he is determined by God's grace out of the holy scriptures, to instruct the people committed to his charge, and to teach nothing as required of necessity to eternal salvation but that which he shall be persuaded may be concluded and proved from the scripture; that he will use both public and private admonitions, as well to the sick as to the whole within his cure, as need shall require and occasion shall be given, and that he will be diligent in prayers, and in reading of the same; that he will be diligent to frame and fashion his own self and his family according to the doctrine of Christ, and to make both himself and them, as much as in him lieth, wholesome examples and patterns to the flock of Christ; that he will maintain and set forwards, as much as he can, quietness, peace, and love among all people, and especially among those that are or shall be committed to lids charge. No person shall disturb or molest any religious assembly; nor shall use any reproachful, reviling, or abusive language against any church, that being the certain way of disturbing the peace, and of hindering the conversion of any to the truth, by engaging them in quarrels and animosities, to the hatred of the professors, and that profession which otherwise they might be brought to assent to. To person whatsoever shall speak anything in their religious assembly irreverently or seditiously of the government of this State. No person shall, by law, be obliged to pay towards the maintenance and support of a religious worship that he does not freely join in, or has not voluntarily engaged to support. But the churches, chapels, parsonages, globes, and all other property now belonging to any societies of the Church of England, or any other religious societies, shall remain and be secured to them forever. The poor shall be supported, and elections managed in the accustomed manner, until laws shall be provided to adjust those matters in the most equitable way.

XXXIX. That the whole State shall, as soon as proper laws can be passed for these purposes, be divided into districts and counties, and county courts established.

XL. That the penal laws, as heretofore used, shall be reformed, and punishments made in some cases less sanguinary, and in general more proportionate to the crime.

XLI. That no freeman of this State be taken or imprisoned, or disseized of his freehold, liberties, or privileges, or outlawed, exiled or in any manner destroyed or deprived of his life, liberty, or property, but by the judgment of his peers or by the law of the land.

XLII. That the military be subordinate to the civil power of the State.

XLIII. That the liberty of the press be inviolably preserved.

XLIV. That no part of this constitution shall be altered without notice being previously given of ninety days, nor shall any part of the same be changed without the consent of a majority of the members of the senate and house of representatives.

XLV. That the senate and house of representatives shall not proceed to the election of a governor or lieutenant-governor, until there be a majority of both houses present.

In the council-chamber, the 19th day of March, 1778.
Assented to.
RAWLINS LOWNDES.
HUGH RUTLEGE,
Speaker of the Legislative Council.
THOMAS BEE,
Speaker of the General Assembly.

E: Pension Claims

The following pension application (and one indent) were transcribed by the author and contain the original spelling and grammatical errors.

Henry Connelly Pension; Andrew Hamilton Pension; Samuel Hammond Pension; William Hillhouse Pension; Charles Holland Pension; John Pickens Widow Pension; Joseph William Pickens Indent; Robert Andrew Pickens Pension; Wiiliam Gabriel Pickens Pension; Wiiliam Pickens Pension; John Wallace Pension; Thomas Young Pension

PENSION APPLICATION, HENRY CONNELLY, FLOYD CO. KY.
(National Archives No. W-8188)
Declaration in order to obtain the benefit of the act of Congress passed June 7th 1832.

Appendix E

State of Kentucky
Floyd County

On this 15th day of August, 1833, personally appeared before me, James Davis, a Justice of the Peace now sitting, Henry Connelly, a resident of Floyd County, and State of Kentucky, aged Eighty one years, who being first duly sworn according to law doth on his oath make the following declaration, in order to obtain the benefit of the act of Congress passed June 7th, 1832: That he entered the service of the United States under the following named officers and served as herein stated: That he entered the service and commanded one hundred men as state troops of North Carolina (called militia) as the Captain thereof on the 7th day of July 1777, for five years or during the war in the County of Guilford, North Carolina. His Col in the first instance was Col John Williams; then under Colonel Pacely [sic]; then by Col John Taylor; and lastly, by Col Billy Washington. This applicant's company was a horse Company & was raised for the especial purpose of keeping down a daring Tory Colonel by the name of Fanning who had made several daring attempts in the neighborhood of Sailsbury [sic] and Charlotte. During the first year of the service of this applicant, by the orders of his Col, the company traversed and marched to Rowan and Guilford in order to keep Fanning and his confederates down. During this year, in the month of October, the company encountered his scouts and routed them with some loss. The general rendezvous of the Tories was in that region of the country called the Haw Ford on the Haw River. These counties and the adjacent neighborhood were assigned to the applicant's charge by His Excellency the Governor of N. Carolina, in the month of June 1778. This this applicant and his company continued to do, during the year 1778 and that winter he and his company rendezvoused at Salisbury. The particulars of this year's service were only a few fights with the Tories. The war was raging in the North, whither that distinguished and active officer, Col William Davidson had gone, and all remained for the constituted authorities to do was to keep down the Tories, which were so numerous in this region of N. Carolina. During this year 1778, the men suffered much for clothes and every necessary, and our forage master frequently had to press forage for our perishing horses. Continental money was then one hundred dollars for one; for this applicant could not get a breakfast for $100 in Continental money. During this year, by order of the Governor, this applicant's company was placed under the direction of Col Davie, who then commanded the North Carolina Cavalry; but he renewed the old orders, and my district still remained as under my former orders. Early in March, 1779, the Tories broke out with great fury at a place called the Haw Fields, whither this applicant and his horse company repaired and dislodged them with the assistance of Colonel Lytle from Rowan who commanded a regiment of militia. During this year the Tories were fast accumulating in Rowan, and this applicant's horse Company was almost withdrawn from Guilford to that section of North Carolina. The Whigs this year took a great many Tories, who were all put in jail and confined at Hillsboro and Salisbury. In the month of November 1779, orders were received by Peasley from Col Davie, the Commanding Col, to rendezvous at Salisbury to start to the South to join Genl Lincoln at Savannah, but about this time news arrived that Genl Lincoln was overtaken at Charlestown, and all were taken prisoners. Genl Davidson now raised several hundred men, and Col Sumner and Pervard [sic], they had several skirmishes with the loyalists, in which this applicant and his company actively participated at Colson's Mills. About this time at a place in the western part of the state the Tories had collected to a great amount and we marched against them and at Colson's Mills, this was in the month of May 1780, as well as this applicant recollects. He recollects well that it was just before or about the time of Gates' defeat at Camden. During this winter and the fall this applicant's company abandoned his district of "protection" and under Col Davie and Genl Davidson opposed the passage of Lord Cornwallis through North Carolina. At the time of approach of Cornwallis to Charlotte, under Col Davie the troops posted themselves to meet the enemy. On the enemy's approach the companies commanded by this applicant received the first onset from Tarleton's Cavalry, and the firing became general on the left wing. The troops were commanded by Col Davie in person, and for three times we succeeded in repulsing the enemy. At length we had to yield to superior numbers. In this battle we had many men killed, several from under this applicant. In December, just before Christmas, Genl Nathanael Greene, from the north, took command of us all. This was in 1780. We all, by his proclamation and the orders of our Governor, were placed under his command, and assembled at Charlotte. From there this applicant was placed under Col Washington and marched to South Carolina to Augusta and Ninety Six. After marching in a southern direction for several days, news came that Tarleton was after us. We were all now under Genl Morgan, and a terrible conflict ensued at the "Cow Pens" between Tarleton's men and the army under Genl Morgan. Here the Americans were victorious and took a great many military stores, cannons, baggage and six or seven hundred British and Tory Prisoners. This was in January 1781. It was cold weather but inclined to be raining during this battle. The company which belonged to this applicant was placed under Col Howard, on

the extreme right of the division, and this applicant commanded a company in the center. Our company, when just about to catch up our horses which were hid about four hundred paces in the rear of the line of battle, fell upon us with great fury, but we were fortunately relieved by Washington's Legion that hastened to our assistance. After this engagement, we all formed a junction with Genl Greene, and retreated with him to Dan and crossed over into Virginia and remaining there but a short period, marched back to Guilford Court house, and this applicant actively participated in that memorable battle, and he had the great mortification to see his men in a panic fly at the approach of the enemy; and although this applicant endeavored to rally them, it was impossible, and many even retreated to their homes, but this applicant remained and continued to fight until the Americans were thrown into disorder and confusion & defeated. At this time or in a few days afterwards, this applicant being unwell, and his company broken, obtained a respite for a while, which was granted him. He remained at home and did not go with General Greene to Ninety Six. During this summer, he did all he could to get his company to assemble. Their cry was "no pay" and our families required them at home. He then went from Guilford over into Virginia, and in September 1781, he raised a small volunteer company for three months, to join Genl Washington at "Little York." "Little York" was, however taken before this applicant arrived. He knew a great many Continental Officers, and regiments, and Militia Officers, during his service. In the Month of October the term of service of the Company from Montgomery County, Virginia, just mentioned, expiring, he gave them their discharges, and he himself returned to N. C., where he received the thanks of the Governor and a certificate stating his services. This applicant knew Genl Smallwood, Genl Davidson, Genl Rutherford, Genl Pickens, Genl Sumner, Genl Otho Williams, Col Cleveland, Colonel Lytle, Col William Washington, Col Malmedy, Col Lee, Genl Gadsom, Col Howard, who commanded the 3rd Maryland Regiment, Captain Holgin, Col Peasley, John Williams. The Baron Dekalb, Colonel Pervard and many other Continental and Militia Officers that he now forgotten. I have now no documentary evidence in my favor, having forwarded my commission about six years ago by General Alexander Lackey to the War Department. It has never been returned to this applicant. He received a letter from the Secretary of War informing him that as he was not a regular. He could not be allowed his commission was from the Governor of N. Carolina. He has made search and inquiry for it for sometime, and he believes the same is lost or mislaid. He refers the War Department to Henry B. Mayo, Esq., The Honorable David K. Harris, to Col Francis A. Brown, to Col John Vanhoose, the Reverend Henry Dixon, the Reverend Cuthbert Stone, the Reverend Samuel Hanna, the Reverend Ezekiel Stone, & Wallace Bailey, to Andrew Rule, Esq., to John Rice, to Jacob Mayo, Esq., Clerk of the Floyd County Circuit Court. These can testify to his character for his veracity and their belief of this applicant's service as a soldier and officer of the Revolution.
Sworn to and subscribed the day and year aforesaid.
S/ Henry Connelly {seal}

Pension Application, Andrew Hamilton, Abbeville Dist. SC.
(National Archives No. S-18000)

Declaration in order to obtain the benefit of the act of Congress passed June 7th 1832.
State of South Carolina
Abbeville District

On this twenty fourth day of October in the year while Lord 1832 personally appeared in open court before the Honorable Richard Gant Presiding Judge of the Court of Common Pleas & General Sessions for the District and State aforesaid now sitting Major Andrew Hamilton a resident of Abbeville District in the State of South Carolina who being first duly sworn according to law, doth on his oath, make the following declaration in order to obtain the benefit of the act of Congress passed 7 June 1832.

That he entered the service of his country the United States as a Captain of a Volunteer company which was raised and organized for the protection and defense of the country at as early a period as the year 1775, at this period the enemies of the country denominated Royalists or Tories, threw every obstacle in the way of their opponents the Whigs against the unjust impositions & exactions of Great Britain to such a violent and insurrectionary length had the Royalists proceeded that the friends of Liberty found it necessary to arm in self defense, and to repel by force, the force of the Royalists, accordingly sometime in the year 1775, Major Williamson who commanded the Whig Militia at the time in the District of Ninety Six ordered a body of the militia to go in quest of some plundering Royalists and ????? retreating into a Stockade Fort in which he & his militia including the applicant and his Company were confined without water for three days when they obtained a scanty supply by digging. The Royalists or Tories obtained possession of the gaol of Ninety Six from which they fired into the Fort, without much effect, after some days the Royalists hoisted a flag and proposed a truce, that object of which was to enable both parties to confer with their respective heads viz. the Loyalist with their Royal Governor and the Whigs with their Council of Safety, then lately organized by the friends of Liberty in South Carolina for the common safety & protection of the Country.

The applicant says that he marched his company in the fall of the year 1776 to the Cherokee nation by order of Major or General Williamson who commanded the expedition in person and to the number of about two thousand men, who were met and opposed by a superior force of Indians, Williamson entered a narrow valley surrounded by mountains, the larger portion of the Indians occupied the mountain heights from which they poured in a constant and well directed fire, orders were given for Detachments of Williamson's Army to gain the heights above the Indians whom being hard pressed by the advances in the valley & those on the mountain sides, betook themselves to flight, Williamson's Army then laid waste to all the Cherokee settlements in that section and the Army disbanded sometime in October.

The Applicant says that he was subsequently in another Indian expedition, but does not recollect the circumstances of it, to state them particularly: —

The Applicant also states that in the year 1779 several hundred Tories embodied and marched along the Western frontiers of South Carolina taking several persons prisoners in their march, and that Colonel Pickens collected a force of three hundred men and followed these Tories to a place called Kettle Creek in the State of Georgia Colonel or General Pickens then disposed his force into three divisions and give the command of the right division to the applicant who acted as Major in this battle, at Kettle Creek, where after an action of some considerable contest, the Tories were completely routed and defeated with a loss of about 40 killed, including their commander Colonel Boyd, — the loss on the part of the Whigs was comparatively small.

The Applicant also states that he commanded a Company at the siege of Ninety Six, in the year 1781, and remained there under General Green in the active performance of Military duty until General Green raised the siege and marched his troops across Saluda River towards North Carolina.

The Applicant also states that at the battle of the Eutaw in the year 1781, he commanded as Major a Battalion of Militia under the command of General Pickens. He also states in conclusion, that he was in several other expeditions or Campaigns, and in several skirmishes as the Captain of a company of Whig volunteers & that from the want of recollection and from there partaking of the Character of partisan warfare at home, and in the surrounding settlements, & borders of South Carolina against Tories, and Indians, he deems it unnecessary to state or to notice as it would be impossible to recapitulate the various diversified scenes he experienced in the defense of his Country, he considers it sufficient to say, that he was almost always employed in the service of his country through the whole revolutionary war, as the commanding Officer of a Company in opposing the Tories, Indians & British and of all enemies he conceived the Tories, most detestable and most obnoxious to the Liberty of his Country.

Answers to certain Interrogatories

Ans to 1st Inty — The Applicant answers & says that he was born in Augusta County in the State of Virginia, and that he was baptized by the Reverend John Craig on the 17th day of July in the year 1741 in the State of Virginia Augusta County.—

Ans to 2nd Inty — The Applicant says the only record he has of his age is a copy of the date of his baptism, which he took from the books of the Reverend John Craig in the State of Virginia.

Ans to 3rd Inty — The Applicant says that he was living in Ninety Six District in the State of South Carolina when he was called into the service of his country, that he has lived since the revolutionary war in the same State, and District, now called Abbeville District, where he now lives.

Ans to 4th Inty — This Applicant answers & says, that he entered the service as a Volunteer and ended his service in the Revolutionary War throughout as a volunteer, he was never drafted, & never was a substitute.-

Ans to 5th Inty — General Green, Colonel Campbell, Colonel Williams, Colonel Lee, — others the Applicant cannot now recollect — the Applicant does not recollect much about the regiments of continentals, or Militia, this much he knows, that both kinds of troops were with him and fought hard at Eutaw, he knew Colonel Hammond, Colonel Washington & General Pickens at Eutaw.

Ans to 6th Inty — The Applicant is known to James Wardlaw, Esquire, Colonel Patrick Noble, Moses Taggart Esquire and to the greater part of the population of Abbeville District he is also intimately known to John C. Calhoun vice president of the United States, and to many distinguished Characters of South Carolina, who can testify as to his character for veracity & their belief of his services as a Officer of the Revolution.

The Applicant hereby relinquishes every claim whatever to a pension or annuity except the present and declares that his name is not on the pension roll of the agency of any State.

Sworn to and subscribed the day and year aforesaid.

S/ Jas. Wardlaw, Clerk S/ A. Hamilton

State of South Carolina Abbeville District: Affidavit of Major Andrew Hamilton amending his foregoing Declaration

Personally appeared before me the undersigned a Justice of the Peace for Abbeville District in the State of South Carolina Andrew Hamilton who being duly sworn deposeth and saith that by reason of old age and the consequent loss of memory he cannot swear positively as to the precise length of his service but according to the best of his recollection he served not less than the periods mentioned below and in the following grades, For at least 3 years I served as a Captain in the revolutionary war in the defense of my country the United States and for at least one year I served as a Major in the revolutionary war in defense of the United States and for which entire service I claim a pension.

Sworn to 9th of April 1833 before me S/ Andrew Hamilton

S/ Geo. Shillito, JP

South Carolina Abbeville District:

I Andrew Hamilton Senior of the District and State aforesaid, as a secondary amendment to my declaration for a pension under the late act of Congress of June 7th 1832 — do hereby solemnly swear that such was the character of the Revolutionary War in the upper sections of South Carolina and particularly in the District of Ninety Six where the deponent principally lived, acted and performed military services in the defense of the United States, that the friends of liberty performed continuous tours of duty from the commencement of the Revolutionary war to its final close, and were constrained to do so, from having to contend with a triple enemy, Indians who were provoked by British influence, to slaughter without mercy the Whig inhabitants and their families, who in many instances suffered as much from Tories who scarcely ever failed to plunder, burn, & destroy the substance & property of Patriots taking their lives if captured and leaving their families widowed & orphans & stripped of everything necessary for their comfort and support to oppose these enemies successfully, the small band of Patriots in this section of the country, were necessarily compelled to perform continuous tours of duty, both by night & by day, the former generally being the most auspicious season for movement from one place to another, whenever duty called, the constant appearance of force served in some measure to intimidate the Indians and Tories, this patriot force were principally volunteers, raised under competent authority — Colonel Pickens had the command of the Military force of Ninety Six District and always aided, in giving authority to any body of Patriots associated together for the defense and security of the Country, whenever they deemed their services necessary to effect that object.— the deponent further says, that, he was a near neighbor & friend of Colonel Pickens, that they lived within 15 miles of the line dividing the Indian land from that of the whites, that Colonel Pickens & himself were almost constantly together, acting for, & in defense of their country, that the deponent derived his authority from Pickens to act as a Captain within his command & subsequently to act as Major under him. The deponent further says, that the following statement will show his actual services in the Revolutionary War.

In 1775 he served 5 weeks as a Captain under Major Williamson against an embodied force of royalist in the Village of Cambridge or Ninety Six.—

In 1775 he served 6 weeks as a Captain under Major or Colonel Williamson against the Cherokee Indians.—

In 1776 he served 6 weeks as Captain under Major or Colonel Williamson being another tour of duty against the Cherokee Indians.

In 1777 & 1778 he acted as Captain under the Authority of Colonel Pickens to perform military services in protecting & defending the frontier of Ninety Six and said District of Ninety Six —

In 1779 — he acted as Captain & as a Major part of this year under the authority & under direct command of Colonel Pickens, with whom, the deponent acted as Captain in the attack upon Carr's Fort in the State of Georgia, where he also bore a flag of truce, to the enemy in the Fort, which was abandoned by Pickens, to meet a Colonel Boyd, the deponent further says that Pickens pursued Colonel Boyd to

Kettle Creek in Georgia & the deponent in this battle, acted as Major & commanded the right wing which killed Boyd the deponent being near, & and eye witness to his fall and death, & whose last expiring words were "that he had this consolation that he died a true friend to his Majesty King George the 3rd" Boyd then give something to Colonel Pickens to forward to his wife & then expired. The deponent further says, that he believes he was in service the whole of this year 1779 but will only said that he was 9 months in actual service as Captain under Colonel or General Pickens during the year 1779 —

In 1780 the deponent acted as Captain under General Pickens in protecting the frontiers against Tory depredations.

In 1781 the deponent acted as Captain under General Pickens at the siege of Ninety Six, and acted under General Pickens as a Major of Militia at the Battle of the Eutaw & must have performed this year at least 6 months of actual service, this deponent further says that from the battle of the Eutaw to the end of the war he acted as Major of Militia under General Pickens.

The deponent further says that he omitted heretofore to mention that Colonel or General Pickens & himself went unaccompanied by others to confer with a Colonel Few from Georgia who had a few troops in the District of Ninety Six, all true Whigs, that when Colonel Pickens & himself /the deponent/ were on their road to see Colonel Few, a private of the Tory stamp directed them to a Camp of British soldiers & Tories by whom Pickens & himself were made prisoners & sent to the Village of Cambridge or Ninety Six, where they remained prisoners one month, under a British officer by the name of Allen, by some means Colonel Pickens obtained his & my release, from imprisonment, while prisoners we were treated with great attention & kindness by the British attributable I believe to the popularity & influence of General Pickens, the deponent further believes that he always acted under competent military authority in the defense of his country, & that he was not employed in any civil pursuit, during the aforesaid services, the deponent says that Patriots of this Section of the Country in the revolutionary war would not with safety appear on their farms to perform one days work. It was principally performed by the women & children, & when the crops were made by them, often plundered & destroyed by the Tories, civil pursuits, could not be attended to by the men, they had to bear arms night & day the militia of other states where there were comparatively few Tories, could attend to their civil pursuits without danger & served their rosary tours of duty, this was not the case here. — To all contained in the foregoing second Amendment of my declaration for a pension under the Act of Congress 7 June 1832, I hereto subscribe my name & affixed my seal, being previously sworn on the Holy Evangelist of Almighty God to the truth of the matters & things therein contained to the best of my belief & understanding & recollection.

Sworn to this 7th of August 1838 before S/ Andrew Hamilton Senior {Seal}
S/ Moses Taggart, JP

State of South Carolina Richland District

I Samuel Hammond of the State and District aforesaid Certify that I became acquainted with Major Andrew Hamilton of the District of Abbeville in the State aforesaid in the year 1779. That he was then called Captain Hamilton and in actual service in Colonel Pickens Regiment of Militia & that he knows he was most of that year and Service. I was afterwards associated with him in general Pickens' Brigade and particularly that he was in the Battle of Eutaw acting as a Major in September 1781 & continued with the Army some time after — I can further Certify that Major Andrew Hamilton whose declaration this is attached was highly esteemed as an Active & zealous officer, & respectable Citizen.

Samuel Hammond
S/ S. Hammond
Sworn to before made this 13th day of October 1833
S/ Chas. L. Hammond, NP

Pension Application, Samuel Hammond, Richland Dist. SC.
(National Archives No. S-21807)

Declaration in order to obtain the benefit of the act of Congress passed June 7th 1832.
State of South Carolina
Richland District

On the 31st day of October & 1st day of November in the year of our Lord 1832 personally appeared in open Court before me Richard Gant now sitting Samuel Hammond at present a resident of the State & district aforesaid now in the seventy sixth year of his age & he being first duly sworn as the law directs, doth on his oath make the following declaration in order to obtain the benefits of the act of Congress passed the 7th June 1832.

Applicant states that according to his father's family Register he was born in Richmond County in the State of Virginia, was baptized and registered in the Episcopal Church of Farnham Parish in said county, that about the commencement of the Revolutionary War he was at school in Prince William County Near Dumfries, that he offered himself as a volunteer in a company of Infantry raised for the purpose of military improvement commanded by Mr. Grayson, afterwards Col. Grayson and a member of Genl. Washington's family, & in which Mr. Leach, afterwards Major Leach, & P. L. Lee, afterwards Major Lee, were lieutenants the Company accrued & equipped themselves & with a part of that Company applicant marched towards Williamsburg, Va., to aid in compelling Lord Dunmore, Governor of the Province to restore to the public Magazine Arms & ammunition which he had taken there from & removed on board a British armed vessel and about 8 miles from Williamsburg met up Col. Patrick Henry who had anticipated us & caused a return of the locks of the muskets & other munitions to be restored to the magazine or arsenal.

Next applicant returned to Richmond County to his Father's residence & enrolled himself in a volunteer Company called minute men in Richmond County Sanctioned by Committee of Safety in 1775. The Company when filled elected their officers & he was elected a Lieutenant. The officers however had no Regular commissions their elections were certified by Col. LeRoy Peachey to others of the Committee. They armed & equipped themselves as a Company of Infantry.

While applicant was attached to said Company he with a part thereof performed some services & in December 1775 was with Major Richard Parker, afterwards Col. R. Parker *killed in Charlestown* in a battle against a detachment of British Troops at a place called the Great Bridge in Virginia where the British were repulsed & defeated, their commanding officer killed & a number of Prisoners taken, the British officer killed, he believes, was a Captain or Major Fondica perhaps memory may have failed as to his real name. Deeming it unimportant to detail all the circumstances in relation to the Services of the applicant always adverse to anything like egotism will only advert to such circumstances as are essential to the establishment of his claim, therefore passing over other services will state that in the years *1777* & *1778*, he was in service in Western Pennsylvania under the command of Genl. Hand of that State, that in the fall of that year he was ordered to South Carolina & joined Genl. Lincoln on Savannah River either the last of December *1778* and 1st January 1779 — that he was immediately after sent to 96 and entered in Service there under the orders of Genl. Williamson & was attached to Col. LeRoy Hammond's Regiment marched with him to Spirit Creek in Georgia about 12 miles below Augusta where they met the British army commanded by Col. Campbell on its march to Augusta.

A warm cannonade took place which was kept up some hours in which time Col. L. H. destroyed the Bridges on the main road upon said creek & also the path ways over Henderson's Mills above by which the British were delayed in their arrival at Augusta two days & gave time for the Troops & public stores to be removed North of the river.

Applicant remained with Genl. Williamson until the retreat of the enemy from Augusta, few days after which he marched under the Command of Col. LeRoy Hammond upon an expedition in Georgia, was with that command in a Battle with the Indians & Tories South of Ogechee on one of its tributary branches — the Indians were defeated, a Chief was killed with several Tories in Indian dress.

On return from that expedition, Applicant was put in charge of a fatigue party & Boat builders to prepare Flats for the Passage of Genl. Lincoln's army across Savannah River. Genl. Prevost crossing that river below and his advance towards Charleston caused a change of purpose with Genl. Lincoln. The Boats were left & your Applicant deposited them where directed, followed on after the Army. But he did not arrive with his command until some days after the Enemy had settled near Stono Ferry, but was in time to take a share in the Battle of Stono about the 20 June 1779 after which his command being composed of volunteers from the militia of Genl. Williamson's Brigade were discharged after being marched to 96 District.

Applicant however continued in Service though without command in some staff employments. In September he marched to Savannah with a Detachment of Col. LeRoy Hammond's Regiment & volunteers of his own enrolling, still acting as Assistant
Quarter Master, he was in the attack upon the British Works upon the left of their line, and attached to Genl. Huger's command.

His senior Brother Charles Hammond commanding a company of Col. L. Hammond's Regiment was wounded but taken off the ground by Applicant when retreat was ordered. In the month of April 1780, was marched into Georgia under the order of Genl. Williamson & was encamped with a detachment of Carolina & Georgia militia on Cupboard Creek a few miles below Augusta on the Savannah roads on the 16th of May on which day Genl. Williamson notified the commanding officer there that he had received official information of the surrender of Genl. Lincoln & garrison at Charlestown to the British Commander Sir H. Clinton. Called upon the officers to attend a council at McLean's above Augusta, attending there Gov. Howley of Georgia, his counsel and officers of State with many others attending nothing conclusive adopted for defenses.

Governor H. retired with counsel & State officers. Williamson discharged Militia & called a council of Officers to attend at White Hall, his residence near Ninety Six. Counsel attended. Advised by a majority to send a Flag & purpose to surrender on terms such as was granted to the militia in Service at Charlestown, Applicant protested against that course, withdrew from there & with a few real Patriots retired to North Carolina. On his way he had one or two skirmishes with the Tories always successful. Passed to the North & on his entering into North Carolina fell in with & joined Col. E. Clark of Georgia with his little band of Patriots & in a few days was joined by Col. Edward Hampton, Col. James Williams & Col. Thomas Brannon in July date not at present known was with Col. Elijah Clark in a Battle at a place called the Green Springs near Burwick's Iron Works in Western part of So. Carolina.

In August 18 or 19 was with Col. Williams of Carolina, Clark of Georgia & Col. Shelby from over the mountains in the Battle of Musgrove's Mills on Enoree River 96 District. The Enemy were defeated, Col. Innis commanding officer of British wounded, Major Fraser 2nd in command killed, a number of prisoners taken who were committed to Applicant's Care & Safety. Conveyed to Hillsborough N. Carolina.

While at that place received the appointment of Major with a Brevet commission as such from Gov. Rutledge with orders to command the militia from Col. L. Roy Hammond's Regiment of 96. Had conference with Board of War & obtained from Mr. Pen an order on the commissaries & Quartermasters for the So. Western frontiers of North Carolina, for Rations of provisions & forage, for the S. Carolina & Georgia militia, who might assemble for active service. Applicant on his return into Roan County established a camp as a rallying rendezvous for the Carolina & Georgia Refugees as they were then called & advertised at public places invitations to join him there. A copy of which being preserved will be found hereunto annexed and marked A.

The number assembled there upon that appeal by the last week in September was considerable & made the largest proportion of Col. Williams' command in the Battle of Kings Mountain 7th of October following. Immediately after the Battle of that day,

Applicant was joined by a number of men from the Regiment to which he had been appointed Major, who had joined Col. Clark in his previous attack upon Huger Sta. & came away with him, with this addition to his command he marched to Mecklenburg & joined Genl. Davidson & served some time with Col. Davy upon the Enemy lines then on retreat, soon after the Applicant joined Genl. Sumter & was with him in the Battle of Blackstock's after which in consequence of wounds received by the General in that affair the State was deprived of his usefulness at the time & Applicant joined his command to Cols. Twiggs, Clark & Sevier was with them in several small engagements which continued until Clark's affair on Long Creek near 96 was not in that engagement being out on command at the time was left behind on their retreat, followed made good his retreat & on his way fell in with & joined Col. William Washington & Col. McCall to whose command he was attached & joined Genl. Morgan next day.

Was in several light skirmishes with the Enemy previous to the Battle of Cowpens & was with the General there. Commanded on the left of the front line as Major of McCall's Regiment. It is here necessary to observe that Col. McCall had been promoted to the command of a Regiment of Cavalry authorized to be enrolled for six months & Applicant appointed to the Majority neither had yet been commissioned & only few armed with swords & pistols.

The Refugee militia attached to their respective commands enrolled in the regiment and were promised by the Governor to be provided with clothing & arms as soon as they could be procured — not a day was lost in recruiting nor was the full number made up before the Battle. The few 25 to 30 that were equipped as Horsemen were placed under Col. McCall and attached to Col. Washington's command. Those who were not so equipped were armed with Rifles & placed under the Applicant. After the action, the Service was so pressing & the movements of the Army so rapid that no recruiting could be attended to out of Camp & the Applicant was kept constantly on Detachments upon the Enemy Lines, so that he could not recruit in the Army as he had previously done.

The evening of the day of the Battle of the 17th he was detached by order of Genl. Morgan to look into Cornwallis' Camp north of the Broad River & to update his movements & communicate with Genl. Pickens and himself daily until further orders.

This service was performed regularly until the British took up Camp at Ramsour's Mills. Thence proceeded on & joined Genl. Greene & reported to him north of Catawba River. Was with the Genl. on his retreat through North Carolina constantly employed command of small detachments until they arrived at Moore's Plantation on the Guilford road, there Genl. Pickens was ordered to pass round the British, fall in their rear & watch their movements & to communicate them to the Genl. Applicant was kept in advance in rear of the British, took many prisoners on the way to the borders of Virginia.

Continuing upon their rear on their retrograde march, until their arrival at Hillsborough.

In conjunction with Col. McCall, took a picket guard at Hart's Mills in full view of the Enemy Camp consisting of one Commissioned officer, 2 non-commissioned Os & 23 privates with some scattering Grenadiers, on plundering expedition.

Prisoners committed to the charge of Applicant, was taken to Genl. Greene & by him ordered to Halifax old Court House Virginia. This duty, irksome as it was, was performed, returned & joined the army in Guilford County prior to the Battle of the 17th of March as memory now serves him — continued with the Army until the pursuit of Cornwallis was given over.

He was there ordered to join Genl. Pickens previously detached to the Western part of North Carolina, to rally the friends of South Carolina & Georgia with those of North Carolina with the view of recovering all the South from the Enemy. Applicant halted on the South fork of Catawba river, several of his men taken with the Small Pox, he had the whole of command inoculated upwards of 100, which detained him sometime, after which, he joined Genl. Pickens & was immediately ordered to prepare for the command of a detachment intended to pass into the District of 96 to cause the people friendly to the cause to join & give them aid to expel the Enemy from Carolina and Georgia — selected for such service & with the assistance of support in Company with Major Jackson of Georgia, an Officer of much popularity & superior military understanding, left Genl. Pickens, date not remembered & not material, passed through District of 96 with one hundred Citizen Soldiers & arrived safe on the margin of the Savannah river near Paces Ferry.

Joined there by Capt. Thomas Kee of Col. L. Hammonds' Regiment & Capt. Henry Graybill of the same with a considerable number of Volunteers, detached Capt. Kee to attack a British post on Horn's Creek commanded by a Capt. Clark. The British party were defeated, the Captain killed & the Company taken & paroled. Major Jackson passed over to Georgia, joined Cols. Baker, Stark & Williamson, who had collected a considerable force of the Georgia militia & were near Augusta, the British outposts were driven in on both sides of the Savannah River & a Siege commenced.

The Georgians under Col. Jackson raided a Battery near Fort Greyonson & the Applicant simultaneously erected a Battery opposite Fort Cornwallis on the North side of Savannah River, & held the Enemy within, cut off from all communication with the Country with the arrival of Genl. Pickens, Col. Clark & Col. Lee.

Applicant continued with Genl. Pickens aiding in the reduction of the British Garrisons in Augusta until Col. Brown surrendered when he was detached towards Orangeburg Co. & then other Troops under Pickens and Lee marched to & joined Genl. Greene at 96. While in front of the British under Lord Rawdon, advancing toward 96, Rec'd by express, ordered to retreat & joined Gent. Pickens west of that place & with him retreated towards the North & rejoined Genl. Greene on the Congaree River below Broad River.

Continued actively employed as a partisan until the Battle of Eutaw the 8th September. That part he acted upon that occasion is matter of Historical record.

After that, say 17 September 1781, he was appointed to the command of a Regiment of Cavalry which he was on that day authorized to raise for three years, or during the War, to be recommended by the Governor to be placed on Continental Establishment as may be seen by a certified Copy of the Governor's letter of that date hereunto annexed marked B.

A member of his Regiment of State Troops who had been long with him first as volunteer, secondly as recollected in six months service reenlisted with them & a detachment from Col. Hammonds Regiment militia he the Applicant, remained in service with Genl. Green, until preliminary articles of Peace were signed & announced, then encamped with Genl. Green's Army near Bacon's Bridge in Cathead Precinct. Ordered to discontinue recruiting for his new Regiment & in a few days after they with a few of his former Regiment of State Troops & a detachment of Col. Hammond's Regiment were discharged. Previously to this, Two Companies of his Regiment of State Troops were detached under the care of Capts. Jesse Johnson & George Hammond with Genl. Pickens in an expedition to the Cherokee Nation of Indians.

Their term of Service was nearly expired but they voluntarily performed the Service — most of them were engaged for the three years, but discharged before joining. It may now be necessary for a clear development of the Applicant's services that he should state some facts not brought into view in the preceding detail.

In the first place then, he states that when he left the State of South Carolina with his few volunteers, they were collected from different Regiments of Carolina militia & a few from Georgia & although he held the commission of Captain, he had no right to command them but by their own consent, but that consent was freely given, but as the numbers increased he did not feel satisfied himself to hold them together as a Company with such precarious powers & one or two Patriotic Lieutenants having joined who might rightfully command a part of them, with the advice of Col. Williams, Clark & Shelby, an election was held & he was elected.

Yet he felt further solicitous better to secure them & his own usefulness & devise Enrollment for their signature (a copy of which will be found hereunto annexed marked B). That Enrollment was signed & resigned by the same men, at different times & for different pensions & were always received at the expiration of their terms until he was authorized to raise the Regiment of Ten months service, when nearly all those who had been with him in the various services before noticed enlisted in the Regiment for 10 months, & served again for three years or during the War.

From the fall of Charlestown in May '80 to the formation of the Regiment of State Troops, Applicant never made a payroll nor did any of his Citizen Soldiers require it to be done for them. They furnished themselves as well as they could with their own clothing which was often very scanty & with their own horses & arms. Applicant also done the same & the only payroll ever presented or signed for payment was for the Ten months Service of the 10-month men State Regiment and all of those, except a few who were very young & came in late, had service from the Fall of Charlestown to that time. Some of Genl. Pickens' letters to Applicant on Public Service have been preserved & will be herewith exhibited to the Honbl. Court plus one of Gov. Rutledge's letters accidentally preserved most of these communications being lost, misplaced or with his commission mistreated by the Hand of Time, so as to be largely unintelligible. He also has relinquished every claim whatever to a Pension or annuity except the Present and Declares that his Name is not placed by himself or any authorized agent on the Pension Rolls of any State.

Sworn to before
Me Richard Gantt P. Judge
S/ S. Hammond

We Harwood Bartly, a clergyman residing in the District of Edgefield, and L. S. Brooks Residing in the same, hereby certify that we are well acquainted with Samuel Hammond who has subscribed and Sworn to the above declaration, that we believe him to be Seventy Six years of Age, that he is Respected and believed, in the neighborhood where he resides to have been a Soldier of the revolution and that we Concur in that Opinion.

L. S. Brooks served under Col. Hammond.
Subscribed the Sworn to the day & year aforesaid.
L. S. Brooks Harwood Bart.

The said court do hereby Declare their opinion after the investigation of the matter and after putting the interrogatories Prescribed by the War department that the above named applicant was a Revolutionary Soldier and served as he states and the Court further certifies that Harwood Bart.— who has signed the preceding certification as Clergyman residing in Edgefield District and that L. S. Brooks— who has also signed thereon is a Resident in the said district — and is a credible person and that their statement is entitled to Credit.

S/ Richard Gantt
P. Judge

I J. Richardson, Clerk of this Court of Common Pleas do hereby certify that the foregoing contains the Original Proceedings of the said Court in the matter of the application of Samuel Hammonds for a Pension.

In testimony whereof, I have hereunto set my hand, Seal of Office this thirty first day of
October A. D. 1832.
S/ J. Richardson
Clerk

South Carolina
Edgefield District
I do hereby certify that I served a short time under Col. Samuel Hammond while he commanded the

State Troops in the revolutionary war, and was with him when we killed a few Tories that were following Lord Rawdon when he relieved Col. Cruger at Ninety Six in June 1781 on their way to Charleston & served with him sundry other times when not under his command.

S/ M. Timkins

State of South Carolina
Laurens District

This day personally appeared James Dillard Senior before me Robert Long Esquire, one of the Justices of the Quorum of the district of Laurens aforesaid, and being duly sworn, on his oath Saith that he was acquaint with Samuel Hammond in the Revolutionary War — that in the year 1780, in or about the month of July, after the reduction of Charleston, he saw him with a small company of men (which he appeared to command) in his neighborhood, on his way to join the American Army, that he had stopped there a day or two to give time for Home Whigs to prepare to go on with him, that he (this deponent) saw several meet, and went away with him; that he passed by the title Captain Hammond; that he has good reasons to believe that he was in Several Battles especially King's [sic] Mountain, Blackstock's & the Cowpens that is Tarleton's defeat, as he was in the command about the times of the same, but does not recollect now of Seeing him in them — He also says that he had command either as Major, or Captain at least in the State Troops under General Thomas Sumter; also that he enlisted two men out of the Militia company commanded by this deponent, then a Captain — That when Tarleton was on his march after General Daniel Morgan, he (Samuel Hammond) and John Greer were sent by General Pickens with this deponent to reconnoiter his line of March & to give such notice of the British march as might appear necessary; that he then was called Captain Hammond; that in the last named Service they the three aforesaid Viz: Captain Hammond, John Greer & this deponent, saw a Tory Colonel near Tarleton's line & took a negro man & two Horses from him and further he does not now recollect.

S/ James Dillard

Sworn to and subscribed the 15th day of May in the year 1833 Before me, S/Robert Long, J.Q. Laurens District:

I Robert Long one of the Judges of the Quorum of the District aforesaid do hereby certify unto all whom it may concern that the above deponent James Dillard Senior is a very old and infirm man generally confined to his house and as Such is unable to go before a Judge of the Court. Given under my hand, the day and year above written.

S/ Robt Long, J. Q.

The State of South Carolina Laurens District

Personally appeared Robert Long before me, Henry S. Neel Esquire, one of the Justices of the Peace of the Said district and being duly sworn on his oath Saith that he was acquainted with Captain Samuel Hammond in the Revolutionary War and more particularly after the reduction of Charleston in the month of July in the year one thousand seven hundred & eighty, he Saw him in the Command of a Small company of men on his way to Join the Whig Refugees and northern army, that he stopt two or three days near where this deponent then lived (& does yet) to give time for Some Whigs to prepare to go on with him in which time he (this deponent) piloted four men to his camp, to wit: James Scott and Isaac Greer, the first day; and Captain Josiah Greer and Samuel Ewing the Second day, the two first went away with Captain S. Hammond; and the two left with James Dillard followed in a day or two after this immediately before the fight at Musgrove's Mill — that Some time after this deponent Saw him in the command of a company in General Sumpter's camp that he must have been in the fight at Blackstock's, as he Saw him in Sumpter's camp but two days before — but this deponent being Sent out in a detachment of fourteen men under Captain Ewing to reconnoiter the post toward the fort on Colonel J. Williams' plantation: This, Immediately after Sumpter had returned (with a good number of his command) from taking a view of Tarleton's camp at Shirer's Ferry on Broad River — So the day following Tarleton pursued General Sumpter in his turn: So by this unexpected movement he got between Sumpter & the above detachment this is the reason why this deponent did not see him (S. Hammond) there that he saw him in a day or two after this he knows that he was in the Battle of Cowpens (that is Tarleton's defeat) but rather believes he was then promoted to Major, believes he commanded on the front line left wing and this deponent was in the center line on the right wing in Captain Ewing's company commanded by Colonel Joseph Hayes, next to Colonel Howard's Infantry. That he Saw him repeatedly afterwards in the American Service under General Pickens both in North and South Carolina till, as this deponent now believes, he was attached to General Sumpter's State Troops, or Cavalry as a Major, or Captain at lest; and of course must have been in the Battle of Eutaw Spring — That the above Captain or Major Samuel Hammond is the Same who is now called Colonel Samuel Hammond.

Sworn to and Subscribed the 10th day of May in the year 1833. S/Henry S. Neel
S/ Robt. Long
Congaree Sept. 17,1781
Sir

I should like to have Such a Corps of Light Dragoons as Col. Maham' s under your command & as I am persuaded that your will exert Yourself to raise and equip Such an one which from Your Zeal & activity I flatter myself that you soon will. I do hereby empower You to do so & request that you will with the utmost expedition. The men to be entitled to the Same Rations & pay as Maham's & enlisting during the war or at least for three years, as State Troops, Subject to Continental Articles, liable to be sooner disbanded by the Legislature or executive authority. If You meet with the Success I expect I will recommend You to be put in Continental Establishment which I think will be done — appoint Your own officers— You are sensible that very thing depends on the officers therefore get good ones.

I am Sir, Yr Very Hble Serv't.
S/ J. Rutledge
Lt. Col. Samuel Hammond
Long Cane 8th Feby 1782
Dear Sir

I received yours of the 6th Inst. respecting the Enemy — tho it was night before the man from Capt. Towls got her, I immediately wrote Cols. Casey and Roebuck. Col. Anderson sets off this Morning with what men he can collect to Norward's Mill on Saludy — and he will wait there for further intelligence. If you can get intelligence as which way the enemy is gone, you will do Every thing in your power to come up with them and send to the Col of Militia between Saludy and Broad Rivers— advising them of the movement of the Enemy if in your power. Likewise to Col. Anderson at Norward's Mill, as I am of opinion they intend for the Cherokee Country — If Cunningham is along and can make their way through — I wait to hear from you as soon as convenient — wishing you success— and am Dr Sir Your most humble Serv't

S/ Andrew Pickens
Col. Hammonds
Long Cane 13th August 1781
Dear Sir

I expect by this you have your men property equipt and your horses in good order and fit for Service — I have ordered Col. Leroy Hammond to meet me at Perkins's Mills on Saludy with part of his Regiment on Thursday the 1st Inst — you will please, likewise to meet me there on that day, with the whole of your Regiment properly mounted — you will get a wagon and bring with you as much provision as will serve your men to the Congaree — there was sent and some other things went in Col. Hammond's wagon when we parted at Kirklands— you will please have them brought on with you.

I am Dear Sir your most obedient Serv't
S/ Andrew Pickens
Lt. Col. Hammonds
P. S.

I wish you to send Capt. Richard Johnson with Twelve good men up here as soon as
possible as I want him for a particular purpose.
To Saml. Hammond
A Call to Arms: Beef, Bread & Potatoes
Higgins' Plantation 23rd Sept. 1780

The undersigned has just returned from Hillsborough to this neighborhood. While there he obtained an order on the Companies and Quartermasters upon this frontier for supplies of provisions and forage for such of the patriotic Citizens of South Carolina & Georgia as might be embodied for actual services and being informed that there is a number of you, resting with patriotic friends in the Two adjoining Counties no doubt anxiously looking for an opportunity to embody for the performance of duty, but without the power or means of supporting yourselves or your horses from you own resources I have thought your wishes would be forwarded by the Establishing of a Camp at a rallying rendezvous at a convenient place for your assemblage, and to be ready when occasion might offer to give our aid for the recovery of Our County.

I have with this view formed a Camp at Higgins' Plantation a few miles from Capt. Brannon's Tavern, near the road leading westwardly to Torrence's Crossroads, where we will be supplied with the needful. I am justified in the expectation of the arrival of a powerful support shortly and that we may return toward home with a strong army. Let us be prepared to do our part, our little force will be important if Combined possessing as we do a better knowledge of the County and its resources. Now is the time to show ourselves and I invite you, both Officers & soldiers to obey the call: I here assure you that I shall cheerfully surrender the Command, and Cooperate fully to and with any Officer of Senior Rank of either State that may think proper to Join; Should an opportunity offer immediately for my advancing toward the enemy with a prospect of doing good an officer will be left at this Camp authorized to obtain Rations for such as may Join there after my departing. I have some other good news. Come and hear it.

S. Hammond Major
Comdg Refugees Lower Regt.
So Carolina 96th Brigd.
Higgins' Plantation near
Brannon's, Roan County, NC
State of South Carolina

Richland District I do certify that the foregoing Is a true and Exact Copy of a paper of very old appearance put into my hands by Col. Samuel Hammond to be copied and Certified.

I have Carefully Compared the Copy with the original And find it Correct.
Sworn under my hand this thirteenth day of October Ano. Domni. 1832
Charles L. Hammond
Notary Public & JP

Pension Application, William Hillhouse, Marengo Co. Al.
(National Archives No. S-7008)

Declaration in order to obtain the benefit of the act of Congress passed June 7th 1832.
State of Alabama
Marengo County

On this third day of February — personally appeared in open Court, before the Hon. William J. Alston Judge of the County Court of Marengo now sitting William Hillhouse Sen. a resident of township 18, range five, East in the County of Marengo and State of Alabama, aged seventy three years on the 18th of March last; who being first duly sworn according to law, doth on his oath, make the following declaration, in order to attain the benefit of the act of Congress passed June 7, 1832.

I entered the service of the United States, in the month of December in the year 1775, under the command of Brigadier General Richardson, in the Regiment of Col. Thomas Neil, as a private soldier in the company commanded by Captain Thomas Kirkpatrick and left the service the first of October 1781.

I resided when I entered the service in York District South Carolina. I entered as a volunteer holding myself ready at all times when ever called to go into service.

The first tour of duty I performed, was for the term of two months, in which tour I marched through the District of York and Union in the State of South Carolina, and Lincoln County North Carolina. During this Campaign I did no service with any Continental troops, nor was I in any battle.

My next term of service commenced about the last of July 1776, and continued two months. This tour was performed principally in the then Indian Country, now the Districts of Greenville, Anderson and Pickens, in the State of South Carolina. In this period of service there was skirmishing with the Indians, some of them, and a few of our soldiers were killed, but there was not what might be called a battle.

I was next called into actual service about the first of December in the year 1777: which service continued as well as I now recollect for 60 days. I was then under the command of Brigadier Gen. Williamson and marched through the Districts of Union, Laurens and Abbeville to 96 White Hall and Fort Independence.

About the last of March in the year 1778 I commenced a tour of military duty, which terminated on the 28th of June following. During this service I was commanded by His Excellency Governor Rutledge: and marched through almost all the low country of S. Carolina, especially those parts watered by Cooper and Edisto rivers. Count Pulaski a Regular officer having under his command a troop of Cavalry, frequently visited the encampment to which I belonged.

In May 1780 I again went into actual service, and continued till October 1781. I entered as orderly Serjeant, in which capacity I served a short time, when I was elected Lieutenant of the Company in which I had hitherto done duty. Brigadier Gen. Thomas Sumpter now commanded the Brigade, and Col. Andrew Neil the Regiment to which I belonged; and Captain J. Jamison the company.

Appendix E

During this campaign I marched through the greater part of the middle and lower sections of S. Carolina, and through a considerable portion of North Carolina. As well as I can recollect, I was, during this term of duty, in the following Battles, viz., at Williamson's plantation in the District of York S. Carolina I was in a battle in which the British and Tories were commanded by the British officers, Captains Huck and Adams, and most gloriously defeated by a few Militia Boys, my Companions in arms, commanded by Col. Neil.

Some time in the same month I was called to face my Country's enemy at Rock [sic] Mount, where my brave and beloved Col. Neil was slain. Eight days after, I was in the battle of the Hanging Rock, in which my Captain was severely wounded, and rendered unfit for service. In the heat of the battle I took command of the Company, which command I held until sometime in the April following when I resigned. Some time in the month of August, on the same day, if I mistake not on which Gen. Gates was defeated, I was in a battle at Campden [sic] Ferry, where our troops captured a British Guard and a number of Wagons. In two or three days after I was in the battle where my brave General Sumpter was defeated.

The next battle in which I was engaged was, I believe, in the month of February 1781 at Granby Fort on the Congaree River. In a few days after, I met and fought the British at a place called the Big Savannah, where our forces captured a large guard and a great quantity of military stores.

Some four or five days after, I was in another engagement at Fort Watson commonly called Wrights Bluff. In a few days, I again fought the enemy near Black River not far from Kingstree Bridge.

In the month of May 1781 I was in a second rencounter [sic] with the enemy at Fort Granby. In the August following the Brigade to which I belonged was marched under the command of Gen. Greene to Orangeburg, in S. Carolina, in a design to draw out the enemy from his entrenchment; but he refused to come out, and there was no battle. During this tour I had the pleasure of knowing Gen. Greene, Cols. Washington and Lee.

I would also state to the War Department, that the British Commander in Chief Lord Cornwallis on his march to Virginia in Jan. 1781 made my plantation his place of rendezvous from Tuesday till Friday, stripping me of all my possessions except the land which he could not destroy.

I have no documentary evidence to offer to the Department in proof of the foregoing declaration, but have procured the testimony of two witnesses, whose certificates are here annexed in proof of my service, and the rank I held, during the Revolutionary conflict. I hereby relinquish every claim whatever to a pension or annuity, except the present and declare that my name is not on the pension roll of any agency of any State.

I became the lieutenant of the company to which I belonged the first of July 1780, and continued in that command about three weeks, when owing to the disability of Capt. Jamison as before stated, I took the command of the company, after Capt. J. with the other wounded were put in a place of safety and the soldiers who had charge of them had returned to camp an election was held for Captain, in which I was unanimously elected.

This election took place about the last of July, which rank I held until the last of

April 1781, under the command of Col. Wm. Bratton at which time I resigned. After my resignation, Frame Woods was elected Capt. under whom I served five months. The Department will therefore discover from this declaration, that I served during the Revolutionary war, fourteen months as private soldier, five weeks as Sergeant, three weeks as Lieutenant, and nine months as Captain.

The answers of the said William Hillhouse Senior to the interrogatories prescribed by the War Department

Answer to the first

I was born in the year 1760 on the 18th day of March near Land's Ford on the Catawba River, in the State of South Carolina and in the bounds of what is now called Chester District as I think.

Answer to the Second

I have no record of my age, as to that, and the place of my birth, I received the information orally from my parents

Answer to the third

When called into service I was living in what is now called York District S. Carolina, since the Revolutionary War, I have lived for the most part of the time in the District of Pendleton S. Carolina, then in Greene County Alabama, and now in Marengo County Alabama.

Answer to the fourth.

I went into service as a volunteer

Answer to the fifth

Gen. Greene, Col. Count Pulaski, Col. Washington and Col. Lee were occasionally with the troops among whom I served. The Continental regiments were those of Col. Washington (horse), Col. Lee (horse) Col. Pulaski (horse) the Militia Regiments were those Col. A. Pickens, Col. John Thomas, Col. Thomas Brandon, Col. Edward Lacey, Col. Richard Wynn, there were others not recollected.

I was in the following engagements, at Williamson's plantation, S. C., Rock Mount,

Hanging Rock, Camden ferry, Sumpter's defeat, Fort Granby, Fort Motte, the Big Savannah, Fort Watson on Santee, near Kingstree on Black river and another on Fort Granby and Biggin Church, near Moncks Corner. As to a more particular detail I beg leave to refer to my declaration.

Answer to the sixth

I never received any written discharges, we were discharged by our Captain verbally. I never received a commission; I was elected by the company owing to the situation of the State during the period that I was in office it being overrun by the enemy the Governor and Council were compelled to suspend the operations of the Executive department and consequently, Officers could not receive commissions. In confirmation of this fact, I would refer to the Department to Ramsey's History of South Carolina from the 12th of April 1780 to May 1781.

Answer to the seventh

I refer to His Excey: John Gayle Col. Patrick Norris (a revolutioner) both of Greene County, the Hon. J. Murphy Representative in Congress from the State of Alabama, Col. James Pickins of Marengo County and Frederick Peck Post Master at Greensborough, Alabama.

Wm Hillhouse

Pension Application, Charles Holland, Tuscaloosa Co. Al.
(National Archives No. S-7027)

Declaration in order to obtain the benefit of the act of Congress passed June 7th 1832.
State of Alabama
Tuscaloosa County

On this 13th day of October 1832 personally appeared in open court, before the Judge of the Circuit Court of Said State now sitting in Said County, Charles Holland, a resident in the county aforesaid, aged Seventy four years on the 2nd day of April last, who being first duly sworn according to law, doth on his oath make the following declaration, in order to obtain the benefit of the act of Congress passed June 7, 1832.

That he entered the service of the United States under the following named officers and served as herein stated: namely, that he volunteered, some time in the month of September (as well as he can recollect) 1776 (*Note: Actually July*), in a company of militia under the command of Captain James McCall, in the District then called Ninety Six, now Abbeville, in the State of South Carolina, that said company was attached to a Regiment, or corpse [sic] of men, under the command of Major Andrew Williamson or Wimson, the Colonel, if any, not recollected; that he continued with Capt. McCall until about the month, July 1777 (Note: 1776), when the Capt. was taken prisoner by the Indians & this relator was transferred to a militia company commanded by Capt. Andrew Pickens, in the same Regiment; that soon after this, Williamson was promoted (*Note: to Colonel*) to the command of the Regiment & Capt. Pickens was made the Major & one Thomas Weems became the Captain, who was previously Lieutenant under Pickens—that after the lapse of two years or more, Captain Weems resigned and one Joseph Pickens was promoted to the Captaincy of said Company, under whom the relator served twelve months & more, until the battle of Ninety Six, in which battle Capt. Joseph Pickens was wounded mortally and died in about three weeks; that some time, say three months, before the battle of Ninety Six, Col. Williamson deserted to the British and Major Andrew Pickens became the Commandant of said Regiment; and one Alexander Noble became Major; that after the death of Capt. Joseph Pickens, one William Strain was promoted to the Captaincy in his place, under whom this relator served until the end of the War with Great Britain;—that during his service, which in all was, as near as the relator can remember, about seven years, he performed the following tours & acted in the battles & skirmishes mentioned below—He volunteered, as before stated, in the District of Ninety Six, at a place of rendezvous about 35 miles from the Town of Ninety Six, he then marched to the town of Ninety-Six to meet & give battle to the Tories who had assembled in the vicinity of that place; that on arriving at Ninety Six the Regiment to which he was attached was met by a Regiment of regular troops from Charleston City, under the command of Colonel Henry William Drayton [author note: William Henry Drayton], at whose approach the Tories dispersed & fled. He & regiment then returned to the neighborhood in which they were raised & in a short time had to return to Ninety Six for the same purpose just mentioned, when a fight ensued between the Regiment and the Tories in which there are were two Whigs wounded & one killed; Some time after this, Captain McCall & a part of his company, including this relator were detailed to go into the Indian Nation in the northern part of the State of Georgia, after some Tories who had retreated there, when the Indians made an attack upon said detachment, killed several men & wounded several others and took Captain McCall & another prisoners; that after the surrender of Charleston (in which battle this relator was not engaged) this relator & about 40 others of the same company retreated for protection into the state of North Carolina where they remained about eight months, during which time they had several skirmishes with the Tories in the upper edge of South Carolina; about this time General Morgan passed into North Carolina & was joined by this relator & those with him who had retreated as aforesaid & shortly after ensued the battle of the Cowpens or Tarlton's [sic] Defeat, in which, he was wounded by a sword thrust through the body, which disabled him for active service for two or three months; previous to Tarlton's [sic] Defeat, (this relator forgot to mention) he partook in the battle of King's [sic] Mountain where Ferguson, the British commander was killed & defeated by the American troops commanded by Colonels Shelby, Cleveland, Sevier, Campbell, McCall and perhaps Clarke; that after Tarlton's [sic] Defeat, the next engagement in which the relator acted, was the battle of Hanging Rock, where he again rec (*Note: received*) a wound, which was a shot-wound in the groin; this proved comparatively slight; next after this, saying nothing of skirmishes at Ramsour's mill, Hammon's (*Note: Hammond's*) old store, William's Fort, &c came the Siege of Ninety-Six, where General Greene commanded, in which this relator took part & it was the last battle in which he was engaged during his service; this claimant is unable to name particularly any of the Continental Regiments or companies with which he served; He has already named several regular officers & now remembers that he did not name that General Sumter commanded at the Hanging Rock; he has no discharge in writing or other documentary evidence of his services. He hereby relinquishes every claim whatever to a pension or annuity, except the present, and declares that his name is not on the pension roll of the Agency of any State.

Sworn to & subscribed the day & year first aforesaid.
Signed John W. Jenkins, Clerk / Charles Holland

Service and Claims of John Pickens

STATE OF SOUTH CAROLINA: Debtor to JOHN PICKENS, deceased for duty as private Col. Anderson's company. Mr. John Pickens, his account for Militia Duty as Private done since the reduction of Charleston, also for a mare lost in service in 1781, the whole acmounting to 41 pounds, 8 shilling and sixpence.

ABBEVILLE COUNTY OF) I do hereby authorize and impower (my present NINETY SIX DISTRICT) husband) WILLIAM BLACK to draw and receive the Indent or Indents with the interest due for the use of my orphan children by my former husband JOHN PICKENS, and which was due to him for sundry militia services of this State as a private, serving mostly as a Horse-man, both before the reduction of Charleston and afterwards, until he was taken prisoner by the enemy and given into the hands of Indians, who in a most barbarous manner put him and others to death. Col. Robert Anderson, Commissioner saith that he returned the accounts of said former husband JOHN PICKENS militia duty or services to the auditor's office. Given under my hand this 3-rd day of February 1790

Signed: *Mary (X) Pickens* The above MARY BLACK signed and acknowledged the above order in my presence and also made oath that neither herself nor any interest in consequence of the above duty or services and that there is not beside this any order out for the same. Sworn to this 3-rd day of February 1790 before me. PAT. CALHOUN, J.P. NOVEMBER 19, 1819. To the Honorable the President and Members of the Senate: Your petitioner humbly sheweth that her former husband JOHN PICKENS was killed in service of this state on the 16-th day of December 1781, and left your petitioner with a family of small and very helpless childen, that your petitioner continued the widow of the said JOHN PICKENS until the 10th day of January 1784 when she intermarried with WILLIAM BLACK who has been dead for many years and your petitioner is now very old and infirm and unable to make a support and prays that your honorable body will place her on your pension list and thereby enable her to drag out the few remaining days which she may have to live and at least she hopes she will not be refused the three years annuity which she might have drawn. She refers for her records of the Treasury office where she did draw for her minor children out did not draw for herself.

MARY (X) PICKENS

Indents and Claims, Joseph William Pickens
South Carolina State Archives
File 5935 Pickens, Joseph

NINETY SIX DISTRICT: Personally came Lieut Joseph Pickens before me and on his oath deposeth that on the eleventh day of February last past [Note: February 1779] he being called out with part of Capt. Thos. Weems' Company of Militia under the Command of Col. And^w Pickens in the Public Service of this state on Savannah River near a place called the Cherokee Ford where Being Engaged in a fight with a large body of disafected armed men called Col. Boyd's Tories, that in said fight he the Deponent lost a Saddle and Saddle Cloth and a pair of Saddlebags and blanket, appraiseth same to one hundred and twenty pound total.

Signed: J^O PICKENS

Sworn to the twenty first day of July 1779, before me,

Signed: PAT CALHOUN

The above certified the 11th of December 1779 by AND^W PICKENS, Col.

Appraisers sworn and signed: THOMAS STRAIN, JA^S STRAIN, WILLIAM STRAIT 12 NOVEMBER 1779) We, William Drannan, James Strain, and Ezekiel NINETY SIX DISTRICT) Evans, Freeholders, do on our Oath value and appraise a certain Bay gelding, pacer, 13 1/2 hands high, six years old, Branded JP on the near Buttock, lost and taken by the Enemy at Savannah on or about 9th of October last, at Two Thousand Pound Currency.

Sworn to be fore me this 12th Nov. 1779,

Signed: PAT CALHOUNSigned: FRANNAN, STRAIN and EVANS

Ninety Six District of S. Carolina

Personnally appeared before PAT CALHOUN, one of the Justices of said District, JOSPEH [sic] PICKENS and maketh Oath that he never hath got said horse or any satisfaction therefor.

Signed: JO. PICKENS

Sworn before me this 12th Nov 1779

Signed: PAT CALHOUN

Certified 11th December 1779, AND^W PICKENS Col.

State of S. Carolina W. No. 37.

D^r [Note: debtor] to JOSEPH PICKENS, Deceas'd for Duty to Col. Anderson's return Waggon Service in 1779 and 1780, 376 days, and a Bay Mare lost in July 1781.

MR. JOSEPH PICKENS, dec. his acco^t of Military Duty as Capt. done before and since the reduction of Charleston; also for Waggon Hire in 1779 & 1780 on Militia acco, & for a Bay Mare lost in 1781, the whole to amo^t to 335–18–6 3/4, Three Hundred and thirty five Pounds, Eighteen Shillings, and sixpence three farlings.

A Waggon and team exclusive of the above amt. Is made no charge of but left to the discretion of the Public to value — see Col. Anderson's Certificate at the bottom of voucher for the which, with the attestation preceeding will justify the party concern in having the same affairs of record in another Acct.

[Signature unreadable]

Stub Entries to Indents
Issued in Payment of
CLAIMS AGAINST SOUTH CAROLINA
Growing Out of the Revolution
Books U-W
Edited by
A. S. Salley, Jr.
Secretary of the Historical Commission of South Carolina
Printed for
THE HISTORICAL COMMISSION OF SOUTH CAROLINA
By The State Company, Columbia, S. C.
1918

Page 290, item 2

No. 634} Issued the 29 Aug^s 85 To for the
Lib W } Est^a.. of Jo^s Pickens for Three hundred & Thirty
Five pound Eighteen & Six pence for Duty as
Captain & for Waggon Master in 1779 & 80 per
A/c from Commissioners Principal 335–18–6 3/4
Annual In^s 23–10–4

GENTLEMEN:

Pleas to deliver the indent that is due my late Husband JOSEPH PICKENS for militia duty and other services to M^r. John Lesley and his receipt shall be of sufficient from,

Gentl^n, Your most humble servant,

ELENEAR PICKENS

To the treasurer of the State of South Carolina, these may certify that I saw Elanor Pickens, widdow and Executor of the late Joseph Pickens, sign the above order, this 21 January 1786

Signed: AND^W PICKENS, JR.

Indented Certificate
SOUTH CAROLINA

PURSUANT to an ACT of the GENERAL ASSEMBLY passed the 16th of March 1783; We the COMMISIONERS of the TREASURY, have this day delivered to *For the Estate of Joseph Pickens*, this our INDENTED CERTIFICATE, for the sum of *Three hundred thirty five pound eighteen shillings & six pence for Militia Duty as Captain, also for Waggon Hire in 1779 & 1780, and for a bay horse lost in 1781 as per account passed the Commission of Accts* the said, his Executors, Administrators or Assigns will be entitled to receive from this office the Sum of *Twenty three pound ten shillings and four pence on demand* one Years Interest on the principal Sum of *Three hundred & Thirty five pound eighteen shillings and six pence* and the like Interest annually....

Given under our hands at the TREASURY OFFICE in CHARLESTON, the *Twenty ninth* Day of *August* One Thousand Seven Hundred and Eighty-*five*.

Signed: J. MITCHELL, Commissioners of the Treasury

EDITOR's NOTE: This indent was cashed by John Lesly, David Lesly, Abram Markley, and was used to purchase 200 acres of land by ANDREW PICKENS, JR. who was a son of Capt. Joseph and Eleanor Pickens. Final payments made August 14, 1787.

Contingent Account passed by the Legislature Nov 23, 1795

Pay Bill of Joseph Pickens, a Spy, Amounting to 2–11–4

Rec. Dec 11th 1795 of S. Theus Treas At Charleston Two pound Eleven & four pence in full of this pay Roll–

I Certify that the Foregoing receipt is a true copy taken from the Original transmitted to Philadelphia.

Signed: *Simeon Theus Treas*

December 14, 1795

Pension Application, Robert Andrew Pickens, Fayette Co. Tenn.
(National Archives No. S-3697)

Declaration in order to obtain the benefit of the act of Congress passed June 7th 1832.

State of Tennessee

Fayette County

On this 23rd day of October, 1832, personally appeared in open Court before Richard Gantt, Judge of the Court of Common Pleas now sitting for the District of Abbeville, Andrew Pickens, a Resident of Fayette County, State of Tennessee, aged seventy nine years, who being duly sworn according to Law, doth, on his oath, make the following declaration in order to obtain the benefit of the Act of Congress, passed on the 7th of June, 1832.

That he entered the Service the United States under the following named Officers, and served as therein stated. That he entered the service as a Volunteer Militia-man under General Andrew Williamson, who commanded on that Expedition; his Captain's name was Robert Anderson, & William Riley was his Lieutenant. That he entered the service on or about the 15th July, 1776, and marched into the Cherokee Nation, in what was called the Cherokee Expedition — that they marched to the Beaverdam creek, where they made a short halt for some days — That they then marched to Seneca river, where they were attacked by the Indians & Tories, & had a battle in which he was wounded in the knee, & carried to Fort Independence on a litter between two horses, where he lay under the Doctors for ten months — that as soon as his wounds would permit him, he again entered the service as a Volunteer with his waggon & team to haul Baggage for General Williamson, as he thinks in the Fall of the year 1777, and continued in that Service about three months, and got a discharge, and left his waggon in in (repeated word in original document) the service, which was taken by the British, near or in Augusta, Georgia.

That he again entered the service as a Volunteer under the command of Capt. Robert Carithers [sic], as a Scout to guard the Frontiers — That he continued to serve in the character of a Guard for the Frontiers, sometimes acting with other Commanders, but generally as a guard — That he was at the siege of Ninety six with General Greene. That he thinks he must have served at least four years, & was acquainted with Colonel Washington & Colonel Lee; & also well acquainted with Colonel Andrew Pickens who was his full cousin, and under whom he performed several Tours of service, and was with him at Sota [sic] & Chota, two towns in the Cherokee Indian Nation. — That he was in the service when peace was made & was then finally discharged — That he resided in Ninety six District, South Carolina, when he first entered the Service, & continued to reside in the said District of Ninety six during the whole War.

He hereby relinquishes every claim whatsoever to a pension or Annuity, except the present; and declares that his name is not on the Pension-roll of any State or Agency of any State, except the Pension-roll of South Carolina; which State has been kind enough to place him on the pension list & allow him sixty dollars per year, ever since about the year 1812; before which time he had 5 pounds allowed him as an Invalid Pensioner from near the close of the Revolutionary War; and that he has no documentary evidence in his possession, nor does he know of any person, who could testify to his Service.

Sworn to and subscribed this day & year aforesaid in Open Court

Test: Signed/ Jas Wardlaw, Clerk / Andrew (X) Pickens, his mark

We, Moses Waddel, a Clergyman residing in the District of Abbeville, and Hugh Mecklin, residing in the same, hereby certify, That we are well acquainted with Andrew Pickens who has subscribed & sworn to the above Declaration — that we believe him to be seventy nine years of age — that he is reputed & believed in the neighborhood where he did lately reside (Say Abbeville District, South Carolina) to have been a soldier of the Revolution, and that we concur in that opinion: And further, that we have been acquainted with him for the space of nearly forty years last past.

Sworn to & subscribed the day & year aforesaid. In open Court

Signed/ Jas Wardlaw, Clk, / M. Waddel, / Hugh Mecklin

State of Tennessee
Fayette County
County Court July Term 1833

Personally appeared in open Court Andrew Pickens, now residing in the County and State aforesaid, who being duly sworn, deposeth and saith, that by reason of old age and the consequent loss of memory, he cannot swear positively as to the precise length of his service, but according to the best of his recollection he served not less than the periods mentioned below, and in the following grades: He entered the service as stated in his former declaration about the first of July 1776 as a private volunteer and was in service until the first of August following, when he was wounded as before stated, and lay in that condition for ten months. In the year 1777 he served as a waggoner as stated in his former declaration for three months. After the expiration of said term he again volunteered as a Scout and served for not less than three months. He then went as a private soldier into the Cherokee Nation under Genl. Pickens and Genl. Clark, immediately commanded by Capt. Carithers [sic] and continued in service not less than two months. After that he was in service under Captain Carithers [sic] not less than one year. Some time after he joined the army of Gen. Greene and was at the siege of Ninety six and remained in actual service, not less than six months. He then went into service under Genl. Clark & Genl. Pickens as a volunteer private and continued in service not less than one month. This is the time of his actual service, though he was subject to be called out at any moment and was very often called out for short periods of which he has no account and can give no distinct statement. And for the foregoing services he claims a pension. He cannot obtain the proof of any living witness within his knowledge who can state that he did actually perform said services.

I hereby relinquish all claim to pension except the present & declare that my name is not on pension roll of any State.

Where and in what year were you born.

I was born in State Virginia in the year fifty three

Have you any record of your age if so where is it

My age is record in my family bible which is now in my possession —

Where were you living when Called into service where have you lived since the revolutionary war and where do you now live

I lived in the State of South Carolina when first called into service Abeville [sic] district I live at the same place in the same State until the 1806 when I removed to the State of Tennessee I now reside in Fayette County Tennessee —

Were you called into service as a volunteer or were you drafted or substituted

I volunteered my services and at time when in service was a volunteer

State the names of some of the officers who were with the troops where you served such continental and militia Regiments as you can recollect and the general circumstances of your services

I cannot answer the last question more fully than by referring to my declarations

Did you ever receive a discharge

I never received a discharge to the best of my recollection if I did it has been lost

Have you any documentary evidence by which you can prove your services

I have none

Signed/ Andw Pickens

Sworn to & subscribed

Signed/ Thos C. Hudson

State of Tennessee
Fayette County
Court of Pleas and quarter sessions
July Term 1833

This day personally appeared in open court Milton Moore a clergaman resident in the County of Fayette and Josiah Higgason & Benjamin Branch who made oath in due process of law that they are well acquainted with Andrew Picking [sic] who singued [sic] the forgoing declaration and that they believe him to have been a revolutionary solder and served as stated ___court in His declaration submitted. He is generally _____ and believed in the neighborhood to have been a revolutionary solder where he stated in which opinion we concur.

Sworn to and subscribed in open court the 8th day of July 1833

Signed/ Thos C Hudson, Clk
Signed / Milton Moore
Signed / B. Branch
Signed / J. Higgason

Pension Application, William Gabriel Pickens, Livingston Co. KY
(National Archives No. S-1244)

Declaration in order to obtain the benefit of the act of Congress passed June 7th 1832.

State of Kentucky
Livingston County

On this 4th day of February 1833 personally appeared in open court, before John Berry, Isham Clement, and Vinson B. Simpson, Esqrs., Justices of the county court for the county aforesaid, now sitting, William G. Pickens, resident of said county aged seventy two years, the 18th October last, who being first duly sworn according to law, doth on his oath make the following declaration in order to obtain the benefit of the act of Congress passed June 7, 1832.

That he entered the service of the United States under the following named officers, and served as herein stated: About the first of October 1775 I first entered the service as a private (in the District of Abbeville (formerly Ninety Six) and as a volunteer under Captain Robert Anderson (afterwards General.) About the 2nd of July preceding my entering the service, the inhabitants along the frontiers and back settlements of Georgia, and the Carolinas, had generally forted up, in consequence of the Cherokee Indians, who were extremely troublesome at this time; having been instigated by the Brittish. To protect themselves from Indian warfare, and to defend the country as much as possible, the frontier inhabitants had constructed a line of forts along the Savannah River and had mustered themselves into companies, stationed principally at these forts. As soon as I joined the service, which was to aid in guarding the frontiers and in repelling these Indians, Captain Anderson stationed himself at one of these forts called Independence, situate on the Savannah, where we remained fourteen months in constant service against these Indians—in scouring the country and protecting the inhabitants. In the latter part of the year 1777 (*Note: Actually 1776*) (I think in December) General Williamson made a campaign into the Indian Country and defeated the Indians first at Sinico [sic] and next at Tomassa [sic], or some such name; which gave the frontier inhabitants an interval of peace, as the Indians were driven off.

A fort was built at Sinico [sic] called Rutledge, which was afterwards left under the command of Captain John Moore, with a company of Independints, as they were called. I was not in this campaign, having been left with others under Captain John Pickens (my brother) to guard the fort. But the most of my company, under Captain Anderson was in this expedition. After the return of Genl. Williamson, which I think was some time in January or February 1778, I was discharged by Capt. Anderson, as our services was not required any longer on the frontier. I think quiet certain that we were discharged in January 1778—having served from the month of October 1776 to January 1778, at least fifteen months. After my discharge, I immediately returned home (Abbeville) and engaged in waggoning for the American Army, and continued it until sometime in 1780, after the fall of Charleston, and the capitulation of Genl. Lincoln; but I am advised that this service (waggoning) gives no claim to a pension, and I pass over it. After the Brittish entered Charleston, they soon established forts throughout the country and seemed to have subjected it to the Brittish Crown. Resistance almost ceased, for the Tories and Brittish together had overrun the country; and, indeed many of the Whigs found it necessary to take protection, it was called under the Brittish—this was matter of necessity; and many of the most devoted Whigs done so, and particularly after the defeat of Gates at Camden in August of that year. Thus things remained until the arrival of Genl. Green [sic] from the North. This gave encouragement to the Whigs, and they began again to take up arms under their several leaders, in defense of their country. If I am not mistaken, Green [sic] arrived late in 1780 or first of 1781. Early in the spring of 1781 (I think in April) I with many others, volunteered under Capt. Caruthers, Major Alexander Noble, and Col. Robt. Anderson (the same who was formerly my Captain) and joined General Green [sic] in May, then before Ninety Six. We continued here with Green [sic], during the siege of this place, and until he was repulsed. Our regiment was actively employed during this siege, the particulars of which I could relate if necessary, but will only mention, that it was Green's [sic] first object to approach cautiously, and take the place by a regular siege, of which he had no doubt if time was allowed him. He pushed the siege rigorously until sometime in June, when he learned that a re-inforcement under Rawdon was hastily advancing to the relief of the place (then under Col. Cruger). This induced Genl. Green [sic] to hazard an assault, as it would be impossible to succeed by a regular siege before the arrival of Rawdon. The troops were immediately disposed for the assault. Col. Lee succeeded in forcing the works assigned to him, but in other parts our troops were repulsed, after much hard fighting and considerable loss, and Genl. Green [sic] called off his troops. The next day he raised the siege, crossed the Saluda and encamped on Little River.

In this siege, my brother in law; Captain Joseph Pickens (who was also a cousin) was killed. I served as a soldier in this siege, and remember the most of the particulars, but it is not necessary to relate them. On the retreat of Genl. Green [sic], the most of the militia dispersed for a few days, but reassembled about fifteen miles above Ninety-Six, and there joined Genl. Pickens (an own cousin to myself, being brother's children, and with whom I had been raised.) After joining Genl. Pickens, we marched toward North Carolina—crossed Broad River at Hamilton's Ford, and proceeded down towards the Congaree. Here I, with others were sent out as spies to ascertain the situation of the enemy then on their march toward Charleston. We (the spy company) came up with the enemy's rear guard, and attacked it; in which we killed five. But we could do no more than harass the rear and flanks, and embarrass their march as much as possible, which we continued to do for ten miles. We were on horse, as were all now under the command of Genl. Pickens. After this we marched up towards the Dutch Fork, into a settlement almost entirely Tories, and who had embodyed in considerable numbers near the line. After marching for sometime in search of them, I came to the determination of quiting the service for a while, as the support of an aged mother and a widowed sister (the wife of Capt. Joseph Pickens, Killed at Ninety-Six) now devolved on me, and required my attention. But at this time Captain Norwood called on me, and earnestly pressed me to join his company, and fill the place of one of his spies, who had been lately killed by the Tories. Although it was almost absolutely necessary for me to quit the service at this time, and attend to the support of mother and sister, who were left quiet destitute, yet as my service as a spy was thought to be of considerable importance, I determined to forego the duty I owed at home, and immediately joined Captain Norwood as a spy, and continued in this service for the term of six months. Captain Norwood was principally stationed on the frontier, between the white settlements and Indian Nation. It would be impossible for me to recount all the circumstances that transpired during this last service. W performed all the duties, and encountered all the hardships. As well as I now remember, I joined Capt. Caruthers as before stated from April 1781 until October of the same year. I served full six months under Norwood as spy, and was discharged sometime in April or May 1782 as well as my memory serves me, and since my papers were sent back for want of dates, etc. I have reflected much on the subject, and I do not think I am much wrong in any of the dates I have mentioned. The length of the tours of duty mentioned, I have put down at least as short as they really were, as I do not desire to receive for more than I deserve.

There is another circumstance which I omitted to mention in its right place: While I served under Colonel Anderson in 1781, we made an expedition to the frontier of Georgia in search of the celebrated Bill Cunningham who commanded a party of Tories and Indians, and also had done much mischief after arriving towards the frontier, Capt. Robt. Maxwell and myself were sent forward to spy out the position, strength of the party. We discovered them encamped on Cane Creek on Tugulo [sic] River. We immediately returned to our main body and gave the information. Colonel Anderson immediately planned the attack by dividing his force into three divisions, the right, left and centre. The right and left were committed to the command of Maxwell and myself, and the centre he commanded himself. In this form we advanced, with the sanguine hope of surprising them; but unfortunately, just before reaching their camp, one of the divisions accidentally met a party driving some cattle to the river, and fired upon them. This gave the alarm to the camp, and they instantly fled. Thus our project was defeated, after we supposed they were within our power.

In the year 1782 the Indians still continued troublesome on the Georgia frontiers. The inhabitants being weak and unable to protect themselves, dispatched messages into South Carolina for assistance. I again volunteered to aid these people, and with a company of volunteers, marched to the Oceony [sic] River, and there had a battle with the Indians across the river. They were defeated and we took several prisoners. We were only about three weeks in this service, and I only mention it as a continuation of events in which I was concerned, not as a part of my service for which I claim a pension, as the term was so short as not to be worth mentioning.

There were many other circumstances I could mention, but perhaps it is not necessary to mention them. Indeed, my memory is a little impaired, and I cannot fix the time, nor describe particularly, all the circumstances of my service; and particularly so at one time. In consequence of over exertions in my younger days, exposure, etc. I became blind, at an early age, and can now scarcely distinguish any object. My claim to pension is now submitted, and if granted, well; and if not, I can make out no better case, nor produce any further proof than that amassed; and would rather live without it than in my old age, and helpless condition, to be applying to the court from time to time to listen to my tale. I have endeavored to supply the details mentioned by the department, as well as my recollection would enable me.

I have no documentary evidence in my possession which would prove my service, nor do I know of any living witnesses by whom I can prove any portion of it, except one Patrick Cain and one John Drennon — the former of whom is so old and infirm that his attendance in court cannot be procured, and Drennon lives in another county (Caldwell) but the evidence of one or both of them I will endeavor to procure before this declaration is sent in. I never received a written discharge for the service that I have any recollection of, nor any pay, except an Indent of my claim against the Government amounting to 208 pounds sterling, which I sold to one Capt. Swift for a trifle as the claim was thought of little value. I surely relinquish every claim whatever to a pension or annuity except the present, and I declare that my name is not on the pension roll of the (?) of any state or territory whatever.

And the said court propounded to said applicant the following interrogations as prescribed by the War Department to which he made the subjoined answers in open court.

Question by the court 1. Where and in what year were you born?
Answer. *I was born in the District of Camden, State of South Carolina, the 18th day of October 1760.*
Question by the court 2. Have you any record of your age, and if so, where is it?
Answer. *I have the family record of my age at my house.*
Question by the court 3. Where were you living when called to service, where have you lived since the Revolutionary War, and where do you now live?
Answer. *When I entered the service I was living in Abbeville District, formerly Ninety Six, whither I had moved at an early age. I remained in that country until the year (?) when I removed to this country where I have lived ever since.*
Question by the court 4. How were you called into service; were you drafted, did you volunteer, or were you a substitute, and if a substitute for whom?
Answer. *All my service was as a volunteer.*
Question by the court 5. State the names of some of the regular officers, who were with the troops when you served, such Continental and militia regiments as you can recall, and the general circumstances of your service.
Answer. *While at the siege of Ninety Six I became acquainted with several regular officers, to wit, Col. Lee who commanded a legion of infantry, and Col. Campbell, Lt. Col. Duvall, and their regiments. The balance of my service was with militia, and I have already mentioned all the militia regiments which I knew as also the general circumstances of my service.*
Question of the court 6. Did you ever receive a discharge from the service and if so, by whom was it given, and what has become of it?
Answer. *I did not that I recollect of. My service was amongst volunteer troops where it was not usual. I received an Indent, as it was called, specifying the pay due me, but no formal written discharge.*
Question of the court 7. State the names of persons to whom you are known in your present neighborhood who can testify as to your character for veracity, and their belief of your services as a Soldier of the Revolution.
Answer. *I am known of a great many. I will name William Thompson, Christopher Haynes, William Gray, Robt. Hodge, James Craw, James Elder, and Joseph Hughes.*
Signed; Wm. G. PICKENS

We James Johnson a clergyman residing in the county of Livingston and State of Kentucky, and James McCawley, and James A. Whyte residing in the same county hereby certify, that we are well acquainted with the above named applicant; that we believe him to be seventy two years of age; that he is reputed and generally believed in the neighborhood where he resides to have been a soldier of the Revolution and that we concur as that opinion.

Sworn and subscribed the day and year aforesaid.
James Johnson
Jas. McCawley
J. A. Whyte

And the said court do hereby declare their opinion after the investigation of the matter, and after putting the interrogatoried prescribed by the War Department, that the above named applicant was a Revolutionary Soldier and served as he states. And the court further certifies that it appears to them, that James Johnson who has signed the presceding Certificate is a clergyman resident in the said county of Livingston and that James McCawley & James A. Whyte who have also signed the same are residents of the same county, and are credible persons, and that their statement is entitled to credit.

John Berry
Isham Clement
V B. Simpson

Pension Application, William Pickens, Mary Co. Tenn.
(National Archives No. S-3699)

Declaration in order to obtain the benefit of the act of Congress passed June 7th 1832.
State of Tennessee
Maury County
On this the 16th day of September, 1833, personally appeared in open court before James Hughes, John Mack, and John C. Wormley Esquires, Justices of said court being the court of Pleas and Quarter Sessions now sitting for the county of Maury in the State of Tennessee, William Pickens aged about

eighty four years who, being first duly sworn according to law, doth on his oath make the following declaration in order to obtain the benefit of the act of Congress passed June 7, 1832.

That he entered the service of the United States under the following named officers & served as herein stated.

That about the first of August 1776 (*Note: actually 1775*) he volunteered in the State of South Carolina, Abbeville (*Note: actually Ninety Six*) District in the company commanded by Thos. Langdon, Wm. Bowles, Lieutenant, and the whole commanded by Col. Drayton. he did not volunteer for any specific time. They marched to Ninety Six at which place they were stationed, or near that place, until the 19th of November of the same year at which time the battle of Ninety Six was fought & which battle this applicant was engaged. After which time they were marched to the Long Fork of Saluda River and were engaged in scouting ___ until they marched to Reedy River & routed the Tories that were encamped there. This was about the last of December in the same year, at which time they were discharged. The discharge was not in writing.

The following year the Indians committed frequent depredations and this applicant together with many families were compelled to erect a fort for their safety and defence called Fort Independence. They remained stationed in this fort about two or three months during which time this applicant was constantly engaged discharging the duties of a spy. Applicant was marched in October 1777 to Seneca as a guard at a treaty with the Indians, remained there a week, no treaty was affected. Returned to Fort Independence and remained there until May 1778. Marched to Due West Corner as guard at a treaty with the Indians, remained there about two weeks, when a treaty was affected with the Indians after which this applicant was discharged.

In February 1779 he volunteered in Abbyville District, South Carolina, in the company commanded by Capt. Robert Anderson, Col. Andrew Pickens & Gen. Andrew Williamson were the officers. Marched to Savana [sic] River, where a battle was fought with the Tories— after the battle they pursued the Tories to Kettle Creek in Georgia when they overtook the Tories and defeated them. He was then discharged but not in writing & returned home. This tour was about a month.

In the spring or early in the summer of 1780 as well as he now recollects this applicant again volunteered under Capt. Robert Anderson and joined Genl. Green [sic] at Ninety Six, remained untill the siege was raised and Green marched to Charleston. This applicant was transferred to a company of Rangers commanded by Capt. Coruthers and Lieutenant Francis Corlish. It was the duty of this company to range upon the frontiers which duty was performed for about five months when he was discharged & returned home. His discharge was not in writing. This was the last duty this applicant performed — that he has no documentary evidence of his services & he knows of no living person by whom he can prove his services. This applicant states that he was born in Virginia in Augusta County in 1749, but what time in that year he does not know. The record of his birth was destroyed by the Indians, but from information from his parents and others he believes that he was born in that year. His father removed to Abbyville district, South Carolina when this applicant was bout 15 years of age at which place he resided until the year 1807 when applicant removed to Maury County, State of Tennessee where he now does and ever since had resided. He hereby relinquishes every claim whatsoever to a pension or annuity except the present & declares that his name is not on the pension rolls of the agency of any state. Sworn to and subscribed the day & year aforesaid.

Thos. A. Porter, Clerk.
Signed his mark
(X)
Wm. Pickens

Supplementary statement (Affidavit) dated April 23, 1834 signed by himself states he served four months in 1776 from August To December. Served four months in 1777, July to October under Capt. John Pickens, and William Bloes, Lieutenant. Served one month in 1779, and five months in 1780.

AFFIDAVIT: We, Andrew Smith, a Clergyman residing in the county of Maury and State of Tennessee, and Ashly [sic] Moore, residing in the same, hereby certify that we are well acquainted with William Pickens who has subscribed and sworn to the above declaration and the we believe him to be about eighty four years of age. That he is reputed & believed in the neighborhood where he resides to have been a soldier of the revolution and that we concur in that opinion.

Sworn to and subscribed the day & year aforesaid.
Andrew Smith
Ashley Moore

Certificate of pension was issued May 16, 1834 at rate of $46.66 per annum, to commence March 4, 1831. Last payment made to ALEX MEECE, attorney, October 1834.

Appendix E

PENSION APPLICATION, JOHN WALLACE, RAY CO. MO.
(National Archives No. S-17178)

Declaration in order to obtain the benefit of the act of Congress passed June 7th 1832.

State of Missouri
Ray County

On this fifth day of August in the year of our Lord 1833 personally appeared in open court before the Justices of the County Court of Ray County in said State, John Wallace a resident of Ray County in the said State of Missouri aged Eighty seven years who being first duly sworn according to Law doth on his oath make the following declaration in order to obtain the benefit of the provision made by the act of Congress passed June 7th, 1832.

That in the month of June 1775 as I believe I entered the Service of the State of South Carolina as a Volunteer Militia man under the Immediate Command of Captain William Bratton. I cannot now recollect who was his Superior Officer: our forces were of Volunteer Mounts. We marched from York town in South Carolina into the then Cherokee County under the Orders of the Governor of South Carolina as I believe consisting of 300 mounted men we penetrated into the then Cherokee County we burnt the Indian towns of Toxaway and Seneca inhabited by the Cherokee Indians and passed through Keowee, Warhatchee and Couhatchee towns owned by the said Indians a distance of Eighty miles after serving in this campaign 60 days and returned to my residence in York County S. C.

And on the month of June 1778 or 1779 (I cannot now precisely recollect owing to the loss of my memory) Captain John Wallace a cousin of mine raised a Company of Rangers of about 26 men with whom I volunteered as I think he was then acting under the Orders of Gov. or Executive authority of the State of South Carolina we marched from York County in said State of South Carolina through the State of South Carolina into the Cherokee County where we were in the hopes of chastising some of the Indians of that nation who had been committing murders in the frontier settlements of South Carolina we fell in with a party of Cherokee Indians near the Parris Mountain we charged on the Indians and rescued the dead body of Mrs. Hight.

The Indians dispersed without much resistance and took refuge in one of their towns I was engaged in this tour of duty 60 days. I then returned to my residence of York County State of South Carolina. I had a discharge given by Captain Wallace which I lost in the manner hereinafter mentioned in crossing the Missouri River. I again entered the Service of the State of South Carolina as a volunteer private Militia man by order of the Executive of that State. We marched to meet the Enemy under the Command as we were told of Colonel Ferguson [Note: Major] who was traversing the States of South and North Carolina. I was in this Campaign commanded by Colonel Neel.

I was then next Engaged under Major Ross of South Carolina Militia by orders of the Government of that State we traversed some time in the month of June (but in what Year, I do not now recollect) into the State of Georgia in reconnoitering the British forces and as neared the British Camp of Briar Creek we were discovered the enemy charged upon us I was dismounted and escaped by swimming Savannah River I made the best of my way on foot to General Williamson's Camp where I joined my former Commander Ross. The situation of the British being now discovered we returned home to York town S. C. after a tour of 60 days on my part as I believe. We marched from York town S. C. and were joined not far from King's [sic] Mountain by Colonels Shelby and Campbell with some Virginia Militia. The result of that action is well known I cannot recollect at what time I entered into the Service in this Campaign. I am Old and have Lost my memory but to the best of my Knowledge I was out in Service in all the full space of 60 days.

I was next a Soldier in Captain William Bratton's Company as a Volunteer by the direction of the Governor of South Carolina. We marched from York town in S. C., in the pursuit of some Tories under the Command of a certain William Cunningham we met them after a march of one day and a night put them to flight at a place called the Snow Camp Battle. I well recollect there was some snow on the ground but what time of the Year I do not know but think it was about Christmas but do not recollect what Year. I was gone in this Campaign 30 days as I do sincerely believe I was Commanded in this Campaign by Colonel Neel as I above mentioned of the S. C. militia soon after my return from the Last mentioned tour I removed to Abbeville S. C. about 120 miles from my former Residence. I was next engaged in Captain Baskin's Company spying. I served with him the full space of six months I believe we went in this Campaign by the order of General Pickens of South Carolina.

Next served under Major Noble who was an officer under Colonel Anderson & General Pickens S. C. Militia we marched from Abbeville in the State of Tennessee with about two or 300 militia under the command of Colonel McCall S. C. Militia and proceeded to Reedy Branch in S. C. we there had a meeting with some British and Tories wherein I was wounded & taken prisoner taken to the post of 96

I staid in close confinement Ironed to the floor of my Dungeon for three months. I was absent at this tour for 14 months from the time I started from Abbeville until I was released as a prisoner & sent to Charleston S. C., and discharged therefrom and sent to Jamestown in Virginia and from there to Williamsburg to an hospital said to be made out of the Governor's house there I was discharged or Exchanged I was absent 14 months as above stated in this Campaign. I remained at my residence in Abbeville S. C. greatly enfeebled by my confinement in prison. I was sent for by General Pickens to keep the Tories from killing me during my absence on the Last Campaign the Tories robbed my house of bed & bedding two Horses and a wagon which property never was restored by me. I have served in all the space of five years putting all my services together there are some Campaigns I have omitted here from the want of memory to trace them more particularly. I am poor and old and needy I came to the State of Missouri about the year 1817 and in the Year 1820 I came to Ray County State of Missouri where I now reside in crossing the River Missouri in the month of May 1820 I lost all my evidence of service with my wife and three Grand children and have neither house nor home wherein to hide my aged head nor can I prove them by any living witnesses.

By reason of the Loss of my Memory

State of Missouri,

County of Ray:

Personally appeared before me the undersigned a Justice of the Peace within and for said County & State John Wallace who being duly sworn deposeth and saith that by reason of old age and consequent loss of memory I cannot swear precisely positively to the precise length of his Service but according to the best of his Knowledge or recollection he served not less than the periods mentioned below and in the following grades for the space of five years I served as a Soldier on the Continental line or South Carolina militia and for such service I claim a pension as a common Soldier and I believe him to be [Note: honest and believable].

S/ Sebourn J. Miller, J. P.

State of Missouri County of Ray

I George Woodward Clerk of the County Court within and for the County of aforesaid do certify that Sebourn J. Miller whose name is attached and subscribed to the foregoing affidavit is a Justice of the Peace duly commissioned & the signature annexed is his genuine Signature.

In Testimony whereof I have set my hand and affixed my seal of Office this 18th day of June in the year A.D. 1833.

S/ George Woodward, Clerk

I John Wallace hereby relinquish every claim whatever to a pension or annuity, except the present, and I do declare that my name is not on the Pension roll of any Agency in any State whatever and during the said time I was not Employed in any civil pursuit nor cannot prove my services by any person living.

S/ John Wallace

In the Ray County Court Missouri August term 1833

Present Henry Jacobs and William Thornton Jr. the Justices thereof which is a Court of record the said Court did propound the following interrogatories to said John Wallace who was present

Question 1st: In what Year and where were you born

Answer: I was born in the year 1746 in the State of Pennsylvania

Question 2nd: Have you any record of Your age and if so where is it —- Ansr: I have none

Quest. 3Rd: Where were you living when called into Service, where have you lived since the revolutionary war, and where do you now live

Answer: I lived in the State of South Carolina when called into action or service: I have since lived in that state and Mississippi and Missouri & now live in Ray County Missouri

ditto 4th: How were you called into Service were you drafted, did you volunteer or were you a substitute and if a substitute for whom

Answer: I volunteered

5th: State the names of some of the regular officers, who were with the troops where you served, such Continental and militia regiments as you can recollect and the General Circumstances of your Services

Answer: I was acquainted with a Captain George Liddle of the regular service who was a prisoner along with me in confinement at post 96 all the others were embodied in my narrative as well as I can recollect

6th: Did you ever receive a discharge from the Service and if so, by whom was it given and what has become of it?

Answer: I have received a discharge from Captain William Bratton, Captain Baskin and General Pickens which discharge is lost together with my wife & three grand children and property in crossing the River Missouri on the 17 May 1820.

7th: State the names of persons to whom you are known in your present neighborhood, and who can testify as to your character for veracity and their belief of your service as a Soldier of the Revolution.

Answer: I am known to General William Thompson who is Brigadier of the State Militia, I am also known to Captain George Woodward who is the Clerk of the County Court of Ray County who can testify to my character for veracity and their belief of my services as a Soldier in the revolution.

We the undersigned residents of Ray County and State of Missouri being called on by the Declarant John Wallace to state here in open Court our Opinions of his character for veracity of said Declarant, do say that we can testify to his character for veracity, and we believe that he served in the Revolutionary war.

Sworn to and Open court.
S/ George Woodward
S/ Wm. P. Thompson
Attest: S/ George Woodward, Clerk
Attest: S/ Wm. Thornton, Jr. Justice R. C.

Pension Application, Thomas Young, Union Dist. SC.
(National Archives No. S-10309)

Declaration in order to obtain the benefit of the act of Congress passed June 7th 1832.

State of South Carolina
Union District

On this to wit the 17th day of April in the year of our Lord 1838 personally appeared in open court before John J. Pratt Judge of the Court of Ordinary of Union District in the State of South Carolina, Thomas Young, a resident of the aforesaid State & District & aged 74 years who being first duly sworn in open Court according to law, doth on his oath, make the following declaration in order to obtain the benefit of provisions made by the act of Congress passed the seventh day of June in the year of our Lord 1832, that he volunteered in the service of the State of South Carolina under Captain Benjamin Jolly of Col. Thomas Brandon's regiment about the last of May or the first of June in the year 1780. At the time of his volunteering he was a resident of Ninety Six District which place of residence is in that subdivision now known by the name of Union District. He marched thence to North Carolina in Rowan County & returned in the latter part of the Summer to York District, or the territory now known by that name, & was engaged in a skirmish with a party of Tories at Stallion's house. He thence returned to North Carolina & met Col. Williams above Charlotte & was united to his Corps & after uniting with other troops proceeded to King's [sic] Mountain & was actively engaged during that remarkable conflict. After this engagement, the Corps to which he was attached returned to their homes or to the neighborhood of their former residences but still remaining on duty subject to the command of their officers. His next adventure was that of uniting under the same officers with General Morgan at Grindal Shoals on Pacolet River & marching thence to Cowpens where he was engaged in that engagement against Col. Tarlton on the 17th January 1781. In this engagement he received many severe wounds & was made a prisoner & carried near the camp of Lord Cornwallis. Whence he made his escape, he was then disabled by his wounds for near one month. He then volunteered under Captain Joseph Hughes & marched to Buck Head & attended the siege of that fort. But before that fort was taken, went off with a detachment against Orangeburg & took that fort under the command of Genl. Sumter. He was thence under the command of Sumter and marched to Granby on Congaree River where he was dismissed from service. He then proceeded voluntarily to Ninety Six & joined his old company under Captain Jolly, who was under the command of Col. Brandon of Pickens' Brigade. He continued in the siege laid to this fort until the siege was raised. He was then detached with the Corps to which he belonged to scour the up country & prevent the mischief & depredations of the Tories, where he continued in service to the end of the War. The Court propounded the following interrogatories:

Where & in what year were you born?
Answer: 17th January 1764 in Laurens District in this State.

Have you any record of your age?
Answer: No, but Christopher Brandon says that he has & that I was born in February 1764.

Where were you living at the time of your volunteering? Where have you lived since the Revolutionary War & where do you now live?

Answer: I have lived since my first recollection in this District & in the same neighborhood.
How were you called into service?
Answer: I volunteered.
State the names of some of the regular officers who were with the troops where you served.
Answer: I have as fully as my recollection will permit answered this interrogatory in my declaration.
Did you ever receive a discharge from the service?
Answer: No. I never did. I continued until the end of the war when I was formally dismissed from service, without any written discharge.

He hereby relinquishes every claim whatever to a pension or an annuity that is incompatible with the present claim and he declares that his name is not on the pension roll of any agency in any State, except that of South Carolina on the Roll of Invalid Pensioners under the Act of Congress passed the 4th day of February 1822.
S/ Thomas Young
Sworn to & subscribed the day & year aforesaid.
S/ J. J. Pratt, judge of the Court of Ordy.

F: Pickens, Hillhouse and the Cherokee Ancestry of the Author

See the following two pages of a genealogy chart.

Appendix F

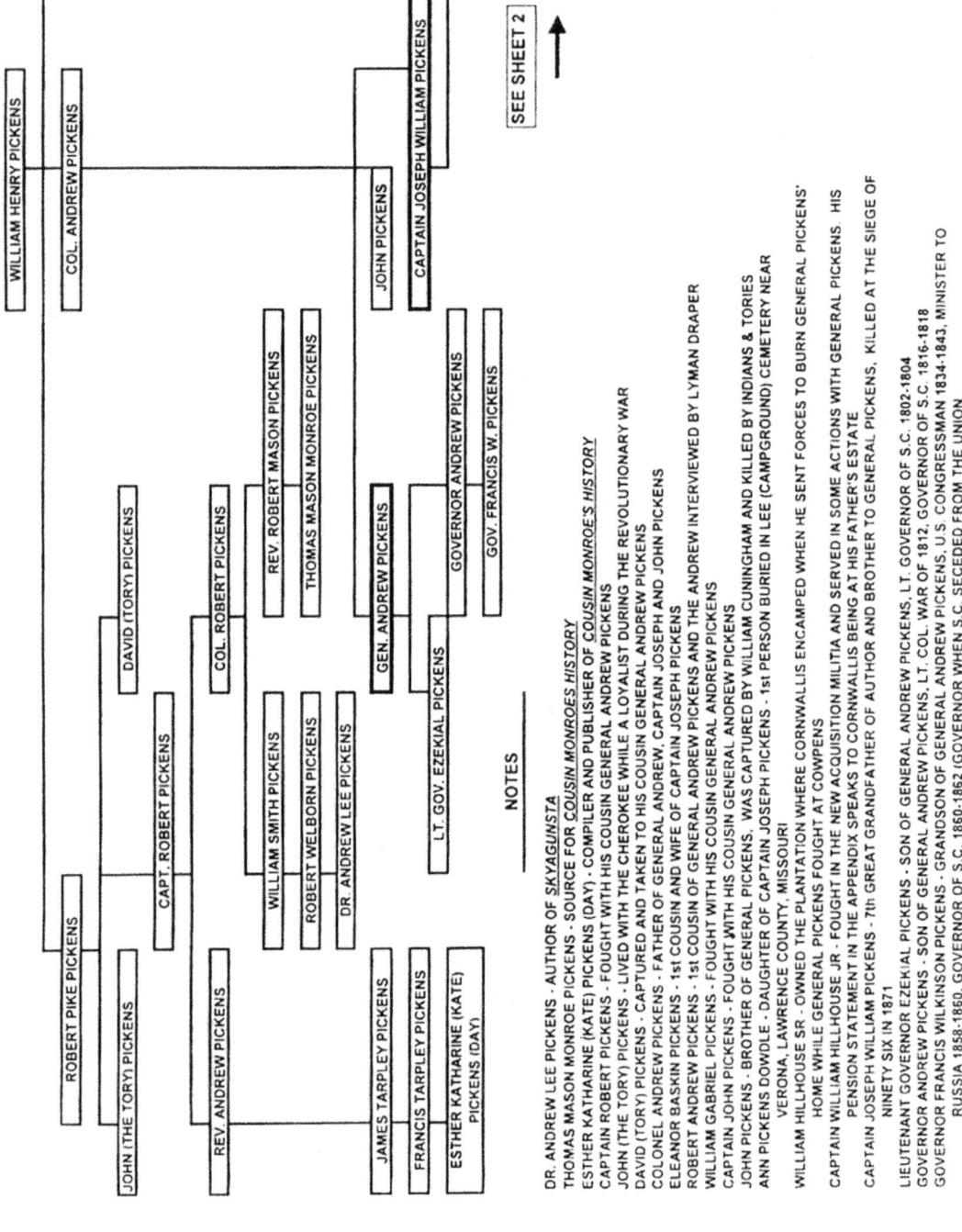

NOTES

DR. ANDREW LEE PICKENS - AUTHOR OF SKYAGUNSTA
THOMAS MASON MONROE PICKENS - SOURCE FOR COUSIN MONROE'S HISTORY
ESTHER KATHARINE (KATE) PICKENS (DAY) - COMPILER AND PUBLISHER OF COUSIN MONROE'S HISTORY
CAPTAIN ROBERT PICKENS - FOUGHT WITH HIS COUSIN GENERAL ANDREW PICKENS
JOHN (THE TORY) PICKENS - LIVED WITH THE CHEROKEE WHILE A LOYALIST DURING THE REVOLUTIONARY WAR
DAVID (TORY) PICKENS - CAPTURED AND TAKEN TO HIS COUSIN GENERAL ANDREW PICKENS
COLONEL ANDREW PICKENS - FATHER OF GENERAL ANDREW, CAPTAIN JOSEPH AND JOHN PICKENS
ELEANOR BASKIN PICKENS - 1st COUSIN AND WIFE OF CAPTAIN JOSEPH PICKENS
ROBERT ANDREW PICKENS - 1st COUSIN OF GENERAL ANDREW PICKENS AND THE ANDREW INTERVIEWED BY LYMAN DRAPER
WILLIAM GABRIEL PICKENS - FOUGHT WITH HIS COUSIN GENERAL ANDREW PICKENS
CAPTAIN JOHN PICKENS - FOUGHT WITH HIS COUSIN GENERAL ANDREW PICKENS
JOHN PICKENS - BROTHER OF GENERAL PICKENS, WAS CAPTURED BY WILLIAM CUNINGHAM AND KILLED BY INDIANS & TORIES
ANN PICKENS DOWDLE - DAUGHTER OF CAPTAIN JOSEPH PICKENS - 1st PERSON BURIED IN LEE (CAMPGROUND) CEMETERY NEAR VERONA, LAWRENCE COUNTY, MISSOURI
WILLIAM HILLHOUSE SR - OWNED THE PLANTATION WHERE CORNWALLIS ENCAMPED WHEN HE SENT FORCES TO BURN GENERAL PICKENS' HOME WHILE GENERAL PICKENS FOUGHT AT COWPENS
CAPTAIN WILLIAM HILLHOUSE JR - FOUGHT IN THE NEW ACQUISITION MILITIA AND SERVED IN SOME ACTIONS WITH GENERAL PICKENS. HIS PENSION STATEMENT IN THE APPENDIX SPEAKS TO CORNWALLIS BEING AT HIS FATHER'S ESTATE
CAPTAIN JOSEPH WILLIAM PICKENS - 7th GREAT GRANDFATHER OF AUTHOR AND BROTHER TO GENERAL PICKENS, KILLED AT THE SIEGE OF NINETY SIX IN 1871
LIEUTENANT GOVERNOR EZEKIAL PICKENS - SON OF GENERAL ANDREW PICKENS, LT. GOVERNOR OF S.C. 1802-1804
GOVERNOR ANDREW PICKENS - SON OF GENERAL ANDREW PICKENS, LT. COL. WAR OF 1812, GOVERNOR OF S.C. 1816-1818
GOVERNOR FRANCIS WILKINSON PICKENS - GRANDSON OF GENERAL ANDREW PICKENS, U.S. CONGRESSMAN 1834-1843, MINISTER TO RUSSIA 1858-1860, GOVERNOR OF S.C. 1860-1862 (GOVERNOR WHEN S.C. SECEDED FROM THE UNION

Appendix F

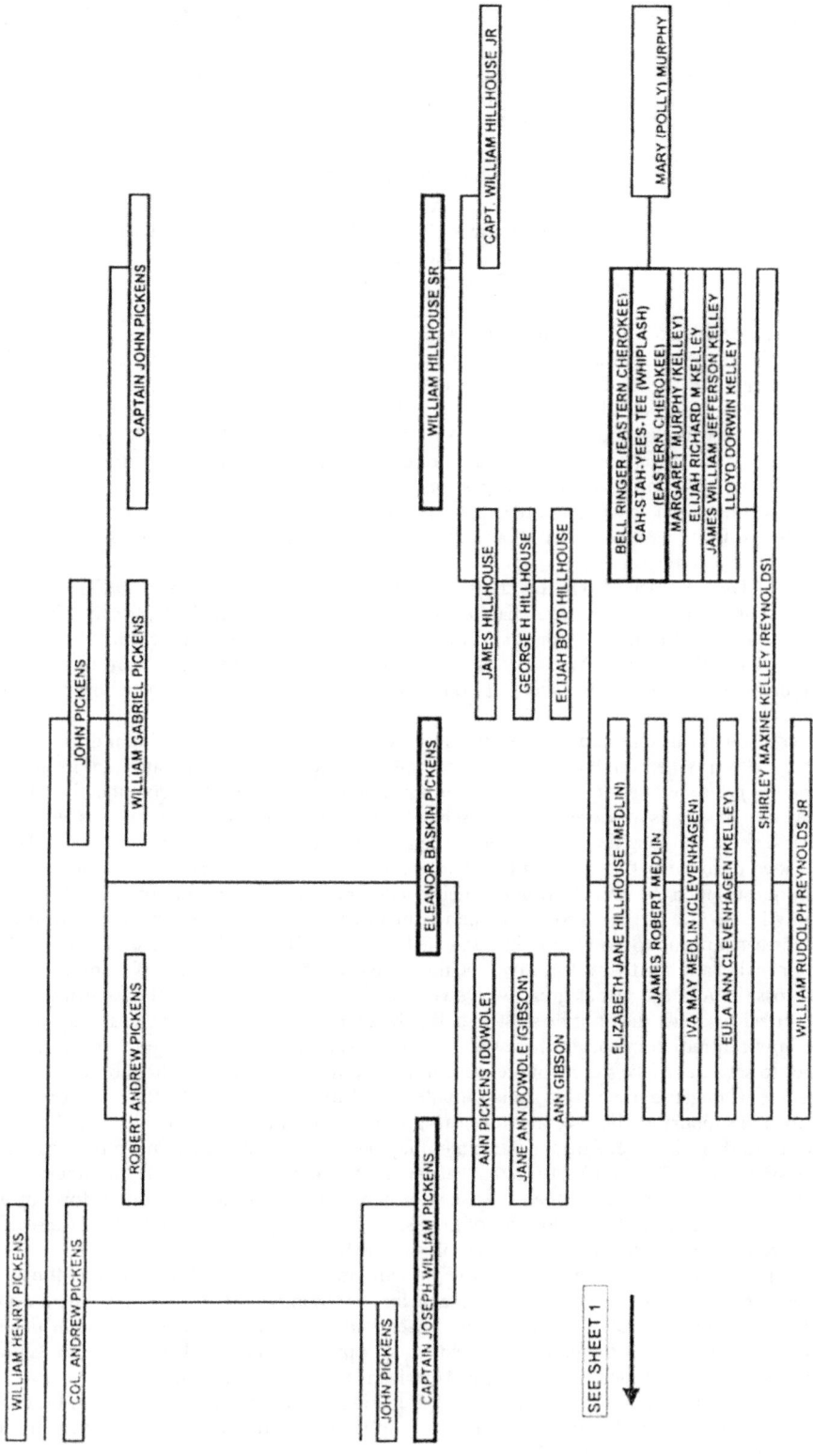

G: Articles from Revolutionary Era Publications

The following articles were transcribed by the author from the original issues. They include the original spellings, grammar, and style, except that the "*ſ*" representing the old style long form of the letter "s" is replaced by the standard "s."

THE LONDON CHRONICLE
VOL. XXXVINo. 2773
From THURSDAY, September 15, to SATURDAY, September 17, 1774
Page 268
To the PRINTER *of the* LONDON CHRONICLE

SIR,

THE inconsistencies of the Boston Agents and American Emissaries are beyond example. For this month past they have been bullying and insulting us with the plenty they enjoyed; boasting that their sheep and their flour, their fish and their rice, came in faster than they could use them. That that was the fortieth day of their ports having been shut, and notwithstanding this they want for nothing, they fear nothing, they will pay nothing for the private property they have destroyed, nor make the smallest submission to our government; but set us at open defiance. After all this, stoutness, the next letters hold them out to us as objects of our compassion; represent the miserable condition they are in, as in danger of starving; wish to set forward a subscription for their relief, and call upon particular New England Merchants by name to begin it; and our Coffee-house Politicians read each of these accounts, and implicitly believe them both.

Still more — The very men who in their letters to America advised the non-exportation scheme, (which in reality means nothing more or less than a resolution not to pay their debts, for they have no other means of paying them but their exports, and which therefore is only a softer term for their resolving to cheat their English Creditors,) these very men, I say, probably are the same persons as now insult our common sense with proposals of a subscription for the relief of these Americans whom they have been advising to cheat us.

However insolent this may appear, it is but similar to many other parts of their conduct. In the beginning of the last war, when the French were attacking the Americans, and threatening, in the phrase of those times, *to push the English into the sea*, then the Colonists were most importunately calling out to us for help; and so long as we were taxing ourselves to pay the interest of all the millions we were spending in their defence, so long they acknowledge themselves to be fellow-subjects and a part of ourselves, and persuaded us to think that fighting for them was only fighting for ourselves. But no sooner had we by our conquests taken the French from off their backs, and placed them in a state of security, but they instantly fly in the face of their Protectors, and tell us that they are different people from us; that our government has nothing to do with them; and that King, Lords, and Commons, have no authority to lay taxes or make laws for them; for, say they, they live three thousand miles off from us. Was not the distance cross the Atlantic just as great twelve years ago as it is now? And, if the Americans were then a part of ourselves, must they not be so still; and subject to our government just as much as they were then? Yet how contradictory soever these two propositions may be, the good people of England believe them; and, to save themselves the trouble of thinking, contentedly swallow them both.

The people of England are at this time annually taxed to the amount of fifteen hundred thousand pounds, for the support of the several American governments, and the payment of the interest of the money spent in their defence. And the Parliament laying taxes on Great Britain for the Americans use, is very consistent with English liberty: But if Parliament think it reasonable, that the Americans should contribute towards the support of their own government, and pay some small duties for that purpose; that, they tell us, is contrary to the liberties of Englishmen; and hoping that we shall prove weak enough to be frighted by it, threaten that they will revolt rather than pay it.

After having run ourselves so many millions in debt, and employed at least thirty of those millions in *their* defence and support, instead of thanking us for the blood and treasure we have spent upon *them*, they upbraid us with our debt; and their chief adviser, bent upon the destruction of the British government, holds up our debt to the view of the world, as a proof of our debility, and as an invitation to French and Spaniards to attack us, and to his Americans to rebel against us.

Yet under all their insults, the good people of England look on with indifference; and are taught to think of an attempt to dissolve and break up the Empire, as nothing more than an exertion of *British liberty, and the rights of Englishmen.* B.C.

THE LONDON CHRONICLE:
OR,
UNIVERSAL EVENING POST.
VOL. XVINo. 1233
From TUESDAY, November 13, to THURSDAY, November 15, 1764
Page 470
Thursday, Nov. 15.
AMERICA
Charles Town, Sep. 13 [1764]

By letters from Fort Boone at Long-Canes we are informed, that on the 24th past Capt. Calhoun [meaning Patrick], of the Rangers, received information from two Cherokee Indians, that they had discovered some Indians, which they took for Creeks, with two horses, at some distance. Capt. Calhoun immediately dispatched his Lieutenant, with a party, accompanied by one of the Indian Informants as a guide; they soon came up with an Indian camp, round which, as there was nobody in it, they placed themselves in ambush, in order to seize the Indians on their return, which happened soon after, when the Lieutenant took and made prisoner the head of the gang, who, to his great surprise, proved to be a Cherokee from Toogoloo [sic], as were likewise the seven others with him: The Lieutenant took the horses, which he knew to be the property of one of the inhabitants near Long-Canes. We are told a very shameful traffick has been carried on with the Indians for horses, which they are induced to steal in the settlements.

The Delawares, shawnese [sic], and other northern tribes of the enemy Indians, continue their incursions on the Cherokees: Two of the enemy were lately killed in the Upper Cherokee Towns.

THE LONDON CHRONICLE:
OR,
UNIVERSAL EVENING POST.
VOL. XVINo. 1233
From TUESDAY, November 13, to THURSDAY, November 15, 1764
Note: The following article concerns property of General Cornwallis' father who died in 1762 — General Cornwallis had been in America to fight the French and Indian War and finally made it home to settle the estate.
Page 469
To be sold at Auction by Mr. PRESTAGE,
On the PREMISES,
On Wednesday the 28th of November instant,
Punctually at One o'Clock.

A substantial, large, and well-built Brick House belonging to the Right Hon. EARL CORNWALLIS, deceased, situated in Hill street, Berkeley Square. Containing three large Rooms on a Floor, elegantly fitted up with Statuary and other Marble Chimney Pieces, rich carved Ornaments, exceeding good Offices, Coach Houses for three Carriages, and Stabling for eight Horses, a large Kitchen, Laundry, and Wash-house, at a proper Distance from the House, with several Fixtures thereunto belonging.

The said Premises are in very good Repair, and held by Lease, Seventy-four Years of which are unexpired, subject to a Ground Rent of 18l. 10s. per Annum.

Likewise on Thursday the 29th Instant, and the following Day, will be sold all the genuine and rich HOUSEHOLD FURNITURE; consisting of Genoa Damask, Mohair, and other Furniture, French Chairs, Sophas [sic], large Pier, and other Glasses, Variety of Mahogany in Presles, Book Cases, Tables, and Chairs, Marble Tables, Screens, Carpets, and a large Quantity of Kitchen Furniture.

The House and Furniture will be publickly viewed on Friday the 23[d] Instant, to the Time of Sale (Sunday excepted.)

Printed Particulars, and the Dimensions of each Room, with a Catalogue of the Furniture, will then be delivered gratis, at the Place of Sale; and at Mr. Prestage's, in Savile Row.

The London Chronicle

VOL. XLIX No. 3797
From SATURDAY, March 31, to TUESDAY, April 3, 1781
Page 313
MONDAY, APRIL 1. (Note: Actually was April 2.)
From the LONDON GAZETTE, *March 31.*
Whitehall, March 31.

BY the Mail of Sandwich Packet, which failed from Charles-Town the 28th of February, Dispatches were this Day received by Lord George Germain, One of his Majesty's Principal Secretaries of State, from the Earl Cornwallis and Lieutenant Colonel Balfour, of which the following are Copies and Extras.

Camp on Turkey Creek, Broad River
January 18.

(NOTE: *This first short note is Cornwallis' cover memo to Lord George Germain to accompany a copy of the Cornwallis letter to Sir Henry Clinton. George Germain was Secretary of State for the American Colonies in the cabinet of Prime Minister Lord Frederick North. There were two other Secretaries of States: one for Europe and one for the rest of the world other than America. The letters from Balfour regarding his Race to the Dan Report are transcribed separately.*)

My Lord,

I THINK it necessary to transmit to your Lordship a Copy of my Letter to Sir Henry Clinton, lest the exaggerated Accounts from the Rebels should reach Europe before your Lordship could hear from New York. I shall only say, in Addition to what I have said to Sir Henry Clinton, that this Event was extremely unexpected, for the greatest Part of the Troops that were engaged, had, upon all former Occasions, behaved with the most distinguished Gallantry.

Extract of a Letter from Earl Cornwallis to Sir Henry Clinton, dated, Camp on Turkey Creek, Broad River, January 18, 1781.

IN my Letter of the 6th of this Month I had the Honor to inform your Excellency, that I was ready to begin my March for North Carolina; having been delayed for some Days by a diversion made by the Enemy towards Ninety Six. General Morgan still remained on the Pacolet; his Corps, by the best Accounts I could get, consisted of about 500 men, Continental and Virginia State Troops, and 100 Cavalry under Colonel Washington, and Six or Seven Hundred Militia; but that Body is so fluctuating, that it is impossible to ascertain its Number, within some Hundreds, for Three Days following. Lieutenant Colonel Tarleton, with the Legion and Corps annexed to it, consisting of about 300 Cavalry and as many Infantry, and the 1^{ft} Battalion of the 71^{ft} Regiment, and 1 Three Pounder, had already passed the Broad River for the Relief of Ninety Six. I therefore directed Lieutenant Colonel Tarleton to march on the West of Broad River to endeavor to strike a Blow at General Morgan, and, at all Events, to oblige him to pass the Broad River. I likewise ordered that he should take with him the 7th Regiment, and 1 Three Pounder, which were marching to reinforce the Garrison of Ninety Six, as long as he should think their Services could be useful to him. The Remainder of the Army marched between the Broad River and the Catawba. As General Green [sic] had quitted Mecklenburgh County, and crossed the Peedee, I made not the least Doubt that General Morgan would retire on our advancing.

The Progress of the Army was greatly impeded by heavy Rains which swelled the River and Creeks; yet Lieutenant Colonel Tarleton conducted his March so well, and got so near to General Morgan, who was retreating before him, as to make it dangerous for him to pass Broad River; and came up with him at Eight o'Clock A. M. on the 17th Instant. Every Thing now bore the most promising Aspect; the Enemy were drawn up in an open Wood, and, having been lately joined by some Militia, were more numerous; but the different Quality of the Corps under Lieutenant Colonel Tarleton's Command, and his great Superiority in Cavalry, left him no Room to Doubt of the most brilliant Success. The Attack was begun by the First Line of Infantry, consisting of the 7th Regiment, the Infantry of the Legion, and Corps of Light Infantry annexed to it; a Troop of Cavalry was placed on each Flank; the 1^{ft} Battalion of the 71^{ft}, and the Remainder of the Cavalry, formed the Reserve. The Enemy's Line soon gave Way, and their Militia quitted the Field; but our Troops having been thrown into some Disorder by the Pursuit, General Morgan's Corps faced about, and gave them a heavy Fire: This unexpected Event occasioned the utmost Confusion in the First Line.

The Two Three-pounders were taken, and I fear the Colours of the 7th Regiment shared the same Fate. In Justice to the Detachment of Royal Artillery I must here observe, that no terrors could induce them to abandon their Guns, and they were all either killed or wounded in the Defence of them. Lieutenant Colonel Tarleton assembled Fifty of his Cavalry, and, being animated by the Bravery of the Officer who had so often led them to Victory, charged and repulsed Colonel Washington's Horse, retook the Baggage of the Corps, and cut to Pieces the Detachment of the Enemy that had taken Possession of it, and, after destroying what they could not conveniently bring off, retired with the Remainder unmolested to Hamilton's Ford, near the Mouth of Bullock's Creek.

The Loss of our Cavalry is inconsiderable, but I fear about 400 of the Infantry are either killed, wounded or taken. I will transmit the particular Account of the Loss as soon as it can be ascertained.

I shall direct Lieutenant Colonel Balfour to transmit a Copy of this Letter, by the first Opportunity, to the Secretary of State.

THE GENTLEMAN'S MAGAZINE
July 1780
Page 339
Advices from America *and the* West-Indies

The Following Letter from Sir Henry Clinton *to Lord* Geo. Germaine *came by Col.* Bruce *in the* South Carolina *packet.*

Charles-Town, June 4, 1780
MY LORD,

I HAD the honour in my dispatch by the Earl of Lincoln to communicate to your Lordship the surrender of Charlestown. I am now able to give your Lordship a return of the prisoners taken, amounting (exclusive of near a thousand sailors in arms) to 5618 men.

I informed your Lordship, that Lieut. Gen. Earl Cornwallis was to march up the north side of Santee, whilst another corps moved up the hither shore of that river, towards the district of Ninety-six. These corps are in motion, as well as one up the Savannah river in Georgia.

The troops immediately under his Lordships command have pressed so effectually upon a body of the rebels which remained in the province, that the Earl, by detaching his corps of cavalry, and with them the legion infantry (mounted), has completed the destruction of every-thing in arms against us in this province.

Lieut.-Col. Tarleton headed this detachment, whose celerity in performing a march of near an hundred miles in two days, was equal to the ardour with which they attacked the enemy. These refusing the terms which were offered them, were charged and defeated, with the loss of one hundred and seventy-two killed, and some taken, together with the remaining field artillery of the southern army, their colours and baggage.

With the greatest pleasure I further report to your Lordship, that the inhabitants from every quarter repair to the detachments of the army, and to this garrison, to declare their allegiance to the King, and to offer their services, in arms, in support of his government. In many instances they have brought prisoners their former oppressors or leaders; and I may venture to assert, that there are few men in South Carolina who are not either our prisoners, or in arms with us.

I have also the satisfaction to receive corresponding accounts that the loyalists in the back parts of North Carolina are arming. I dare entertain the hopes that Lord Cornwallis's preference on the frontier, and perhaps within the province, will call back its inhabitants from their state of error and disobedience. If a proper naval force can be collected, I purpose sending a small expedition into Cape Fear river, to savour the revolution I look for higher in the country.

I am, with the troops I could take, quitting the harbour of Charles-Town, on my way to New-York, hoping no foreign armament can yet have reached the coast, or have been able to attempt any-thing in our absence against that place.

Lieut.-Col. Bruce, my aid de camp, will have the honour of presenting these dispatches to your Lordship. He has served with distinction during the whole war, and is well able to satisfy your Lordship in any inquiries you may be pleased to make concerning the late operations in Carolina.

Your Lordship will receive by Major-General Prevost, who fails in a few days, the account from Earl Cornwallis of what shall have occurred to that time.

I have the honour to be, &c.
H. CLINTON

The London Chronicle
VOL. XLIX No. 3762
From TUESDAY, January 9, to THURSDAY, January 11, 1781
Page 39
AMERICAN NEWS
From the ROYAL SOUTH CAROLINA GAZETTE
Charlestown, Nov. 17 (NOTE Meaning 1780)

LAST Saturday, Lieut. M'Leod, of the Royal Artillery, arrived in town from the camp at Wemyss-borough, and brought with him the following agreeable and important intelligence:

That the Earl Cornwallis having dispatched Lieutenant Colonel Tarleton with part of the legion, and 63^d regiment, in quest of Sumpter, that active and enterprising officer, on the 20th inst came up with Mr. Sumpter's rear guard on the Enoree; they were immediately attaked, and cut up to a man. Colonel Tarleton having discovered Sumter's tract, immediately pursued him with a great rapidity, and came up with him at Black Stolks [sic] on Tyger River. The force of the rebels consisted of about 1000 men, headed by Sumpter, Clarke, Lacy, and Brennan, who were posted on advantageous ground. All the force Colonel Tarleton could bring up, was, 190 cavalry, and 90 infantry. The attack commenced, and notwithstanding the superior numbers of the rebels, and the advantage of the ground, they could not withstand the ardent bravery of the King's troops, but after some resistance were totally defeated and dispersed; and their horses, waggons, &c all taken.—The slaughter amongst them, which was very great, would have been much more so, if the night had not favoured their escape. Sumpter is dangerously wounded, and it is thought must long before this have fallen into Colonel Tarleton's hands. Our loss consists of fifty killed and wounded. Amongst the former are, Lieutenants Gibson and Cope, of the 63^d; and among the latter, Major Money, and Mr. Monro, of the legion, but neither of them dangerously. Mr. M'Leod was just upon the point of setting off when Col. Tarleton's dispatches to Lord Cornwallis arrived; so it is propable our next advices from the country will bring further particulars of this interesting and fortunate event.

By late advices from the back country we are informed, that Major Wemyss, with 160 men in the sixty third regiment, on the 9th inst. Came up with a Mr. Sumpter who had about 400 men with him, near Fish Dam Ford: The rebels were surprised and put to the route, and several of them who fled towards the Ford were pushed into the river; but it unfortunately happened, that, at the very beginning of the action, Major Wemyss was so badly wounded, that he was obliged to be carried to the rear. By this time the rebels had fled on all sides, and the King's troops formed upon the ground; but it being thought disadvantageous, it was resolved to quit it, and Major Wemyss's situation not admitting of his removal, he was left at a farm house in the neighborhood. The next morning the rebels, not finding themselves pursued, began to collect themselves, and with great caution appeared on their old ground. Mr. Sumpter having received information where Major Wemyss had been left, came to him about twelve o'clock and gave him a parole. We are happy to inform the Public, that the wound Major Wemyss has received is not dangerous, and he hath arrived at the camp at Wemyss-borough. Our loss upon this occasion, was 1 serjeant and 5 rank and file killed; and, besides the Major, 1 serjeant and 15 rank and file wounded. The rebels say they had near 20 killed, and fifty-two wounded.

The London Chronicle
VOL. XLIX No. 3766
From THURSDAY, January 18, to SATURDAY, January 20, 1781
Page 65
For the London Chronicle
To Lieut. Gen. Sir W———M H———E
LETTER IV.

In my former Letters (See Dec.30, 1780, p. 617; Jan. 6, 1781, p. 17; and Jan. 13, p. 41) I have said, that the great rule, which you laid down to yourself, seems to have been, to gain the confidence of your Sovereign, by repeating declarations of your zeal in his service: by shewing to him in all your letters, that you perfectly well knew your duty; and what was proper to be done for subduing the rebellion; and thereby leading his Majesty to conclude, that you intended to do it. In all your Letters, previous to the campaign of 1776, both while you was at Boston, and after you was driven out of it, you are perpetually writing, that nothing was more to be desired by you, than to bring the rebels to a decisive action.

In words, it is impossible for you to express a more determined resolution to do so: By your actions, Sir, it seems impossible for you to shew a more fixed and determined resolution not to do it. Five times did the rebels put it in your power to shut them up, and force them to a decisive action: five times did your superior care provide a way for them to escape without any decisive action at all. To this end, I have said, you invariably attacked them on the side opposite to that by which only they could escape. These are facts, Sir, which have already been established by your conduct at Bunkers Hill, and at Long Island. In the first, Col. Abercrombie founded the water near the causeway before-hand, as if from a presentiment of his own and a thousand other brave men's fall, if you did not go thither. Every mariner in Boston could have told you there was depth enough. But you must then have shut the rebels up, and not a man of them could have escaped. You chose therefore to attack them on the opposite side; and left the way open for them to go quietly off.

At Long Island your good disposition towards the American brethren was still more apparent: you promised his Majesty, that upon any advantage gained, you would pursue the rebels *immediately*: You had gained the *greatest* advantage; and stood still for three days, to give them time to collect their boats, and to take themselves away from the destruction they expected.

There is a third instance, in your permitting the rebels to be taken off from the Governor's Island, in open day-light, and in the sight of your fleet and army, which has been more fully stated in Three Letters to Lord Howe, printed for Wilkie, and a fourth, in your landing near the South end of New York Island, and suffering Putnam with 3000 men to march quietly by you.

But your conduct at White Plains seems to be a demonstration of all that I have said. Your letter of the 16th January 1776, is written professedly to explain your ideas about the operations of the next campaign; and the force you judged necessary to render them effectual. In that letter you write thus: "If a respectable supply of troops from Europe does not arrive soon in the Spring, another defensive campaign I conclude will be the consequence; for by want of a force to act early, the rebel army will have full time to entrench, in every strong position their Commanders may fix upon: In which case, though we should get possession of new York without resistance, we must not expect to carry their entrenched camps, but with considerable loss. *Whereas, on the contrary, the army on the opening of the campaign being in force, would probably by rapid movements bring the rebels to an action upon equal terms, before they could cover themselves by works of any signification.*"

You then, Sir, specify the force requisite for this purpose: "I beg leave to remark, that with a proper army of 20,000 men; having 12,000 at New York, 6000 at Rhode Island, and 2000 at Halifax, the present unfavourable appearance of things would probably wear a very different aspect before the end of the ensuing campaign." I have before quoted two other letters of the like import. Was it possible, Sir, for his Majesty or his ministers to doubt of the sincerity of these, and many more such repeated declarations? You accordingly gained their full confidence; and, far from stinting you in the force you demanded, instead of 20,000 they gave you 30,000*; and instead of 12,000 at New York, you had 24,000 to attack the rebels at White Plains. Washington, on the other hand, it appears from Gen. Robertson's evidence, instead of 50,000, as you wildly write home, never had above 16,000 men with him: and of these, 3300 had, you say, been killed and taken at long Island; 300 of them in York Island; and 2700 had been left in Fort Washington. The reminder that had not deserted, you yourself tell us were dispirited by their late defeats.

But, Sir, beside your immense superiority of force, the situation of the rebel army gave you every circumstance of advantage. The Hudson's River, and an arm of the Sea called the East River, contain between them a large peninsula, surrounded on the east, west, and south sides, and open only on the north side. The rebels were encamped at Kingsbridge, in the midst of this peninsula. The troops were embarked, and set off early in the morning of the 12th of October. You had only twenty-five miles to go to New Rochelle, where the posting them on the only outlet, would have given you the entire command of the rebel army.

For eight months together, you had been telling his Majesty, that your *chief hopes were in bringing the rebels to decisive action. That nothing was more to be desired, or fought for by you, than a decisive action:* And July 7th, that *you was still of opinion that peace would not be restored, till the rebel army was defeated.* True, to the very last minute, to the same deception, you begin your letter of 30th of November, with telling his Majesty, the very strong positions the enemy had taken on this island, and fortified "with incredible labour, determined me to get upon their principal communication with Connecticut, with a view of forcing them to quit their strong holds in the neighbourhood of Kingsbridge, and, if possible, *to bring them to action.*"

You knew, Sir, the rebels only road of communication with Connecticut, was by Rochelle; and had you intended what you wrote, you had only to have landed at Rochelle, as you might have done in five or six hours; and have posted your army to the north of the rebels, and you could not possibly have avoided bringing them to action. The efficacy of this measure was obvious, and for that reason it suited your party, that you should not do it. In conformity therefore to the constant course of your proceedings, instead of landing to the northward of the rebels, to shut them in, you stopped half way, and let them see whither you was going, and at nine o'clock in the morning landed on the remotest point of the coast, to the southward of them, to let them out. You wrote to his Majesty, that you was determined to get upon their principal communication with Connecticut: That you knew was by Rochelle: And you landed at Frog's Neck, at the greatest possible distance from it; and at a place, too, from which you never could possibly march to it. You tell his Majesty, that you was determined to bring the rebels, if possible, to a battle; and you took care to leave open for them the only possible road to avoid it. Such, Sir, was the performance of twenty different promises, continually repeated in your letters, during the whole course of your command.

The two principal requisites to the successes of every military operation, are secrecy and expedition. You took effectual care that yours should have neither. By stopping half way, you told the rebels whither you was going; and by remaining six days there, you gave them time to quit their camp, and take themselves out of danger. This, Sir, is one of your *rapid movements*; by which you promised his Majesty to prevent the rebels from fortifying any new camp. I just mention it at present, because this landing at Frog's Neck is only the first stage of your gross, and seemingly, wilful failures. The merits of the other two (your march to White Plains, and your standing still there three days within cannon shot of the rebels, after you had half routed them on the 28th) shall be stated in my next.

I call them, Sir, *seemingly wilful failures*; for unless you give better reasons than you have hitherto done, how is it possible for us to judge otherwise? The reason you give for thus stopping half way, is (a pretence you always have had) the want of provisions. The army, you write, *remained in this situation, until the stored and provisions could be brought up.* Judge for your own self, Sir, whether it is possible for us to believe, that you landed at Frog's Neck, instead of Rochelle, for want of provisions. You had a fleet of two or three hundred transports, with all their boats, which could have victualled you for six months; and yet, you could not hold out a voyage of six hours. These provisions and stores could have been brought for you to Rochelle, more easily than to Frog's Neck. And, if they were landed for you at Frog's Neck, you must have shipped them again, to be carried for you, to Rochelle; for your men, and much more for your baggage, could not get out of Frog's neck by land. You importantly tell us: *All previous arrangements being made,* the army embarked on the 12th of October in flat boats and other craft, and landed at Frog's neck about nine in the morning. Is it possible for us to suppose, that you, whose letters are full of concern about provisions, could, *with all your previous arrangements,* have embarked your troops so utterly destitute, as that they could not have held out till dinner-time, which would have carried them to Rochelle? Gen. Robertson tells us, that Lord Amhherst's troops often marched with 14 days provisions on their backs. Your men had only to sit at their ease, and to be rowed in their flat boats about as far as from London to Garvesend, and yet could not hold out the whole voyage; but, after having been rowed for two or three hours, landed at Frog's Neck, and staid there six days to get their breakfast. Had you, Sir, given no reason at all, your friends might have fancied one for you; but it is impossible for us to conceive, that this was your *real* one. You had performed the longest, and only difficult part of the voyage, by nine o'clock in the morning. But had you gone on the other ten miles to Rochelle, you might have shut up the rebel army, without having given them any warning. And the North River being guarded by your ships, they must have laid down their arms, or have fought you under every possible disadvantage. The most sensible and best informed writers among the rebels acknowledge this, and laugh at you for not having done it. The loyal part of the Americans saw, and mourned it. His Majesty, from all the solemn allurances of your Letters, could not but judge, that you would do your best in his service: But a leader of the party seems to have known you better, when he said of you, He is one of us, and will do the Americans no harm.

ARISTIDES

* The numbers are taken from your own correspondence.

Halifax army	8000	
First division of Hessians		8200
Guards		1098
Highlanders	3466	
Second division of Hessians	4000	
Clinton's corps		3000
Sixty-fifth regiment	400	
Waldeckers	500	

German recruits		402
British		500
Roger's corps and Provincials	1000	
Sixteenth and seventeenth light Dragoons		888
		31454
Deduct for the betrayed into Boston, by your not fortifying George's Island, as you promised to do	600	
		30854

THE LONDON CHRONICLE
VOL. XLIX   No. 3762
From TUESDAY, January 9, to THURSDAY, January 11, 1781
Page 39
Charlestown, Nov. 13 (NOTE Meaning 1780)
Extract of a Letter from Camden, dated the 13th instant

On the evening of the 9th instant, came in a deserter from the rebels. He informs, that General Morgan having received intelligence that our troops had evacuated this town, marched from North Carolina with 300 foot, and 75 horse, in order to take possession; but on his approaches, as far as the Waxaws [sic], distant 35 miles from this, he was informed, that we still kept possession, and meant to defend the place, let the consequence be what it would, which induced him to retreat with precipitation to his former station.—We have thrown up works all round the town, and at several places about a mile distant.—We are under no apprehensions of having a visit paid us by the Americans. They have nothing, for miles round, to subsist on; and their only incitement for coming into the country is plunder. Lord Cornwallis is perfectly recovered, and his army in high spirits.

THE LONDON CHRONICLE
VOL. L   No. 3866
From SATURDAY, September 8, to TUESDAY, September 11, 1781
Page 241
AMERICAN NEWS
From the NEW YORK and the WEEKLY MERCURY EXTRAORDINARY
Extract of a Letter from Major General Green [sic], dated Camp at Little River, near Ninety-six, June 20, 1781, to Gen. Washington.

In my letter of the 9th, I informed your Excellency, that the enemy had received a considerable reinforcement at Charlestown, and that I was apprehensive they would march out and interrupt our operations. On the 11th, I got intelligence they were advancing; I immediately advanced all the cavalry, with orders to General Sumpter, to collect all the force he could and keep in their front, and by every means in his power to retard their march. The enemy passed him at Congaree before he got his troops in motion; afterwards he found it impracticable to gain their front. It was my intention to have fought them before they arrived at Ninety Six, could I have collected a force sufficient for the purpose.

We had pushed on our approaches very near to the enemy's works, our third parallel was formed round their abbatis, a mine and two approaches were within a few feet of the ditch. These approaches were directed against the Star Fort, which stand upon the left of the town, as we approached it from the Saluda. On the right, our approaches were very near the enemy's redoubt; this was a strong stockade fort, with two blockhouses in it. These two works flanked the town, which is picketed in with strong pickets, a ditch around the whole, and a banked raised near the height of a common parapet. Besides these fortifications were several little flushes in different parts of the town, and all the works communicated with each other by covered ways. We had raised several batteries for cannon, one upwards of 20 feet high, within 140 yards of Star Fort, to command the works, and a rifle battery also within 30 yards, to prevent the enemy from annoying our workmen. For the last ten days not a man could shew his head but he was immediately shot down, and the firing was almost incessant day and night. In this stage of the approaches I found the enemy so near us that it would be impossible to reduce the place without hazarding a storm. This, from the peculiar strength of the place, could only be warranted by the success of a partial attempt to make a lodgment on one of the curtains of the Star redoubt, and a vigorous push to carry the right hand work. The disposition was formed, and the attack made; Lieut. Col. Lee, with his legion infantry, and Captain Kirkwood's light infantry, made the attack on the right; and Lieut. Col. Campbell with the first Maryland and the fifth Virginia regiments, was to have stormed the Star redoubt, which is their principal work, and stands upon the left: The parapet of this work is near 12 feet high, and raised with sand bags near three feet more. Lieut. Duvall, of of (repeated word original) the Maryland Line, and Lieutenant Selden, of the Virginia Line, led on the forlorn hope, followed by a party with hooks to pull down the sand bags, the better to enable them to make the lodgment. A furious cannonade preluded the attack. On the right, the enemy were driven out of their works, and our people took possession of them; on the left never was greater bravery exhibited then by the parties led on by Duvall and Selden; but they were not to be successful. They entered the enemy's ditch and made every exertion to get down the sand bags, which, from the depth of the ditch, height of the parapet, and under a galling fire, was rendered difficult. Finding the enemy defended their works with great obstinancy, and seeing but little prospect of succeeding without heavy loss, I ordered the attack to be pushed no further.

The behaviour of the troops on this occasion deserves the highest commendations; both the Officers that entered the ditch were wounded, and the greater part of their men were either killed or wounded. I have only to lament, that such brave men fell in an unsuccessful attempt.

Capt. Armstrong, of the first Maryland regiment, was killed, and Capt. Benson, who commanded the regiment, was wounded at the head of the trenches. In both attacks we had upwards of 40 men killed and wounded; the loss was principally at the Star Fort, and in the enemy's ditch, the other parts being all under cover. The attack was continued three quarters of an hour; and as the enemy was greatly exposed to the fire of the rifle-battery, and artillery, they must have suffered greatly. Our artillery was well served, and I believe did great execution.

The troops have undergone incredible hardships during the siege; and though the issue was not successful, I hope their exertions will merit the approbation of Congress.

We continued the siege until the enemy got within a few miles of us, having previously sent off all our sick and wounded, and spare stores.

Return of the Killed, Wounded, and missing, during the Siege of Ninety Six, in South Carolina.
Total. Killed 57; wounded 70; missing 20.

Capt. Armstrong of the Maryland Line, killed; Capt. Benson, and Lieut. Duvall, wounded; Capt. Bentley, of the Virginia Line, prisoner; Lieutenants Evans, Miller, and Selden, wounded. Colonel Koscuitzko [sic], Chief Engineer, was slightly wounded.

O. H. WILLIAMS, D. A. G.
Published by order of Congress
CHARLES THOMPSON, SECRETARY.

THE LONDON CHRONICLE
VOL. XLIX No. 3762
From TUESDAY, January 9, to THURSDAY, January 11, 1781
Page 39
AMERICAN NEWS
From the ROYAL SOUTH CAROLINA GAZETTE
Charlestown, Nov. 8 [1780]

In consequence of the powers to me vested by the Right Honourable Lord Cornwallis, and warrants received from his Lordship and the Commandant of Charlestown; I do hereby make public to all whom it may concern, that I have given orders for the seizure of the estates, both real and personal, of those persons whose names are under mentioned, excepting such property in Charlestown, as is secured to those who were in the town at the time of capitulation. And I do hereby strictly prohibit all and every person or persons from attempting to conceal, remove, or in any way injure the said property, on pain of being punished, as aiding and abetting rebellion. JOHN CRUDEN

John Rutledge	John Harleston, jun.
Henry Laurens	Isaac Harleston

Thomas Ferguson	Isaac Motte
Christopher Gadsden	Nicholas Eveleigh
William Moultrie	John Lewis Gervais
Pierce Butler	Stephen Bull
Ralph Izard	Peter Horry
Arthur Middleton	Hugh Horry
Charles Cotesworth Pinckney	Thomas Heyward
Francis Marion	William Clay Snipes

THE LONDON CHRONICLE
VOL. XLIX   No. 3797
From SATURDAY, March 31, to TUESDAY, April 3, 1781
Pages 313–314
MONDAY, APRIL 1. (Note: Actually was April 2.)
From the LONDON GAZETTE, *March 31.*
Whitehall, March 31.

BY the Mail of Sandwich Packet, which failed from Charles-Town the 28th of February, Dispatches were this Day received by Lord George Germain, One of his Majesty's Principal Secretaries of State, from the Earl Cornwallis and Lieutenant Colonel Balfour, of which the following are Copies and Extras.

(NOTE: These are two letters from Balfour to Germain. George Germain was Secretary of State for the American Colonies in the cabinet of Prime Minister Lord Frederick North. There were two other Secretaries of States: one for Europe and one for the rest of the world other than America. The letter from Cornwallis is transcribed separately as Cornwallis' Cowpens Report.)

Extract of a Letter from Lieutenant Colonel Balfour to Lord George Germain, dated CharlesTown, February 18, 1781.

BY the Letter in which I had the Honor to address your Lordship on the 16th of January last, you will have been informed of the Situation of Affairs here to that Period, and by Lord Cornwallis's Dispatch, dated the 18th of the same Month, of Lieutenant Colonel Tarleton's unfortunate Action on the preceding Day: I am now to give your Lordship such further Information as have been received since, either immediately from Earl Cornwallis, Lord Rawdon, or Major Craig, or by Intelligence through the Country.

Notwithstanding the unexpected and untoward Event of the 17th ultimo, Lord Cornwallis still continued his forward movements, and pressed hard on General Morgan, without being able to come up with him, who, with his Prisoners, pushed for the Catawba, and by crossing that River high up, there is Cause to believe, accomplished his Junction with General Green [sic] Army. It was not till the 1st instant that Lord Cornwallis could pass it; this he then did at a private Ford, four miles below Bratty's [sic], though strongly opposed by a Body of Militia, who were routed, and General Davidson, who commanded them, killed. On this Occasion, his Lordship observes, "The Guards behaved gallantly, crossing the River under a heavy Fire, without returning a Shot, until they were over and formed."

On the same Day Colonel Tarleton had the good Fortune to defeat another Corps of the Enemy's Militia, that had assembled under Colonel Pickings [sic], killing and taking many, and entirely dispersing the rest.

In relating these Circumstances to your Lordship, it is no small Satisfaction to add, that on both Occasions the Loss sustained by the King's Troops is inconsiderable; and that, except Colonel Hall of the Guards, who is killed, no Officer was hurt.

After gaining these Advantages, Lord Cornwallis proceeded to Salisbury, of which Town he possessed himself in the 4th instant.

Hitherto, General Green [sic] had remained in his Position on the Eastern Banks of the Peedee; and by thus hanging on the Frontiers of the Province, and having with him a Force in Cavalry, was enabled to make Inroads into the Heart of it, which were greatly distressing to the Inhabitants, and obliged me to detach, to cover the Communications between this and Camden, prevent the Enemy's taking Post on this Side of the Santee, and hinder Insults in our Vicinities; but on the News of Lord Cornwallis's late Successes, he called in his Out-Parties, and by a precipitate Movement reached the Moravian Settlements in North Carolina, where, by the last Accounts, he has taken a Station to cover a Passage of the Yadkin.

From this View of the Situation of both Armies we may expect soon to hear of some Event of Moment, and which I hope will give Occasion to congratulate your Lordship.

By my last Letter your Lordship was informed of an Expedition being then to fail under Major Craig, of the 82^d Regiment. The force employed on that Service, and the Objects of it, I have now the Honour to communicate to your Lordship; his having taken Possession of Wilmington without Opposition, on the 29th ultimo: But finding that a Body of the Enemy had posted themselves at Heron's Bridge, about twelve Miles from that Town, to cover as well this Pass as the Shipping in the River, and shew a Force for the Militia to form on, Major Craig, by an immediate and well timed Exertion, surprised the Rebels in this very strong Position and, by dislodging them from it, has cleared that Part of the Country, gained, in Co-operation with his Majesty's Ships of War, Possession of their Vessels, and taken on board them and in their Camp several military Stores, the Want of which may be much felt, should they attempt again to raise any Force in these Parts.

Major Craig further informs me, that he is exerting every Means to put the very essentual Post of Wilmington into a State of Defence, and eventually to communicate with the Army under Lord Cornwallis.

Extract of a Letter from Lieutenant-Colonel Balfour to Lord George Germain, dated, Charles Town, Feb. 25, 1781.

SINCE the date of my Dispatches, No. 2,

Captain Barkley, with the Blonde [a ship], arrived here from Cape Fear, where he left every Thing in a State of Security, and the Works for the protection of Wilmington nearly perfected.

No Accounts since my last have been received immediately from Lord Cornwallis; but Lord Rawdon has favoured me with some further Intelligence respecting the Operations of the Army, which his Lordship derived from a Man who quitted it on the 9th instant, and who is come into Camden.

At the Period it appears, Lord Cornwallis was advanced six Miles beyond Salem, the farthest of the Moravian Settlements in North Carolina, and to the Eastward of the Yadkin, which points out by what uncommon Exertion and rapid Movements his Lordship must have reached that Distance, in so small a Space of Time, through a strong and intricate Country.

By crossing the Yadkin so high up, the Army has got above Green's [sic], which, by this Intelligence, was advancing on Deep River, and some Way removed to the Rear of Lord Cornwallis's Right; General Morgan, with his Corps, being advanced, and on the Left. With this last there were some Hopes Lord Cornwallis would soon be able to come up; and, on the Whole, it will be clear to your Lordship, that, by this Movement, the Junction of the Enemy's Force, of which in my last I was apprehensive, is for the present frustrated.

I must not omit informing your Lordship of the Arrival of the Assurance [a ship], with the Fleet of Victuallers from Corke, after a Passage of twelve Weeks, the Length of which obliges them to water before they can proceed on their Voyage to New York, during which Time the Assurance will remain at Beaufort, being of too large a Draft to pass this Bar.

THE LONDON CHRONICLE
VOL. XXXVI   No. 2773
From THURSDAY, September 15, to SATURDAY, September 17, 1774
Pages 270–271
Saturday, Sept. 17.
LONDON

Yesterday arrived a mail from South Carolina, brought by the *Swallow* packet-boat, Captain Copeland, in 35 days to Falmouth.

From the SOUTH CAROLINA GAZETTE

Charles-Town, July 11. In consequence of the advertisements lately published by the General Committee, and other proper means used, to obtain the sense of the whole Colony on the present alarming state of American affairs; on Wednesday last, the 6th inst. The largest body of the most respectable inhabitants that had ever been seen together upon any public occasion here, or perhaps any where in America (for Gentlemen of the greatest property and character, animated with an ardent zeal to relieve their suffering brethren, and to preserve their own freedom, and the birthrights of their posterity, notwithstanding the extreme inconvenience of the season, from even the remotest parts of the country, attended) met at the exchange in this town, in order to "consider of the papers, letters, and resolutions, that had been transmitted to the said Committee from the Northern Colonies; and also of the steps necessary to be pursued, in union with the inhabitants of our Sister Colonies on this continent, to avert the dangers impending over American liberties in general, by the late hostile Act of Parliament against Boston, and other arbitrary measures of the British Ministry;"— and, after choosing the Hon. Col. Powell (who had presided at all the former general meetings) for their Chairman, and the *fame* Secretary as had hitherto served, continued in solemn deliberation upon these important matters on that and the two succeeding days, during which several resolves were unanimously entered into.—[The resolutions agreed to on Wednesday, are in substance the same as those entered into by divers places in America, which have already appeared in this paper].

Thursday, July 7. Resolved, That Henry Middleton, John Rutledge, Thomas Lynch, Christopher Gadsden, and Edward Rutledge, Esqrs. Be and they are hereby nominated and appointed Deputies, on the part and behalf of this colony, to meet the Deputies of the several Colonies of North America, in general congress, the first Monday in September next, at Philadelphia, or at any other time or place that may be generally agreed on; there to consider the act lately passed, and bills depending on Parliament, with regard to the port of Boston and province of Massachusetts-Bay; which act and bills, in the precedent and consequences, affect the whole continent — also the grievances under which America labours, by reason of the several acts of Parliament that impose taxes or duties for raising a revenue, and lay unnecessary restraints and burdens on trade — and of the statutes, parliamentary acts, and royal instructions which make an invidious distinction between his Majesty's subjects in Great Britain and in America — with full power and authority, in behalf of us and our constituants, to concert, agree to, and effectually prosecute, such legal measures (by which we, for ourselves and them, most solemnly engage to abide) as in the opinion of the said Deputies so to be assembled, shall be most likely to obtain a repeal of the said acts, and a redress of those grievances.

Resolved, That we do agree to pay the expence of the five Gentlemen now chosen, to be sent upon the above business.

Resolved, That while the oppressive acts relative to Boston are enforced, we will cheerfully, from time to time, contribute towards the relief of such poor persons there, whose unfortunate circumstances, occasioned by the operation of those acts, may be thought to stand in need of most assistance.

Resolved, That we will, by all means in our power, endeavor to preserve harmony and union amongst all the Colonies.

Friday, July 8. Resolved, That copies of all the resolutions entered into by the Inhabitants of this province at the present meeting be transmitted to every colony on this continent, from Canada to West Florida; accompanied with a letter to each respectively, signed by the Chairman, inviting them to unite with us: And that as Capt. Hunt had voluntarily detained his vessel for some days on purpose to carry the transactions of the present meeting to New York, in order to forward his departure, the Chairman be desired to quit the chair, and immediately dispatch copies of the resolutions now entered into by Capt. Hunt; and that the thanks of the meeting be given to Capt. Hunt.

Resolved, That a Committee of 99 persons be now appointed, to act as a general Committee, to correspond with the committees of the other colonies, and do all matters and things necessary to carry these resolutions into execution; and that any 21 of them meeting together may proceed on business, their power to continue till the next general meeting. And in case of the death, departure from the province, or refusal to act, of any or either of them, the parish or district for which such person (dying, removing, or refusing to act) was chosen, shall fill up the vacancy.

The colony was ready to go into resolutions of non-importation and non-exportation if it had been found absolutely necessary; but it was thought most proper to invest our Deputies with absolute power to agree with the other Members of the congress in any measures; that so they might take place from one end of this extensive continent to the other, on one and the same day: And several of the principal Merchants made a public declaration, in behalf of the rest, that, in order to quiet the minds of the People, they were ready and willing to enter into any agreement, not only to desist importing British or East India goods, wines, and slaves, but also to countermand all orders already sent, till the event of the congress should be known; which declaration was received with a loud and general plaudit.

Three hundred and fifty more barrels of rice are now ready to be shipped as soon as a proper vessel can be procured to carry it, for the relief of the poor sufferers in Boston.

Charles Town, July 25. Last Tuesday morning, at eleven o'clock, the General Committee met, in consequence of their adjournment the day before, to see Capt. Maitland destroy some tea that had been landed the preceding day: When, upon re-considering the matter, and that it could not be got out of the Collector's custody, without violence or paying the duty, both which the Committee were equally disposed to prevent, it was agreed, that the said tea should remain as a seizure, under the same circumstances as the India Company's, not to be sold in this colony, unless the duty thereon should be repealed.

But Capt. Maitland being looked upon as a man who, by his conduct, had grossly imposed on and deceived the Committee, and insulted the people, it was resolved to appoint a Sub-Committee to wait on all importers, and request that they would not hereafter ship or receive any goods whatever, in any bottom wherein he was or should be concerned; and a Committee was accordingly appointed.

The people in general being much disappointed in their expectations of seeing Capt. Maitland burn the tea that day, they were so much enflamed at his conduct, that it was impossible to prevent a considerable number of them going in quest of him that evening. What they might have done, had they met with him, it is impossible to tell; but they seemed inclined rather to make a public exhibition of him, than to do him a bodily injury: However, he eluded their search, by slipping away, and remaining on board his Majesty's ship the *Glasgow*, in Rebellion Road, whether his ship soon followed him, and now lies Windbound, since which he has not thought proper to appear on shore.

Capt. Urquhart having brought five chests of tea, one for Mr. Tunno, and four to Mess. Johnston and Simpson (for Mr. Penman at St. Augustine) those Gentlemen attended the meeting of the General Committee last Wednesday evening, when Capt. Urquhart declared that he knew not of his having any on board, till he examined his cockets on the day of his arrival, before he before he brought his ship up to town, upon being informed of what had happened to Capt. Maitland. He was requested to bring none in future, unless the duty should be repealed, and very readily answered he would not.

Messrs. Johnston and Simpson, and Mr. Tunno, respectively behaved upon this occasion as worthy citizens, and declared, that they would not receive the said tea, not having ordered any. As the 20 days within which the duty is required to be paid, will expire on the 7th of next month, it is presumed the said tea will be seized by the Collector on the 8th, and stored with the rest.

The Gentleman's Magazine
For July 1780
Page 339
Advices from America *and the* West-Indies
Romulus off Charles-Town Harbor,
June 5)

MY LORD [Lord George Germaine],

I Have just received from Earl Cornwallis a letter, including a more particular report than had yet been received from Lieutenant-Colonel Tarleton of the affair at Wacsaw.[sic]

H. CLINTON

Lieutenant Colonel Tarleton's *Letter to Earl* Cornwallis

I Have the honour to inform you, that yesterday at three o'clock, P. M. after a march of 105 miles in 54 hours, with the corps of cavalry, the infantry of the legion mounted on horses, and a three pounder, at Wacsaw [sic], near the line which divides North from South Carolina, the rebel force, commanded by Colonel Buford, consisting of the 11th Virginia, and detachments of other regiments from the same province, with artillery, and some cavalry, were brought to action.

After the summons, in which terms similar to those accepted by Charles-Town were offered, and positively rejected, the action commenced in a wood: the attacks were pointed at both flanks, the front and reserve by 270 cavalry and infantry blended; and, at the same instant, all were equally victorious, few of the enemy escaping, except the commanding officer, by a precipitate flight on horseback.

It is above my ability to say any thing in commendation of the bravery and exertion of officers and men. I leave their merit to your Lordship's consideration.

I have the honour, &c, &c.
BAN. TARLETON
Lt.-Col. Comm, Br. Legion
Liet.-Gen. Earl Cornwallis,
Return of rebels killed, wounded, and taken, in the affair at Wacsaw [sic], *the 29th of* May, *1780.*

1 lieutenant-colonel, 3 captains, 8 subalterns, 1 adjutant, 1 quarter-master 99 serjeants and rank and file killed.

3 captains, 5 subalterns, 142 serjeants and rank and file, wounded, unable to travel, and left on parole.

2 captains, 1 subaltern, 50 serjeants and rank and file, prisoners.

Taken, 3 stand of colours , two brass six-pounders, 2 royals, 2 waggons with ammunition, 1 artillery forge cart, 55 barrels of powder, 26 waggons loaded with new clothing, arms, musquet-cartridges [sic], new cartridge-boxes, flints, and camp-equipage.

(Signed)B. TARLETON, Lt.-Col.

Return of British *killed and wounded in the affair at* Wacsaw [sic], *the 29th of* May, *1780.*

Cavalry. 2 privates, 11 horses, killed; 1 subaltern, 8 privates, 19 horses wounded.

Infantry. 2 subalterns, 1 private killed; 3 privates wounded.

N.B. Lieut. Pateschall, the 17th dragoons, wounded; Lieut. Lauchlin Macdonald, of the Legion Infantry, killed; Ensign Campbell, of the Legion Infantry, serving with the cavalry, killed.

(Signed)B. TARLETON

Chapter Notes

Preface

1. *The Old Stone Church — Oconee County — South Carolina*, page 130.
2. *The Old Stone Church*, page 106.
3. *The Old Stone Church*, page 140.

Prologue

1. E.M. Sharp, *Pickens Families of the South*, page 12.
2. Sharp, page 25.
3. *The Old Stone Church*, page 137.
4. David Freeman Hawke, *Everyday Life in Early America*, pages 111–113, 150–153.
5. General Andrew Pickens, *Letter to General Henry Lee*, 28 August 1811.
6. Sharp, appendix II, item 4, page 137.
7. Henry Jones Ford, *The Scotch-Irish in America*, Chapter 1 "The Plantation of Ulster," LibraryIreland.com; McAdams Historical Society, "The Scotch-Irish in America," mcadamshistory.com; Matthew A. C. Newsome, *The Migration of the Scots-Irish to Southwestern NC*, albanach.org; S. Clark Pickens, *Pickens Genealogy*, scpickens.tripod.com; Christine R. Swager, *Heroes of Kettle Creek 1779–1782*, page 13.
8. Swager, page 13–14.
9. S. Clark Pickens, *Pickens Genealogy*; Sharp, 'Pickens Origins' annotated following the Table of Contents.
10. McAdams Historical Society; Newsome; S. Clark Pickens, *Pickens Genealogy*; Swager, page 15–18.

Chapter 1

1. *The Old Stone Church*, page 137.
2. Kate Pickens Day, *Cousin Monroe's History of the Pickens family*, chapter 2, page 25; Sharp, page 3.
3. Sharp, page 3.
4. Sharp, appendix II, item 4, page 137.
5. Sharp, end of appendix II, page 141.
6. Sharp, appendix II, item 6, page 138.
7. Sharp, end of appendix II, page 141.
8. Day, chapter 2, page 26; A. L. Pickens, *Skyagunsta, The Border Wizard Owl*, page 1; Sharp, appendix I, page 135.
9. Sharp, page 4.
10. Michael C. Scoggins, *The Scotch-Irish on the American Frontier*, newacquisitionmilitia.com.
11. Hawke, pages 88–100.
12. Day, chapter 2, page 26; A. L. Pickens, *Skyagunsta*, page 2; Sharp, page 11.
13. Day, chapter 4.1, page 38.
14. Day, chapter 2, page 28.
15. Pickens, *Letter*.
16. Day, chapter 4.1, page 38 and chapter 2, page 28; A. L. Pickens, *Skyagunsta*, page 2.
17. A. L. Pickens, *Skyagunsta*, page 2; Sharp, page 11.
18. Robert D. Bass, *Ninety Six: The Struggles for the South Carolina Back Country*, page 30; Old Waxhaw Presbyterian Church Bulletin.
19. Day, chapter 4.1, pages 38–40; Old Waxhaw Presbyterian Church Bulletin.
20. Day, chapter 4.1, pages 38–40; Sharp, page 11.
21. Day, chapter 2, page 28.
22. A. L. Pickens, *Skyagunsta*, page 2; Sharp, page 11.
23. A. L. Pickens, *Skyagunsta*, page 2.
24. Bass, *Ninety Six*, page 38.
25. Day, chapter 4.1, pages 38–40; A. L. Pickens, *Skyagunsta*, Page 2; Sharp, pages 11–12.
26. Hawke, pages 31–46.

27. A. L. Pickens, *Skyagunsta*, page 2.
28. Pickens, *Letter*.
29. Swager, page 36.
30. Henry Lee, *The Revolutionary War Memoirs of General Henry Lee*, edited by Robert E. Lee, page 595, appendix N.
31. Bass, *Ninety Six*, pages 38–39; Day, chapter 2, pages 30–31.
32. Jerome A. Greene, "Ninety Six, A Historical Narrative," pages 1–3.
33. Jerome A. Greene, pages 9–10.
34. Jerome A. Greene, *pages 6–7*.
35. Chuloch-Culla is generally accepted as Attakulla Kulla who accompanied Old Hop (Connecorte) and acted as his spokesman; Attakulla Kulla was born approximately 1710 on an Island (possibly Sevier Island) in the French Broad River of the over mountain region in Virginia (now eastern Tennessee). He, then known as The White Owl (Okoonaka), was one of seven Cherokee selected to visit London in 1730. He was kidnapped by the Ottawa, allies of the French, in 1740 and held until 1748. He spent his life for the good of his people, the Ani-Yunwiya (the Real People); Some have recorded that Oconostota and Attakulla Kulla were cousins rather than uncle and nephew, and that Attakulla Kulla was born of the sub-tribe Nipissing, captured by the Cherokee when an infant, and adopted into the tribe.
36. Jerome A. Greene, page 18; J. B. O. Landrum, *Colonial and Revolutionary History of Upper South Carolina*, pages 23–24; Robert D. Bass, *Ninety Six: The Struggles for the South Carolina Back Country*, page 41; Louise Manly, *Southern Literature from 1579–1895*, pages 105–106.
37. This event was known popularly in America as the French and Indian War because it began in the American Theater two years before the encompassing world war was declared. The American Theater of the conflict lasted from about 1754 until 1763 involving the British army, the colonial militias, and their Cherokee allies against the French and their Indian allies of the northern tribes. The actual declaration of war by Britain against France on May 18, 1756, marks the beginning of the Seven Years' War that ended with the Treaty of Paris on February 10, 1763. This also officially ended the war in the American Theater.
38. Day, chapter 2, pages 30–31.
39. Bass, *Ninety Six*, pages 43–44.
40. Landrum, pages 28–30.
41. Bass, *Ninety Six*, page 42–44.
42. Jerome A. Greene, pages 29–30.
43. Bass, *Ninety Six*, page 44; Day, chapter 2, pages 30–31; Jerome A. Greene, pages 27–28; A. L. Pickens, *Skyagunsta*, page 3.
44. Jerome A. Greene, pages 27–28.
45. Bass, *Ninety Six*, page 45–46; Jerome A. Greene, pages 30, 32.
46. Descriptive information used for the brothers is taken from family history passed down through Joseph Pickens' line. His daughter, Ann Pickens Dowdle, moved to Lawrence County, Missouri to live with her daughter's and granddaughter's families. Ann Pickens Dowdle died in 1841 and was buried in Lawrence County. Her granddaughter, Ann Gibson, married Elijah Boyd Hillhouse and is the four-great-grandmother of the author, William R. Reynolds, Jr., who was born in Lawrence County.
47. Bass, *Ninety Six*, pages 50–51; Day, chapter 2, pages 30–31.
48. Pickens, *Letter*.
49. Bass, *Ninety Six*, pages 50–51; Day, chapter 2, pages 30–31.
50. Day, chapter 4.1, pages 38–40.
51. Bass, *Ninety Six*, pages 50–51; Jerome A. Greene, page 39.
52. Bass, *Ninety Six*, page 51.
53. Landrum, page 35.
54. Bass, *Ninety Six*, page 51; Jerome A. Greene, page 39.
55. Pickens, *Letter*.
56. Bass, *Ninety Six*, page 53; Jerome A. Greene, page 39–40; Landrum, page 35.
57. Janie B. Cheaney, *Charles, Earl Cornwallis*, jrshelby.com/kimocowp/cornwal.htm, 1998; *The London Chronicle*, Volume XVI, No. 1233, Thursday, November 15, 1764, page 469.
58. A. L. Pickens, *Skyagunsta*, page 4.
59. *The London Chronicle*, Volume XVI, No. 1233, Thursday, November 15, 1764, page 470.
60. Brian Scott, *Military and Political*, July 15, 2009, *Calhoun Burial Grounds Marker*, hmdb.org; *The London Chronicle*, Volume XVI, No. 1233, Thursday, November 15, 1764, page 470.
61. Day, chapter 4.2, page 41; *The Old Stone Church*, pages 138–139; A. L. Pickens, *Skyagunsta*, page 4.
62. Jerome A. Greene, pages 41–42.
63. *The Old Stone Church*, page 139.

Chapter 2

1. Cheaney.
2. Jerome A. Greene, page 47–57.
3. *The Old Stone Church*, page 139.
4. A. L. Pickens, *Skyagunsta*, page 39.
5. Bass, *Ninety Six*, pages 59–61; Jerome A. Greene, pages 47–48.
6. Bass, *Ninety Six*, page 53; Robert M. Dunkerly and Eric K. Williams, *Old Ninety Six, A History and Guide*, page 20; Jerome A. Greene, page 41.

7. William M. Dabney and Marion Dargan, *William Henry Drayton & the American Revolution*, page 89.
8. Charles Woodmason, *The Carolina Backcountry on the Eve of the Revolution: The Journal and Other Writings of Charles Woodmason, Anglican Itinerant*, edited by Richard Hooker, pages 27–28.
9. Bass, *Ninety Six*, pages 61–63; Dunkerly and Williams, *page 20;* Jerome A. Greene, page 48.
10. Woodmason, page 175.
11. Woodmason, pages 175–176.
12. Woodmason, page 176.
13. Woodmason, page 57.
14. Woodmason, pages 176–177.
15. Bass, *Ninety Six*, page 63–65.
16. Jerome A. Greene, page 49.
17. Bass, *Ninety Six*, page 67; Dunkerly and Williams, *pages 20–21;* Jerome A. Greene, pages 49–50.
18. Bass, *Ninety Six*, page 66; Swager, page 21.
19. Thomas G. Rodgers, "Colonials Collide at Bloody Marsh," *Military History*, Volume 13, Number 4 (October 1996), pages 38–44.
20. Bass, *Ninety Six*, pages 72–74.
21. William Tennent III, *Album, 1758–1777 (Anonymous letter to the Ladies of South Carolina)*, undated but likely December 1773 (Excerpts), William Tennent papers, South Caroliniana Library, University of South Carolina, Columbia SC.
22. *The London Chronicle*, Volume XXXVI, No. 2773, Thursday, November 17, 1774, pages 270–271.
23. Bass, *Ninety Six*, pages 75–76.
24. Bass, *Ninety Six*, page 77; Dabney and Dargan, pages 66–67; Jerome A. Greene, page 58.
25. John W. Gordon, *South Carolina and the American Revolution*, pages 19–20.
26. Bass, *Ninety Six*, page 81; Gordon, page 20; Jerome A. Greene, page 58.
27. Jerome A. Greene, page 58.
28. Bass, *Ninety Six*, page 81; Jerome A. Greene, page 58.
29. Pickens, *Letter;* Andrew's recollections, much as Robert Andrew Pickens' (related in Chapter 1), had apparently suffered somewhat with time. He wrote above to General Lee in 1811 that both Cunningham and Kirkland "immediately took the other side" but Kirkland actually took a little time before he made the switch. While Cunningham left the Whigs in a huff, Kirkland apparently kept his cards close to his chest and waited for a time when a switch of sides would be more dramatic and detrimental to the cause of the Provincial Congress. Throughout the Revolutionary War, many of the militia rank and file seemed to switch loyalties depending on convenience. These interchanges by Cunningham and Kirkland are perfect examples, each seeming to crave political futures dependent upon his military rank; thus, each decided it would be to his advantage to become a Tory. Regarding Andrew's recollection, it is noted that he wrote of "four regiments." However, only three regiments were organized at the time, including the two lowland infantry regiments, and the three men were only being considered for the backcountry Ranger Regiment. He was likely recalling the formation of three militia companies in the backcountry about two months after the Cunningham/Kirkland fiasco (related later in chapter 2) along with the Ranger Regiment; however, the three militia companies made up one regiment equivalent to the Ranger Regiment.
30. Bass, *Ninety Six*, pages 82, 85; Dunkerly and Williams, pages 22–23, 28, 46–47; Jerome A. Greene, *Ninety Six: A Historical Narrative*, pages 58–59.
31. Bass, *Ninety Six*, page 85; Dunkerly and Williams, pages *23–24;* Jerome A. Greene, page 59.
32. Bass, *Ninety Six*, pages 85–86; Dunkerly and Williams, pages *23–24;* Jerome A. Greene, page 59.
33. R.W. Gibbes, *Documentary History of the American Revolution*, Volume I, pages 128–133.
34. Gibbes, Volume I, pages 134–135.
35. William Tennent III, *Travel Journal, 1775*, August 13, 1775, entry, William Tennent papers, South Caroliniana Library, University of South Carolina, Columbia SC.
36. Gibbes, Volume I, page 142, from report Drayton to the Council of Safety dated August 16, 1775.
37. Landrum, page 48.
38. Gibbes, Volume I, page 157, from report Drayton and Tennent at Enoree to the Council of Safety dated August 24, 1775.
39. Gibbes, Volume I, pages 150–151, from report Drayton at Lawson's Fork to the Council of Safety dated August 21, 1775.
40. Tennent, *Travel Journal, 1775*, August 25, 1775, entry.
41. Gibbes, Volume I, pages 164–165, from report Tennent at Long Canes to the Council of Safety dated September 1, 1775; Jerome A. Greene, pages 60–61.
42. Bass, *Ninety Six*, pages 95–98.
43. Tennent, *Travel Journal, 1775*, August 31, 1775, entry.
44. Tennent, *Travel Journal, 1775*, September 2, 1775, entry.
45. Bass, *Ninety Six*, page 98; Jerome A. Greene, page 61.
46. Tennent, *Travel Journal, 1775*, September 3, 1775, entry.
47. Tennent, *Travel Journal, 1775*, September 4, 1775, entry.
48. Jerome A. Greene, page 62; Landrum, pages 55–57.
49. Tennent, *Travel Journal, 1775*, September 11, 1775, entry.
50. Bass, *Ninety Six*, page 100.
51. Bass, *Ninety Six*, page 100; Dunkerly and Williams, pages 25–26.
52. Gibbes, Volume I, pages 180–183.
53. Bass, *Ninety Six*, page 101; Jerome A. Greene, page 63.

54. Gibbes, Volume I, pages 194–195.
55. Bass, *Ninety Six*, pages 103–108; Jerome A. Greene, page 64.

Chapter 3

1. "Drumming out a Tory," *Harper's Weekly, Journal of Civilization*, February 3, 1877, page 90.
2. Gibbes, Volume I, pages 191–192.
3. Gibbes, Volume I, page 200.
4. Gibbes, Volume I, pages 207–208.
5. Bass, *Ninety Six*, page 124.
6. Bass, *Ninety Six*, pages 110–111; Jerome A. Greene, page 64.
7. Jerome A. Greene, page 66.
8. Bass, *Ninety Six*, pages 111–112; Gordon, page 29; Jerome A. Greene, pages 65–66; Landrum, pages 64–65; A. L. Pickens, *Skyagunsta*, pages 8–9.
9. Gordon, page 29.
10. Jerome A. Greene, pages 66–67; A. L. Pickens, *Skyagunsta*, page 9.
11. Bass, *Ninety Six*, page 117; Jerome A. Greene, page 65.
12. Bass, *Ninety Six*, page 112; Gibbes, Volume I, page 221; Gordon, page 29; Jerome A. Greene, pages 66–67; A. L. Pickens, *Skyagunsta*, pages 9–10.
13. Jerome A. Greene, page 67; A. L. Pickens, *Skyagunsta*, page 10.
14. Bass, *Ninety Six*, page 113; Dunkerly and Williams, pages 22–23; Gordon, page 30; Jerome A. Greene, page 67; Landrum, page 66; A. L. Pickens, *Skyagunsta*, pages 10–11; Swivel guns were small cannons, usually less than 3 feet long, and a maximum bore of 1-1/4 inches. They were muzzle-loaded usually with small shot called "grape shot," thus rendering the cannon a large shotgun-type weapon. However, it could be loaded with two or three large caliber balls. The motive force was supplied by a fused powder bag placed behind the shot. They were affixed with a clevis atop a stake that could be placed within any base having a properly-sized mounting hole.
15. Bass, *Ninety Six*, page 113; Dunkerly and Williams, page 23; Gordon, page 30; Jerome A. Greene, pages 69–70; A. L. Pickens, *Skyagunsta*, page 12.
16. Gibbes, Volume I, page 218, from report Williamson at Whitehall to Drayton dated November 25, 1775; A. L. Pickens, *Skyagunsta*, page 13.
17. Gibbes, Volume I, page 218, from report Williamson at Whitehall to Drayton dated November 25, 1775.
18. Bass, *Ninety Six*, pages 114–116; Dunkerly and Williams, page 23; Jerome A. Greene, page 70; A. L. Pickens, *Skyagunsta*, pages 12–13.
19. Gibbes, Volume I, page 218, from report Williamson at Whitehall to Drayton dated November 25, 1775.
20. Bass, *Ninety Six*, page 114; Gibbes, Volume I, pages 216–219, from report Williamson at Whitehall to Drayton dated November 25, 1775; Jerome A. Greene, pages 70–71; Landrum, pages 68–69; A. L. Pickens, *Skyagunsta*, page 13.
21. Gibbes, Volume I, pages 215–216, from report Major Mayson at Ninety Six to Colonel Thomson dated November 24, 1775.
22. Bass, *Ninety Six*, pages 114–115; Gibbes, Volume I, pages 215–216; Gordon, page 30; Jerome A. Greene, pages 71–72; A. L. Pickens, *Skyagunsta*, pages 13–14.
23. Bass, *Ninety Six*, pages 117–118; Gordon, page 31; Jerome A. Greene, page 73; Landrum, page 72; A. L. Pickens, *Skyagunsta*, page 14.
24. Landrum, pages 48, 76. According to Richardson, Fletchall was found in a cave above the junction of Fair Forest Creek with the Tyger River. However, Drayton indicates that he received a letter in later years that Fletchall was captured at his regular hiding place in a hollow sycamore tree, about eight feet in diameter, on the north side of Fair Forest Creek and two and one-half miles from Brandon's mill.
25. Gibbes, Volume I, page 225.
26. Gibbes, Volume I, page 241, from letter Colonel Richardson at Camp Great Survey, Duncan's Creek to Honorable Henry Laurens dated December 12, 1775.
26. Bass, *Ninety Six*, pages 119–120; Gordon, page 31; Landrum, pages 72–76; A. L. Pickens, *Skyagunsta*, page 15.
28. Landrum, pages 78–79; A. L. Pickens, *Skyagunsta*, page 15.
29. Bass, *Ninety Six*, pages 119–121; Gordon, page 31; Jerome A. Greene, page 74; Landrum, page 79; A. L. Pickens, *Skyagunsta*, page 15.
30. Gibbes, Volume I, page 247.

Chapter 4

1. Jerome A. Greene, page 42; Swager, page 24.
2. Gibbes, Volume I, pages 254–255.
3. Landrum, page 83.
4. American Archives Series 4, Volume 5, Page 582, Documents of the American Revolution, 1774–1776, South Carolina Provincial Record, February 27, 1776, Lincoln.lib.niu.edu.
5. Bass, *Ninety Six*, pages 123–132.
6. Swager, page 22.
7. Henry Lumpkin, *From Savannah to Yorktown*, page 12.
8. Washington Irving, *Life of George Washington*, Volume II, pages 201–202.

Notes — Chapter 4

9. Bass, *Ninety Six*, page 129–130; Gordon, page 36; Jerome A. Greene, page 77.
10. Irving, Volume II, page 289.
11. Irving, Volume II, page 289.
12. Irving, Volume II, pages 291–292.
13. Gibbes, Volume III, pages 19–21.
14. Bass, *Ninety Six*, pages 132–135; Gordon, pages 36–39; Irving, Volume II, pages 292–293; A. L. Pickens, *Skyagunsta*, page 35.
15. A. L. Pickens, *Skyagunsta*, page 35.
16. Gibbes, Volume III, page 28.
17. Gibbes, Volume III, pages 22–23; A. L. Pickens, *Skyagunsta*, page 18.
18. Gibbes, Volume III, pages 25–26.
19. Michael Stephenson, *Patriot Battles, How the War of Independence Was Fought*, page 194.
20. Gordon, page 47; A. L. Pickens, *Skyagunsta*, page 17; Swager, page 24.
21. Sharp, page 48.
22. Sharp, appendix II, paragraphs 2, 6–10.
23. A. L. Pickens, *Skyagunsta*, page 17.
24. Gibbes, Volume III, page 24.
25. Bass, *Ninety Six*, page 135; Gordon, pages 47–48; A. L. Pickens, *Skyagunsta*, page 18; Sharp, appendix II, paragraph 2.
26. Bass, *Ninety Six*, page 135; A. L. Pickens, *Skyagunsta*, page 18; Landrum, pages 89–90.
27. Landrum, pages 90–95; A. L. Pickens, *Skyagunsta*, page 18.
28. Gibbes, Volume III, pages 30–31.
29. Sharp, appendix II, paragraph 1.
30. Bass, *Ninety Six*, page 135; Jerome A. Greene, pages 78–79; A. L. Pickens, *Skyagunsta*, pages 18–19.
31. Gordon, page 48; Jerome A. Greene, page 78.
32. Gibbes, Volume III, pages 24–25.
33. Gibbes, Volume III, pages 26–27.
34. Gibbes, Volume III, pages 30–31.
35. Bass, *Ninety Six*, page 135; Jerome A. Greene, page 79; A. L. Pickens, *Skyagunsta*, page 19.
36. Gibbes, Volume III, pages 24–26.
37. Gibbes, Volume III, pages 26–27.
38. Gibbes, Volume III, pages 28–29.
39. A. L. Pickens, *Skyagunsta*, page 23.
40. Gibbes, Volume III, pages 24–26.
41. Gibbes, Volume III, pages 28–30.
42. Bass, *Ninety Six*, page 136; Gordon, page 49; Jerome A. Greene, page 79; Cameron Judd, *The Overmountain Men*, page 72; A. L. Pickens, *Skyagunsta*, pages 20–21.
43. Gibbes, Volume I, pages 125–126.
44. Cameron Judd, *The Border Men*, pages 137–147; A. L. Pickens, *Skyagunsta*, pages 21–22.
45. Gibbes, Volume I, page 126.
46. A. L. Pickens, *Skyagunsta*, page 21.
47. A. L. Pickens, *Skyagunsta*, page 21.
48. Bass, *Ninety Six*, pages 136–137; Gibbes, Volume I, page 126; Gordon, pages 50–51; Jerome A. Greene, page 79; A. L. Pickens, *Skyagunsta*, pages 21–22.
49. "Francis Salvador, 1747–1776," jewishvirtuallibrary.org/jsource/biography/Salvador.html.
50. "Francis Salvador, 1747–1776," jewishvirtuallibrary.org/jsource/biography/Salvador.html.
51. Gibbes, Volume I, page 126.
52. A. L. Pickens, *Skyagunsta*, page 24.
53. Pickens, *Letter*. This is the first of three instances that Joseph Pickens family lore credits Robert Anderson with rescuing Andrew Pickens when he was either shot off his horse or had his horse shot from under him. The other two are found in Chapters 6 and 13.
54. A. L. Pickens, *Skyagunsta*, page 24.
55. Bass, *Ninety Six*, page 137; A. L. Pickens, *Skyagunsta*, page 26.
56. Bass, *Ninety Six*, page 137; Gordon, pages 52–53; A. L. Pickens, *Skyagunsta*, pages 23–25.
57. A. L. Pickens, *Skyagunsta*, page 24.
58. Bass, *Ninety Six*, pages 137–140; Gordon, pages 51–52; Jerome A. Greene, page 79; A. L. Pickens, *Skyagunsta*, pages 25–27.
59. Gibbes, Volume III, page 32.
60. Stephenson, pages 8, 11.
61. A. L. Pickens, *Skyagunsta*, page 27.
62. Lumpkin, pages 24–25; The author, William R. Reynolds, Jr., has Cherokee ancestors from this region around Murphy, such as, 4th great grandfather CahStahYeesTee (KunSteeNeeStah), meaning Whiplash, born about 1796. He married Polly Murphy and took the name Martin Murphy — his father, Bell Ringer, the author's 5th great grandfather, was born about 1775 and married Rachel Riley.
63. Gibbes, Volume III, pages 28–30.
64. Bass, *Ninety Six*, pages 141–143; Gordon, pages 54–55; Jerome A. Greene, page 79; A. L. Pickens, *Skyagunsta*, pages 26–32.
65. Landrum, page 12; Lumpkin, page 26.

Chapter 5

1. A. L. Pickens, *Skyagunsta*, page 35.
2. Woodmason, pages 27–28.
3. Bass, *Ninety Six*, page 146.
4. Tennent, *Speech to the South Carolina General Assembly (Excerpts)*, January 11, 1777.
5. A. L. Pickens, *Skyagunsta*, pages 32–33.
6. Stephenson, pages 190–191.
7. Bass, *Ninety Six*, page 143; Jerome A. Greene, pages 42, 79–80.
8. Jerome A. Greene, page 80.
9. Gibbes, Volume III, page 88.
10. Bass, *Ninety Six*, page 146.
11. Irving, Volume III, pages 47–48, 252–253.
12. Irving, Volume III, pages 47–48, 254–271.
13. John Ferling, *Almost a Miracle*, pages 239–241, 260; Gordon, pages 56–61; Lee, page 83.
14. James Smart, "Fort Mifflin's Stubborn Stand," *Military History*, Volume 14, Number 5 (December 1997), pages 35–40.
15. *The London Chronicle*, Volume XLIX, No. 3766, Saturday, January 20, 1781, page 65.
16. Ferling, pages 262–263.
17. Ferling, pages 295–297; Lee, page 105.
18. A. L. Pickens, *Skyagunsta*, page 34.
19. Bass, *Ninety Six*, page 147; Woodmason, pages 27–28.
20. Michael C. Scoggins, *Early Usage of the Term "Scotch-Irish, 1500–1800,"* newacquisitionmilitia.com.
21. Bass, *Ninety Six*, page 147; Gordon, pages 54–55; Jerome A. Greene, page 80.
22. A. L. Pickens, *Skyagunsta*, page 35.
23. Bass, *Ninety Six*, page 148; Jerome A. Greene, page 80; A. L. Pickens, *Skyagunsta*, page 35.
24. A. L. Pickens, *Skyagunsta*, page 35.
25. Bass, *Ninety Six*, pages 148–149; A. L. Pickens, *Skyagunsta*, pages 35–36.
26. A. L. Pickens, *Skyagunsta*, page 36.
27. Stephenson, page 8.
28. Stephenson, page 6.
29. Gibbes, Volume III, pages 94–95.
30. Bass, *Ninety Six*, page 147; A. L. Pickens, *Skyagunsta*, pages 35–36.
31. Gibbes, Volume III, page 96.
32. Irving, Volume III, page 480.
33. Gibbes, Volume III, page 99.
34. Gibbes, Volume III, page 96.
35. A. L. Pickens, *Skyagunsta*, page 38.
36. Bass, *Ninety Six*, page 150; Irving, Volume IV, page 478.
37. Swager, page 26.
38. Bass, *Ninety Six*, pages 150–155; Lumpkin, pages 27–28; Swager, page 26.
39. Irving, Volume III, pages 478–479.
40. Bass, *Ninety Six*, page 152; Gordon, page 62; Irving, Volume IV, pages 478–479; Lee, pages 118–119; Swager, pages 26–28.
41. "The Capture of Savannah," theamericanrevolution.org/battledetail.aspx?battle=22; Cecil B. Hartley, *Heroes and Patriots of the South: Comprising Lives of General Francis Marion, General William Moultrie, General Andrew Pickens and Governor John Rutledge*, page 229.
42. Bass, *Ninety Six*, page 152; Lee, page 120; Lumpkin, pages 28–29.

Chapter 6

1. Bass, *Ninety Six*, pages 154–155.
2. Gordon, page 63; Lee, page 122.
3. Bass, *Ninety Six*, pages 155–156; Swager, page 28.
4. Pickens, *Letter*; A. L. Pickens, *Skyagunsta*, page 40.
5. Bass, *Ninety Six*, page 156; Lee, pages 120–121.
6. Stephenson, pages 55–58.
7. Bass, *Ninety Six*, page 156; Swager, page 29.
8. Pickens, *Letter*; Swager, page 41.
9. Pickens, *Letter*.
10. Bass, *Ninety Six*, pages 156–157.
11. A. L. Pickens, *Skyagunsta*, pages 39–40.
12. Bass, *Ninety Six*, page 157; Lee, pages 120–121; Pickens, *Letter*; A. L. Pickens, *Skyagunsta*, page 40; Swager, pages 29, 41.
13. Bass, *Ninety Six*, page 158; Gordon, page 63; Pickens, *Letter*.
14. *The Old Stone Church*, pages 139–140.
15. Gordon, page 64; Pickens, *Letter*.
16. A. L. Pickens, *Skyagunsta*, page 39.

17. A. L. Pickens, *Skyagunsta*, page 41.
18. Pickens, *Letter*; A. L. Pickens, *Skyagunsta*, page 40.
19. A. L. Pickens, *Skyagunsta*, page 40.
20. Pickens, *Letter*.
21. Lee, page 120.
22. Pickens, *Letter*.
23. Pickens, *Letter*; Historic Washington, Georgia, WashingtonGeorgia.net/history.html.
24. Pickens, *Letter*.
25. Bass, *Ninety Six*, page 158; Pickens, *Letter*; A. L. Pickens, *Skyagunsta*, page 40; Swager, page 36.
26. Bass, *Ninety Six*, page 159; Pickens, *Letter*.
27. Bass, *Ninety Six*, page 159; Pickens, *Letter*; A. L. Pickens, *Skyagunsta*, page 41; Swager, page 43.
28. Bass, *Ninety Six*, page 159; Pickens, *Letter*; A. L. Pickens, *Skyagunsta*, page 41; Swager, page 43.
29. Lee, page 120.
30. Pickens, *Letter*.
31. Bass, *Ninety Six*, page 159; A. L. Pickens, *Skyagunsta*, pages 41–42; Swager, pages 43–44.
32. Bass, *Ninety Six*, page 159; Pickens, *Letter*; A. L. Pickens, *Skyagunsta*, pages 42–43; Swager, page 44.
33. Pickens, *Letter*.
34. Pickens, *Letter*.
35. Bass, *Ninety Six*, page 160; Pickens, *Letter*; A. L. Pickens, *Skyagunsta*, page 43; Swager, page 46.
36. Pickens, *Letter*.
37. Bass, *Ninety Six*, page 160; Pickens, *Letter*; A. L. Pickens, *Skyagunsta*, page 43; Swager, page 47.
38. Pickens, *Letter*.
39. Bass, *Ninety Six*, pages 160–161; Crystal Owens, "Kettle Creek Dig Providing New Insights into 1779 Battle"; Pickens, *Letter*; A. L. Pickens, *Skyagunsta*, pages 43–44; Swager, pages 48–52. Although Joseph Pickens' family lore indicates the incident leading to Joseph Pickens Indent Application occurred at Kettle Creek (as presented), and the Indent itself indicates it occurred at Cherokee Ford just before the Battle of Kettle Cree, it is more likely to have occurred at the action of defending Vann's Creek Ford from Boyd's crossing. The Vann's Creek action was essentially a continuation of the Cherokee Ford action and was a part of the Kettle Creek campaign.
40. A. L. Pickens, *Skyagunsta*, page 45.
41. A. L. Pickens, *Skyagunsta*, page 46.
42. Bass, *Ninety Six*, page 161; Jerome A. Greene, page 81; Lumpkin, page 30; Pickens, *Letter*; A. L. Pickens, *Skyagunsta*, pages 45–46; Swager, page 53.
43. Pickens, *Letter*.
44. Bass, *Ninety Six*, page 161; Gordon, page 63; Jerome A. Greene, page 81; Lee, page 121; Pickens, *Letter*; A. L. Pickens, *Skyagunsta*, page 45; Swager, page 53.
45. Gibbes, Volume III, page 109; A. L. Pickens, *Skyagunsta*, page 48.
46. Pickens, *Letter*.
47. Pickens, *Letter*.
48. Gibbes, Volume III, page 106; A. L. Pickens, *Skyagunsta*, page 48.
49. Bass, *Ninety Six*, pages 161–162; Jerome A. Greene, page 81; Lee, pages 123–124; Lumpkin, page 30; Pickens, *Letter*; A. L. Pickens, *Skyagunsta*, pages 48–49; Swager, pages 54–55.
50. Gibbes, Volume III, page 109; A. L. Pickens, *Skyagunsta*, page 48.
51. Gibbes, Volume III, page 113; A. L. Pickens, *Skyagunsta*, pages 48–49.
52. Pickens, *Letter*.
53. Bass, *Ninety Six*, pages 161–163; Jerome A. Greene, page 81; Pickens, *Letter*; A. L. Pickens, *Skyagunsta*, pages 50–51; Swager, pages 55–56.
54. Pickens, *Letter*.
55. Lee, page 121.
56. Gibbes, Volume III, page 113; Gibbes, Volume III, page 24; A. L. Pickens, *Skyagunsta*, pages 51–52.
57. Bass, *Ninety Six*, page 165.
58. Bass, *Ninety Six*, pages 161–166; Gordon, pages 65–68; Pickens, *Letter*; A. L. Pickens, *Skyagunsta*, pages 51–52; Swager, pages 55–56.
59. Grasshopper cannons had barrels made of bronze rather than iron which rendered them "light cannons." Bronze is less brittle than cast iron, allowing the barrels to be thinner and lighter than on cast iron guns. They were easily maneuvered around a rocky or rutted battlefield because of their lightness and their large wheels. The grasshopper was a "three-pounder" referring to the heaviest weight of ball it could successfully fire. Sometimes, when used at close range, the crew would fire three pounds of canister shot rendering the cannon like a huge shotgun. The cannon jumped backwards in recoil when it was fired. That, plus its physical appearance, led to the nickname of *Grasshopper*.
60. Pickens, *Letter*.
61. Bass, *Ninety Six*, page 166.
62. Bass, *Ninety Six*, pages 166–167; Gordon, page 68; Lumpkin, pages 31–32; Pickens, *Letter*; A. L. Pickens, *Skyagunsta*, page 52.
63. A. L. Pickens, *Skyagunsta*, page 54.
64. Bass, *Ninety Six*, pages 166–167; A. L. Pickens, *Skyagunsta*, pages 52–54.
65. Charles Colcock Jones, *The Siege of Savannah, in 1779*, pages 17–30; Swager, page 58.
66. *Siege_of_Savannah*, en.wikipedia.org/wiki/.
67. Robert D. Bass, *Swamp Fox: The Life and Campaigns of Francis Marion*, page 25.
68. *Siege_of_Savannah*, en.wikipedia.org/wiki/.

69. Bass, *Swamp Fox*, page 27; Hartley, pages 104–105; The carronade was a short smoothbore, cast iron cannon designed as a short-range naval weapon with a low muzzle velocity. Originally designed for ships, the carronade was capable of firing large projectiles for short distances. They were of limited use in the ground war during the American Revolution. They were found only in the northern theater, usually a six-pounder, and fired canisters of musket balls. Carronades were the stubby cannons often seen aboard ships in old pirate movies.

70. Bass, *Ninety Six*, pages 168–171; Bass, *Swamp Fox*, pages 24–27; Hartley, pages 101–108, 242–243; Lumpkin, pages 33–40; Swager, pages 57–58.

71. Bass, *Swamp Fox*, page 25; Hartley, pages 104–105; Jones, page 30; Lumpkin, page 37; sciway3.net/proctor/marion/military/revwarsc; Swager, page 58; The 1st and 2nd South Carolina Militia Regiments were organized as state infantry troops on June 6, 1775. The 1st Regiment was commanded by Colonels Christopher Gadsden and Isaac Huger, and the 2nd by Colonels William Moultrie and Isaac Motte. They were created with 10 companies each of militiamen. They were originally coastal regiments and had nothing to do with Andrew Williamson. On November 4, 1775, they were each assigned to the Continental army to satisfy the state requirement to fill a quota of Continental soldiers. On November 23, 1776, they were, respectively, adopted into the 1st and 2nd South Carolina Brigades of the Continental army. On August 26, 1778, the former 2nd Regiment was moved to the 1st Brigade with the former 1st Regiment. On February 7, 1779, the former 1st regiment was assigned to the South Carolina Brigade where they remained at the Siege of Savannah under Brigadier General Isaac Huger. On June 15, 1779, the former 2nd Regiment was assigned to Lachlan McIntosh's Brigade at Augusta, and they were reassigned to Brigadier General Isaac Huger's Brigade on September 14, 1779, just prior to the Siege of Savannah. In the 19th century, Charles Colcock Jones wrote of Williamson's militia being at Savannah; others later specified Williamson's 1st and 2nd Regiments. Given the history of those regiments, it is easy to understand why they would be mistaken for militia troops at the time of the Savannah siege. There were a few coastal South Carolina militia companies that departed Charleston with Major General Lincoln. Bass and Hartley made it clear which South Carolina militia were involved in their above references. Bass states, "Lincoln mustered the American Army. He ordered Colonel Marion and the Second Regiment from Fort Moultrie, called in his other Continentals and the Charleston militia, and set off for the rendezvous" while Hartley adds, "About...one thousand Americans, of whom between six and seven hundred were regulars, and the residue militia of Charleston, advanced in three columns.... The Continental troops lost two hundred and thirty-four men, and the Charleston militia, who, though associated with them...had one captain killed, and six privates wounded." The record is clear that Brigadier General Williamson and his militia left Lincoln's force before the Battle of Stono Ferry, and Colonel Pickens followed suit after that battle leaving only the Charleston militia available to Lincoln.

72. Pickens, *Letter*; A. L. Pickens, *Skyagunsta*, page 54.

Chapter 7

1. Gibbes, Volume III, pages 180–181.
2. Bass, *Ninety Six*, pages 174–176; Bass, *Swamp Fox*, pages 28–29; Gordon, pages 74–79; Hartley, pages 110–112; Lumpkin, pages 42–46; A. L. Pickens, *Skyagunsta*, pages 55–58.
3. Hartley, page 245.
4. Bass, *Ninety Six*, page 176; Bass, *Swamp Fox*, pages 29–30; Gordon, page 80; Lumpkin, pages 46–47.
5. Lee, page 158.
6. Lee, page 158. Hornwork: A work made up of a bastion front, two half bastions and a curtain and two long sides termed branches. It functioned to enclose an area immediately adjacent to a fort or citadel and create another layer of defense.
7. Lee, page 158.
8. John Buchanan, *The Road to Guilford Courthouse: The American Revolution in the Carolinas*, page 67.
9. Lee, pages 150, 157 (note), 161.
10. Bass, *Ninety Six*, pages 177–179; Bass, *Swamp Fox*, pages 29–30; Gordon, pages 82–86; Hartley, pages 244–252; "Lincoln, Benjamin," historyofwar.org/articles; Lee, pages 157,160–161; Lumpkin, pages 46–50; Swager, page 59.
11. *The Gentleman's Magazine*, July 1780, page 339.
12. A. L. Pickens, *Skyagunsta*, pages 57–58.
13. Colonel William Hill, *Col. William Hill's Memoirs of the American Revolution*, page 8.
14. Bass, *Ninety Six*, page 180; Lee, pages 162–163.
15. Robert D. Bass, *Gamecock: The Life and Campaigns of General Thomas Sumter*, pages 51–53; Bass, *Ninety Six*, pages 181–182; Gordon, page 86; Lee, pages 163–164.
16. Lee, page 164.
17. Lee, page 166.
18. Bass, *Ninety Six*, pages 181–182; Gordon, pages 86–87; Lee, pages 164–166.
19. Stephenson, page 317.
20. Bass, *Ninety Six*, page 182.
21. Stephenson, page 315.
22. *The Gentleman's Magazine*, July 1780, page 339.
23. Lyman C. Draper, *King's [sic] Mountain and Its Heroes: History of the Battle of King's Mountain, October 7th, 1780, and the Events Which Led to It*, page 497; A subaltern was any British commissioned officer below the rank of captain.
24. Bass, *Ninety Six*, pages 249–251; Jerome A. Greene, page 82; Lee, page 163 A. L. Pickens, *Skyagunsta*, pages 55–58.
25. Bass, *Ninety Six*, pages 186–189; Gordon, page 96; Jerome A. Greene, pages 82–84; Lumpkin, page 120; Swager, page 60.

26. Ilene Jones Cornwell, "Three South Carolina Sites Associated With Revolutionary 'Feminist' Jane Black Thomas (1720–1811)."
27. Bass, *Ninety Six*, page 189.
28. Bass, *Ninety Six*, pages 190–193; Gordon, pages 87–88; Jerome A. Greene, page 82; Lee, page 168; A. L. Pickens, *Skyagunsta*, pages 58–60; Swager, page 61.
29. A. L. Pickens, *Skyagunsta*, pages 59–60.
30. Hill, page 7.
31. Hill, pages 7–8.
32. Bass, *Ninety Six*, pages 190–202; Gordon, pages 96–108; Jerome A. Greene, pages 83–84; Lee, pages 163–167; Lumpkin, pages 51–54; Michael C. Scoggins, *Three Months in 1780*, newacquisitionmilitia.com; Swager, page 72.
33. A. L. Pickens, *Skyagunsta*, page 55.
34. Bass, *Ninety Six*, page 206.
35. Hill, page 6.
36. Bass, *Ninety Six*, page 206; Draper, page 499; Jerome A. Greene, pages 84–85.
37. Draper, page 499.
38. Bass, *Ninety Six*, pages 203–208; Jerome A. Greene, pages 84–85; Hill, pages 7–9; Lee, pages 163–167; Lumpkin, pages 81–83; Scoggins, *Three Months in 1780*.
39. Bass, *Ninety Six*, pages 213–218; Cornwell, ; Draper, pages 74–75; Gordon, page 89; Landrum, pages 110–112; Lumpkin, page 83; Scoggins, *Three Months in 1780*.
40. Bass, *Ninety Six*, page 218; Gordon, page 89; Hill, pages 9–11; Lumpkin, page 83; Scoggins, *Three Months in 1780*.
41. Hill, page 10.
42. Draper, page 500; A subaltern was any British commissioned officer below the rank of captain.
43. Bass, *Ninety Six*, page 219; Draper, pages 78–81; Landrum, pages 112–125; Lumpkin, page 83; Scoggins, *Three Months in 1780*; Swager, page 63.
44. William R. Davie, *The Revolutionary War Sketches of William R. Davie*, pages 8–10; Scoggins, *Three Months in 1780*.
45. AAA Native Arts, aaanativearts.com/Cherokee/dragging-canoe.htm; Dallas Bogan, "Dragging Canoe & the Chickamauga Cherokees," tngenweb.org/Campbell/hist-bogan/DraggingCanoe.html; Judd, *The Overmountain* Men, pages 343–359; D. Ray Smith, "Dragging Canoe, Cherokee War Chief," smithdray.tripod.com/draggingcanoe-index-9.html.
46. Bass, *Ninety Six*, page 227; Gordon, page 108; Landrum, pages 128–129; Lumpkin, page 87; Scoggins, *Three Months in 1780*; Swager, page 64.
47. Irving, Volume IV, page 75.
48. Bass, *Ninety Six*, pages 227–233; Cornwell, ; Gordon, pages 90–91; Hill, pages 12–14; Irving, Volume IV, pages 90–92; Landrum, pages 129–134; Scoggins, *Three Months in 1780*; Swager, page 64.
49. Bass, *Ninety Six*, page 226; Jerome A. Greene, page 85; A. L. Pickens, *Skyagunsta*, pages 3, 60.
50. Buchanan, *The Road to Guilford Courthouse,* page 162.
51. Buchanan, *The Road to Guilford Courthouse,* page 162.
52. Buchanan, *The Road to Guilford Courthouse,* page 162.
53. Bass, *Ninety Six*, pages 230–239; Gordon, pages 91–94; Hill, page 14; Irving, Volume IV, pages 92–98; Lee, pages 183–186; Lumpkin, page 86; Scoggins, *Three Months in 1780*.
54. A. L. Pickens, *Skyagunsta*, page 60.
55. Davie, page 4.
56. Irving, Volume IV, pages 102–103.
57. Bass, *Ninety Six*, page 240.
58. Bass, *Ninety Six*, pages 239–240; Gordon, pages 94–105; Lee, pages 189–190; Lumpkin, pages 86, 118–119.
59. Landrum, page 155.
60. Landrum, page 155.
61. Bass, *Ninety Six*, pages 240–242; Draper, pages 103–115; Gordon, page 108; Hill, pages 24–29; Landrum, pages 147–163; Lumpkin, pages 87–88; Swager, pages 66–69, 76–78.
62. Peter Force, *Marion, Francis. Peter Force copies of Peter Horry's transcripts of Francis Marion letters, 1779–1782.* N.p.: 1846, microfilm reel, P900013, South Carolina Department of Archives and History, Columbia SC.
63. Bass, *Ninety Six*, pages 243–245; Gordon, pages 109–110; Lumpkin, pages 72–73.

Chapter 8

1. Ferling, page 460.
2. Bass, *Ninety Six*, pages 243–251; Gordon, pages 113–114; Landrum, pages 175–179; Lumpkin, pages 88–89; A. L. Pickens, *Skyagunsta*, page 3; Swager, pages 70–78; "The Battle of Kings Mountain," Tennessee History Classroom, tennesseehistory.com/class/KingsMt.htm.
3. Draper, page 508.
4. Draper, page 508.
5. Draper, page 200.
6. Draper, page 509.
7. Bass, *Ninety Six*, pages 243–254; Gordon, pages 113–114; Landrum, pages 180–183; Lee, page 200; Lumpkin, page 89; Swager, pages 70–78; "The Battle of Kings Mountain," Tennessee History Classroom.
8. "Black Mingo," www.carolana.com/SC/Revolution/revolution_black_mingo.html; Gordon, pages 110–111.

9. Draper, page 195; Landrum, pages 186–187.
10. Draper, page 195.
11. Draper, pages 195–196.
12. Bass, *Ninety Six*, page 253.
13. Landrum, page 194.
14. Bass, *Ninety Six*, page 259; Landrum, page 192.
15. Draper, page 510.
16. Bass, *Ninety Six*, pages 252–259; Landrum, pages 181–187; Swager, pages 75–78; "The Battle of Kings Mountain," Tennessee History Classroom.
17. Bass, *Ninety Six*, page 262; Landrum, pages 193–196; Swager, page 77; "The Battle of Kings Mountain," Tennessee History Classroom.
18. Bass, *Ninety Six*, pages 249–250, 259–262; Hill, pages 17–25; Landrum, pages 188–190, 194; Swager, page 77; "The Battle of Kings Mountain," Tennessee History Classroom.
19. Bass, *Ninety Six*, page 261; Draper, pages 211, 224; Landrum, page 192.
20. Lee, page 200.
21. Landrum, page 207.
22. Bass, *Ninety Six*, pages 261–262; Ferling, pages 460–461; Gordon, pages 114–115; Hill, page 23; Landrum, pages 192, 194, 207; Lee, page 200; Lumpkin, pages 91–96; "The Battle of Kings Mountain," Tennessee History Classroom.
23. Bass, *Ninety Six*, pages 262–263; Landrum, page 199.
24. Landrum, pages 199–200; Lumpkin, page 99.
25. Bass, *Ninety Six*, pages 261–262.
26. Landrum, page 201.
27. Bass, *Ninety Six*, pages 262–263; Gordon, pages 114–117; Landrum, pages 197–201; Lee, page 200; Lumpkin, pages 98–99; Swager, page 77; "The Battle of Kings Mountain," Tennessee History Classroom.
28. Thomas Young, "Memoir of Major Thomas Young," *Orion Magazine*, October-November 1843.
29. Bass, *Ninety Six*, page 263; Landrum, page 202.
30. www.carolana.com/SC/Revolution/revolution_battle_of_kings_mountain.html.
31. Draper, page 247.
32. Draper, page 247; Lumpkin, page 100.
33. Draper, page 249.
34. Draper, page 252.
35. Thomas Young, "Memoir of Major Thomas Young."
36. Draper, page 254.
37. Draper, page 268; Lumpkin, page 102.
38. Draper, page 273.
39. Landrum, page 209.
40. Draper, page 281.
41. Draper, page 282.
42. Draper, page 284.
43. Bass, *Ninety Six*, pages 263–268; Draper, pages 232–290; Ferling, pages 461–463; Gordon, pages 115–117; Hill, pages 16–25; Landrum, pages 201–212; Lumpkin, pages 99–103; Swager, page 78; "The Battle of Kings Mountain," Tennessee History Classroom.
44. Draper, page 510.
45. Draper, page 270; Thomas Young, "Memoir of Major Thomas Young."
46. Draper, page 510.
47. Draper, page 308.
48. Draper, pages 287–309; Landrum, pages 212–215; Lee, page 201; Lumpkin, pages 103–104; "The Battle of Kings Mountain," Tennessee History Classroom.
50. Hill, page 24.
51. Draper, page 277.
52. Draper, page 323.
53. Draper, page 297.
54. Bass, *Ninety Six*, page 256.
55. Draper, page 326.
56. Draper, page 327.
57. Draper, page 511.
58. Draper, page 331.
59. Draper, page 338.
60. Draper, page 348.
61. Draper, pages 316–360; Landrum, pages 214–220; "The Battle of Kings Mountain," Tennessee History Classroom.
62. Draper, page 360.

Chapter 9

1. Irving, Volume IV, page 200.
2. Babits, *A Devil of a Whipping — The Battle of Cowpens*, page 5; Edwin C. Bearss, *Battle of Cowpens — A Documented Narrative and Troop Movement Maps*, Chapter 1, page 1; Gordon, page 125; Irving, Volume IV, pages 200–201.

3. Buchanan, *The Road to Guilford Courthouse*, pages 336–337.
4. Bass, *Ninety Six*, pages 269, 277–283; Babits, page 3; Landrum, pages 237–238; Lumpkin, page 105; Swager, page 79.
5. Bass, *Ninety Six*, pages 276, 279; A. L. Pickens, *Skyagunsta*, page 60.
6. Bass, *Swamp Fox*, pages 76–77; carolana.com/SC/Revolution/revolution_tearcoat_swamp.html; Gordon, pages 117–118.
7. Bass, *Ninety Six*, page 280; Jerome A. Greene, pages 91–92, 111–112.
8. Alexander Garden, *Anecdotes of the American Revolution, Illustrative of the Talents and Virtues of the Heroes of the Revolution, Who Acted the Most Conspicuous Parts Therein, Volume II*, page 271.
9. Bass, *Gamecock*, pages 96–99; Bass, *Ninety Six*, pages 282–285; Bass, *Swamp Fox*, pages 79–83; Gordon, pages 119–120; Landrum, pages 238–242; Lee, pages 205–206; Lumpkin, pages 107–109; Swager, page 81.
10. Bass, *Gamecock*, pages 102–111; Bass, *Ninety Six*, pages 282–287; Gordon, pages 120–122; Landrum, pages 243–253; Lumpkin, pages 105–115; Swager, pages 81–83.
11. Bass, *Gamecock*, page 109.
12. William Johnson, *Sketches of the Life and Correspondence of Nathanael Greene, Major General of the Armies of the United States in the War of the Revolution, Vol. 1*, page 337.
13. Irving, Volume IV, page 202.
14. Irving, Volume IV, page 204.
15. Landrum, page 266.
16. A. L. Pickens, *Skyagunsta*, page 61.
17. Bass, *Ninety Six*, page 299; Bearss, Chapter 1, page 1; Gordon, pages 123–125; Jerome A. Greene, page 95; Irving, Volume IV, pages 200–204; A. L. Pickens, *Skyagunsta*, pages 61–63; Swager, pages 73–84.
18. A. L. Pickens, *Skyagunsta*, pages 58–62; Swager, pages 84–85.
19. A. L. Pickens, *Skyagunsta*, page 63.
20. A. L. Pickens, *Skyagunsta*, page 63.
21. Bass, *Ninety Six*, pages 305–306; Jerome A. Greene, page 96; Lumpkin, page 123; A. L. Pickens, *Skyagunsta*, pages 62–63; Swager, page 85.
22. Landrum, page 267.
23. Bass, *Ninety Six*, pages 301–306; Bearss, Chapter 1, pages 1–2; Gordon, pages 126–127; Jerome A. Greene, page 96; Johnson, page 362; Landrum, pages 260–265; Lumpkin, page 123; *The Old Stone Church*, pages 140–141; A. L. Pickens, *Skyagunsta*, pages 63–64; Swager, page 85.
24. Carolana.com/SC/Revolution/revolution_battle_of_hammonds_store.html.
25. "Col. Thomas Waters, 1738–After 1818," jeanday1.tripod.com/Waters_Thomas_Col_.htm.
26. Bass, *Ninety Six*, page 307.
27. Babits, page 9; Bass, *Ninety Six*, pages 306–307; Bearss, Chapter 1, page 2; Gordon, pages 126–128; Jerome A. Greene, page 96; Johnson, page 362; Lumpkin, pages 120–121; A. L. Pickens, *Skyagunsta*, page 65; Swager, page 85.
28. Babits, page 49; Bass, *Ninety Six*, pages 306–308; George Washington Greene, *The Life of Nathanael Greene, Major-General in the Army of the Revolution*, Volume 3, Chapter VIII, page 134; A. L. Pickens, *Skyagunsta*, pages 63–65.
29. Babits, page 49.
30. Landrum, page 271; John Robertson, "An Effort to Locate the Mill Morgan Called 'Burr's Mill,'" gaz.jrshelby.com/burrs-mill-locating.pdf, November 10, 2010.
31. Johnson, page 341.
32. Johnson, pages 370–371; A. L. Pickens, *Skyagunsta*, page 66.
33. Bass, *Ninety Six*, page 322.
34. Babits, pages 53–55.
35. Babits, pages 8–9, 50–54; Bass, *Ninety Six*, pages 306–322; Bearss, Chapter 1, page 2, Chapter 2, pages 1–3; Gordon, pages 127–129; Johnson, page 362; Landrum, pages 268–272; Lumpkin, pages 121–124; *The Old Stone Church*, pages 140–141; A. L. Pickens, *Skyagunsta*, pages 65–67; Swager, page 85.
36. Babits, pages 61–65; A. L. Pickens, *Cane-Brakes as Key to Cowpens*, Meridian States Research, Volume X, Number 1, 1951.
37. Babits, page 65.
38. Bearss, Chapter 2, page 4; Landrum, pages 275–276.
39. Thomas Young, "Memoir of Major Thomas Young."
40. *The Old Stone Church*, page 141; Lee, Editor's note, page 226.
41. A. L. Pickens, *Skyagunsta*, page 68.
42. A. L. Pickens, *Skyagunsta*, pages 68–69.
43. Ferling, page 455.
44. Thomas Young, "Memoir of Major Thomas Young."
45. A. L. Pickens, *Skyagunsta*, page 69.
46. Babits, pages 53–56, 61–65; Bass, *Ninety Six*, page 321; Bearss, Chapter 2, pages 3–5; Gordon, page 129; Landrum, pages 275–277; Lee, Editor's note, pages 225–226; Lumpkin, pages 124–126; A. L. Pickens, *Skyagunsta*, pages 68–69; Swager, pages 87–89.
47. Thomas Young, "Memoir of Major Thomas Young."
48. Thomas Young, "Memoir of Major Thomas Young."
49. Babits, pages 56–80; Bass, *Ninety Six*, pages 322–323; Bearss, Chapter 2, pages 3–8, Chapter 3, pages 1–2; Gordon, pages 129–133; Irving, Volume IV, pages 235–239; Landrum, pages 275–281; Lee, Editor's note, pages 227–228; Lumpkin, pages 126–128; A. L. Pickens, *Skyagunsta*, pages 69–70; Swager, page 97.
50. A. L. Pickens, *Skyagunsta*, page 70.

51. Thomas Young, "Memoir of Major Thomas Young."
52. Babits, page 99.
53. A. L. Pickens, *Skyagunsta*, page 73.
54. Babits, page 127.
55. Pickens, *Letter*.
56. Thomas Young, "Memoir of Major Thomas Young."
57. *The Old Stone Church*, page 140.
58. A. L. Pickens, *Skyagunsta*, page 76.
59. A. L. Pickens, *Skyagunsta*, page 76.
60. A. L. Pickens, *Skyagunsta*, page 71.
61. Lee, Editor's note, page 230.
62. Gordon, page 137.
63. A. L. Pickens, *Skyagunsta*, page 74.
64. A. L. Pickens, *Skyagunsta*, page 76.
65. Landrum, pages 290–291; A. L. Pickens, *Skyagunsta*, page 77.
66. A. L. Pickens, *Skyagunsta*, page 77.
67. Draper, Introduction, page vi.
68. Babits, pages 81–133; Bass, *Ninety Six*, pages 323–325; Bearss, pages 2–10; Ferling, pages 483–486; Gordon, pages 133–135; Irving, Volume IV, pages 239–242; Johnson, pages 368–384; Landrum, pages 281–291; Lee, Editor's note, pages 228–230; Lumpkin, pages 128–133; A. L. Pickens, *Skyagunsta*, pages 70–75; Swager, pages 99–101.

CHAPTER 10

1. Pickens, *Letter*.
2. Thomas Young, "Memoir of Major Thomas Young."
3. A. L. Pickens, *Skyagunsta*, page 75.
4. A. L. Pickens, *Skyagunsta*, page 75.
5. Bass, *Ninety Six*, page 323; Irving, Volume IV, pages 242–243; Johnson, page 385; A. L. Pickens, *Skyagunsta*, pages 74–75; Swager, pages 101–104.
6. Johnson, pages 368–369.
7. Pickens, *Letter*.
8. Johnson, page 427.
9. A. L. Pickens, *Skyagunsta*, page 81.
10. Johnson, page 403.
11. Bass, *Ninety Six*, pages 329–330; A. L. Pickens, *Skyagunsta*, page 76.
12. Bass, *Ninety Six*, pages 313–332; Ferling, pages 488–490; Gordon, pages 128–143; George Washington Greene, Volume 3, Chapter VIII, page 134-Chapter IX, page 153; Irving, Volume IV, pages 246–248; Johnson, pages 368–390, 412 footnote, 427; Lee, Editor's note, pages 223–225; A. L. Pickens, *Skyagunsta*, pages 75–81; Swager, page 104.
13. Bass, *Ninety Six*, page 334; Ferling, page 490; George Washington Greene, Volume 3, Chapter IX, pages 155–157; Irving, Volume IV, page 249–251; Johnson, pages 414–415; Lee, Editor's note, pages 233–235; A. L. Pickens, *Skyagunsta*, page 81.
14. Bass, *Ninety Six*, page 334; Ferling, page 490; George Washington Greene, Volume 3, Chapter IX, pages 157–159; Irving, Volume IV, page 251; Johnson, pages 416–417; Lee, Editor's note, page 234; A. L. Pickens, *Skyagunsta*, pages 81–82.
15. Monica Mary Gardner, *Kosciuszko: A Biography*, Chapter II.
16. David T. Zabecki, "In The Cause of Freedom — Tadeusz Kosciuszko Fought for Freedom in America and Poland," *Military History*, page 55.
17. Gardner, Chapter II.
18. Bass, *Ninety Six*, pages 334–335; Ferling, pages 492; George Washington Greene, Volume 3, Chapter IX, pages 159–162, Chapter X, pages 163–166; Irving, Volume IV, pages 252–253; Johnson, pages 418–423; Lee, Editor's note, page 236; Lumpkin, pages 164–166; A. L. Pickens, *Skyagunsta*, page 82.
19. Bass, *Ninety Six*, pages 335–337; Ferling, pages 491–494; George Washington Greene, Volume 3, Chapter X, pages 167–175; Irving, Volume IV, pages 253–259; Johnson, pages 424–433; Lee, Editor's note, pages 243–250; A. L. Pickens, *Skyagunsta*, page 82; Swager, page 105.
20. Johnson, page 435.
21. Bass, *Ninety Six*, pages 334–335; Gordon, page 143; George Washington Greene, Volume 3, Chapter XI, pages 179–183; Irving, Volume IV, pages 259–262; Johnson, pages 433–435, 452–457; Lee, Editor's note, pages 251–263; Lumpkin, pages 166–167; A. L. Pickens, *Skyagunsta*, pages 83–86; Swager, page 106.
22. Lee, Editor's note, page 263.
23. Johnson, page 457.
24. Johnson, page 457.
25. Pickens, *Letter*.
26. Bass, *Ninety Six*, pages 337–351; Gordon, page 148; George Washington Greene, Volume 3, Chapter XI, pages 183–188; Johnson, pages 457–472; Lee, Editor's note, pages 263–271; Lumpkin, pages 167–169; A. L. Pickens, *Skyagunsta*, pages 87–89; Swager, page 107.
27. Johnson, pages 469.
28. Bass, *Ninety Six*, pages 342–351; Gordon, pages 142–146; George Washington Greene, Volume 3, Chapter XI, pages 189–202; Jerome A. Greene, page 115; Irving, Volume IV, pages 262–271; Lee, Editor's note, pages 272–286; Lumpkin, pages 163–175; Swager, page 110.

29. Colonel Morton Wilkinson served as an officer in the Colleton County South Carolina militia. This was also Colonel Isaac Hayne's militia regiment. The Colleton County Regiment often worked closely with Brigadier General Francis Marion. The regiment would have been contemporary with the forces of Georgia Colonel Elijah Clarke, one of the eleven colonels listed as having joined with Brigadier General Andrew Pickens. Colonel Morton Wilkinson married Susannah Smith. Their daughter Susannah Wilkinson married Francis Wilkinson. Francis' and Susannah's daughter, Susan Smith Wilkinson, married General Pickens' son, South Carolina Governor Andrew Pickens, Jr. Then followed their son, South Carolina Governor Francis Wilkinson Pickens. Thus, Governor Francis Wilkinson Pickens was not only the grandson of General Andrew Pickens, but he was also the great-grandson of Colonel Morton Wilkinson.

30. Bass, *Ninety Six*, pages 346–357; Gordon, page 147; George Washington Greene, Volume 3, Chapter XI, pages 203–217; Jerome A. Greene, pages 116–117; Lee, Editor's note, pages 315–326; Lumpkin, page 176; A. L. Pickens, *Skyagunsta*, pages 89–93; Swager, pages 108–109.

31. Bass, *Ninety Six*, page 359.

32. Bass, *Ninety Six*, pages 357–367; Gordon, pages 148–149; George Washington Greene, Volume 3, Chapter XIV, pages 230–238, Chapter XV, pages 240–253; Jerome A. Greene, pages 117–118; Irving, Volume IV, pages 320–321; Lee, Editor's note, pages 327–339; Lumpkin, pages 176–185; A. L. Pickens, *Skyagunsta*, page 92.

33. Bass, *Ninety Six*, pages 371–381; Gordon, pages 151–153; Jerome A. Greene, pages 117–119; Irving, Volume IV, page 322; Lumpkin, pages 176–185; A. L. Pickens, *Skyagunsta*, pages 93–94; Swager, page 110.

Chapter 11

1. Bass, *Ninety Six*, pages 380–383; Gordon, page 153; Jerome A. Greene, page 119; Irving, Volume IV, page 322; Landrum, pages 319–321; Lee, Editor's note, pages 353–355; Lumpkin, pages 186–187; A. L. Pickens, *Skyagunsta*, page 94; Swager, pages 110–111.
2. Landrum, pages 320–321 267; A. L. Pickens, *Skyagunsta*, page 94.
3. A. L. Pickens, *Skyagunsta*, page 94.
4. Tarleton Brown, *Memoirs of Tarleton Brown a Captain in the Revolutionary Army*, page 44.
5. Brown, pages 44–45.
6. Lee, Editor's note, pages 367–369; A. L. Pickens, *Skyagunsta*, page 95.
7. A. L. Pickens, *Skyagunsta*, page 96.
8. Lee, Editor's note, pages 367–369; A. L. Pickens, *Skyagunsta*, page 96.
9. Lee, Editor's note, pages 367–369; A. L. Pickens, *Skyagunsta*, page 97.
10. Lee, Editor's note, pages 367–369; A. L. Pickens, *Skyagunsta*, page 97.
11. Brown, page 46.
12. A. L. Pickens, *Skyagunsta*, page 100.
13. Lee, Editor's note, page 371.
14. Bass, *Ninety Six*, pages 390–394; Gordon, pages 154–155; Landrum, pages 319–323; Lee, Editor's note, pages 354–371; Lumpkin, pages 188–192; A. L. Pickens, *Skyagunsta*, pages 94–101; Swager, pages 112–118.

Chapter 12

1. Bass, *Ninety Six*, pages 386–387; Bass, *Swamp Fox*, pages 198–203; Gordon, pages 153–158; Jerome A. Greene, page 119; Irving, Volume IV, page 322; Landrum, page 323; Lumpkin, page 186.
2. Bass, *Ninety Six*, pages 377–385; Jerome A. Greene, pages 101–125; Irving, Volume IV, page 322; Landrum, pages 324–327; Lumpkin, pages 192–196.
3. Jerome A. Greene, pages 136–137.
4. Bass, *Ninety Six*, pages 387–395; Gordon, pages 155–157; Jerome A. Greene, pages 127–137; Irving, Volume IV, page 322; Landrum, pages 324–327; Lumpkin, pages 192–199.
5. Jerome A. Greene, page 140.
6. Bass, *Swamp Fox*, page 212.
7. Bass, *Ninety Six*, page 395; Jerome A. Greene, pages 138–141; Irving, Volume IV, page 322; Landrum, pages 324–327; Lee, Editor's note, pages 370–372; Lumpkin, pages 192–199; A. L. Pickens, *Skyagunsta*, page 101.
8. Stephenson, pages 163–164.
9. Stephenson, page 170.
10. Sharp, page 33.
11. Sharp, appendix II, item 1, pages 136–137.
12. Day, chapter 4.5, pages 75–76.
13. Day, chapter 4.1, page 40. Interestingly, the source for this citation is the same as for the citation at the previous note, which declared that John Pickens had been killed at Ninety Six.
14. Lee, Editor's note, page 371.
15. Lee, Editor's note, page 371 footnote.
16. Thomas Young, "Memoir of Major Thomas Young."
17. Jerome A. Greene, pages 153–154.
18. Gibbes, Volume II, page 94.
19. Gibbes, Volume II, pages 95–97.
20. Lee, pages 373–374.
21. Bass, *Ninety Six*, pages 396–398; Gordon, page 157; Jerome A. Greene, pages 141–158; Irving, Volume IV, pages

322–323; Landrum, pages 327–329; Lee, Editor's note, pages 371–374; Lumpkin, pages 199–202; A. L. Pickens, *Skyagunsta*, pages 101–102; Alice Noble Waring, *The Fighting Elder: Andrew Pickens, 1739–1817*, pages 81–83.
    22. Jerome A. Greene, page 157.
    23. Jerome A. Greene, page 175; Waring, page 87.
    24. Bass, *Ninety Six*, pages 400–410; Gordon, page 158; Jerome A. Greene, pages 158–175; Irving, Volume IV, page 323; Landrum, pages 329–332; Lee, Editor's note, pages 374–379; Lumpkin, pages 202–205; A. L. Pickens, *Skyagunsta*, page 102; Swager, page 118; Waring, pages 83–87.
    25. Jerome A. Greene, page 175.
    26. Gibbes, Volume II, pages 100–101.
    27. Bass, *Ninety Six*, page 415.
    28. A. L. Pickens, *Skyagunsta*, page 105.
    29. Bass, *Ninety Six*, pages 408–427; Gordon, page 158; Jerome A. Greene, pages 168–175; Landrum, pages 332–334; Lee, Editor's note, pages 378–387; Lumpkin, page 205; A. L. Pickens, *Skyagunsta*, pages 104–105; Swager, page 118.
    30. Landrum, page 335.
    31. Bass, *Ninety Six*, pages 427–428; Gordon, pages 159–162; Lee, Editor's note, pages 387–394; Lumpkin, pages 206–211; A. L. Pickens, *Skyagunsta*, pages 104–105; Swager, page 118.
    32. Jerome A. Greene, page 173.
    33. Bass, *Swamp Fox*, page 213; Lee, Editor's note, page 455.
    34. Bass, *Ninety Six*, pages 428–430; Gordon, pages 159–163; Jerome A. Greene, page 173.
    35. Lee, Editor's note, page 458.
    36. Lee, Editor's note, page 457.
    37. Lee, Editor's note, page 458.
    38. Lee, Editor's note, page 457.
    39. Bass, *Ninety Six*, pages 429–430; Bass, *Swamp Fox*, pages 212–215; Gordon, pages 162–163; Lee, Editor's note, pages 447–459; Lumpkin, pages 212–213; Swager, pages 118–119.
    40. A. L. Pickens, *Skyagunsta*, page 106.
    41. A. L. Pickens, *Skyagunsta*, page 106.
    42. A. L. Pickens, *Skyagunsta*, page 106.
    43. Carolana.com/SC/Revolution/revolution_battle_of_eutaw_springs.html.
    44. Virtual War Museum, virtualolgy.com/revolutionarywarhall/battle/eutawsprings.
    45. Virtual War Museum, virtualolgy.com/revolutionarywarhall/battle/eutawsprings.
    46. Bass, *Swamp Fox*, page 217.
    47. Bass, *Ninety Six*, pages 430–432; Bass, *Swamp Fox*, pages 215–219; Gordon, pages 164–167; Lee, Editor's note, pages 463–475; Lumpkin, pages 213–221; A. L. Pickens, *Skyagunsta*, pages 106–108; "Southern Campaigns of the American Revolution," newsletter, Volume 3, Number 9, Southerncampaign.org; Swager, page 119.

Chapter 13

    1. Gibbes, Volume II, pages 162–163; A. L. Pickens, *Skyagunsta*, page 108.
    2. Bass, *Ninety Six*, page 434; A. L. Pickens, *Skyagunsta*, pages 108–109; Swager, pages 119–123.
    3. Landrum, page 348.
    4. Landrum, page 350.
    5. Bass, *Ninety Six*, pages 434–435; Gordon, page 171; Landrum, pages 347–348; A. L. Pickens, *Skyagunsta*, page 109.
    6. A. L. Pickens, *Skyagunsta*, page 109.
    7. A. L. Pickens, *Skyagunsta*, page 110.
    8. A. L. Pickens, *Skyagunsta*, page 110.
    9. A. L. Pickens, *Skyagunsta*, page 113.
    10. Bass, *Ninety Six*, page 435; Gordon, pages 172–173; A. L. Pickens, *Skyagunsta*, pages 109–113; Swager, pages 120–125.
    11. Gibbes, Volume III, pages 210–211; A. L. Pickens, *Skyagunsta*, pages 115–116.
    12. Gordon, page 176; A. L. Pickens, *Skyagunsta*, pages 114–116; Swager, pages 124–125.
    13. Gibbes, Volume III, pages 220–221; A. L. Pickens, *Skyagunsta*, page 116.
    14. Pickens, *Letter*.
    15. Pickens, *Letter*.
    16. A. L. Pickens, *Skyagunsta*, page 116.
    17. A. L. Pickens, *Skyagunsta*, page 116.
    18. A. L. Pickens, *Skyagunsta*, page 116.
    19. A. L. Pickens, *Skyagunsta*, page 116.
    20. A. L. Pickens, *Skyagunsta*, page 119; Sharp, appendix II, paragraph 3, page 137.
    21. Gordon, page 176; A. L. Pickens, *Skyagunsta*, pages 114–116; Gordon B. Smith, "The British Evacuate Savannah Georgia," *The SAR Magazine*, Vol. 100, No. 4 (Spring 2007), Georgia Society of Sons of the American Revolution; Swager, pages 124–125.
    22. A. L. Pickens, *Skyagunsta*, pages 110–122; Swager, page 125.

Epilogue

    1. A. L. Pickens, *Skyagunsta*, pages 123–158.
    2. *The Old Stone Church*, pages 142–143; A. L. Pickens, *Skyagunsta*, page 143.

3. A. L. Pickens, *Skyagunsta*, pages 124–127.
4. A. L. Pickens, *Skyagunsta*, page 125.
5. A. L. Pickens, *Skyagunsta*, page 125.
6. A. L. Pickens, *Skyagunsta*, page 125.
7. A. L. Pickens, *Skyagunsta*, pages 132–133.
8. Fergus M. Bordewich, "Opening Salvo," *Smithsonian,* April 2011, page 89.
9. A. L. Pickens, *Skyagunsta*, pages 122–123.

Bibliography

AAA Native Arts, aaanativearts.com/cherokee.
American Archives, Documents of the American Revolution. lincoln.lib.niu.edu.
The American-Israeli Cooperative Enterprise, jewishvirtuallibrary.org.
The American Revolution, theamericanrevolution.org.
Babits, Lawrence E. *A Devil of a Whipping — The Battle of Cowpens.* Chapel Hill: The University of North Carolina Press, 1998.
Bass, Robert D. *Gamecock: The Life and Campaigns of General Thomas Sumter.* Lexington, SC: The Sandlapper Store, 1961.
_____. *The Green Dragoon: The Lives of Banastre Tarleton and Mary Robinson.* Lexington, SC: The Sandlapper Store, 1957.
_____. *Ninety Six: The Struggle for the South Carolina Back Country.* Lexington, SC: The Sandlapper Store, 1978.
_____. *Swamp Fox: The Life and Campaigns of General Francis Marion.* Lexington, SC: The Sandlapper Store, 1974.
"The Battle of Kings Mountain." Tennessee History Classroom, tennesseehistory.com/class/KingsMt.htm.
Bearss, Edwin C. *Battle of Cowpens — A Documented Narrative and Troop Movement Maps.* National Park Service, reprinted by Overmountain Press, 1967.
Bender, Albert. "Dragging Canoe's War." *Military History*, Volume 28, Number 5 (January 2012): 68–75.
Blankenship, Bob. *Cherokee Roots, Volume 1.* Cherokee, NC: Bob Blankenship, 1992.
Bodie, Idella. *The Wizard Owl.* Orangeburg, SC: Sandlapper Publishing, 2003.
Bogan, Dallas. "Dragging Canoe & the Chickamauga Cherokees." tngenweb.org/Campbell/hist-bogan/DraggingCanoe.htm.
Bordewich, Fergus M. "Opening Salvo." *Smithsonian,* April 2011: 76–99.
Brown, Tarleton. *The Memoirs of Tarleton Brown a Captain in the American Revolutionary Army.* New York: privately printed by Charles I. Bushnell, 1862.
Buchanan, John. *The Road to Guilford Courthouse: The American Revolution in the Carolinas.* New York: John Wiley and Sons, 1997.
Calloway, Colin G. *The American Revolution in Indian Country.* New York: Cambridge University Press, 1995.
Cann, Marvin. *Old Ninety Six in the South Carolina Backcountry 1700–1781.* Eastern National, 2000, reprinted 2005.
Carolana.com, carolana.com/SC/Revolution.
Cheaney, Janie B. *Charles, Earl Cornwallis.* jrshelby.com/kimocowp/cornwal.htm, 1998.
Clark, Murtie June. *Loyalists in the Southern Campaign of the Revolutionary War, Volume 1.* Baltimore: Genealogical Publishing, 1981.
Coffin, Charles Carlton. *The Boys of '76 — A History of the Battles of the Revolution.* New York: Harper & Brothers, 1876.
"Col. Thomas Waters, 1738–After 1818." jeanday1.tripod.com/Waters_Thomas_Col_.htm.
The Connecticut Journal [New Haven], No. 728, Thursday, October 11, 1781.
Cornwell, Ilene Jones. "Three South Carolina Sites Associated with Revolutionary 'Feminist' Jane Black Thomas (1720–1811)." sciway3.net/clark/revolutionarywar/JaneBlackThomas.
Curtis, Edward E. *The Organization of the British Army in the American Revolution.* New Haven: Yale University Press; London: Humphrey Milford Oxford University Press, 1926.

Dabney, William M., and Marion Dargan. *William Henry Drayton & the American Revolution.* Albuquerque: The University of New Mexico Press, 1962.
Davie, William R. *The Revolutionary War Sketches of William R. Davie.* Edited by Blackwell Robinson. Raleigh, NC: Dept. of Cultural Resources, Division of Archives and History, 1976.
Day, Kate Pickens. *Cousin Monroe's History of the Pickens Family.* Compiled by Thomas Mason Monroe Pickens. Revised by Kate Pickens Day. Easley, SC: self-published, printed by Hoitt Press of Greenville, SC, 1951.
DeSaussure, Gen. Wilmot G. *An Account of the Siege of Charleston, South Carolina in 1780.* Charleston, SC: The News and Courier Book Presses, 1885.
Draper, Lyman C. *King's [sic] Mountain and Its Heroes: History of the Battle of King's Mountain, October 7th, 1780, and the Events Which Led to It.* Cincinnati: Peter G. Thomson, Publisher, 1881.
"Drumming out a Tory." *Harper's Weekly, Journal of Civilization,* February 3, 1877.
Dunkerly, Robert M., and Eric K. Williams. *Old Ninety Six: A History and Guide.* Charleston, SC: The History Press, 2006.
Edgar, Walter. *Partisans & Redcoats.* New York: HarperCollins, 2003.
Ferling, John. *Almost a Miracle.* New York: Oxford University Press, 2007.
Force, Peter. Marion, Francis. *Peter Force copies of Peter Horry's transcripts of Francis Marion letters, 1779–1782.* N.p.: 1846. Microfilm reel. P900013; Columbia: South Carolina Department of Archives and History.
Ford, Henry Jones. *The Scotch-Irish in America.* 1915. Libraryireland.com.
Garden, Alexander. *Anecdotes of the American Revolution, Illustrative of the Talents and Virtues of the Heroes of the Revolution, Who Acted the Most Conspicuous Parts Therein, Volume II.* Brooklyn, NY: The Union Press, Reprinted 1865.
Gardner, Monica Mary. *Kosciuszko: A Biography.* London: George Allen & Unwin; New York: Charles Scribner's Sons, 1920.
"General Sir Banastre Tarleton, Bart., G.C.B." *Baily's Magazine,* April 1908: 282–285.
Gibbes, R. W. *Documentary History of the American Revolution.* Volumes I to III. Spartanburg, SC: Reprint Co., 1972.
Gordon, John W. *South Carolina and the American Revolution.* Columbia: University of South Carolina Press, 2003.
Greene, George Washington. *The Life of Nathanael Greene, Major-General in the War of the Revolution, Three Volumes.* New York: Hurd and Houghton, 1871.
Greene, Jerome A. "Ninety Six, A Historical Narrative," National Park Service brochure.
Harper, Josephine L. *Guide to the Draper Manuscripts.* Madison, WI: State Historical Society of Wisconsin, 1983.
Hartley, Cecil B. *Heroes and Patriots of the South: Comprising Lives of General Francis Marion, General William Moultrie, General Andrew Pickens and Governor John Rutledge.* Philadelphia: G. G. Evans, Publisher, 1860.
Hatcher, Patricia Law. *Abstract of Graves of Revolutionary Patriots, Volume 3.* Dallas, TX: Pioneer Heritage Press, 1987.
Hawke, David Freeman. *Everyday Life in Early America.* New York: Harper and Row, 1988; Perennial Edition, HarperCollins Publishers, 2003.
Hill, Colonel William. *Col. William Hill's Memoirs of the American Revolution.* Edited by A. S. Salley, Jr. Columbia, SC: The Historical Commission of South Carolina, The State Company, 1921.
Historic Washington, Georgia, washingtongeorgia.net/history.html.
Irving, Washington. *The Life of George Washington (1st edition).* Vols. II–IV. New York: G. P. Putnam & Co., 1855.
Johnson, William. *Sketches of the Life and Correspondence of Nathanael Greene, Major General of the Armies of the United States in the War of the Revolution, Vol. 1.* Charleston, SC: Originally printed by A. E. Miller, 1822; reprinted by Whitefish, MT: Kessinger Publishing.
Jones, Charles Colcock. *The Siege of Savannah, in 1779.* Albany, NY: J. Munsell, 1874.
Judd, Cameron. *The Border Men.* Nashville, TN: Cumberland House Publishing, 2000.
_____. *The Overmountain Men.* New York: Bantam Books, 1991.
Lampman, Charles R. "The Battle of Cowpens, South Carolina." *The SAR Magazine,* Vol. 100, No. 3 (Winter 2006), Sons of the American Revolution.
Lancaster, Bruce. *The American Revolution.* New York: American Heritage, 1971, 1987.
Landrum, Dr. J.B.O. *Colonial and Revolutionary History of Upper South Carolina.* Greenville, SC: self-published, 1897.

Lee, Henry. *The Revolutionary War Memoirs of General Henry Lee.* Edited by Robert E. Lee. New York: Da Capo Press, 1998.
Leyburn, James G. *The Scotch-Irish: A Social History.* Chapel Hill: The University of North Carolina Press, 1962.
Logan, J. H. *History of Upper Country South Carolina.* Austin, TX: DMK Heritage, pdf file.
The London Chronicle, Volume XVI, No. 1233, Thursday, November 15, 1764.
The London Chronicle, Volume XXXVI, No. 2733, Saturday, September 17, 1774.
The London Chronicle, Volume XLIX, No. 3762, Thursday, January 11, 1781.
The London Chronicle, Volume XLIX, No. 3766, Saturday, January 20, 1781.
The London Chronicle, Volume XLIX, No. 3797, Tuesday, April 3, 1781.
The London Chronicle, Volume L, No. 3866, Tuesday, September 11, 1781.
Lumpkin, Henry. *From Savannah to Yorktown.* Lincoln, NE: to Excel Press, 1987, 2000.
Manly, Louise. *Southern Literature from 1579–1895.* Richmond, VA: B.F. Johnson Publishing Company, 1900.
McAdams Historical Society. "The Scotch-Irish in America," mcadamshistory.com.
McAlister, Evelyn. "Set in Stone." *Country Extra*, July 2009: 27.
McCall, Hugh. *The History of Georgia.* Atlanta, GA: Cherokee Publishing, 1909.
McCullough, David. *John Adams.* New York: Simon & Schuster, 2002.
McGraw-Hill Education, teachingushistory.org.
McMeekin, Isabel McLennan. *Journey Cake.* New York: The Junior Literary Guild & Julian Messner, 1942.
_____ . *Juba's New Moon.* Eau Claire, WI: Cadmus Books by E. M. Hale and Company, 1944.
Military History Encyclopedia on the Web, historyofwar.org.
Moss, Bobby Gilmer. *Roster of South Carolina Patriots in the American Revolution.* Baltimore, Genealogical Publishing, 1983.
Newsome, Matthew A. C. *The Migration of the Scots-Irish to Southwestern NC*, albanach.org.
The Old Stone Church—Oconee County—South Carolina. Collected and edited by Richard Newman Brackett. Published by The Old Stone Church and Cemetery Association with the Cooperation of the Andrew Pickens and Cateechee Chapters of D. A. R. Columbia, SC: The R. L. Ryan Company, 1905.
Old Waxhaw Presbyterian Church Bulletin.
Owens, Crystal. "Kettle Creek Dig Providing New Insights into 1779 Battle." *Athens [Georgia] Banner-Herald*, July 3, 2008, OnlineAthens.com.
Pickens, Dr. A. L. *Cane-Brakes as Key to Cowpens.* Meridian States Research, Volume X, Number 1, 1951.
_____ . *Skyagunsta, The Border Wizard Owl.* Greenville, SC: Observer Printing Co., 1934; reprinted Ann Arbor, MI: University Microfilms, 1966.
Pickens, General Andrew. *Letter to General Henry Lee*, 28 August 1811. Included in *The Sumter Papers, Volume I*; of The Draper Manuscripts, Series VV, Sumter County Genealogical Society Research Center, Annex to Sumter County Museum, Sumter Carnegie Public Library, Sumter SC.
Pickens, S. Clark. *Pickens Genealogy*, scpickens.tripod.com.
Piecuch, Jim. *The Battle of Camden: A Documentary History.* Charleston, SC: The History Press, 2006.
Rhoden, Nancy L. *Revolutionary Anglicanism.* Hampshire, England: Macmillan, 2010.
Robertson, John. "An Effort to Locate the Mill Morgan Called 'Burr's Mill.'" gaz.jrshelby.com/burrs-mill-locating.pdf, November 10, 2010.
Rodgers, Thomas G. "Colonials Collide at Bloody Marsh." *Military History*, Volume 13, Number 4 (October 1996): 38–44.
Salley, A. S., Jr. *Documents Relating to the History of South Carolina During the Revolutionary War.* Columbia, SC: Historical Commission of South Carolina by The State Company, 1908.
Scoggins, Michael C. *Early Usage of the Term "Scotch-Irish," 1500–1800.* York County [South Carolina] Historical Center, newacquisitionmilitia.com.
_____ . *The Scotch-Irish on the American Frontier.* York County [South Carolina] Culture and Heritage Commission, 2003, newacquisitionmilitia.com.
_____ . *Three Months in 1780.* York County [South Carolina] Culture and Heritage Commission, June 2003, newacquisitionmilitia.com.
Scott, Brian. "Military and Political." Calhoun Burial Grounds Marker, hmdb.org, July 15, 2009.
Sharp, E.M. *Pickens Families of the South (incl. Excerpts from the Draper Papers).* Memphis, TN: E.M. Sharp, 1963. Annotated by John Carr Pickens, 1995.
Sheriff, G. Anne. *Sketches of Cherokee Villages in South Carolina.* Easley, SC: Forest Acres Elementary

School Schoolwide Enrichment Program, sciway3.net/scgenweb/pickens-county/images/sheriff-01.pdf, c. 1990.

"Siege of Savannah," en.wikipedia.org/wiki/siege_of_savannah.

Smart, James. "Fort Mifflin's Stubborn Stand." *Military History*, Volume 14, Number 5 (December 1997): 35–40.

Smith, D. Ray. "Dragging Canoe, Cherokee War Chief," smithdray.tripod.com/draggingcanoe-index-9.html.

Smith, Gordon B. "The British Evacuate Savannah Georgia." *The SAR Magazine*, Vol. 100, No. 4 (Spring 2007), Georgia Society of Sons of the American Revolution.

South Carolina Genealogical and Historical Websites, Sciway3.net/proctor/marion/military/revwarsc.

"Southern Campaigns of the American Revolution" newsletter, Volume 3, Number 9 (September 2006), Southerncampaign.org.

Stedman, Charles. *The History of the Origin, Progress, and Termination of the American War, in Two Volumes.* London: J. Murray, 1794.

Stephenson, Michael. *Patriot Battles, How the War of Independence Was Fought.* New York: HarperCollins, 2008.

Swager, Christine R. *Heroes of Kettle Creek 1779–1782.* West Conshohocken, PA: Infinity Publishing.com, 2008.

Tennent, Reverend William III. *Album, 1758–1777.* William Tennent papers, South Caroliniana Library, University of South Carolina, Columbia SC, sc.edu/library/digital/collections/tennent.html.

_____. *Travel Journal, 1775.* William Tennent papers, South Caroliniana Library, University of South Carolina, Columbia SC, sc.edu/library/digital/collections/tennent.html.

Virtual War Museum, virtualolgy.com/revolutionarywarhall/battle/eutawsprings.

Waring, Alice Noble. *The Fighting Elder: Andrew Pickens, 1739–1817.* Columbia: University of South Carolina Press, 1962.

Woodmason, Charles. *The Carolina Backcountry on the Eve of the Revolution: The Journal and Other Writings of Charles Woodmason, Anglican Itinerant.* Edited by Richard Hooker. Chapel Hill: The University of North Carolina Press, 1953.

Young, Bessie Hillhouse, and Ruth Mackey Young. *A Genealogy of the Hillhouse-Dickey Families; 1639–1972.* Aurora, MO: self-published, 1972.

Young, Thomas. "Memoir of Major Thomas Young." *Orion Magazine*, October-November 1843.

Zabecki, David T. "In the Cause of Freedom — Tadeusz Kosciuszko Fought for Freedom in America and Poland." *Military History,* November 2011: 52–57.

Index

Numbers in *bold italics* indicate pages with photographs.

abatis 127–129, 176, 253, 262, 273
Abbeville, South Carolina 17
Abbeville Courthouse 296
Abbeville District (County), South Carolina 18, 51, 63–64, 301, 320–323, 330, 332–333, 335–336, 338, 340–343
(Old) Abraham (Abram), Chief 302
Action Committee 37
Adams, Capt. 155, 331
Adamson, Lt. John 154
Aiken, Pvt. Hugh 271
Alatamaha River, Georgia 92
Alexander, Capt. James 124, 257, 260
Alexander's Old Field, South Carolina 148–149
Allaire, Lt. Anthony 146, 153, 155, 169–170, 173, 183–184, 186
Allegheny River 19
Allen, Lt. Col. Isaac 160, 169, 200, 205–206, 285, 323
Alligator Creek, Florida 9
Anderson, Capt. Richard 227–228
Anderson, Col. Robert F. 4, 57, 94, 105–106, 148, 203, 206, 242, 250, 294–298, 333–334, 336, 338–339, 341–342; at Eutaw Springs 285–286, 288; Kettle Creek campaign 111–112, 122, 351; at Kings Mountain 180; at Ninety Six (1775) 50, 106, 268; at Ninety Six (1781) 263–264, 234; promoted to Colonel 237; at Stono Ferry 130; Williamson's Cherokee campaign 67, 69, 73–76, 330
Anderson District, South Carolina 69, 335
Anderson's Fort *see* Fort Thicketty
Anglicanism 8, 29–31, 81–82, 104, 145, 150, 163, 279; disestablished 91
Ani-Yunwiya 158, 364n35
Anson County, North Carolina 14–15, 308, 310
Arbuthnot, Adm. Mariot(t) 134, 137, 139–140
Aristeides *see* Aristides

Aristides 88, 354
Armstrong, Capt. 275, 356
Armstrong, Capt. James 257, 279, 284
Arnold, Brig. Gen. Benedict 85–86
Ashby, Capt. Anthony 169
Ashe, Gen. John 104, 113, 122–125
Ashley River, South Carolina 140
Association Resolution 37, 40–42, 44
Attakulla Kulla, Chief 18, 24, 83–84, 157, 364n35
Augusta, Georgia 20, 41–43, 99, 101–105, 111, 113, 123–125, 131, 133, 146–147, 205, 262–263, 295–296, 302, 319, 324–326, 336, 370n71, 320, 327, 329, 344; Siege of 1780 160, 168–170, 250; Siege of 1781 254–262, 266, 269, 274, 288, 307
Augusta, Treaty of 300
Augusta County, Virginia 11–14, 309, 321, 323, 341

backwater men *see* over mountain men
backwater settlements *see* over mountain settlements
Baird, Capt. Sir James 97
Baker, Col. 326
Balfour, Lt. Col. Nisbet 146–147, 152, 160, 167, 192–195, 197, 200, 207, 232, 240, 250, 263, 280–282, 288, 350–351, 357, 357–358
Ball, Col. John Coming 171
Baptist(s) 31, 82; Association of 82
Barker's Creek, South Carolina 67–68, 95
Barrett, Col. Thomas 93
Baskin, Capt. 111–112, 122, 342–343
Bass, Robert 185
Battle of Blackstock's Estate 195–197, 271, 325, 328, 352
Battle of Brandywine 87
Battle of Brier's Creek 122–123
Battle of Bunker's Hill 88, 132, 353

Battle of Carter's House *see* Turner House Massacre
Battle of Carter's Old Field *see* Turner House Massacre
Battle of Clapp's Mill 247
Battle of Cloud's Creek *see* Turner House Massacre
Battle of Concord 37
Battle of Eutaw Springs 283–284, *287–288*, *291*, 307, 321
Battle of Freeman's Farm *see* Battle of Saratoga
Battle of Guilford Courthouse 248–250
Battle of Kanawha *see* Battle of Point Pleasant
Battle of Kettle Creek 105, 111, 113, *114–119*, 120, *121*, 122–125, 133, 149, 151, 180, 199, 200, 236, 307, 321, 323, 341
Battle of Lexington 37
Battle of Lick Creek *see* Turner House Massacre
Battle of Musgrove's Mill, South Carolina 164–165, 171, 174–175, 180, 325, 328
Battle of Point Pleasant 157
Battle of Saratoga (First) 85–87, 95, 158, 162, 189
Battle of Stono Ferry 126, *127–129*, 130–131, 133, 149, 160, 286, 324, 370n71
Battle of the Great Cane Brakes *see* Reedy River Fight
Battle of the Rice Barges 57
Battle of Ticonderoga 85
Battle of Yorktown 3, 292
Beard, Lt. Col. Jonas 93–94
Beard, Sgt. William 310
Beattie's Ford of the Catawba River 239–240
Beattie's Mill 250
Beaufort, South Carolina 53, 131, 147, 303, 358
Beaufort District 32; mililtia 53
Beaver Creek Ford (South Carolina) 157
Beaverdam Creek 72, 108, 333
Beech Island of the Savannah River 124, 257

Bell, Lt. 20, 222, 225
Bell, Thomas 32
Bell Ringer 367n62
Benoit, Esther Jane (Jean) 9
Benson, Capt. 275, 356
Benson, Solomon 178
Beverly Mills Place, Virginia 13
Bibby, Pvt. John 187
Bickerstaff's Old Fields 186, 192
Big Home Plantation 48, 51
Biggin Church (South Carolina) 278–279, 332
Biggin's Ferry on the Catawba 202
Birmingham, James 51
Bise's Mill *see* Burr's Mill
Bishop, Mr. 66
Bishop, Mrs. 66
Black Hole of the Coweechee 78
Black Mingo Creek 170–171
Blackstock, Capt. William 195
Bledsoe, Pvt. 293
Bloodsuckers *see* 63rd Regiment of Foot
Bloody Marsh 34
Blue Savannah (South Carolina) 166
Boise's Mill *see* Burr's Mill
Boone, Daniel 157, 198
Boone, Gov. Thomas 21, 29
Border Reevers 8, 11
Boston Tea Party 35
Bowie, Maj. John 49–50, 192, 203, 205
Boyd, Lt. Col. John (James) 101–106, 109, 111, 119–122, 124, 180, 334; at Kettle Creek 113–118, 307, 321–323, 334; mortally wounded 116, 324; skirmish at McGowan's Blockhouse 111–112; skirmish at Vann's Ford 112, 369n39
Boyd, Mrs. 101, 118–119
Boyd's Ferry of the Dan River 243
Braddock, Gen. Edward 19
Braddock's Defeat 19
Brandon, Christopher 344
Brandon, Col. Thomas 93–94, 149–150, 174, 180, 186, 195, 216, 220, 222, 250, 270, 332, 344
Brandon's Mill 366n24
Bratton, Mrs. Martha 154
Bratton, Robert 154
Bratton, Lt. Col. William 148–150, 153–155, 331, 342–343
Bratty's Ford *see* Beattie's Ford
Brennan (half-breed scout) 74
Briar Creek *see* Brier Creek, Georgia
Brier('s) Creek, Georgia 122–123, 133, 342
Brierly's Ferry on the (Carolina) Broad River 206–207
Bristol, Tennessee 168
British fleet 58–59, 61, 89, 131, 134
British Legion *see* Tarleton's Legion
British outpost at Ninety Six 146–148, 150, 152–154, 156, 158, 160, 163, 165, 168–170, 174–175, 187–188, 191–193, 195–197, 200–203, 205–208, 210, 231–232, 236, 238, 248, 250, 254, 255, 260–278; *see also* White Hall
British provincial forces 198; *see also* Volunteers of Ireland
British ships: *Acteon* 60; *Anne* 34; *Blonde* 358; *Bristol* 56, 58–59; *Experiment* 60; *London* 35; *Tamar* 43–44
British Southern Army 134, 145, 191, 235, 351
Broad River (Carolinas) 4, 14, 101, 148, 150, 156, 158, 164, 170, 174, 177, 186, 194, 202, 207–208, 210–212, 214–215, 217, 231–234, 236, 251, 275–276, 296, 313–314, 326, 328–329, 338, 350
Broad River (Georgia) 107, 112–113
Broadmouth River 66
Brown, Bartlett 257
Brown, Col. Francis A. 320
Brown, Hugh 57, 67
Brown, Capt. Tarleton 257, 260
Brown, Thomas 17–18
Brown Bess musket 225
Brown(e), (Lt.) Col. Thomas "Burn Foot" 41–42, 44, 91–92, 96, 103, 124, 146–147, 150, 168–170, 188, 205, 255–260, 263, 294, 326
Brownfield, Robert 196
Brown's Fort, Georgia *see* Fort Cornwallis
Bryan, Col. Samuel 159
Buchanan, Capt. Patrick 215, 222
Buck's Creek (South Carolina) 215, 225
Buffalo Creek (North Carolina) 186
Buffalo Ford of the Deep River 153
Buffington's Ironworks *see* Speedwell's Ironworks
Buford (Beauford), Col. Abraham 142–146, 148, 150, 183, 360
Buford's Play 183
Bull, Brig. Gen. Stephen 53, 91, 193, 357
Bull, Acting Gov. William 21, 29–31
Bull Town, South Carolina 42
Bullock Creek, South Carolina 210
Bullock's Creek (South Carolina) 148, 150–151, 210, 232, 351; Nathan's Branch of *see* Turkey Creek
Burdell's Tavern (South Carolina) 284, 287–288
Burgoyne, Maj. Gen. John 85–87, 95
Burke, Edmund 11
Burke County, Georgia 102; Militia Regiment 102, 131
Burke County, North Carolina Militia Regiment 173, 215
Burlington, North Carolina 246–248

Burr's Mill (South Carolina) 208, 214, 233, 373n30, 381
Bush River (South Carolina) 204
Butler, Sen. Andrew Pickens 304
Butler, Capt. James 292–293, 297
Butler, Pvt. James, Jr. 293
Butler, Pierce 193, 303, 357
Butler, Capt. William 297–298, 304
Byas Mill *see* Burr's Mill
Byce's Mill *see* Burr's Mill

CahStahYeesTee 367n262
Caldwell, Maj. John 39, 43, 47, 291; death of 294
Caldwell, Mrs. 294
Caldwell, Pvt. Robert 310
Calhoun, Catherine (grandmother of Rebecca Calhoun) 15, 20
Calhoun (Noble), Catherine (sister of Rebecca Calhoun) 48
Calhoun, Ensign (first name unknown) 62
Calhoun, Ezekial 15, 20, 26
Calhoun, James 15
Calhoun, Vice Pres. John C. 321
Calhoun, Mary 15
Calhoun, Mr. (first name unknown) 151
Calhoun, Patrick 15, 18–19, 21, 25–26, 32–33, 37, 42, 121, 333–334, 349, 364
Calhoun (Pickens), Rebecca 20–21, 24, 26, 151, 201, 210, 296; death of 304
Calhoun, William 15, 26
Calhoun family 17–22, 24–25, 27, 105, 203
Calvinist Protestants *see* Huguenots
Camden, South Carolina 90, 142–143, 145–146, 149–150, 152, 154–156, 159–167, 189, 191, 193, 197–198, 203, 207–208, 237–238, 247, 250–253, 319, 338, 355, 357–358
Camden District 32, 340; militia 48, 51, 279
Camden Ferry 332
Cameron, Agt. Alexander 39, 42, 44–45, 47, 61–63, 65, 70–71, 73, 83, 130
Cameron, John 94
Campbell, Capt. Archibald 283
Campbell, Lt. Col. Sir Archibald 95–105, 113, 122–126, 133, 191, 324
Campbell, Lt. Charles 142–143
Campbell, Capt. Colin 279
Campbell, Lt. Col. George 238
Campbell, Capt. Peter 273
Campbell, Col. Richard 264, 273–274, 285, 250, 350, 356
Campbell, Col. William 168, 171–172, 174–175, 177–178, 186, 188, 192, 244, 321, 324, 333, 342; attains command of over mountain militia 172; Battle of Kings Mountain 179–183
Campbell, Gov. Lord William 39,

44–45, 47, 50, 58; mortally wounded 59
Canada 57, 85, 359
Candler, Maj. William 173–174, 177, 180
Cane Creek (Georgia) 295, 339
Cane Creek (North Carolina) 202
Canusee (Cherokee Village) 78
Cape Fear, North Carolina 58, 61, 358
Cape Fear River 351
Carleton, Maj. Gen. Sir Guy 297
Carr (Kerr), Robert 107
Carrington, Col. Edward 243
Carrington, Lt. George 279
Carroll, Pvt. John 155
carronade 132, 370n69
Carr's Fort 107–109, 322
Carruthers, Capt. Robert 298
Carter, Mr. 293
Casey, Col. Levi 94, 296, 329
Caswell, Maj. Gen. Richard 156, 243
Catawba, North Carolina 236
Catawba River 19, 151, 154, 156, 160, 174, 191, 202, 232, 236–240, 314, 326, 331, 350, 357
Catawba Indians 156
Cathead Precinct 326
Cathead Swamp, Georgia 92–93
Catholicism 8–9, 283; Order of Cistercians of the Strict Observance (Trappist) 283
Cayuga Indians 83
Cedar Shoals of Fishing Creek, South Carolina 148
Cedar Shoal(s) of the Savannah River 111
Cedar Springs (South Carolina) 154; battlefield 154
Chambers, Pvt. Samuel 172–173
Chandler, Raymond 305
Chapman, John A.: *The History of Edgefield County, South Carolina from the Earliest Settlements to 1897* 268
Charles I 9
Charles II 300
Charles Town, South Carolina 4, 18–19, 22–23, 25, 28–29, 31–36, 39–40, 43–44, 47, 50–52, 54–57, 61, 68, 79, 84–85, 90, 96, 99, 104, 125–127, 130–131, 133, 147, 149, 152, 160, 165, 193–194, 197–198, 206–207, 238, 240, 250, 253–254, 262, 267–268, 270–271, 275–277, 279, 280–283, 288–292, 295–298, 300, 324, 349–352, 355–360; attack of (1776) 58–60; fall of (1780) 134–**138**, 139–142, 147, 152, 167, 188, 191, 199, 267, 280, 325, 327, 351; Harbor 35, 37, 47, 137–138, 264, 351, 360
Charles Town Road 127, 275
Charleston, South Carolina 104, 133, 138–141, 152, 209, 249, 260, 264, 276, 278, 281, 295, 300,
309, 313–314, 316, 324, 328, 332–335, 338, 341, 343, 370
Charlestown *see* Charles Town
Charlotte, North Carolina 143, 145–146, 149, 151, 156, 161–162, 164, 167, 170, 173–176, 190, 197–198, 200, 202, 240, 247, 252, 273, 277, 319, 344
Charlottesville, Virginia 237
Chattahoochee River 17, 298
Chattooga River 80
Cheraw, South Carolina 32, 146, 202, 207, 237
Cheraw Hill *see* Cheraw
Cherokee 17–19, 24–27, 33–34, 38–39, 42, 44–45, 47–48, 53, 55, 79, 83–85, 91, 95, 103–106, 124, 130, 133, 144, 146, 156–158, 169, 183, 238, 259, 286, 289, 298–300, 302–304, 307–308, 321–322, 326, 329, 336, 338, 342, 349, 364n35, 37, 367n62; lower villages 17, 19, 23, 39, 62–63, 75, 77, 130, 300; middle villages 23, 77, 79; over mountain villages 17, 23, 33, 47, 83, 144, 349; uprising (1759–1761) 19–23; uprising (1776) 61–79
Cherokee Ford of the Broad River (Carolina) 158, 164, 173, 177, 210
Cherokee Ford of the Savannah River 105, 111–112, 121–122, 298, 334, 369n39
Chesney, Lt. Alexander 150
Chester District (County), South Carolina 18, 154, 331
Chew, Lt. William 267
Chickamauga Cherokee 83, 130, 158
Chickamauga Creek 83
Chickamauga villages 83
Chitwood, Capt. James 187
Chronicle, Maj. William 175, 177–181
Chullochcullak *see* Chuloch-Culla
Chuloch-Culla 18, 364n35; *see also* Attakulla Kulla
Church of England 8–11, 29–31, 46, 82, 104, 120, 317–318; disestablished 91; *see also* Anglican
Circuit Court Act 32–33
Clark, Capt. John 251, 326
Clarke, Brig. Gen. Alured 297
Clarke (Clark), Col. Elijah 34, 92, 106–107, 155–156, 158–159, 165, 194, 196, 198–201, 250–251, 298, 300, 333, 352, 375n29; at Battle of Kettle Creek 114, 116–117, 200; at Battle of Musgrove's Mill 164–165; at Siege of Augusta (1780) 168–169; at Siege of Augusta (1781) 255–256; 30 man detachment to Kings Mountain 173–174; trek to over mountain settlements 170
Clem's Branch of the Catawba River 154
Clemson University 70, 302
Cleveland, Col. Benjamin 171–174, 177, 179–180, 188, 320, 333
Clinton, Maj. Gen. Sir Henry 44, 58–61, 88–**90**, 95, 134, 136–142, 145–147, 149–153, 163, 170, 175, 231–232, 235, 290, 292, 297, 325, 350–351, 354, 360
Clinton, South Carolina 204
Coates, Lt. Col. John 278–279
Cobb, Pvt. 250
Coffin, Maj. John 284–285, 287
Colcock, Hon. John 281
Coleridge, North Carolina 153
Colson, Capt. James 50
Colson's Mills 319
Conaste *see* Canusee
Congaree River 40, 247, 265, 276, 326, 329, 331, 338, 344
Congaree Store, South Carolina 40, 290, 329, 355
the Congarees 45, 51–53, 152
Conklin(g), Capt. Thomas 136
Connecticut 85, 176, 353–354
The Connecticut Journal 280
Connelly, Capt. Henry 12, 215, 222–225, 318–320
Constitutional Convention (United States) 90–91
Continental Army 1, 4, 60, **62**, 70, 76, 81, 87, 90–93, 95–97, 99, 104, 120, 125–126, 128–131, 133–135, 137–140, 142, 145, 152, 156, 161–164, 166, 172–173, 188–189, 197–198, 202–203, 205–209, 211, 213, 215–217, 219–222, 225–227, 230–231, 234, 236–238, 241–244, 248–249, 251, 254, 256, 263, 265, 268, 271, 275–276, 281, 285–287, 290, 292, 311, 320–321, 330–331, 333, 337, 340, 343, 350, 370n71; Northern Department 57, 60, 85, 87, 189, 268; Southern Department 4, 57–58, 60, 81, 85, 91, 93, 95, 99, 125, 131, 152, 158, 162–163, 176, 188–189, 197–198, 202, 234, 237–238, 243, 263, 274–275, 277, 281, 289
Continental Congress(man) 35–36, 37, 47, 56–57, 60, 81, 85, 87, 93–94, 96–99, 138, 140–142, 149, 151, 158, 162–163, 181, 189, 197, 268, 275, 281–283, 289; Andrew Pickens member of 301, 304, 308; authorizes sword for Andrew Pickens 231, 307
Continental scrip 87, 319
Cooper, James Fenimore: *The Last of the Mohicans* 19
Cooper, Maj. Samuel 282–283
Cooper River 137, 330; West Branch (Fork) 278–279
Cork(e), Ireland 268, 358
Corn Tassel, Chief 18, 302
Cornstalk, (Shawnee) Chief 157
Cornwallis, Charles "1st Earl" 25
Cornwallis, Lt. Col. Charles Lord 25, 27–28, 52, 56, 58–60, 89, **92**,

134, 142–143, 145–153, 160–163, 165–171, 173–176, 178, 184–185, 188–198, 200, 202–203, 205–208, 210, 228–245, 247–250, 253–254, 263, 265, 267, 277, 280–282, 290, 319, 326, 331, 344, 349–352, 355–358, 360; Battle of Guiford Courthouse 249–250; bivouac at Turkey Creek 150, 210, 228–236; Race to the Dan 236–243; surrender at Yorktown **292**
Coronaca, South Carolina 65–66
Coronaca Creek, South Carolina 65
Court Days 32–33
Court of Common Pleas 30, 320, 327, 335
Cowan's Ferry of the Savannah River 106, 109, 123, 125
Cowan's Ford Dam 240
Cowan's Ford of the Catawba River 239–240
Cowee 78
Coweechee (Cherokee Village) 78
Coweechee Branch of the Tennessee 78
Cowpens, Battle of 3–5, 52, 212–*213*, *217*–*221*, 222, *223*–*224*, 225, *226*–228, *230*–232, 235–238, 240, 244, 249–250, 252, 262, 274, 288–289, 307, 325, 328, 333, 344, 357; remarks about Andrew Pickens after the battle 229–231, 307; Tarleton & Washington duel 228–*229*, Washington Light Infantry Monument **216**–**217**
Cowpens, South Carolina (village) 174, 209
Cowpens Battlefield 204, 210–211, 214, 233–234; topography of 15, 211–212
Cowpens Centennial Committee 7, 26, 28, 104, 301; *Cowpens Centennial, 1781-1881* 7, 229, 301
Cowpens Creek 208–209
Cowpens over mountain militia encampment 174–175, 177, 185
Coytmore, Capt. Richard 20
Crawford, Pvt. James 172–173
Crawford, Joseph 25
Crawford, Maj. Robert 25, 156
Creek Indians 26, 34, 123–124, 303, 349; at Brown's Augusta Garrison 146, 256, 259
Creswell, Rev. James 66–67
Crockett, Cpl. Alexander 310
Crockett, Pvt. Arche 310
Crockett, Davy (Davy's grandfather) 172
Crockett, Davy (famous) 172
Crockett, Ens. John 310
Crockett, Pvt. John 172
Crockett, Pvt. Robert 310
Croft State Natural Area 147
Cross Anchor, South Carolina 164
Cross Hill, South Carolina 203
Cruden, John, Esq. 193, 356

Cruger, Lt. Col. John Harris 131, 163, 165, 169–170, 175, 188, 191–193, 195–197, 200–203, 205–206, 210, 250–251, 253, 255, 274–277, 328, 338; abandoned Ninety Six 277–278, 290; at Eutaw Springs 285–286; rescues Brown at Augusta 169; takes command at Ninety Six 150, 160; under siege at Ninety Six 262–273
Culbertson, Josiah 147
Cuningham, John 292
Cunningham, Lt. Col. Andrew 300
Cunningham, Maj. John 217–218, 295–296
Cunningham, Lt. Col. Patrick 40–42, 44, 46–53, 55, 57–58, 67, 111, 276, 291, 295, 300; captured 57
Cunningham, Brig. Gen. Robert 29, 38–42, 44, 46–47, 57–58, 68, 111, 153, 193, 195, 203, 205–206, 235, 263, 276, 263, 295, 300, 365n29; commissioned Brigadier General 197; jailed 47
Cun(n)ingham, Maj. William "Bloody Bill" 111–112, 149, 153, 188, 276, 282, 291–298, 300, 302, 329, 339, 342
Curling, Capt. Alexander 35

Dan River 238, 241–244, 247, 276, 320, 350
Davidson, Brig. Gen. William Lee 151, 174, 209, 214, 237–239, 319–320, 325; death of 239–240, 357; dual command of 209; regiment of 238, 240–242
Davie, Maj. Andrew 130
Davie, Col. William R. 156–157, 161–162, 319
Davies, Pvt. George 310
Davies, Pvt. John 310
Davies, Pvt. Moses 310
Davies, Pvt. Robert 310
Davies, Pvt. William 310
Davis, Pres. Jefferson 304
Davis (Pickens), Nancy Ann 7, 13, 15–16, 22, 26, 308, 311
Davis, Major William 13–15, 308, 311
Davy Crockett Birthplace State Park 172
Dawson, Maj. Thomas 285
Day, Kate Pickens: *Cousin Monroe's History of the Pickens Family* 12, 311
Declaration of Independence 1, 60, 76, 81, 90, 106
Deep River (North Carolina) 153, 358
de Grasse Tilly, (Marquis) Francois-Joseph Paul 281
de Kalb, Maj. Gen. Johann 152–153, 156, 158–159, 161, 149; death of 162
DeLancey's Brigade 160, 273, 285

Delaware Continentals 161, 215, 285–287
Delaware River 87
Delaware Indians 19, 83, 349
DeLoach, Mr. 298
de' Medici, Marie 8
Dennard's Ford of the Broad River (Carolina) 174, 234
De Peyster, Capt. Abraham 165, 180–182, 184
Deshaser, Pvt. 233–234
d'Estaing, Adm. Comte Jean Baptiste Charles Henri Hector 131–133
Dewitt's Corner, South Carolina 65, 67, 83
Dickie, Hector 310
Dickie, Robert 309
Dickie, Susanna 310
Dickson, Maj. Joseph 246
Dillard, James 328
Dillard, Mrs. Mary 195
Dinning Creek (South Carolina) 206
Dinwiddie, Lt. Gov. Robert 19
Doak, Rev. Samuel L. 172
Dollard's Tavern, South Carolina 171
Dolly, Quanimo "Quash" 97
Domesday Book 8
Dooley, Col. John 34, 103–104, 106–107, 123, 124, 131, 156; at Battle of Kettle Creek 114, 116–117
Doublehead, Chief 157
Downs, Maj. Jonathan 57, 67, 75
Doyle, Lt. Col. Welbore 249
Dragging Canoe, Chief **83**–84, 157–158, 172; death of 84
Draper, Lyman C. 4, 7, 12–14, 63, 65–66, 69, 178, 181, 184–185, 268–269, 312; on Andrew Pickens 231
Drayton, Hon. William Henry 4, 40–48, 50–51, 56–58, 60–62, 65–73, 76, 79, 82, 84, 101, 332, 341, 365 n36 & 38–39, 366n16–17 & 19–20 & 24
Due West, South Carolina 67, 250
Duggins, William 57
Dumas, Alexandre 106
Duncanson, Capt. Robert 145–146, 227
Dunlap, Maj. James 156, 173, 193, 200–201, 204–206, 210, 251; death of 250
Dutch 13, 40
Dutch Fork 52, 276, 339
Duval(l), Lt. William 273–275, 340, 356

Earl's Ford of the Pacolet River 156
Earlsville, South Carolina 156
The East India Tea Company 34–35, 359
Easterwood Ford on the Pacolet River 209
Eaton, Maj. Pinkertham "Pink" 256–257

Eaton's Station, Tennessee (#1 at Long Island of the Holston River) 83
Ecochee (Cherokee Village) 78
Edgefield County (District), South Carolina 18, 268, 327
Edgehill Plantation (South Carolina) 293
Edgemoor, South Carolina 153
Edgeville, South Carolina 251
Edict of Fontainebleau 9
Edict of Nantes 7–9
Edisto River (South Carolina) 282–283, 298, 330; North Fork 314
Eggleston, Maj. Joseph 246, 256
Eighteen Mile Creek 70
Elbert, Col. Samuel 92, 97
Elizabethton, Tennessee 157
Emistisiguo, Chief (Creek) 124
Enoree, South Carolina 40, 365n38
Enoree River (South Carolina) 41, 164, 196, 275, 325, 352
Estatoe (Cherokee Village) 68, 73, 75
Europe(ans) 1, 7, 11, 20, 76, 82, 88, 231, 350, 353, 357
Eustash (Cherokee Village) 75
Eutaw Springs (South Carolina) 283, 284, 287–291, 307, 321, 323, 326, 328
Eutawville, South Carolina 166, 283
Eveleigh, Nicholas 193, 357
Ewald, Capt. Johann 140

Fair, Col. 220
Fair Forest, South Carolina 151, 164–165, 203, 206
Fair Forest Creek 52, 101, 147, 149, 156, 167, 366n24
Fair Forest Militia 151, 203, 208, 216
Fairfield District (County), South Carolina 18, 154
Falconer, Will 59
Farar, Lt. 71
Federalist 90
Ferguson, Col. James 150, 153; death of 155
Ferguson, Maj. (Lt. Col.) Patrick 100, 137, 146–147, 152–153, 155, 164–174, 185–187, 192, 214, 262, 342; death of *182*, 184, 333; at Kings Mountain 175–178, 180–184, 189, 190, 191, 208, 333
Ferguson, Thomas 193, 357
Ferguson's Hill (Ridge), North Carolina 168
Few, Col. Benjamin 102, 124, 131, 160, 194, 196, 199–200, 323
Few, Col. William 102
1st Regiment of Foot 285–286
Fish Dam Ford on the (Carolina) Broad River 194–195, 251, 275, 352
Fish Dam Ford on the (Georgia) Broad River 113
Fisher, Col. John 254

Fishing Creek, South Carolina 148, 164–165, 167; Lower 150; Upper 149–150
Fletchall, Col. Thomas 39–41, 43–44, 46, 52, 56, 300, 366n24
Florida 34, 39, 45, 91, 99, 359; General Howe's Foray 91–97; General Lee's foray to 60–61
Floyd, Capt. 151
Floyd, Col. Matthew 150
the Flying Army 198, 203, 209, 238
Folsom's Fort, Georgia 124
Forest City, North Carolina 174
Fort Anderson see Fort Thicketty
Fort Boone 26, 349
Fort Carr see Carr's Fort
Fort Caswell see Fort Watauga
Fort Charlotte 29, 39–43, 63, 109–111, 122
Fort Cornwallis, Georgia 255–258, 260, 326
Fort Defiance, Virginia 13, 19
Fort Dreadnought see Fort Galphin
Fort Duquesne 19
Fort Galphin, South Carolina 255–256, 262
Fort Gilpin see Fort Galphin
Fort Granby, South Carolina 254, 256, 331–332; see also Granby Landing
Fort Grierson, Georgia 255–256
Fort Independence, South Carolina 64–65, 67, 69, 72, 105–106, 109, 330, 336, 341
Fort Johnson, South Carolina 44, 47, 135
Fort Mercer, New Jersey 87
Fort Mifflin 87
Fort Morris, Georgia 96, 99, 131
Fort Motte, South Carolina 147, 253–254, 277, 284, 332
Fort Moultrie 135, 137–138, 370n71
Fort Mud 87
Fort Necessity 19
Fort Prince, South Carolina 156
Fort Prince George, South Carolina 18, 20–24, 29
Fort Rutledge 76, 78, 338
Fort Thicketty 159
Fort Tonyn, Florida 92–93
Fort Washington 353
Fort Watauga, Tennessee 83
Fort Watson, South Carolina 147, 247, 251, 257, 331–332
Fort Williams see Williams' Fort
four-pounder cannons 43, 111–112
Fraser, Maj. Charles 280–281
Fraser, Maj. Thomas 252, 278–280, 282–283, 325
Fraser's Highlanders 134, 227
Frazer (Fraser), Brig. Gen. Simon 86
Frederick County, Virginia 11–12, 93
Freeman, John 85
Freeman, Thomas 85
Freeman, Capt. William 109
Freeman's Farm 85–86

French 7–8, 18–19, 57, 89–90, 141, 225
French, Capt. Thomas 273
French Broad River 364n35
French Charleville musket 198
French fleet 89, 131–132, 292
French and Indian War 18–20, 25, 27, 61, 216, 349, 364n37
French troops 19, 36–37, 79, 131–132, 284, 348
Furman, Rev. Richard 82
Fuser, Lt. Col. Lewis 95–96

Gadsden, Lt. Gov. Christopher 36, 38, 57, 138, 193, 357, 359, 370n71
Gaffney, South Carolina 158–159
Gage, Gen. Thomas 45
Gaillard, Isaac 55, 84
Gaillard, Tacitus 55, 84
Gaines, Capt. William 285
the Gallows Oak 187, 192
Galphin, George 255
Garden, Lt. Alexander 77, 122, 311
Gardner, Monica Mary 241
Gardner, Maj. William 104
Gaston, Hon. John 82, 90, 148–150
Gates, Col. Benjamin 237
Gates, Maj. Gen. Horatio 162–167, 174, 176, 185, 188–189, 191, 197, 209; at Camden 159–162, 191, 197, 237, 319, 331, 338; commander of the Southern Department *158*; at Saratoga 85–87, 95
Gates, Robert 189, 197
General Committee 35–37, 358–360
General Meeting of Citizenry 35–36
The Gentleman's Magazine 141, 145, 351, 360
George II 18, 21
George III 18, 21, 27–29, 39, 32, 35, 40–41, 45, 48, 59, 87, 97, 99–100, 104, 120, 141, 147, 151, 187–188, 194–196, 200, 258–260, 267, 317, 323, 351–352, 357
Georgetown, South Carolina 146, 165, 170–171, 238, 254–255, 262, 277
Georgetown District 32
Georgia(ns) 3, 20, 34, 47–48, 57–58, 63–65, 80, 83–84, 91–134, 136, 141–142, 151, 158, 165, 168, 170, 212, 232, 237–238, 251, 295, 297–300, 303, 308, 324, 333, 338–339, 342; Continentals 97, 292; history of 34; Rangers see King's Carolina Rangers; State Militia 34, 63, 76, 92–93, 102–133, 136, 155–156, 158, 160, 164, 174–175, 177, 194–196, 199–200, 204–205, 209, 211, 217–219, 229, 233, 242, 244, 247–248, 250–251, 255–256, 260, 262, 295, 298, 323–327
Germain(e), Sec. of St. Lord George 87–89, 141, 145, 231,

235, 240, 350–351, 357–358, 360
Germany 10, 13, 34, 40; troops 297, 355; *see also* Hessian Jäger Corps
Gervais, John Lewis 32, 193, 357
Gethsemani Abbey (South Carolina) 283
Gibbes, R.W. 4, 73
Gibson, Ann *see* Hillhouse, Ann (Gibson)
Gibson, Gideon 31
Gibson, Lt. 352
Gilbert Town, North Carolina 165, 168, 170, 172–174, 186–187, 236
Gilkey, Capt. Walker 187
Gilmer, Pvt. Enoch 177–178
Girardeau Plantation, Georgia 97
Glen, Gov. James 18–19, 83
Glendale, South Carolina 154, 209
Glynn, Col. David 285
Gooch, Lt. Gov. Sir William (Virginia) 11
Goodwin (Goodwyn), Col. Robert 39, 93–95
Goucher Creek (South Carolina) 159
Goudelock, Adam 233
Goody *see* Gouedy
Gouedy, James 309
Gouedy, Kiunagree 309
Gouedy, Mary 309
Gouedy, Nancy 309
Gouedy, Peggy 309
Gouedy, Robert 18, 20, 32–33; will of 309
Gouedy, Sarah 309
Gouedy's trading post 26
Gould, Col. Paston 268
Grafton, Duke of 190
Graham, Capt. Joseph 239–240, 244, 246–247
Graham, Col. Joseph 53
Granby Fort *see* Fort Granby
Granby (Landing), South Carolina 147, 152, 272, 277, 344
Grant, Lt. Col. James 22, 30, 75; Andrew Pickens comments about 23, 46, 79; Expedition (Indian War) 4, 22–23, 46, 61, 70, 79
grasshopper cannons 128, 164, 369n59
Gray, Capt. Robert 262
Gray, William 340
Graybill, Capt. Henry 326
Grayson, Col. 324
Great Falls, South Carolina 164
The Great Law of Peace of the Longhouse People 83
Great Rocky Creek, South Carolina 64–65
Great Wagon Road 10, 12, 105
Greene, Colonel Christopher 87
Greene, Maj. Gen. Nathanael 3, 77, 158, **190**, 197–200, 202–203, 206, 207, 209, 211–212, 229, 236–237, 244–249, 251–257, 260, 275–278, 280–283, 290, 292, 298, 301, 304, 326, 331; Eutaw Springs 284–288; Guilford Courthouse 249–250; Hobkirk's Hill 252; letters about Andrew Pickens at Eutaw Springs 289; Race to the Dan 238–244, 276, 320; selected as Commander of the Southern Department 189, 319; Siege of Ninety Six 262–275, 320, 326, 333, 336
Greene River, North Carolina 170, 173
Greensboro(ugh), North Carolina 242, 332
Grierson, Col. Benjamin 260
Grierson, Lt. Col. James 255–257, 260
Grimes, Capt. 187
Grindal Shoals on the Pacolet River 101, 202–203, 206, 208–209, 344
Guilford County, North Carolina 319, 326
Guilford Courthouse, North Carolina 241–243, 248–250, 320
Guilford Courthouse National Military Park 242
Gully Hole Creek 34

Habersham, John 303
Haddrell's Point, South Carolina 140
Hager, Frederick 239
Haldane, Lt. Henry 197, 201–202, 206–207
Hall, Col. 357
Hall, Rev. James 78
Hambright, Col. Frederick 175, 177–182
Hamilton, Capt. Andrew 94, 159, 192; jailed at Ninety Six 160, 168; pension of 318, 320–323; siege of Ninety Six (1781) 264
Hamilton, John 18
Hamilton, Maj. (Lt. Col.) John 100–101, 103–104, 106, 108, 112–113, 124, 134; at Carr's (Kerr's) Fort 109–111
Hamilton's Ford (Broad River) 232–234, 264, 276, 338, 351
Hammond, Capt. Charles 324
Hammond, Capt. George 326
Hammond, Capt. John 69
Hammond, Col. LeRoy 37, 43, 53, 68, 70–72, 76, 78–79, 124, 147, 152, 237, 250–251, 255, 260, 324–326, 327, 329
Hammond, Col. Samuel 174, 180, 200, 217–219, 222, 242, 244, 250, 285, 295–296, 318, 321, 323–324, 327–330
Hammond's Mill 251
Hammond's store 204, 333
Hampton, Col. Andrew 143, 157, 171
Hampton, Anthony 66, 78
Hampton, Capt. Edward 66, 78, 156, 325; death of 292
Hampton, Col. Henry 66, 196
Hampton, John 66
Hampton, Mrs. 66
Hampton, Preston 66
Hampton, Lt. Col. Wade 66, 285–252
Hanging Maw, Chief 303
Hanging Rock, South Carolina 146, 156, 159, 161–162, 331–333
Hannon, Edwin 66
Hannon, John 66
Hannon, Mr. 66
Hannon, William 66
Hannon, Winnie 66
Harden's Ferry 42
Hardin (Harden), Col. William 237, 250, 257, 281–283
Harleston, Isaac 193, 356
Harleston, John, Jr. 193, 356
Harper's Weekly, Journal of Civilization 46
Harris, Hon. David K. 320
Harris, Rev. John 94
Hart, Mr. 42
Hart's Mill (North Carolina) 244, 326
Hayes, Col. Joseph 205–206, 216–217, 220, 222, 250, 285, 293, 328; death of 294
Hayes' Station, South Carolina 293–294
Hayne, Lt. Col. Isaac 149, 267, 280, 282, 288, 375n29; death of 281; plantation 282
Haynes, Christopher 340
Heard, Stephen 107
Heard's Fort 107, 113
Heinrichs, Capt. Johann 91
Henderson, Richard 157–158
Henderson, Col. William 78; at Eutaw Springs 284–286
Henderson's Mills 324
Hendrix's Mill 41
Henry IV 8–9
Hesse-Hanau Jäger *see* Hessian Jäger Corps
Hessian Jäger Corps 87, 91, 126–127, 129, 134, 140, 254, 282, 300, 354
Heyward, Thomas 193, 357
High Hills of the Santee 278, 281, 289
Hight, Col. 69
Hight, Mrs. 69, 75, 342
Hill, Colonel William 'Billy' 142, 148–152, 154–155, 174–175, 177, 184–185, 209
Hillhouse, Ann (Gibson) 52, 210, 364n46
Hillhouse, Elijah Boyd 52, 210, 364n46
Hillhouse, James 52, 210
Hillhouse, Capt. William, Jr. 52, 69, 150–151, 155, 159, 192, 210, 318, 330–332
Hillhouse Estate 52, 150, 210, 234; used by Cornwallis 210, 234

Index

Hill's Estate 149–151
Hill's Iron Works 149–151, 153–154
Hillsboro(ugh), North Carolina 142, 152–153, 156, 162–165, 174, 185, 188–189, 191, 244–246, 319, 325–326, 329
Hiwassee River 78
Hobbs, Pvt. Augustine 187
Hobkirk's Hill, South Carolina 252–253
Holland 283
Holland, Pvt. Charles 63, 77, 121, 318, 332–333
Hollingsworth, Ben 181
Hollingsworth's Mill 53
Holmes, James 84
Holston River 157; South Fork of 168; lower 172
Holston settlements 168
Hopewell (South Carolina) 302–304, 308; *see also* Treaty of Hopewell
Hopkins, Capt. 84
Horner's Corner, South Carolina 251, 326
Horner's Creek *see* Horner's Corner
Horn('s) Creek *see* Horner's Corner
Horry, Col. Hugh 165, 193, 357
Horry, Col. Peter 132–133, 142, 156, 159, 161, 165–166, 193, 357
Horse Creek (South Carolina) 165
House of Commons 25, 89
House of Lords 25, 27
Hous(e)man, Col. 147–148
Houston, Gov. John 92–93, 303
Howard, Lt. Col. John Eager 145, 202, 212–213, 215, 221–224, 227, 231, 234, 236, 243, 319–320, 328
Howe, George 302
Howe, Adm. Lord Richard 87
Howe, Maj. Gen. Robert 60–61, 81, 91–95, 99, 113, 162, 176, 211; loss of Savannah 96–98
Howe, Maj. Gen. Sir William 58, 60, 87, 89; Aristides editorial letter to 88, 352–355
Huck, Capt. Christian 147, 150–151, 153–154, 331; death of 155
Huger, Brig. Gen. Isaac 21, 56, 97, 128, 131, 133, 137, 142, 198, 202, 241–242, 324, 370*n*71
Hughes, (half-breed trader) 63–64
Hughes, Pvt. Benjamin 293
Hughes, Hon. James 340
Hughes, Capt. Joseph 340, 344
Huguenot(s) 8–9, 90, 278
Hunt, Capt. 359
Hunt, Lt. 155
Huron Indians 19
Hyrne, Maj. Edmund (Edward) M. 125, 237, 289

Inman, Capt. Joshua 136
Inman, Capt. Shadrick (Shadrack) 136, 164; death of 165

Inman, South Carolina 156
Innes, Lt. Col. Alexander 147–148, 150, 156, 164; death of 165
Ireland 7, 9–11, 28, 82, 166, 268
Iroquois Confederacy 18, 83, 157
Irvin(e), Capt. John 94, 101, 120, 122–123, 125
Irvine's Ferry of the Dan River 243
Irwin, Col. Robert 156
Island Creek (South Carolina) 211
Island Ford of the (Carolina) Broad River 210
Island Ford of the Catawba River 236
Island Ford of the Saluda River 43, 48, 50, 273
Island Ford Road 263, 265, 269
Izard, Ralph 193, 357

J. Strom Thurmond Reservoir 39, 109
Jack, Col. Samuel 76
Jack's Creek, South Carolina 51
Jackson, Pres. Andrew 130; captured by the British 159–160, 253
Jackson, Pvt. Hugh 130, 160
Jackson, Maj. James 227, 233, 242, 244, 326
Jackson, Dr. Robert 228
Jackson, Pvt. Robert 159–160
James I/VI 8
James Island, South Carolina 44, 126–129, 134, 140
Jamison, Capt. James 151, 155, 330–331
Jarvis, Lt. Stephen 283
Jefferson, Pres. Thomas 275
Jenkinsville, South Carolina 207
Jocassee (Cherokee Village) 75
John Prince's Fort *see* Fort Prince
Johnnycake *see* Journey Cake
Johns Island, South Carolina 126, 134
Johnson, Rev. James 340
Johnson, Capt. Jesse 326
Johnson, Capt. Richard 329
Johnson, Capt. Stephen 174
Johnson, Dr. Uzal 184
Johnson, William 197; on Andrew Pickens 246–249, 304; on Banastre Tarleton's defeat at Cowpens 236
Johnsonville, South Carolina 31
Jolly, Maj. Benjamin 212, 215, 228, 270, 344
Jones, Col. John 156
Jonesborough, Tennessee 168, 172
journey cake 70, 171

Kanawha River 157
Kelly, Capt. Dennis 285
Kemp family 66
Kennedy, Squire 270
Keowee (Cherokee Village) 17–18, 25, 47, 71, 75, 342
Keowee River 17–18, 23, 70
Ker(r), Capt. George 201
Kerr, John 12

Kerr, Joseph 175
Kerr's Fort *see* Carr's Fort
Kershaw, Capt. Ely 39
Kershaw Militia Regiment 156
Kettle Creek, Georgia 111, 113
Key, Capt. Thomas 251
King of England 9, 87; *see also* Charles I; Charles II; George II; George III; James I/VI
King of France 132; *see also* Henry IV; Louis XIII; Louis XIV
King of Scotland *see* James I/VI
King's Carolina Rangers 91, 169, 255–260
King's Creek, South Carolina 40
King's Florida Rangers 91, 98, 134
Kings Mountain 22, 173, 175–178, 186, 207, 210, 342; Battle of 4, 151, 169, 178–*179*, 180–*182*, 183–186, 188–191, 208, 228, 231, 250, 277, 293, 328, 333, 344
Kirkland, Lt. Col. Moses 29–30, 32, 39–45, 56, 61, 146, 192, 195, 300, 329, 365*n*29; appeal 55; becomes a Tory 40; jailed 45; passed over for regimental major 38–39
Kirkwood, Capt. Robert 274, 285–286, 356
Kosciuszko, Col. Thaddeus 241–*242*, 264–265
KunSteeNeeStah *see* CahStah-YeesTee

Lacey, Col. Edward 154, 174–175, 177, 180, 184, 196, 279, 285, 332
Lafferty, Lt. 187
Lake Hartwell 70
Lake Keowee 18
Lake Marion (South Carolina) 166, 247, 249, 283
Lake Norman (North Carolina) 240
Lake Norman Regional Medical Center 240
Lake Reidsville (North Carolina) 250
Lake Secession (South Carolina) 65
Lake Wylie, South Carolina 149
Lancaster County, Pennsylvania 7
Lancaster County, South Carolina 14
Land, Capt. Benjamin 150
Landrum, J.B.O. 53, 177, 198
Landrum, South Carolina 156
Lane, Maj. Joseph 99
Laurens, Lt. Col. Henry 21, *23*, 55–57, 193, 356, 366*n*26; imprisoned in Tower of London 283; plantation 283; president of Council of Safety 55; president of Provincial Congress 37, 39, 47; vice-president of South Carolina 58, 72
Laurens, Lt. Col. John 126
Laurens County (District), South Carolina 18, 328, 330, 344
Lawson, Capt. John 215, 222

Lawson's Fork (South Carolina) 209, 365n39
Leach, Maj. 66, 324
Lee, Maj. Gen. Charles 57–58, **59**, 60–61, 81, 91, 158, 162
Lee, Lt. Col. Henry "Light Horse Harry" 2–4, 7, 13, 22–23, 46, 74, 77, 79, 97, 99, 102–104, 106, 112, 122–123, 130, 133, 144, 188, 227, 233, 236, 238, 242–**245**, 247–248, 251–252, 260–263, 275, 277–279, 283, 289, 298, 299, 304–305, 320–321, 331, 336, 340; about Abraham Buford 144; about Andrew Pickens at Cowpens 230; about Andrew Pickens at Kettle Creek 111, 124; about Charles Town 140–141; about Kings Mountain 177; about Kosciuszko 270; Eutaw Springs 284, 286–287; Fort Motte 253–254; Fort Watson 251; Pyle's defeat 245–246; the Siege of Augusta with Andrew Pickens 254–**261**, 267, 274, 326; the Siege of Ninety Six 269–273, 274, 326, 338, 356
Lee, Maj. P.L. 324
Lee, Gen. Robert E. 304; on Andrew Pickens 17
Lee's Legion 77, 144, 238, 243–247, 252–253, 256–257, 259–260, 272, 274, 278–279, 284, 286–287, 340, 356
Leslie, Maj. Gen. Alexander 207–208, 210, 236, 297
Lewis, Col. Andrew 76, 157
Lexington, South Carolina 294
Limestone, Tennessee 172
Lincoln, Pres. Abraham 304
Lincoln, Maj. Gen. Benjamin 95, **96**, 97–99, 101, 104, 122, 125–126, 140–142, 152, 158, 162, 176, 211, 319, 324, 347; fall of Charles Town 134–140, 325, 338; at Savannah 131–133, 370n71; at Stono Ferry 74, 127–130
Lincoln County, North Carolina 330
Lincolnton, North Carolina 152
Lindley's Fort, South Carolina 67–68
Little, Capt. James 112
Little Carpenter *see* Attakulla Kulla
Little Pee Dee River 166
Little River, Battle of 75, 311
Little River (Georgia) 108, 120, 123
Little River (South Carolina) 41, 74–75, 94, 250, 269, 273–274, 294, 338, 355
Little River Militia Regiment (District) 56, 216, 293, 313–314
Little Thicketty Creek (South Carolina) 209
Livingston, William 18
Locke, Col. Francis 125, 151, 244
The London Chronicle 25–26, 36, 88, 193–194, 196, 198, 231, 235, 240, 274, 348–360
The London Gazette 350, 357
Long Canes Creek 18, 20, 25, 42
Long Canes Massacre 20, 26
Long Canes settlement 4, 15, 17–18, 22, 24–27, 39, 42, 63, 78, 94–95, 105, 109, 111, 196–197, 199–200, 203, 205–206, 296–298, 301–302, 312, 329; Cherokee attacks within 20, 26, 65, 349
Long Creek 138, 328
Long Fellow, Chief 302
Long Fork of the Saluda River 51, 341
Long Island, New York 59, 88, 353
Louis XIII 8
Louis XIV 9
Love, Capt. Andrew 150
Love, Pvt. 294
Lowndes, Pres. Rawlins 90–92, 96, 98, 312, 318; promoted Andrew Pickens to colonel 91
Lowndesville, South Carolina 64
Luce, Claire Booth 283
Luce, Henry R. 283
Luper, Capt. 51
Luther, Martin 8
Lyles, Col. James 52–53
Lynch, Dep. Thomas 36, 359
Lynches Creek 31
Lynches River 31
Lyttleton, Gov. William Henry 19–20

Mackay's Trading Post *see* Fort Cornwallis
Mackenzie, Lt. Roderick 196
Madison, Pres. James 141
Maham, Lt. Col. Hezekiah 252, 279, 329
Maham tower 252, 257–258, 271–273
Maitland, Capt. 359–360
Maitland, Col. John 126, 131
Major Brown's Crossroads 153
malaria 34, 93, 167–168, 189–190, 207, 289
Malmady *see* Malmedy
Malmedy, Col. Francis 284–285, 289, 320
Malmody *see* Malmedy
Maple Swamp (South Carolina) 211–212, 215, 225, 227
Marchand, Sehoy (Creek) 124
Marion, Brig. Gen. Francis "Swamp Fox" 2–4, 21, 23, 38, 44, 59, 72, 135, 142, 156, 159–160, 164–166, 189, 192–194, 198, 238, 248, 250–251, 255, 257, 262, 264, 267–268, 270–272, 274, 276–283, 289–291, 296, 305, 357, 370n71, 375n29; Black Mingo Creek 170–171; broke leg at Charles Town 136; Eutaw Springs 284–286; Fort Motte 253–254; Fort Watson 251–252; named "Swamp Fox" 193–**194**; Savannah 132; Wyboo Swamp 249
Marion, Virginia 168
Marjoribanks, Maj. John 285–287
Marrow, Sam 64
Marr's (Mars) Bluff 31
Martin, Andrew 309
Martin, Edward 154
Martin, Lt. Col. James 53
Martin, Brig. Gen. Joseph 302–303
Martin, Capt. Salathiel 240
Martin, Capt. William 257
Martin, Rev. William 150
Mason, Rev. William 145
Mat(t)hews, Gov. John 142, 298
Maude, Rev. Robert 279
Maxwell, Maj. Andrew 254
Maxwell, Capt. Robert 260, 295, 298, 300, 339
Mayson, Maj. James 30, 32, 37–40, 48–51
McAden, Hugh 14
McArthur (MacArthur or MacCarthur), Maj. Archibald 134, 146, 170, 207; speaking of Tarleton 234; surrendered sword to Brig. Gen. Andrew Pickens 227
McArthur, Lt. Gen. Arthur, Jr. 134
McArthur, Douglas 134
McBride, William 72
McCafferty, William 191
McCall, Col. James 42, 48, 50, 70–72, 76, 94, 105–106, 148, 158, 160, 168, 194, 196, 199–200, 204–206, 242, 244, 248, 250–251, 326, 333, 342; attack Brown at Augusta 168–169; Battle of Cowpens 215, 217, 325; Battle of Kettle Creek 114–117; captured by Cherokee 62–63, 79, 106, 83, 97, 104, 332; death of 251, 272, 304
McCall, Mrs. 200
McClenachan, Robert 25, 308
McClure, Lt. Hugh 148–149
McClure, James 154
McClure, Capt. John 148–149, 153–155
McClure, Mrs. John 154
McClure, Mary 154
McCowan's Ford *see* Cowan's Ford
McCrady, Edward 231
McDaniel's Ford of the Greene River 170, 173
McDonald, Capt. Adam 44
McDowell, Col. Charles 155–156, 158, 164–165, 168, 171–173, 187, 192, 236
McDowell, Capt. Joseph 215
McDowell, Col. Joseph "Joe" 172–173, 177, 187, 192, 236; Cowpens 212, 215, 217–219, 221–222, 225–227; Kings Mountain 180
McDowell, Mrs. 187–188
McFall, Pvt. John 187

McGillivray, Chief Alexander (Creek) 124, 303
McGillivray, Lachlan 124
McGirth, Col. Daniel 96, 102–103, 105, 136
McGowan's blockhouse *see* McGowen's blockhouse
McGowan's Ford *see* Cowan's Ford
McGowen's blockhouse 108
McGuire, Pvt. 269
McIntosh, Brig. Gen. Lachlan 96, 131, 302–303, 370n71
McKay, Lt. James 251–252
McKissick, David 231
McLauren, Capt. Evan 49–50, 52, 55, 146
McPheeters, John 309
McPheeters, William 14, 309
McPherson, Lt. Col. Donald 221
McQueen, Capt. Alexander 136
McRary, Lt. Col. Robert 93–94
Mecklenburg County, North Carolina 25, 151, 232, 325, 350; militia 156, 248
Mecklin, Hugh 336
Mepkin Abbey (South Carolina) 283
Mepkin Plantation (South Carolina) 283
Mercer, Brig. Gen. Hugh 87
Miami Indians 19
Middle Tyger River, South Carolina 66
Middleton, Arthur 141, 193, 357
Middleton, Henry 36, 359
Middleton, Lt. Col. Hugh 285
Middleton, Capt. James 50
Middleton, Colonel Thomas 21–22
Midway, Georgia 95–96
Midway, North Carolina 250
Mifflin, Maj. Gen. Thomas 90
Miller, Capt. 111–112, 122
Miller, Pvt. David 310
Miller, Jean *see* Pickens (Miller), Jean
Miller, Lt. 275, 356
Miller, Mr. 66
Miller, Robert 14
Miller, Samuel 72
Miller, Hon. Sebourn J. 343
Miller, William 72
Mills, Col. Ambrose 156, 187
Mine Creek, South Carolina 47
Mingo Indians 19
Missouri 2, 15, 123, 342–344, 364n36
Mitchell, J. 335
Mitchell, Capt. John 297
Moderators 32, 37
Mohawk Indians 57, 83
Monck's Corner, South Carolina 22, 137, 254, 278, 283, 332
Money, Maj. John 196, 352
Monongahela River 19
Montagu, Gov. Charles 29–30, 32, 37
Montgomery, Gen. Richard 77
Moore, Ashley 341

Moore, Capt. 96
Moore, Pvt. Elijah 120
Moore, Pvt. James 310
Moore, Col. John 101, 104–105, 147, 152–153, 180, 338
Moore, Rev. Milton 337
Moore, Mr. 72
Moore, Col, Patrick 147, 159, 180
Moore, Pvt. Samuel 120, 292
Moore, Capt. William 183, 310
Moore's Plantation 326
Morgan, Brig. Gen. Daniel 3–4, 86, 198–**199**, 202–203, 206–210, 234–240, 249, 252, 274, 307, 328, 350, 355, 357–358; Andrew Pickens implores him to fight at Cowpens 212–213; arthritis, sciatica, and hemorrhoids 198, 209, 237; comments on Andrew Pickens at Cowpens 229; comments on Andrew Pickens to General Greene 209; Cowpens 145, 210–234, **239**, 319, 325, 333, 344; requests Andrew Pickens' presence at Grindal Shoals **203**; retired 242; at Saratoga 86
Morgan's Hill 225
Morganton, North Carolina 155
Motte, Col. Isaac 193, 357, 370n71
Motte, Jacob 253
Motte, Mrs. Rebecca B. 253–254, 277
Moultrie, Maj. John 21–22
Moultrie, Maj. Gen. William 21, 38, 42, 44, 58–60, 97, 101, **103**–104, 125–130, 136, 140, 193, 357, 370n71
Mt. Carmel, South Carolina 39, 109
Mount Mourne, North Carolina 240
Mt. Zion Academy 190
Mt. Zion College 277
Mt. Zion Society 90, 190, 277
Mud Island of the Delaware River 87
Mud Lick Creek (South Carolina) 203
Murphy, Hon. J. 332
Murphy, Martin *see* CahStahYeesTee
Murphy, Polly 367n62
Murphy North Carolina 78, 367n62
Murray, Dr. John 18, 26
Muscle Shoals Council 83–84
Muscle Shoals of the Tennessee River 83
Musgrove's Mill, South Carolina *see* Battle of Musgrove's Mill
Myddleton, Col. Charles Starkey 196

Nash, Gov. Abner 174
Nathan's Branch of Bullock's Creek *see* Turkey Creek
Neel, Capt. 112
Neel, Capt.: death of 75
Neel, Hon. Henry S. 328–329

Neil (Neal, Neel), Col. Andrew 149–151, 154–155, 330–331, 342; death of 159, 331
Neil (Neal, Neel), Col. Thomas 42, 52–53, 73, 76, 78, 330; death of 129–130, 149
Nelson's Ferry on the Santee, 165–166
New Acquisition District 192, 277, 314
New Acquisition Loyalist Militia 48
New Acquisition Militia Regiment 42, 51–52, 129, 148–151, 159, 174, 192, 210, 277
New England 36, 82, 88, 140, 348
New Era Iron Works *see* Hill's Iron Works
New Era Ironworks *see* Hill's Iron Works
New Jersey Volunteers: 2nd Battalion 160, 200, 285; 4th Battalion 176
New Rochelle, New York 58–60, 85, 89, 101, 134, 141, 149, 353–354
New York City 92, 101, 124, 129, 136, 176, 231, 297, 350–351, 353, 355, 358–359
New York Island 353
New York (Provincial) Volunteers 155, 160, 191, 285–286; *see also* DeLancey's Brigade
Newberry County, South Carolina 18
Newriver, (Catawba) Chief General 156
Ninety Six, South Carolina (village) 17–18, 25, 32–33, 37, 39–44, 46–48, 50, 52, 55, 63, 65–67, 69, 105–106, 123–125, 130, 133, 146–148, 150, 152–154, 156, 158, 160, 163, 165, 169, 170, 174–175, 187, 191–193, 196, 200–201, 203, 205–208, 210, 220, 231–232, 236, 238, 250–255, 260–261, 277–278, 291–292, 296, 299, 309, 319, 322, 325, 328, 332, 338, 350, 355; Articles of Cessation of 51–52; courthouse 32–33, 49; jail 33, 49–50, 67–68, 84, 123–125, 154, 160, 168, 321, 354; Siege of (1775) 48–52, 322, 351; Siege of (1781) 4–5, 262–264, **265–267**, 268–276, 288, 295, 307, 320, 321, 332–333, 336, 338–341, 344, 356; Treaty of (1775) 44, 46
Ninety Six District, South Carolina 17, 21, 26, 29–30, 32, 37, 41, 44, 51, 57, 63, 84–85, 92–93, 103, 105, 121–122, 133, 146, 160, 193, 195, 197–198, 200–201, 248, 253, 278, 290, 297, 300–301, 307, 314, 320–323, 332–334, 336, 338, 340–341, 344, 351; Militia Regiment (Tory) 48–51, 121, 153–154, 160, 169, 188, 193, 195, 197, 200, 205–206, 291, 300;

Militia Regiment (Whig) 3, 12, 38, 48–51, 53, 56, 76, 93–95, 107, 125–126, 133, 146, 151–152, 174, 180, 200, 203, 206, 250, 292, 320, 332
Ninety Six, Fort (Gouedy's) 20–22, 24–26, 37
Noble, Maj. Alexander 48, 203, 205, 263–264, 332, 338, 342
Noble, Pvt. James 72
Noble, Col. Patrick 321
Nolichucky River 157, 168, 172
Nolichucky settlements 168, 171
Non-importation resolution 35, 37, 40, 44, 359
North, P.M. Lord Frederick 87–89, 235, 350, 357
North Augusta, South Carolina 251
North River, New York 88, 354
North Tyger River, South Carolina 66
Norward's Mill (South Carolina) *see* Norwood's Mill
Norwood, Capt. John 67, 268, 298, 339
Norwood's Mill (South Carolina) 296–297, 329

Oconee (Cherokee Village) 71–73
Oconee County, South Carolina 80, 363, 381
Oconee Creek 70
Oconostota (Chief) 18, 20, 79, 157, 364n35
O'Donnell clan 8
Ogeechee River, Georgia 124, 136
Oglethorpe, Gen. James 34
O'Hara, Brig. Gen. Charles 190, 249
Ohio River 19, 157
Ohio Valley 19
Old Tassel *see* Corn Tassel
Oneida Indians 83
O'Neill clan 8
Onondaga Indians 83
Orange County, Virginia 11
Orangeburg, South Carolina 41, 51, 147, 152, 254, 277–278, 295, 331, 344
Orangeburg District 32, 314, 324; militia 51
Orr, Mr. 66
Ostatoy (Cherokee Village) 73
Ottawa Indians 19, 83, 364n35
over mountain (militia)men 157–158, 164–165, 168, 170–171, 173–175, 178, 181–183, 185–186, 188, 190, 192–193, 207–208, 214, 244, 250; scream or yell 180, 183; *see also* Yellin' Boys
over mountain settlements 83, 157, 164, 168, 170–171, 364n35
Owens, Maj. John 155

Pacolet Mills, South Carolina 202
Pacolet River 101, 148, 150, 156, 202–203, 208–209, 231, 234, 344, 350; North 66
Page's Creek (South Carolina) 46

Parata, Pvt. 299
Parker, Cdre. Hyde 95–96, 99
Parker, Cdre. Sir Peter 56, 58–60, 137
Parker, Col. Richard 324
Parker's Ferry of the Edisto River 282–283
Parliament(arian)(ary) 11, 28, 34–36, 348, 359
Patterson, Brig. Gen. James 134, 136
Pattinson, Lt. Col. Thomas 146
Pearis (Paris), Capt. Richard 32, 44–45, 48–50, 52–53, 68–69, 83, 146–148, 150, 260
Pee Dee, South Carolina 31
Pee Dee River 31, 166, 232, 350, 357
Pendleton District, South Carolina 66, 301, 303, 307–308, 331
Penn, William **9**
Penn family 10
Pennsylvania 7, 10–12, 87, 324, 343
Petigru, James Louis 28
Peyton, Pvt. Bailey 181
Philadelphia 36, 60, 87, 89, 91, 95, 140–141, 151, 301, 303, 335, 359
Phillips, Samuel 168, 171
Picken (Picon), Robert 8; brothers Andrew, Johnne, and Peter 8
Pickens, Andrew (son of Robert Picken) 9
Pickens, Brig. Gen. Andrew (unhorsed) 74, 130, 286
Pickens, Gov. Andrew, Jr. 301, 304, 375n29
Pickens, Captain Andrew, Sr. 7–9, 11–15, 308–309, 311–312
Pickens, Andrew L. (A.L.) 29, 53, 60, 81, 91, 105–106, 122, 130, 141, 148, 162, 203, 231, 240, 284, 294–295, 301–302, 311–312; *Skyagunsta, the Border Wizard Owl* 3, 12, 302, 311
Pickens (Davis), Catherine 12–13, 15, 311–312
Pickens, Mrs. Dorcus 296
Pickens, Eleanor Baskin 14, 335–343; marriage 21
Pickens, Lt. Gov. Ezekial 304
Pickens, Gov. Francis Wilkinson 304
Pickens, Gabriel (brother of Andrew Pickens, Sr.) 12, 311
Pickens (Kerr), Lucy 12
Pickens (Miller), Jean 12, 14–16, 308, 311
Pickens, John, Sr. (brother of Andrew Pickens, Sr.) 12–15, 64, 105, 308–309, 311
Pickens, John (brother of Brig. Gen. Andrew Pickens) 4, 12, 14–16, 269, 295, 308, 312, 318; death of 4, 256, 294–296, 333, 375
Pickens, Capt. John (cousin of Brig. Gen. Andrew Pickens) 14, 65, 69, 203, 310–311, 338, 341
Pickens, Capt. Joseph William 3–4, 7, 10, 12–17, 21–22, 25–27,

38, 46, 51–52, 63–66, 69, 77, 78, 94, 105–106, 109, 111–112, 118, 120, 148, 203, 206, 210, 242, 273, 295, 308, 310–312, 332, 364n46 367n53, 369n39; correct rank 6, 12, 66, 77, 105, 112, 118, 121–122, 332; at Cowpens 217–222; death of 4, 268–269, 272, 332, 338–339; indents and claims 318, 334–335, 369n39; marriage 14, 21; promoted to captain 203; at the Ring Fight 74, 106, 130; at the Siege of Ninety Six 263–269, 332, 338–339
Pickens, Robert (grandfather of Andrew Pickens, Sr., and son of Robert Picken) 9
Pickens, Capt. Robert (cousin of Brig. Gen. Andrew Pickens) 14, 203, 225, 296, 311
Pickens, Robert Andrew 7, 12–14, 63–66, 69, 72, 268–269, 312, 318, 335, 365n29
Pickens, Robert Pike 12, 14, 17, 22, 25
Pickens, Thomas Mason Monroe 12, 15, 311–312
Pickens, William (brother of Brig. Gen. Andrew Pickens) 12, 15, 310–312
Pickens, William (cousin of Brig. Gen. Andrew Pickens) 51, 53, 65, 69, 111, 264, 311, 318, 340–341
Pickens, William Gabriel 65, 69, 263, 269, 276, 295, 311, 318, 337
Pickens, William Henry (father of Andrew Pickens, Sr.) 9–11
Pierce, Maj. William 275
Pike (Pickens), Margaret 9, 11
Pinckney, Gov. Charles Cotesworth 37–**38**, 56, 90–91, 125, 193, 303, 357
Pinckney, Prov. Marsh. Roger 31
Pinckney, Maj. Thomas 134–135, **137**
Plantation of Ulster 8–9, 11
Point Pleasant, West Virginia 157
Polk, Capt. Ezekial 39
Polk, Col. Thomas 52–53, 68
Ponder, James 178
Powell, Col. G. G. 31, 35, 359
Pownall, Gov. Thomas 21
Presbyterianism 7–8, 10–13, 17, 24, 26, 30–31, 35, 40, 46, 82, 90–91, 104, 150, 153, 163, 213, 301–302, 308; Bullock's Creek Presbyterian Church 148; Fair Forest Presbyterian Church 206; Ninety Six Presbyterian Church 277; Old Hopewell Presbyterian Church 304, 308; Old Stone Presbyterian Church (Virginia) 13, 19; Old Waxhaw Presbyterian Church 14–15, 145; Upper Fishing Creek Presbyterian Church 149
Preston, Col. William 247–248
Prevost, Maj. Gen. Augustine

91–92, 95–96, 99–102, 104, 122, 125–126, 130–134, 324, 351
Prevost, Lt. Col. John Mark 95–96, 122, 125–126, 131
Prince, Capt. 68, 71
Prince, John 156
Prince of Noth (Cherokee) 302
Prince of Wales American Regiment 166
Pucksinwah, (Shawnee) Chief 157
Pulaski, Gen. Kazimierz 131–132, 330–332
Pur(r)ysburg (Landing), South Carolina 99, 125–126
Purves, Capt. John 39
Pyle, Col. John 245–246
Pyle's Defeat 245–246
Pyle's Massacre *see* Pyle's Defeat

Quaker Meadows, North Carolina 155, 165, 171–172, 187, 192, 236
Quakers 13, 189
Qualhatchee (Cherokee Village) 75
Quebec 19
Quinby Bridge (South Carolina) 279

Ramseur's Mill, North Carolina 152–153, 236–237, 326, 333
Rawdon, Lt. Col. Francis Lord 137, 146, 149, 155, 160, 162, 190–193, 207, 250–255, 262–263, 265, 267–268, 271–272, 274–278, 280–281, 283, 326, 328, 338, 357–358
Rawdon Town 291–292, 294
R. B. Russell Dam 111–112
Red House *see* Dollard's Tavern
Red House (Andrew Pickens' last home in South Carolina) 304
Reed, James 66
Reedy Branch 247–248, 250, 342
Reedy River 53, 341
Reedy River Fight 53–54, 341–342
Regulators 1, 30–32
Reidsville, North Carolina 250
Rhems, South Carolina 171
Rice Kings 27–28
Richardson, Capt. Edward 39
Richardson, J. 327
Richardson, Brig. Gen. Richard 48, 50–55, 67, 73, 76, 91, 330, 366n24 & 26
Richardson, Capt. Richard, Jr. 52
Richland District (County), South Carolina 18, 323, 330
Richtex, South Carolina 207
Riddle, Capt. William 172
Rimini, South Carolina 48
Ring Fight 4, 74–75, 106, 130–131; rumored in 1776 4, 130–131, 133
Ritchie, Capt. William 292
Roan County, North Carolina 325, 330
Roan Mountain, Tennessee 172
Robbins, Maj. John 49
Roberts, Col. Owen 47
Robertson, Maj. Charles 157, 159
Robertson, Gen. 353–354

Robertson's Creek (North Carolina) 186
Robinson, Maj. Joseph 40–41, 48–51
Roche, Patrick 283
Rochelle *see* New Rochelle
Roche's Plantation 283
Rocky Mount, South Carolina 146–147, 149–152, 155, 159, 161, 191
Rocky River (South Carolina) 64–65
Roebuck, Col. Benjamin 195, 216, 220, 222, 250, 296, 329
Rogersville, Tennessee 172
Roney, Lt. John 264
Ross, Col. 69, 75, 78
Ross, Maj. Francis 122, 124, 342; death of 124
Rowan County, North Carolina 319, 344; militia 105, 152, 248
Rowarth, Capt. Samuel 255
Roworth *see* Rowarth
Royal Assent 28
Royal Gazette (South Carolina) *see* *Royal South Carolina Gazette*
Royal Gazette (New York) 141
Royal South Carolina Gazette 20, 193–194, 196, 267, 352, 356, 358
Rucker's Mill, North Carolina 170
Ruckersville, Georgia 112
Rudolph, Capt. Michael 256, 259–260, 273
Rugeley, Col. Henry 143, 150
Rugeley's Mills (South Carolina) 143, 150, 253
Rugley Mill *see* Rugeley's Mills
Russell Lake 111–112
Rutherford, (Loyalist) 257
Rutherford, Brig. Gen. Griffith 53, 76, 78, 125, 151–152, 320
Rutherfordton, North Carolina 165, 168, 186
Rutledge, Edward 36–37, 359
Rutledge, Gov. John 36–37, 56–**58**, 76, 84–85, 90, 104, 125–127, 134, 137, 142–143, 151, 159, 164–165, 174–175, 185, 189, 193, 230, 237, 247–248, 254, 289–291, 296, 307, 325, 327, 329–330, 356, 359

Safford's Creek (South Carolina) 209
St. Augustine, Florida 34, 39, 44, 92, 95–96, 360
St. Catherine's Sound, Georgia 96
St. John's River, Florida 96
St. Ledger, Capt. Hayes 285
St. Mary's Church Road, North Carolina 155
St. Mary's River, Georgia/Florida 92
St. Simon's Island, Georgia 34
Salem, North Carolina 242, 358
Salisbury, North Carolina 146, 237–238, 240, 242, 249, 319, 357
Saluda, South Carolina 294
Saluda River (incl. Upper, Lower,

Little, etc.) 39, 43–44, 48, 50–51, 53, 65–67, 99, 101, 147, 153, 206, 263–264, 269, 273–274, 240, 258–259, 295–296, 313–314, 321, 329, 338, 341, 355
Salvador, Capt. Francis 42, 62, 65, 67–69, 73, 76, 79, 132; death of 71–73
Santee National Wildlife Refuge 249
Santee River (South Carolina) 142, 161, 165, 265, 277, 281–282, 332, 351, 357; Great Savannah of 165; High Hills of 253, 278, 281, 289; upper 165
Santee River State Park 247
Saratoga National Historic Park 86
Sattilla River, Georgia 92
Saunders, Mr. 174
Saunders Creek (South Carolina) 161
Sauta (Cherokee Village) 299
Savage, Ann (Gaillard) 55
Savage, Col. John 26, 32–33, 38, 49–51, 55, 84, 220
Savage, Pvt. Nathan 254
Savage's Old Field 51, 106, 152, 192, 300
Savannah, Georgia 4, 34, 39, 57, 63, 91–93, 95–99, 101, 104, 113, 123–124, 126, 130–131, 134, 136, 141, 152, 258–260, 319, 324; British and Tories evacuate 297; fall of (1778) 96–97, 101, 191; Siege of (1779) 131–133, 191
Savannah River 17, 34, 39, 42–43, 64–65, 69, 80, 95–96, 99, 101–103, 105–107, 109–113, 121–125, 131, 134, 155, 169, 205, 251, 255, 298, 314, 324, 326, 334, 338, 342, 351
Schofield, Col. John 31–32
Schofieldites 31–32, 38, 67
Scopholites *see* Schofieldites
Scotland 7–9, 34, 59, 82
Scots-Irish (Scotch-Irish) migration 7–10
Scott, Capt. 60
Scottish Lowlanders 7–9, 11
Scovilites *see* Schofieldites
Screamin' Boys *see* Yellin' Boys
Sedition Act 84
Seldon, Lt. Samuel 273
Seneca (Cherokee Village) 62, 64, 68, 70–71, 73, 75–76, 302, 308, 341–342
Seneca Indians 83
Seneca River 64, 72, 336
Seven Years' War 18, 27, 57, 79, 123, 131, 364n37
17th Dragoons 143, 214, 217, 219, 222, 225, 361
71st Grenadiers 145, 227
71st Regiment of Foot (Highlanders) 97, 126–127, 129, 134, 146, 162, 170, 178, 207, 214, 220, 225–228, 234
Sevier (Xavier), Col. John 157,

164–165, 168, 171–173, 177, 180–183, 188, 214, 325, 333
Sevier, Joseph 183
Sevier, Capt. Robert 171, 178; death of 182–183
Sevier Island of the French Broad River 364n35
Shankland, Capt. Thomas 111, 298
Shanklin, Capt. Thomas *see* Shankland
Shawnee Indians 19, 83, 157, 349
Shelby, Col. Isaac 157, 159, 164–165, 168, 171, 173–174, 177, 179–183, 186–188, 214, 244, 325, 327, 333, 342
Shelby, Capt. Moses 171
Shelby, North Carolina 173
Shelby's Fort 168, 171
Shepherd's Ferry at Black Mingo Creek 171
Sheridan, Maj. Henry F. 285–287
Sherral(d)'s Ford *see* Sherrill's Ford
Sherrill's Ford of the Catawba River 236–238
Shubrick, Capt. Thomas 280
Shubrick's Plantation (South Carolina) 279–280
Simons (Simmonds), Crnt. James 205
Simpson, Rev. John 150
Simpson, Mr. (first name unknown) 360
Simpson, Judge Vinson B. 337, 340
Simpson, William 18
Sinquefield, Capt. Francis (Frank) 50
Six-and-Twenty Mile Creek 70
six-pounder cannons 146, 270, 285, 361, 370n69
64th Regiment of Foot 137, 285–286
63rd Regiment of Foot 166, 191, 195–196, 285–286; mounted 191
Skiuka, Chief 63–65, 71
Smith, Capt. Aaron 65, 71
Smith, Rev. Andrew 341
Smith, Capt. John 65–66, 71
Smith, Capt. John C. 97
Smith, Mrs. 65
Smith, Capt. Robert 256–257, 260
Smith, Pvt. Roger 310
Smith, Susannah 375n29
Smith, Pvt. William 165, 310
Smith's Ford of the Broad River 164
Snipes, William Clay 193, 357
Snoddy's Bridge 66
Snow Campaign *see* Reedy River Fight
Snow's Island (South Carolina) 249
South Boston, Virginia 243
South Carolina Constitution: (1776) 57, 81; (1778) 81–82, 90–91, 95, 312–318
South Carolina Gazette see Royal South Carolina Gazette
South Carolina General Assembly 21, 32–33, 57–58, 81–82, 85, 90–91, 134, 137–138, 143, 307–308, 312–313–315, 317–318, 335
South Carolina Provincial Congress(men) 37–38, 40, 44, 46–48, 51, 53, 55–58, 62, 70, 72, 365n29
South Carolina Provincial Militia: 1st Infantry Regiment 38, 285–286, 370n71; 1st Rifle Regiment 56; New Districts (1776) 56; reorganized 91; 2nd Dragoon Regiment 196; 2nd Infantry Regiment 38, 42, 132, 159, 370n71; 2nd Rifle regiment 56; 3rd Regiment of Rangers 38–39, 48, 51–52, 291, 341–342
South Carolina Royal provincial government 55
South Carolina Royal Provincial law 31
South Carolina Royal Provincial Militia 21–22, 31–32, 38–39; Rangers 279
South Carolina School for the Deaf and Blind 154
southern campaign (theater) 3–4, 58, 93, 125, 146, 167, 181, 188, 198
southern colonies (provinces) 84–85, 87–89, 95, 106, 120, 131, 133–134, 141–142, 230
Southern Department of the Continental Army 4, 57–58, 60, 81, 85, 91, 93, 95, 99, 125, 131, 152, 158, 162–163, 176, 188–189, 197–198, 202, 234, 237–238, 243, 263, 274–275, 277, 281, 289
Spain (Spanish) 8, 34, 231
Spartanburg, South Carolina 101, 156, 209
Spartanburg District (County), South Carolina 18, 216
Speedwell's Ironworks (North Carolina) 250
Speedwill Ironworks *see* Speedwell's Ironworks
Spring Branch (South Carolina) 49, 153, 192, 270
Spurgin, Maj. John 124
Spurgin (Spurgen, Spurgeon), Maj. William 105, 114, 117, 120
Stallings, John 150
Stallings, Mrs. John 150
Stamp Act 27–28
Star Fort 262–274, 355–356
Star Redoubt *see* Star Fort
Staunton, Virginia 13, 19
Step, James 170
Stevens, Brig. Gen. Edward 161, 237
Stevenson, Thomas 95
Stevenson, Lt. William 170
Stewart, Lt. Col. Alexander 277–278, 281–289
Stono Ferry, South Carolina 74, 126–131, 133, 136, 149, 160, 286, 324, 370n71
Stono River 127, 129, 140
Strong, Mrs. Janet 150
Strong, William 150
Stuart, Maj. John 39, 42, 44–45, 47, 124
Suck Creek (South Carolina) 211, 215, 219
Sugar Town (Cherokee Village) 61, 68, 73
Sullivan's Island, South Carolina 47, 58–60
Sumner, Brig. Gen. Jethro 128, 285–286, 319–320
Sumter, Mary 143–131
Sumter (Sumpter), Brig. Gen. Thomas "Gamecock" 3–4, 30, 54–56, 58, 72, 78, 91, 142–143, 151–**152**, 153–154, 156, 158–161, 164–165, 167–168, 174–175, 185, 189, 191, 193–196, 198, 209, 212, 237–238, 247–248, 250–252, 254, 256, 264, 268, 270–272, 274–280, 284, 298, 303–305, 325, 328, 333, 344, 352
(Port of) Sunbury, Georgia 96, 99, 131
Surry County. North Carolina militia 172, 240
swivel guns 43, 49–51, 111, 132, 366n14
Sycamore Shoals, Tennessee 157, 172; over mountain militia rendezvous (1780) 171; Treaty of (1775) 157–158

Taitt, Agt. David 124
Tamassee *see* Tomassee
Tarcoat River *see* Tearcoat River
Tarleton, Lt. Col. Banastre "Bloody Ban" 100, 136–137, **143**, 153, 155, 162–164, 183–184, 186–187, 190, 193, 197, 207–208, 210–211, 232–235, 240–241, 245–248, 319, 328, 350; at Blackstock's 195–196, 352; Buford's defeat 144–146, 150, 351, 360–361; at Cowpens 145, 211–229, 231–232, 234, 236, 252, 262, 307, 350–351, 357; yellow fever 167, 169–170, 190
Tarleton's Legion 100, 136–137, 143–145, 147, 151, 154, 162–163, 165, 167, 173, 193, 195–196, 208–209, 212, 214, 227–228, 232–233, 236, 238, 240, 243–245, 247–248, 319, 350
Tarleton's quarter 145, 183, 227
Tarrant's Tavern (North Carolina) 240–241
Tarrar's Spring 293–294
Tate, Capt. 68
Tate, Capt. Edmund 215, 227
Taxation of the Colonies Act 89
Taylor, Col. John 319
Taylor, Maj. Samuel 168
Taylor, Col. Thomas 194, 254, 279
Tea 27–28, 34–35, 359–360
Tea Act 28, 34–35; repealed 89, 98
Tearcoat River (South Carolina) 192

Tearcoat Swamp (South Carolina) 192
Tecumseh, (Shawnee) Chief 157
Tennent, Rev. William 35, 40–43, 82, 365n21, 35, 38, 40–41, 43–44, 46–47, 49, 368n4
Terry, Maj. Champness 42
Thicketty Creek (South Carolina) 159, 208
Thicketty Fort see Fort Thicketty
3rd Regiment of Foot 285–286
30th Regiment of Foot 247
33rd Regiment of Foot 137, 161
Thomas, Col. (Tory) 102
Thomas, Jane (Black) 147, 154, 159–146
Thomas, Col. John, Jr. 147, 154, 156, 216, 220, 222, 250, 332
Thomas, Col. John, Sr. 51–52, 68, 73, 76, 147, 154, 160
Thomas, William 147
Thompson, Lt. Col. Benjamin 296
Thompson, Hon. Charles 275, 356
Thompson, Brig. Gen. William P. 340, 344
Thomson, Col. William 4, 38, 51–53, 58, 73, 366n21
three-pounder cannons 128, 218–219, 229, 285, 350, 369n59
Tilicho see Little Telliquo
Timossee see Tomassee
Tomassee (Cherokee Village) 69, 75, 78, 106, 130, 302, 304, 308, 338
Tomochichi (Yamacraw Indian) Chief 34
Torrence's Tavern see Tarrant's Tavern
Tory, Drumming of **191**
the Tory Oak 172
Towles, Oliver 293
Towles' Blacksmith Shop (South Carolina) 293
Towls, Capt. 296, 329
Townshend Acts 28, 34, 89, 104
Toxaway (Cherokee Village) 75, 342
Treaty at Dewitt's Corner (1777) 79, 83
Treaty of Hopewell: (1st — 1785) 302–303; (2nd — 1786) 303; (3rd — 1786) 303
Treaty of Paris: (1763) 25, 364n37; (1783) 300
Trenton, South Carolina 251
Triplett, Maj. Francis 'Frank' 215, 222
Troublesome Ironworks see Speedwell's Ironworks
Troy, South Carolina 20
Tryon, North Carolina 175
Tryon County, North Carolina 236
Tsi'yu-gunsini see Dragging Canoe
Tuckaseegee Ford of the Catawba River 151–152
Tugaloo (Cherokee Village) 63–65, 73, 75

Tugaloo River 73, 75–76, 78, 80, 106
Turkey Creek, South Carolina 150, 210, 231, 233–234, 350
Turnbull, Lt. Col. George 146–147, 149–150, 153, 155, 159, 191
Turner, Capt. Sterling 293
Turner House Massacre 293–294
Tuscarora Indians 83
Tutt, Capt. Benjamin 47
23rd Regiment of Foot 161
Twiggs, Col. John 102, 124, 131, 136, 194, 196, 199–200, 325
Twitty's Ford of the Broad River (Carolina) 170
Tybee Island, Georgia 134, 297
Tydiman's Plantation (South Carolina) 296
Tyger River (incl. North & Middle), South Carolina 66, 156, 195–196, 352, 366n24
Tyger settlement, South Carolina 66

Union, South Carolina 206
Union County (District), South Carolina 18, 215, 330, 344
United States National Whitewater Center 151

van Keppel, Gov. Willem Anne (Virginia) 11
Van(n)'s Creek, Georgia 112, 369
Vann's Creek Ford of the Savannah River 112, 369
Virginia 10–14, 19, 57–58, 60, 76, 93, 134, 158, 168, 171–172, 188, 197, 207, 210, 232–233, 237–238, 242–244, 248, 250, 253, 275, 292, 309, 320–321, 324, 326, 331, 337, 341, 343, 364; Continentals 57, 134–135, 142, 145, 198, 231, 285, 360; General Assembly 11; Whig militia 63, 128, 157, 161–162, 177, 211, 215, 222, 231, 237, 243, 247–248, 263–264, 273–275, 285
Volunteers of Ireland 137, 162
von Borck, Lt. Col. Ernst Leopold 282–283
Von Stedingk, Count Curt 132

Wadesboro, North Carolina 14, 308
Walker, Pvt. George 310
Walker, Pvt. James 310
Walker, Col. John 186
Walker, Pvt. Nethanel 310
Walker, Pvt. Philip 310
Wallace, Capt. Andrew 215, 222, 225
Wallace, Capt. John 342
Wallace, Pvt. John 123, 318, 342–344
Walpole, Horace 145
Wambaw Bridge (South Carolina) 296
War Hill 113
Wardlaw, James 321–322, 336
Wardlaw, Lt. W. 95, 123

Waring, Alice N.: *The Fighting Elder: Andrew Pickens (1739–1817)* 3
Waring, Robert 309
Washington, Augustine 63
Washington, Gen. George 19, 57–58, 85, 87, 89, 131, 149, 152, 158, 163, 189, 197, 292, 303, 320, 324, 353, 355
Washington, Lt. Col. William 137, 203–204, **205**–206, 233–234, 246, 271–272, 274–277, 285–287, 319–321, 325, 331, 336, 350–351; at Cowpens 213–232; duel with Tarleton 228
Washington, Georgia 107–108
Washington County, Virginia 168, 171
Watauga River 157–158, 171
Watauga settlements 157, 173, 250
Wateree River 51, 207–208, 265, 314
Waters, Col. Thomas 203–205, 298, 300
Watkins, Pvt. George 178
Watson, Lt. Col. John W. T. 249, 251–252
Watson, Col. Samuel 148
Waxhaw, North Carolina 146, 252
Waxhaw Creek 14, 25, 156–157
The Waxhaws 13–15, 17, 19, 21–22, 24–25, 105, 145–146, 156, 183, 355
Webb's Ferry of the (Georgia) Broad River 113
Webster, Lt. Col. James 137, 239
Weems, Capt. Thomas 81–82, 96–97, 104, 113, 338, 341
Weitzall's Mill see Whitesell's Mill
Weitzall's Mill see Whitesell's Mill
Welch, John 63–64
Wemyss, Maj. James 163, 191, 193–194, 352
Wemyss-borough, South Carolina 352
Wetzall's Mill see Whitesell's Mill
Wetzell's Mill see Whitesell's Mill
Whaling, Sgt. 272
Whiplash see CahStahYeesTee
Whirl of the Tennessee River 83
White, George 231
White Hall 61, 65–66, 84, 95, 122–123, 325, 330, 350, 357, 366n16–17, 19–20; British outpost 148, 200–202, 206; Pickens' command post 277
White Plains, New York 88, 353–354
Whitesell, Pvt. Henry 248
Whitesell's Mill 247–248
Whitsell's Mill see Whitesell's Mill
Wiboo Swamp (South Carolina) 249
Wilfong, George 172
Wilkes County, Georgia 103–104, 124; militia 95, 131, 255
Wilkes County, North Carolina 171; militia 171

Wilkinson, Francis 375n29
Wilkinson, Col. (Morton) 250, 375n29
Wilkinson, Susan Smith 375n29
Wilkinson, Susannah 286n29
Willanawaw (Willinewah), Chief 157
Willett, Col. Marinus 303
William the Conqueror 8
Williams, Capt. Daniel 183, 293–294
Williams, Pvt. Edward 310
Williams, Col. Hezekiah 292, 300
Williams, Brig. Gen. James 164–165, 174–175, 180, 184–186, 293, 325; death of 185–186; mortally wounded at Kings Mountain 183; promoted to Brigadier General 174
Williams, Col. John 319–320
Williams, Joseph 183, 293–294
Williams, Maj. 260
Williams, Brig. Gen. Otho H. 161–162, 242, 247, 249, 265, 267, 284–285, 320, 356
(Col. John) Williams' Fort, South Carolina 203, 328
(Col. John) Williams' Plantation 203, 328
Williams Road, South Carolina 294
Williamsburg, Virginia 324, 343
Williamsburg County, South Carolina 159
Williamson, Brig. Gen. Andrew 4, 18, 38, 47–48, 52–53, 84, 92–95, 99–104, 111, 113, 122–123, 125, 130, 151–152, 197, 199, 201, 277, 311, 320, 324, 330–331, 341–342; ambushed at Seneca 70–73; Augusta 99–113; captured at Charles Town by Isaac Hayne (1781) 267, 280; (not at) Charles Town (1780) 126, 136, 325; Cherokee Campaign of 61–79, 106, 268, 291, 307, 321–322, 332, 336, 338; kidnapped by Whigs 200; Ninety Six (1775) 48–51, 322, 324; parole 147–148, 153, 327; promoted to brigadier general 91, 95; promoted to colonel 76, 332; Provincial Congress 37; Royal Militia 38; (not at) Savannah 133, 370n71; suspicious actions 104, 133, 152–153, 160, 195, 199, 201–202, 206; Treaty of 1777 79; Whig Militia 39
Williamson, James 154; plantation 154–155, 332, 337
Williamson, Lieutenant Colonel Micajah 255–256
Williamson's Fort 49–50, 192, 262
Williamson's (Andrew) Plantation see White Hall
Will's Creek (Maryland) 19
Willtown, South Carolina 171
Wilmington, North Carolina 250, 358
Wilson, Capt. 187
Winn, Lt. Col. John 93–94
Winn, Col. Richard 154
Winnsboro, South Carolina 190–191, 193, 202–203, 207, 231, 276–277

Winston, Col. Joseph 172, 177, 180, 188
Winter Quarters, Pennsylvania 87
Winyah Bay (South Carolina) 262
Wise, Capt. Samuel 39
Witherspoon, Pvt. David 184
Wofford's Iron Works 209
Woodmason, Rev. Charles 29–31, 82, 90
Woods, Capt. Frame 331
Woods, Dep. Sheriff John 30
Woods, Robert 310
Woodward, Capt. George 343–344
Woodward, Capt. Thomas 30, 39
Wright, Sgt. Thomas 310
Wrights Bluff, South Carolina 331
Wrightsborough, Georgia 113, 117, 123–124
Wyboo Swamp see Wiboo Swamp

Yadkin River (North Carolina) 241–242, 357–358
Yellin' Boys 158, 180
yellow fever 167, 190
York District (County), South Carolina 18, 148, 154–155, 330–331, 342, 344
York Town, South Carolina 342–354
Yorktown, Virginia 3, **292**
Young, Maj. Thomas 178, 181, 183, 185, 204, 212–213, 215, 220, 228, 233, 270, 293, 318, 344–345

www.ingramcontent.com/pod-product-compliance
Lightning Source LLC
Chambersburg PA
CBHW081533300426
44116CB00015B/2618